*The Journals of*

# WOODROW WYATT

*Volume One*

# *The Journals of*

# WOODROW WYATT

*Volume One*

Edited by Sarah Curtis

MACMILLAN

First published 1998 by Macmillan

an imprint of Macmillan Publishers Ltd
25 Eccleston Place, London SW1W 9NF
and Basingstoke

Associated companies throughout the world

ISBN 0 333 74166 8



1 3 5 7 9 8 6 4 2

A CIP catalogue record for this book is available from
the British Library.

Phototypeset by Intype London Limited
Printed and bound in Great Britain by
Mackays of Chatham plc, Chatham, Kent

# *Contents*

# *List of Illustrations*

SECTION THREE

# *Introduction*

When Woodrow Wyatt, Baron Wyatt of Weeford, died on 7 December 1997 only a handful of professional advisers knew that he had been keeping a journal for twelve years.

In October 1985 he began writing (or rather tape-recording) an uninhibited commentary on his life and times. He had published his autobiography, *Confessions of an Optimist*, in 1985 and that may be one reason why few suspected he would be keeping a journal, although Jo Grimond, the Liberal politician, told him in November 1986 that he should keep a record of his conversations with the Prime Minister: 'It would be very valuable historically.' His obituaries noted his special relationship with Margaret Thatcher and the *Times* said he exercised far more influence than many more successful political figures. However, there was little recognition of the importance of his network of friends and contacts.

During the three years covered in this first volume of his journals (1985–8) we find Wyatt talking to the Prime Minister on most Sunday mornings and on other days when he thought she needed his support. Their discussions cover major political issues from day to day. Some matters, like the Westland affair or the modernization of the newspaper industry, captured the headlines for a time and then were over. Others, from the handling of political leaks, to cabinet government, to public sector pay, to political bias in the media, to the privatization of the Tote (of which he had been chairman since 1976), still resonate today.

Wyatt channels to the Prime Minister not just his own views but the opinions of others he meets in his busy working and social round – it is amazing how many politicians are to be found on the racecourse – and especially the concerns of his two great friends, Rupert Murdoch, the newspaper and media proprietor, and Arnold Weinstock of GEC. If the journals were a novel, the heroine would be Margaret Thatcher (with a special starring role for Queen Elizabeth the Queen Mother, whom he knew through racing and adored) and the heroes would be Rupert Murdoch and Lord Weinstock.

How did Wyatt's relationship with Lady Thatcher begin? Inserted in the typed-up pages of the journal, at October 1988, I found the following handwritten note: 'In these diaries Mrs Thatcher is a principal figure, possibly the principal figure. I knew her slightly when I was in the Commons and thought her an energetic conventional party point-scoring Tory inclined to a tiresome bossiness which males find irritating in female politicians. At that time I doubt if she was sufficiently mature politically to have begun to formulate her grand design for reviving Britain and untying the strangling cords of Socialism gone too far or she would then have supposed that she would be the instrument for destroying the soggy consensus which had lain like dank fog over Britain and her politicians since 1951.'

By the time these journals begin he delights in what he sees as her feminine qualities. 'Margaret is all woman,' he says in November 1985. He is devoted to her as a woman as well as a politician whose agenda for change is his agenda. Again and again he makes the point that he is not a Tory and his allegiance is not to the Conservative Party. In a letter he wrote in 1993 to Martin Gilbert, the Churchill historian, he says, 'I would not like posterity to believe I ever joined the Tory party which has been anathema to me all my life.' When to his joy Mrs Thatcher makes him a life peer in 1987, he sits on the crossbenches from where he can more effectively support her but be selective in his support of some government measures. He even tells the Duchess of Beaufort in June 1988 that Mrs Thatcher is not a Conservative either: 'She's a radical making a revolution which horrifies many Conservatives.'

The journals offer compelling evidence of the importance of the press to politicians, of how much it mattered to Mrs Thatcher not only to have Rupert Murdoch's newspapers on her side but also to have government policies explained clearly to the electorate by a journalist with a readership like Woodrow Wyatt's, at both ends of the newspaper spectrum: he was proud that his 'Voice of Reason' column in the *News of the World* had as many as seventeen and a half million readers. She is delighted when he tells her before the 1987 general election that he will be writing every Saturday in the *Times* during the campaign 'so I could keep the muddled eggheads in order in the *Times* and the masses in the *News of the World*'. Anyone who thinks Tony Blair was the first prime minister to invite Rupert Murdoch to Chequers can read the accounts here of Murdoch's visits to Chequers with Wyatt and Arnold Weinstock too.

However, it is clear that Mrs Thatcher was very much her own woman, listening to what Wyatt canvassed but sometimes demurring – and he was his own man. In November 1987 he is outraged when Joan Ruddock, the former Campaign for Nuclear Disarmament leader, suggests he has written an unfavourable review of a book by Peter Jenkins, the political commentator, at Rupert Murdoch's behest: 'In fact I have never written anything which I did not believe in any newspaper since I first began to write for them.' He tells Alan Clark, politician and diarist, in December 1987: 'Sometimes I may mention to her that I'm thinking of writing on a particular topic and she may say, "Oh that's a good idea. I hope you do." Otherwise we never talk about my articles before they're written. Only afterwards.' This approach is confirmed by the journals though it is clear that he often decides his subject after talking to her and he also provides her with material for her speeches.

Wyatt's political interests go beyond the Conservative Party. He still has friends – and enemies – from the twenty-one years he was a Labour MP. As early as March 1986 he meets the late John Smith, then Labour spokesman on trade and industry, spots his quality, thinks he ought to be Labour Leader and hears from him that Labour is planning a changed approach. 'If you are going to sound too moderate,' he says to Smith, 'people will say what is the point of changing as you sound like Mrs Thatcher.' His election at the end of 1986 to The Other Club, with its membership of political figures of all hues, is a bountiful source of political gossip.

Once he is in the House of Lords we see him energetically pursuing the interests of the Tote and racing, marshalling their lordships to vote to allow betting on racing on Sundays. He is also able to continue his life-long commitment to reforming the trade unions through successful amendments about the conduct of ballots. With or without forewarning, he never misses an opportunity to promote his causes. In December 1988, towards the end of this volume, he rushes to the rescue and intervenes in a debate when the topic of the restoration of Heveningham Hall, built by his forebear James Wyatt, is raised.

But in the end it is Woodrow Wyatt as a person, as a character on his own stage, who captures and envelops the reader of these journals. They were written for publication, as a nest-egg, he tells us, for his widow and daughter. It is not just the breadth and bustle of his activities which impress. Here is the public man, the politician, the journalist, the representative of racing interests and the playwright *manqué* – his valiant efforts to get performed the play he has written are an endearing, comic thread throughout. But he is also a friend to many. These journals give more intimate portraits than have hitherto been published of the two powerful media and business magnates to whom he is devoted. There is a galaxy of other friends besides, for whom he is a generous host and appreciative, if sometimes critical, guest. He is rarely discreet about them, he is sometimes biting but there is nearly always some warmth in his appraisals. He must have been a skilful listener to judge from some of the conversations and confidences he records.

It is curious that someone so active and ebullient should characterize himself as lazy. His self-doubt shows how high his standards – and his ambitions – were. But above all it is his appetite for life which emerges from his journals. I think he would agree with the Roman writer Terence who said, '*Homo sum; humani nil a me alienum puto*' ('I am a man; there is nothing in human existence I think foreign to me').

*

I met Woodrow Wyatt three times in 1994 with Diana Rawstron, his lawyer from Goodman Derrick. She had asked me if I might be interested in editing his journals and I had spent a day sampling the boxes of them at his solicitors' offices. At that stage my involvement was only a distant possibility: I was fully employed editing the *Journal* of the Royal Society of Arts. We had lunch twice, a glass of champagne first, at the Waldorf Hotel where Lord Wyatt always had his hair cut, and met once for a drink, champagne again, at the RAC Club where he swam. The talk ranged from the politics of the day (mine are different from his), to South Africa, to his negotiations with his publishers, to P. G. Wodehouse. (Did I like Wodehouse? I felt that was a trick question.)

I had little opportunity to discuss with him any aspect of the journals, which I had only glimpsed. I signed the contract with Macmillan to edit the journals in October 1997, by which time he was gravely ill with cancer of the throat. I did not see him again but in the course of our brief, convivial conversations in 1994 he pinpointed the main problem for any editor: the length of the journals. He wrote on average 250,000 words a year. This volume covers over three years and over three-quarters of a million words. What the reader sees here is a third of what he wrote.

At a lunch party in April 1988, Sir Isaiah Berlin, the philosopher, says about the historian Macaulay, 'You can't fault him for accuracy.'

Wyatt replies, 'You can fault him for selection.' I have tried to the best of my ability to select for this volume what I think Woodrow Wyatt would have chosen, cutting the length but giving a correct balance of all he wrote. Only a few minor incidents or characters have been totally omitted.

It was comparatively easy to cut about a third of the manuscript. Repetition had to go. Wyatt recorded his entries several times a week, daily at times, and his secretary typed them up regularly. The importance of his journals lies partly in the fact that they are contemporaneous. We have the Benn, Crossman and Clark diaries recorded as events happened, but many political memoirs are written through the filter of time. Perhaps because he dictated the entries (though he dictated his newspaper articles, too), or perhaps because as a veteran of daily and weekly journalism he was used to explaining everything afresh to the reader, he often repeated conversations. The reader needs the complete story only once.

I have also cut entries which did little more than list those who were at race meetings or dinner parties. I have not elided paragraphs where there have been cuts, and have only on a few occasions deleted a word on its own, when it might be libellous or give unacceptable offence.

It is always difficult with a journal of this kind to decide what are the boundaries of taste and discretion. I have tried to be scrupulous in not bowdlerizing Wyatt who often gleefully epitomizes all that today is politically incorrect. He prefaced nearly all his remarks about women with an appraisal of their looks. This was his way and I hope that the subjects will remember that beauty is in the eye of the beholder. (For the record, when he met me in 1994 he recorded, 'She seems pleasant in appearance, with remnants of a type of prettiness which does not appeal to me.')

Some passages have been cut which would give lasting pain to people who are still alive. There are doubtless other passages which will cause irritation and embarrassment but to have excised them would have changed the nature of the journals and given a false impression of their author. His friends enjoyed his sallies about others and will doubtless take in good part what he says about them.

Journals by their nature often contain gossip which the writer believes at the time but others may not. One person may interpret a conversation at a dinner party differently from another. Woodrow

Wyatt gives his spontaneous responses to everything he sees and hears.

I most regret having to omit for reasons of space his accounts of little excursions he sometimes made to places he found beautiful and his descriptions of buildings (not always ones built by a member of the Wyatt family). It is a pity, too, that there cannot be a wine appendix. He noted down all the wines he was offered or gave. For the average reader it would be tedious to scan them all but for the aficionado it would be marvellous.

If he had lived, I would have asked him about the style he used for the journals. A true professional, he clearly adapted his style for the very different newspapers he wrote for (leaving aside the efforts of sub-editors). I am confident, however, that the ambling, discursive style he mainly uses here was intentional. He was presenting himself as a contemporary Pepys, with an easy flow of wit and observation.

One small but important point. WW, as I call him in the notes, read through the typescript most weeks, making in his small handwriting an occasional addition which I have included. He also corrected the odd literal but time and again names are spelt wrongly, with different spellings given in different sections. I have checked as far as possible every name but I apologize if any spelling is wrong.

Biographical details of some of the principal figures in the journals are given at the end of this volume on pp. 706–15. An asterisk at the end of a footnote refers the reader to the biographical notes the first time such a person is mentioned.

*

Some personal thanks. First, to Diana Rawstron who suggested me for this project and encouraged me throughout with her enthusiasm and sound judgement. Lady Wyatt, whom I met after Lord Wyatt's death and who has not at the time I write seen the manuscript, has been most helpful. Mrs Wendy Tamborero, Lord Wyatt's secretary from 1989 until his death, was most efficient and kind, finding newspaper cuttings and other information. Mr Geoffrey Webster, public relations director at the Tote for the years WW was chairman, answered many questions about racing. I could not have completed the editing of this volume in the short time since WW's death without the forbearance and support of my husband, Anthony Curtis. I should also like to thank my sons: Job for loan of political memoirs of the period, Charles for information about racing and business, and Quentin for books on politics and sport and for many helpful discussions about the editing process.

SARAH CURTIS

*June 1998*

# *Woodrow Wyatt*

Baron Wyatt of Weeford in the County of Staffordshire (knight 1983, life peer 1987) was born Woodrow Lyle Wyatt on 4 July 1918, son of Robert Harvey Lyle Wyatt (d 1932), founder and headmaster of Milbourne Lodge School, Esher, and Ethel, née Morgan (d 1974). He was descended from Humphrey Wyatt (d 1610), ancestor of the Wyatt architects, painters and sculptors.

Woodrow Wyatt was educated at Eastbourne College and Worcester College, Oxford, where he took a second in law.

He married 1 (1939–44) *Susan* Cox, an Oxford contemporary; 2 (1948–56) Nora (*Alix*) Robbins; 3 (1957–66) Lady *Moorea* Hastings, now Black (daughter of the 15th Earl of Huntingdon, *Jack*, (d 1990) and his first wife *Cristina* (d 1953), daughter of the Marchese Casati, Rome) by whom he had a son, *Pericles*, b 1963; 4 (in 1966) *Verushka*, née Racz, widow of Baron (Hungary) Dr Laszlo Banszky von Ambroz, by whom he had a daughter, *Petronella* (b 1968), and a stepson, *Nicholas* Banszky von Ambroz (b 1952), merchant banker, m (1984–95) *Caroline* née While (two daughters Genevra, b 1985, Antonella, b 1987).

Major *Robert* David Lyle, WW's older brother (d 1989), owned the family estate Bonython in Cornwall, his son and heir being WW's nephew *Robert* Lyle, b 1952, m (1991) the Hon. Tessa Mayhew.

After serving throughout the 1939–45 war (he was mentioned in dispatches in Normandy in 1944), during which time he founded and edited the magazine *English Story*, WW entered Parliament in 1945 as Labour MP for Aston, Birmingham. He was personal assistant to Sir Stafford Cripps on the Cabinet Mission to India to prepare for independence in 1946. He lost the Aston seat in 1955 through redistribution but was returned as MP for Bosworth (1959–70) and was Parliamentary Under-Secretary of State and Financial Secretary, War Office, from May 1951 until October 1951 when Labour lost power.

While still an MP he opposed his party on some issues, voting with Desmond Donnelly to hold up the nationalization of steel when Labour had a tiny majority, and once out of Parliament he moved further to the right. However, he never joined another party and when Mrs Thatcher made him a life peer in 1987 he sat on the crossbenches.

Throughout his career WW was an active journalist, on the *New Statesman* (1947–8), as a weekly columnist on *Reynolds News* (1949–61), the *Daily Mirror* (1965–73) and the *Sunday Mirror* (1973–83). He was under contract to BBC Television (1955–9) and a regular presenter of *Panorama* in the days of its early fame. It was through television as well as when an MP that he fought Communist domination of the unions, particularly the engineering union (AEU) and electricians' union (ETU). In the 1960s he owned a chain of Midlands newspapers and the Banbury Press, introducing non-heat-set web-offset colour printing to England in 1962. He was a member of the Council of the Zoological Society of London (1968–71, 1973–7).

In 1983 WW joined Rupert Murdoch's newspapers with a fortnightly column in the *Times*, book reviews and a weekly column called 'The Voice of Reason' (not his title) in the *News of the World*. He was chairman of the Horserace Totalisator Board (first appointed by Roy Jenkins when Home Secretary) from 1976 until 1997, the year of his death. He wrote for the *Times* until the close of May 1997 when his contract was ended; his last column for the *News of the World* was on 30 November 1997. By then he was ill with cancer of the throat. He died of a burst artery on 7 December 1997.

His books include the ten volumes of *English Story* he edited (1940–50); an edition of the short stories of O. Henry (1967); *What's Left of the Labour Party?* (1977); *To the Point* (1981), a collection of short *causerie* pieces; two children's books about Mr Saucy Squirrel (1976 and 1977); his autobiography *Confessions of an Optimist* (1985); a selection from *English Story* (*The Way We Lived Then*, 1989); and a play, *High Profiles* (1992).

*Names in italics are of people WW mentions in this volume.*

# 1985

**Saturday 19 October**

Some people have terrible manners. I thought Geoffrey Wheatcroft, now in charge of the Diary in the London *Standard* and an accomplished author,[1] was civilized when I met him previously. He arrived an hour and twenty minutes late for the lunch before the Tote Cesarewitch[2] at which there were fifty guests all seated at different tables according to a careful plan – there were so many that Verushka[3] had to sit on a stool.

He did not sit at his allotted place because he brought, uninvited and without warning, a woman who looked like a bedraggled, tired prostitute for whom there was no room. They stood at the drinks bar, he still wearing his hat and mackintosh. Isabel Derby,[4] sitting next to me, said, 'Who are those two dreadful people? Why doesn't he take his hat off? You ought to have them sent away.'

The woman turned out to be Germaine Greer.[5] He neither apologized for being late nor for bringing an uninvited guest.

Robert Sangster[6] brought his latest wife. The previous one, Susan, was a jolly talkative blonde girl with the agreeable openness of a barmaid. She would leap up to rush eagerly to get to the winners' enclosure to lead in any horse with a Sangster connection which won.

The new wife is another version of the same thing, with long blonde

---

1. His book *The Randlords: The Men Who Made South Africa* was published in 1985.
2. Race run annually in October at Newmarket, sponsored this year by the Tote of which WW had been chairman since 1976 – see Appendix on racing.
3. WW's fourth wife (m 1966), née Racz, widow of Baron Dr Laszlo Banszky von Ambroz.*
4. Countess of Derby (1920–90).*
5. Journalist and academic; author of *The Female Eunuch* (1969) and other books.
6. Chairman, Vernons Organisation, 1976–88, Sangster Group Ltd, 1988–91; leading winning racehorse owner 1977, 1978, 1982, 1983 and 1984 seasons.

hair, who sat next to Hugh Trevor-Roper (Lord Dacre)[7] who had Petronella[8] on the other side. I was told she was very dull and had nothing to say so Hugh Trevor-Roper spent nearly all the time telling Petronella Oxford jokes: 'The Lord God is everywhere. The Lord Briggs[9] is everywhere except Worcester' and 'Lord Briggs can't see a Concorde in the sky without thinking he ought to be on it.'

Night at Hatley Park with Jakie Astor[10] who is more or less over Susie's desertion which hit him hard. She was attractive and much younger, wanting to go to parties and dances which, even before he got Parkinson's disease, Jakie detested. Two or three years ago we sat in their kitchen while she listed her complaints, the chief of which was that Jakie always wanted to go home at 10.00 p.m. and to stay later than 11.00 was a rarity. He also wouldn't go to London often enough.

Jakie said he would try to do better but Verushka and I could see he wouldn't and that the end was approaching. Despite violent days hunting she felt more was needed for her to be fulfilled. She was ready to flirt with anyone including the highly intellectual Wynne Godley[11] when he came to dinner at Hatley Park one evening and who liked the look of her, as I did too, but he never did anything about it. She used to say 'Jakie always likes it when boredom is in the house.'

Jakie asked if we minded going to bed at 9.45 p.m. and was ready to go at 9.15. He was apologetic that we had to be at Victor Rothschild's[12] in Cambridge where we were all having lunch the next day by 12.00 because Princess Margaret was coming for drinks before lunch. However, there would still be time to play our annual game of croquet on Jakie's beautifully kept croquet lawn.

**Sunday 20 October**

Two rounds of croquet with Jakie giving me a shot a hoop but still winning. His Parkinson's disease is stabilized. It is a large, pretty Queen

---

7. Regius Professor of Modern History, Oxford University, 1957–80; Master, Peterhouse, Cambridge, 1980–7; life peer 1979 (Lord Dacre).*
8. Daughter of WW and Verushka (b 1968).*
9. Asa Briggs, historian; Provost, Worcester College, Oxford, 1976–91, life peer 1976.
10. The Hon. Sir John Jacob Astor, son of 2nd Viscount Astor, m 2 (1976–85) Susan, née Eveleigh.*
11. Professor the Hon. Wynne Godley, director, Department of Applied Economics, University of Cambridge, 1970–85.
12. 3rd Baron Rothschild (1910–90), scientist, m 2 Teresa (Tess) (1946).*

Anne Georgian house though I feel Jakie's loneliness as he walks through the empty rooms. Kind and thoughtful, a loyal friend with no bitterness, he deserved better. As Astors do, he generously endowed his errant wife.

We found Victor sitting gloomily in the hall wearing a strange pair of blue trousers looking like a shopkeeper waiting for customers. A good deal of cursing that it was all Tess's fault. She should have rejected Professor Plumb's[13] wish to include his house in Princess Margaret's Cambridge tour. He had been forced to put on a coat and tie which did not redeem the odd belt which failed to hold his trousers up accurately. 'You'll have to amuse her,' he told me grumpily.

Princess Margaret arrived with Roddy Llewellyn[14] and his wife, who seemed charming, and the Tennants (Glenconners).[15]

Colin Tennant said at dinner recently Claire Ward[16] had complained the whole evening that Tony Lambton[17] would not marry her and added that she thought he would in the end but I said he wouldn't, having always used his promise to Bindy never to divorce her to ward off the other women in his life.

I definitely did not amuse Princess Margaret. I explained to her my theory that the reason why Cambridge had spies and Oxford didn't was because Cambridge people were clever but isolated and unworldly, believing that what they thought was right took precedence over any worldly duty to their country. Oxford undergraduates are closer to London and country houses and are ambitious. It's a university of the metropolis and social life. No intellectual from Oxford would damage their career by treachery. Cambridge is a little country market town and once the train stops there you have nowhere to go on to. 'Not at all,' Princess Margaret said. 'It goes on to Sandringham.'

Despite the doctors Princess Margaret smoked steadily but looked

---

13. Professor Sir John Plumb, Professor of Modern English History, University of Cambridge, 1966–74; Master, Christ's College, Cambridge, 1978–82; knight 1982.
14. Designer, close friend of Princess Margaret, m 1981 Tatiana née Soskin.
15. Sir Colin Tennant, 3rd Baron Glenconner, m (1956) Lady Anne (Veronica), née Coke.
16. Claire Ward, née Baring, m (1956–74) the Hon. Peter Ward (son of the 3rd Earl of Dudley).*
17. Viscount Lambton, m (1942) Belinda (Bindy) née Blew-Jones; MP 1951–73; Parliamentary Under-Secretary of State, Ministry of Defence, 1970–3; he resigned from the Commons in 1973 after photographs of him with a prostitute were offered to the press.*

healthier than I had seen her for some time. She is still pretty with a lovely complexion. She can never reconcile herself to being number two and has always reached for something to lift her life to where she wouldn't mind. It was an impossible dream.

Because she has no inner repose I find her difficult to be with. Sometimes she is very gay and friendly, encouraging you to make jokes and treat her as though she were an ordinary human being. Then suddenly you may feel her psychologically draw herself up with the unspoken 'I am the sister of the Queen' which is instantly crushing. Yet though I am nervous of her, I like her and am sorry she has had so little happiness.

'You were a fat lot of help,' Victor said and he took off his coat and tie. We had a very good blanc de blancs for lunch. I chided Victor for preferring Evelyn[18] to his son Jacob[19] whom he calls Granite. It was not as simple as that, he said. Victor is Chairman of the holding company which owns N. M. Rothschild. When a split came between the two cousins he stayed at N. M. 'I have my living to earn.'

Shortly after the War when N. M. Rothschild was restructured Victor was still a Socialist and could have held the great majority of the shares but allowed nearly all of them to go to Evelyn's father because Victor thought otherwise he would have more money than a Socialist should. He thus deprived Jacob of his birthright.

When I first met Victor he told me he was disappointed in his son who had little brains. Later I knew Jacob. I found he not only had much of the financial flair of the original N. M. Rothschild but that he got a First at Oxford. Underneath Victor is very proud of Jacob but, as sometimes happens between father and son, they cannot make warm contact.

**Thursday 24 October**

Douglas Logan-Kalis came.

He is the wine steward at the restaurant where Pericles[20] works as a waiter. Every two months or so he finances a flight to London out of visiting Christie's and buying ancient bottles of first growth claret

18. Son of Anthony Gustav de Rothschild.*
19. Succeeded as 4th Lord Rothschild on Victor's death in 1990.*
20. Son of WW and his third wife (now Lady Moorea Black), b 1963, working in the US.*

for hundreds of pounds and carrying them back to America where he sells them for three times or more what he paid for them.

He was friendly and obviously fond of Pericles whose ability to attract numerous pretty girls he admired, while lamenting the lack of a similar ability in himself. Pericles seems happier and is going into the property business as a side line via the buying of derelict property, resurrecting it and then selling it on. At last he, at twenty-two, is beginning not to regard being a waiter as his final career.

**Monday 28 October**

Laurence Fitch came to lunch. He is the agent for my play *A Thoroughgoing Woman*. Peter Saunders,[21] who said he would put it into rehearsal next Monday if Diana Rigg would take the leading part, brought us together.

Peter Saunders, whose *Mousetrap* has been running for thirty-five years and has owned or owns other triumphant successes, is not keen to launch into new ventures at the age of seventy-three, as he has quite enough money coming in already. Diana Rigg, for whom I wrote the play, liked it, thought it was very funny and the characters marvellous but said it all depended on Michael Codron [impresario] whose judgement she accepts. He rejected it but Laurence Fitch, who is jolly and laughs a lot, believes in it.

When Bernard Levin[22] heard that I had written a play he demanded to see it. I had not shown it him before because I was afraid that he would say it was rubbish, as he would not hesitate to do if that was what he thought. I heard nothing for a week and then a familiar voice on the telephone began: 'Is that W. Wyatt masquerading as W. Shakespeare? . . . It's amazing that you should sit down at the age of sixty-seven and calmly write such a remarkable play.'

I wrote it between the 4th August and the 4th September in Italy. Laurence Fitch says I mustn't be too impatient. It sometimes takes two years to get a play put on.

---

21. Impresario, m 2 (1979) Catherine Baylis (Katie Boyle), actress and TV personality; knight 1982.
22. Journalist, critic and author.

**Tuesday 29 October**

Went with 'Monkey' Blacker[23] to see the new Home Secretary Douglas Hurd. He was more sympathetic than I expected and agreed that before Sunday racing could happen the 1780 Lord's Day Observance Act would have to be repealed.

I put it to him that the racing industry is public spirited. It did not, as all other major sports do without interference from the police, put on its events on Sunday because we know that if betting were not allowed officially it would take place illegally on the course or off the course. So we were being discriminated against by the law not allowing betting shops to be open on a Sunday or to allow betting on the racecourse, though betting by credit for those rich enough to have credit accounts and telephones would be legal.

It will be a long haul. He recommended us to make a commotion when our Working Party report was ready and try to get public steam behind the idea which in turn would affect MPs.

**Thursday 31 October**

Verushka was a great success at the 10 Downing Street dinner given in honour of Kádár[24] and his Hungarian entourage. 'This is the lady who told me what to expect when I went to Hungary,' Margaret[25] told him.

It was strange for Verushka meeting the people at No 10 who had imprisoned several of her family and dispossessed them of their property. She sat next to a Hungarian General who told her that he was equivalent to the head of what would be the Household Brigade in England but it transpired that he was actually head of the Secret Police.

Tom Stoppard[26] was there, with his wife Miriam, presumably because the state of English ignorance is such that someone at No 10 thought that a Czech would get on well with Hungarians whereas they hate each other, the Hungarians despising the Czechs as miserable cowards. I told him about my play and that it had gone to Michael

---

23. General Sir Cecil Blacker, deputy senior steward of the Jockey Club, then heading the Jockey Club working party on Sunday racing; WW is in his capacity of Chairman of the Tote.
24. János Kádár, Hungarian General Secretary, 1956–88.
25. Margaret Thatcher, Prime Minister, 1979–90.
26. Playwright, m 2 (1972–92) Dr Miriam Moore-Robinson, née Stern, medical journalist.

Codron. 'I'll tell him to read it seriously,' he said. I wished I hadn't mentioned it, fearing that his incredulity that I should suddenly write a play which might be good would impart itself to Mr Codron.

Mrs Thatcher made an excellent speech and looked beautiful. I wish she could be seen like that on television where she often doesn't convey her real warm self as she is too keen to get the impression right. Kádár made a too long typically Central European speech of which a printed translation was provided, not making me think I would have enjoyed the speech any more if I had understood Hungarian.

Kádár is the man who said, 'He who is not against me is with me,' standing Jesus Christ on his head but the Hungarians have understood that he has got the best terms obtainable from the Russians for a tolerable existence, despite occupation by Russian divisions which one of the Hungarians I spoke to tried feebly to play down as being merely the same as British occupation by American air bases.

Kádár once out of favour was imprisoned by brother Communists and was reputed to have had his finger nails pulled out. I looked at his hands for evidence but never caught sight of his finger nails.

**Monday 4 November**

Sat next to Sir John Greenborough[1] at one of Edwin McAlpine's[2] monthly lunches. He ran Shell and must know more about oil than most. No cause for alarm, he thought, about North Sea oil. New fields could and would be developed but more expensive than the earlier ones, requiring the government to allow the oil producers to keep more of the profits if they are to have the incentive to continue producing. He thought we would be all right for at least twenty years.

Michael Havers,[3] recovering from a heart bypass operation which he told me was bigger than Robin Day's,[4] had said he would not say anything. However, his normal loquacity and indiscretion overcame him and he explained to the lunch party [about] the nine airmen involved in the Cyprus secrets trial.

'On the conclusive evidence we were bound to prosecute the aircraftmen. The difficulty is getting a jury willing to convict on the facts in Official Secrets cases.'[5]

Edwin McAlpine said he had liked my book[6] so much he'd bought ten copies to give away. Very pleasing.

---

1. (1922–98); deputy chairman, Shell UK, 1976–80; deputy chairman, Bowater Industries, 1984–7 knight 1979.
2. (1907–90); partner, Sir Robert McAlpine, from 1928; chairman, Greycoat London Estates, from 1978; racehorse breeder, member of the Jockey Club, life peer 1980.
3. (1923–92); Conservative politician; Solicitor General, 1972–4; Attorney General, 1979–87; Lord Chancellor, July–Oct. 1987; life peer 1987.
4. Television and radio journalist; knight 1981.
5. During 1984–5, when Michael Havers was Attorney General, nine British servicemen stationed at communications units in Cyprus were acquitted of alleged offences under the 1911 and 1920 Official Secrets Acts. The Interception of Communications Act was passed in July 1985 to clarify the law in this area.
6. *Confessions of an Optimist* published by Collins (1985, paperback 1987).

**Wednesday 6 November**

Dinner at Alastair Horne's.[7] On my left his pretty girlfriend whom he hopes to marry, previously daughter-in-law of smartie-boots Eccles,[8] famous for congratulating the Queen on being such a good leading lady in the arrangements he made for her coronation, the success of which he mainly attributed to himself.

Somehow I was involved talking longer than I should with the divorced wife of Rodney Elton[9] whose father was a distinguished historian and a Labour peer. She is very County and a substantial land owner.

Boredom seemed to be the cause of the end of the twenty-one year marriage in 1979.

She is what Jung would call an *anima* woman whose men can rarely survive the realization that they are not the heroes they were constructed as in her imagination.

**Friday 8 November**

Reginald Bennett, former Tory MP and keen drinker, and Dr Hugh Sinclair came to lunch.

Hugh some twenty-two years ago told me the best diet to eat to avoid lung or any other form of cancer, coronaries, strokes and other rampant killers. Saturated fats as in butter, full milk and cream, lard, lamb and sugar are out as far as possible. All game, fish, chicken if free range, vegetables, even pork if it is from free range pigs, polyunsaturated fats from the appropriate margarines and oil like sunflower or soya oil are in. I have done my best and am still alive, aided also by at least eight grams of ascorbic acid (vitamin C) a day and for the last three years a daily packet of 'Hiptolec' containing six grams of enriched lecithin which I hope will arrest the senility which afflicted my mother in her last years after she was seventy-five.

Hugh Sinclair runs the International Nutrition Foundation at his house near Oxford. He wants £2 million to build a laboratory and he

7. Historian and biographer, m 2 (1987) Sheelin Ryan Eccles.
8. Viscount Eccles (created 1964), Conservative politician; he was Minister of Works at the time of the Coronation.
9. 2nd Baron Elton, Conservative minister 1979–86, m (1958–79) Anne Frances, née Tilney; his father was a Fellow of The Queen's College, Oxford, and biographer of Ramsay MacDonald.

hopes I can set him on the way to it with somebody like Lord Forte[10] or Lord Wolfson[11] who would be allowed to give their name to the laboratory.

Hugh maintains that those who eat the right food could probably inhale cigarettes all day but never get lung cancer because the cell walls of their lungs would have been made with the right fats and would withstand any attack, in place of being made with saturated fats which collapse at the first onslaught.

**Tuesday 12 November**

Lunch at George Weidenfeld's[12] for Mrs Kirkpatrick, the US Ambassador at the United Nations who was against us over the Falklands.[13] She arrived an hour and ten minutes late and we had already got to our second course. She was not as waspish as I expected. She spoke at length to the fifty or so guests and answered questions. Like most Americans in public life she found it difficult to say anything briefly or with elegance. She gave her banal view that at the Geneva Summit Gorbachev[14] would test the ground to see how far Russia could go without disturbing the possibly better relations with Reagan.[15]

**Wednesday 13 November**

A proper dinner at George Weidenfeld's. The food, as usual, execrable and the wine the same. Most of his life George drank no alcohol, though lately he drinks brandy but still knows nothing about wine. The dinner was for Kurt Waldheim, one-time Secretary General of the United Nations.[16]

At the end of it George tinkled on his glass and made a little speech welcoming him, saying they had been educated together before George left Vienna and that this was the fortieth anniversary of his starting his publishing firm. Kurt Waldheim responded with a rambling

---

10. Charles Forte, chairman, Trusthouse Forte; life peer 1982.*
11. Leonard Wolfson, son of Sir Isaac Wolfson, chairman, Great Universal Stores; chairman and founder trustee, Wolfson Foundation; life peer 1985.*
12. Publisher; life peer 1976.*
13. The war to recover the Falkland Islands after the Argentine invasion, 1982.
14. Mikhail Gorbachev, Soviet President, 1985–91.
15. Ronald Reagan, US President 1981–9.
16. UN Secretary General, 1972–81; President of Austria, 1986–92; allegations had been made about his wartime activities.

onwards and upwards speech describing himself as having been in the eye of the storm and full of amiable hope for the future despite having watched and been unable to stop many disasters.

Immediately after he finished Shirley Maclaine,[17] who used to be very pretty and was enchanting as an actress in her earlier films, got up. No one had asked her to but she is one of those tiresome ladies, the worst editions of whom are in America, who think that they know how to put the world right on flimsy foundations of ill-digested and inaccurate information.

She told us, though nobody cared, that she had been much encouraged by Kurt Waldheim's optimism considering that he had been a close observer of dangerous situations. It did not occur to her how boring she was being; an actress should be more sensitive.

**Monday 18 November**

Ian Chapman,[18] Chairman of Collins, to lunch. We agreed that I would drop the racing book which I feared would not be sufficiently original and would not repay the work already gone into it nor the considerable work before completion. I offered to return the £12,000 advance but he was not keen. Instead he is pushing the idea of a book of the history of the press brought up to date for which he thought we might get a bit more in serial rights in the *Sunday Times*. He will speak to Rupert[19] about it. I am writing an article for the *Times* this week on the current commotion in Fleet Street.[20]

**Thursday 21 November**

Queen Elizabeth the Queen Mother came to dinner. José, our Portuguese butler for eighteen years, returned to help with another Portuguese who comes when extra staff are needed, Stephan.

José at once wanted to take over the decanting of the 1940 Château

17. American film actress and Democrat Party activist.
18. Ian Chapman Senior, chairman and group chief executive, William Collins 1981–9; chairman, Harvill Press, 1976–89, Hatchards, 1976–89; co-chairman and acting chief executive, Harper & Row NY 1987–9; subsequently chairman and managing director, Chapmans Publishers, 1989–94, deputy chairman, Orion Publishing Group, 1993–4.
19. Rupert Murdoch, newspaper proprietor.*
20. 'How the press could prosper', 23 November 1985, about the introduction of modern electronic technology with direct input of copy by journalists, eliminating the expensive process of typesetting and the jobs which went with it.

Latour but as Flavio, the present butler, would have been put out, I wouldn't let him but continued to do it with Flavio, though José was put in charge of serving the wines throughout the dinner. 1940 Château Latour was in strange white and green bottles with makeshift capsules. Hitler's army was occupying France while it was growing and being made so Château Latour could not get their usual bottles, capsules and corks.

One of the labels had slipped off when I gave some to Roy Jenkins[21] when he came to lunch at Conock[22] in the late seventies. It led him to believe that it was a very young wine not of the first growth but 'It must be good or you wouldn't have given it me.' He mused that nothing so grand as first growth would have been in such peculiar bottles. It gets better every time I try it.

Queen Elizabeth had never drunk Tokay until I gave it her here before. We spoke then of an 1889 Tokay which I told her, as she drank a 1964 Tokay Eszencia, 'I was reserving for a special occasion,' then realizing what I had said added hastily, 'but of course this is a special occasion.' She agreed so it was brought up from the cellar and she enjoyed it considerably.[23]

Quite the best I could find tonight was a 1957 Tokay Eszencia. With the first course we had a Premier Cru Chablis 1958. Queen Elizabeth always begins with a dry Martini which I make and which she always says is too strong and we add more ice. It was the same again this evening. The port was Cockburn's 1960 and very good. Before dinner there was either 1979 Bollinger or Perrier-Jouët 1953 for those who prefer older champagne.

Mrs Jeffrey Archer[24] arrived only a few seconds before Queen Elizabeth after an accident as she drove from Cambridge. Queen Elizabeth, as ever, arrived on the dot at 8.15. As we came up the steps together she said, 'I love this house. It is so welcoming and warm.' Both the front doors were open and it did look far more imposing than it is.

---

21. Politician and historian, life peer 1987.*
22. WW's former country house in Wiltshire.
23. Tokay comes from a small district in Hungary about thirty miles from the Russian border. Michael Broadbent in *The Great Vintage Wine Book* (Mitchell Beazley, 1980) says the 1889 Eszencia is not unlike an old oloroso sherry: 'sweet, fairly full bodied, wonderfully rich flavour with excellent acidity . . .'
24. Mary Archer, scientist, m (1966) Jeffrey Archer (Conservative politician and best-selling novelist); Fellow, Newnham College, Cambridge 1976–86.*

The morning had begun with a disaster. Isaiah Berlin[25] was struck speechless and his wife crippled with sciatica. That was about 9.10 a.m. Marcelle Quinton[26] nobly cancelled her arrangements and with Tony prepared to fill the gap. I try to arrange that at these dinners no one should have been before to give Queen Elizabeth new people to meet but Tony Quinton had scored brightly with Queen Elizabeth on an earlier occasion and it was an emergency. She likes clever men who make jokes. All intellectuals with any spirit fall in love with her immediately, prisoners to her charm and held by her intelligence and a knowledge of books which they had not expected.

I asked her to explain why she had once told me she was not as nice as I think she is. I think she had meant that she could sometimes be unkind in her mind and a little malicious in a harmless way. But this time she said it was because she was lazy. A surprising verdict. She felt she wasted too much time frivolously instead of spending it purposefully. It's the old Victorian ethic which makes you feel guilty if you're not filling Kipling's 'unforgiving minute' with something constructive or self-improving. It is that spirit over the shoulder always ready to condemn any deviation from duty which has kept her honouring engagements, writing letters, touring, etc.

Tony Quinton on her left talked about P. G. Wodehouse whom she loves and made jolly jokes. I talked to her about Barbara Pym[27] and *A Very Private Eye* which I promised to send her. She laughed to hear that Jay, an early Barbara Pym lover, is Julian Amery.[28] I told her that C. Gordon Glover, the great love of Barbara Pym's life, was married to my cousin Honor and that my brother and I as children used to hide giggling behind the sofa in the drawing-room on a Sunday afternoon when they were canoodling.

She said again that it was quite untrue that she ever hated Mrs Simpson or that she had anything to do with her not being called 'Her Royal Highness'. 'Of course I was upset at the time but I would never demean myself to hate her. I don't think I've ever hated anyone.' She

---

25. Sir Isaiah Berlin OM (1909–97), philosopher.
26. Sculptor, m (1952) Anthony (Tony) Quinton (President, Trinity College, Oxford, 1978–87; chairman, British Library, 1985–90, life peer 1982).*
27. Novelist (1913–80). *A Very Private Eye: an autobiography in letters and diaries* edited by Hazel Holt and Hilary Pym was published in 1984.
28. (1919–96); Conservative politician; m (1950) Catherine Macmillan (d. 1991), daughter of Harold Macmillan (Prime Minister, 1957–63, 1st Earl of Stockton).*

was clearly very fond of the Duke of Windsor and detested the way he was portrayed as a silly ass in the television series by Edward Fox because he was intelligent and hard-working and not at all a playboy. It was just unfortunate that he fell in love with Mrs Simpson.

I complimented her on her necklace. 'Your wife has a very beautiful one,' she said. 'But hers isn't real,' I replied. She said no one says such lovely things to her as I do but I said that couldn't be possible; everyone must always have done.

She stayed until 12.00 a.m. looking as lively at the end as she had at 8.15 p.m. Verushka organized the alternating guests to talk to her beautifully. Jeffrey Archer, who had to arrive after dinner because of a speech he had been making at Croydon, said proudly to me as he left, 'I had half an hour with her. It was a great experience.' I had told her that he was like Arnold Bennett's Card.[29]

**Saturday 23 November**

At Newbury [racecourse] I went to the Directors' Box for some tea and found Queen Elizabeth there. She was full of talk about the dinner. 'All those intellectuals are so tall.' 'They have the best food in London,' she was telling the others.

'Have you been there?' she said to Priscilla Hastings,[30] who is on the Tote Board. 'No, Ma'am, I haven't had that honour.' Queen Elizabeth held her racecard up to her face and giggled. 'Oh dear, what have I said?' She said she woke up feeling very well though she had drunk quite a bit of Tokay. As the Tsars found, it is a royal health drink.

Dinner at Asa Briggs' at Worcester. It turned out to be their thirtieth wedding anniversary. I sat next to Simone Warner[31] and promised to send *The Way of All Women* by Esther Harding.[32] She'd never recovered from having two or three affairs when she was eighteen and hearing that people talked about her. She needs the book to get her balance back.

Asa said, 'I want to get your archives into the college.' 'At the

---

29. The eponymous hero of Arnold Bennett's 1911 novel.
30. A director of Newbury Race Course; widow of Captain Peter Hastings-Bass, mother of the 16th Earl of Huntingdon.
31. Née Nangle; m (1971) Sir Fred Warner, diplomat; formerly married to Basil de Ferranti MEP.
32. *The Way of All Women: a psychological interpretation*, published in 1933, introduction by Jung with whom Esther Harding studied and worked.

moment,' I replied, 'I'm keener on getting Petronella into the college.' He took the hint and said that he was doing his best and he hoped Harry Pitt (in charge of History) would do the same. 'We all want her here.' Patronage is not so easy as it was.

**Monday 25 November**

Memorial Service for Charlie Douglas-Home[33] at St Paul's. I decided that if there was a memorial service for me[34] I should like to have sung the Toreador's song, written as for the all black modern version *Carmen Jones*,[35]

> Stand up and fight until you hear the bell,
> Stand toe to toe, trade blow for blow,
> Keep punching till you make your punches tell,
> Show that crowd what you know,
> Until you hear that bell, that final bell,
> Stand up and fight – like hell!

and have read the parable of the talents (St Matthew 25) and the whole of the last chapter of Ecclesiastes including 'Vanity of vanities saith the preacher, all is vanity' (it must be in the Authorized version). For another hymn the 'Battle Hymn of the Republic'[36] would be nice and 'Onward Christian Soldiers'. And they must play 'Dear Little Buttercup' from *HMS Pinafore*.[37]

I speculated once more on the absurdity of believing in an after-life which most of the congregation gave every sign of doing. I wish I could

33. (1937–85); Editor, the *Times*, 1982–5.
34. WW's memorial service was held at St Margaret's, Westminster, on 1 April 1998. Before the service the organist played music from operettas by Arthur Sullivan; Petronella Wyatt read Ecclesiastes 12:1–7 and Rupert Murdoch the parable of the talents (Matthew 25:14–30 – 'For unto everyone that hath shall be given, and he shall have abundance: but from him that hath not shall be taken away even that which he hath'. 'Stand up and fight' was sung by Blair Wilson. Lord Runcie, formerly Archbishop of Canterbury, led the prayers and Lord (Roy) Jenkins gave the address. The final hymn was the 'Battle Hymn of the Republic'. See also 4 December 1986 and 29 October 1987.
35. Oscar Hammerstein's 1943 version of Bizet's opera *Carmen*.
36. By Julia Ward Howe (1819–1910), popular among Union partisans in the US Civil War, sung to the tune of 'John Brown's Body'.
37. Gilbert and Sullivan's 1878 opera; Buttercup was a pet name for Verushka.

say to a Pope or an Archbishop after he was dead, 'There you are. There's nothing. You've wasted your whole life on an illusion.'

Prince Charles read the lesson in a clear voice and then added an unannounced passage, saying, 'It meant a lot to Charlie.'

**Tuesday 26 November**

Dinner at Olga Polizzi's.[38] She says she's now put Norman Lamont[39] out of her mind. After he got his black eye from Richard Connolly, we had lunch and Lamont came to see me several times for advice on what to do.[40]

I told him he should concentrate on his career. He'd been lucky not to be removed at the last government reshuffle and if he kept out of the gossip columns for a couple of years he might well get promotion.

Annunziata[41] was there, who I had not seen for several years. She is a beautiful girl, now thirty-seven, who has never found anyone worthy of marrying although she had many admirers. Her first love when she was at Oxford was Randall Crawley[42] and Virginia was very worried that they might get married absurdly young. But it wore out and Virginia and Aidan more or less treated her as one of the family thereafter, with her in partnership with their children in their antique and art objects international business.

She said she didn't respond to flattery about her looks and liked to be made to laugh. I said, 'That's just as well since you're so ugly.' She sat next to me at the buffet dinner and I promised her, too, that I would send her a copy of *The Way of All Women*. Like many women open to receive men's *anima* she is not sure who she is.

---

38. Née Forte.*
39. Conservative politician, at this time Minister of State, Department of Trade and Industry (DTI).*
40. An article by Simon Freeman in the *Sunday Times* of 14 July 1985 quoted Nigel Dempster of the *Daily Mail* as saying that Richard Connolly, art dealer friend of Lady Olga Polizzi, told the *Mail* 'how he had been dining with Polizzi on Wednesday, how she had gone home early to her house in Bayswater, how he had returned later to find Lamont there, how he had chased the minister and how he had thumped him. But the background to this remained vague.'
41. Lady Annunziata Asquith, writer and journalist, daughter of the 2nd Earl of Oxford and Asquith, granddaughter of Raymond Asquith and Katharine, née Horner.
42. Son of Aidan Crawley (1908–93), journalist, and his wife Virginia, née Cowles (d 1983).*

**Wednesday 27 November**

Lunch at Hambros Bank with Chips Keswick[43] who arranged it for me to meet Michael White, the theatrical impresario. He had not read my play but promised to ring me on Monday after he had. He seems interested.

He had just got himself a new wife[44] and described a visit to her awful northern businessmen parents and their dreadful house at Formby in Lancashire. It turned out that she was one of the Littlewood family, enormously rich from the pools business, so it may not keep him hungry enough to want to try my play. He had been in Los Angeles making a film in which he acted and for which he was paid more, he said, than he got from producing plays.

Petronella's second day of her Oxford exam. She wrote nine pages on her current hero, Peel, finished a question on the causes of the First World War and had no time to do more than a short piece for the third question she chose on Napoleon III, another favourite. She's been taut with anxiety for weeks.

Worcester has become too egalitarian. Asa Briggs and Harry Pitt both say they can't get her a place unless she beats the competition.

Petronella, relaxed from moodiness with her examination completed, happily came to Christie's with me for an evening tasting of old Tokay in which she has some experience. We sampled every one of twenty bottles and one of them twice and left bids for a Muskotaly 1963 and 1958 which I had not tasted before.

Bron Waugh[45] was there and did the usual 'Haven't seen you since you were so high', putting his palm to the ground to Petronella. When I said we were only interested in Tokay because of Verushka, and Petronella being half Hungarian, he said, 'But I remember you drinking it long before you were married to Verushka.'

When we got back Verushka, who always resents anybody amusing themselves if she is not there, used one of her favourite phrases, 'There is a punishment on you'. The punishment was that a call had come from 10 Downing Street, which wasn't a punishment at all.

When the Prime Minister heard I was not there she asked to be put

---

43. John Chippendale Lindley Keswick, chairman, Hambros Bank, since 1986, knight 1993.
44. Louise, née Moores; her father, Nigel Moores, died in 1977.
45. Auberon Waugh, novelist, journalist and wine connoisseur; son of the novelist Evelyn Waugh.

through to Lady Wyatt. 'I've rung to find out if there's anything wrong. Woodrow always rings me on a Sunday and he didn't this Sunday. Is there something wrong? He looked thin when I saw him last.'

(This has happened before when I haven't rung her at least once in the week. I don't always if I have nothing original to say. When I explained that previously she said, 'Never mind. I like you to ring me for a chat.' Caroline Ryder[46] told me that I am the only person in the country who regularly rings her and is put through at once. In response to my disbelief she said, 'Work it out. How on earth would she have time to speak to other people the way she does to you?')

Margaret is all woman. So is Verushka. After she had enquired whether Verushka's eyes were now all right Verushka told her that she had fallen off a ladder (untruthfully because it was off the back of a sofa when trying to shut the french windows, which had blown open in her bedroom, without stepping on the burglar alarm pads beneath the windows) and was going to the physiotherapist daily for her painful shoulder. 'You must have it x-rayed at once.' In Verushka's judgement this means that she and the Prime Minister think I don't pamper her enough.

**Thursday 28 November**

A dinner party at Cavendish Avenue.[47] Sir Peter and Lady Saunders (Katie Boyle, once famous on television as presenter of the Eurovision Song Contest), Bruce Matthews (Managing Director of News International),[48] Bernard Levin, Caroline Searby (wife of Richard Searby, Chairman of News Corporation[49]) and Petronella. Château Latour 1965 on the theory that Château Latour never put out a bad wine for fear of damaging their reputation so it would be good even in a poor year and it was.

Bruce Matthews thought Eddie Shah[50] knew too little about news-

46. Mrs Thatcher's political secretary.
47. No. 19; WW's house in St John's Wood, London, where he lived from 1970.
48. 1926–96.
49. Chairman, News Corporation Ltd, Australia, since 1981, News Ltd, since 1981, *South China Morning Post*, since 1987.
50. After the victory of his free-newspaper group over the NGA at Warrington in 1983, allowing the direct input of copy by journalists, Shah was planning a new national daily newspaper without union labour. *Today* was launched in March 1986, taken over by Lonrho in 1987 and then by News International, as will be seen.

papers to make a success of the daily he is launching next March. News International's own projected *London Post* seems to be a serious venture and will be a twenty-four hour newspaper.[51]

Peter asked for reassurance that Mrs Thatcher would win the next election. I gave it him.

**Saturday 30 November**

Went to the 5.00 p.m. performance of *The Dragon's Tail* in which Penelope Keith acted the principal part. Her part was too long and she was talking nearly all the time. However, she did it well and made almost bearable a pathetic play.

I decided to write her a letter congratulating her on her performance in making so much out of so little and commending to her my play which they have now had for two weeks, as providing a much better part for her with better supporting characters and rather better jokes as well as a plot.

---

51. It was never launched; see 19 January 1986.

**Sunday 1 December**
Rang Margaret.

She was put out by the Church's report on the Inner Cities[1] but I told her not to bother as it was clearly a somewhat left-wing stereotyped committee that had composed it and it was bound to contain nothing of value but would automatically blame the government.

'They seem to be more interested in Mammon than in God,' I said. 'They think you can just solve everything by chucking money at it.' 'Yes,' she said. 'There's nothing about self-help or doing anything for yourself in the report.'

I told her that her interview two Sundays ago with Brian Walden[2] was one of the best I had seen her do, though he laboured the question whether she really cared about the unemployed rather too heavily. I said she looked much more at ease with herself without the little bit of tension she sometimes has, wondering whether she is going to be able to deal with the questions all right. She is a great perfectionist. I also told her that she looked pretty. 'Not bad for sixty,' she replied.

One of the reasons why I hadn't rung her the previous week was that I tend not to ring her so much when things are going well. It's when I feel that she is a bit down because of attacks on her that I ring her more to cheer her up. She is more vulnerable than the world at large thinks. She has to steel herself to many tough decisions and it is difficult to do that without seeming tough which underneath she is not.

She was just working on the papers for her Luxembourg meeting with the Common Market leaders the next day. She never stops work but that is her oxygen.

I once more urged on her that she should try to make the privatization of gas much more competitive within itself than British Telecom has been. There is a danger that privatization of big monopolies will be seen as substituting one unresponsible monopoly for another.

---

1. Church of England report, *Faith in the Cities*, on urban deprivation.
2. Former Labour MP, television journalist and presenter, ITV's *Weekend World*.

As ever, she enquired about Verushka's eyes and was disturbed about her fall from the sofa. 'You must make sure she has it x-rayed.'

**Monday 2 December**

In the evening I went to see John Willoughby[3] with a bottle of Irish whiskey, a bottle of champagne and a bottle of Chilean red wine. His wife Rachel was one of the most beautiful women in London. Aly Khan once said she had the prettiest breasts he'd ever seen. I understand he saw them quite often.

John is the oldest surviving member of the Jockey Club. He is now vague in his memory even from one part of the conversation to another. He sits in his little room in a nursing home near Notting Hill Gate watching television and gazing at the *Daily Telegraph*. He left the television on with *Crossroads* which he couldn't understand and said he'd never seen before.

He was a wild gambler on horses. Now the money is fairly tight, otherwise Rachel would have him at home where he needs twenty-four hour attention being, poor soul, incontinent. He said that Rachel had told him the lights in Regent Street were quite good this year but he had been too lazy to get up and see them which showed some misunderstanding as to his position, as he certainly would not be able to get up to see anything.

He asked me several times if I would like a drink and I said no and finally I said yes. He said he would like some of the Irish whiskey so I asked the nurse for it. She came back and said, 'Lord Willoughby, you can't have any whiskey. You've only just had your tablets. They don't go together.' 'I insist on having my whiskey.' I had to say, 'John, you mustn't insist on it. It simply wouldn't do you any good. Have it tomorrow.' So he subsided.

It is a decent nursing home and they are clearly fond of him but it is a sad ending for a lively life full of fun.

**Tuesday 3 December**

Atlantic Richfield dinner at Claridge's given by Bob Anderson.[4] Having bought the *Observer* and found it not profitable, he sold it to Tiny

---

3. Lord Willoughby de Broke, 20th Baron (1896–1986).
4. Chairman, Atlantic Richfield, an American citizen.

Rowland,[5] keeping a small stake in it. For him the *Observer* was a social power base in Britain.

Kenneth Harris[6] works closely with him and organizes the dinners for him. The invitations go out so many months ahead that few can think of any adequate reason for refusing. As I left he told me that December 4th was the date of next year's dinner, would I be sure to be there.

In my case I would not like to hurt Kenneth Harris' feelings. I've been fond of him for years and he is a great flatterer. He told me *Confessions of an Optimist* is a classic and he bought twelve copies of it.

That night I learned from him that when the chairmanship of the *Observer* was being decided on some years ago it was offered to Roy Jenkins who could not take it because he was President of the EEC Commission at the time. Roy suggested that I should be asked and the others agreed but Arnold Goodman[7] vetoed it because he thought I was too pro Arab which is strange as I have always been rather more pro Israeli.

The gathering was large, containing the well-known in politics, business and journalism. We were subjected to a boring speech from Bob Anderson who told us that he'd invested £100 million in Britain recently and would invest more and how much he admired the British. He also greatly enjoyed proposing the health of the Queen at unusual length.

Willie Whitelaw[8] spoke in his amicable waffling way telling us that he was very pleased to thank Mr Bob Anderson for his hospitality as anyone could see from his (Willie's) appearance how much he enjoyed eating and drinking. This must be the fourth time I have heard him make this joke at different occasions.

Interview at Cavendish Avenue for the Queen Mother's obituary on

---

5. (1917–98); chairman, Lonrho Group.
6. Journalist and writer; director, the *Observer*, since 1978.
7. (1913–95); solicitor, Master of University College, Oxford, 1974–86, chairman, Observer Editorial Trust, 1967–76; life peer 1965.*
8. Viscount Whitelaw (created 1983), Conservative politician, at this time Conservative Leader, House of Lords; Lord President of the Council and Leader House of Commons, 1970–2; Secretary of State for Northern Ireland, 1972–3; Secretary of State for Employment, 1973–4; Home Secretary, 1979–83; m (1943) Cecilia, née Sprot.

TV AM in the same room she had recently sat in and I wondered whether I would ever see the obituary as she seems likely to outlive me.[9] When I was asked how I would remember her I said as someone I had loved as much as anybody I had ever loved.

**Thursday 5 December**

Spoke to Arnold Weinstock[10] about his bid to take over Plessey. 'They can't say any more that you're not using your cash mountain or not trying to do for electronics what you did for electrical equipment.'

Suddenly the gloom with which he often surrounds himself had gone with the excitement of great things beginning.

He wants me to speak to Mrs T to make sure the government won't oppose the merger. He read me his entire speech in the House of Lords debate on Tuesday. It was a mixture of wanting fierce competition, cohabiting with a government determination to buy British equipment from him rather than foreign, even though it may be cheaper.

Dinner at Leonard Wolfson's. First time I had seen Clarissa Avon[11] since my book was published and was nervous about her reaction to my unflattering comments on Anthony over Suez. She said she'd enjoyed the book and didn't mind what I had said about Anthony.

Arnold Goodman was there and once again asked me when we were going to have dinner with him at University College, Oxford, which he will be leaving soon, and once again I said 'When you ask us.' He too had liked my book though he was more tolerant of George Wigg[12] than I am and was in the book.

Ruth Wolfson said she was producing again the Mouton Rothschild 1970 which five years earlier I had told her was too young to drink when she gave it me. She was proud of having decanted it carefully back into the original bottles, as I had instructed her, at about five o'clock that evening but that was too early. It was very good but still too young, having some years to go before it reaches it best.

---

9. WW was right. He died aged seventy-nine on 7 December 1997 when the Queen Mother was ninety-seven years old.
10. Managing director, GEC 1963–96; racehorse owner, member of the Jockey Club, life peer 1980.*
11. Widow of 1st Earl of Avon (Sir Anthony Eden, Prime Minister, 1951–5) and niece of Sir Winston Churchill.*
12. (1900–83); Labour politician, Paymaster-General, 1964–7; member, Tote Board, 1961–4; chairman, Horserace Betting Levy Board, 1967–72; life peer 1967.

**Saturday 7 December**

Went down Jermyn Street looking for some handkerchiefs. All were foreign made. If we cannot even sell handkerchiefs made in Britain unemployment is not surprising.

Lunch with Harold Lever.[13] Ed Streator, once Minister at the American Embassy in London and now US Ambassador to the OECD, told me how much he had enjoyed my book but was apologetic at not having bought a copy. He'd been lent it by Peter Carrington[14] with a high recommendation.

Harold Lever dominated the conversation with his theories on exchange rates, interest rates, international loans and their need to have a fixed currency rate for each country and the desirability of our joining the European Monetary organization. He was boring on the topic and the ladies had to listen. He is an old friend so must be forgiven for these monologues and conviction that he knows more than anybody, though some who are knowledgeable doubt it.

Dinner with Irwin Stelzer[15] and his wife Cita. He had some excellent 1971 Château Mouton Rothschild which he had not decanted and perhaps did not taste as well as it would have done if it had been looked after better. People who buy very expensive wines often think that is sufficient in itself but it is the way the wines are laid down and the length they are laid for without disturbance and the even temperature in which they should be kept and the decanting of them at the appropriate time before drinking which prevents them being not as good as they should be.

Cita is a discriminating addict of books, museums, pictures. She was delighted when I read her Stephen Pile's introduction to *Secret Lives*[16] which I had given her. They are Americans who prefer England to live in to their own country. Other Americans were there who felt the same but what they really like is that people here are not so

---

13. (1914–95); Labour politician; Financial Secretary to the Treasury, 1967–9, Paymaster General, 1969–70; Chancellor of the Duchy of Lancaster, 1974–9; life peer 1979.*
14. 6th Baron Carrington, Conservative politician; Foreign Secretary, 1979–82; Secretary General, NATO, 1984–8; chairman, GEC, 1983–4; director, *Daily Telegraph* 1990– .
15. American-born economist and journalist; *Sunday Times* columnist.*
16. *Secret Lives* (1932) by E. F. Benson was republished by The Hogarth Press in 1985 with a new introduction by Stephen Pile.

ambitious or keen on money as they are in America because we are slowly subsiding.

As I said to my neighbour, 'It is the iridescence of decay which makes us so attractive.' To the English it is not so appealing and if I were eighteen I would emigrate to America where expansion and excitement and high rewards are much more possible.

**Sunday 8 December**

Arnold Weinstock telephoned to talk to me again about his fear that the government would oppose the merger he wants between GEC and Plessey and would refer it to the Monopolies Commission. He was upset by a long article in the *Sunday Times* saying that the fizz had gone out of GEC, as his profits were down and perhaps his empire was stagnant and drifting. He was afraid he was out of favour with Mrs Thatcher.

When I rang Mrs Thatcher she had gone to church, perhaps to pray against the Archbishop of Canterbury and Commission on the Inner Cities which is more of a political attack on the government than a call to spiritual values.

She said, 'Of course I'm not turning against Arnold. Tell him how much I still admire him. He's marvellous. I must get him in. Let me look at my engagement book.'

On the question of the Monopolies Commission she said, 'I suppose they have to refer it, it's such a big thing.' When I said 'No, not necessarily,' she said, 'Well this is a quasi-judicial decision of Leon Brittan's.[17] He will have to make up his mind.'

I told her that the Department for Industry was reputed to be in favour of the proposed merger which was in answer to various previous appeals from the government for Arnold to rationalize the electronics industry as he had once done the electrical industry.

She had no criticism, though she had evidently not seen a letter he had sent her complaining about the attacks on the torpedo that GEC are making for the Ministry of Defence because of the harm they do to GEC getting exports for the torpedo.

When I reported the conversation to Arnold he said, 'But surely no one can believe that her Ministers don't do what she tells them. If she tells Leon Brittan not to refer it to the Monopolies Commission, he won't.' I said, 'Maybe. But she asked me not to ring Leon Brittan as

17. Secretary of State for Trade and Industry, since September 1985.*

it might turn the decision the other way.' Arnold was cheered up by her obvious warmth towards him.

I also told her about Chips Keswick's worries about the international metal market because of the failure of the twenty-six countries, apart from Britain, to honour their obligations to pay up over the guarantees to maintain the tin price, which has caused the closure of the international tin market for several weeks. 'We regard them as legal obligations. Almost every day I say can't we do more to get these governments to honour their obligations.' There is very little she is not well informed about.

'We're doing well aren't we?' she asked, speaking of the general situation politically.

Before breakfast I went to Gerald Road[18] after my Sunday morning swim at the RAC still wearing my dressing-gown and nothing else to deliver the cheque to Irwin for the fifteen hundred dollars he had wired to Pericles in Philadelphia for a tumble-down house he wants to develop. I felt virtue at having got up before 7.15 a.m. and swum a third of a mile before eating haddock and two poached eggs instead of fried eggs, sausages and bacon which I usually have on Sunday when I indulge myself in dangerous saturated animal fats.

During the afternoon Nigel Lawson[19] rang. 'How could you of all people write that about Sedgemore?'[20] In the *News of the World* I had suggested that wild though many of his allegations were, he had provoked a more rigorous investigation of possible frauds.

Lawson said it was not true. The Fraud Squad had already been at work before Sedgemore began his smear campaign which was hindering police investigations by alerting suspects so that they would run away or destroy the evidence. Lawson has been riled by Sedgemore particularly when he said in November that Lawson had 'perverted the course of justice' and was suspended from the Commons for refusing to withdraw the allegation.

---

18. The Stelzers' house in Belgravia, London SW1.
19. Chancellor of the Exchequer, since 1983.*
20. Brian Sedgemore, Labour MP, had made allegations in the House of Commons about corruption at Lloyd's and in the City.

**Monday 9 December**

My nephew Robbie Lyle[21] brought Miss Brown to dinner. My brother is alarmed that she is a tough American after Robbie's money. She worked in a circus when she was nineteen and has been making video films which she describes as horror films but my brother thinks they are pornographic.

Verushka talked to her alone and said Robbie has no money but a huge appetite for extravagance and that if she married him she would have to see that he did not lose the property (Bonython) and overspend.

He is like Great Uncle Joseph who nearly lost Bonython entirely and had to sell a life interest in it to pay his debts, including damages in a breach of promise action brought against him by a tobacconist's daughter he met at Cambridge.

I promised his mother in the last few days before she died that I would try to see that he did not make a fool of himself but it is not easy and when he resents my questions I say, 'I'm sorry but I promised your mother.' He is irritated that his mother left some £300,000 to his sister plus the mews house in London worth around another £350,000 (which has now been sold) and not to him but I think his mother knew what she was doing.

I told him that I would have to reconsider being buried in the family vault in Cornwall because I was not convinced that Bonython would stay in his hands for long after I was dead so there would be no one to look after it and I might as well arrange to have myself buried at Weeford among the Wyatts who began the architectural dynasty and who were major contributors to the rebuilding of the church by James Wyatt. He wasn't sure whether I was serious or not.[22]

He is a nice boy, full of charm but without a methodical brain. He has already cost his father a great deal of money in paying debts over and above all the property he has given him.

It's possible, as Miss Brown has a strong character, that she might actually save Robbie from self-destruction if she married him but I imagine the sex would not last long, particularly on her side as he is no Adonis.

---

21. Son of WW's older brother, b 1952; heir to the family house, Bonython, in Cornwall.*
22. WW was buried at Weeford in December 1997.

**Tuesday 10 December**

Gimcrack[23] Dinner at York. I proposed the toast of the Jockey Club. I hate these speeches. I have a reputation for making very funny ones as well as for having some serious content so I have to put in work to keep up the standards for a racing audience. I always fear that one day my speech will be a flop but this time it went well.

Stayed with Rupert Manton[24] whose money comes from soap. He has an agreeable house and pretty garden but the central heating either doesn't work or wasn't on. He has just finished his period as Senior Steward which he did competently. My praise at the dinner for the modernization of the Jockey Club was genuine.

**Wednesday 11 December**

York University. Christopher Hill,[25] who has written a book about the racing industry, not yet published, is a lecturer in Politics. The Tote contributed £1,000 to his writing the book. I felt I could not refuse his plea that I should talk to some twenty of his students in a seminar about the trade unions. He warned me that they would be very left but they did not seem so.

One was a young Army officer who had precise views on greater democracy in the election of party leaders and why did the Tory Party demand that every union member should have the right to elect in a secret ballot his national executive council whereas the Tories elected their leader only by their few Members of Parliament?

A married branch official of the Transport & General Workers Union was also on the course. He was not at all hostile at my having written that the current elections in the TGWU were outside the law because they did not provide either for postal ballots or for voting at workplaces, many being required to go to their branches at inconvenient times – that is if they ever heard about the elections at all.

I spent a jolly hour and three-quarters with the group who seemed surprised that I was not a fascist beast.

---

23. The Gimcrack Stakes for two-year-olds take place each August.
24. 3rd Baron Manton, senior steward of the Jockey Club, 1982–5.
25. Not to be confused with the Oxford historian of the same name. His book, *Horse Power: The Politics of the Turf*, was published in 1988.

**Thursday 12 December**

Petronella off to Oxford for her interview at Worcester.

Lunch with Jeffrey Archer in his heavily windowed flat near the top of Alembic House on the Albert Embankment. Splendid view of the Thames in both directions. A large number of ostentatiously expensive pictures and everything in the worst of good taste. Despite the view I would hate to live there.

Jeffrey Archer asked everyone as they arrived whether they would like a glass of Krug to make sure that they would understand it was not ordinary champagne.

John Wakeham, Government Chief Whip, was there. He looks well but limps from the after-effects of the Brighton terrorist bomb explosion[26] in which his wife was killed. He was cross with the *Times* for printing his name and that of other Tory MPs connected with syndicates at Lloyd's, suggesting that in some way they were involved in the various Lloyd's scandals.[27] 'But if there's anything wrong with a syndicate, we're the victims and lose our money. We don't run them and we can only lose money out of fraud, not make any.'

Charles Price, the American Ambassador, told me that their feedback is that the Russians believe Reagan is sincere about having no hostile intentions but their worry remains over SDI.[28] They are afraid it would give the Americans a permanent advantage. 'But', I said, 'Reagan promised them that once the research was completed and you are ready to deploy SDI, you would share it with the Russians.'

'He said that,' Price agreed, 'but it is not true. We would never share it with the Russians.' So the Russians have got a legitimate anxiety. They may trust Reagan but they don't know who his successors will be.

---

26. At the Grand Hotel during the 1984 Conservative Party Conference.
27. Members of Lloyd's, Lloyd's 'names', without investment of capital in good years receive dividends in exchange for unlimited call on their resources in bad years. Many 'names' at this time were being called on for their total resources when syndicates crashed through a combination of massive losses on the insurance markets and alleged incompetence or fraudulent conduct of those who ran the syndicates.
28. The Strategic Defence Initiative (nicknamed 'Star Wars') proposed by President Reagan in March 1983 to defend America against nuclear attacks by using laser weapons orbiting in space to shoot down missiles.

**Sunday 15 December**

Irwin Stelzer came to talk about his plans for making money and some for me too. As he sold, with his former partner, NERA[29] for $22 million, he may be right.

I want Arnold to let him do some work for GEC either to help prevent his take-over bid for Plessey being referred to the Monopolies Commission or to help present the evidence if it is.

Arnold is excited now about the approach Heseltine[30] has made to him to come in behind the European consortium trying to stop the American firm Sikorsky getting control of Westland.[31] He thinks Mrs Thatcher is on the other side.

When I spoke to her she said several times it is John Cuckney's[32] affair. They must decide whatever is in the best interests of their shareholders. (When I told Arnold this he said that the shareholders have not got anything: the banks have got the lot.) Mrs T said if the Europeans were so keen to help Westland why didn't they order a helicopter from them years ago when they could have done? She didn't seem as put out by Heseltine's intervention as had been suggested, believing that it is for Westland to choose the best offer.

We talked about Lloyd's. She said they (Denis and she) had never

---

29. National Economic Research Associates, international economic consultants, established in New York in 1961 and in London in 1984, now part of the Mercer Consulting Group, the consulting division of Marsh & McLennan Companies.
30. Michael Heseltine had been Secretary of State for Defence since 1983.
31. This entry marks the beginning of the explosive sequence of events over the Westland helicopter company which culminated in the resignation of two cabinet ministers, Michael Heseltine and Leon Brittan. The US helicopter firm Sikorsky was trying to take a substantial stake in Westland, a comparatively small company by international standards but Britain's only major helicopter manufacturer, based in Somerset with a turnover of about £300 million. In April 1985 Alan Bristow, chairman of Bristow Helicopters, had made a bid for Westland, which was in financial difficulties, seeking assurances from the Ministry of Defence that the company would receive government orders. When these were not forthcoming, despite the government's wish to avoid Westland going into receivership, Mr Bristow withdrew his bid. Sir John Cuckney took over as chairman of Westland, Sikorsky showed its interest and Heseltine championed a counter-bid by a European consortium for control of the company. See Margaret Thatcher's *The Downing Stret Years* for her account of the events.
32. Chairman Westland Group 1985–9, Thomas Cook Group 1978–87, John Brown 1983–86, Royal Insurance Holdings 1985–94, 3i Group 1987–92; The Orion Publishing Group since 1994 (knight 1978, life peer 1995).

become a 'name' though invited to more than once. She felt there was something vaguely wrong about it.

**Tuesday 17 December**

Harry Pitt, Vice Provost of Worcester, rang in the morning to say that Petronella had got a place at Worcester. I left her a note beginning 'Dear Miss Wyatt' in the style in which Harry Pitt had asked.

Cut the Levy Board dinner for tedious Gordon Haddon, now retiring after thousands of years of mediocre service, in favour of a Jeffrey Archer party. Bumped into Ian Hay Davison who is leaving his job as Chief Executive at Lloyd's. He reminded me, getting it wrong, that his accountancy firm had once acted when I floated a publishing company. Reminders of that always embarrass me because of our going bust in 1982.[33]

Mary Archer was there looking very pretty with beautiful white shoulders. She lives in the Old Vicarage next to the Grantchester church made famous by Rupert Brooke's 'Stands the Church clock at ten to three? / And is there honey still for tea?' I said I would come and have tea with her and she said, 'Why not come to dinner with me at Trinity?' where she is a Fellow as well as being a Fellow of Newnham. I shall try to do it. She said she met the Queen Mother for the second time when she came to the Fitzwilliam Museum and they talked about me, the Queen Mother saying 'His articles are full of fire.'

It was very crowded. At one point I was trying to get through the long room to collect some food and Jeffrey Archer said, 'No, I'll bring it to you. We can't have you shuffling along to get food.' It is true that when I have not been swimming (the roof at the RAC swimming pool has fallen in) I tend shamefully to shuffle when moving through a lot of people.

Geoffrey Pattie, formerly at the Ministry of Defence in charge of procurement and now at Trade & Industry as Minister for Information and Technology, introduced himself. Another person who thinks Arnold is not efficient and only wakes up when complaints are made against him because he has had it too easy as a more or less monopoly supplier to the Ministry of Defence.

On the way home called in at the Café Royal where a large number

---

33. WW's ownership of the *Banbury Guardian*, the start of other weekly papers and eventual collapse of his print business are described in *Confessions of an Optimist*, pp. 323–7, 350.

of racing people, looking very bored and boring, were still entertaining Gordon Haddon who was pleased that I had looked in, though I think he doesn't like me any more than I like him for his past endeavours to frustrate the Tote in their legitimate activities at racecourses.

**Wednesday 18 December**

Another impresario, Ray Cooney, has turned down my play.

Penelope Keith has also written saying she is committed for two other plays.

Lilli, Verushka's sister, and Witold her husband arrive to stay until 7 January.

**Thursday 19 December**

Lunch with Hugh Thomas[34] at the Centre for Policy Studies. In the dining-room photographs of Keith Joseph[35] and Mrs Thatcher looked down upon us. Her presence is everywhere, making it like a holy shrine which I don't mind though it is slightly comical.

The thinkers of the Centre believe that they persuaded her to start taking credit for over-spending in place of harping on cuts. I think it was more myself that suggested that to her than the Centre but I did not say so.

Archie Hamilton,[36] a Tory MP who has been a Minister dealing with defence procurement and now a government Whip, was much against Arnold. He said that he ran a very inefficient business only interested in the bottom line of profit and loss, not keeping them on their toes in meeting their commitments to specifications or to time and within the right price. 'He's been whingeing about British Telecom because he and Plessey no longer have a monopoly for supplying but have to beat foreign competition. That's the only reason he wants to take Plessey over.'

---

34. Historian; chairman (1979–90), Centre for Policy Studies, a Conservative 'think-tank' founded by Sir Keith Joseph in 1974; life peer 1981.
35. (1918–94); Sir Keith Joseph Bt, Conservative politician, Secretary of State for Social Services, 1970–4, for Industry, 1979–81, for Education and Science, 1981–6; Fellow of All Souls College, Oxford, 1946–60, life peer 1987.
36. An assistant government Whip 1982–84, at the Treasury, 1984–6; Parliamentary Under-Secretary of State for Defence Procurement 1986–7.

**Sunday 22 December**

Tried to persuade Mrs T that Heseltine and Brittan taking different positions over Westland was healthy, open government and the public were intelligently informed rather than dismayed by it. She was not convinced and thought it appalling that two Cabinet Ministers should be quarrelling in public. She reiterated it was for the shareholders and the company to decide whether to take the Sikorsky or the European offer and not the business of any Minister.

I told her the public would accept stronger action against the teachers[37] and that those who won't work normally should be dismissed, as there were many willing to take their place who could easily be trained. She had been horrified to learn that many Labour councils didn't even dock their pay when they went on strike and maybe some Tory councils.

She also agrees there is a danger in pouring money into the Inner Cities where there are no votes to be had and taking it away from other areas who are asked to bail out inefficient Labour councils making a mess of the Inner Cities.

Nigel Lawson was delighted with what I had written about Sedgemore and the City in the *News of the World*. 'You have made handsome amends.' I suggested he should consider Chips Keswick to be on the advisory panel to supervise banks but he had not yet made up his mind whether the panel or board should consist solely or partly of those who have retired from banking recently; otherwise it might be said there was a conflict of interest.

**Monday 23 December**

Norman Lamont brought me a box of Davidoff cigars.

Interesting about Heseltine's obsession with Westland. He speaks of nothing else and says he'll resign if he doesn't win. Winning means defeating the Sikorsky bid with the European consortium.

He's gone way past the point of neutrality, of leaving it to Westland to decide. He's been bullying banks and Westland to get them to give in and has persuaded Arnold to join in which he says he is doing because GEC makes the electronics for the helicopter and Sikorsky probably wouldn't let them.

He said Heseltine keeps saying that he would never have made any

---

37. Teachers had been militant since the National Union of Teachers' rejection of the local authorities' pay offer in October 1985.

fuss if Mrs Thatcher had allowed him to discuss it in Cabinet and he was angry that she didn't. Now he says that he'll resign if he doesn't win. Lamont pointed out to him that if his ground for wanting to resign is that Mrs Thatcher snubbed him in Cabinet, he should resign now whatever happens to Westland if he feels so strongly about it.

But, no, Heseltine is out to demonstrate what a powerful fellow he is and support a claim for the leadership. Even his civil servants are utterly fed up with him and think he's quite wrong anyway about Westland.

Lamont made another point, saying the Sea King, the best helicopter made by Westland, was under licence from Sikorsky.

**Tuesday 24 December**

Relayed the gist of Lamont's account of Heseltine to Mrs T, adding that Lamont wished that she had put her foot down at the beginning to stop the quarrelling. As to the charge that Heseltine was not allowed to discuss the matter in the Cabinet, she said, 'But he never put a paper in.'

I now sympathize with her in being angry with Heseltine. She said Brittan has played it absolutely straight, leaving it to the shareholders and the company to decide but they (meaning herself and other Ministers) can't answer Heseltine, who is intriguing and trying to force the company to do what he wants, without making the quarrel worse in public.

I told her that Heseltine thinks he's on a winner because there's a thirteen per cent shareholding by Libya in Fiat and Fiat is part of Sikorsky's offer; but that is all nonsense because Fiat components are already included in a number of vital weapons made for the Ministry of Defence.

**Wednesday 25 December**

In the morning we went to the Grosvenor Chapel where John Wilkes is buried and there is a tablet to 'John Wilkes. The friend to liberty' on the wall. Twenty-seven people in the congregation. We came in very late but the earnest, intelligent, very high church priest (practically a Roman Catholic) who preached quite a sensible sermon about not succumbing to depression was clearly pleased to see us.

We wondered whether he would have been had he known that the sole reason for us being in his church was to honour the libertine John

Wilkes, founder member of the Hellfire Club[38] of Medmenham Monks who died on Boxing Day 1797.

We then went to see Irwin and Cita Stelzer because it was their first Christmas in England and Cita had asked for a copy of my play which I took to her.

**Thursday 26 December**

Kempton Park. The King George VI Chase. A very early lunch (11.45) because Queen Elizabeth had a runner in each of the first two races.

As she went off to the paddock for the second race I said, 'Please tell Insular I have 5p each way on him. It might encourage him.' When she came back I said, 'Did you tell him?' She said, 'Well I whispered it – but obviously not loud enough.' Though the favourite, it came in fifth. A very good result for our betting shops and credit business. I passed the news on to Queen Elizabeth. 'They always do back my horses. Isn't it embarrassing? But I'm glad your business did well out of it.'

At lunch she sat next to Evelyn de Rothschild who is very cross with me because I am trying to get United Racecourses, of which he is Chairman, owned by the Levy Board, handed over to Racecourse Holdings Trust, owned by the Jockey Club, because United Racecourses (Epsom, Sandown and Kempton) have been so badly run.

He was even more cross when Queen Elizabeth kept waving to me at the end of the table and talking to him about me and the marvellous articles I write and he had to pretend he agreed. Unlike Queen Elizabeth he doesn't read the *News of the World*, only my articles in the *Times*.

She was full of liveliness, as ever. I admired her brooch: diamonds and some black objects. I enquired what they were. 'It was given me by the King[39] and they are sapphires.'

We chatted about books as well as about the racing and I told her what Heseltine was up to – she is always interested in the gossip of politics.

---

38. Sir Francis Dashwood founded a mock brotherhood, The Hellfire Club, at Medmenham, near Wycombe, Buckinghamshire, the site of a twelfth-century Cistercian abbey; their motto was 'Fay ce que voudras' ('Do as you please') and the original members included Wilkes.
39. Her husband, King George VI (d 1952).

**Friday 27 December**

A lot of bridge playing. Witold is determined to make me into a bridge player and writes out instructions on how to bid which I find hard to follow as his English is not good. I fear he is trying to make a bridge player out of someone who is illogical, not methodical, and has a poor memory for what cards have been played. But it all passes the time and Lilli and Verushka enjoy it.

**Sunday 29 December**

A jolly lunch at Bowden Park.[40] Sat next to Princess Michael.[41] Obsessed by the dislike she thinks the Family have for her.

She had told me before that, when Maxwell[42] was hounding her, she had written to Prince Charles complaining he was not gallant or chivalrous and didn't behave like a gentleman in allowing Robert Maxwell to come to tea with him at Kensington Palace in connection with some charity affair. 'My husband would have written out a cheque for £7,000 if Prince Charles had let him so that he need not invite the Maxwell but he refused.'

I said, 'He has to see people like Maxwell. He can't suddenly withdraw an invitation.' 'It's hypocritical!' she cried. I said, 'Yes, but the whole of Britain is founded on hypocrisy. The place wouldn't work otherwise.'

'Why do they attack me? Princess Anne has had at least five affairs. Prince Philip has had lots of affairs. The Duchess of Kent has had a lot too.' I said, 'Because you're on the fringes of the Royal Family and whereas the press don't like to attack the centre they think it fair game to have a go at you.'

She's a good-looking girl with a bright face and nice eyes. Her figure is reasonable but her legs are too large so she wears skirts which come well below the calf. She's very sexy. Referring to the Hunt[43] affair and the *News of the World* description of her entering an apartment block to see him, wearing a wig, she said, 'I've never worn a wig in my life.'

---

40. Lord and Lady Weinstock's house in Wiltshire.
41. Princess Michael of Kent, née Baroness Marie-Christine von Reibnitz, m (1978) HRH Prince Michael, cousin of the Queen.
42. Robert Maxwell (1923–91), newspaper proprietor and former Labour MP.
43. Princess Michael has always denied that her association with Ward Hunt (a property dealer from Texas, in his early forties, divorced 1984, cousin of the oil tycoon Nelson Hunt) was an affair.

She asked if I had read the account of her early life by somebody called Everingham[44] which was so bad and boring even the *News of the World* rejected it and never printed it. I said I had read a bit of it. It didn't seem very interesting, saying she had had boyfriends when she was young in Australia. 'But you're a healthy girl and why shouldn't you have boyfriends?'

After she'd eaten some sticky chocolate she said her fingers were sticky, would I lick the chocolate off for her, whereupon she stuck three fingers one after the other into my mouth and I obligingly licked them. It was, I suppose, intended to be erotic.

She said Mrs Thatcher had been very nice to her and rung her up when all the trouble was going on about her father's Nazi past. She will probably get into more scrapes. She is a restless girl and her husband has little money when she would like to have lots.

Arnold said to me after they'd gone, 'Why don't you put him on the Tote Board?' I said, 'But it's only £5,000 a year.' 'Yes, but he has to eat.' I said 'Yes, but my darling Queen Mother might not like it.' However, it is an idea as Andrew Devonshire[45] is leaving in September and Prince Michael could perform some stately functions. Netta[46] says Princess Michael wants Arnold to give him a job.

When I said goodbye to Princess Michael she gave me warm kisses. I said, 'If you have any problems don't hesitate to ring,' and she said, 'But I haven't any now.' I said, 'Good, but if you do have any . . .'

During the summer she rang me a lot, sometimes after midnight, first about her father and getting an interview in the *Times*, which I organized with Rupert, for her mother in Australia though she said today, 'They only put it on the back page,' and second about the *News of the World* running the story of her association with Hunt, the American of the Baker Hunt family.

The *News of the World* told me of the detailed evidence they had even from her own friends.[47] She is dreadfully indiscreet. However, there was nothing I could do about it.

I told Mrs Thatcher how pleased Princess Michael had been at her

---

44. *The Adventures of a Maverick Princess* (1985) by Barry Everingham, Bantam Press.
45. 11th Duke of Devonshire, former Conservative minister, member of the Tote Board 1977–86.*
46. Lady Weinstock.
47. See note 43 above for Princess Michael's denial of this allegation.

kindness. 'I don't like people being kicked when they're down,' she said.

Mrs Thatcher had not read my article about Heseltine's machinations over Sikorsky. 'Tell me what's in it.' I did, and she seemed pleased. Before I left Bowden I told Arnold that he should keep a low profile over Westland otherwise he would not do himself any good in certain quarters.

I congratulated Mrs T on her article in the *News of the World* which was way above the normal stuff produced by her or her office or both. 'You'll be taking my job.' 'No, no one has such a lucid way of getting to the nub of the point in as few words as you do,' she said.

I [had] tried to get her two or three times but she had not arrived back from Chequers. Then she rang when we were playing bridge. I turned the others out of the room and she talked for twenty minutes.

She had come back to deal with the Westland affair instead of staying at Chequers.

She wanted to know why Arnold was involved and I said, 'It must be partly because he's having trouble with the Ministry of Defence over Nimrod.[48] It is a way of keeping on the side with Heseltine.'

I asked her whether she would like to come to dinner again. She said 'Very much.' 'Who would you like to have with you?' 'Oh, just one or two people, but I love having dinner with you. They're the most stimulating dinners I ever have.' Then she said, 'What about Rupert Murdoch? I like talking to him. And also Andrew Knight[49] and his wife.'

Then she said she felt very sad about Michael Hartwell[50] and the *Telegraph*. 'The last gentleman left running his own newspaper.'

**Monday 30 December**

Arnold rang in the morning and said again that he was concerned about Sikorsky not allowing GEC to put their electronics into the

---

48. The Nimrod Airborne Early Warning System being produced by GEC.

49. Editor, the *Economist*, 1974–86; he became chief executive and editor-in-chief of the *Daily Telegraph* in 1986.

50. Lord Hartwell (life peer 1968, formerly the Hon. Michael Berry), second son of first Viscount Camrose; chairman and editor-in-chief, *Daily Telegraph* and *Sunday Telegraph*, 1954–87. Conrad Black, the Canadian newspaper proprietor, acquired control of the *Telegraph* titles in December 1985 after sixty years of ownership by the Berry family.

helicopters. I had forgotten he'd said that the night before so I rang Caroline Ryder, Mrs T's political secretary, and asked her to give a note to correct the wrong impression I have given. 'Oh, the Prime Minister's just outside. You'd better speak to her yourself,' which I had not intended to do.

I was put through and she said, 'Yes, but it's not a take-over bid. That's where they're all getting it wrong. Westland continues in its own right whatever happens.' She was pleased I had rung and we wished each other a happy New Year.

# 1986

**Thursday 2 January**

An article for the *Times* about Westland.[1] Frequently they cut my articles about and shorten them without consultation, although renewed promises of good behaviour are given after each breach, so I rang the editor to ask particularly that no cuts should be made in this one without reference to me because it was unusually important.

The affairs of this little company have been seen by Heseltine (Secretary for Defence) as a chance to project himself as a front runner for the Tory leadership banging the patriotic drum. Though why a European consortium should be more patriotic than Sikorsky (US) and Fiat (Italy) coming to the rescue, particularly as the US connection gives a greater chance of getting NATO work, is hard to see. There is latent anti-Americanism always ready to be tapped.

Had much help from Sir John Cuckney, Chairman of Westland, but Arnold W says he's no good which is his regular comment on anyone who may be opposing him at the moment.

**Saturday 4 January**

A jolly tour with Cita [Stelzer] and Petronella to Apsley House where they had moved the portrait of the Duke of York by Henry Wyatt and considerable investigation was needed to find out where it was hanging. He was one of the leading portrait painters of his day and was assistant to Thomas Lawrence, painting a number of pictures now attributed wrongly to Lawrence. I have a little oil painting he did of my great-great-grandfather and lots of drawings from his sketch book.

**Sunday 5 January**

Could not speak to Mrs Thatcher in the morning because there was a meeting of Ministers, presumably discussing what to do about Heseltine.

She rang back in the evening. 'What a splendid article in the *Times*.

---

1. Published 4 January 1986.

I don't know all those facts. How did you find them.' I said, 'But surely you must know them?' She said, 'No, I have a Minister of Defence and a Secretary for Industry instead. Poor Leon is frightfully bad at public relations. You are the only person who ever gives me the facts.'

I told her the latest news from Cuckney and she asked me to find out a number of facts which she could not get from her own Ministers. I said, 'Aren't you in touch with Cuckney and Gordon Reece (who is dealing with Westland's public relations)?'[2] 'No,' she said, 'I have to be seen to be absolutely neutral.'

So I rang Cuckney and told him I wanted some more facts and clarification in case the article in the *Times* was challenged and also for future reference. But I think he may have guessed why I wanted to know some more, though on the whole my relations with Thatcher are fairly secret. Gordon Reece has an idea about them.

Cuckney had been delighted with the article. He'd spent the whole Sunday with the figures etc. preparing the board's final recommendation to Westland shareholders to go the Sikorsky route. 'But if the European consortium comes up with a better offer, even though so late, I am legally committed to recommend it to the shareholders.'

After speaking to Cuckney I rang Mrs Thatcher again telling her the latest information. She is furious with Heseltine but agrees with me that she should not sack him: 'I don't want to look petty.'

**Monday 6 January**

The third in command at Westland rang up with the answers to Mrs Thatcher's questions though he thought they were mine.

She was very interested to know that the Sea King helicopter, made under licence from Sikorsky and which was so successful in the Falklands, is really the basic structure of a helicopter and the system was developed by Westland in Britain, which is why it was such a valuable weapon for our services. I said, 'It is rubbish to say that Sikorsky would stop our technology. The main reason they are interested in Westland is because the technology is so good. The European consortium would only let Westland make little pieces of helicopters and the technology would be lost, contrary to what Heseltine's putting about.' She said, 'Why don't they put that out in their public relations material?'

---

2. Public relations consultant and former journalist; director of publicity, Conservative Central Office, 1978–80; adviser to Mrs Thatcher, 1975–9; knight 1986.

She was also interested that Aérospatiale, the French company, was told by its auditors they must have thousands of redundancies but the French government will not allow it for political reasons and instead orders helicopters they probably don't need for the French Army.

She was sorry for Sir John Cuckney who is having a hell of a battering from the Heseltine faction and the bankers and has been attacked again in this morning's newspapers on misinformation from Heseltine's sources. I said, 'I don't think Heseltine'll win,' but she understands the point that if the European consortium do offer a substantially better deal which is verifiable, Westland will have to accept it.

Rang Gordon Reece and told him to get Cuckney at his press conference this afternoon to emphasize the amount of British technology that went into Sea King; also, the point about Aérospatiale's redundancies making the European consortium a very shaky provider of work for Westland.

Cuckney met Arnold and Jim Prior[3] and two from British Aerospace. Cuckney said Arnold was unusually charming. To his, 'You mean you don't like us?', 'That's right,' Cuckney replied.

I told Margaret of the Cuckney conversation, I saying he sounded a good egg. She enthusiastically agrees. I repeated my advice that she should be above the battle like Reagan who indicates 'boys will be boys' when there is a quarrel among his senior colleagues and stands back to leave them to sort it out.

**Tuesday 7 January**

Arnold rang in full force. 'I can see why you were taken in by Cuckney. He's very plausible. It took me some time to realize that he doesn't know what he's talking about. Margaret's making a great mistake. If they go the Sikorsky route there's no guarantee they will get any work and they will be swallowed.'

'But what is the guarantee they'll get any work from a lot of loss-making firms in Europe?'

---

3. Chairman, GEC, 1984–98; Conservative politician; Parliamentary Private Secretary (PPS) to Edward Heath as Leader of the Opposition, 1965–70; Minister of Agriculture, Fisheries and Food 1970–2, Lord President of the Council and Leader of the House of Commons 1972–4 in the Heath government, then Secretary of State for Employment, 1979–81, for Northern Ireland 1981–4 under Mrs Thatcher; life peer 1987.

'British Aerospace can put pressure on them to keep the consortium up to the mark. They won't get their seventy-five per cent vote on the 14th.'

'Why don't you and British Aerospace make a proper bid to take the whole thing over?'

Pause. 'We don't want it. Margaret's in serious danger. If Heseltine resigns it will do a lot of damage with the backbenchers. Here's Jim Prior who's just walked in.'

'That's right,' says Jim.

'Why should it affect her? Her position is absolutely neutral – leaving it for the board and the shareholders to decide.'

Prior: 'She should tell Bernard Ingham.[4] That's not the press stories he's putting out – they are all anti-Heseltine and anti-European.'

Prior was indignant with the *Times* for saying in its leader this morning that he'd been sacked. I said, 'I know that's not true' and he said, 'Yes, when I resigned Margaret said, "I'd always give you a job again if you want one."' He added, 'Why are they so malicious?' I said, 'It's more like carelessness.'

Cuckney rang just before lunch. He is afraid that they are going in for wrecking tactics to prevent the Sikorsky arrangement going through next Tuesday. When I said to Arnold that if they did this the company would collapse into receivership, he said it would not matter.

Earlier Julian Amery rang. He was Minister of Aviation for several years. Mr Bristow, who once made a £150 million offer and withdrew it when he saw the books but is still a shareholder in Westland, had told him that he thought the European route was the right one and not the Sikorsky one.

**Wednesday 8 January**

Told Margaret what Arnold and Jim Prior had said, including the point Jim Prior made that Heseltine would resign on the constitutional issue of not being allowed to raise the matter properly in Cabinet, to which I had said, 'Have you got a copy of the British constitution? I would like to see one.' She said, 'But it was discussed in Cabinet twice.'

Suggested to Gordon Reece that they should have a Gallup poll of all the Westland employees if they thought they would get the right answer.

---

4. Chief Press Secretary to the Prime Minister, 1979–90.

**Thursday 9 January**

Heseltine resigns, complaining about the unanimous Cabinet decision that further statements by Ministers on Westland should be cleared centrally by the Cabinet Office to prevent Ministers publicly hurling incorrect or misleading statements and facts against each other.

Speak to Norman Lamont in his car driving on his way to see his constituents at Kingston. He thinks that resignation will do great harm to Mrs T and to the government, and that the constitutional point made by Heseltine that he was not allowed to discuss the matter, as arranged at a Cabinet meeting on a Friday before Christmas, has to be answered. Also his point that Leon Brittan asked him to organize a European consortium.

Heseltine gives a long press conference speech at 4.00 p.m. on TV which he must have prepared before the Cabinet meeting which he did not leave until about 12.00 p.m. Full of detail and noble sentiments. Rather boring unless you are a Parliament aficionado.

Rang Mrs T and told her that Lamont thought she must answer the two points he had raised with me. She said, 'I'm not going to speak about it on Monday in the House. Why should I? Just because a Minister resigns.'

It was odd that Heseltine made his resignation speech not in the Commons but to a press conference made in the room lent him by the Ministry of Defence where he is no longer a Minister. For someone who is so keen on the constitution he might have observed its conventions.

Chips Keswick to dinner. We drank a 1961 Château Neuf du Pape Domaine de Mont-Redon. It was very good. Chips brought a bottle of Crystal champagne and a magnum of Château Lafite 1970 which must have been worth at least £185.

**Friday 10 January**

7.15 a.m. Cuckney told me that Bristow's intervention in buying about eleven per cent of the shares could mean that only the resolution allowing Westland to borrow to reconstruct its capital would be passed, and that the other resolution about taking in Sikorsky as a partner would have to be postponed perhaps for a week when there had been time for emotions to settle down and both the European and the Sikorsky propositions would be put to the shareholders. 'I expect there'll be some horse-trading with Bristow during the day so I'm not quite sure what will happen.'

Cuckney said that most institutions he had visited during the day thought the European consortium was really a blocking move.

Margaret was a bit worried as she sometimes is when there is a crisis. At such times I ring her more often to cheer her up. I said it would be a seven-day wonder. Heseltine would not get much backing among Tory MPs except for those already malcontents. Far from being autocratic many thought (as Chips Keswick did last night) that she had been too tolerant and should have got rid of Heseltine earlier.

Asked Arnold again why GEC and Aerospace did not buy Westland as they had oodles of money. 'It's not worth the money,' he said. 'You mean you'd still rather it went into receivership.' 'Yes, that's the best answer.' 'Not very nice for the workers.'

**Saturday 11 January**

Rupert Murdoch says in the evening that Mrs Thatcher has got a bad press in the Sunday papers tomorrow. Much concentration on Leon Brittan threatening British Aerospace if they do not go the Sikorsky way. There must be a good answer to show that he was not breaching neutrality in the manner that Heseltine was.

Spoke to Mrs Thatcher and afterwards rang Leon who says he had officials present making a complete record and he did not say what he was supposed to have said. I said, 'It is quite legitimate for you to have an opinion as I have said in the *News of the World* tomorrow. That is very different from threatening anybody with loss of orders if they don't do what you tell them.' He pointed out that British Aerospace's own subsidiary or associate firm in America were themselves worried at their losing orders because of the anti-American turn the Sikorsky affair had taken in Britain.

On Brittan she says, 'He's a very good lawyer you know and I'm sure he would have taken care.'

Cuckney still confident that something can be done by some form of rearrangement of the deal which might require only fifty-one per cent and not the seventy-five per cent needed in its present form.

**Sunday 12 January**

Margaret much more cheerful and relaxed. The *Mail on Sunday* had been fairly beastly and of course the *Observer*. The *Observer* ran some story about Mark Thatcher[5] and Fayed,[6] the man who took over Harrods. It is Tiny Rowland's spite for not being allowed to proceed with his take-over bid for Harrods.

Later in the day she tells me that Fayed is issuing a statement that he has never even met Mark Thatcher.

Cuckney tells me that Heseltine hired a helicopter to go to Yeovil on Saturday where he was going to parade the streets and visit the Westland works. He cancelled his flight when he heard that the workers had got flags and placards out in a great demonstration to tell him to go away as he wouldn't help them when they needed it and they didn't want his help now.

Arnold surfaced late afternoon. He had come back to London early. 'I wish Margaret had told me at the beginning what she wanted done and I would have arranged it.' This is not really true as he knew perfectly well what she wanted done when he followed Heseltine into the European consortium.

His explanation is that he had to because Aerospace is one of their biggest customers and they wanted him to do so and it would have been difficult for him not to. However, he had been talking to John Agnelli who owns Fiat. The idea is that Sikorsky-Fiat should join the European consortium with everyone diluting their stake and no further squabbles and rows. Westland could go on taking their Sikorsky licences. No one would try to block Westland from European projects and all would be a great united family.

First he said could I speak to Margaret to put some pressure on Cuckney and Sikorsky-Fiat about it. I said that is quite impossible as she doesn't speak to Cuckney or even to Gordon Reece who is acting as their public relations officer. He would not believe it but I said, 'It is true. She has been maintaining a strict neutrality whatever her feelings have been.'

During the conversation he veered between his wanting me to tell her and not wanting me to tell her. He is terrified that something might get out and make the approach still-born. I said, 'Do you think she can't keep a secret? We have shared many secrets about other matters much more serious that this in the past.' He said he thought it would be nice for her to feel that she's not isolated and there is someone out there working for her. I said, 'Fine. Carry on.'

---

5. The Thatchers' son, a businessman based in the US.
6. Mohamed Al Fayed.

Margaret was delighted. 'A glow of light.' I said, 'If we could organize this, Heseltine would disappear in a puff of smoke.' She said she would keep it absolutely under wraps and speak to no one, not even Leon Brittan.

Arnold has obviously been getting worried, as I hoped he would be, by having put himself into a position of quarrelling with Mrs Thatcher. He doesn't understand much about politics and thinks that Heseltine can rock the government and possibly get the party defeated at the next election. But he's more concerned about his relations with Margaret which might rebound badly on GEC.

It seems the European consortium are now fed up with Heseltine. They thought he should have stayed on to fight his case or at least waited to see what happened. They now feel out on a limb and naked. Lygo[7] is also furious with Heseltine for revealing what Brittan said to him. It was intended to be private and he thought it very ungentlemanly of Heseltine to make political capital out of it. 'Whoever thought Heseltine was a gentleman?' I asked.

Obviously the European consortium, as I told Margaret, are worried as to where they've got themselves, too. The salient fact remains that no one in their right minds would buy Westland outright. The shares were today (Sunday) changing hands at about 135p, valuing the company at around £90 to £100 million. Anybody who bought it would still have to find an extra £60 million immediately and a lot more later. They would be paying up to £200 million for something which is just about bankrupt and in no way can be worth more than £25 million, if not zero. Everything has got into a marvellous tangle.

Heseltine goes banging on about the situation and how he has been outraged by Mrs T's behaviour towards him, though he cannot explain why the twenty other members of the Cabinet were against him on the day he resigned. I still think that Heseltine will do little damage after a week or so. Tory backbenchers don't like him and he has been so palpably dishonest.

After I had spoken to Margaret I told Arnold. He was clearly relieved that bridges which might have been burned seemed to be under repair so far as Margaret was concerned.

He has been too much under the influence of Jim Prior. Of course if Cuckney rearranges his scheme so he only needs a fifty-one per cent

---

7. Admiral Sir Raymond Lygo, formerly Chief of Naval Staff, Royal Navy; managing director, British Aerospace, 1983–6, chief executive, 1986–9.

majority it could become unnecessary for the European consortium to join with Sikorsky-Fiat, though it might be happier for everyone all round.

Saturday night Rupert Murdoch had been worried that his newspapers might not come out because of the announcement in the *Sunday Times* that next week the *Sunday Times* would be even bigger, with an extra section printed at Tower Hamlets. Lawyers and management stood by as the presses began, fearful that a strike would be called, but in the event it all passed off without commotion.

Looked at Dick Crossman's *Diaries*[8] and his lectures in America in 1970 on the British constitution. Mrs Thatcher, as I had told her, had done nothing unusual for a Prime Minister.

'The real criticism of you', I told her, 'is you have been far too tolerant and you should have acted sooner.' She said, 'I suppose you are right. He is saying that I constructed a trap for him which caused his resignation. If I had done that he must have been a fool to have fallen into it, mustn't he? I gave him all the rope he could possibly have and it is not my fault if he hangs himself on it.'

**Monday 13 January**

Arnold says Bristow, the man who has been buying a key share, has to be squared in some way and offered the chairmanship. I said that wouldn't matter because all that Cuckney is trying to do is to stabilize Westland and then move on to other things where he has plenty to do.

Commotion in the House. Brittan makes a sensible statement about Westland and what he had said to British Aerospace. Heseltine should have been on the run but he asked whether a letter had been received from Sir Raymond Lygo. There had been a letter from Sir Austin Pearce, the Chairman of British Aerospace, but not from Lygo, marked Private and Strictly Confidential to the Prime Minister.

Brittan, instead of saying there was a letter in existence though the contents could not be divulged, said he had had no letter from Lygo and no letter from British Aerospace – which was true as it had gone to the Prime Minister but it gave the impression there was no letter from British Aerospace which was silly as Heseltine obviously had been told the letter was on its way. It had arrived shortly before lunch.

Brittan had to return to the House late in the evening for a fairly

8. *The Diaries of a Cabinet Minister* by Richard Crossman, vols. 1–3, published 1975–7.

muddled apology acknowledging the existence of the letter but not revealing the contents.

Bad day for the government. They look confused.

Rupert to dinner. Could I write his biography? At first he says no, then he becomes interested, reciting his early days in Australia and how he came to take over the *News of the World* when the wily old men in the City thought he was too young to have it and could be prevented.

I said, 'You're a child of nature, an elemental force. You have very little guile. You love danger. Anyone with sense would have stopped years ago and sat safely on the vast empire you had. But not you. You must go on and on and on until you have a debt bigger than the national debt of South Africa.' 'Not quite,' he said. 'At the moment we've got our borrowings ($1.5 billion) down to match our assets.'

He's in the middle of a high risk manoeuvre to stop the printing unions from printing the *Times*, *Sunday Times*, *News of the World* and the *Sun*. He wants them to go on strike at a moment which will suit him, not just on a Saturday evening mucking up the *Sunday Times*. He has a new problem in that the unions are scared and reluctant to strike. If they did he can sack everyone and print with five hundred and twelve people he has lined up who have already learned to work the presses at Tower Hamlets. That would be instead of the four to five thousand currently employed. I am sure he will win but not without hiccups.

I asked him to put in a word with the *Sunday Times* about my wish to write a feature on my South African trip as there will be much more material than I need for an article in the *Times* and in the *News of the World*. I could do with the money, perhaps £2,500, if it comes off.

I asked Rupert if he thought it would be a good idea to put Prince Michael on the Tote Board. He said, 'No. He's getting mixed up with very doubtful people like Jonathan Aitken: he can't help it as he has no money. Quite apart from Princess Michael he might get into some scandal which would reflect badly on you and the Tote.'

**Tuesday 14 January**

Arnold says he has heard nothing definite yet from Agnelli.

Mrs Thatcher deals effectively at Question Time with the ridiculous issue of the private and strictly confidential, saying that she treated such things as private and strictly confidential including their existence and hoped others would. She has now got the authority of Sir Austin

Pearce to publish his letter and her reply tomorrow morning before the debate.

Gordon Reece says it is extremely unlikely that the Westland board will get their seventy-five per cent at the adjourned shareholders' meeting on Friday. It will probably become a matter of shifting the goal posts so that the scheme is based on something like a loan stock, not requiring more than a simple majority. It could take weeks. Cuckney is the type of chairman not to give in to the European consortium. Someone has been buying shares sympathetic to the Westland board but not enough to win on Friday.

A Levy Board dinner to say thank you to the committee who made a report on the National Stud. I have not read the report, though I should have done, as the subject was boring and the committee was unnecessary.

Rupert rang and said he was trying to organize Sikorsky (Rupert is a director of United Technologies) into doing a deal with British Aerospace and GEC and leaving out the European elements. What would Arnold think? Bound by secrecy I couldn't tell him what Arnold was trying to arrange.

'Would you like to speak to Arnold?' 'Could you ask him?' So I rang Arnold who was very keen to talk to him. Rupert said, 'We've got to get her out of this jam somehow. It's looking very bad.' Arnold agrees as he is partly responsible for the jam she is in. I rang Rupert back. 'How did he respond?' 'Very well,' I said. 'Ring him at once.' I gave him Arnold's telephone number.

The desperate attempts to solve the situation with so many people whose honour needs to be placated continue. Arnold says he advised Bristow not to sell his shares and now he can't let him down. Nor can Arnold switch without looking an idiot. Rupert said he was going to try and act as an honest broker which I suppose is what I am doing all the time.

**Wednesday 15 January**

Rupert rings from his motor car. I wish he wouldn't as it is frightfully difficult to hear what he is saying with the noise of the car and the traffic. Despite BT being privatized their mobile telephone is ghastly.

Rupert says that Sikorsky has not got properly the message which Arnold had been trying to pass through Agnelli Fiat. He will now see that they do get the message. There's not much time left.

Ring Margaret at 7.45 a.m. to wish her luck in the debate this afternoon. I told her that I have put Rupert and Arnold together. Also that it's extremely unlikely that the Westland board can win what it wants on Friday. 'Oh Lord. The longer this drags on the more damaging it is. It's now doing harm to sterling and the economy as well as to the government' (which is what Rupert thinks as well and so does Arnold).

'My difficulty today is that I can't attack Heseltine without making everything worse. I don't want to look as though I am attacking a colleague and giving him an excuse to do even more harm.' I said, 'You should remain cool and distant in sorrow not anger.' She said she will try to do this.[9]

'What about the charge that Brittan leaked the letter from Patrick Mayhew (the Solicitor General)[10] to Heseltine telling him he had been inaccurate?' 'There'll be the usual leaks procedure but there have been a lot of leaks all round in this affair,' she said, sounding rather dismal. She will get her energy back by this afternoon and no one will know she has been feeling somewhat low.

Tell Arnold that Rupert said that his messages to Sikorsky via Agnelli had got snarled up on the way. He said he wasn't surprised. He is still on the idea that the European consortium should join with Sikorsky-Fiat, all reducing their shares proportionately. Like Rupert he said, 'A possible solution would be to make Bristow the Chairman.'

Rupert had said to me, 'Why not make him Chairman for a year and offer him a knighthood which he badly wants.' I told Rupert she could not possibly do that. 'But can't some of their friends put their arms round him and say, "I'm sure you'll get a knighthood if you behave well"?'

Listen to debate on wireless, Kinnock[11] deep out of his depth. He cannot or will not work on his speeches to make them authoritative. Nye Bevan[12] would never have missed such a chance to lacerate M.

She was splendid with a well marshalled convincing factual speech.

---

9. In her memoirs *The Downing Street Years*, published in 1993, she says, 'My speech was low-key and strictly factual' and comments that it was not well received: 'The press were expecting something more fiery.'
10. Sir Patrick Mayhew QC, Solicitor General, 1983–7, Attorney General, 1987–92; he wrote to Heseltine on 6 January about 'material inaccuracies' of Heseltine's on what would happen if Westland chose Sikorsky rather than the European consortium.
11. Leader of the Labour Party and the Opposition, 1983–92.
12. Aneurin Bevan (1897–1960), Labour politician and creator of the National Health Service, famed for his Welsh oratory.

Heseltine was fair but no new shafts worth anything. His rot about 'constitutional outrage' wouldn't stick. He sounded just peeved he hadn't got his way. Callaghan[13] was effectively avuncular. (Arnold told me before the debate that C had rung him asking if GEC were discontented. He was anxious I should know he had said no and the Sikorsky route was a reasonable option.)

Dinner at Cavendish Avenue. Clarissa Avon said how much more restricted girls were when she was young. 'How old were you when you had your first affair?' 'Seventeen,' she replied. 'You don't sound to have been very restricted.' She had pleasant memories of it. Said the man was quite well-known and is still alive.

Much talk about Westland. Kenneth Baker, Secretary for the Environment, had to leave at 9.30 p.m. for the vote.

Arnold very argumentative. When I teased him on his part in damaging the government he said that if he was provoked he would reveal a great deal more. I said, 'You are doing a "heavy" as Brittan is accused of doing with Lygo.'

Elaine Rawlinson,[14] exceptionally pretty, said she would get private names and addresses of friends and relations of hers in Philadelphia and Washington for Pericles to see.

Irwin did his usual piece about everyone being anti-American in Britain, strongly refuted by Arnold. George[15] looked bemused by all the political discussion over Westland and its consequences.

Arnold assumed that the latest mystery buyer of fifteen per cent had been put up to it by Sikorsky. Peter Rawlinson said Patrick Mayhew, Solicitor General, should never have written the letter to Heseltine saying he'd got his statement about the effects of the Sikorsky route on European co-operation wrong. A Law Officer should only write a letter if asked and in this instance should only have been asked by No 10 and should have resisted.

**Thursday 16 January**

Arnold despite his boast that he would get it all settled by Friday has got nowhere. Nor has Rupert. The latest mystery buyer is disclosed as

---

13. James Callaghan, Labour Prime Minister, 1976–9; life peer 1987.
14. Wife of Lord (Peter) Rawlinson (life peer 1978, lawyer and Conservative politician, Solicitor General, 1962–4, Attorney General, 1970–4).
15. Weidenfeld.

James Hanson.[16] 'He must have been put up to it by Margaret,' says Arnold.

Government has another bad press though Brittan's effective speech in the debate is given some recognition. The newspapers would like another resignation – so much more fun.

Decide to write an article for the *Times* about the constitutional rights and powers of a Cabinet Minister being a big zero. All the talk about constitutional outrage is idiocy as there is no constitution and, as Callaghan said on Wednesday, Cabinet government is what the current Prime Minister decides to make it.

Tim Neligan, Managing Director of United Racecourses, came to tea. Asked him whether he would mind Racecourse Holdings Trust taking over. He thought it quite a good solution but would be sorry if they threw Evelyn de Rothschild out. I told him there was no need for that. He could still go on receiving the Queen when she arrived at the Derby which is really what he minded about.

Alexander Ward[17] came to dinner. Tracy is hoping to marry Harry [Marquess of] Worcester. Petronella would not like that as all women who don't want someone are annoyed if the admirer takes somebody else. Admirers, potential or otherwise, should remain sadly on safari in Africa if rejected.

**Friday 17 January**

James Hanson rang. After my article on 4 January he had written to the *Times* saying how much he agreed with me and that I was right.[18] The *Times* didn't publish the letter. 'They missed a scoop now that I'm revealed as the mystery buyer of fifteen per cent.' I said, 'Perhaps they will publish it now.' He said, 'They can't because I withdrew it yesterday.'

British Aerospace now concede there was a genuine misunderstanding between Lygo and Brittan. The poor man now has one less obstacle to cross. The inquiry into who leaked the Solicitor General's letter will not publish its report, Margaret saying that that has often been previous practice.

---

16. Chairman, Hanson PLC and Hanson Transport Group Ltd; life peer 1983.
17. Son of the Hon. Peter Ward and Claire Ward; younger brother of Tracy Ward.
18. WW had argued Heseltine's intervention was on the wrong side: 'He has bullied and blackmailed Westland. In short, he has got himself into a regular tantrum about nothing at all.'

Heseltine seems to have achieved nothing as blocking the Sikorsky-Fiat rescue does not enable the European consortium to get theirs through. Just more delay while Cuckney works something out requiring only a simple majority of shareholders' votes. His vindictiveness against the Prime Minister is upsetting more Tories.

**Saturday 18 January**

Quite pleased with myself. Not a bad review in the *Times* on Thursday.[19] A good article in the *Times* on Saturday about the constitutional powers and rights of Cabinet Ministers being zero and quite a good article for the *News of the World* tomorrow.

Rupert in high spirits. Rang about 9.00 a.m. to say he'd been up till 2.45 a.m. overseeing the printing of the extra section of the *Sunday Times* at Tower Hamlets. A great new plant with maximum security. He said the police were ready in case there were pickets and they had riot shields stored in the warehouse nearby and every now and again a police helicopter came over to see that there was no trouble. 'I really felt secure.' So far he has got away with it brilliantly.

Norman Willis, General Secretary of the TUC, wanted to see him tomorrow. He said that was impossible, he'd have to see O'Neil in charge of the negotiations for News International. Actually he's coming to Chequers[20] with us so he wouldn't have been there anyway.

Verushka told him she bought some of his News Corporation shares. 'Great!' He had told her that if he gets away with what he is doing by reducing the printing staff from around four thousand to five hundred or so, the shares will double.

Rupert has been too busy to pursue his plan to try to bring Sikorsky-Fiat together with the European consortium. Arnold very grumpy this morning. Everybody has behaved dishonourably. He and Jim Prior have been threatened at least five times. If they refer the GEC takeover bid for Plessey to the Monopolies Commission, it will be a political act directed against him and he will spill the beans and reveal the terrible threats he has been subjected to at the Select Committee of Defence at the Commons.

I said, 'Don't be silly. You'll only make matters worse.' 'I don't care. Why didn't she tell me what she wanted at the beginning? I would never have got involved in it.'

---

19. He reviewed *Making Sense of Europe* by Christopher Tugendhat.

20. The British Prime Minister's official country residence in Buckinghamshire.

He's furious with Heseltine. How could he walk out and leave them in the lurch? The European consortium won't withdraw. He doesn't care what happens.

I said, 'Have you rung Margaret?' 'I haven't rung her since before Christmas to thank her for helping us get the great Chinese export deal of £500 million. She knows I'd come and see her immediately if she wants to see me. She doesn't ask me to.' From the way he's talking perhaps it's just as well.

Cuckney is worried that there is still something to come out about the Solicitor General's letter to Heseltine. Maybe it will be shown that it was leaked by somebody in Brittan's Department or even Brittan. I said, 'Yes, but the report of the internal inquiry is not going to be published.' 'No matter. It'll leak. Somebody will give it away. It's still very bad for Brittan and Margaret if anything comes out.'

I think they're all wrong. The public is beginning to get bored with the whole affair and, as I explained in the *Times* this morning, Harold Wilson himself said when a leak has the approval of the Cabinet it is no longer an official secret.[21] That does not apply to Heseltine any more because he has no official position and his leaks are not official.

Cuckney thinks it will take about six weeks to rearrange the scheme for Sikorsky to come to the rescue in a legal fashion and get it through. All very damaging.

Cuckney feels British Aerospace has not got much heart in it now and probably would like to go. Indeed they may even do so. He says Arnold is wrong in believing that Hanson's buying of the shares (fifteen per cent) made all the difference. How does he know that they wouldn't have voted that way in any case? But Arnold says at least five per cent were bought from Robert Fleming's[22] who were going to vote against the Sikorsky route and the result would then have been fifty-fifty.

Cuckney is very worried because he says Brittan is now trying to dig up everything he can to hurl at Heseltine and it's going to make the fight nastier and bloodier. I think Brittan ought to restrain himself now but obviously he is feeling vicious against his enemies. Cuckney seems to be remaining cool. Whatever Arnold says he has dealt with

21. WW wrote: 'Wilson also established the doctrine in 1969 that "where the Cabinet agrees to information being made available, then from that moment it is no longer regarded as an official secret". That was to cover unattributable leaks, at which Wilson was a dab hand.'
22. A merchant bank.

the situation well. What annoys Arnold is that he is opposed to him and he is persuasive.

Rupert is nervous for such a powerful man about how he should speak to Mrs Thatcher whom he has met before once or twice with me at lunch or dinner. I said tell her exactly what you think as you told me about her not getting a grip on the Westland affair much earlier. 'Would she mind?' 'Of course not. What's the point of talking to her if you're not going to tell her what you think?'

I have been wondering whether to tell her about Arnold's threats if the GEC bid for Plessey is referred to the Monopolies Commission. Decided to leave it and see if there is an opportunity on Sunday. I don't want Arnold to get estranged irrevocably from Mrs Thatcher. He's being very childish. Anyone who disagrees with him is a villain. He cannot see that sometimes people have to take action other than that he prefers.

**Sunday 19 January**

As Chequers comes into view we agree how easy it would be for a helicopter or armed assassins to land despite the odd police car dotted around the park. Only ten minutes late.

Denis and Margaret waiting on the doorstep outside the front door, having been alerted by police at the lodge. She was delighted with my *News of the World* article this morning. It cheered her up. 'It's been a bad week.'

It's always very hot inside with a log fire burning high to which Margaret adds logs often. 'Would you like some champagne?' Denis asks. When I say yes he said, 'I thought you would. We have some ready.' It's quite good but Rupert has his mixed with orange juice. He has really given up drinking altogether.

I told her of Arnold's threats and how he will make all kinds of revelations if his bid for Plessey is referred to the Monopolies Commission (which I don't believe: I think he'll calm down eventually). She says, 'But we haven't even had a recommendation from Borrie[23] yet' (Office of Fair Trading). I say I think it will be difficult not to refer such a gigantic merger to the Monopolies Commission: the decision is Leon Brittan's whom Arnold now detests. If Arnold weren't a Jew I would think he was anti-Semitic from the way he talks about him.

23. Sir Gordon Borrie QC (knight 1982), director-general, Office of Fair Trading, 1976–92.

I say a remaining worry is the leak of the Solicitor General's letter. 'Are there precedents for the internal inquiry report not being published?' Margaret said, 'Yes.' 'Well I think someone ought to assemble them very carefully now because it will look bad if, as I assume, it was a leak from the Department of Trade and Industry.' She looks worried but I think is reluctant to say much more in front of Rupert, probably thinking erroneously he might put something in his newspapers.

I drink champagne throughout lunch, the bottle having been brought in for me to finish, so I'm drinking more than usual, particularly at lunch time. Rupert saw the cigar in my breast pocket on the way down. 'Why are you bringing that? Don't you get a cigar at Chequers?' 'Sometimes,' I said 'but sometimes it comes very late.' This time no cigar came so I was right to have brought my own.

Margaret lamented the fact that nurses on £140 a week pay £40 tax. The difficulty is that lowering the top rate of tax would cost a piffling amount. Unfortunately, drastically to cut basic rates for nurses and all people in such a position would be more than the nation could afford.

We talk about Puritans and Cavaliers. She says she must be a bit of a Puritan, particularly as she doesn't draw her full salary as Prime Minister but now they've bought Dulwich[24] she rather wishes she had. I say that that is one of the great problems of England. Everyone even within themselves is part Puritan and part Cavalier. 'I'm a Cavalier,' says Denis. 'Yes,' I say, 'but it's more finely balanced in most people. The Civil War of the 1640s has never ended.'

Denis says he wished he could go and live in Dulwich now. I said, 'Margaret can't resign for least ten years and certainly not until I'm dead.' He says it's near a very good golf course.

I tell Margaret that Cuckney thinks it could be six weeks before they get the new Sikorsky-Fiat scheme through. 'Oh dear.' I tell her that Arnold thinks she put James Hanson up to buying fifteen per cent. She hasn't spoken to him or to Cuckney.

I wouldn't like to live at Chequers. I hate these leaded-window, Elizabethan-type buildings, though the hall between the sitting room we were using and the dining-room is very fine. 'Yes,' says Margaret, 'Ted Heath was responsible for making it like this.' It must be a long time since she paid him a compliment.

---

24. The Thatchers had bought a house in Dulwich, south-east London, for their retirement.

Instead of going straight home we call at Tower Hamlets. Rupert gives us a tour inside and outside the vast new printing works. Part of the operation is in a listed warehouse which has been beautifully done up with lovely brickwork outside and inside in many places except for where some chumps have painted it white. We have coffee in the deserted canteen which V says is so attractive it is as good as the Churchill[25] where she often has coffee and sandwiches. Rupert very happy as he tows us round.

I say, 'You're not really serious are you about the *London Post*?' He says, 'No, of course not. It's just a ploy.' I said, 'It was so convincing it almost had me fooled.' The *London Post* was the vehicle used for him to employ his five hundred plus electricians as printers at Tower Hamlets, ready to advance to about eight hundred when all the titles could be printed there.[26]

Netta told V that Arnold is now subscribing to the SDP. He may be able to run a great business but emotionally and politically he's a child. But I remain devoted to him, anxious to stop him going too far.

10.30 p.m. Rupert rings. 'I've had an idea. I think I shall try to get United Technology to buy fifteen per cent in Westland. That should fix the vote permanently in favour of the Sikorsky-Fiat deal. Will it provoke Arnold and make him worse?' I said, 'I don't think so. He may be relieved not to have to do anything more. He keeps telling me that it would be dishonourable of him to withdraw now but if victory is hopeless what would be the point of going on?'

It is really unbelievable that so much time has been spent on Westland during this extraordinary period. As poor Margaret was saying, how on earth can we have been wasting so much time and effort on this tiny little company which is of no account in our affairs?

**Monday 20 January**

Get home to find Arnold has been ringing. The GEC bid for Plessey has been referred to the Monopolies Commission. Now he will reveal everything but what I do not know. I suppose he means all about the times that he thought GEC were leaned on and Prior was leaned on and so forth.

Again I say, 'Don't be an ass. Calm down.' 'No, they're ruining my

25. Hotel in Portman Square, London W1.
26. See 28 November 1985.

business. We have to have a different government.' 'Even Kinnock?' 'Yes, that would probably be better for GEC.'

Jim Prior breaks in on a three way telephone system. I asked him, 'If you had been in the government, would you have supported a referral to the Monopolies Commission of the GEC/Plessey bid?' 'Probably. I didn't know anything about it then.' I said, 'Well how could the government on such a huge matter fail to refer it to the Monopolies Commission? There would have been the most violent criticism.'

Arnold butts in. 'Oh, but it's all politically directed against me.' I say, 'Brittan would have been much more cunning. He could have bought you off by not referring to the Monopolies Commission. It was a quasi-judicial decision.' Prior says, 'Oh no. He's just weak and took the easy way out.'

Arnold is furious because the Permanent Secretary at Trade and Industry had previously said for goodness' sake merge with Plessey.

I said, 'Well, it can't make all that much difference if you have to wait six or nine months.'

Crispin and Prue Odey come to dinner. She is Rupert's daughter.[27] When they were in Italy with us she was complaining every day that her marriage was not working and taking the temperature hour by hour. 'How is the marriage going?' I asked. 'Quite well at the moment,' she said. 'Are you going to have a baby?' 'I'll just see how he behaves himself.' Without thinking hard I called Crispin 'Pipkin' which delighted Prue. She says she'll go on using the nickname.

When I was talking with Arnold Weinstock on the telephone today Arnold said, 'I'm going to go and live in Switzerland. I'll pay no taxes there.' 'What about the racing?' I ask. 'Oh I can come to England for ninety days.' 'But I can't let you do that,' I say. 'What should I do without you?' 'You can come with me. Make friends with the Prime Minister and write a column in the local *Wittenberg Chronicle* or whatever it may be called. I may be too old to go on with this sort of thing.'

**Tuesday 21 January**

The print unions have decided to give their executives the power to call a strike at all Rupert's titles. We may lose the *News of the World* most likely in the London area this week-end. Rupert wants them to go on strike so he can sack the lot.

---

27. By his first marriage.

Rupert asked me did I think the strike would last long and be very bitter. I said, 'No. It's not like the coal strike when rightly or wrongly Scargill's miners thought they would win. This time the print workers begin knowing they're already beaten and have very little heart for it.'

Verushka opens a letter to Petronella from Worcester, Oxford. There's a copy of the letter they wrote on December 19th which never arrived because of the Christmas post and which says that she has to have an O level in mathematics or a science subject or she can't go. Panic all round. I spend half the morning ringing Oxford speaking to Harry Pitt, St Paul's[28] and to Dr Andrew Lintott who says, 'Why doesn't she try human biology? My science friends say it isn't a subject at all. Anybody can learn it in a fortnight.'

I say, 'She has a blockage about mathematics. What happens if she doesn't get one of these damn O levels?' He says, 'We'll go into action straight away in August and say there are exceptional circumstances, though unfortunately Worcester has been one of the colleges most keen on insisting on the minimum standards for entrance to the University.' I said, 'What would the exceptional circumstance be?' 'An unhappy childhood, perhaps.'

More realistically he said, 'We could perhaps say if she goes in for biology and doesn't pass she didn't have enough time in switching from mathematics.'

At lunch today I was at the South African Embassy. A number of dim Tory MPs were there about to go on a tour of South Africa, examining their programmes. They and the programme both dull.

I keep agitating Mr Evans, the Minister, to send me the books he promised me so I can read up about South Africa before I go.

I said, 'I hope you're going to make all the arrangements for me to see Chief Buthelezi, Bishop Tutu, President Botha and so on. Perhaps even Mrs Mandela.'

When I told him in the evening of the programme arranged by the Oppenheimers[29] he said, 'That'll fit in very well.' I told him I thought the white wine was very nice we had at lunch. 'Oh, I'll send you round a bottle.' I said, 'For goodness' sake don't.'

They keep on wanting to pay all or part of our trip and I keep telling them if they did that it would vitiate anything good I said about

28. St Paul's Girls' School which Petronella attended.
29. Sir Philip Oppenheimer (knight 1970), industrialist and racehorse breeder, of the South African diamond industry family.

them and not only that I'd be bound to say more horrid things about them than I otherwise would. They cannot get the point. The MPs are all having a free tour.

Go out to dinner without Verushka to Andrew Knight's. His wife is a beautiful Indian part-Persian, half-Muslim girl. Her mother lives in Rajasthan. She tells me she was married when she was seventeen, her father having unwisely let her go to Brussels. She was terrified always of her father who taught her English by reading Shakespeare to her and making her read it. She speaks beautifully. She has read my book and liked it. She said she doesn't believe there's all that much difference between men and women except women like to have some understanding and sympathy.

Also present was Peregrine Worsthorne[30] and I tell him what rubbish he wrote on Sunday in the *Sunday Telegraph* about a coalition government being more or less inevitable. I said it was one of his perverse articles where he thinks the opposite of what is likely and then writes it up for a journalistic stunt. His wife[31] wasn't very pleased.

On the other side of me to Mrs Knight at dinner is the wife of a famous pianist (Alfred Brendel: she is surprised I have never heard of him) who is on the board of Covent Garden. 'Why don't they put on Gilbert and Sullivan?' I ask. 'It's only because it's English. The only English modern opera they like is by Benjamin Britten and that's because he was queer.'

The American Ambassador, Charles Price, and his wife Carol are there. She is very affectionate and rather pretty. 'We've been feeling so sorry for Mrs Thatcher. I admire her enormously but we're in a difficult position and can't ring up and say how much we support her. Perhaps you could let her know.'

Talking to Charles Price after dinner I said, 'It's no good asking the British to go in for sanctions against Libya. As I wrote in the *News of the World*, Higgins says to Alfred Doolittle the dustman, "Have you no morals, man?" to which Doolittle replies, "I can't afford them, governor. Nor could you if you were as poor as I am." That's the point.' I ask him why the USA doesn't use the Israelis to take out

---

30. Deputy editor, *Sunday Telegraph*, 1961–76, associate editor, 1976–86, editor, 1986–9, knight 1991.
31. His first wife, Claudie, née de Cólasse, who died in 1990.

terrorist bases in Libya and assassinate Gaddafi.[32] He's not sure they would agree.

Andrew Knight is very clever but remote and slightly forbidding. He takes over running the *Telegraph* on February 1st. He tells me that they're losing circulation by the tens of thousands every week. I say, 'That's strange. I think it's such a good paper.'

Imran Khan, the famous Pakistani cricketer, comes in with his girlfriend. He asks me do I think Botham[33] is good? 'He's not a quality player.' He agrees. He seems very pleasant. 'What do you think about all this fuss about people playing in South Africa?' He said he thought Bangladesh took an absurd attitude against the England B team but he wouldn't play in South Africa. 'I would only be an honorary white because I'm good at cricket. Otherwise they would look down on me because of my colour.'

This colour thing is ridiculous. Mrs Knight, a couple of shades whiter, would look exactly like a beautiful English girl. Imran Khan would also look like an English boy, a couple of shades whiter. All they've done is sit in the sun about a hundred thousand years longer than we have, we all having started from the same point. We arriving late found all the best places occupied and moved on to the ghastly climate of Europe, naturally staying or turning white or pink.

Mrs Knight says she had so been looking forward to meeting Verushka and trying to make a friend of her as she was rather frightened of her.

I said, 'She may frighten the family but she doesn't frighten anybody else. The reason I love her so much is she makes me laugh.'

Carol is a frisky girl. I had been sitting next to her after dinner. After she had left the room to go with her Ambassador husband she turns back again and presses her finger on my nose with a mischievous grin.

**Wednesday 22 January**

Rupert says he has spoken to Andrew Neil[34] and he's just considering whether or not to do my extra piece about South Africa in the magazine or the front page of the review so I must ring him and sort the matter out.

---

32. Libyan ruler since 1969.
33. England cricketer who played in ninety-four test matches 1977–87, twelve times captain.
34. Editor, *Sunday Times*, 1983–94; executive chairman Sky TV, 1988–90; editor-in-chief, European Press Holdings, since 1996; editor, the *European*, since 1997.

Charles Wilson[35] rings to say he can come to dinner on February 12th with Sir Geoffrey Howe[36] but his wife can't which is rather a relief as she's a real fright. He's thinking of asking Christopher Tugendhat[37] whether he'd like to be political editor and asked me whether I could find out more about him.

Charles also was wondering why *Private Eye* is attacking him so much which they did again this morning. Was it, he wondered, because he doesn't come from the usual sources, meaning that he's not grand socially like Douglas-Home.[38] I said, 'Well they always like to have a character to pursue. They do it with lots of people and then they get bored.'

He was clearly referring to the suggestion in today's *Private Eye* that when he saw a pretty girl working in one of the departments he was supposed to have remarked 'What do I have to do to get my c . . . up that?' Not usually the sort of language associated with the editor of the august *Times*.

The leak of the Solicitor General's letter is identified as from the Department of Trade and Industry. She promises a full statement about the leak inquiry conducted by Sir Robert Armstrong[39] for tomorrow. What a lot of nonsense about an unimportant letter which should have been published anyway.

V dashes off with Petronella to school, then goes down to Sloane Street to talk to Jane Churchill[40] about wallpaper for the new Tote rooms at Newmarket. Gets herself 'clamped' and complains bitterly to me as though it were my fault. She also arrives over half an hour late at Nicholas'[41] for onward transmission with myself to Caroline's mother who'd been cooking a special dinner of stuffed pheasant.

---

35. Editor, the *Times*, 1985–90.
36. Secretary of State, Foreign and Commonwealth Affairs.*
37. Former *Financial Times* journalist; Conservative MP, 1970–6, British EEC Commissioner, 1977–81, Vice-President, European Commission, 1981–5; knight 1990.
38. The late Charles Douglas-Home, whom he succeeded as editor of the *Times*, was a member of the family of the Earl of Home, former Prime Minister.
39. Secretary of the Cabinet, 1979–87, Head of the Home Civil Service, 1983–7; life peer 1988.
40. Interior decorator; m (1970) Lord Charles Spencer-Churchill, son of the 10th Duke of Marlborough.
41. Verushka's son by her first marriage, Nicholas Banszky von Ambroz, merchant banker at this time with Charterhouse J. Rothschild Group; m (1984) Caroline, née While, an executive at N. M. Rothschild & Sons.

**Thursday 23 January**

Rupert on the telephone at 7.30 a.m. She (Margaret) must tell the absolute truth without any deception. He's off to meet the unions to talk about the possibility of some of them remaining at the old printing centres but it will have to be on a seventy-five per cent reduction of staff. I ask if Eric Hammond[42] is standing steady and he says yes. He doesn't mind if the TUC do expel the electricians though he'd rather this had been caused by Scargill[43] than on an issue like this.

It was last summer that I put Eric Hammond together with Rupert and Bruce Matthews of News International, having sounded Eric out first if he'd be willing to let electricians run the works at Tower Hamlets. The secrecy had been kept perfectly since.

I had tried her [Margaret] earlier but she was in the bath. After a while I try again to find that there's something wrong with her telephone in the marvellous era of the new British Telecom. Eventually they ring back and we get through.

I gave her the message from the American Ambassador and Carol Price of support and affection which he felt that as Ambassador he could not put in writing or speak to her on the telephone about. She was delighted: 'How sweet of them.' She seemed confident though worried. 'I'll need your prayers around about 3.30 this afternoon.' I told her not to worry. Everything would be all right.

At Wood Lane BBC television centre I see the *Panorama* film which occupied the whole programme which I had made in June 1957[44] – except that they hadn't got all the parts there and I now have to go back again on another day. It was nostalgic to see myself as young, lean and sprightly, with dark black hair, interviewing Strijdom, the Prime Minister, and many others. Soweto was shacks and corrugated iron then. I want to see what it looks like now.

In the evening Kinnock said it was like the start to the Watergate scandal which he would like the Solicitor General's letter to become in

---

42. General Secretary, Electrical, Electronic, Telecommunication and Plumbing Union (EETPU), 1984–92; the electricians were co-operating with Murdoch to introduce the new printing technology.
43. President of the National Union of Mineworkers who led the 1984 miners' strike.
44. WW was a regular presenter of *Panorama* at this period. The South African government protested to the British government and the BBC because blacks were interviewed in the same programme as their Prime Minister, J. G. Strijdom (*Confessions of an Optimist*, pp. 247–8).

Britain. I think the country must soon get bored. Margaret in some respects was thin, not explaining when she first knew that the Solicitor General's letter had been leaked (she had not been consulted) and why she had set up an inquiry when she must have been told, so there was nothing to inquire about, as Brittan had authorized the leak. She is not free from her pursuers yet.

Rupert thinks Brittan must go. 'But that would be disloyal of her. They would say that she has let him down though he had stood by her.' Rupert says, 'Perhaps he has something on her and might make a commotion if he was forced to resign.'

His meeting with the unions had been highly satisfactory. They've refused to negotiate on lower numbers at the old centres and he refused to discuss any of them going to Wapping. So the strike looks almost certain. Rupert is hoping to get his papers out with most of their pages using Tower Hamlets and Glasgow if they won't print at Manchester.

A lot of wild rumours about the majority of the 1922 Committee saying they won't support Margaret on Monday unless Brittan goes. They want somebody's blood. If they fail to back her many of them will lose their seats and they'll lose the general election.

Andrew Neil says they pay £5,000 if they use one review piece and £8,000 if they use two about South Africa.

**Friday 24 January**

David Montgomery, the editor of the *News of the World*, and John Smythe, deputy editor, cancel their lunch at Cavendish Avenue. They're too involved in trying to get the papers out in Tower Hamlets as a fall-back if the strike comes.

I write an article dwelling partly on Kinnock's lie about his age making himself sound older because he was so young when he was first adopted as a Labour candidate at Bedwellty. How can a man who will tell a lie under those circumstances lead a witch hunt about leaks and misrepresentations?

Robbie [the chauffeur] comes in to say he's heard on the wireless that Leon Brittan is intending to resign.[45]

Nicholas Soames[46] says that he was at the 1922 Committee and the reports were absurd. Most of those who spoke wanted Brittan to resign

---

45. He did, that day.
46. Conservative MP since 1983, son of Lord (Christopher) Soames and grandson of Sir Winston Churchill.*

but the majority did not seem to be so agitated. Nearly all are convinced they have to support Margaret or be done for themselves. He thought her statement was feeble in the House that afternoon. Nicholas was not staunch himself.

**Saturday 25 January**

'How can I best help her?' I asked Willie Whitelaw. 'By encouraging her.'

She has to meet the awkward questions. People find it hard to believe she wasn't told about the leak of the Solicitor General's letter immediately it happened or before it happened, or soon after it happened. If she wasn't when did she know? And when did she know that Brittan or the DTI had authorized the leak? If it was pretty soon after the leak why did she authorize an inquiry? What was the point of it if she knew the answer already?

Willie says she must be seen to be telling the truth and he hopes there is nothing she could not answer satisfactorily. 'If she can't?' 'Well,' said Willie, 'God knows what happens.' He said, 'Of course Brittan had to go. He should never have seen Lygo. He made a dreadful muddle of everything.'

Speak to her. She repeats that until she saw the report of the inquiry on the 22nd she didn't know eighty per cent of the facts. 'Truth is stranger than fiction,' she said several times.

I said, 'Is your answer to setting up the inquiry about a leak, though you would have known it had been authorized, that there were so many facts which were unresolved or unknown that you thought an inquiry was needed to clear them up?' 'Yes,' she said. 'Look at how many differences of opinion there were over what Lygo said and what Brittan said to Lygo. Lygo had one version, the civil servants and the Ministers had another version: truth is stranger than fiction.'

I was getting the impression that there is some dispute between No 10 and the DTI offices about what exactly did happen over that week and who authorized what and who did what. In which case she can justify the inquiry.

I asked her why she didn't answer more fully the questions when she made her statement on Thursday. 'I had to be absolutely meticulous in what I said. I didn't want to answer anything off the cuff.'

'Don't worry,' I said. She said, 'Of course I worry. Did you see what Willie said about Heseltine in the House of Lords yesterday?' I said, 'Yes. And I have used it in my *News of the World* article.' 'When you have a rogue elephant in the Cabinet,' I said, 'collective responsibility becomes impossible.'

Rupert very joyous. The arrangements are going well. The journalists of the *Sun* and the *Sunday Times* and the *News of the World* are all prepared to work at Wapping. The doubters and dissenters are among the *Times* which has been somewhat left-wing and bolshie for years among its journalists and to some extent in the stuff they produce.

He says, 'There's an unfortunate cartoon in the *News of the World* showing Mrs Thatcher choking on leek soup. Do you think she'll mind?' I said, 'I suppose not. It's not worse than all the other things she has to put up with.'

In the evening it is announced that Paul Channon[47] has taken Brittan's place as Secretary for Trade and Industry. That's scraping the barrel. He's a shallow uninteresting man with no ballast or authority, merely the Guinness millions behind him. I've never liked him though his wife is jolly.

Originally she was married to Jonathan Guinness who lived in my Bosworth constituency. She left him to go off with Paul Channon, prompting me to say, 'She was the girl who thought that more than one Guinness was good for you.'

Caroline[48] says that when Tony [Lambton] rang up the other day, she told him we were coming. He gave as his reason for the great row[49] that we didn't pay our bills. I said, 'That's monstrous. We paid everything we were asked to by Hugh Hamilton and he charged us for things he should not have charged us for in Italy such as replacement of a swimming pool motor. Verushka thinks probably the real reason was that his book[50] received very few reviews and mine was reviewed everywhere in large space. Caroline says that probably didn't help.

In May or June he'd been very friendly. It was only when we arrived in August I realized he was determined to be hostile and get rid of us. I told her about [how] he excused the filthy condition of the swimming pool – blossoms from the ilex trees which if they did have them at all

47. Son of Sir Henry (Chips) Channon MP, and a member of the Guinness family on his mother's side.
48. Duchess of Beaufort (1928–95).*
49. Over La Cerbaia, the villa on Lambton's Cetinale estate near Siena in Italy rented by the Wyatts from Lambton.
50. His *Elizabeth and Alexandra* was published in 1985.

were tiny and came in March and not August or July. Anyway, they're too far from the pool.

I said, 'The trouble with Tony is he has enthusiasm for people for a bit and then he turns against them.'

When I spoke to Margaret I asked her who was going to wind up for the opposition on Monday. She said, 'Don't say anything, it's not known yet, but John Biffen.[51] He's on our side.'

When I spoke to Rupert I said I had two friends in difficulties, him and Margaret, and he said, 'Yes, but I'm winning.'

**Sunday 26 January**

The trouble with staying deep in the country in places like Badminton[52] is that you don't get the newspapers early enough. I hadn't seen one by half past ten. When I went down to get my breakfast I poked my nose into the kitchen and found about eleven servants sitting around the table just like *Upstairs, Downstairs*. They now have far more servants than when I was last here. David is doing very well with the estate and of course has his own art gallery business which pumps in the money.

Michael Tree[53] rings while we are having breakfast (just David and I). He speaks on his walkie-talkie telephone. Julian Amery is staying with the Cranbornes.[54] Hannah asked Catherine would she like some coffee in the morning? She said, 'No, I've already had two Bloody Marys.' Julian for breakfast had three-quarters of a bottle of claret, a large brie and then went on to large quantities of brandy.

I said, 'He did that once when he was staying with us in Italy. The servants said that's what peasants have for their breakfast, wine and cheese.'

Robert Cranborne says that they're all fed up with Mrs Thatcher in his constituency and I say, 'That's because he tells them to be.' Anne Tree comes on the telephone. 'What are they doing to my heroine? All those Tory MPs are turds.'

Rupert rings. He says she must admit to fallibility if there is any.

51. Leader of the House of Commons, 1982–7.

52. The Beauforts' seat in Avon.

53. Son of Ronald Tree (Conservative politician (d 1976)); m (1949) Lady Anne, née Cavendish, daughter of the 10th Duke of Devonshire; see 19 July 1986.*

54. Viscount Cranborne, heir to the Marquess of Salisbury; Conservative MP for Dorset South 1979–87; m (1970) Hannah, née Stirling.*

She must tell all the truth however difficult. He says the *Times* will be friendly tomorrow probably and the *Sun* will be very friendly saying 'Well, what do you want, somebody like Galtieri[55] to run the country?'

Rupert this morning enjoying his triumph. 'The journalists from the *Times* are rolling in now this morning (he was at Wapping). I rather wished they hadn't been. We could have produced the paper better with about thirty executives. I'm inclined to sack all the *Times* journalists who don't turn up except one only creates large numbers of enemies on television.'

I'm worried. I have a feeling there's something Margaret is still afraid of. She was good on the Tyne Tees 1.30 programme, but she's skating around something.

After getting back from Badminton I speak to her. 'You must at least answer when you first knew that the famous letter had been leaked and why you set up an inquiry when you must have known who leaked it.' As she had done earlier the day before, she said again, 'Well the truth is stranger than fiction,' a phrase she used on Tyne Tees television. I am very worried. She may not satisfy the mob yet.

When I spoke to Nicholas Soames today he said that a group of them had been to see the Chief Whip on Thursday morning and had demanded that in her statement that afternoon she should deal with everything so explicitly that they would never hear about Westland again but she didn't do so. He said a lot of the backbenchers were very unhappy and barely willing if at all to support her. He reminded me that a while back he had said that many of them are inexperienced and afraid of gunfire and run for cover when they hear it. He didn't sound very robustly behind her either.

For the first time there is semi-serious talk of her having to go which would be a disaster for the Tory Party as well as for the country.

I was asked what I would do then. I said I would never support the Tories. I would join the SDP and support them. I only support Mrs Thatcher who is not a real Tory. If they were such fools and cowards as to get rid of her they would be my enemies.

Arnold rings up and says he's been badly treated by Rupert in the *Sunday Times* Business News. Several attacks on GEC. One may have lost a contract in Oman because they published details which should have remained secret as Oman hates anything being published. There were also one-sided onslaughts on his merger bid with Plessey. I said,

55. Argentine President, 1981–2, during the Falklands War.

'Why don't you speak to Rupert about it?' He said, 'Oh, well, he'd only say he can't interfere with his editors. Andrew Neil is hostile to me. I don't know why.'

**Monday 27 January**

I think we should go to the American system where there's an official government spokesman and although there may be some leaking, a hell of a lot is given to the press by the government on matters of current interest. However, this, I suppose, might be held to conflict, if done too openly, with collective Cabinet responsibility.

Kinnock made a feeble speech. He was put off early on by young Winston Churchill,[56] who had picked up the point from my *News of the World* article, asking him why he was talking about honesty when he had falsified his age for the selection conference which made him an MP.

Mrs Thatcher very effective. Much fuller than before. She conceded matters could have been handled better. Heseltine, who thought it time to try to restore some credit with the Tory Party particularly, congratulated her on conceding that some matters could have been better handled and came out in support. Tories are altogether happier and apart from a few professional malcontents are satisfied.

Before leaving for dinner Arnold rings up. Still full of fury about Mrs Thatcher and Leon Brittan. Insists that the government are hopelessly corrupt and doesn't believe a word of what Margaret has said. Says she's finished and will now be out of office within three months. He cites in particular a decision of the DTI to reject the official recommendation of the Monopolies Commission that BT shouldn't be allowed to supply MITEL equipment in the UK. He says it's all political and directed against him.

A boring dinner with Sir Gordon Brunton[57] and some bookmakers discussing the new *Racing Post* they intend to start in March or thereabouts. We as bookmakers explained to them that the format they propose would not be any good for display in the small space we have in our betting shops. Therefore we could not guarantee to remove the *Sporting Life* in its favour.

---

56. Conservative MP, grandson of Sir Winston Churchill.
57. Newspaper executive and horse breeder; chief executive, Thomson Organization, 1968–84; chairman, Bemrose Corporation, since 1978; knight 1985. The *Racing Post* is still in publication but the *Sporting Life* folded in 1998.

Despite all their boasts I have a feeling that the paper will be a disaster though one of the Makhtoums[58] is putting up all the money. If they can't get rid of the *Sporting Life* he is in for a long ride of heavy losses.

Rupert rings from his car at nearly midnight. 'I'm just going through the picket lines. There are about a hundred pickets here. Some of them are shouting "I hate you." Oh, one has just said, "Good evening, governor."'

Rupert is sticking injunctions on SOGAT [Society of Graphical and Allied Trades] and anyone else who holds up the distribution of his papers. He thinks Mrs Thatcher has done well and says that the *Times* is favourable for tomorrow.

**Tuesday 28 January**

Told Margaret she did very well and that I'm sure the great bulk of the Tory Party are happy.

On Heseltine I said, 'At least he tried to make some amends.' She said in a slightly unforgiving way, 'Well it was all his fault in the first place.'

I wanted to find out from Peter Stothard – he is going to be deputy editor of the *Times*[59] – whether he was still coming to lunch and whether he would come on his own steam. I didn't want my precious 1962 Léoville-Barton opened for nothing.

We couldn't get through on the only telephone number they have at Wapping, a very insufficient switchboard, always engaged, which takes calls for the *Times*, *News of the World* and the *Sun*. So I rang Rupert's private number. He answered the telephone himself and immediately sent messengers out to Stothard to ring up which he did. He was astonished to get a message from the great man to ring me about lunch.

Peter Stothard said, 'Where are your books? I thought this house would be full of books. In none of the rooms I've been in have I seen any books.' So we took him upstairs and he was fascinated by some of the first editions which he has a weakness for collecting. He is very nice. His wife, Sally Emerson, was editor of *Books and Bookmen* for a long time.

I told Stothard I was delighted to see the *News of the World* and

---

58. Racehorse-owning family.
59. He became editor of the *Times* in 1992.

*Sun* journalists working side by side with the grandees of the *Times* and the *Sunday Times* because the *Times* certainly has been depending on the immoral earnings of the *Sun* and the *News of the World* for its existence. Alas, I can't go on teasing my friends on the *Times* with this because with the new arrangements at Wapping the *Times*, nearly in profit now, is going to make a large amount of money on its own.

**Wednesday 29 January**

To National Coal Board for lunch with Mr Ian MacGregor.[60] I was met by the chauffeur who took us to Nottingham where we had the meeting with the executive board of the NCB in my campaign to get the working miners better treated after the strike.

MacGregor very affable. Told me a true story about a speaking engagement he had with a large organization in the north. When it was over he was asked how much money he would like for his speech. He said, 'I don't make speeches for money. I came as a friendly gesture for you and that's it.' So then they wrote to him and said they were very grateful for his generosity. They were sure he would like to know that the £100 he would have been given had been put into a fund so that they might be able to get better speakers in future.

Though he is due to retire from the Coal Board in August he says he is willing to go on or to do anything which *she* would like him to do. I think he intended for me to give that message to her. I congratulated him on how brilliantly he had now turned the Coal Board round and apparently he is due to be making an operating profit before long. In five years he said the NCB or coal will be ready for privatization.

He says there is one advantage in a nationalized industry. You can plan way ahead into the future because you are being subsidized by the public.

He thought very soon now steel could be privatized. It was going the right way. But he was worried about those who run the unions. I said that the new one man, one vote laws for union executives should produce at the end of five years or so different types of executives, far more like the electricians and the engineers now have.

I said, 'The battle is between the old reactionaries and the modern approach. The modernizing element of the TUC will realize that no-strike agreements, higher pay and modern technology are in the

---

60. (1912–98); chairman, National Coal Board, 1983–6; chairman and chief executive, British Steel Corporation, 1980–3; knight 1986.

interests of their members and the other semi-Communist ones are the true conservatives who cannot change their ideology – and in any case want power by getting their posts in undemocratic ways.'

We parted with great cordiality. Many congratulations from me and many tokens of appreciation from him, having made various suggestions for articles I should write which I'm afraid I forgot almost as soon as I left the door.

Apart from sitting next to the lovely Elaine Rawlinson (he is Chairman of some Australian concrete company),[61] the dinner [that night], which was some thing to do with Australia Day and the approaching bi-centenary of Australian existence, was boring. During the tedious speeches (only Hugh Casson[62] was amusing), I pushed my chair back so that I could look at her profile – she has pretty moles on her back.

Tim Rathbone, Conservative MP I met at the dinner, says that for the first time there are serious moves afoot to challenge Mrs T for the leadership next autumn and that Francis Pym[63] is a possible candidate. I said, 'He would get nowhere. He's useless.' 'Yes but it's a sign of her diminished authority that anybody should challenge at all.'

Peter Rawlinson maintains she lied throughout the whole of the Westland saga. Elaine says that she hates Mrs Thatcher because she has been so horrid to Peter not making him Lord Chancellor and saying to people that he would never get anything as long 'as I am here'. She would dearly like her destruction, but she is a gentle woman, saying that she thinks it is wrong for women to be Prime Ministers and that men should have the power and be above all women.

**Thursday 30 January**

While I am trying to write an article for the *Times* about the need for a better system of divulging government views and policies than the furtive one we have now,[64] Arnold rings up.

---

61. Lord Rawlinson was chairman of the UK subsidiary of Pioneer International, Sydney.
62. Sir Hugh Casson, architect and illustrator; president, Royal Academy 1976–84.
63. Foreign Secretary, 1982–3.
64. WW wrote in the *Times* of 1 February 1986: 'I cannot see why Bernard Ingham, the Number 10 press secretary, is unable frankly to say what it is he and the government want the media to understand. If he could, the surreptitious atmosphere which has led to much of the difficulty over Westland would not exist.'

'It is now sworn enmity against her. I was told at the Ministry of Defence yesterday from somebody who really knows and one of your people', he says, 'that she herself has given orders to cancel the great Nimrod[65] project which GEC was working on.'

I said, 'But there's been difficulty about this for a long time. I thought you blamed the Ministry of Defence for continually altering their specifications.' He said, 'Ah yes, but she's now taking it all on herself and is giving orders that it's to be cancelled and another project which I can't tell you about. It's all because of my taking up with the European consortium. Why didn't she tell me she didn't want me to or ask me to withdraw?'

I said, 'She didn't know you were in it until she read about it in the newspapers.'

'She didn't even ask me to dinner at 10 Downing Street when the Israeli Prime Minister Peres was there. It's very extraordinary. She obviously hates me. I'm going to volunteer to go to the Defence Committee Inquiry at the Commons and say everything. I'm going to damage all I can.'

I say, 'But there's a bigger issue involved than this. The most important thing is that she should be the Prime Minister.' 'Not to me it isn't.' 'You're taking a narrow view.' 'Yes I am taking a narrow view. The view of what is best for my business. Any Prime Minister would be better than her now.' I say, 'Don't be hasty and do silly things. I'll talk to you about it tonight.' He is taking me to dinner at Gray's Inn where he is a bencher.

Rupert on breakfast television and on BBC Radio 4 around 7.30 a.m. The Radio 4 Brian Redhead,[66] taking his usual very left-wing line, told him he was packing Wapping with Australian and American journalists, which is quite untrue, and he had behaved badly towards the unions, which is also quite untrue.

The BBC is hopelessly biased against private enterprise and the government because it is a loss-making nationalized industry which exists on public subsidies, apart from most of its producers and commentators being Kinnockites or worse. The wretched Stuart

65. The Nimrod Airborne Early Warning Missile System project was cancelled in December 1986 after £660 million had been spent on it.

66. (1929–94); journalist and broadcaster; presenter BBC Radio 4 *Today* programme, 1975–94.

Young,[67] the Chairman, is a very good accountant but knows nothing whatever about politics and is bamboozled by his staff all the time.

Rupert is firing injunctions at all concerned. He is going to use the law to its ultimate to win his battle. He will win. Eric Hammond is considering taking the TUC to the Monopolies Commission for making a monopoly in labour and refusing to allow competition which is the effect of their saying that the electricians cannot rival the print workers without expulsion from the TUC. Last night at the Australian dinner Sir Geoffrey Howe and the High Commissioner referred glowingly to the enterprise of this Australian down at Wapping.

Lunch with Charles Moore[68] of the *Spectator* at the St Quentin Brasserie, Knightsbridge. Robert Cranborne was there. I taxed him with having said his constituency didn't want Mrs Thatcher any more. He said it was quite true. Many constituencies in the south and south west felt the same.

He had been satisfied with her statement on Monday night but the backbenchers are not. The more they read her statement the thinner they think it is. He said that it reminded him of the 1950/51 Labour government which got tired and irritated. He thinks there's only a 2 to 1 chance of her remaining the Leader of the party. I said, 'Well, that is better than evens.'

I told him that Tim Rathbone had said she'd be challenged for the leadership in the autumn and he said he believed that to be true. He said, 'There is a feeling that her time has come and she'd better decide which title she wants as a Countess and go off with Denis somewhere. Of course everybody would say how marvellous she had been but now she's lost her touch.' It's more serious than I had thought, though as I said to Robert, 'You're very hostile to her and probably exaggerate the feeling against her.'

To dinner at Gray's Inn. It was quite amusing. I picked up Arnold at GEC HQ and found Jim Prior sitting in his office. I said, 'We're not going to talk about Westland or anything to do with it this evening.' Jim said, 'I'll bet you can't get through the evening without that.'

We went in Arnold's curious cab with chauffeur to Gray's Inn.

---

67. (1934–86); senior partner, Hacker Young, Chartered Accountants; chairman, BBC, 1983–6.
68. Editor, *Spectator*, 1984–90, *Sunday Telegraph*, 1992–5, *Daily Telegraph*, since 1995.

Inside it is luxuriously fitted up with extremely comfortable padded seats and prettily covered. There's a wireless and everything else except that Arnold couldn't get the wireless to turn on to Radio 4 for the news.

We saw the Dame Justice Heilbron,[69] now a judge, whom I used to gaze at before the War in the Inner Temple Library when we were both reading for our Bar finals. She was one of the most beautiful girls I have ever seen, her beauty increased by the intelligence of her face. Her face is still beautiful though in a different way. She's four years older than me. I told her that I loved her from a distance and she said, 'I heard about that. A friend of mine sent me an extract from your book.' She seemed very pleased though she's a grand mature judge.

After dinner, in what is the equivalent of a Fellows' common room, a judge from the Court of Appeal (Sir Ian Glidewell) who came and sat next to me for a while said we were both at Worcester College. What did I think of this dreadful man Rupert Murdoch? I said, 'Well he's one of my greatest friends. There's nothing dreadful about him at all. He's first class. He has the nature of a child and is full of friendliness and loyalty to his friends. He's just very good at business. He has sorted out the unions with great dash and skill.'

Many people don't like Rupert. No doubt it is the envy of success syndrome. The English are so set in their declining ways they don't like a man who brings a new world in. They don't like change.

---

69. Dame Rose Heilbron was Treasurer, Gray's Inn, in 1985.

**Saturday 1 February**

When talking to Margaret I told her that MacGregor said that he was quite willing to go on at the Coal Board after August or to do anything else she would like as he loved this country. She said, 'Oh, how nice.'

I told her he said he would soon have coal in profit and ready for privatization in five years' time. 'I should hope he would,' she said.

I also canvassed with Margaret the possibility of having some form of a Ministry of Information but she reasonably said that had never worked in the past and anyway Willie Whitelaw is supposed to be in charge of co-ordinating information. I said, 'Yes. But he's no good at it.'

I wanted her to get Ian Gow[1] back in some capacity as he was very loyal to her. 'Your present PPS may be very agreeable or good but you need as a PPS the kind of person to whom people instinctively say what they're thinking and confide in them because they like him or trust him or both.' This sort of person has to be warm and inviting not slightly cold and forbidding as her present PPS is. He is called Michael Alison,[2] Barley Alison's[3] brother. She has hung around the fringes of literary society in London for years and is unmarried and now seems a bit crabbed. He is too similar to his sister in persona.

Wet and raining at Sandown. But quite a good crowd. Joe Gormley[4] at lunch, now a director of United Racecourses. 'Which union would

1. Conservative politician, PPS to the Prime Minister, 1979–83, Minister of State, HM Treasury, 1985; resigned December 1985 in protest at the Anglo-Irish Agreement; murdered by the IRA 1990.
2. Conservative politician, PPS to the Prime Minister, 1983–7.
3. Barley Alison was a publisher who nurtured many talents; she was a director of Weidenfeld & Nicolson; then from 1968 she had her own imprint, the Alison Press, in association with Secker & Warburg, publishing among others Saul Bellow in this country, Piers Paul Read and David Cook; she died in 1989.
4. (1917–93); President, National Union of Mineworkers 1971–82; life peer 1982; the Union of Democratic Mineworkers was formed by miners who continued working during the 1984–5 miners' strike.

you belong to? The NUM or the UDM?' I asked him. 'If I'd still been there, there would have only been one union and no UDM.' Poor man. He had a terrible stroke a year or so ago. He's speaking a little better now but he's lost his alertness.

**Sunday 2 February**

Spoke to Margaret again about my idea of making Bernard Ingham's lobby meeting open.

She said, 'It would be a great blessing not to have these lobby correspondents coming in to No 10 every morning.'

She said, 'But I don't want him to think I don't trust him and that he's somehow being demoted.' I said, 'That doesn't arise. One of the reasons I love you is that you don't have enough cunning and you're not a devious person.' She said, 'Yes. Ingham and the other officials say that I'm the most honest Prime Minister they've ever dealt with.'

I asked her if Hurd was OK. I thought he might be slightly trying to get at her with his remarks about getting back to real Cabinet government and so on. She said, 'I think he only meant we couldn't have collective Cabinet responsibility while Heseltine was roaming around.' I said, 'I hope that was what he meant and I think it probably was.' She said, 'I find him very loyal and he's an honourable man.'

I said, 'The papers are not too bad this morning. Peregrine Worsthorne, I suppose because he thought it was going slightly against the fashionable grain, decided to say how awful life would be without you. Could anybody contemplate such a thing?' 'Yes, that was marvellous,' she said.

I wish I worked harder. Fundamentally I'm lazy and never want to get started. When I've got under way it's not so bad. I'm behind with learning about South Africa. I have not yet started on my article about the difference between the 1960s and today for the *Mail on Sunday* colour supplement *You*. I excuse myself by saying I must read the newspapers or listen to something on the television or radio. Consistent hard work is something I have never been able to do, though I do more of it now knowing that I have less and less time to live and that my brain may go at any minute.

Rupert very effective on the Dimbleby programme at one o'clock. Brenda Dean, the SOGAT leader, looks as though she wished she had not led her members out on strike and into the loss of their jobs and their redundancy.

Rupert had wanted to take his family (Anna and his two boys are over from New York for the week-end) into Wapping but the security people wouldn't let him because the pickets were much more violent than the previous night.

**Monday 3 February**

At the Working Party on Sunday Racing at the Jockey Club backsliding was evident. The bookmakers' representative wanted to know what guarantee there was of increased betting turn-over.

Monkey Blacker, Deputy Senior Steward of the Jockey Club, is far more go-ahead than the others in the Working Party, anxious to get Sunday racing going. But the Jockey Club wanted to lay down a criterion for how many Sunday race meetings there should be for an experimental period.

I said, 'No. It is for the racecourses to decide their own business. Those who wish to try it should be allowed to try it provided we don't have more than three or four meetings on any Sunday.'

The Westland affair rumbles on. Arguments about whether or not the Private Secretary at No 10 and the Press Office and Private Secretary etc. at the Department of Trade and Industry should appear or be compelled to appear as witnesses to the Defence Select Committee. All very tiresome for poor Mrs T.

**Thursday 4 February**

Laurence Fitch announces the gloomy news that Frith Banbury, having read the play again, thinks it not quite suitable and is too short. This is very odd as everyone else has been telling me it was too long and it certainly is about the same length as *You Never Can Tell*[5] which I measured carefully when I was writing my own play in Italy.

Dinner at the South African Embassy. The Ambassador, Dr Denis Worrall, annoyed Verushka by making attacks on Rupert, saying he'd handled Wapping too ruthlessly. Julian Amery was there with Catherine who looks much better though she is smoking far too much.

The Ambassador is in real life a professor and would like to go back to being a professor. He is gentle and civilized and knows as well as anyone that change must come fast in South Africa, but how? We were taken there by the Minister, Leo Evans, and his wife who live next door.

---

5. Comedy by George Bernard Shaw.

Catherine talks about Antonia Fraser.[6] It was her flaunting of her love affair which so annoyed her and others. It's all right to have love affairs but you don't have to flaunt them in the face of your lover's wives and everyone to show off.

We talked of the unhappiness she caused Hugh who loved her to the end. Catherine said, 'Yes. When he was dying he wanted to see her.'

The Ambassador was surprised and interested to hear us talking about Antonia who I said was a very bad writer and historian. 'But she's very good on some word game on the wireless,' the Ambassador said. 'Yes, that's just about her mark.'

A strange girl: voraciously lustful, rapacious, determined to be a figure of fame or notoriety, not minding which; yet with sensitivity and intelligence. I kissed her once after the races at Salisbury twenty-five years ago; it was pleasant but I never followed it up.

**Thursday 6 February**

There is a new twist to Westland. The ghastly Mr Bristow announced that two peers 'eyeball to eyeball' had offered him a knighthood if he would abandon his support of the European consortium.

He said he was also offered a £2 million profit from the fifteen per cent shares he bought in order to muck up the Sikorsky-Fiat rescue.

Actually he wanted the chairmanship and got into pique when they told him they wouldn't let him have it.

He's only become respectable in Arnold's eyes since he began to support Heseltine and subvert Margaret.

**Friday 7 February**

No 10 issued a denial of any authorization or of any authorization being sought for a knighthood for Mr Bristow. Kinnock jumped in: 'Only one thing is certain: the Prime Minister cannot be believed about anything in connection with Westland.' He foolishly pretends that he believes Mr Bristow and not Margaret.

I am surprised to find that a knighthood is considered to be such a prize.

---

6. Lady Antonia Pinter, writer, daughter of the Earl and Countess of Longford, m (1956–77) Sir Hugh Fraser, Conservative MP (d 1984), m (1980) Harold Pinter, playwright.

**Saturday 8 February**

Arnold says that Bristow was definitely approached by Lord King;[7] by Gordon White who is the right-hand man of James Hanson who is a peer, Lord Cayzer[8] and Charles Forte[9] who is another peer. Bristow says he told people immediately after and Arnold can confirm that. Each of them said to him they would see that he got a knighthood if he withdrew from the European consortium or backed the Sikorsky deal.

Arnold says that the whole thing will be stalemate. The Europeans will still sit on thirty per cent of the shareholding and they will block everything and be a great nuisance. But he did say that the consortium are not getting all the acceptances they hoped for and it looks as though they won't get enough. So maybe they won't be able to prevent the Sikorsky-Fiat route, merely cause a lot of damage afterwards.

Arnold now says he's not going to offer to go to the Select Committee on Defence but he'll have to go if he's asked. I said, 'Well that's an improvement on what you were saying before when you were going to volunteer.' He said, 'Well, I was very cross then. But as the time goes on the pain gets less.'

Heseltine he has not spoken to since he had rung him up and said, 'Why don't you put GEC money into buying Westland shares?' and Arnold had said, 'Why don't you put your own in? You've got plenty of money.' 'Ah yes, but that would be my money. Yours is only the company's money.' To which Arnold replied, 'I take as much care of my shareholders' money as I would of my own, even more so.'

I said, 'I told you he was that kind of a person. He doesn't understand that you regard your shareholders' money as a trust; whereas you might play the fool with your own you wouldn't do it with the shareholders' money.'

I told him that I didn't suppose that any of these people he referred to had really offered Bristow a knighthood. The most they would have done would have been to say that if you behave yourself and withdraw from the consortium, then we'll do what we can for you and we might even see if we can get you a knighthood, or words to that effect.

---

7. Chairman, British Airways 1981–93; life peer 1983.
8. Chairman, British and Commonwealth Shipping Co, 1958–87, Cayzer, Irvine & Co, 1958–87; life peer 1982.
9. Chairman and president, Forte plc, retired 1996; life peer 1982.*

**Sunday 9 February**

Mrs T rang early. She was going to start on a speech in about an hour and thought I might be ringing later when she was busy. Usually she waits for me to ring her so I think she is a little flurried this morning.

'I am not going. I will fight them all the way.' She was referring to the Tory dissidents and the disloyal elements who are making noises more violently about getting rid of her. I said, 'Absolutely right. There's no question of your going. If they force you out I will support the SDP.' 'Oh, that's even worse. Owen is the worst rat in politics.'

She thanked me for my *News of the World* article in which I had supported her vigorously against the traitors. She said, too, that the government had made a very wrong decision in climbing down over the Ford approach to British Leyland.[10] 'It would have been a wonderful opportunity for them all at BL,' she said. She had no choice in the present climate. But she hopes it might not stay that way.

I said, 'All your Cabinet ought to be loyally backing you and making speeches about it. Why do you think Geoffrey Howe doesn't?' 'At the back of his mind I think he hopes to be Leader himself. But they would never make him it.' 'He should remember,' I said, 'that those who remain loyal to their leader to the last are the most likely to succeed. Winston Churchill went on supporting Neville Chamberlain even through the adverse vote in the Commons in 1940.'

She said, 'Howe has not got the calibre to be Prime Minister.' At the Commonwealth Conference it was she who had to fight the forty-six other countries over the South African sanctions. He was feeble.

I said that I didn't really detect solid criticism of Tebbit or herself in what Biffen is reported to have said. 'But he ought to realize by this time,' she answered, 'how what he is going to say will be interpreted.'

I forgot to mention to her the silence of Mr Hurd in the last two days. He could make it to the top but I doubt it.

She said she wished the BBC could be made to know that she doesn't listen to them because they all think she does and doesn't like it and that's why they do it.

I told her Arnold believed she now hated him and was engineering all kinds of awful things against him like the cancellation of Nimrod.

She said, 'Of course I don't hate him. I never hate anybody. I admire

---

10. The government's secret negotiations with Ford were revealed in the press. Lady Thatcher explains in *The Downing Street Years* (p. 440) that the Cabinet decided on 6 February not to go ahead with a deal with the American company.

and respect him. I have a very high regard for him.' I said, 'He had been a bit upset because he had rung and asked to see you but you wouldn't see him.' She said, 'I cannot see anyone until the whole of this Westland affair is over. I have only seen Sir John Cuckney in the presence of Ministers at No 10 in the Cabinet Committee. I have not spoken [to] or seen anybody else connected with Westland on one side or the other.'

Margaret said, 'I was even-handed. I am still even-handed. It was Heseltine who destroyed all that. He wasn't even-handed. That is what all the trouble was about.'

I told her that Arnold said Bristow was claiming that Charles Forte, Lord Cayzer, Gordon White (I forgot about Lord King) had all offered him a knighthood.

She was full of fire. 'It's absolutely ridiculous. As anybody who knows anything about how honours are given would know straight away.'

When I asked her why she thought Lawson didn't speak up she said, 'Well he is very pre-occupied with his Budget. I think he's absolutely sound but that will be the explanation.'

I said I was worried that she hadn't got enough new people coming on, younger ones. She said she had got some good ones coming up. I said, 'Well I don't know them. I don't see much of them so I wouldn't know.' I nearly said 'and that's because you won't put me in the Lords where I would be able to keep an eye on the up and coming' – but I didn't wish to add to her feeling of being crowded by referring to that again.[11]

She will fight to the end to stay Leader of the Tory Party. Thank goodness. No sign of wavering. The more she's attacked the more she'll fight back.

Spoke to Arnold. Told him that Margaret would be glad to see him when the Westland thing blows over but she was not seeing anyone till it was.

What a feeble crew the Tories are. They are nasty and back-biting. Some of them, the more aristocratic ones, can't forgive Mrs Thatcher for being lower middle class. They pretend they are not snobs but they're the worst of the lot, covering it up by saying that they get on better with the working classes and miners than the middle classes do.

---

11. WW did not have long to wait before he reached the Lords; he was made a life peer in the 1987 New Year's Honours.

Dinner at Stelzers for 7.00 p.m. Earlier than I would have liked, leaving me not having done enough homework on South Africa. But nice pink champagne and Château Latour 1971 which had been probably kept badly (forty degrees in cellar under road) and had not been decanted so there was sediment in it.

Andrew Neil present with a dusky-looking, tart-like lady with tight white skirt hitched up well above her knees. She was Sinhalese, agreeable to talk to, working on one of the give-away magazines called *Boardroom*. Evidently Andrew's new girlfriend (he changes them about once a month).

Rupert was also there at dinner looking a little tired but in good spirits.

Rupert got the whole of his *Sunday Times* out today but one and a half million copies short on the *News of the World* because Manchester NGA refused to print it. He is suing them next week and SOGAT tomorrow in the courts.

Petronella more adult than ever, amusing and pretty. Her excitement at going to Rome by herself this weekend for the great Forte[12] wedding is mounting. Dressed by Chanel for dancing, reception, dinners and lunches. She will be about the most elegant person there, seeming immensely rich with no one knowing it was a total outlay of £200 for dresses which last year cost some £3,000 or £4,000.

**Monday 10 February**

This morning, as Arnold had said it would be on Saturday, the European consortium have not got enough acceptances for their twenty per cent of the vote at the shareholders' meeting on Wednesday. It looks as though the Sikorsky-Fiat rescue offer is now likely to triumph, though Arnold says, 'We'll still have thirty per cent and can cause a lot of trouble.'

I don't know why he won't leave the damn thing alone.

Put on another pound in weight yesterday. Can't understand it. Had 6 ounce mackerel for lunch and one piece of toast and margarine and one apple. For breakfast two pieces of toast and margarine and sugar-free marmalade. It must have been my second helping of veal and eating the fruit salad plus all the drink at dinner last night, together with the 1955 Taylor's port which was very good.

---

12. The Hon. Rocco Forte, son of Lord Forte, married Aliai, daughter of Professor Giovanni Ricci of Rome, on 15 February 1986.

**Tuesday 11 February**
Encouraged by a poll or straw sample of Tory MPs on Channel 4 last night (saying that sixty-two wanted Mrs Thatcher to lead the party at the next election and only three didn't, of whom one said he would like to be the Leader), I rang Mrs Thatcher this morning. I told her that my instincts were that the worst of the squall was now blowing out and that the dangers were receding.

She ended with her usual 'God bless you.' She seems to be more her old self again.

Spoke to Julian (Amery).

He said it was very unusual for senior Cabinet Ministers to be talking about a replacement for the Prime Minister. I said, 'But Biffen surely cannot think that he would succeed her?' 'No, but he sees himself as a Kingmaker.'

**Wednesday 12 February**
Arnold in a fury.

They have referred GEC's bid for Plessey to the Monopolies Commission but now they've just announced they are not referring Hanson's bid for the Imperial Group. That's because he bought the fifteen per cent or thereabouts of Westland shares to get the Sikorsky-Fiat deal through and he gives more money to the Conservative Party than anybody. The whole thing is totally corrupt.

I said, 'Wait a moment. I thought the Imperial Group and Sir Hector Laing of United Biscuits want to get together and they won't be able to now.' 'Yes,' he said. 'That's right.'

I said, 'Well, he's a great friend of Margaret's. He's been a supporter for many years and he's even written a letter to the *Times* this morning backing her up, so if it has all been directed against people like you who back the European consortium, why wouldn't she, if she had anything to do with it, have seen to it that he was allowed to do his deal with Imperial from United Biscuits?' 'I expect Hanson gives more money,' was Arnold's answer.

The shareholders at the Westland meeting carried the new proposal with Sikorsky-Fiat by two to one, with the losers complaining at the irregularities under which shares had been bought by supporters of Sikorsky-Fiat's deal. They seem to hope that the Stock Exchange will do something about it. However, the matter at last seems finally settled.

Geoffrey Howe and his wife, David Somerset,[13] Rupert Murdoch, Charles Wilson (the editor of the *Times*), Olga Polizzi, the Stelzers, Margaret Stuart[14] and Chips Keswick to dinner.

Elspeth Howe complained that we stayed in the dining room after the women had left for an hour. Irwin also commented on this strange English custom. I told Elspeth that it was impossible to conduct a general conversation with thirteen people in the room unless I banged on the table and took the chair. Therefore it was sensible that the women should go away and rearrange themselves and talk about what they wanted to while the men had a serious conversation much of which would be boring to women, as I know very well.

She was not satisfied, saying she used to be Chairman of the Equal Opportunities Commission,[15] to which I replied 'Oh, I thought we'd got you out of that.' She then said Geoffrey had said he was going at half past ten because he had to work on his boxes, but he was still here at well after 12.00. I said, 'Well, he must have found it worthwhile talking to Rupert and the editor of the *Times* and others.' She is very loyal to Mrs Thatcher and she wanted me to realize that they both were.

Though the others found Geoffrey unimpressive they underestimate him. He was a good Chancellor of the Exchequer and in many ways is a good Foreign Secretary.

Rupert was arguing that America should support Marcos and we should support America in doing so.[16] It is a great dilemma of who is more likely to stop the Communists winning in the Philippines. I think we should support Mrs Aquino and the USA just hang on to the bases, as they do in Cuba which most people have forgotten. Geoffrey seemed inclined to agree but was rather hesitant about it – perhaps they've not made up their mind what to do.

The Léoville-Poyferré 1950 was very good and tasted full of body and strong. So was the Perrier-Jouët 1953 champagne. The dinner was

---

13. Duke of Beaufort.
14. Viscountess Stuart, interior designer; née Du Cane, m (1979) 2nd Viscount Stuart of Findhorn (son of 1st Viscount Stuart and Lady Rachel, née Cavendish, daughter of the 9th Duke of Devonshire).
15. She was deputy chairman, 1975–9.
16. Ferdinand Marcos had been President of the Philippines since January 1973 when he declared himself President for life. He fled the Philippines on 24 February 1986 when Mrs Aquino took over; he died in 1989.

good with an avocado mousse with shrimps, properly cooked fillet of beef and mushroom salad as well as the ordinary vegetables and a very good prune mousse.

Geoffrey told V that he was sure that Michael H did not arrive on the fateful morning intending to walk out of the Cabinet.

**Thursday 13 February**

Went to see Ewan Fergusson at the Foreign Office.

He was Ambassador in South Africa and is somewhat an expert.[17] Very pessimistic about any peaceful solution. Botha[18] too old and arthritically set in his ways to make real concessions of equality to the blacks. Witness his rebuff to Pik Botha, his Foreign Secretary, for saying that one day a black would be President of South Africa.

Maybe one solution was the military autocratic dictatorship which might remove colour bars but keep the lid on. The alternative Athenian system of the élite democracy ruling the rest would not last. He expects nothing but a little delay from the 'eminent persons' sent by the Commonwealth to South Africa when they arrive in two weeks or so.[19] Buthelezi was not fully in control of the six or seven million Zulus and he doubted whether Inkatha[20] had a million members.

Fergusson stressed the importance of religion among Africans and what the Christian missionaries did to educate them. He thinks that the Afrikaners distrust the English because of their liberalism. It's the Great Trek all over again.

**Friday 14 February**

Valentine's Day. Thought not much point in getting the usual red roses for Verushka as we'll soon be gone. But got a Valentine card with champagne glass bubbling away for her and one for Petronella. Unfortunately they're well aware of where they come from.

Said goodbye to Margaret. Told her that I thought all looked reasonably safe though there were still a few mutterers around. 'Who are

---

17. Ambassador to South Africa, 1982–4, Deputy Under-Secretary of State (Middle East and Africa), FCO, 1984–7; Ambassador to France, 1987–92; knight 1987.
18. P. W. Botha, South African Prime Minister, 1978–84, President 1984–9.
19. The Commonwealth heads of government at their 1985 Nassau meeting had decided to send a group of 'eminent persons' to report on the South African situation.
20. Chief Buthelezi's political movement.

they?' she asked. 'Oh the usual ones, malcontents, the ones you didn't give jobs to, the one's who've lost jobs, and so on. But I think they're scurrying back again now.'

I told her that Geoffrey and Elspeth Howe were one hundred per cent behind her, to which she made no comment.

*From Saturday 15 February until Thursday 27 February 1986 WW was in South Africa with Verushka, making his own eminent person's visit, nearly thirty years after the reports he did in June 1957 for the BBC* Panorama *programme. His encounters and views on the situation as he saw it were published on 31 March 1986 as the lead article in the* Sunday Times *Review section, entitled 'South Africa in Black and White'.*

*In diary form he told how he stayed with the Oppenheimers near Johannesburg, and went on his first day to the multi-racial races at Gosforth Park. Graham Beck, chairman of the Gosforth Park, owner of coalmines, is the first of many he meets who accepts 'the prospect of one man one vote over a period' but 'deplores the folly of sanctions and disinvestment by sanctimonious foreign banks, which cause additional unemployment among blacks, making them easier recruits for the revolutionary African National Congress'.*

*He flies to Bophuthatswana, 'one of the four Homeland states given independence by South Africa but not recognised internationally' where he meets cabinet ministers and students at the university, some of whom favour the banned ANC (African National Congress) 'despite its commitment to violence'. He learns from Mike Rantho of the Urban Foundation about the pass laws which the police use to harass alleged troublemakers. He meets Tertius Myburgh, editor of the* Sunday Times, *'a civilised Afrikaner liberal veering from optimism to hopelessness', and Dr Motlana, chairman of the Soweto Committee of Ten, who is connected with the ANC and tells him of his treatment in prison: 'Curiously, he thinks the Botha reforms may be genuine though they won't go far enough.'*

*At a game reserve he watches black and white children playing together: 'They are comrades. Oh, if the rest of South Africa could be like that.' He lunches with Harry Oppenheimer at the headquarters of Anglo-American. 'He, seventy-seven, has spent much of his life urging fairer treatment of the blacks and providing decent working conditions and pay for black employees.' John Kane-Berman, director of the*

*Institute of Race Relations, tells him that 'The apparatus of apartheid has built up elaborately over many years. It is crumbling fast but will take a few years to disappear completely.'*

*To his surprise, most of the businessmen he meets at a race meeting at Kenilworth Park near Cape Town think it would be a good idea to unban the ANC and bring it out into the open but they reject the idea of one man one vote. He thinks Dr Treurnicht, Leader of the Conservative Party, is a tough customer, indicative of the problems Botha has to his right.*

*He has dinner with Professor Cillié, chairman of the largest group of Afrikaner newspapers and magazines, who thinks there is force in the idea that the ANC should be unbanned and loathes Treurnicht. Dr Allan Boesak, 'soft spoken eminent coloured divine', thinks the ANC would come to a conference if it was a genuine offer to transfer power to them. 'Wait a moment,' WW says, 'no one group can dominate all the others.' Boesak demurs: 'You've got to have the blacks predominate.'*

*Finally, on 26 February, he met President Botha but before then there was an incident with the* News of the World.

**Saturday 22 February**

Last night great commotion from the *News of the World*. The editor hysterical, saying I painted too rosy a picture of South Africa. I said, 'Have you ever been there?' He said, 'No,' but he had relations there. I said, 'Well I have. I am here. I can see what I can see with my eyes.'

At one point I said, 'Well leave the article out then' because he was trying to make me write in a whole lot of extra stuff about what I was going to put in next week. He said, 'You're not to write an article next week about South Africa.' I said, 'But you agreed before we went that I would be writing a part of my second article about South Africa but not the whole of it. That was the part in which I wanted to deal with the grievances which have to be dealt with.'

He said, 'I am the editor. Are you going to obey my instructions?' I said 'If that's how you are going to talk, then you'd better leave the article out – and I've never been censored before.' 'I resent being told I'm censoring you.' 'That's exactly what you are doing,' I said.

John Smythe, Nick Lloyd and Bruce Matthews all rallied round. Very difficult on the long-distance telephone. Somehow at the end we agreed that I would have a longer article than usual. Previously they were going to give me less than usual, getting me to take great chunks out of the piece about Soweto.

I think this is a very serious matter. David Montgomery was absolutely hysterical. 'I can't stand any more of it,' he was screaming. 'I never wanted you to go to South Africa.'

I'm sorry if he hadn't been consulted. Bruce Matthews knew about it, Rupert Murdoch knew about it. I had no idea he hadn't been consulted. In any case, as I told John Smythe, we tried to arrange to have lunch to talk about it and for various reasons he hadn't been able to come. It wasn't my fault.

I have now had to put in [that] the government must recognize the ANC, intended for next week.

**Wednesday 26 February**

*Interview with President Botha*

Danger of Mandela being killed if released and he being accused of it.

Would hand over Namibia now to the five nations but they don't want to take it.

Blacks will talk when they want to. Buthelezi's manoeuvring and he understands it.

Media build up ANC. It's not as strong.

Power sharing absolutely genuine. No problem about Army and police. He'd been promoting black officers, some of them are Colonels now.

It is a nation of minorities, whatever the ANC says. Feels silent majority are on his side.

Absolutely adamant about getting rid of the pass laws and having common identity cards for whites and blacks. Population Registration Act to go.

Agrees that everything does not have to be done by tomorrow afternoon. Seems to think my time scale of about two years was OK.

Afraid that the whites might want to try and take the law into their own hands and demand a lot of shooting. Not at all cross when I put to him my unbanning ANC idea. But he doesn't know that he can do that. He's already said if they will renounce violence they can all come back, the exiles and all, and engage in the council where he is determined on genuine power sharing. Of course all they are saying is hand over power to them which is ridiculous. Nor will they renounce violence.

Very affable. Interview began at about seven minutes to ten, didn't finish until thirteen minutes past eleven.

He told me to tell Mrs Thatcher how much he admires her and give her his regards. He is obviously very grateful for what she made happen at the Commonwealth Conference about the sanctions.

He pointed out the dangers to the economy of not being able to get foreign aid. They need foreign money to do their urbanization programme to build businesses and factories etc. for the blacks.

I discussed with him the morality position of the banks. I said I thought it [their lack of investment] was due more to their fearing South Africa was not a good place to invest in at the moment and said that the media, television scenes of violence, etc. provoke that feeling.

I told him I thought he was right to have banned TV crews from the violent areas. He said yes, and the other day they did take pictures in Soweto which must have been pre-arranged because they were taken from high buildings. It all must have been fixed before the riots began and they must have known when and where the riots were going to be.

He said how he had addressed a meeting of about two million blacks and nobody reported it in the press because it was so friendly. It was not sensational.

Botha said he didn't mind my referring to what he said in general terms but not to quote him directly.

He thought much of the unrest was due to the unemployment. If they could cure that it would take a lot of the sting out of the tail. He was convinced that the majority of blacks were really, the silent majority, behind him.

He says that much of the police and Army presence is as much to protect the moderate blacks from the riots and troubles.

He said, 'Yes, the Group Areas Act is dissolving but it is very difficult to do it all overnight,' and there were certain problems about people not wanting to lose the value of their houses and so forth.

He said it was unfair to go on with boycotts of sport when they have done all they have been asked to. There is no apartheid in sport.

He said he is certainly on the level about educational standards, though it would take time. He was very interested in vocational training for blacks so they could get jobs and not just the academic stuff which was not going to help them get jobs when they left school.

Buthelezi would come along when he thought he had the right

moment to do it without being accused of letting the side down by the other Africans.

He wants a no holds barred discussion of the possibilities in a real constitutional conference.

He struck me as a very honourable man. He agreed with me that many whites in South Africa of the liberal kind did not want to believe him and he agreed that the ANC did not want any reform. He said I was right when I said the world was out of date about South Africa.

He said that if he released Mandela he had very good information they were going to kill him and say he had done it. I said, 'Can they be as devilish as that?' He said, 'Oh yes, quite.'

**Friday 28 February**

Told Mrs Thatcher I was back.

Told her that Botha had sent her his best regards and that he admired her greatly. He also had been very grateful about her stand about sanctions at the Commonwealth Conference.

She asked if I had seen anything of the Eminent Persons' team touring South Africa. I said 'No. I don't think they're going to do any good.'

She liked my article in the *News of the World*. I told her how difficult Montgomery had been, trying to shorten it and censor it. I said, 'It's incredible how people are brainwashed in England about the state of South Africa.'

Spoke to Rupert and wondered why the police or his lawyers did not take more action against the illegal pickets.

Asked him whether the morale was good. 'Not so good on the *Times*,' he replied. 'They are all wets.'

Told him I had an up and downer with Montgomery of the *News of the World* over my column from South Africa.

I said, 'What's the matter with the man?' He said, 'Oh, he's got a white left-wing South African girlfriend.' Thus are policies of newspapers shaped. Good heavens.

**Sunday 2 March**

Lunch with Willie Whitelaw at Dorneywood.[1] He agrees the early warning political system of the government has not been working well. They only knew, that is Ministers, at a very late moment that negotiations had been going on with General Motors and Ford with regard to Austin Rover and British Leyland Land Rover and Trucks. It is now politically impossible to let General Motors take over because of the anti-Americanism sweeping the country.

The lunch was rather good with a hot kind of grapefruit to begin with, pork and very good crackling and a beautiful blackcurrant mousse which looked the colour of magenta, very pretty. The view out of the window over park lands with bare trees, Shakespeare's ruin'd choirs,[2] was lovely with the sun shining on the snow.

Willie says he's never smoked anything in the whole of his life except once in Germany when at his regiment. They said if Hitler dies in his bunker will you smoke a cigar? He said yes and when he went to bed he was woken up to be told the announcement had come that Hitler had killed himself in his bunker. They said you've got to come to breakfast smoking a cigar. He did it. He didn't enjoy it and that was the last and first time he ever smoked anything.

My neighbour, Lady Swinton [Baroness Masham], at lunch said that about one in sixteen of the population is now on drugs. She is an expert on the subject. I said, 'This can't be true. It would mean that one in every eight of all the young were on drugs.' She said, 'Well maybe they are.'

I said, 'What would happen if we legalize the stuff and you can buy a penny packet which would normally cost several hundreds of pounds?' She said, 'That has been an argument advanced but it is rather a dangerous step to take.' I said, 'It might take the glamour out

---

1. Country house near Burnham Beeches, Buckinghamshire, owned by the National Trust and used by the government for entertaining.
2. Sonnet 73.

of it all. So much of the young are attracted by anything which seems illegal and is against authority.'

Willie and Alan Clark[3] were exercised about the Sunday Shopping Act.[4] Clark said he thought that there ought to be a free vote. Willie said no, he didn't think so.

Willie said his advice on Sunday racing was still the same as he had given me a couple of years or so ago when he was Home Secretary. Wait two years until the Sunday shop trading thing has settled down and then try. He thought it was bound to come.

It's extraordinary how intelligent and supposedly well-informed people are so totally ignorant of conditions in South Africa. When I told Cecilia Whitelaw how I had walked through the course with 14,000 people half black at races near Johannesburg she said, 'I suppose they were all separated?' I said, 'No, of course not. All that has gone. We are completely out of date in our views about South Africa.'

James Hanson's helicopter landed on the lawn to take him away. Very smart.

**Sunday 8 March**

Tell Mrs T that I've never felt so ill for thirty years. After my Tote Annual Luncheon speech I had to go back to bed with a temperature of a hundred and one. 'Neither of us can be ill,' she says. 'We have to keep on fighting.'

I told her that her seeing Peregrine Worsthorne, new editor of the *Sunday Telegraph*, evidently paid off judging from his article this morning. 'I don't know why he says I did all the talking. He asked me questions all the time.'

She is having Max Hastings, new editor of the *Daily Telegraph*, to lunch today which I think is a good idea. We wonder what is the matter with David English, editor of the *Daily Mail*, who is unremittingly hostile these days. I said it was because Vere Harmsworth[5] is too disinterested and lazy to interfere. I suggest not seeing David English to talk him round, as he might take it as a sign of weakness.

---

3. Conservative politician and diarist.
4. The Shops Bill would have eased restrictions on Sunday opening imposed by the 1950 Shops Act, now regarded as unenforceable and flouted in most high streets.
5. (1925–98) 3rd Viscount Rothermere, chairman, Associated Newspapers (*Daily Mail*, *Mail on Sunday* etc.), since 1970.

**Saturday 11 March**

Dinner given by Mr and Mrs Richard Searby for Rupert's birthday (fifty-five).

Rupert is looking tired and thin. The strain of all the Wapping move has obviously told on him. Still the picket mob outside.

Charles Wilson, editor of the *Times*, and his wife Sally,[6] who edits a thing called *Options*, are also there. He has rashly bet the owners of Dawn Run, with whom he stayed in Ireland, £100 to £500 Dawn Run won't win on Thursday. He's a great gambler and uses the Tote a lot.

He is also turning out to be an excellent editor of the *Times*. Quite firm and knows what a newspaper should be like.

**Thursday 13 March**

Tote Gold Cup Day at Cheltenham.

Queen Elizabeth looks extraordinarily pretty as ever and wears one of her favourite sapphire brooches. At lunch she speaks about the Penelope Mortimer book published that day which is an acid unpleasant attack on her.[7] I tell her that I knew her a bit some years ago and she was always very bitter and neurotic and she obviously said to herself 'How can I say the opposite of what is generally believed when I write this biography?'

Queen Elizabeth says to me, 'I'm going to write a record of what really happened. The King was not a weak man. He was very strong. I want to put down all the events of that time.'

She said, 'I shall put it in the archives at Windsor and they can decide what to do about it years ahead.' She added, 'This is between you and me. Nobody else knows that I'm going to do this.'

Later at tea she told Piers Bengough[8] that she is always saying indiscreet things to me.

She says the Royal Family when they're alone together often drink a toast at the end of dinner to Mrs Thatcher. She adores Mrs Thatcher and thinks she is very brave and has done tremendous things. She is

6. Sally O'Sullivan, journalist and magazine editor.
7. *Queen Elizabeth: A Life of the Queen Mother*, a biography by the author of *The Pumpkin Eater* and other novels.
8. Colonel Sir Piers Bengough, Her Majesty's Representative, Ascot, 1982–97; Jockey Club steward, 1974–7 and 1990–2; Jockey Club representative on Horserace Betting Levy Board, 1978–81; former amateur jockey riding in four Grand Nationals; knight 1986.

very pleased with what I have written about South Africa. She thinks it is awful how the BBC and media misrepresent everything that Botha is trying to do.

The race is a great race. Four coming up almost together. First Wayward Lad heads Dawn Run by three lengths just towards the top of the hill and Dawn Run recovers and comes back again. A pity for the Tote as we lost £2,500 ante post on Dawn Run. And a pity for me as I had £10 each way on Coombs Ditch which comes nowhere.

A vast crowd swarms round Dawn Run and nearly smothers the horse. The Queen Mother looks over the balcony and says, 'Can't we go down?' Miles Gosling, the Chairman, says, 'Oh no. It is far too big a crowd. You'll get mobbed.' 'Oh,' she says, 'I don't mind. I like it.'

So off we go before the crowd has settled down in any degree. Huge cheers for her. People reaching out to touch her. She loves it all.

At lunch David Stevens,[9] Chairman of a company which now owns the *Daily Express*, and his wife Melissa arrive about an hour late and come up to Queen Elizabeth in great confusion. She was very polite and gracious about it and said to me, 'How awful for them to be late,' but I think they are just very silly and didn't start soon enough.

She is an unattractive lady, stout with thick legs, who makes a good deal of fuss of her short husband, treating him as though he were Napoleon. We once had dinner there when she smothered him in kisses and adulation to the general embarrassment but to his great satisfaction. She claims to be the daughter or granddaughter of a Hungarian Count but Verushka says that is nonsense, she is really Yugoslav.

**Sunday 16 March**

A long talk with Mrs T. Congratulate her on her yesterday's robust speech in which she attacks those who think new policies are required of a softer kind.

She is very touched when I tell her that Queen Elizabeth the Queen Mother said to me on Thursday that when the Royal Family are together they often drink a toast at the end of dinner to her as they think she is marvellous. 'It's all rubbish these stories that the Queen doesn't like you. They all think you are wonderful.'

---

9. Chairman, United Newspapers, since 1981, *Express* Newspapers, since 1985; m 2 (1977) Melissa Milicevich (d 1989); life peer 1987.

She thinks quite highly of Kenneth Baker[10] and thinks he could get to the very top. I said, 'He's a sturdy fellow.' She said, 'I put him in to defeat Ken Livingstone[11] and I think he did.'

One day last week Ronnie Grierson,[12] who deals with the arts and raising money for it and running the South Bank and is closely connected with Paul Getty, said to me that Paul Getty very much wants an honorary knighthood.[13] He's given away millions upon millions and he's got to give away about £30 million a year but is reluctant to do so any more in Britain because he feels he's not getting any recognition. Could I do something about it?

I tell her and she says, 'Well there are problems. First of all there is Bob Geldof.[14] We didn't give him an honour. And secondly we have got to avoid it looking as though you can just buy knighthoods.' I said, 'It's only an honorary one.'

She said she understood that but the connection between the money and the honour doesn't want to be as obvious as it sometimes has been.

I said, 'Was he not getting his honour because he used to be on drugs and so on, because he's not on them any more. He's quite a good fellow.' She said, 'No. It's nothing to do with that. I am watching it and something will be done when it seems the right time.'

**Saturday 22 March**

In the evening a supper with the South African Ambassador. The chief guest is Koornhof.[15] He says how much the President liked me and enjoyed my conversation with him. Says that yes, the pass laws will be abolished by July though there is some delay by resisters on technical points but think they will clear it all up. Says the Group Areas is really

---

10. Conservative politician, at this time Secretary of State for the Environment.
11. Labour politician; leader of the Greater London Council, which was abolished on 1 April 1986 under the Local Government Act 1985.
12. Vice-chairman, GEC, 1968–91; chairman, GEC International, since 1992; member, Arts Council of Great Britain, 1984–8; chairman, South Bank board, then South Bank Centre, 1985–90; knight 1990.
13. John Paul Getty Junior; he was awarded an honorary KBE later in 1986.
14. The pop singer who organized Band Aid, Live Aid and Sport Aid to raise funds for Ethiopa; he was also awarded an honorary knighthood later in 1986.
15. Piet Koornhof, Chairman of the President's Council in South Africa and a former Rhodes Scholar at Oxford; WW had met him on 25 February.

the thing which annoys people a great deal. It is going to take some time to get rid of it.

We were given our supper and a plate was put in front of me and I began to eat. Then the Ambassador said to Koornhof, 'Would you like to say grace?' so to my embarrassment grace was said after I'd started eating. I apologized and Koornhof said, 'It's all right. I had started to eat too.' These Afrikaners are dreadfully religious.

We all went off to see *The Apple Cart*[16] with Peter O'Toole and Susannah York. It was quite good except that I felt the thing was somewhat dated and had far too much talk and too little action and the plot is somewhat ridiculous. Koornhof and the others lapped it up and said how marvellous and democratic it is to be able to show it in England.

'Aren't you proud of it?' I said, 'Why should I be proud of an Irishman? Though of course I think Shaw is marvellous.' Susannah York, very pretty, might have stopped acting if she'd known the South African Ambassador and Koornhof were in the audience. She is both left wing and CND.

**Sunday 23 March**

The *Mail on Sunday*, edited by Stewart Steven, has plastered across its front page 'Premier Faces a New Storm' and underneath in huge headlines 'Exposed: Maggie's Share Dealing'. It is about some shares which she apparently bought or sold or both and made a profit of £2,300 on in Broken Hill Property in Australia. There was nothing secretive about the transaction. Her name was on the Register.

Speak to Harold Lever who says there are no guidelines or rules, as alleged in the *Mail on Sunday*, governing what Prime Ministers or anybody else does and the idea they have to set up trustees is ridiculous. When he was first in the Cabinet at the Treasury he said to Callaghan[17] 'I've got a very large interest' (he has several million pounds) and Callaghan said 'Don't worry. We know you will behave honourably,' which of course he did.

During the afternoon Rupert rings from Beverly Hills, California, and asks about it. I had not then rung Mrs T but I did so.

She says that the shares were bought, as far as she can remember, before she became even Leader of the Opposition and the little bits

16. By George Bernard Shaw, a burlesque of parliamentary governments.
17. Prime Minister, 1976–9.

they were referring to where she made a profit were new share issues or share rights issues as time went by. She didn't even know they'd been sold and she supposed that the professional man who manages her little bits of shares (and she hasn't got many) just altered the address from Flood Street where she used to live to 10 Downing Street at the last transaction.

She says, 'If they haven't got anything better to throw at me, I don't think much of that.' She wasn't taking it at all seriously. I hope she is right. I think she probably is.

**Tuesday 25 March**

A lunch for *The Mousetrap*[18] to celebrate its third of a century run.

I arrived a bit late with Verushka because the Levy Board meeting had gone on longer than usual and I felt it necessary to stay to protest at the idiotic way in which they were adding members to the board of United Racecourses, commentators and race goers who know nothing about running a racecourse. They wouldn't accept my idea that John Sanderson, who runs York and is on our board, should be asked to join United Racecourses.

Sit next to Peter O'Sullevan[19] at the *Mousetrap* lunch. He says I was a bit generous to Lester Piggott[20] in my review of the Dick Francis book[21] which appeared in the *Times* yesterday. He said he's not as honest as I thought he was. He got involved with a lot of bookmakers and at one time early on he had difficulty paying off his gambling debts.

However, he agreed that he was a great genius and it was perhaps OK that I had been fairly free with my praise. I had, however, pointed out his plea of poverty was bogus and that he put on his deafness when it suited him: he was always able to understand on the telephone anyone who was offering him a riding engagement.

**Wednesday 26 March**

Ian Chapman at Collins. Show him my synopsis about the book on the press. He seems very pleased.

---

18. Thriller by Agatha Christie, still running.
19. Racing commentator.
20. Champion jockey, a trainer since 1985.
21. *Lester: The Official Biography* by Dick Francis.

I let him look quickly through the diary[22] which I began on 19 October last. I wanted to know whether he thought it was worth going on writing it. He is strong in praise of it. 'Marvellous' and 'Outrageous.' He says that I must go on with it. He could get me some money for it now.

I said, 'You can't because it has to be a total secret that this diary exists and you are never to breathe a word about it. You must regard yourself as a doctor or a Roman Catholic priest. If you start trying to pay me people will want to know what it is for and the cat will be out of the bag.'

I was a bit worried at seeing Mark Bonham-Carter[23] in his room when I arrived. He is a gossip.

We discussed what is to be done with my diary. I say there would have to be something in instructions to a literary executor. It obviously can't be published until after Mrs Thatcher's death, and one or two of the other characters.[24] Or there would have to be some negotiation. I cannot let Mrs T down: she thinks I don't keep a diary because I told her that ten years ago, when it was true.

I say that I'm really writing it to try and leave something substantial to Verushka and perhaps Petronella so they can make a bit of money out of it in the future. I thought if Crossman[25] could do it, I could write just as good a diary as his, though of a different kind.

He is quick and efficient and I think has good judgement, though he had thought *Confessions of an Optimist* would sell at least ten to fifteen thousand copies and so far it has only sold six thousand plus. He couldn't quite understand why. It may be that the *Sunday Times* serialized too much of it and everybody thought they'd already read the book. He also said it was almost entirely a London sale, hardly anybody had bought it north of Watford.

---

22. These journals; the secret of their existence was well kept until after WW's death.
23. (1922–94); Liberal politician and publisher; first chairman of the Race Relations Board, 1966–70; vice chairman, BBC, 1976–81; former director and at this time editorial consultant at Collins; life peer 1986.
24. WW subsequently decided he wanted his memoirs published on his own death.
25. Richard Crossman, Labour MP, 1945–74; Minister for Housing and Local Government, 1964–6; Leader of the House and Lord President of the Council, 1966–8; Secretary of State for Social Services, 1968–70; he was also a prolific writer and journalist. The three volumes of his diaries were published posthumously.

Irwin Stelzer and Cita come [to dinner] early because I have to talk to Irwin about the famous newsletter[26] with Andrew Neil.

Irwin has got a mailing list of fifteen thousand people, mainly compiled by Cita. He intends that we should sell it at £1,500 for a year's subscription of ten issues whose cost can be put against tax. I am very doubtful whether people could be such mugs as to buy something which, although it is called 'Confidential' and will be well done, is very short and could really be put together by any intelligent person.

However, he says if only one per cent accept the proposal on receiving a free copy of the first issue, we would make £225,000 a year income.

After a year or so we would have something valuable to sell at ten times earnings. The three of us are to share in the proceeds but he has put up the money. I think he has spent some £25,000 on it already.

We get down to a paper on which we intend to base our questioning of John Smith[27] when he comes to Cavendish Avenue at 9.30 a.m. on Thursday morning. John Smith is Labour's Shadow Trade and Industry Secretary. Denis Healey said he thought he was the most able of them and I would do well to talk to him about what was really likely to happen, if there's a Labour government, on the industrial and economic front.

When I told Smith Andrew Neil was one of the three, he said it would be awkward to meet him because of the ban the Labour Party's put on News International journalists but he does not seem to connect me with News International, though I write fortnightly in the *Times* and once a week in the *News of the World* and numerous book reviews in the *Times*.

So we exclude Andrew from the meeting for tomorrow. A car has been arranged to collect John Smith. Irwin wanted to send his Rolls Royce but I thought that inappropriate so he is sending a BMW instead.

**Thursday 27 March**

John Smith arrives at 9.30 a.m., saying he must leave at about 10.15 to have a caricature drawn of him by Mark Boxer[28] who is coming to see him at the Commons. We pack all in very fast trying to get as

26. The newsletter was called *Britain Confidential*.
27. (1938–94); he succeeded Neil Kinnock as Leader of the Labour Party and the Opposition in 1992.
28. (1931–88); magazine publisher and cartoonist, on the *Guardian* at this time.

many questions [as possible] answered in a very short time. He is highly intelligent and thoughtful and honestly says, 'Everybody should understand that parties have political interests. There are some things we can do and some things we can't.'

If there is a Labour government and he and his friends are in control of it, it should be a very moderate one, no nationalizing. They would try to punish the rich but not so badly as the noises made by Hattersley[29] and others would suggest. There is a realization by John Smith at any rate that to take away all incentive even from inheritance is counterproductive.

He is hesitant about what they will do on the unions. I say, 'You owe Mrs Thatcher a great deal. She has made it possible for unions to become led by moderates who will support the Labour leadership and you will hold the Conference and stop them passing dotty things.' He agreed.

I say to him, 'If you are going to sound too moderate, people will say what is the point of changing as you sound like Mrs Thatcher.' He said, 'Yes. There is that danger. You have to balance it rather carefully.' He then rings up at 11.40 to tell his office he is going to be late and is told that Mark Boxer is ill and has cancelled the appointment so he stays another three-quarters of an hour.

A very helpful talk for our purpose. He understands we are trying not to do propaganda in this newsletter but to tell foreign investors and people interested in investing what the industrial and economic climate of Britain is likely to be if Labour wins.

Smith says on no account would Labour form a coalition with the Alliance. So it would be a forlorn hope for Labour to form a government if they don't have an overall majority of their own.

**Sunday 30 March**

I told her about my meeting with John Smith.

I say, 'You've shifted the centre about two hundred miles to the right.' She said, 'Yes but not far enough yet.'

I say, 'I quite like John Smith. I'd never met him before and I talked to him for an hour and a half. He seemed fairly reasonable.' She on

---

29. Roy Hattersley, Labour politician and newspaper columnist; deputy leader, Labour Party, 1983–92; chief Opposition spokesman on Treasury and economic affairs 1983–7, home affairs 1987–92; life peer 1997.

the other hand clearly dislikes him. 'He looks very sinister on television,' she says, 'doesn't come over at all well.'

She thinks, like me, that they would not be able to control their Militants, Trotskyists and other extremists, however confident they are.

'However, I don't think all this arises, because you're going to win anyway.'

I tell her that I am worried about the possibility that her backbenchers will prevent the Sunday Shopping Bill going through. 'There are a lot of votes for you in this. You'll look very weak if you have to drop it or emasculate it. Why don't you put on a three line whip and force them to vote for you?'

She said, 'I don't think that would work. I think too many would rebel. My idea is that for four weeks we should apply the law in its full rigour to show them what it's like.'

**Monday 31 March**

Arnold's house in Wiltshire. He is at his most jocular and insulting. Said what I had written in the *Sunday Times* about South Africa was predictable; I looked very old and much too thin and needed to eat more and didn't look well at all. Some delicious pink Pol Roger champagne.

Arnold's butler is going to work for the Duke of Westminster. When I said goodbye I said, 'I'm sorry I shan't be seeing you again' and he said, 'Oh but you will if I can get you an invitation from the Duke and Duchess of Westminster. I'm sure they would like to see you.'

I thought they probably wouldn't as I wrote a very rude review about the book on Bendor.[30] I said the Grosvenor family was the most useless ever to be rich in England having contributed nothing to the State or to the arts or any other useful occupation and even the architecture they have presided over in London has been of very poor quality.

---

30. (1879–1953); Bendor was the 2nd Duke of Westminster, a notable pleasure-lover. In Noël Coward's *Private Lives*, Amanda asks, 'Whose yacht is that?' Elyot replies, 'The Duke of Westminster's I expect. It always is.' WW reviewed *Bendor: the Golden Duke of Westminster* by Leslie Field in the *Sunday Times*, 4 Sept. 1983.

**Tuesday 1 April**

The bookmakers are paranoiac about the Tote. Any sign of increased Tote activity and they go rushing to the Levy Board demanding that the Tote be curbed. They are particularly worried about our credit offices now because these are smart, well-built, comfortable with television sets and protected from the weather. Also they have boards showing the results of away meetings.

This afternoon Len Cowburn, who runs William Hill[1] and is now the representative of the Bookmakers' Committee on the Levy Board, came to Cavendish Avenue with Alfie Bruce who used to be on the Levy Board, a small-time bookmaker. Plus a man called Air Commodore Brooks who used to work for William Hill and is now working for BOLA,[2] having been Secretary of the Racecourse Association.

I give them a short lecture on the penalties put on the Tote by Parliament when they allowed thirteen thousand, five hundred bookmakers to set up in the High Street in betting shops and the Tote wasn't allowed to do it until ten years later, in 1972 when all the best positions had been taken.

Anyway, we got down to brass tacks and agreed not to press for the creation of a new credit office in the Members' [enclosure] at Goodwood (which we didn't want and only Lord March[3] wants us to have) in return for their not opposing one which we do want at Bath. We told them of our future plans about credit offices which do not amount to very much and they were quite pleased at being told in advance.

---

1. One of the 'big four' bookmakers; see Appendix on racing.
2. Betting Offices Licensees Association.
3. The Earl of March and Kinrara, son of the Duke of Richmond, of Goodwood House.

**Wednesday 2 April**

A jolly board meeting at the Tote.

Andrew[4] looked much better as I told him. 'Oh I live a virtuous life now.' 'Do you enjoy it?' 'Not much.'

He had been to Pratt's Club the night before. He said, 'We have an innovation at the Club now. We have a stewardess. I wanted her called Mrs George by the members but they refused so she is called Georgiana.' (Not inappropriate considering the famous Georgiana, Duchess of Devonshire.)[5] It is a curious custom by which whatever their names may be, the stewards are always summoned under the name George.

Earlier that day Charles Moore had rung up from the *Spectator* saying I couldn't write the diary which he wanted me to write in June (as they had suggested on a postcard) because he had got Debo[6] to do it for June. After a time I said well I'll do it for you in July then.

I don't know why I've agreed to do it because it's quite a nuisance.

He is a very nice man, just thirty years old. Very bright with a pretty wife who is a don at Cambridge, Peterhouse.

At the board meeting this morning I said to David Montagu,[7] 'Would you like a decent cigar? I'll have one brought in.' At the previous meeting he said he didn't get a decent cigar unless the Chairman was there.

He is a very jolly man, very kind and sociable. He has had bad luck and was rottenly treated by Jacob[8] on whom he is to some extent dependent now as he threw in his lot with him – under the impression that he was going to be running Charterhouse Bank which Jacob decided to sell out of because Jacob got bored with the administration.

Jacob has been very kind to me and I have always liked him, and I particularly like Serena. I precipitated their marriage and was the best man or only witness at the Registry Office when they got married. Serena has on the whole been very happy and been tolerant of Jacob's many infidelities. He in his way is devoted to her.

---

4. Duke of Devonshire.
5. Wife of the 5th Duke, daughter of the 1st Earl Spencer, leader of fashion and supporter of Charles James Fox in the election of 1784.
6. Duchess of Devonshire, née Mitford (Andrew's wife).*
7. (1928–98); The Hon. David Montagu; he succeeded his father as 4th Baron Swaythling in 1990.*
8. Rothschild, m (1962) Serena, née Dunn.*

**Thursday 3 April**

I reply to the letter from Princess Michael. It was kind of her to write in praise of my South African Review section in the *Sunday Times* last Sunday. She said she had lived in South Africa for a year when she was seventeen. That was with her father who had caused her so much trouble by being disclosed as a Nazi and possibly a member of an SS unit which I don't think he was.

She says the hypocritical Foreign Office won't even let them stop off in Johannesburg on the way to Swaziland where they have to represent the Queen at the coronation of the new King. This tinpot place has far less right to be considered an independent country than Bophuthatswana.

Spend the morning preparing a reply to the idiotic man who complains at my fomenting racial prejudice by an article in the *News of the World* some time back. He has got the Press Council to take up his complaint. The country is quite dotty in the way it panders to anybody who utters the word 'racist' or 'racial prejudice'. It is like McCarthyism[9] in reverse.

Have lunch with David Montgomery at the Savoy Grill.

It was only just before we left that I said to David Montgomery, 'I'm sorry about the altercation we had. It was all rather unnecessary. I think you were under some strain being sued for libel or whatever by the ex lover of Miss Ferguson.' He said, 'Yes. But not only that, there's trouble with a footballer we have been exposing. It was all very late and I was rather tired.'

We agreed to think no more of it.

David M says they have a marvellous story building up about Ian Botham. There's a girl who supplied him and took cocaine with him. They have all the evidence. He has not just been on cannabis but on the hard stuff. I think it is reasonable of the *News of the World* to expose this sort of thing.

I said to him it was very wrong of the cricket authorities to allow him to go on playing for England after he had been actually convicted of being in possession of cannabis. He is a great hero to the young who think he is a good cricketer whereas he is not. And they assume that if it is all right for him to take drugs it must be all right for them as the cricket authorities overlook it.

---

9. The anti-Communist witch-hunt conducted 1950–4 in America by Senator Joseph McCarthy.

I say, 'Was that photograph on the front page of the *News of the World* with Sarah Ferguson[10] depicted as rolling a cigarette meant to indicate it was not really a hand rolled cigarette but hand rolled cannabis or another drug?' He said, 'Yes, of course. We've all the evidence and McNally,[11] her previous lover, threatened us with a libel action and he is still leaving it on the table because we said that she was involved in cocaine parties and the like in his Swiss chalet when she lived with him.'

I said, 'Well, you could call her in evidence and show that photograph and ask her to deny or otherwise.' He said, 'Exactly. That's why the action will never be brought. We would be bound to subpoena her as a witness and everybody knows that.'

I asked Montgomery whether Princess Anne had really had an affair with her detective in a sexual sense. What they had published left the question slightly open. He said, 'Yes. It was a full-blown affair.' They had slightly played that aspect down giving, they thought, enough hints to the reader to make it pretty obvious.

The *News of the World* is rather careful of what it publishes and it always has supporting evidence, with corroborative signed statements and all the rest of it, and they did I am afraid in the case of Princess Anne. Poor girl. She must have been very lonely and I suppose bored with that rather dim husband of hers.

It is extraordinary that a girl in her position should have no one else to turn to but a common 'lady-killer' detective whose behaviour afterwards shows how low level he was, boasting of his sexual conquests including sweet Princess Anne. The *News of the World* paid him £20,000.

**Friday 4 April**

Lord Goodman at dinner. He tells me he is writing his memoirs[12] and at least five publishers are offering him enormous sums for them. They all think it's going to contain sensational inside stuff concerning the celebrated clients he has dealt with like Harold Wilson, Marcia Williams[13] and so forth but there are going to be no revelations. Only

---

10. Engaged to the Duke of York since 19 March 1986.
11. Paddy McNally, racing driver.
12. *Tell Them I'm on My Way* was published in 1993.
13. Harold Wilson's political secretary; life peer 1974 (Lady Falkender).

his reflections on the world and incidents not involving breaches of confidence.

He confirms to me that he told Rowland[14] that he was not fit to be proprietor of the *Observer* and if he became such he, Goodman, would resign from the board which he did. He rejected Maxwell's offers to hire him as his solicitor, saying that his business affairs were too complex and of a kind that he didn't deal with. 'Oh will you deal with my personal affairs, then?' Maxwell asked. The answer was no. He told him he didn't think his personal affairs were of the kind he would like to handle either.

He also told James Goldsmith[15] that he was not fit to be the owner of the *Observer*, not a suitable person. Goldsmith was very upset. At that time Goodman was able to prevent him.

He dislikes Kenneth Harris intensely because he was the one who got Bob Anderson of Atlantic Richfield to come into the *Observer* which Goodman disapproved. He, Kenneth Harris, said, 'I think I would either like to be managing director or editor of the *Observer.*' Goodman replied, 'You are not capable of being either.'

**Saturday 5 April**

Grand National. Call in at the Racecourse Holdings Trust tent, leave Petronella and Verushka. Refrain from drinking champagne. Go out round the course looking at Tote installations and waving the flag. The new County Stand is good, with fine Tote positions.

Repair to the Derbys' box which is really a little house, '1 Acacia Avenue' as I described it to Isabel [Derby]. There's an upstairs and a downstairs and a roof view of the course as well, a dining-room, a comfortable sitting-room. You can see the winners' enclosure from one side where the Grand National winners are always greeted by huge crowds and see the racecourse from the other side, as well as being able to watch it on television.

A favourite near the top this year is Door Latch owned by Jim Joel. He is ninety-one years old and comes in with his trainer to watch the race on the television. He says Door Latch is running a year too early but it might be a year too late for me next year so we have put him in

14. Tiny Rowland of Lonrho.

15. (1933–97); industrialist, environmentalist, member (for France) of the European Parliament; campaigner against political integration of Europe; Leader of the Referendum Party in the 1997 general election; knight 1976.

now. Alas, the race starts and in a few moments Door Latch falls at the first fence and the poor old boy, who is thin and old, puts his hands over his eyes and doesn't say a word. After a while he takes his hands away and starts looking at the race which he may never see again, and his horse is not in it.

Sit next to Rachel Dacre[16] and Sarah Keswick.[17] Sarah says she agreed with three-quarters of what I had written in the *Sunday Times*. I said, 'What is the quarter you don't agree with?' She said, well, she is not quite sure but she thought I was too kind to the blacks though agreed it was a balanced picture.

Several people who have read it say they did not realize what South Africa was like till then and Ian Trethowan[18] said what a balanced account, not polemical as some of my writing is. I say I have sent it to the BBC Chairman, Stuart Young, and asked him to adjust his reporting accordingly.

Isabel and I do our ritual examination of the horses about which I know nothing but she likes the funny remarks I make about them.

In the RHT [Racecourse Holdings Trust] tent Rocco Forte and his pretty young wife who is lonely already. When Petronella went to see her the other day, she said, 'He only knows old people like Charles Churchill[19] and Chips Keswick' and she gets very bored with them, though Petronella rather likes Charles and Chips Keswick.

Rocco is agreeable but not intelligent, though he may be good at running the Trust House Forte empire with his father. Olga, his sister, is the lively one.

They offer to take Verushka and Petronella, and me if I like, back to London in his jet but I decline, leaving the other two to go. I want to see more of what the Tote is doing.

I am very fond of Isabel. She was once engaged in a dramatic episode shortly after the War when they had not been long married, involving their two butlers and a shooting affray.

---

16. Baroness Dacre, wife of the Hon. William Douglas-Home, playwright brother of Sir Alec Douglas-Home, former Prime Minister.
17. Wife of Chips Keswick.
18. (1922–90); Director General, BBC 1977–82; chairman, Horserace Betting Levy Board, from 1982; knight 1980.*
19. Lord Charles Spencer-Churchill (b 1940).

Winston Churchill remarked, 'I'm glad there are people who still have two butlers in the same household.'[20]

Charlie Morrison[21] in the Derby box with comparatively new wife, pretty. Somehow he managed to extricate himself from his miserable marriage perhaps using Sara,[22] his long-standing wife, as the guilty party. She, Sara, is niece to Annie who married Lord O'Neill, then Lord Rothermere and so on until she married James Bond.[23] I loved her dearly.

Annie's sister was Laura[24] who finished up marrying the aged Duke of Marlborough when she was pretty aged herself.

Of the two sisters Annie was much the nicer. The daughter of Laura, Sara, who I think was her daughter by a man called Lord Long, one of Laura's early husbands, has the same sort of features as the two older ones and a sharp brain but more masculine.

[Arnold] made her a director of GEC which she still is and works there in the office every day.

**Sunday 6 April**

Rupert has a big advertisement in the newspapers putting the News International case about Wapping in a clear and simple form.

I congratulate him on his imaginative stroke in offering the old Grays' Inn [Road] printing works to the unions, plus the contract to print the *Guardian* which brings in £1 million a year, saying he would give them managerial help as well if they want to take the works over, particularly if they would like to print a Labour daily, which the Labour Party is always complaining they lack.

They are now on the spot. Kinnock and Co. seem very keen

---

20. See 17 October 1987 for the full story.
21. The Hon. Sir Charles Morrison, Conservative MP, 1964–92; m 1 (1954–84) the Hon. Sara Long (daughter of 2nd Viscount Long and Laura, née Charteris), m 2 (1984) Rosalind, former wife of Gerald John Ward; knight 1988.
22. The Hon. Sara Morrison, vice-chairman, Conservative Party Organization, 1971–5; chairman, National Council for Voluntary Organisations, 1977–81; director, GEC, since 1980.
23. I.e. Ian Fleming, James Bond's creator: Anne, née Charteris (1913–81), m 1 (1932–44) 3rd Baron O'Neill, m 2 (1945–52) 2nd Viscount Rothermere, m 3 (1952) Ian Fleming.
24. Laura Charteris (d 1990), m 1 (1933–43) 2nd Viscount Long (one daughter, Sara), m 2 (1943–54) 3rd Earl of Dudley, m 3 (1960) Michael Temple Canfield of New York and London, m 4 (1972) 10th Duke of Marlborough (d 1972).

something should be done about it. Rupert says Miss Brenda Dean is also quite keen but she has lost control more or less of her union with a very left-wing executive.

This afternoon the biggest march on Wapping ever is planned, starting in Trafalgar Square with a great mass meeting. 'How will you get your papers out?' He said, 'It will be very difficult if twenty thousand come. I was praying that the West Indies would finish beating England last night, which they did, so there is no news today. We are going to start printing at about 4.00 p.m. so by the time the marchers get here they will be unable to stop the papers going out as they will have mostly gone out by then.'

I tell Mrs Thatcher of Rupert's plans and she laughs. She says of his offer to the union, 'Do congratulate him for me. It is not only a stroke of genius but very generous too.'

I tell her that I hope my saying that Rhodes Boyson[25] ought to be the next Secretary for Education won't put her off him. She said, 'No, that won't. But he really wasn't very good when he was at the Ministry of Education; he never made any robust speeches at all or constructive thinking. And now look what he's doing in Northern Ireland. There he is a Minister and you never hear him saying anything. He seems to have lost interest.'

She says, 'When do you think I should ask Keith [Joseph] to go?'

I say, 'In May, June or July. It ought to be fairly soon but you've got to think of the right person first. He has to be very tough, able to be persuasive.' She says, 'Yes. I'm afraid although Keith's speeches read very well, he is not able to get them across.'

I say, 'I sometimes think that all education ought to be run by the state and having local authorities doing it is absurd.' She says, 'Some local authorities do it quite well. It isn't really so much that. The problem is the Department of Education & Science itself which is absolutely hopeless, completely sold on comprehensive schools which have ruined education.'

I say again, 'We need a very tough person. I suppose Christopher Patten[26] who made a good speech the other day might do it.' She says,

25. Conservative politician and former headmaster, at this time Deputy Secretary for Northern Ireland, Parliamentary Under Secretary of State at the Department of Education & Science (DES), 1979–83; knight 1987.

26. Minister of State, DES, at this time.

'I don't think he's got enough experience. If you have any ideas please let me know.'

I see that the *News of the World* has done its several page exposé of Botham, drugs and his girlfriends. In the leader David Montgomery has taken up my point at lunch with him on Thursday that the worst of Botham's offence is that he is regarded as a hero by the young and is setting them an appalling example.

**Monday 7 April**

Dinner with Clarissa Avon in her pleasant apartment at Bryanston Square.

She used to have a house with Anthony in Wiltshire, a Queen Anne one, but she has had to give it up.

She has gone to some expense hiring two butlers or waiters. The champagne before dinner is in magnums, rather good. The white wine is good too, at the start of dinner. Château Cantemerle 1967 for claret. Excellent. She says Anthony thought 1967 was a good year and he had bought the Château Cantemerle we were drinking. He had very good judgement in all matters like wine and pictures and books – not so good in matters like Suez.

Next to me on the right is Mrs Halpern, married to a man[27] who owns or controls Burtons the tailors. When I ask her what her husband does she says, 'He runs Burtons.' I say, 'That's a brewery isn't it?', thinking she was talking about Burton-on-Trent. But we established that it was in fact a chain of tailors' shops.

As we are leaving Clarissa asks me if I have seen the Duff Cooper book.[28] I tell her that I have reviewed it. It's rather good. 'Nonsense,' she shouts and goes and gets the book, 'Look at this' – and one of the photographs says 'Duff Cooper with a friend.' 'That's Liz.[29] Why doesn't it say so?'

It's so badly written and it makes him out to be nothing but a sex fiend.

I say, 'Did you ever have an affair with him? I didn't think you did from the way you were written about in the book.' She said, 'No. He used to say that I was the only woman who he never got more than a

27. Ralph Halpern; knight 1986.
28. *Duff Cooper* by John Charmley.
29. Lady Elizabeth von Hofmannsthal, wife of Raimund von Hofmannsthal, son of the Austrian playwright, poet and librettist Hugo von Hofmannsthal.

peck on the cheek from. But I liked him. He was always trying to get me to go to bed with him but I wouldn't.' He, Duff, died at the beginning of '54. Thirty-two years ago Clarissa was a lovely girl.

**Thursday 10 April**

Dinner with Rocco Forte and his twenty-year-old bride. Prince Khalid bin Abdullah was there. Charming. Says that privately all the Arab leaders wish that the Americans would just destroy Gaddafi but what they are doing is foolish and dangerous. Instead of destroying him they are making little attacks which build him up as a great hero throughout the Arab world and no one dares do other than support him.

Israel, he says, wants Gaddafi to remain in power and that is why the Americans do not topple him. For Israel Gaddafi is simply the visible sign by which they hope to prove to the world the Arabs are awful and therefore they need money and support from America to keep going.

The Prince expects the cut in the oil prices to last for four or five years.

I say to the Prince, 'Will Arabs have to pull out of British racing with the less money available to them from oil?' He says, 'They could not disentangle themselves easily and it would be a very slow process if they tried. They couldn't sell their great strings of horses (he has two hundred himself) because the price would be negligible.'

He has the favourite in the Derby at the moment and also the second favourite in the 2,000 Guineas. I promised not to back either because if I do they are bound to lose.

Aliai, Rocco's wife, is pretty and not a fool. She and Petronella talk about Byron, the poets and books they read and history. I ask her if she is enjoying her marriage and she says, 'So far.' She is going to Italy in a few days. She will have been three times already since she was married which was only while we were in South Africa, something like February 20th.

It is extraordinary this child has so much money. She is looking for houses because they consider their quite substantial house in Lowndes Place too small.

**Sunday 13 April**

Mrs Thatcher sounds brisk and cheerful. 'I read what you said about Fulham.[30] You are quite right.' I say, 'The trouble with the Tories is they are too idle and do not get across their achievements enough nor what is intended for the future.'

Actually we agree for private consumption that the result was not as bad as might have been feared and that things look fairly bright. She is enthusiastic about the economic prospects.

She says, 'I've got to leave now.' It's about ten past five and we've been talking for twenty minutes. 'I have to go to my constituency to read the lesson.'

I've been thinking of how to review the last four volumes of Bagehot by Norman St John-Stevas[31] – a review he hoped I would write for the *Times*. He is a strange likeable person but over-feminine, which led him into making catty remarks about Mrs T who had liked him and promoted him to the Cabinet and Leader of the House, a job which he adored. His cleverness is not balanced by enough ballast.

He has been twenty-five years editing the works of Bagehot which is a long time to spend on somebody else's work, though the result is worthwhile.

Arnold fetches me for dinner with Sara Morrison driving her car, covered in some peculiar fur for her black mongrel dog.

We go to the Capital Hotel with its one-star restaurant. Arnold takes a very long time choosing his food, refusing to have the set menu and ordering backwards and forwards. He says his blood pressure has gone up. Ours go up waiting for him to order his dinner so we can get ours.

**Tuesday 15 April**

Rupert enthusiastic about Mrs Thatcher allowing the Americans to use the air bases to send their F1 Elevens to bomb Libya.[32] On Sunday shopping he makes the comment that Douglas Hurd has made a mess

---

30. The by-election which the Conservatives lost on the previous Thursday.
31. Conservative politician, lawyer and writer; Chancellor of the Duchy of Lancaster, Leader of the House of Commons and Minister for the Arts, 1979–81; at this time chairman, Royal Fine Art Commission; life peer (Baron St John of Fawsley) 1987.
32. The raid was early that day.

of it, which will take some of the aura away from him and put him out of the running for the leadership – so maybe there's a bonus.[33]

Dinner with Julian Amery.

Before dinner there is a 1979 Pol Roger which Julian is mixing with orange juice. I say, 'Is there something wrong with the orange juice that you have to dilute it with this vintage champagne?'

Ian Gow comes in.

He was her PPS and a Minister. Foolishly he resigned because he disapproved of the agreement with Dublin under which Dublin was allowed to take some interest in the affairs of Northern Ireland.

I said, 'She was very sorry that you left her. She needs you and I think it was unnecessary. Why are you making such a fuss about such an unimportant matter as Northern Ireland which will never be solved anyway?' 'I was a soldier there.' I said, 'Well that seems a very trivial ground on which to mount a great resignation. You must not build a tortoise shell round yourself and become rigid. You must make overtures and get back again.' He says, 'Exactly what my wife says.'

On the way in Catherine[34] opened the door because I had been ringing all the bells, hearing no answer. She was in bedroom slippers, looking dowdy. I say, as a joke, 'Are you going to be at dinner with us?' 'No,' she says, and is already drunk, I fear. She then says, 'Do you tie your own ties?' and to prove it I undo my tie in the hall and put it on again which she thinks a remarkable feat because Julian cannot tie a bow tie.

It is very sad that Catherine drinks so much. It is a Cavendish failing. Her first cousin, Andrew Devonshire, has been made hopeless by drink. Her own brother Maurice[35] had to be dried out after years of ghastly behaviour caused by drunkenness. He was resolute enough to stop drinking after his final dry-out and didn't drink for several years until he died. His death was brought on by excessive cigarette smoking and inhaling which he was warned against by the doctor but took no notice. Catherine has also been warned against smoking repeatedly but she too takes no notice.

She had some fearful operation to her legs which have got tubes in

33. The bill was defeated after a backbench revolt on its second reading on 14 April 1986.
34. Julian Amery's wife, née Macmillan; she died in 1991.
35. Viscount (Maurice) Macmillan (1921–84), Conservative politician; son of Harold Macmillan, the former Prime Minister, 1st Earl of Stockton.

them now but still she won't stop smoking or drinking though it seems occasionally she stops for a week or two. She's even been convicted for drunken driving.

Her father adores her. She is his favourite child. I too am very fond of her. She was a very beautiful girl when Julian married her thirty-six years ago. Outgoing, amusing and lively. But all that has gone.

**Thursday 17 April**

Evening – reception for Lord Goodman at Painters Hall, celebrating his fifty years as a solicitor. Vast concourse soon started to arrive.

Havers, the Attorney General, and I discussed the Botham situation. He brought a libel action against the *Mail on Sunday* for saying he took drugs, and the Attorney General had applied to the courts for an injunction to stop the *News of the World* printing any more articles on matters which affected or concerned the nature of the libel action against the *Mail on Sunday.*

The *News of the World* had been printing a series of articles about his torrid affair with a beauty queen in the West Indies when he was supposed to be playing cricket and them taking drugs together, Botham possibly on the field as well. He was supposed to be taking cocaine while fielding. At first the Attorney General had succeeded but today the *News of the World* got another court to reverse the decision and they can now print more, which they will probably do this Sunday.

Michael Havers told me that they had masses more evidence about Libyan terrorist plans than they could publish including details of plots against ten European capitals.

Alexander Macmillan[36] says his mother has become totally impossible, even more than before. If she comes to see them she interferes even before she's got into the door, having given different instructions to the gardener to those already being given by Birgitte and himself.

I asked him how his grandfather was surviving. 'I find it politic to fall in with her views,' is what Harold Macmillan says about his daughter-in-law.

While I was talking to Michael Havers, Peter Rawlinson came up. They pretended to be friendly but as Peter knows that he is likely to

36. Grandson of Harold Macmillan, son of (Viscount) Maurice Macmillan (d 1984) and Katherine Viscountess Macmillan (Katie); becomes 2nd Earl Stockton on his grandfather's death later in 1986; chairman, Macmillan Publishers, 1980–90, president, Macmillan Ltd, since 1990.*

get the job of Lord Chancellor which he would like, and as Michael knows he would like it, the friendliness was not deep.

Kenneth Robinson[37] is there. He was once Minister of Health and became a quango chairman. He said he couldn't open a newspaper now without seeing a review by me. I say, 'There would be one of a book of yours if you wrote another one. You haven't written one since *Wilkie Collins*.' 'How clever of you to remember.' 'No, it was a very good book. You should write another.'

On the way out I see Michael Heseltine and his wife on the doorstep. We exchange smiles and hellos and how are yous. Michael Heseltine, after what I wrote about him when he made his bogus resignation over Westland, could hardly have been pleased to see me. But politicians are inured to smiling at those who have insulted them.

**Friday 18 April**

A letter comes from Irwin saying because the Italians prefer the Libyans to the Americans he is now cancelling his holiday with us in Venice. He means the Italians would not allow overflying rights and gave no support to Reagan. He must mean that he won't get to Paris again either, or to Germany because they were against the Americans on overflying rights or any support. The only places he can go to are Britain, Canada and Israel who backed America.

He also says he is going to sell the house they have just bought in Gerald Road because he finds the English inhospitable and aloof and he had looked forward to having a lovely intellectual or social circle and it didn't materialize, although we have been very kind inviting him to function after function, as he put it.

He asks me also to get a letter from the Prime Minister saying how good *Britain Confidential* is, indicating that he thinks I won't want to because the British have an aversion to making any effort in the interests of their own livelihood. But he does not understand that my relationship with the people he wants me to get endorsements from would be quite changed if they thought I was touting for that kind of support.

I hope a breach is not coming between Irwin and ourselves. I like getting the £5,000 every six months for helping him. Verushka says he

---

37. Labour politician, chairman of the Arts Council of Great Britain, 1977–82; his *Wilkie Collins: A Biography* was published in 1951; knight 1983.

made you leave NERA[38] because he had a row with the parent company so you had better be prepared.

He proposes that we should go to Venice by ourselves at his expense and have the holiday just the same or go to America at his expense to New York and they would arrange to be there while we were there. Neither prospect appeals to me partly because it's too much like charity and I don't care for it. Partly because, as I said to Verushka, I would get bored with her alone in Venice because she would never go to museums or cathedrals or old buildings with me. She is then very hurt and says our marriage is at an end, but as she says that quite often I am not taking it too seriously.

**Saturday 19 April**

Badminton Horse Trials.

Speak to James Lees-Milne[39] and we agree that the Duff Cooper book by Charmley is excellent and I tell him that Clarissa was picking holes in it. Caroline's mother Daphne[40] had also read the book. She appeared in it considerably. She was at one time a lover of Duff. She thinks it's very good too.

I ask Daphne how old she is. 'Eighty-one.' I said, 'I hope I shall be as sprightly as you if I live as long as that. Do you still think as you did when you were eighteen?' She says, 'Yes, exactly. The only difference is that I can't move so well and the body is no longer what it was.'

I bump into somebody on my right-hand side. I cannot see out of my right eye. It turns out to be Andrew [Devonshire] who says, 'I thought you were going to cut me.' I said, 'No, I didn't notice you there.' He says, 'You didn't seem very pleased to see me.' I said, 'I am delighted to see you but I couldn't see you in the light. I have something to raise with you. Very serious for the Tote.'

He looks worried. I say, 'When you were photographed recently in some magazine in your sitting-room at Chatsworth you had an enormous calendar headed "Ladbroke's" with great letters on your table.'

---

38. National Economic Research Associates.

39. (1908–97); architectural and cultural historian, on the staff of the National Trust, 1936–66.

40. The Hon. Mrs Daphne Fielding (1904–97), writer, daughter of 4th Baron Vivian; m 1 (1926–53) Viscount Weymouth (succeeded as 6th Marquess of Bath in 1946, d 1992); their daughter, Lady Caroline Thynne, m (1950) David Somerset, now 11th Duke of Beaufort; m 2 (1953–78) Xan Fielding, travel writer.*

'Oh dear,' he said, 'but I'm not allowed to bet with the Tote,' which is quite a good point as I have had to lay down that board members may not have credit accounts with the Tote for fear of the evil-minded writing or gossiping that they get special terms or something crooked has happened.

They have the great entrance hall open today and are not merely using the side entrance. The hall is where the strange game of Badminton was invented and first played. I suppose they wanted those soft missiles to avoid damaging the pictures and sculptures. So that's how another great international game was started in England.

Watch the South African *Witness to Apartheid* programme which talks about a thousand people being killed in the Townships without referring to them as mainly the victims of blacks against blacks. I think I should try and do the *Right of Reply* offered by George Thomson[41] last week and which the South African Ambassador is so reluctant to do because he doesn't want himself to be put in the dock.

**Sunday 20 April**

Speak to Mrs T and congratulate her on her speech on Libya to the House. She says she's been feeling very lonely. The four she had to make the decision with all backed her up and agreed with her but one or two of the others were wobbly. She said, 'As I go on in this job I sometimes think I can't go because who on earth is there to succeed me.' 'You can't resign unless I give you permission,' I say and she laughs.

I say, 'Can something be done about Ian Gow? He's a very good egg.' She says, 'I do keep in touch with him.' 'But if you can get him back it would be a great help to you.' She says, 'Yes. But of course he's gone and resigned from the Treasury which is the one job he wanted and how could he come back since the policy on Northern Ireland hasn't changed at all?'

I say she ought to do something about direct grant schools between now and the next election.

She says, 'I agree with you but the trouble is dear old Keith is so much governed by his officials.' I said, 'Well I think you'll have to grit your teeth and remove him soon.' She said, 'Yes, but when something like Libya happens he's absolutely reliable and solid.'

I said, 'I see the difficulty. I still think Christopher Patten might be

---

41. Chairman, Independent Broadcasting Authority (IBA), 1981–8; life peer 1977.

a good idea,' and she says, 'He's very young. I don't want to over-promote him. That's what I did with Leon Brittan and look what happened. He was too young and not experienced enough.'

Rupert has been magnificent. I told her that he had rung saying how much he had admired what she had done. She commented on the *Times* and the *Sun* giving 'wonderful support'.

On Sunday shopping I said, 'I don't think the defeat will hurt you at all. The general public will realize you were trying to modernize and you've been let down by a number of silly Tory MPs as well as the Labour Party.' She said, 'Yes they get frightened by a few letters.'

Another point she makes is her worry that it isn't just anti-Americanism, she is told by some of her colleagues, but anti-Reagan feeling that is gripping the country. I'm not sure this is true but it can be cleared up by results, particularly if terrorism dies down a bit from Libya. I think I shall write an article for the *Times* for this coming Saturday on the subject.

Nicholas and Caroline come to lunch, in their beautiful red Mercedes. It cost about £20,000, paid for by his new firm. Promises to get me a list of stock exchange people to whom we can send the famous *Britain Confidential*.

**Monday 21 April**

I speak to Bernard [Levin] who is a little aloof these days. I think he may be put out a bit by what I've been writing about South Africa which he continues to regard as the devil in his (B's) last shred of left-wing clothing. He also seemed glum when I say that I've resigned from the National Union of Journalists in protest against the NUJ Conference sending a message of condolence to Colonel Gaddafi.

However, he is very helpful with suggestions about the play which he still maintains is very good. I arrange for Mr Fitch to ring him immediately which he does. From this it emerges that a man at Chichester, who was very prominent in the West End but has been at Chichester for a little while, may like to return to London. Mr Fitch tells me that he is writing to this man, his name is Gale.[42]

I ring Caroline and thank her for the lunch.

She says Tony [Lambton] is coming to stay this weekend.

'Would you cut him in a narrow room if you met him?' I said, 'No.

42. John Gale, theatrical producer; director, Chichester Festival Theatre, 1985–9.

I still quite like him. I think he is untrustworthy, though he has enough charm when he wants to put it on.'

I thought I should give her something of our side of the story and I told her how he said we didn't pay the servants and explained how after giving them eight hundred thousand lire for August we simply arranged that the balance for clearing up, which is about thirty thousand lire or £12, we would give them at Easter. They were quite happy about it.

I think I shall make him the centre of a play if I write another one.

**Tuesday 22 April**

Ring Henry Anglesey[43] to ask him to dinner on June 10th. When he answers I hold my nose in my fingers to disguise my voice: 'Can you tell me what time you close tonight?' I was going to say, when he wondered what I meant, 'Oh aren't you the Marquess of Anglesey public house?' But instead he says, 'We're open to you at all hours, my dear Woodrow,' and then adds, 'Your inimitable voice cannot be disguised.'

**Thursday 24 April**

A glimmer of good news. Mr Fitch says that the man at Chichester is keen to see the play and he wants to get back to London to manage. He put on *No Sex Please, We're British* so he is not hi-falutin'.

**Friday 25 April**

Peter Hillmore, the gossip columnist of the *Observer*, rings about *Britain Confidential*. I do not speak to him but prepare a statement saying that it cannot be discussed because it is confidential. Plus a warning that it is copyright and any quotations or summaries or paraphrases of it may result in legal action. It is not a document offered to the media for comment or review.

A bad tempered letter from Stuart Young, Chairman of the BBC. He resents my telling him that he knows nothing about politics and that his staff are biased in favour of the Communist dominated ANC in South Africa. He is a fool who ought never to have been made Chairman of the BBC, knowing nothing about politics whatever.

---

43. 7th Marquess of Anglesey.

**Saturday 26 April**

Go to Sandown to see how the new Tote betting shop in the members' area is getting on.

I didn't expect the Queen Mother to be there as she had no horse running in the Whitbread[44] which she won two years ago.

I ask her if the name Augustus Hare[45] means anything to her. I am reviewing a book about him. 'Oh yes, he was the man who made sketches and went to stay with lots of people and wrote about what he heard at their houses. I've got a sketch he did of our house near Durham. Osbert Sitwell[46] gave it to me.'

We discuss his curious life and upbringing by his mother who doted on him and thought his spirits should be broken because that is how you should bring children up and engaged his uncle to whip him, sending for him from the nearby Rectory. I said, 'Perhaps it made him homosexual.' She said, 'Do you think that's true? Lots of people say that about people who don't get married but it isn't always true.' 'No,' I say, 'it isn't true of Ted Heath.'[47]

'What do you think of the US raid on Libya?' 'Between us I think it was a mistake. They were not very accurate with their bombing and I can't see how it's going to do any good in stopping terrorism.' That is probably the view of the Queen too. She agrees that Mrs Thatcher was put in a very difficult position and probably made the right decision.

I ask her whether her kind of mauve and blue outfit, which is attractive, is half mourning[48] and she says, 'Yes.' She didn't want to put on black.

She says they have revived all the old stories about Mrs Simpson now that she's dead. She reiterates that she never hated and never had any spite against her and it was all rubbish. She thinks it was very fortunate that Mme Blum was so devoted to her and looked after her. For the last five years Mrs Simpson had made no sense at all and without Mme Blum she would have just lain derelict somewhere. She says it is all nonsense about her having gone off with the Royal jewels: 'It is an invention.'

---

44. A steeplechasing event.
45. Writer of travel books and conversationalist (1834–1903).
46. Sir Osbert Sitwell, writer (1892–1969).
47. Margaret Thatcher's predecessor as Prime Minister.
48. The Duchess of Windsor had died two days previously, on 24 April.

Several times she says, 'You're looking very natty today. I like those gold buttons.' I am wearing a new blazer which I got at Nicholas' tailor near Wapping. Evelyn de Rothschild also remarked on it and said I ought to be on a boat, 'Where's my yacht?' and various rather feeble jokes of that kind.

She picks up my glass of half finished champagne which I don't want. 'I'll carry this in for you,' as we move back from the balcony. Eventually I go after she has gone to the paddock. When I say goodbye to her she seems quite disappointed: 'I do so enjoy talking to you.' I say, 'I adore it' and kiss her hand.

While we are on the balcony we also talk about Liz von Hofmannsthal. Queen Elizabeth says, 'A very beautiful girl, one of the most beautiful I've ever seen.' I tell her how I went to see her the day before she died and said, 'Liz you look more beautiful than you ever did' and how pleased she was. I said it was true. Queen Elizabeth thought that was very touching and understood how pleased she must have been.

**Sunday 27 April**

Mrs T says that Chirac[49] whom she saw yesterday for lunch is a very determined and ambitious man. 'If he wants to be President, he'll get it.' He had said to her that if the Libyan raid had been successful they would have supported it and she had said, 'How can you tell before you do it?' I ask her if she can get along with him all right and she thinks yes, she can.

She also said how irritating it was to her that Chirac was doing all the things which she had done and acquiring a novelty value from it. 'They've denationalized thirty-seven industries simply by decree.'

I ask her how she got on with Conrad Black who went to lunch with her last week. She says he is very firm about supporting her. He thinks that Max Hastings, the new editor of the *Daily Telegraph*, has made a number of mistakes. It will take at least until September before he (Black) gets the place better organized. The management have been spending most of their time on labour problems which prevents real thought being given to the editorial side.

I say to her that I don't think much of the Labour Party going grey. It's not very convincing. She says, 'No they're still red, as red as anything.' I don't think she would like *Britain Confidential* which

49. French Prime Minister, 1974–6, 1986–8; President since May 1995.

suggests Labour would be rather a moderate affair if they became a government.

There is a tease in the Pendennis column of the *Observer* this morning about *Britain Confidential* which is really quite funny and not particularly harmful.

She agrees when I say that the Westland affair killed the privatization of BL.[50] She adds, 'It finished Michael Heseltine, too.'

**Tuesday 29 April**

Jacob Rothschild's fiftieth birthday party at 27 St James's Place which is a magnificent house, now the centre of his financial transactions. Beautifully stuffed with flowers from the Clifton Nursery including whole trees just coming out in blossom. Given a very nasty drink which is champagne with some raspberry in it and sugar round the edge at the top of the glass.

Mary Campbell,[51] the mother of Serena and Nell, is here and makes a great show of affection in greeting me but I know she doesn't like me and I don't like her.

It was a joy to see Nell [Dunn] whom I haven't seen for years. She wrote another play after *Steaming* but no one would put it on which I found strange because *Steaming* ran for two years and was a tremendous success here and in America. Amateur dramatic societies are now beginning to perform it. I say, 'Yes, particularly those with girls in the Amateur Dramatic Societies who fancy their breasts.'[52]

Though the rooms are enormous it is hard to move for the crush of people. Andrew Devonshire lifts Verushka into the air when he sees her. Margaret Anne [Stuart] says to him, 'Why don't you ask me out to lunch?' and he says, 'I'm too busy, I've got so many girlfriends.'

Andrew Parker-Bowles tells Verushka how attractive Petronella is but she won't take any notice of him because she likes Charles Churchill which is quite untrue. Andrew Parker-Bowles' wife Camilla was the Prince of Wales' mistress and was the girl on the train when the *Mirror*

---

50. News of the negotiations with the American firm Ford for British Leyland was leaked at the height of the Westland crisis; see 9 February 1986.

51. Lady Mary Dunn, daughter of 5th Earl of Rosslyn, m 1 (1933–44) Sir Philip Dunn; m 2 (1945–59) Robin Campbell; remarried 4, 1969, Sir Philip Dunn (d 1976).

52. *Steaming* was set in a Turkish bath.

first began by saying it was Diana and referring to the mystery girl just before he got married. He, Andrew, is agreeable and a good soldier.

**Wednesday 30 April**

Mrs T says that she had a very jolly evening at the centenary dinner given by Arnold for GEC people. 'He made a lot of jokes though he seemed to think he had angina. Is he really ill? I thought he had a brother much older than himself. Why does he think he's going to die?' I say, 'Because he's a hypochondriac. Don't take him seriously. He's all right really.'

I add, 'He is much more worried about whether you'll still hold the Westland affair against him. I warned him at the time that I could not tell him what you thought. I said to him, "Keep out of it Arnold, have nothing to do with it" but he was overwhelmed or taken in by Heseltine.' 'Back in the fold now,' she says. 'I like him.'

**Thursday 1 May**

Arnold rings about 11.00 a.m. 'It's a sunny day. I don't feel like work. Why don't we go to Newmarket in my helicopter and watch the 1,000 Guineas?' It is the warmest day of the year. We leave GEC in South Audley Street at 12.45 for the Battersea heliport. At 1.25 we land on the Newmarket racecourse.

During the day Arnold and I talk about his relations with Mrs Thatcher. He is now happy that there is a reconciliation.

He says Sara[1] would help her and do anything for her but Margaret has been dismissive of her. She ought to have sent her to the Lords when she finished her stint of voluntary work which was normal for the post she had.

**Friday 2 May**

In the evening to Channel 4 studios in Charlotte Street to record a *Right to Reply* programme. Sharon Sopher is the American Jewish very liberal producer of the outrageous *Witness to Apartheid* programme which had been shown not the previous Saturday but the Saturday before.

It was an appalling shambles. She insisted on trying to stick to talking about torture, particularly of children, by South African policemen and tried to stop me explaining that the courts forbade such action by the police and so did the government. There had already been ninety-three convictions of policemen for brutality in 1985 so it was not a thing organized by the South African government as she pretended.

**Saturday 3 May**

Last lunch party in our entertainment room at Newmarket which is being destroyed for the rebuilding of stands.

---

1. The Hon. Sara Morrison; she was chairman, National Council for Voluntary Organisations, 1977–81.

The delightful Prince Khalid Abdullah comes in to lunch very punctual (unlike the rude Rocco). He says he has come because he knows it is the only sure way he can win the 2,000 with his horse Dancing Brave. The trainer or owner of the winner usually stands by me watching TV.

Mrs Hurd's brother-in-law, Jeremy Hindley, has a horse which is very much fancied called Huntingdale. He and his wife have lunch with us too. So does Robert Sangster who has another horse, Tate Gallery, with a chance of winning.

When the race actually starts the two owners of Huntingdale and the trainer stand by me but Robert Sangster doesn't (which he did when Lomond won).[2] Prince Khalid thinks it is sufficient to win that he has had lunch with us.

Huntingdale comes in third which is the best I can do with my aura for his connections. Khalid Abdullah wins with Dancing Brave. After all the ceremonies and prize giving are over he comes back and charmingly thanks Verushka and myself for giving him the luck needed to win. But it wasn't luck: it was a very good horse.

We return to watch the *Right to Reply* programme. I should have cornered the ghastly lady earlier but it was difficult to stop her flow of torture stories. After the programme is over somebody rings up and says they met me years ago and she just wanted to say that she thought it was appalling I hadn't let that poor woman speak so I say, 'Goodbye, goodbye' and put the telephone down.

**Sunday 4 May**

Dinner with Andrew Knight and his wife.

At dinner the men, beginning with Andrew, are served first. I turn to my neighbour and try to get her given my plateful but Andrew explains, 'No. This is a Muslim household and my wife insists on the men being served first.' How nice. I wish I had a Muslim wife who believed in that kind of thing.

Max Hastings, editor of the *Daily Telegraph*, is there with a pretty wife who has broken her foot or ankle or leg skiing and is on crutches. He says that when he went to Chequers to have lunch with Mrs Thatcher, he talked to her [for] about an hour but she just went through all the things she said in public, didn't ask his views and he wondered what the point of it was.

2. In 1983.

Then he asks, 'Should I know politicians well or not as an editor?' I say, 'Know them only distantly so that you can be rude about them without you or they feeling that you let them down. Of course once you become a great editor and have been an editor for ten or fifteen years, you can be very friendly with them and give them advice and tick them off in public because your status will allow you to do so, but not yet.'

A jolly man called Tony O'Reilly is one of the guests. He was a famous rugger player for Ireland though I'd never heard of him. He had read all my book *Confessions of an Optimist* and said he used to keep three pages a day only to read so he would get some chuckles each day. He is a great admirer of my cousin Bob[3] and says that when he played cricket for the Gentlemen of Ireland Bob once captained an MCC team against them. I asked him to come to our cricket lunch on June 5th and he said he would if he could.

He runs the whole of the Heinz organization throughout the world. Jack Heinz has done nothing about it for fifteen or twenty years except draw money from it, he explains. He also owns the newspaper in Ireland called the *Independent*.[4]

There is some conversation about Rupert Murdoch.

Mr O'Reilly at first begins to wonder whether he hasn't over-stretched himself too much in buying television stations in America without the money to pay for them because of the huge interest he has to pay out. But he recognizes that he is so brilliant and remarkable he will probably get away with it.

He is concerned that Rupert has left a field he really knows about, newspapers, and gone into television which he doesn't know about and may come a cropper and the same applies to his buying the film company [Twentieth Century] Fox, though it has got a large library of films which may be lucrative.

I am asked what I think about Aidan Crawley by Andrew Knight. I say, 'He is beta minus rather than alpha as a politician and the same as a writer. He is very good though at friendship and social intercourse and is a decent man with good instincts. His wife Virginia Cowles was

---

3. Bob Wyatt (1901–95) first captained England against Australia in 1930.
4. O'Reilly was at this time president and chief executive, H. J. Heinz Co.; chairman, Independent Newspapers, the newspaper group in Ireland which obtained a controlling interest in the UK *Independent* newspaper in 1998; he played rugby for Ireland twenty-nine times.

much better than he was intellectually and as a writer.' I think that their family is remarkable; Randall, Andrew and Harriet keep him going financially by having started their own import-export business in which is included Annunziata Asquith.[5]

They are a remarkably close family which Andrew thought was bad because it prevents them having proper relationships with other people.

Harriet had never got married though she is thirty-eight. She is the girl who Victor Rothschild was very much in love with and she wrote a novel about it which upset him a good deal.[6] When I asked her about her relations with Victor she said she had thought of him only as a kind of friendly uncle who gave her presents and took her out to lunch and dinner and had not realized that he felt about her 'in that way'.

As I was giving my description of Aidan as being beta minus or plus politically and as a writer, I thought to myself that that description fitted me also and nearly said so, but decided not to.

Andrew says how sad it is about Michael Hartwell.[7] He comes in once a week now and occasionally asks to see the editor or him and they don't take any notice of him. He just never got the hang of the business side of it right and Andrew said he was also getting the newspaper wrong as well.

I said, 'If Pamela Berry had lived I'm sure she would have averted the catastrophe. I know she had nothing to do with the running of the newspapers but she had a very strong character and would have thought something up and prevented him ending his days in misery.' Andrew said all his money has gone in trying to avert the take-over by Conrad Black. He may have a house or two but the fortune has vanished.

Andrew Knight is greatly enjoying running the whole of the Telegraph group on behalf of Conrad Black. He and Max Hastings think he is somewhat simplistic in his views, as one would expect a Canadian to be, but that he is good at business. He expects a turn round of the fortunes of the *Telegraph* (that is Andrew does) round September when they force the unions to agree to realistic manning levels.

---

5. See 26 November 1985.
6. *The God-daughter* (1975).
7. Lord Hartwell, former proprietor of the *Telegraph* newspapers (see note 29 December 1985); his wife, Lady Pamela Berry, daughter of Lord Birkenhead (F. E. Smith), died in 1982.

Andrew thinks that Rupert has been marvellous and laid the way for Fleet Street and made everything possible for a profitable future.

**Tuesday 6 May**

David Montagu very pessimistic about the next election. Convinced that an irreversible trend has now set in against Mrs T. Chips Keswick and Alan Hare[8] disagree. So do I.

Petronella finds Leonard Wolfson interesting on history.[9] She enjoys talking to him, though Chips says to me that he is a typical Jewish tycoon, can't think about anything but himself. Not a fair comment I feel.

I had forgotten that Alan Hare was coming when I got out my 1956 Château Latour. Alan now is Chairman of Château Latour and travels all over the world selling this highly priced stuff. 1956 was not one of the best years but it tasted superb. Each bottle was slightly different to the other though bottled, doubtless, side by side because the ageing of the cork is always slightly different one from another.

**Thursday 8 May**

Dinner at Kensington Palace with Prince Michael and Princess Michael. I sit next to her. She talks much about herself and her recent trip to Swaziland where they attended the coronation of the new King on behalf of the Queen. Fun for the Prince with hundreds of naked virgins prancing around but not much fun for her.

She says that Rowland of Lonrho is now conducting a vendetta against them because he was not on the podium for the opening of some bridge he had built. But it was not their fault. They had nothing to do with the arrangements and didn't know one person from another.

On my other side was Valerie Hobson, married to Jack Profumo.[10]

Valerie Hobson is interesting about going to RADA at ten and leaving at fourteen and going straight into a film, followed by Hollywood, before returning to England at about eighteen. She knew Noël

---

8. The Hon. Alan Hare (1919–95), chairman, *Financial Times*, 1978–84; director, Pearson Longman, 1975–83, *Economist*, 1975–89; president, Société Civile du Vignoble de Château Latour, 1983–90.*
9. He founded the annual Wolfson History Prize.
10. Conservative politician, Secretary of State for War, 1960–June 1963; his lie to the House of Commons about his association with Christine Keeler precipitated the fall of the Macmillan government; m (1954) Valerie Hobson, actress.

Coward well and appeared in his *Private Conversations*.[11] He was very kind and thoughtful. By her first marriage she had a mentally retarded son, now aged forty-two. Noël Coward was always concerned about him, sending him presents for his birthday and Christmas. The two men he left his fortune to,[12] both homosexuals I presume, continue the practice to this day, enquiring first what [he] would like for each present.

Prince Michael is still very keen to join the Tote Board. He has heard that enquiries are going on at the Palace and hopes all will be well. The Home Office takes a long time to go through its bureaucratic machinery. I wrote to Douglas Hurd the Home Secretary in early March with this suggestion and we are now in May before anything has been finalized.

Also at the dinner at Kensington Palace were Henry Keswick[13] and his new bride, Tessa Reay.

Tessa Reay says to Verushka, 'How extraordinary that Tony should give fish pie to the Prince of Wales when he went to lunch at Cetinale.'[14] Verushka said, 'How do you know?' She said, 'I heard three hours later and the fish pie was brought out deep frozen from Marks & Spencer's, put in a deep freeze and thawed out for the Prince of Wales.'

The food at Cetinale is absolutely appalling. They don't even have Italian pastas which at least are reasonable. Tessa said that when there are shooting parties at Durham and Bindy Lambton supervises the food it is delicious but Claire is obviously incapable or uninterested. Which makes it a mystery as to how she got so fat.

**Saturday 10 May**

Lunch with Ted Heath at Arundels in The Close at Salisbury. I've always thought an ideal existence would be to live in a handsome house in the Close there. Ted's house is partly 1430 and partly Queen Anne. It has a lovely front and a very pretty back with the façade composed of flint stones moving to brick and stone.

The garden is large and well planned with shrubs and trees and lawns. It leads down to the river where the Avon meets the Bourne

---

11. WW must mean either *Private Lives* or *Conversation Piece*.
12. Cole Lesley and Graham Payn.
13. Banker, brother of Chips Keswick, m (1985) Tessa Lady Reay; at this time she was director, Cluff Investments and Trading, and a Conservative councillor.
14. Tony Lambton's house in Italy.

and the Madder in a swirl which is mildly exciting but not alarming, certainly not to the swans which float contentedly. Across the river are the meadows which presumably can never be built on.

From the front of the house there is a wonderful view of Salisbury Cathedral which is even better from the upper rooms. James Wyatt made it float on a lawn which was not there before. He removed the excrescences around the Cathedral so that it could stand in all its glory.

At the front of the house looking towards the Cathedral and to the left is an outbuilding, itself old. Ted has all his archives stored in it. One of the rooms in his house is given over to his research assistant. He is writing his memoirs.[15] I tell him to tell everything, which he says he will do. And not to be pompous and do the kind of boring stuff that Macmillan and Eden did.

I'm not sure he is quite capable of this but I think he will have a go. The book will probably be good because it will be animated by his hatred of Mrs Thatcher and the feeling that he was a great Prime Minister done down by her and the Tory Party. Certainly his achievement in getting Britain into the Common Market was monumental. Macmillan couldn't do it, Churchill couldn't do it and Mrs Thatcher probably would not have done it from lack of enthusiasm.

At lunch there is naturally some talk of the loss of Ryedale[16] on Thursday, a Tory seat with a sixteen thousand majority. I wonder why they didn't like Neil Balfour, the Tory candidate, who was a good one. Ted says, 'Perhaps they didn't like her.'

On the right as you come through the front door he has put up a splendid show case in which are contained models, beautifully executed, of all his yachts.

His writing desk was handsome. 'Are you in a confidential mood?' he asked me. He pulled open a drawer of the writing desk in which there was a typed notice on the bottom proclaiming that the desk had belonged to Lloyd George. 'What is confidential about that?' I asked. Ted replied, 'The Tories would use it against me if they knew that I had the dreaded Lloyd George's writing desk and worked at it.'

He said there was a very close life in The Close, apologizing for the pun. It is still Trollopian.

He recounted a marvellous set of arguments about where facilities for coach parties were to be provided, lavatories and all that. It was

15. Due to be published ten years later, autumn 1998.
16. The Liberal Party won the Ryedale by-election on 8 May.

first of all suggested that they should be outside the Bishop's house. The Bishop manoeuvred to get that altered. It was then proposed that they should be outside the Archdeacon's house. And the Archdeacon successfully manoeuvred to get that stopped. It was then proposed that they should be outside, I think it was a row of houses occupied by canons. They successfully stopped that. Finally it was decided this year there would be no coaches allowed into The Close and that the lavatories and facilities for coach parties should be provided by the council outside The Close. Everyone was happy.

When I remarked how quiet it was and what a wonderful place to work in Ted said, 'Yes. Dulwich is not so quiet,' and grinned.[17]

He's only been there four months. It was very kind of him to ask us to come so soon but we've always been fond of each other since we first met at Oxford.

**Sunday 11 May**

I have said this morning in the *News of the World* that the successful Tory act was in danger of becoming boring. I say to Margaret that we want to present her as new and exciting which she is, and Kinnock as old fashioned with no new policies but going back to the sixties and seventies, old-fashioned and imitative of her in fact, trying to say that he would not undo most of what she had done.

I ask, 'Is Tebbit's brain all right? He seems to me to have lost his edge. He's all right on attacking the Labour Party but he seems to have nothing to say of much consequence about the future.' She says, 'He is still under terrible stress.'[18]

I say, 'What a pity we can't bring back Parkinson.[19] I'm sure it would be OK now.' She says, 'Well I don't think I can at the moment but after the next election, when he's been re-elected, then it would be a different matter.'

I tell her that I saw Biffen on *Weekend World* with Brian Walden just before lunch. He was saying that the Tories need a balanced ticket and that although she is a conviction politician she has her liabilities, perhaps particularly because she is.

---

17. The Thatchers had bought a house there.
18. He was injured and his wife crippled in the IRA bomb attack at the 1984 Conservative Party Conference.
19. Cecil Parkinson had resigned from the government in 1983 on the revelation of his affair with his secretary, Sara Keays.

I said, 'He's coming to dinner with me on Wednesday night. What shall I say to him?' She said, 'Why don't you say to him what I shall say to him, which is you're one of the cast, not one of the spectators or a detached observer: you have to play in a team.' She is very annoyed about it.

She's always been quite fond of him. When they were in opposition she gave him quite a big leading Shadow Spokesman post and he said he was mentally exhausted and could not carry on with it. Instead of throwing him into outer darkness when there was a government, she gave him an important job, and now as Leader of the House of Commons he doesn't seem to have enough to do except for little intrigues and pushing himself along and being disloyal.

Andrew Neil tells me that the morale of the journalists particularly on the *Times* and to some extent on the *Sunday Times* is getting lower. They didn't leave until 3.15 a.m. on the night of Saturday/Sunday. They could not get away because of the mobs. There is a feeling that Rupert doesn't give a damn about the journalists and they don't like it. He says the quality of the management has not matched the new opportunities.

He goes on, 'The only person capable of making a decision is Bruce Matthews.'

When Rupert rings I tell him something of what Andrew Neil has said and he remarks that Bruce Matthews although very good and works all the hours of the day, is not really as good at making decisions as Andrew Neil thinks he is. He also thinks Andrew Neil has considerable defects.

He raises the question of *Britain Confidential* and I tell him what it is all about. He says, 'Well I didn't see it. I knew nothing about it. And Andrew Neil shouldn't be doing it because that gets him into bad odour with the journalists who think he ought to be devoting his energies, his thoughts and his discoveries to the *Sunday Times*, not *Britain Confidential*.'

He is still very supportive of Mrs Thatcher and thinks Biffen is a twerp. Perhaps he will tell him so on Wednesday night when they are both here for dinner.

**Tuesday 13 May**

A jolly lunch. Philip Howard, literary editor of the *Times*, and Tony Howard, deputy editor of the *Observer*. We remember early days at *Reynolds News* when I was writing a column for it and he was a starter on the staff.

Philip thinks that the writers in the *Times* are all too one-sided. There's not enough from the left. This is partly because the Labour Party people are not allowed to write for the *Times* at the moment.[20]

There is a suggestion that Rupert interferes which surprises me. I ask for illustrations and they say when he is on Concorde he marks things in the *Sunday Times* and the *Times*. I say, 'Well I don't think he can interfere much. The editor of the *Times* is now in a very strong position and so is the editor of the *Sunday Times*. He can't get rid of two more so soon because of the restrictions put on him when he bought the newspapers.'

It seems the morale is somewhat down at the *Times*. People are leaving for the *Observer*, they tell me. And also for the new *Telegraph* set-up, and for this new paper called the *Independent* which is being started as a high quality weekly with the ambitious target of four hundred thousand but they'll be lucky, thinks Tony Howard, if they get a hundred and sixty thousand.

Philip Howard is dressed eccentrically with some kind of sneakers and what looks like a barman's coat, light. He is very agreeable. We talk about Tom Driberg[21] and how he taught me not to use the word 'although' and how the *Times* insists on making my word 'though' into 'although'. We discuss the merits of although and though.

Tony and I talk a bit about John Freeman[22] and his curious career. He says that he now wishes to stay in California for the rest of his life. He also wrote to Tony Howard to get references to make sure the authorities would allow him to stay in America. We both thought it very odd considering that he'd been Ambassador in America.

I explained how I had known him since 1944 and that he had once gone very left at the time he resigned and how, when I came back from India, he said, looking mysterious, that he'd become great friends with Tom Driberg while I had been away. They had been very thick together and undoubtedly Tom had influenced John into a nearly Communist line for a period. He could have been Leader of the Labour Party if he had not thrown it all up because of his dislike of political intrigue.

---

20. Because of their opposition to the Murdoch manoeuvres against the print unions.
21. (1905–76); Labour politician and journalist; life peer 1975 (Lord Bradwell).
22. At this time Visiting Professor of International Relations, University of California, Davis; former Labour politician and journalist; British Ambassador in Washington, 1969–71.

**Wednesday 14 May**

An amusing dinner at 19 Cavendish Avenue. Mrs John Biffen sits between Arnold Weinstock and myself. She is very conscious of her charms. She leans back in her chair flirting with Arnold Weinstock, pushing her breasts up in the air, though they are modestly covered.

At the other end of the table John Biffen is buttering up Rupert Murdoch.

Biffen goes at 10.15 to vote and wants to take his wife with him. She says, 'No I'm enjoying the brilliant company. You can send the car back for me.' He meekly goes out.

It is quite clear who runs that household. She was divorced and has two children of sixteen and fourteen. She is now forty-one. She was never interested in politics before but she got a job as a secretary at the House of Commons when she was broke after her divorce and she came to find herself working for John Biffen, and married him. He had never been married before. How lovely sex is in determining the fates of men.

Before dinner I said to John Biffen, 'Has she spoken to you?' (by her meaning Mrs Thatcher). He said, 'No she hasn't.' I said, 'I'm surprised. I know Willie Whitelaw told you he thought your behaviour was very bad in your television interview.'

As Biffen leaves to go and I see him off I say, 'Now don't do it again,' and he says, 'No. I won't.' I think that is probably true. I think he's been alarmed at the reaction to his disloyalty on Sunday and will now be more in line.

**Saturday 18 May**

'Did you read the Audit Commission on the schools?' 'Yes,' she replied. 'I don't know who you're going to make Secretary for Education but he should get on with cutting out this appalling waste in the schools, closing down unnecessary ones and saving no end of money on cleaning, heating and maintenance. Have you thought of Kenneth Baker?' Mrs Thatcher said, 'He's a good propagandist. He's not bad.'

I ask her whether she has spoken to Biffen. She says she hasn't because she didn't want to commit herself. She is now considering what to do, perhaps in a September reshuffle which she is going to have.

We had a mild brush about the government's intention to pay only half the mortgage payments for those on the first six months of supplementary benefits. I say, 'People will believe that the government is not a caring government which is what we want to avoid.' She then explained in some detail how the £30 million is important to save and how unfair it is on other taxpayers.

She is not dismayed by the Gallup poll showing Labour at thirty-seven per cent and the Alliance[23] at thirty-two and Tories at twenty-seven. She regards it, as I do, as a temporary effect of the local elections.

Of course in my little argument with Mrs Thatcher she reveals how she believes only in doing what is right. She ignores the conventional approach to catching votes.

**Monday 19 May** ***New York***

I find New York rather exhausting.

We go to the ballet at the Metropolitan Opera House. Irwin is some kind of a patron, being a heavy benefactor with his name on the programme and acting as a host for a party of sponsors, some of whom have lapsed and whom he was trying to get to subscribe again. *Les Sylphides* was all right but I hate ballet on the whole.

Then came a Requiem written by Andrew Lloyd Webber for his father. It was devised around a brother and sister in Cambodia. The brother was to be put to death if his sister was to live and the other way round. Writhings all over the floor in somewhat incestuous manner.

Dinner at Twenty-One Club. I first came here in 1952. The food has not improved nor has the ambience.

**Tuesday 20 May**

'Soup' Campbell James[24] gives us lunch at the Knickerbocker Club. Irwin says this is a very grand club into which he would not be admitted. They won't have Jews. Again there is the chip on the shoulder.

First question I ask Soup is 'Do you allow Jews in this club?' so he says, 'One of the founder members in my great-great-grandfather's time was a man called Belmont who was a Jew. We have a number of Jews who are members.'

When I tell this to Irwin later he says, 'Oh but only a very special type of Jew. A Jew like me couldn't get in.' I tell him also that Soup's

---

23. The Social Democrat and Liberal parties had formed the Alliance before the 1983 general election.

24. Worked for the CIA attached to embassies overseas; a cousin of Edward James (1907–84), the wealthy half-American art collector who lived in Sussex.

grandfather or great-grandfather founded a golf club in Long Island because the one he used to play at wouldn't admit Jews and he had some great Jewish friends he liked to play golf with. Now ironically the club bars Jews.

**Wednesday 21 May**

Go to see Pericles in Philadelphia. Two of his restaurant friends, both chefs and both managers, who are going to start a new restaurant together. One of them has cooked or prepared a very good lunch. Will Pericles join them in the restaurant? He would have an option to buy shares. Pericles feels uncertain as he has now been made what he calls 'Maitre De' at another restaurant where he went because his friends hadn't got their liquor licence transferred in time.

**Thursday 22 May**

We had tea, Petronella and I, with Kenneth Galbraith[25] and Kittie and Kenneth's sister. She was violently anti Mrs Thatcher and said, 'Are you waiting now for the retribution to fall upon you for Mrs Thatcher foolishly helping Reagan with his bombing raid on Libya?'

Kenneth says he has read my memoirs and finds them remarkably accurate so far as he was involved in any of the events.[26] 'You realized before all of us that the mood of the times was changing. I stuck rigidly to my old Social Democratic ideology but you were not so stuck. I cannot change now.'

Irwin quarrels with most people in the end about something. He quarrelled with NERA and made me leave them, saying 'Don't you trust me? I will make you rich,' but he is now worried about *Britain Confidential*, which we aim to sell at £1,500 a shot and only got seven subscriptions for, instead of the hundred which was necessary.

I say to him at lunch that of course I would not like to hold him to his arrangement to give me £10,000 a year if *Britain Confidential* doesn't go on. Instead of saying, 'Nonsense, I will certainly go on with our arrangement', he says, 'Oh thank you. I will note that.' So as I feared from my trip to New York, there would not only be a very

---

25. Former Professor of Economics, Harvard University; US Ambassador to India under the Kennedy Administration; his best known book is *The Affluent Society*.
26. WW first met Galbraith when travelling in the US on his Smith-Mundt Fellowship in 1952 and 'was dazzled by him'; see *Confessions of an Optimist*, p. 190.

tiresome week for me, though Petronella and Verushka adore it, but the loss of my £10,000 a year.

**Friday 23 May**

Dinner with Rupert, Anna and Liz.[27]

Rupert is off to London in the morning to deal with the Wapping situation. He thinks he may have something which will work. He has been having secret discussions with Brenda Dean and she has been waiting for the right moment to put his proposals to her members.

Before going to the restaurant we drink champagne at Rupert's *New York Post* office from which he conducts most of his American affairs. He shows us a picture of a fabulous house overlooking Los Angeles which he is buying for about £5 million or thereabouts, including the furniture and the *objets d'art*. He is going to get rid of Aspen in a year or so which will also upset the Stelzers as they have been enlarging their house partly to rival Rupert.

**Sunday 25 May**

At last we go from New York. Once again Irwin kindly sends us with a car to the airport. He is an extraordinarily generous man and I like him greatly. I often get ideas from talking to him.

**Monday 26 May**

It is in the newspapers that Rupert has offered a final deal of £50 million plus the Gray's Inn Road buildings to the unions to call off their pickets and bring an end to the dispute. Miss Dean obviously wants to do it but is meeting a lot of opposition from members. Tony Dubbins, who now heads the NGA, is bitterly against the deal and obviously hopes the NGA members affected will vote against it. Print unions are so used to striking and getting everything they want and being reinstated they cannot believe that the future they look forward to of permanent jobs not only for themselves but for their children has gone.

**Wednesday 28 May**

Talk to Mrs Thatcher after her return from Israel. She has had a good press for it though some criticism for suggesting to the Israelis that

---

27. Daughter of Rupert and Anna Murdoch.

they allow the Arabs in the Occupied Territories at least to hold local elections.

The last time we talked I said, 'Have you thought of Kenneth Baker for Education Secretary?' By this time she had appointed him.[28] 'He said he would need more money to spend on education. I told him to read the Audit Commission Report first to see how much was being wasted. There's plenty there already.'

She was riding on a wave of energy. Where it all comes from is amazing. It is the adrenaline of power which keeps her going. She says, 'I have been hinting strongly that I won't necessarily have an election until the last moment. I don't want a run on the pound by people thinking there is going to be an election any moment and Labour might win.' We talk for twenty minutes. I really love that woman.

**Saturday 31 May**

A lovely letter from Queen Elizabeth the Queen Mother. It was in return for my sending her the book about Augustus Hare. She does not write an ordinary thank you letter, a perfunctory note. She covers two pieces of paper on both sides in her very readable well-formed handwriting. Her thank you letters are a model. For some reason all her letters come by registered post and she writes out the envelope herself and puts her initials in the corner.

To Stratford-on-Avon where I have to open a building for the Tote.

I am given a presentation which is unusual. It is a solid silver horse and hound (it is Horse and Hound Day at Stratford) with a little plaque on it with my name etc. Inscribed. I am touched.

A dreadful lunch which I suppose was the best they could manage in a marquee. I sit next to the Chairman of a local district council who is something to do with the Stratford Conservative Party. He says they do not have any problem on the doorstep about the unpopularity of the Prime Minister. Over Libya the question was 'Why didn't they give them a harder bang?'

On the other side is the Chairman of the racecourse. He before we sit down for lunch asks everyone to stand for one minute to remember John Willoughby de Broke[29] who was the patron of the racecourse. He speaks movingly about him.

---

28. In a ministerial reshuffle on 21 May 1986.
29. He had died on 26 May.

**Monday 2 June**

To the Stafford Hotel, 11.00 a.m. Meeting with conspirators. Brian Crozier,[1] Julian Lewis[2] and a man from Aims of Industry whose name I've forgotten and another man who I never identified. How to make the public realize that Labour is still dominated by the extremists, Militants, Communists and Marxists. Some consternation at the beginning because of a reprint from a page of the *Socialist Worker* which had got hold of a copy of *Britain Confidential* in which we had said the Labour Party intended to run a moderate government if it got in.

A lot of work has been done on bias in the media and there will be a report coming to me soon I hope. It covers BBC and Independent TV. Brian Crozier is to do a Who's Who in book form of people on the left so that they might be identified. We want to test the proposition that it is libellous to call someone a Communist. Why should it be? It is not libellous to call someone a Conservative.

**Wednesday 4 June**

Dinner with Diana and John Wilton.[3]

John says, 'Margaret Anne rang up this morning and said you told her a very good story about Harold Macmillan being expelled for buggery from Eton.' I say, 'It is quite true. J. B. S. Haldane[4] wrote it to me. He was in the same house at Eton. Harold Macmillan has never been back as a former Old Boy who had become Prime Minister would have been.'

---

1. Journalist and author, in the *Guinness Book of Records* as the writer who has interviewed the most heads of state and government.
2. Elected Conservative MP, 1997.
3. 7th Earl of Wilton; m (1962) Diana, née Galway, previously m to David Naylor-Leyland.
4. (1892–1964); geneticist and popular science writer; Professor of Genetics, 1933–7, Professor of Biometry, 1937–57, London University; he became a Marxist in the 1930s and joined the Communist Party in 1942, resigning in 1956.

Rosita [Duchess of Marlborough] to whom I sit next asks, 'Are you going on the luxury cruise paid for by Vivien Duffield (Charles Clore's daughter)?' I say, 'I haven't been invited.' 'Would you have gone if you had been?' 'No, I don't like the sound of the people.'

**Sunday 8 June**

She is worried. 'We've only got a year to pull up on the opinion polls.'

I comment on Hurd's speech in which he urges more public spending while putting in the perfunctory obligatory statement about the need to cut taxes as well. 'Why do they do it? Are they putting down a marker?' She thinks that may be it. 'He knows it's not your policy. If they disagree with you your Ministers should send you a note or speak to you, not air it. The Cabinet is not supposed to be a public debating society.'

I go on, 'Do you ever say anything in the Cabinet about it or send them a note?' 'If I did that I would be told I was being headmistressy again.'

**Monday 9 June**

Ring Robin Day to find out when the *Tonight* programme started and to check with him that it did not begin the hard-hitting television interview, as is said by Michael Leapman in his new book.[5]

He says he has a dreadful time with his programme *Question Time*. They keep putting on these terrifyingly boring left-wing women. There is no proper balance. They say to him, 'Why do you complain to your friend Woodrow Wyatt? He's always attacking us.' He says, 'I haven't spoken to him for six months,' and adds to me this morning, 'and I'm not speaking to you now, am I?'

The poor fellow has to go back into hospital at the end of July because his bypass operation has not been a hundred per cent effective. 'A girl's head resting upon me – naturally we were discussing the problems of public spending – and she said "You're clicking." I went to the doctor and I've got a broken or split sternum.'

Dinner for Mr Hu Yaobang, General Secretary of the Chinese Communist Party at No 10. He is tiny, smaller than most jockeys. He is either Number Two or Number Three in China and will rise higher as he is very young, being only seventy-two or thereabouts.

---

5. *The Last Days of the Beeb* (1986).

My neighbour is Li Zhaoxing, Deputy Director of the Information Department of the Chinese Ministry of Foreign Affairs.

He says they will keep their word about Hong Kong because there is a Chinese proverb that if you make a promise you are not a man if you don't keep it. I say to him, 'Perhaps you will be bolstered in your promise by the thought that if you treat Hong Kong badly, Taiwan will never be induced to return to the Motherland.' He conceded there was a good point there but said Hong Kong was needed as part of the double economy to show what can be done by capitalism.

Opposite me sits Stuart Young.

Stuart Young is friendly. He said, 'We took a lot of notice of what you wrote to me about South Africa. Do you think our news reporting from South Africa is now improved?'

I thought to myself, 'Well, if you'd said that to me a few days ago I might not have written a somewhat tart review I have written in the *Times* for Thursday which weighs into you pretty strongly.'

Eric Hammond assures me that the Wapping electricians will not vote to go on strike. He thinks that the whole affair will drift on in an unpleasant way but will eventually come to an end. His people are earning some £30,000 and why should they want to strike or lose their jobs? And he won't throw them out of the union and the TUC can now do nothing further to him.

The Château Mouton Rothschild 1970 was splendid. It hurt me to see that more was left undrunk than was drunk of this highly valuable wine. My Chinese government neighbour said he preferred beer when I asked him what he would like to drink.

I persuaded him to drink some of the Château Mouton Rothschild and tried to explain how good it was to him. He did try it but left most of it.

When I got back Verushka told me that it had been on the news that the *Sun* journalists had voted not to continue working at Wapping. I rang Rupert in New York to find that he was in London, where I got hold of him. He was wounded and sad though he did not think they would actually go on strike.

When I was talking to Rupert he said that Owen ought to be offered the job of Deputy Prime Minister by Mrs Thatcher. He says he thinks he would take it. He's obviously realizing that the SDP has nowhere to go and wants the top job with the Tories.

I said, 'I think that's unlikely. Anyway she doesn't like him at all.' 'But it would be a very good move,' he says. 'Think of the commotion,'

I say, 'if it got out that she made such an approach.' 'It could all be done secretly.'

**Tuesday 10 June**

When I get back home about 6.15 p.m. Rupert rings. Can I do something to make sure that any attempt by Maxwell to buy *Today* is referred to the Monopolies Commission to give Rupert a chance to bid as well or to get a third party interested? I promise I will enquire.

Andrew Neil rings to say that he can't come to the dinner party. Trouble with the journalists at the *Sunday Times*. A little later Rupert rings and says, 'Is your dinner a black tie affair?' On being assured that it is not he says, 'Then will you take me as a replacement for Andrew Neil as he's going to be tied up here?' Dinner party saved if not enhanced.

1967 Château Lascombes. Top of the second growth. Excellent. And the 1978 Chablis Premier Grand Cru which is running out.

Rosie d'Avigdor-Goldsmid[6] smokes a largish cigar. She adores cigars. At one time I used to buy cigars with her at sales. Very lively. I don't know how old she is. Must be over seventy. Plants warm kisses on my mouth.

On my left is Mrs Hurd. We discuss the motives of people going into Parliament.

I say, 'They all want to be Prime Minister otherwise they wouldn't be there.' She asks if I think that her husband wants to be Prime Minister. I say, 'I assume so. Though he doubtless went into Parliament with some high motives, probably because he was brought up in a political household, his father being an MP.[7] I imagine he has a reasonably high desire to serve people and be useful.' 'He's very cynical,' she says.

Harold Lever in good talking shape. After the women have gone he speaks very much to the right of Douglas Hurd about Mrs Thatcher and can be assumed to be more desirous of her success at the next election than Douglas is.

Rupert attacks Hurd for not clearing the streets and keeping the highways open properly around Wapping. Hurd replies by saying, 'Our

---

6. Widow of Major Sir Henry Joseph d'Avigor-Goldsmid, Conservative politician (d 1976); she was seventy-five (b 22 July 1910).

7. Sir Anthony Hurd (1901–66; life peer 1964), Conservative MP for Newbury (1945–64) and journalist.

main concern is that it is very expensive. It's costing £5 million so far and we can't afford it.' I say, 'Does that mean we can't protect people from being murdered because it's too expensive?'

I say to Rupert, 'I think you really must try to get injunctions like Shah did in Warrington'[8] and he promises he will.

**Thursday 12 June**

Ring Mrs T just after 8.00 a.m. I say, 'We don't want *Today* to fall into the hands of our enemy Maxwell.' She advises Rupert to ring Shah and say that he is willing to make an offer for the paper and try to get a third party interested as well.

Tell Rupert who says he is having lunch with [Kerry] Packer, the extraordinary Australian businessman, and will urge him to put in a bid for it. I say to Mrs T the reason why it should be referred to the Monopolies Commission, if it is Maxwell alone, is that whereas Rupert was the only person offering to save the *Times*, a number of people are prepared to have a go at saving *Today.*

The trouble with Shah's paper is, as Rupert and I thought [it] would be long ago before he started it, that there is no journalistic flair in it. It is not sufficient to put some smudgy colour pictures in a newspaper and write in a provincial uninteresting style. That is not journalism. In the end people are captured or put off by what the words are.

**Friday 13 June *Bordeaux***

In the cellars[9] or in the *chais*[10] everything is clean like a chemical factory almost. The smell from the barrels is very rich and strong.

We saw the 1985 in casks. They were getting ready to move it on. They have different cellars for each manoeuvre. We tasted the '85 and the '84. '85 seemed very strong and almost spicy. We were told that it was a good year, somewhere between '82 and '83.

The head man said really Château Latour mostly should be drunk ten, twenty or thirty years after it has been made. In fact thirty years is a good time to start.

He said the corks still do age differently. There's nothing they can

---

8. Eddie Shah, who pioneered newspapers produced in Warrington by the new technology.
9. Of Château Latour which WW is visiting with a view to writing an article for the *Sunday Times*.
10. Wine stores.

do about it, not at this stage anyway. So it is true that after many years each bottle will taste slightly differently.

A very pretty house, steps either side circular going down, built 1870.

Wonderful views across the vineyards and to the River Gironde. The tower is more like a pagoda. It's said to have once been used for doves. Not at all like the original tower on the picture they put on the labels of Château Latour.

We walk down to the river and across the water is a great nuclear power station. Nobody seems to be bothered about these things in France. The fishermen have their huts which stand up over the water and their nets and they fish for a fish called *lotte* without worrying about pollution from the effluent of the nuclear power station.

The house is decorated internally by John Fowler and Fowler & Colefax. Tom Parr redid it. The rooms are small in a small house, beautifully shaped and everything, every detail has been thought of and everything is perfect

The meals are arranged to fit the wine not the other way round. No garlic. No herbs, nothing with a strong taste.

No smoking is allowed in the dining-room. The servants are horrified if anybody tries to smoke, even at the end of the meal, as it sullies the atmosphere which would disturb the bouquet and taste of the wine. Ladies discouraged from using strong scents.

Every year during the picking (*vendange*) two hundred people including their families eat lunch for a fortnight. A good one with wine. The man in charge of organizing the pickers blows a whistle when he thinks they have had enough. I enquire whether productivity is as high after lunch as before but no one seems to know.

The same people come year after year. Because of that they select the grapes more carefully, they don't put leaves in with them, they don't put ones that are bad or look as though they are not quite ripe so the end result is slower, not so economical but more like having a hand-made car. The product is absolutely unadulterated.

**Saturday 14 June**

This morning I have a tummy ache.

The French are just as bad as us for liking ceremonial. At the end of our tour of the bottles in the cellars, where there seemed to be about a million bottles of Château Latour, there was an induction of some people into the Society of the Caves de Mêdoc. Alan[11] seemed to be in charge, dressed up in his robes which looked something like the Garter robes. He had a cap. His face immediately became mediaeval and Norman-looking but then so did the other people's.

**Sunday 15 June**

The Barton house built in 1756; Léoville-Barton, Langoa-Barton [made here]; bought by the Bartons who were already in Bordeaux and had been for about a hundred years in 1820. One of them escaped from the French Revolution. A great new *chais*, that is to say cleaned up out of an old one, disclosing the original beams.

The rooms are good proportions. Nothing like the lavish furniture of Château Margaux where there is a pianola, a mechanical organ, given by Napoleon to Murat, and all the furniture is French Empire. But at Barton they have lovely roses growing in enormous profusion.

There was a sort of joke which goes on between the great proprietors. When you invite one of them to dinner you always have to give him one of his wines as well as one of your own. The joke is to select one of his wines but not of his best years and then one of yours at one of your best years so that he is mildly discomfited but cannot say anything about it. They vary from year to year in superbness from château to château.

Anthony Barton is youngish, good looking. His wife is Danish. Very acid about the Petits,[12] saying her father only had grocery stores and knows nothing about wine. They are the aristocrats having been holding their châteaux since before the 1855 classification. The only other family to do that is the Rothschild family which had their Mouton in 1853.

All the other estates in the 1855 classification have been disbursed to other owners, mainly through the Code Napóleon.[13] There were a hundred and twenty owners of Château Latour when it was bought by Pearson in '63.

Margaux has been restored to its original acreage exactly the same as the old 18th century map.

---

11. The Hon. Alan Hare was president, Société Civile du Vignoble de Château Latour, 1983–90.
12. Owners of Château Margaux.
13. The complex laws on inheritance which disperse property between all the children of a marriage and other relations.

At lunch the Pavillon Blanc 1978 was the same as we had at Château Margaux the day before. The Latour '67 was very good which makes me think of my Margaux '67 and the Latour '55 is also excellent. Lots of learned noises made about each. The white Sauternes at the end, Château Coutet 1966, is one I don't mind if I never drink again.

Bron[14] is quite annoyed when I say at the Barton place what does he think of the 1985 Léoville and Langoa? 'Oh dear, I wish you wouldn't keep making me out to be the expert.' Teresa[15] says, 'I've never heard you be so modest before' but he does talk very knowledgeably about wine, and entertainingly. He may be unpleasant but he's never dull.

The Great Growths must sink or swim together. They are very careful not to knock each other, just to suggest every now and again one of their years may be better than the same year of one of the others. The 1953 Margaux we had at lunch on Saturday was written up in *Wines of the World*, latest edition, [edited by] André Simon, as one of the best they ever had so it was a great honour to be given it. When the opinions were being asked for I simply said, 'Bloody marvellous.'

**Tuesday 17 June**

The effects of all the grand claret have not yet worn off. Dizzy with the memories of the vintages.

Leave early for Ascot so that I can walk round before having lunch with Piers Bengough. I sense a certain coolness but I may be mistaken. Perhaps he has heard that on the Levy Board I continually demand that we should be allowed to see the accounts of the Ascot racecourse to which the Levy Board gives more money than any other racecourse.

**Wednesday 18 June**

Lunch in the Tote entertainment room. On my right is Mrs Thomas, the wife of the Austrian Ambassador. She is agreeable. She disagrees

---

14. Auberon Waugh.
15. Novelist and translator; daughter of 6th Earl of Onslow; m (1961) Auberon Waugh.

with the version of Mayerling in my book[16] which I got from Nadjie (Mrs Racz) my mother-in-law, who got it from her uncle who was legal adviser to the Hapsburgs. He was told it by the Crown Princess. Mrs Thomas thinks the affair was political to which I say, 'Nonsense.' She says her family knew people who were at the hunting lodge and they never said anything. 'Of course not. It was hushed up as best they could.'

Peter Winfield, one of the Tote Board members, has a horse called The Patriarch. It wins the Royal Hunt Cup at 20 to 1 with the Tote paying 24 to 1. He comes in with his trainer and the great gold cup. I pull the lid off and knock it on the floor. I wanted to fill it with champagne which I then did. He is delighted. Great applause all round led by Sonny Marlborough. Peter Winfield is immensely happy, and particularly pleased at being applauded by a Duke.

**Thursday 19 June**

Another lunch party to which all but Mr and Mrs Arnott[17] arrive punctually. He explains he had to conduct two eye operations in the morning which I thought was a very poor excuse.

Elaine Rawlinson sits on my left looking very pretty in black and white. There is an outbreak of black and white among the ladies this day.

On my right at lunch is Jane Spencer-Churchill. She tells me she has written to Mrs Thatcher to thank her for the help the government's start-up for businesses had given her. I think she borrowed £50,000 and she has made a great success out of her shops selling materials and so forth for decorating. She got a letter back in typed form but at the bottom Mrs Thatcher wrote in her own handwriting, 'You are the only person who has bothered to write in and thank us for the help they got from the government start up scheme.' That's extraordinary. People just take everything for granted.

Ted Heath was at the lunch enjoying everything hugely. As his old PPS when he was Prime Minister, Timothy Kitson, and his wife are

---

16. *Confessions of an Optimist*, p. 330; in this version the rejected mistress of Crown Prince Rudolf of Austria (1858–89, son of the Hapsburg Emperor Francis Joseph) cut off his penis whilst he slept in his hunting lodge at Mayerling; he then shot her and himself.

17. John Arnott, ophthalmologist specializing in cataract and lens implant operations.

also there, plus his Attorney General Peter Rawlinson, I said, 'I thought we would reassemble your government for you' which delighted him.

**Friday 20 June**

Ring Mrs Thatcher to find out whether she is weakening on sanctions. 'No, but we may have to make a few gestures.' She wishes that Botha would do what I have been suggesting and release Mandela, unban the ANC and start some talks. He is making it very difficult for her to go on resisting sanctions.

She will have a tough battle with the EEC next week. She says France and Italy are in favour of banning fruit and wine imports from South Africa. I laugh and say, 'Typically cynical.' She will not agree to international air flight bans so the press comment that she is going to is quite wrong.

When I remark that it doesn't matter if some of these countries like India and Zambia leave the Commonwealth she agrees but says, 'Other people would mind.' She means the Queen.

I ring Leo Evans after I have spoken to her. Not to tell him anything of what she said but to say off my own bat that I thought it was insulting of Botha to say that the only reason Mrs Thatcher was against sanctions was because she is frightened of unemployment in Britain.

I said, 'I think you should tell him he will lose his only friend if he goes on talking like that.'

**Monday 23 June**

Ring Mrs Thatcher at 7.45 a.m. She is having her hair done. She rings back just before 9.00.

When I say that I think the South African government has now gone too far in repression,[18] she comments that they had to in order to prevent the violence which had been planned for last Monday.

Princess Michael is on the telephone and I cannot get her off it.

'Why is there so much aggression to me from the Murdoch press and all the press? It was an error of a typist that the engagements for the month were circulated to the *Times* and included Ascot last Thursday. They made out that I was being Princess Pushy and there

---

18. On 12 June hundreds of anti-apartheid activists were arrested and held incommunicado under the South African emergency regulations, with a ban on the press reporting the activities of the security forces.

was a huge cartoon in your paper, the *News of the World*. Will you buy it for me?'

'What do you want it for?' 'I don't want it hanging in some bar for everybody to goggle at.' 'Anybody can hang it up as a cutting from the newspaper. I didn't notice it myself. How did you see it?' 'My husband cut it out for me.' 'Did you read my article underneath it?' 'I didn't notice it.' 'I didn't notice the cartoon.'

I said I couldn't buy the cartoon: they would know why I wanted it.

She is very aggrieved that she was reported as snubbing guests at some *Emmerdale Farm*[19] lunch in aid of leukaemia research at Birmingham.

Though the Chief Barker, organizer of the proceedings, wrote to the *Times* and they published the letter to say she had not snubbed anybody as they always knew she had to go early, nevertheless the *Times* Diary repeated the accusation.

'I don' t know why they go at me and put newspaper reporters on aeroplanes to pursue me. What about that Sarah Ferguson, there must be plenty to write about her?'

She then asked me could I get her book serialized by the *Sunday Times*. That would be some recompense for what they have done to her. She is also worried that when she starts giving interviews in October about her book the press will be after her again. 'Why give the interviews?' 'I must, to sell the book. The *News of the World* has already said it's about Royal sex scandals and it isn't true.'

**Tuesday 24 June**

Norman Lamont came to lunch at Cavendish Avenue. He is very chuffed at being promoted to F.S.T.[20]

I warned him not to get into any more trouble.[21] It would be letting down Mrs Thatcher who had been very decent to him. He agrees he owes all to her.

He feels that the government must make more of the defence issue and the Labour Party's abandonment of the nuclear deterrent. At a dinner with Christopher Soames, Willie Whitelaw said he didn't think it was a major issue: the country was only interested in the economy.

---

19. Television series.
20. He was appointed Financial Secretary to the Treasury in the May reshuffle.
21. A reference to the gossip columns; see 26 November 1985.

This is nonsense. There is a deep patriotism in Britain. The Tories must play on it. Michael Heseltine used to do it very well.

Rupert rings from Aspen. Very alarmed by a report in *Today* saying that the government was weakening in its support for him at Wapping, believing that his use of the law makes it likely that the Labour attack will be more credible on the new trade union laws. Eric Hammond and others are flying out to see him. Would I find out whether there is a weakening or not? I say I will try.

**Wednesday 25 June**

Speak to Mrs T who has not heard of the report in *Today* and is horrified. 'I will make an enquiry, and if there is anything in it I will squash it. Our position is perfectly clear. We think Rupert has made a very generous offer and we are right behind him. Anything to the contrary is untrue.' I rang Rupert, woke him up presumably in the middle of the night but he was greatly relieved.

A pleasant memorial service for John Willoughby at St Mary Abbots Church which I had never been in before and had hardly noticed going down Kensington High Street.

Rachel looked dignified and sad and still beautiful. Poor John. I was thinking of him lying for months in the tiny nursing home room saying how good the corned beef and sausages were. That after a life of luxury during which he gambled away fortunes.

Later at lunch at the Levy Board. Tristram Ricketts, Chief Executive, said that one of the reasons why the Tote didn't get a Tote monopoly in 1960 was because John Willoughby, important in the Jockey Club (twice Senior Steward), was so much in debt to his bookmakers and preferred to keep them going unassailed by a Tote monopoly. I forgive him because he was gentle and friendly and often very funny.

Home Secretary at the Levy Board lunch. The more I see and hear him talk the less stature I think he has. He is forecast, or was, as a Prime Minister to succeed Mrs Thatcher. He'd be no good. He measures his language carefully and it sounds quite impressive but the content is vague. He sounds tough but isn't.

More discussion about Sunday racing and I explain that Monkey Blacker and I are seeing Lord Brentford[22] and later the Bishop of Birmingham to try and cobble something together. He agrees that if there was something that they would not wholly object to, a private

22. 4th Viscount Brentford.

member would be a vehicle to get a Bill through and it might not be too difficult.

**Thursday 26 June**

A drinks party at the American Embassy in Regent's Park. We were evidently put on the smart list. The Duke of Marlborough and his wife are there, Sir Francis Dashwood, Edward Montagu[23] and a lot of socialites as well as Callaghan. We both avoid each other. Rosita[24] looks a little less pretty now and her legs are a tiny bit thick. But she was jolly.

Moorea[25] looks elegant in a pink and white flowery kind of light dress. I hardly recognize Brinsley who looks so much older with grey hair. Moorea is looking much older too. Verushka says, 'I hope I don't look as old as her.'

We have quite a long conversation about Pericles and she gives me a kiss.

Go to Gray's Inn Hall for anniversary EETPU dinner given by Lawford's.[26] They and the union have provided the dinner for the members and friends of the ETU (which they call now the EETPU because it's got the plumbing union in it as well). It is the anniversary of the twenty-fifth year of winning the famous court case which got the Communists out of the union. They were convicted of ballot rigging fraud and of doing it in the interests of the Communist Party. They had been doing it for twenty years or so.

Eric Hammond made a speech; so did Frank Chapple.[27] There was considerable praise for me, how I had early on exposed the machinations of the Communists and made it possible for the support to be gathered and the court case to succeed. I enjoyed that bit.

Most touching were the Branch Secretaries, some of them now very old and retired. They had risked their livelihoods by coming forward to give evidence that the ETU Communists were lying when they said that their ballot papers had been posted to head office late.

---

23. Lord Montagu of Beaulieu.
24. Duchess of Marlborough.
25. Lady Moorea Black, WW's former wife, m 2 Brinsley Black.
26. Lawford & Co. was established in 1952 to provide legal services to trade unions and their members. See *Confessions of an Optimist* for WW's account of the court case and his role in fighting Communist dominance of the union.
27. General Secretary of the Electrical Trades Union (ETU), 1966–84; life peer 1985.

Before the dinner I was asking Eric Hammond what he was going to do when he saw Rupert in Los Angeles on the coming Saturday. He said he hoped to work out something by which there would be a recognition of the actual fact that for a year or more, when they were setting up the printing operation at Wapping, there were members of the NGA and SOGAT there. Something perhaps might be built on their recognition as members of the union without admitting the union in properly. Certainly his members in the electricians are not willing to give up their five hundred jobs; how on earth could that satisfy the demands of the five thousand, sacked because they went on strike, that they should all have their jobs back?

When I asked him a bit more he said, 'I'm not going to put all my cards on the table now.' Frank Chapple said I would ring Rupert and tell him what Eric said. I didn't actually, though I tried to get him on Friday afternoon when he had already left for Los Angeles.

It was very nice to see all those ETU people again. And to see how proud they were of having got rid of the Communists. That is the reason why they are always attacked in the TUC by the others. Not because they produce unorthodox and modern policies but because they can never be forgiven for having got the Communists out. The same happened to me in the Labour Party. Once I had done that my career was over in the party. It was resented by the Labour MPs and by all the trade union bigwigs that I had interfered and got democracy into the ETU.

**Friday 27 June**

I was thinking of Diana Cooper[28] who died this week. I used to see her at Zell-am-See with Liz and Raimund [von Hofmannsthal] and we went for walks together. For long she and Liz quarrelled but they got on better in later years.

The last time I saw her she said, 'Why don't you come and have tea with me or a drink?' I said, 'I will soon.' She said, 'The time is getting short you know.' I kick myself that I didn't go.

It wasn't just that she was a beauty always – that was obvious. She had knowledge and wit but especially a grandeur.

28. Lady Diana Cooper (widow of Duff Cooper, 1st Viscount Norwich, diplomat and writer).

**Saturday 28 June**

A letter from Irwin. After a long period of vacillating he now writes that he does not want to continue our business relation because he sees no hope for *Britain Confidential.*

**Sunday 29 June**

'That was a good week's work,' I said to her. I was referring to the way she had got the EEC at The Hague not to put on new sanctions against South Africa but to give South Africa three months to release Nelson Mandela, to start meaningful dialogue with the black leaders and to make general advances.

I say that Geoffrey Howe could do some good in persuading Botha to advance when he goes there as representative of the EEC, if his heart is in the right place. 'Is it?' I ask. 'Is he under the influence of the Foreign Office?' She says, 'I fear he is.' 'It is hopeless then because they believe in one man one vote which is ridiculous in South Africa.' 'Yes,' she said, 'but I think he will try and carry out his brief sincerely while he is there.'

We discuss briefly the next election.

'I want to try and get the mood set not only for what we have achieved but what we are going to try and do.'

She was greatly disappointed in the Peacock Committee[29] which has not recommended advertising by the BBC on their television programmes.

The trouble with these committees is they are always weak and give in to the conventional views.

I say that it is absolute rubbish there wouldn't be enough advertising for both the BBC and commercial television. She says that was what they said about the effect on the newspapers when commercial television was introduced, that it would ruin the newspapers who'd lose advertising but it didn't. There's enough to go round.

---

29. The Peacock Committee on Broadcasting, set up in March 1985.

**Tuesday 1 July**

Monkey Blacker (Deputy Senior Steward of the Jockey Club) and I go to see Lord Brentford. He is the good-looking lugubrious leader of the Keep [Sunday] Special campaign. I ask his advice on how we could meet or neutralize opposition to the Sunday opening of racecourses. He is surprisingly forthcoming. He is going to discuss with his colleagues the possibility of allowing racecourses to open on Sunday because they are not in shopping areas and so long as we don't try to open the betting shops in the high streets.

Dinner at David Metcalfe's.[1] About twenty people.

The guest of honour is a Mr Walter Annenberg who used to be US Ambassador in Britain. I am asked to sit next to Mrs Annenberg at dinner and talk to her about South Africa. She turns out to be intelligent and hadn't realized a great deal of what is going on.

She is well-preserved, not bad looking. I suppose she has had a face lift or two.

Sally Metcalfe said, 'I'm sorry I couldn't come to the Ascot lunch.' 'David always brings some lady with him now but I don't think you've any cause for worry because they are not anything like as pretty as you are.' She doesn't seem to mind him going around with a lot of other ladies. Verushka would be furious.

I took too much fish and it looked as though there wasn't enough to go round. Fortunately there was another large dish available.

I quoted Dr Johnson: 'I am not hungry but thank God I am greedy.'

**Wednesday 2 July**

Told the board meeting at the Tote that Prince Michael is joining the board on October 1st, succeeding Andrew. Said that the Home Secretary decided to put him on the board which they know is a joke but

1. Director, Sedgwick James Management Services (insurance brokers); m 3 (1979) Sally Cullen Howe; son of Major Edward 'Fruity' Metcalfe, best man at the Duke of Windsor's wedding.

can't say so because I select the members of the board though I have to get the Home Secretary's approval.

David Montagu was against it (not at the board meeting) because he felt that he would not be an asset and in fact advised him against it, I gather. The others don't say anything but I don't think they are displeased. Andrew says, 'In case you think you're going up in the social scale, I would like to say that when I went to Cuzco in Peru the Mayor said I have met many Princes but I have never met a Duke before.'

John Heaton (Secretary to the Tote) and Brian McDonnell (Chief Executive) both feel the staff will like it very much. Will Princess Michael wash about, causing chaos? I think Verushka will stop her. They are both from the old Austro-Hapsburg Empire.

**Friday 4 July**

Lunch at Barclays Bank headquarters. I think of the last visit I paid there some four or more years ago trying to save Banbury[2] and with myself in danger of going bankrupt. This time it is the Chairman, Sir Timothy Bevan, who is my host with four or five others concerned with South Africa, including Johnnie Henderson.[3]

I had written to Bevan telling him that in announcing Barclays Bank's policy of disinvestment or not investing more in South Africa he should not have included a statement implying that nothing was being done about apartheid when it is.

A very friendly discussion. Barclays measure their future to some extent in Britain by the number of new students they get taking out accounts every year. The usual run is that some years they are two per cent higher than National Westminster and some years the same or a little lower. Last year they were nineteen per cent below. A survey they did showed that this was because students don't like their involvement in South Africa. They are also owed about £70 million by South Africa and they want to feel they are able to get it out. If they feel they are able to get it out, it means they won't take it out.

Nicholas and Caroline come to dinner for my birthday. We start with a 1937 Pichon-Longueville and follow it with a 1925 La Tour Carnet (a fourth growth). According to my new policy learned via

2. WW's newspaper and printing business.
3. Chairman, Henderson Administration, 1983–90.*

Professor Peynaud adviser to Margaux and the visit to Bordeaux, I open both of them at the table.

**Saturday 5 July**

A trip to the International Nutrition Foundation Council of Management and Annual General Meeting, etc. at Sutton Courtenay. The members of the Council of Management are very aged. It is strange how so many of the old are determined to do good for a future they will never see.

I am trying to go through Anthony Smith[4] at the British Film Institute, a great friend of Getty, to raise money for the International Nutrition Foundation. Smith thinks I ought to write an article in the *Times* or *Telegraph* explaining it all to get an approach forward to Getty.

I think to myself what would any visitor here make of it all. The laboratories are fine but the house in which we have the board meeting and where Dr Sinclair lives is filthy. At the lunch indescribably dirty tablecloths are put out on the side-board and on the little table off which we eat. The glasses look as though they have not been washed.

The place looks as though it has not been dusted this century. The garden is a wilderness. The lawn looks like a hay field just cut. Neglect is everywhere.

There are two lavatories side by side in the house itself. Both pans are filthy. It looks as though no disinfectant had been on them for thirty years. The wash basins are yellowed and rimmed. I think anybody on being asked to give money who saw these surroundings would think how can they deal with research into food in such premises. That will be a mistake because the laboratories are scrupulously clean and the research is brilliant.

Sir Reginald Bennett, who acts as Chairman in the absence of the Chairman himself, keeps calling champagne shampoo. 'Have some more shampoo.' 'This is very good shampoo.' He is extremely fat, used to be an MP,[5] drinks a great deal and though agreeable is not a person with a high reputation.

Today I received a letter from Irwin saying that our relationship in business ceases on July 1st and I will just have to think of him in future

---

4. Director, British Film Institute, 1979–88; President, Magdalen College, Oxford, from 1988.
5. Conservative MP, 1950–74.

as a friend. The letter has evidently crossed with mine in which I ask for a final payment of £5,000 as he had said he would be guided by me on this matter.

**Sunday 6 July**

Rang Mrs Thatcher. We talk about reports in the *Telegraph* this morning that Geoffrey Howe is threatening to resign if Mrs Thatcher won't put on sanctions after he has come back from South Africa. I say, 'I cannot believe that he would ever do a thing like that' and she said, 'No, nor could I.' It sounds to her like tittle tattle.

I say we have to bring the law up to date on the unions. It is not sensible to expect a member of a union always to go to the Certification Officer to make a complaint. They are often very frightened with good reason of losing their livelihood or being victimized.

I also say that it is intolerable that we don't have postal secret ballots. That is why a Militant has won the General Secretaryship of the CPSA[6] by a hundred and twenty-one votes. It's so easy to fiddle them and they have fiddled them. 'We'll deal with it all after the next election.'

**Tuesday 8 July**

Lunch at Sedgwick House, the headquarters of Sedgwick International, the second largest insurance brokers of the world.

At lunch there is Kenneth Keith[7] who asks what am I doing now? I say, 'I write a weekly column in the *News of the World*.' 'Oh I never see that.' 'I write fortnightly in the *Times*.' 'Oh I haven't read it.' 'And I am Chairman of the Tote and I do book reviews for the *Times*.' 'Oh,' he says, 'I can remember you as a printer.'

Rather irritated I say very pointedly, 'Are you still running Rolls-Royce?' I know of course that he left it years ago when he had made a terrible mess of it. That discomforts him and makes it clear that I do not know what he is doing or he thinks it does. 'I am running Beechams now.' 'Oh, you're selling those pills. "Worth a guinea a box" they used to advertise before the War.' Still discomforted he said, 'We do lots of other things besides that now.'

6. Civil and Public Services Association.
7. Lord Keith of Castleacre; life peer 1980.

**Monday 14 July**

Lunch with Sir Brian Cubbon[8] at his small flat at Ashley Gardens. He brought in the melon and the chicken salad and chopped up peaches for pudding himself. He had three young civil servants he wanted me to meet to give them an idea of what goes on in the rest of the world.

One, Vivien Dews, was in charge of immigration at Croydon. She says that the Minister, Waddington, at the Home Office answers seventeen thousand letters a year. These letters are to MPs.

Another was Paul Bolt who is dealing with the Criminal Justice Bill. His mother is Indian. Bright and lively.

The third was dealing with public order, Robert Hazell.[9] They are producing a new Act with a provision against disorderly behaviour and finding it hard to define.

Should journalists be allowed to talk direct to civil servants? The three young ones thought yes. Brian was slightly hesitant on the grounds that it's all right in America, where civil servants are really running departments much more than they do here where there are political Ministers.

Should there be cabinets, on the French lines, of political advisers of the same persuasion as a Minister? It was thought not because the Junior Ministers now have much power and act as a political cabinet all the time for the top Minister.

An intelligent jolly crew.

**Thursday 17 July**

The day for the *Times* fortnightly article. I had to start it early to be ready to leave for lunch on time with Queen Elizabeth the Queen Mother at Clarence House. So naturally I got behind and in a panic.

Queen Elizabeth was standing in her 'drawing-room'.

The space under the tree was arranged like a real drawing-room with little tables with dishes and vases of flowers. She delighted in talking about it in a happy girlish way. 'Is it all right to have a picnic like this?' she asked, pointing at her 'dining-room' under an adjoining plane tree where the table was laden with precious silverware and beautiful plates and other objects. Both the 'drawing-room' and 'dining-room' have ceilings of plane tree branches which come almost to the ground on either side from a fair height.

---

8. Permanent Under-Secretary of State, Home Office, 1979–88.
9. He became director of the Nuffield Foundation in 1989.

She tells me how much she liked Gingo Sanminiatelli.[10]

Martin Gilliatt, the Private Secretary, showed me my place on the board. I was pleased to find I was sitting next to her. Angela Oswald[11] said to me, 'She's put me on your other side because she knows that we like each other' which I thought sweet.

Before lunch I was introduced about three times to Nicholas Soames' wife whom I have met once or twice including at Ascot. When we finally went I said to her, 'No one has tried to introduce me to you for the last five minutes.' She is tall, fairly pretty.

Angus Ogilvy[12] came in, having been Queen Elizabeth's representative at the memorial service for Diana Cooper so he was a bit late. After lunch he engaged Nicholas and myself in conversation about the need to provide business opportunities for young unemployed and did not seem to understand that a lot is being provided already. He wants the Prince of Wales to set up some new trusts but I suppose it's the more the merrier.

Young Viscount Linley[13] was there, who seemed charming, Queen Elizabeth telling me more than once how well he was doing. During lunch I saw her raising her glass to him and he to her half the length of the table. It is the sort of charming gesture she makes. She does it to me sometimes when we are having lunch at a racecourse sitting at separate tables.

Douglas Fairbanks Jnr was there and I said we last met twenty years ago, 'I expect you've forgotten it.' 'No, no. I remember it well. Kind of you.' It was at lunch at the House of Commons with Tom Driberg of all people and I think it was more like thirty or forty years ago. Douglas Fairbanks was sitting on Queen Elizabeth's right.

Queen Elizabeth and I talk about the sense of duty which she has which won't let her rest. Even though she is bored and exhausted, she carries on. I said, 'Yes, but you have a journalist's mind. You're curious and inquisitive about people and things. You have such an enormous zest that you actually enjoy nearly all of it even if it does get tiring.' She agreed. She said, 'I suppose you've got your sense of duty from your father.' I said, 'Curiously yes because he was very lazy.' 'Oh but didn't he do a lot?' I said, 'As little as possible apart from weeding his

10. Count Sanminiatelli, an Italian friend of WW.
11. Woman of the Bedchamber to Queen Elizabeth the Queen Mother.*
12. Husband of Princess Alexandra, the Queen Mother's niece.
13. Son of Princess Margaret and the Earl of Snowdon.

own tennis lawn because he thought nobody else could do it. He was headmaster of his own private school basically because he liked the long holidays.'

Without prompting from me she said, 'How disgraceful it is that the press and people are trying to involve the Queen in the row about sanctions and whether some states might leave the Commonwealth. It is cheek for them to say what she thinks.' I say, 'Is there any truth in the story that she's at odds with Mrs Thatcher?' 'None whatever, of course not.' I ask, 'Will you all mind much if some of those black countries do leave the Commonwealth?' She said, 'Not at all, if that's what they want to do.' She thought it was terrible, the blackmail they have been putting on the Commonwealth Games organizers to get rid of Zola Budd and Annette Cowley[14] and so forth. She agrees with just about everything I write.

Somehow we came to discussing Kenneth Kaunda, President of Zambia. 'He's an idiot,' she said. She was glad she didn't have to meet them at dinner when they come to the Commonwealth Summit at the beginning of August. 'Poor Queen,' she said. 'She will have to.' I suspect she wants me to let Mrs T know the Queen is not against her.

I say to her, 'You never look a day older' and she smiles a little, pointing her hands down to the ground: 'One day suddenly I will be down there, gone.' Previously I had admired her brooch saying how beautiful it was. 'Are they rose diamonds?' 'Oh no, they're real diamonds.' 'I thought rose diamonds were old English diamonds?' 'Yes, but it's the way they are cut and these are real ones.' I said, 'Yes much more valuable. How old is it?' She said, 'I think it came via Queen Mary, like a number of my things. I'm very glad you like it.' She patted it and smiled appreciatively.

It got a bit chilly. 'Oh the English climate,' she said as I tried to light my cigar and it kept blowing out. 'Shall we go in?' I said, 'Oh no, not unless you're cold.'

Martin Gilliatt says should Queen Elizabeth get the *Racing Post*. I explain why the *Sporting Life* is probably better and certainly better for us in the betting shops. 'However,' I say, 'there is an interview I gave appearing in the *Racing Post* soon, I gave it to a journalist.' Queen Elizabeth says, 'Is it one of your funny ones? I must see it.'

---

14. Young athletes living in Britain at the time; they came under the ban against South Africa in sport because they had been born there.

At lunch I had said, 'There's a new Barbara Pym out.[15] I'll see if it's any good and send you one.' She said, 'Oh I didn't thank you properly for the book you sent me about Augustus Hare.' I said, 'On the contrary you wrote a lovely letter. I showed a couple of your thank you letters to Petronella and said. "Now that's how you should write a thank you letter."' 'Oh dear,' she said, 'That won't make me very popular. But what I meant was I didn't explain enough how grateful I was for that book. It was so interesting reminding me of so many things.'

Dinner at Andrew Knight's.

The dinner was boring. The food was execrable. The white wine was nothing in particular.

On Sabihah's [Knight's] other side is Garrett Drogheda[16] who had told me before dinner how terrible it was with Joan his wife now. She has senile dementia. He has to employ four nurses in shifts. She is tiring him out. She utterly depends on him but can't remember who he is half the time. She can't even remember what he has said from one moment to the next. A brilliant concert pianist, she still plays pieces often not making a wrong note for long periods. She can remember that much. She was the girl who inspired Maschwitz,[17] who was in love with her, to write 'These Foolish Things'.

Norman St John-Stevas is there and thanks me effusively for the nice things I said about his editing of Bagehot. It seems that the latest set of volumes has already sold out at £160 the four volumes.

After dinner Conrad Black comes to talk to me. He says he's the youngest newspaper proprietor ever in England at forty-one years old. He owns the *Telegraph* business now. His wife is a bit younger and very pretty.[18] He asks me a great many questions about who are the cleverest people I knew, what were Churchill, Attlee and so forth like and knows his history remarkably.

That contradicts the nasty things which are written about him as a rough untutored wheeler-dealing Canadian with no culture. He cer-

---

15. *Civil to Strangers and other writings*, published posthumously.
16. 11th Earl of Drogheda (1910–89); chairman, *Financial Times*, 1971–5, managing director, 1945–71; chairman, Royal Opera House, Covent Garden, 1958–74; director, Times Newspapers, from 1981; m (1935) Joan, née Carr, pianist.
17. Eric Maschwitz (1901–69), head of light entertainment, BBC Television, 1958–61, playwright and songwriter.
18. He married 1 (1978–92) Shirley Gail Hishon, 2 (1992) Barbara Amiel.

tainly has got a lot. We talk about Beaverbrook. I tell Black that he has some of Beaverbrook's charm which lies in skilful flattery which no one can ever resist. In return for my flattery he keeps telling me how much he admires what I write. He has a strong face.

'Why did you buy the business? For money or because you wanted the power of being a publisher of great newspapers?' 'As an investment and for the other reason you give,' he says. He admires Rupert. He believes that the *Telegraph* will before long be making money. He was amazed to see what a mess they got it into financially. I say, 'Andrew is very good.' He says, 'Yes but he needs help on financial matters, on the business side.' Andrew thinks it is Black's duty to speak to other guests but he insists on continuing to talk to me till we leave.

**Saturday 19 July**

To Donhead St Mary [to stay with the Trees]. Anne Tree[19] has not been well for some months. Hepatitis. Doesn't know where she got it. It could have been from eating vongole in Italy. She has good days and bad ones. Gets tired very easily. Today is quite a good one. She is even fiddling with plants in the garden.

The garden which I remember as nothing, non-existent when they moved in, is now beautifully planned with lakes and a vista of a waterfall going down to a statue with a hill behind.

Stanley Olson[20] who wrote a book about Sargent the painter came to stay on Friday night. He felt ill. Later it emerged he had been to his doctor before coming down who had diagnosed a mild stroke but said it was all right to go to the country – which seemed eccentric. He has been in bed ever since he got here. He came to England from America because he was keen to follow up the activities of the Bloomsbury set to which he is much attracted. He appeared sometime after lunch and had tea in the garden. I met him briefly. He said I'd met him before which I do not recollect and put down to his mind being in disorder.

---

19. The Lady Anne Tree, née Cavendish, daughter of the 10th Duke of Devonshire, sister of the 11th Duke (Andrew); m (1949) Michael Tree, son of Ronald Tree (Conservative politician (d 1976); see note on Marietta Tree below) by his American first wife Nancy, and brother of Jeremy Tree, racehorse trainer.
20. Born Ohio, 1948, educated in the US and then at London University where he wrote a thesis on the Hogarth Press; he had published a study of the American novelist and poet Elinor Wyle, and edited a condensed edition of Harold Nicolson's diaries and letters (1980) as well as writing the book on Sargent.

A little later he got worse. The local doctor was summoned, an NHS one who said that the doctor who sent him to the country telling him it would be all right was criminal. He was rushed off to hospital by Michael and Anne to Salisbury. The specialist said he didn't like at all what was going on in the young man's head, something very nasty. We await the outcome.

He is very young. He lives by himself in London. Anne had met him at Lismore.[21]

Michael rings Andrew [Devonshire] but nobody it transpires knows anything about him, who his parents are or indeed whether he has any which is doubtful, whether he has any next of kin or what. Could be an Agatha Christie mystery story.

Marietta Tree[22] is staying. She married Ronnie Tree and became Michael's step-mother though not much older. She thought the food at the Knights the other evening was rather good apart from the scallops and the summer pudding.

We told her that Sabihah had rung up the next day to ask if we were all right as she hadn't eaten the scallops because she thought they were bad and hoped that the guests who had eaten them suffered nothing. Petronella said it's like Lucrezia Borgia ringing up after a party to find out whether the poison worked or not.

I said to Michael when he told me that the young man had written a book about Sargent, 'Interesting subject.' 'Not at all,' said Michael, 'a very dull man. Did nothing but paint. Had no private life. The critics said the book was bad.'

**Sunday 20 July**

The tiresomeness of staying away is one can never get breakfast when one wants it. All the arrangements are different. The bed was uncomfortable. I woke up early because the curtains didn't keep the light out.

---

21. House of Lord (Charles) Cavendish, second son of the 9th Duke of Devonshire, in Co. Waterford, Eire.
22. Marietta Tree (1917–91), née Peabody, born in Boston, m 1 Desmond Fitzgerald, m 2 (1947) Ronald Tree, Conservative MP, friend of the Astors, with homes at Ditchley Park, Oxfordshire, and in Barbados. She had an affair with the film director John Huston and campaigned for Adlai Stevenson, the Democrat contender for the US presidency in 1952; he facilitated her appointment as US representative to the UN Human Rights Commission.

On the news the lead story is the *Sunday Times*' sensational detailed account from 'unimpeachable sources' from the Palace of the Queen's disapproval of Mrs T because she is uncaring; handled the miners' strike divisively; should not have allowed Reagan to fly from England to raid Libya; is undermining the cosy consensus in British politics and is wrongly busting up the Commonwealth opposing tough sanctions on South Africa.

The poor young man Stanley Olson who is truly thirty-seven has edited Harold Nicolson's diaries and letters. He is writing a book about Rebecca West. I looked at his book on Sargent which is not perhaps exciting but workmanlike. How sad he may never write anything more. The news this morning is not good. The specialist said they can do nothing for him at the hospital near Salisbury, he must go to Southampton or London, and Anne went off in a taxi to transport him to either destination as required.

Verushka broke a huge china lamp in her bedroom, one of a pair which had come from Chatsworth. It wasn't her fault. Her heel caught in a wire left outside the bottom of the curtain.

Anne says, 'Tell her not to mind. It was my fault. I'm a bad housewife. I should have seen there was a wire sticking out. Tell her not to mind about unimportant material things' and I said, 'Particularly as it's Sunday' and she laughed. It was calamitous but it all added to the general excitement.

Anne told me something which really made me hate the English. Ted is maligned in The Close at Salisbury. The catty women say that he must be corrupt, where did he get all that money to spend £260,000 on the house? Only a building labourer's son. Why should he have all that money?

As I explained, the house did not cost £260,000 but he spent a lot doing it up. He has a long lease on very favourable terms from the Cathedral. Also he has written books which have been quite successful.

He's done extensive lectures. He has been connected with business enterprises. Why shouldn't he have some money?

The real nastiness is in all those narrow minded beastly little people, clergymen's wives, deans' wives and so forth who are so utterly absurdly snobbish and can't bear it that Ted started as working class, became Prime Minister, Conservative, and then apparently had enough money to live in some style, followed by his detective, in Salisbury. Good luck to him.

Another nasty trait is thinking that people from modest

backgrounds ought not to be Prime Minister, particularly Conservative. That is part of the dislike the Tories in the upper reaches have for Mrs Thatcher. Like Ian Gilmour[23] who when I pressed him to ask Mrs Thatcher to dinner when she was first Leader of the Tory Party said, 'Oh she's not the sort of person one asks to dinner.' We are off the Gilmour list now because of my love for Margaret Thatcher.

The claret was very good at lunch yesterday, 1978 Branaire Ducru. It was too young to drink but it is a good year. Michael said, 'Well how long should I wait to drink it?' 'About twenty years' time,' I said. 'But we'll both be dead.'

Marietta Tree tells us in the car up to London that she appeared once as an actress in the film called *The Misfits* which was Marilyn Monroe's last. Marietta had a short appearance as the mistress during which she was repeatedly kissed by Clark Gable. She pronounced St Louis in an un-American way, using a West Indian accent where she had spent a lot of time. Again and again there were shouts of 'Cut and retake.' I said, 'Oh you did it so that you could get more kisses from Clark Gable.'

Marilyn Monroe was always very late on the set and much time was lost as shooting had to be stopped or held up. It was because she was always drugged on barbiturates and was in a dreadful mess.

To Mrs T, 'How are you?' 'A bit battered.'

I say that I had lunch at Clarence House on Thursday and sat next to Queen Elizabeth the Queen Mother. I say it is all absolute rubbish the story that is emanating apparently from the Palace.

'Will you raise it with the Queen when you have an audience with her on Tuesday?' 'No, I don't think so.' 'But you get on with her all right?' 'We get on very well. The Royal Family are always very considerate to me and thoughtful.'

'It's the silly season,' I said. 'No one's going to take it very seriously. It's very unfair on the Queen because she can't state clearly what her views are and disassociate herself.' 'It's unfair on me. The Queen doesn't have to fight an election. I do. On Tuesday at Question Time I'll have to say in answer to the usual questions about my engagements for the day that this evening I have an audience with the Queen; then there'll be raucous laughter from the Labour benches.'

We discuss the BBC. She says that Stuart Young is only there an

---

23. Sir Ian Gilmour (3rd baronet, life peer 1992), Conservative MP, 1962–92, and journalist.

hour a day now because he is ill again. I said, 'He wasn't very good before but to try and control the Management Committee who are utterly defiant of the governors is ridiculous on an hour a day.'

I say the structure of the governors is hopeless for running anything with a common objective as each governor represents a different interest. She mentioned putting Joel Barnett[24] on, who is Labour. I said, 'That was a good idea because he is more sensible than most but he won't be able to do anything.'

'When will Stuart Young give up?' 'I think in about a year's time.' 'If anything is going to do you down for the next election it will be the behaviour of the BBC which we have never paid enough attention to.'

**Monday 21 July**

I call Rupert and catch him in New York at about 7.15 a.m. just about to go out to a business breakfast. I ask who was responsible for the story from the Palace which I believe to be total rubbish. He says, 'No, it was very carefully checked.' He thinks it could have been the Prince of Wales but he will let me know later in the day.

Rupert rings back at 6.45 p.m. from Hertford, Connecticut, where he had gone on business. It was not the Prince of Wales or any ordinary courtier. It was a high official. I said, 'Well it couldn't have been Heseltine, the Queen's Private Secretary.'[25] 'No,' he said, 'but go on.' I said, 'Surely not Michael Shea, the Press Secretary?[26] He was the one who issued the denial saying the story was utterly without foundation.' He said 'Yes. You can take it as ninety-nine per cent certain it was Michael Shea. It was him. They checked the story back with him several times. Two experienced journalists (Simon Freeman and Michael Jones) were in the room, reliable people. They read it all back to him and he agreed it all.'

I said I did not believe that the Queen knew anything about it. I didn't believe they were her views either, judging from what the Queen Mother said to me at Clarence House when I sat next to her at lunch last Thursday. 'Why would he do such a thing?' 'I think he has megalomania,' Rupert says. When I had said earlier in the morning to

---

24. Labour politician, Chief Secretary to the Treasury, 1974–9; life peer 1983.
25. Sir William Heseltine, Private Secretary to HM the Queen, 1986–90.
26. Press Secretary to HM the Queen, 1978–87.

Rupert that Mrs Thatcher thought it would harm her at the next election he cheerfully said, 'Oh no, it will do her a lot of good.'

Rupert said the newspaper had to protect its sources and the fact that Michael Shea was the man must remain secret.

He said I was not to tell anybody. I said, 'Can't I tell her?' He said, 'Well you can hint at it.' Shea being the culprit was why Neil refused to print the statement Shea issued that the *Sunday Times* report was entirely without foundation.

I rang Mrs T at 10 Downing Street. I told her it was very delicate as she was not to know who the person was but I was told I could hint at it, which I did in such a way that she knew perfectly well who it was.

I said, 'When you have to answer your questions in the House I should merely say it's the silly season.' 'No,' she said, 'I will say that a denial has been issued from Buckingham Palace and I have nothing further to say. I never answer questions affecting the Queen.'

**Wednesday 23 July**

Told Mrs T that I thought she was very effective at Question Time yesterday and dealt with the questions about the Queen extremely well, as well as others. She had the raucous laughter from the Labour benches which she had predicted to me on Sunday but she rode above it. She said she was determined to grit her teeth and not show any dismay which she didn't. People don't realize that she's very sensitive underneath and it takes a lot for her to screw herself up to face all the hostility she is getting unjustly.

I asked her what happened at her audience last evening. She said, 'That is always something I cannot say, even to you Woodrow but it was a normal friendly meeting.'

**Thursday 24 July**

Cricket lunch on the first day of the test match against New Zealand at 19 Cavendish Avenue. The cricketers are Bob [Wyatt] and Aidan Crawley, once twelfth man for England. He used to play for Oxford and Kent. Laura Grimond[27] also present.

---

27. (1918–94); Liberal politician; daughter of Sir Maurice Bonham Carter and Lady (Violet) Bonham Carter (later Baroness Asquith), granddaughter of Lord Asquith, Liberal Prime Minister, 1908–16; wife of Lord (Jo) Grimond (1913–93), Liberal Leader, 1956–67.

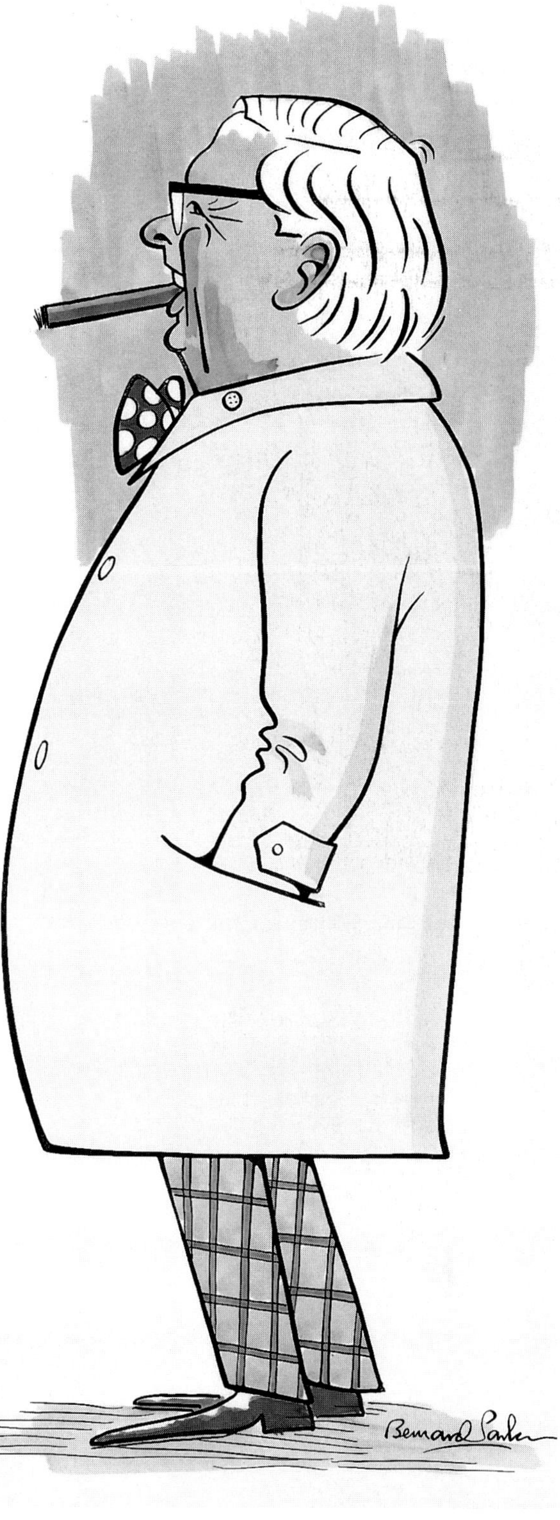


A caricature of Woodrow Wyatt by Bernard Parkin.

Lady Wyatt cuts the ribbon for the Tote with WW and Petronella.

La Cerbaia, Lord Lambton's house in Italy.

Lord Lambton at La Cerbaia.

Petronella in 1985.

Lady Wyatt, her arm in plaster, with Pericles, Woodrow Wyatt's son, in Italy in 1988.

Margaret Thatcher in October 1985.

Rupert Murdoch at Wapping with the *Sun* and *The Times* in January 1986.

WW with Irwin and Cita Stelzer in Venice in 1988.

Lord (Arnold) Weinstock,
Managing Director of GEC.

Lord (Arnold) Goodman,
lawyer.

Michael Heseltine leaving
10 Downing Street after
resigning from the Cabinet,
9 January 1986.

Leon Brittan
facing the press
after his resignation
from the Cabinet,
24 January 1986.

Intermittent talk about cricket and Laura's grandfather H. H. Asquith. Mrs Thatcher has still to overtake his record of seven plus continuous years as Prime Minister.

My cousin explained why England cricket is no good. It was because the Leg Before Wicket rule, accepted only for England, had curbed the scope in playing back and playing forward. 'The wicket should have been widened. That would have been the way to curb excessive run getting. Every time the wicket has been widened it has been good for cricket.'

In the afternoon see Ian Chapman at Collins. He does not want a collection of my previous writings which we were beginning a search for in the attics. He says such books don't sell enough. They are doing a paperback of my *Confessions of an Optimist* next year. I have to make one or two corrections by October.

He agrees reluctantly not to go ahead with the press book. My heart is weary at the idea of writing a general appraisal of the press and trying to make it lively. However, I return to his original suggestion of writing a book about women. We think about this and he is keen and I promise to do a synopsis while on holiday.

**Friday 25 July**

Sir Peter Leng, Chairman of the Racecourse Association, John Sanderson on my board and on the RCA board, and Christopher Sporborg of Hambros come to Cavendish Avenue to talk to Peter George and myself on behalf of the bookmakers [about a satellite information service].

Two hours are spent with the RCA reiterating that they could not allow the bookmakers to control the programme or have control of the company which does. Alan Ross who is there to take the notes for Peter George says, 'Can we ask why don't the racing industry like the bookmakers?' I say, 'Why don't Hindus like Muslims?'

Eventually it emerges that for a very huge sum the RCA would agree to anything we wanted so I say, 'Oh you mean all this moral stuff is total rubbish? What you are saying is if the price is right you have no principles?' Christopher Sporborg laughed and he said, 'Yes, that is correct.' Peter Leng, whom I call the Chinese General, spluttered with dismay. But Sporborg said, 'Yes, of course. If you gave us some very large sum like £20 million we could sell it to the racecourses; they wouldn't mind who controlled the company if you paid us enough for the pictures you want from the racecourse.'

The meeting which we had assumed was going to break down into nothingness suddenly woke up as a result of my saying that it was like Beaverbrook and the Lady; he offered first £20 to go to bed with him which she rejected – 'Do you think I am a prostitute?' – but became interested when he mentioned £20,000.

So that will be the way forward and all the talk about a carefully constructed company which gives the RCA control of the programmes is nonsense.

Dinner at Drue Heinz's,[28] Ascot Place. For her a small event with only some sixty people at tables inside the house except for two or three on the porch.

Next to me is a largeish, charming woman, Lady Mary Coleman. She is a niece of Queen Elizabeth the Queen Mother. She was at Balmoral at a house party on an occasion when Mrs Thatcher had been visiting various things in Scotland and arrived two or three days after the house party had begun. Everyone was beastly to her, some of the guests asking her silly questions about what was she going to do about unemployment to which she gave her stock answer.

She said the Queen was horrid to Mrs Thatcher. They were talking about the Falklands and the Queen sharply in a loud voice said, 'I don't agree with you at all' and Mrs Thatcher went red and looked very uncomfortable. Lady Mary Coleman felt that the Queen was trying to put Mrs Thatcher down all the time knowing that she was unaccustomed to the kind of society which is upper class and surrounds the Queen.

Denis Thatcher survives much better in these circumstances than Margaret. He makes jokes and laughs uproariously and is quite oblivious of Queen's unpleasantness.

Talking to my neighbour I begin to wonder whether there is not some truth in what Michael Shea has issued as the Queen's views to the *Sunday Times* though she may have changed in the last few years. Was Queen Elizabeth the Queen Mother accurate talking to me Thursday, last week?

The Queen has no feelings. I'd always felt that on the brief occasions I have spoken to her. I see why Isabel Derby dislikes the German (Hanoverian) family.

The dancing proceeds apace on the terrace with an awning and a

28. Wife of Henry John Heinz II ((1908–87), chairman, H. J. Heinz Company; Hon. KBE, 1977).

band. Verushka enjoys it. She dances with Tony Quinton and others. I see John Baring. Years ago he sat next to Verushka at dinner and said, 'My name is John Baring and I am very boring,' and he then proceeded to prove it at length.

John Wells[29] and his wife are there. She says, the other day they had been at a dinner and there had been a discussion of the word 'ebullient' and what it meant and who one could apply it to and everybody said the only person you can really apply the word ebullient to with accuracy is Woodrow Wyatt.

While my meeting was going on with the bookmakers in the afternoon just before I had to get changed, the *News of the World* said their libel lawyers couldn't print part of my piece about Maxwell and the BBC and advertising. Would I write another hundred and sixty words to fill in the gap?

**Saturday 26 July**

Wake up at 5.00 a.m. and then at 6.00 a.m. Feverishly agitating about what I have to write for the *News of the World* and also to fit in my hair cut at 8.45 a.m. at the Waldorf Hotel in the Aldwych, and then to be ready in time to go to the Ascot racecourse for lunch with the Oppenheimers, sponsors of the King George VI and Queen Elizabeth Stakes. This is to be a great race with the Derby winner challenged by Dancing Brave who was thought to have been unluckily second through bad riding by his jockey.

When I get back I find a letter from the Tuynhus, President Botha's headquarters. Viviers, his head of the office, says the State President has asked him to write and thank me for putting an honest account of South Africa in my newspaper articles. 'It is rare that we are given credit for what has been achieved in the socio and economic field and for our sincerity in wishing to bring about more equity and to broaden democracy in our fair country.' In particular the State President thanked me for the trouble I took to debate and correct 'the blatant bias of the programme *Witness of Apartheid* . . . I feel we are indebted to you for taking up the cudgels on behalf of justice and fairness.'

The great race is won by Dancing Brave so my little friend Prince Khalid Abdullah will be happy.

---

29. (1936–98); writer and humourist; m (1982) Teresa, daughter of Sir Christopher Chancellor.

**Sunday 27 July**

'It's been an awful week. Something to be got through.' I told her that Jock Bruce-Gardyne[30] said her 1922 Committee speech went well. She was pleased. She said, 'I told them that if they rally round together and don't quarrel we will certainly win the next election. I am confident of it.' 'I have been all the time,' I say.

I tell her that the Queen ought to sack Shea or get him to resign for he had put her in a difficult position. She said, 'Well I can't do anything about that. It's up to her. But we will have to see whether new arrangements are made to prevent such a thing happening again. I think they will be.'

She is disinclined to comment any more about Shea.

I ask her whether she would like to see Rupert while he is over here next week and tell her that he is coming to stay with us in Italy on August 7th. She said, 'Yes, of course, but I don't want him to think that I'm twisting his arm over the *Sunday Times*.' I said, 'Perhaps I won't suggest it to him on his first trip here but when I am in Italy.'

She agreed that was the right way round to do it. 'I'm always very happy to see Rupert. He has been so supportive.'

After the dreadful Commonwealth mini Summit conference she goes into the King Edward VII Hospital for Officers to have an operation done to her hand for some strange though common disease which has been contracting the use of her fingers for a few years, but it can be cured immediately. After that for a few days she will go to Cornwall, Constantine, to stay with David Wolfson.[31]

I say I think that Geoffrey Howe is probably plodding away quite well in South Africa. He cannot expect to get immediate results. 'You've got plenty of time to manoeuvre with the Commonwealth mini Summit[32] by saying that Howe doesn't even report to the EEC until the end of September.'

---

30. (1930–90); Conservative politician and journalist; life peer 1983.
31. Chief of staff, Political Office, 10 Downing Street 1979–85; director, Great Universal Stores, 1973–8, chairman since 1996; chairman, Alexon Group, 1982–6, Next since 1990; knight 1984, life peer 1991.
32. The Special London Commonwealth summit on South Africa opened on 3 August 1986.

**Monday 28 July**

Andrew Neil tells me he is certain Prince Charles was behind the story of Michael Shea, or at least was one of the contributors. Had I seen the *Economist* profile of Prince Charles which had been supplied by Michael Shea? He gave all the information in which it said that Prince Charles was like a member of the SDP, rather wet and very liberal. He would be a natural to dislike Mrs Thatcher. I am still convinced the Queen knew nothing whatever about the story being given by Michael Shea or even the contents of it. Andrew Neil is not so convinced, thinking that it probably reflects her views whereas I do not.

**Wednesday 30 July *Italy***

Rupert rings from England. Had I seen Andrew Neil's letter to the *Times* of yesterday in which he refuted all that William Heseltine said? I had. Had I left before the poll in the *Evening Standard* on Tuesday evening came out? It said the Tories were only one point behind Labour now. 'I always said the row with the Queen would do Mrs Thatcher good. You fought a civil war about this once.'

I think it is more likely people are annoyed with the black Commonwealth countries from Africa and elsewhere who sabotaged the Commonwealth Games. They are probably secretly in favour of the whites in South Africa and certainly don't want sanctions of a punitive kind which might lose jobs here.

Rupert says he thinks he will ring Mrs Thatcher and say has she got ten minutes to see him. I say, 'That'd be fine. I have suggested she might get hold of you but she said she didn't want you to think she was twisting your arm about [the] *Sunday Times*.'

It is very agreeable staying at Perignano[33] with its green lawns, watered lavishly all day and every day making them look almost English except the grass is not cut so short. The sun is out all the time. The food is too good and I eat too much of it. The white sparkling local wine which Gingo has at lunch time is excellent, more agreeable than the Italian champagne.

33. With Count Sanminiatelli (Gingo).

**Friday 1 August**

Arrive at Villa la Valletta, Cala Piccola. It is gorgeous. A beautifully kept garden with lawns twisting and winding along. One side you can go down to the sea and the other side ends in a circle with chairs nice for lovers overlooking the sea. About three terraces all overlooking the sea as do all the bedrooms. Marble floors and beautiful tiles in the bedrooms. Telephone by the long snaking swimming pool which is sea water. But I find it more difficult to swim in sea water as I can't turn so fast on to my back or front.

I have got the kitchen table or one of them brought in for me to write at where I can look out over the swimming pool and the sea.

Speak to Rupert and tell him to come earlier. I say there is a barbecue with lots of instruments and one of these open air dining-rooms. He says it sounds too luxurious for him.

'Any news?' He says there is another poll out today by the same people who did the favourable one and this is bad, giving Labour forty-one per cent but they claim it is something to do with the Queen. I said I was always afraid that a number of people potentially thinking of voting Tory might think to themselves if the Queen doesn't like her, why should I?

I said, 'You think it's Prince Charles behind it all.' He said, 'No, I think it's more likely Prince Philip. He is the one it seems who is mad keen about the Commonwealth. It's something that makes them feel different from other Royal families.'

I said 'Well they still have Australia, New Zealand and Canada.' He said, 'They won't last for ever.' 'But you're not going to push them out of Australia, are you?' 'Oh no. No government would do that, it will just fade away in fifty years' time.'

**Saturday 2 August**

Ring Mrs T to wish her luck for the mini Summit conference.

I don't suppose the Queen would mind a bit if there were a Labour government. They would suck up to her no end and parade their loyalty to her. She's the richest woman in the world. I suppose she must have at least £5,000 million. She pays no tax and no Labour government would make her, not even death duties.[1] And when it came to putting up the Civil Lists they would do it automatically to show how loyal they are to the Crown.

I don't think the Queen is the wise experienced woman people write about, I think she is very stupid and only concerned with her own interests. She is also somewhat stubborn. She is not a bit like her mother; she lacks the sensitivity and genuine feelings. It doesn't matter to her if Britain goes into a decline and never pulls out of it because she'll be sitting pretty at the top the whole time.

Dinner with Lolli Ricci and her husband who is a specialist in neurology and brain scanning and ascertaining what really happens in people's heads. He sounds as though he has laryngitis but that is because he has had cancer of the throat.

Little Aliai Forte is the second daughter of the house, pregnant, married in February, not anxious to be with her husband. As pretty as a little angel but feminine elemental.

Last year before the marriage she was happy to go grouse shooting and follow all the sports and interests of Rocco in England. Now she is married she feels it unnecessary to pretend any more.

**Thursday 7 August**

Rupert and Anna arrive.

He looks a little tired. Anna is full of life. Rupert's energy soon asserts itself and he bubbles away.

Anna brings me a book as a present. 'I got it at Hatchards before I came out today.' It is *Power of the Sword* by Wilbur Smith. Extremely heavy and thick. I glance through its pages. It is one of those shallow international adventure stories which make an enormous appeal to the illiterate. How could she bring me such a book? Her own book is not literature but is fairly well written. Does she think I read this kind of thing?

Prue Murdoch and Crispin have separated. They find themselves incompatible and he has not turned out to be the gentle dependable man she was going to rely on. It was hopeless from the start.

Anna thinks it better to let them part in peace while Rupert is inclined to urge a reconciliation or trying to stick together.

---

1. HM the Queen started to pay tax on 6 April 1993.

Prue has never got over her mother going slightly batty. She is devoted to her father and looks for a husband like him which Crispin certainly is not, though he is quite intelligent and apparently working well at some merchant bank.

**Sunday 10 August**

Rupert and Anna vigorously enjoying themselves swimming and then sun bathing. Rupert already looks far more relaxed and less tired. The telephone rings for him incessantly and when it doesn't he rings Australia, America, England. Verushka is worried about the telephone bill which they are going to deduct from her deposit without her having paid any money into the bank. I imagine he's spent about £600 on the telephone while he has been here.

Rupert has some film just out costing millions called *Aliens*[2] which was panned by the critics but is doing enormous business; he will more than get his money back. He has a gift for making money out of anything. He says his television stations are beginning to turn the corner though his newspapers in America don't make much.

'Why do you keep the *New York Post*? You'll never make anything with it.' 'Because I like to have my New York office on the top of it. It feels real.' Rupert thinks the American economy is falling out of bed and the British will soon follow. Mrs Thatcher should have the election while the going is good.

The first night Nicholas and Caroline are here Caroline makes no attempt to help clear away the things after the dinner – the cook having gone home. Verushka gets up and clears them away and is helped by Anna. Petronella does nothing either and lets the two older ladies do it all. The nanny has her meals with us. So does the baby. I find it irritating.

**Monday 11 August**

Rupert and Anna leave in the morning from Rome in their own private jet.

They both like my article in the *Sunday Times* about Château Latour and Bordeaux. He had brought out the proofs in which there are massive cuts. He thinks it's a pity but he cannot really interfere. Though I got £5,000 I'm mildly distressed by losing so much of it.

---

2. Directed by James Cameron.

**Thursday 14 August**

Clarissa [Avon] arrives. The day before there had been a row when I said at lunch time that it was impossible to have the baby sitting having its lunch with us when Clarissa came. It cries and yells and there is no adult conversation possible. Nicholas became very pompous and said he would leave at once and go back to England because I'd insulted his daughter aged sixteen months.

When I said that Arnold Weinstock didn't have his own grandchild whom he adores to lunch with other people, he said, 'Arnold is dead, finished, hopeless. He's an old man. Your generation has failed the world, failed the country. We are trying to save Britain with our work.' By which he means getting in on the big bang which is transforming the Stock Exchange and giving vastly overpaid jobs to very young men like Nicholas with a few skills while the big bang lasts.

Ask Clarissa again whether she is going to write her memoirs including what she had told me of the contempt with which the Churchill family held Winston before the War when he was clearly a failure and would get no further. 'Oh that's all been done already,' but it hasn't been really. But she has kept a diary of her life with Anthony particularly the Suez crisis. That she is keeping for publication after her death. Maybe Collins would like to get hold of it. I don't know if she has arranged a publisher. When I told them that they had missed Ted Heath's autobiography they were not at all dismayed, believing that it would not sell and be very dull.

The baby does not come to lunch. It has its lunch before we do.

Clarissa takes the old fashioned view that women should not have careers, but they should be wives and mothers and look after their homes like Verushka does, who also agrees with Clarissa.

**Friday 15 August**

Rupert rings in agitation because the Attorney General may prosecute Kelvin MacKenzie the editor of the *Sun* and he may go to jail for breach of the race relations laws in having published a cartoon about the Libyans, after one of those in the Embassy when the policewoman Fletcher was murdered came back to England because he is married to an English girl. They referred to him in the headlines as an Arab pig and the following day or thereabouts the cartoonist had put a picture of a lot of pigs demonstrating at Wapping demanding to see the editor to complain that they'd been called Arabs.

He wanted me to get Mrs Thatcher to intervene. I said, 'I cannot possibly do that. It is such a delicate matter. These are judicial or quasi-judicial decisions that have to be taken by the Attorney General without interference. There would be a fearful row if it got out.' He said, 'Can you ask her if she knows anything about it?'

Bruce Matthews says that it has been agreed with Rupert that my salary or pay for contributions would go up to £40,000 a year which is very little more than I am getting now. Did I have any reactions? I said, 'Is it subject to the normal annual review still?' and he said, 'Oh yes.' I said, 'I suppose that's all right.' I thought it was rather stingy and I believe Bruce Matthews thought it was too. Verushka thought I ought not to press the matter. With the loss of the Stelzer connection I'm short of £10,000 a year. Difficult with a house to run, Petronella going to Oxford, servants to pay, and expenses ever larger.

We took Clarissa to see the Riccis in their strange house, modern concrete and glass.

I asked him, as he is the world's greatest brain specialist and theoretician and researcher, about myself.

'A touch of Parkinsonism,' he said, which gave me some alarm as I've always thought I might have been made of the same material as my brother who has been acutely afflicted with Parkinson's disease for some years.

Professor Ricci wrote out some names of pills and injections and said I should see a top neurologist when I went to England.

It turns out to be very trivial and he says my brain will last another twenty years (if I do) in its present condition. The pills should improve my health and make my locomotion, walking about, better than it is and stop it deteriorating faster thereafter.

**Friday 22 August**

In a café overlooking the harbour at Porto Santo Stefano I talked to Clarissa about her diary.

She doesn't want any thirty year rule applied after she is dead when she doesn't mind publication.

Of young Winston[3] she thinks Minnie, his wife, is a saint who now looks as though she's been worn out by his behaviour. Young Winston is not very bright, has energy and forcefulness and of course his name.

I said, 'I asked Mrs Thatcher to include him in her government

---

3. Winston Churchill MP, son of Randolph Churchill (who was Clarissa Avon's first cousin); m (1964–97) Mary (Minnie), née d'Erlanger.

when it came to the time as a link with the past. She had done her best by making him a Shadow Minister but he blew it by voting against his own party over Rhodesian sanctions. Later he blew it again with Mrs Kashoggi. Was he left much money by his grandfather or in a trust?' 'I don't think he was much. I think the aeroplane and his new house come via his mother[4] and Averell Harriman which I suppose must have stopped now that Harriman is dead.'

Talked to Arnold Weinstock. He is depressed. Everybody now attacks him, says his business is no good and is declining. The government in the name of competition have rejected his wish to take over Plessey. The pretence is that more competition is needed not less and the Monopolies Commission took that line backed by the Minister, Paul Channon.

It is all due, according to Arnold, to a man called Levene[5] who is in charge of buying arms for the Ministry of Defence and he thinks he can get them cheaper. Arnold also says that Andrew Neil, editor of the *Sunday Times*, hates him and is always running pieces about how awful Arnold and GEC are. There was a three page article on the subject in the last issue of the *Sunday Times*. Arnold says Rupert must know about it. He must read his own newspapers.

Now Arnold wants to join in with the Satellite Racing Service which he had tried to get me to abandon earlier. I told him at the outset that it would succeed, that the alternatives, Extel, Cable and Wireless, Mercury, could produce nothing to equal the work we had already done.

I speak to the others at the major bookmakers and they think it is an interesting concept. As they also do the idea of the participation by Rupert which I have interested him in out here. Now they are moving, however, to having a selling document prepared by merchant banks, perhaps Schroder's. Then those who want to join in, we having borne the brunt of the day, would be able to see what they could contribute and would be considered on their merits.

Rupert talks of bringing in sporting events from overseas and gadgets to make sure that the sets would be personal, which we can do

---

4. The Hon. Pamela, née Digby (1920-97), was Randolph Churchill's first wife (1939–46); she married 3 (1971) Averell Harriman, US diplomat, and became US Ambassador to France in her seventies.
5. Peter Levene, Chief of Defence Procurement, Ministry of Defence, since 1985; knight 1989.

ourselves anyway. What the bookmakers are worried about is anybody getting hold of these continuous transmissions of racing and setting up illegal betting centres, particularly in working men's clubs and in grander establishments like casinos.

The Press Council has censured me for irresponsible remarks about a large chunk of the W. Indian/African coloured population because I said they were lawless, drug-taking and violent. I was referring to the West Indian section and there is ample evidence. I shall write on the Sunday after I return to England an attack on the Press Council for trying to suppress freedom of speech.[6]

If Rupert had been more generous with my pay and had put it up to £45,000 or even £42,500, I would have been keener to help him with his problem about the editor of the *Sun*. As it is I rang Mrs Thatcher desultorily and didn't try to get her very hard when I heard she had gone to Dulwich looking at her new house and taking furniture and effects there.

Superstitious, I am worried about her very definite moves to make Dulwich a real home already. Does she subconsciously believe she won't win the next election? Or is it just an insurance? Or is it that she really just wants an alternative place like Flood Street? From the pictures of the neo-Georgian house and the neo-Georgian estate it is on, with houses fairly close together, it is unattractive. But she has no taste. Nor does Denis. Proximity to a golf course is his desideratum.

**Sunday 24 August**

Mrs T sprightly. Hand almost recovered. Busy rushing between Dulwich and No. 10 rearranging her effects, getting ready the new house. Has never heard about the problem of Kelvin MacKenzie and the Attorney General and the possibility of him going to prison. 'It's

---

6. WW wrote in the *News of the World* on 7 September 1986 (his italics): '. . . *Inadequate evidence? Which country is the Press Council living in?* Those of West Indian/African origin are between one and two per cent of the population of England and Wales. Now look at the Home Office statistics published on June 18. Eight per cent of the male prison population are West Indian/African . . . I argued that all our coloured citizens should behave like the white British . . . If they drag me to the Tower of London I shall continue to tell the truth. *The British are entitled to know what's happening in their own country. If they find they've been hoodwinked that really will invite racial prejudice.*'

an absolutely independent decision. No one can interfere with it.' I agree.

**Monday 25 August**

Andrew Knight has arrived. Two charming little daughters, seven and nine. The nine-year-old is Amaryllis and the other girl's name is Afsani. Girls of nine and seven are easier to talk to and much less nuisance than a baby of sixteen months.

Spoke to Rupert to tell him that Mrs Thatcher said there was no way in which anybody could interfere with the decision of the Attorney General and that she'd never heard of the matter. Rupert said, 'Oh, that's fine because the prosecution has now been stopped. We've been told that by the Attorney General's office.'

He seemed to think that perhaps Mrs Thatcher had mentioned it and that my speaking to her had led to their not prosecuting. I shall never know the answer to this but I think it unlikely because the time factor wouldn't have been right. However, it may not be a bad thing for Rupert to think I had a hand in it.

**Friday 29 August**

Stuart Young aged fifty-two, Chairman of the BBC, has died. Andrew says why not make Frank Chapple Chairman? I think, well maybe, or perhaps Robin Day or Chips Keswick? I ring Mrs T and urge her to make Frank Chapple Chairman, she and I both having rejected Chips Keswick as she thinks he wouldn't know enough about communication.

I say that Frank is nominally Labour still, they couldn't say you have packed it. He would know how to rout out these Communists and Marxists, starting with all the current affairs programmes.

She said she would think about it but she hadn't actually started considering it yet.

When I tell Andrew Knight that he says, 'Good heavens, I would have thought that would be the first thing she would be trying to decide.'

**Saturday 30 August**

Tonight I realize the Knights are not going to tip the servants which is extraordinary.

**Tuesday 2 September**

Spoke about five past eight. Said I was anxious that we get the BBC Chairman right this time.

I had read in the *News of the World* that she was thinking of Lord King. She made no comment on that. I said, 'He would be very good probably if he understands enough about politics. He is certainly tough and would sort them out, no doubt.'

I suggested Robin Day but maybe he's not strong enough. He's had his bypass operation. He certainly knows his way around the BBC. She said she wasn't too keen on that idea. I mentioned Frank Chapple again but there was not much of a response.

She said, 'Who is responsible for seeing that the rule about impartiality is observed?' I said, 'Theoretically the governors but they are such a disparate lot they have no cohesion and the board of management runs everything, openly defies them.' I added, 'Did you not know that the governors are not even allowed to see a programme before it goes out?' 'Good Lord,' she said.

I continued, 'Of course it's difficult to get the right man. He doesn't get paid very much. I think it's about £30,000. It needs to be a very rich man or somebody who doesn't need the money. Lord King perhaps would fit that bill.'

I said, 'You really can't expect a Chairman to dominate or even level peg with a Chief Executive who is being paid over double or three times himself.'

Hear that Diana at the pre-wedding ball of Sarah Ferguson at Windsor met the sister of my informant whom she'd invited, being an old friend. Her husband was there, very tall, very good looking and a marvellous dancer. Diana danced with him for quite a long time then said 'Oh, I've got to go now otherwise Charles will be wondering what's happened to me.' She was then overheard saying to Sarah Ferguson, 'I met the most marvellous man who dances divinely but the first thing he did was introduce me to his wife.'

She told the man how lovely it was to have Sarah as a 'mate' in the Royal Family. Now she doesn't feel so lonely.

She adores dancing, particularly with good looking young men. This one was described to me as a very pelvic dancer. There is trouble ahead.

**Tuesday 9 September**

I rang Kingsley Amis to tell him that not only had I got my first edition of *Lucky Jim* without a dust wrapper for him to sign but his latest book *The Old Devils* which is published next Thursday. I said, 'Will you write some jolly message in them?' He wrote only 'Kingsley Amis' having scratched out his name on the title page of *Lucky Jim* but he wrote 'One for you and one for me Woodrow' or words to that effect on the new book.

When I told Saumarez Smith of Heywood Hill's[1] this he said, 'Oh that's fine because people might think unless they are handwriting experts that his signature of the first book *Lucky Jim* was contemporary with publication.' I gather my book is now worth about £140.

**Wednesday 10 September**

Andrew's last board meeting. At the beginning I said how sad it was and we would miss him, that I had tried to persuade him not to resign but he insisted on it which I wished he hadn't. I think now he wishes he hadn't too.

He did it in a mood of despondency over the court revelations of his signing blank cheques for girls and the butler selling his diary to the *News of the World* and the *Sun* and friends being pestered by those newspapers, or at least the *News of the World*. He thought he was held up to mockery. I told him not to bother, it would all blow over but he had insisted on resigning.

At the end of the meeting before lunch I thanked Andrew for arranging for a party of forty Tote workers in the north to go on a tour of Chatsworth next Monday.

'Are you going to take them on a guided tour?' 'No. It's such a dreary house.' 'How can you possibly say that. It's a very beautiful house, built by Jeffry Wyatville.' 'Oh dear, of course it was. I don't really think that but one can't say about one's own house that it's splendid.'

He asked me again what relation Jeffry Wyatt was to James Wyatt

---

1. The fashionable bookshop in Curzon Street where Nancy Mitford worked during the Second World War.

so I said, 'His nephew. George III made James his architect. George IV hated his father and when he took control he made Jeffry Wyatt his architect and wouldn't have anything to do with James Wyatt much. Though by the time Windsor Castle was built by Jeffry Wyatt, James Wyatt was already dead.'[2]

'What about his name Wyatville?' 'That was a decision of George IV to distinguish Jeffry Wyatt from all the other Wyatt architects.'

I told Andrew he should look for the plaque above Colefax & Fowler[3] which I unveiled a year or two ago in honour of Sir Jeffry Wyatville. That was his house. He built a studio there and had a lovely garden.

**Thursday 11 September**

Met Norman Lamont at the RAC to talk about ways of having a management buy out for the Tote and creating a form of trust, to make sure that it continued to have enough money to help racing and that it could not sell itself – because shareholders would only be able to sell through the trust to members of the staff who would be unable to sell outside. He thought it a good idea. He said the government have admitted internally that the Tote does not belong to them, though doubtless they would try to get some money out of us for it.

He said he had been to Greece for a holiday with his family. He is living a model life. I said, 'You're becoming so respectable that your expectations from your aunt are solid.' He said, 'You remember everything and know more about me than anybody else.'

Afterwards I went to Pratt's.

Just before I went Charles Churchill came in. Went on about Prince Michael again.[4] Why had I appointed him and why not Princess Anne? He is pleasant but stupid with a loud voice. I said to the charge that

2. James Wyatt was killed in a carriage accident on 4 September 1813. The origins of Windsor Castle go back to the twelfth century but the buildings were extensively altered by both Wyatts.
3. The interior decorators at 39 Brook Street, London W1.
4. Lord Charles Spencer-Churchill had written to WW on 21 August 1986, copying to him a letter he had intended to send in an abbreviated form to the editor of the *Sporting Life*. The letter protested about the appointment of Prince Michael to the Tote Board: 'He has no knowledge of racing or the betting industry, and besides he is on enough city boards to keep his limited talents occupied. I am also led to believe that he is being paid £5,000 per year of the tax payers money for his advice on racing. This is a total scandal . . .'

Prince Michael knows nothing about racing, 'Nor does Frank Chapple, who is on the board as well.'

**Wednesday 17 September**

After Levy Board meeting which ended an hour earlier than usual caught hold of Ian Trethowan.[5] 'What do you think about the chairmanship of the BBC?' 'Come into my office.' We talked for three-quarters of an hour.

He thinks it should be somebody like John Hunt,[6] Robert Armstrong,[7] somebody who understands politics but is not blatantly pro Mrs Thatcher. He thought John King would be a mistake but he has in any case now withdrawn. Frank Chapple he rates as not big enough, unable to carry the day with the staff, a view which I'm now sharing. He would be unable to say to a producer, 'I've read Proust too so don't come that one on me.'

Ian was also in favour of Joel Barnett. I disagree. He is too much for a quiet time although level headed and sensible.

It emerges that there is no real need to restructure the organization and constitution of the BBC. The governors are all powerful and can be all powerful if they have a good chairman whom everybody respects.

However, the convention has grown up that the governors never see anything now until after it's put out. Ian says that is really quite new. When he was Director-General of the BBC he used to discuss no end of things with Michael Swann[8] who was then the Chairman and they weren't taken by surprise the whole time. Nor had this trench warfare begun between the Board of Management and the governors which ought not to be because the Board of Management and the governors are two facets of the same thing.

At the moment the governors are weak and not high quality. Curiously, Ian thought that Mark Bonham-Carter[9] was one of the best

---

5. Chairman, Horserace Betting Levy Board, at this time and Director General, BBC, 1977–82.*
6. Conservative politician; member, General Advisory Council, BBC, 1975–87; knight 1989.
7. Secretary of the Cabinet, 1979–87; Head of the Home Civil Service, 1983–7; life peer 1988.
8. Scientist; chairman, BBC Board of Governors, 1973–80; life peer 1981.
9. Vice chairman, BBC Board of Governors, 1975–81.

governors they had had and he should have been given the chairmanship and not George Howard.[10] He thought it was perfectly easy but would take some time to correct the slant of some of the left-wing programme makers. He thought that Brian Redhead always had been a bit on the left on the *Today* programme and that John Timpson[11] previously had been moderate and right-wingish but that now John Timpson seemed to have gone overboard too. He thought that the *Today* programme had gone mad. 'It is right to be challenging the government. But it is not right to be condemning it.'

He saw Ian Jacob[12] the other day whom he said rather bitterly to me, 'You describe as the last good Director-General of the BBC in your book'. I smiled and said, 'Bar one, you, of course' but Ian is not very pleased about my having written him down as not much good.

He thinks that Alasdair Milne[13] is intelligent but hasn't got the relationship right at all and quarrelled all the time with Stuart Young. Stuart Young could have been killed, possibly was, by the strain of it all. Alasdair Milne is far too pleased with himself and not good enough.

When Ian Trethowan said that he thought Stuart Young's troubles with Alasdair Milne had led to his early death, I felt very bad that in one of my last letters to Stuart Young I had said that as he was out of his depth there was no point in my writing to him. Ian Trethowan agreed with me that it had been beyond him. Good accountant and so forth but not understanding the political side of it.

**Thursday 18 September**

Kingsley Amis to lunch. Arrives on the dot. Refuses champagne unless it is old.

The young men, George Brock, features editor of the *Times*, and Peter Stothard, deputy editor, arrived half an hour late saying it was a long way.

Kingsley said he'd given up sex long ago. Elizabeth Jane Howard (his last wife) cured him of it. She was too intense. Kingsley is an

---

10. Chairman, BBC Board of Governors, 1980–3; life peer 1983.
11. Television journalist and broadcaster.
12. Lieutenant General Sir Ian Jacob (1899–1993), Director General, BBC, 1952–60; see *Confessions of an Optimist*, p. 250. What WW actually said was that no subsequent DG would have backed his programme of 14 May 1956 exposing Communist infiltration of the unions.
13. Director General, BBC, 1982–7.

excellent mimic, taking off people he's met in pubs, imitating their conversation and accents. I said, 'You're very observant. There was a great deal of acute and clever observation in your last book. You must have a marvellous memory.' He said, 'I don't think one realizes what is in one's memory until you start to write and things you haven't thought about come tumbling out. Or perhaps you are inventing them based on what has really happened.'

It was 4.00 p.m. and he still hadn't gone, though the two young men went shortly after half past two, having stayed but an hour for a lunch which was excellent with the egg mousse and the veal with the tarragon sauce and the bread and butter pudding, to say nothing of the 1964 Cos Labory, followed by half a bottle of 1937 Pichon-Longueville. Before we'd had an excellent Chablis Premier Cru 1978.

Kingsley said, 'I don't really like claret. One doesn't realize until one comes to this house how good it is when you get a decent one. Of course you have to be rich like you for that.' I asked him if he would like some sweet white wine and he said he would with his pudding and we had a bottle of the Graves Royale 1947 which is well-nigh perfect. Then Kingsley drank the best part of half a bottle of port or a little more by himself, no one else touching it. He left at about twenty to five.

Verushka came back and was amazed to find him there when she asked for her tea. He was fairly drunk. He said he's got to the age where he can say no. 'When you asked me if I'd like to come to dinner I said no. I'd rather come to lunch.' He doesn't go out much in the evenings now. He's glad not to have a wife who would probably try to make him. His favourite thing is to sit down and watch some programme like *Kojak* with a glass of whisky, read the odd book and not get involved.

I said, 'But you still go to pubs?' 'Not so much as I did. Hardly at all now. But I go to the Garrick Club. Will you have lunch with me there?' I said, 'Yes, I will.' I dare say it will be long and boozy. I sent him home with Robbie, the chauffeur.

**Friday 19 September**

Told her about my conversation with Ian Trethowan. The structure doesn't need changing you've just got to have a good chairman. Suggested to her Robert Armstrong whom I suppose she wouldn't want to lose or John Hunt which she thought was a frightfully good idea. So we'll see how that goes.

She said, 'You are thinking aren't you about my speech for the Party Conference?' I said, 'Yes,' but I haven't really done much thinking about it at all at the moment. I must get on with it.

**Saturday 20 September**

Rupert says he found Mrs T in good shape, more confident. He told her he thought she would be all right and that he felt the tide was moving in her favour. He now sounds confident that she will win again.

Quite contrary to what he was saying to me in Italy and just before he came out there when he had been talking to his clever journalists at the *Times* who told him that everyone (including themselves) was against her and she couldn't possibly win.

Now it is as though he had never doubted. Then he wanted her to change her style.

He asked how I got on with Andrew Knight. I said, 'He is very prim.'

'I feel about twenty years younger than Andrew when I talk to him though he is only forty-six. When I talk to you I think you're about twenty. You are a child of nature. Not in the least pompous.'

Rupert thought that Peregrine Worsthorne had made the *Sunday Telegraph* livelier and that Max Hastings might be a success with the *Daily Telegraph* though it is too early to tell. He thinks Andrew is able which I do too.

Rupert says, 'I hear Conrad Black has run out of money and can't develop the *Telegraph* properly.' I said, 'That's not the impression I get from Andrew Knight but you may be right. He is certainly worried that the circulations keep slipping.'

**Sunday 21 September**

Admiral Sir Raymond Lygo, the head of [British] Aerospace, was there.[14] He said about the famous meeting with Leon Brittan during the Westland affair, the misunderstanding that he pretended to agree to was that Brittan said to him, 'You should withdraw' and that could have meant him personally rather than Aerospace itself. When he had spoken to Michael Heseltine about his building up of the European consortium and asked whether that wouldn't be politically damaging to Leon Brittan, Michael Heseltine had said, 'That would be a very good thing. I can't think of anything better.'

---

14. For lunch at Arnold Weinstock's house Bowden in Wiltshire.

**Monday 22 September**

Early to the Tote to drill the various heads of divisions into what they should say to Prince Michael of Kent who comes to lunch. I tell Brian McDonnell and John Heaton that people keep saying to me that he's an idiot, even board members. 'He is not an idiot. You will find that when you meet him.'

I get various people to explain what they do during lunch. He asks intelligent questions.

During the tour round the building lasting until about a quarter to four he is very polite and does exactly the right things and speaks to the right people in the right and friendly way.

**Tuesday 23 September**

Ian Chapman says the synopsis which I sent on Friday for the book about women is 'super'.

Nicholas Soames comes to lunch. He thinks the prospects for Mrs T are very good. He hopes she won't slow down her radical reforming. He says there are still two vacancies in the government Whips' office and he would like one of them but he said he won't be terribly distressed if he doesn't get one.

Robert Cranborne, he thought, was far too pleased with himself, thinking he had an automatic entrée into the higher echelons of the Conservative government, like all the Cecils. He is now resigning as MP, seeing that he hasn't. I said, 'He would keep taking the mickey out of Mrs Thatcher and he was very foolish to be a PPS for one day and resign in the evening.'[15]

Nicholas asked how I got on with Andrew Neil. I said, 'Fairly well.' He said, 'He's a liar.' I asked, 'Why do you say that?' 'Because he lied about the story about the Queen, I know he did. It was all made up.'[16] I said, 'They read the story to Michael Shea and he OK'd it.' He said, 'No he didn't. The story was different from the front to the back.' I said, 'It wasn't substantially because I read them both.' He said, 'Yes but the interpretation put on it and the headline, with things like the Queen being worried about the Commonwealth and the effect of not

15. He was PPS to the Minister of State at the Foreign Office, April–May 1982, resigning to be free to criticize the government's Ulster plans.

16. See Andrew Neil's book *Full Disclosure*, chapter 8 'The Queen and I' (pp. 195–228) for his denial of this view and his account of what happened.

having sanctions on the members of it, he never said that and she has never said it in the way she is supposed to.'

I think he may really know because he's very close to the Palace. He wouldn't trust Andrew Neil and advised me not to.

**Wednesday 24 September**

I fear we may make a bad decision about the BBC. She is havering a bit. She thinks John Hunt might have too many commitments, though I say somebody as big as he is could cope with the BBC as well.

I tell her that Nicholas Soames came to lunch and thinks she is marvellous. 'He is very much hoping he might get one of the two last jobs in the Whips' office. It's really not for me to recommend people for jobs.' She laughed, 'You can and do.'

I told her I am worried about a poll done by Mori recently for the CND. It showed that only forty-six per cent were in favour of keeping our nuclear deterrent whereas forty-four per cent said they were prepared to give it up even if other countries didn't. I say, 'We have some work to do on this. Maybe the Liberal/SDP confusion[17] may help and give an opportunity to hammer home the facts.'

Philip Howard[18] rings. He says he will give me a rest after I have reviewed the three books he's sent me.

I've got Jim Prior,[19] the Kilroy-Silk book[20] and the Dictionary of National Biography. The last is much more fun. Philip Howard says he has written a piece about Ivor Brown[21] in it so I suppose I'd better mention it. He says, 'I know you've written one entry,' which is true. It was about Tom Harrisson[22] and has a piece in it on how he used to eat human flesh to please his cannibal hosts in Borneo when he was organizing them to fight against the Japanese. It tasted sweet like pork and was called Long Pig.

---

17. They had voted for nuclear disarmament at their conference, against the advice of their leadership.
18. Journalist, on the *Times* since 1964, literary editor, 1978–92.
19. *A Balance of Power.*
20. *The Political Diary of Robert Kilroy-Silk*; Kilroy-Silk, television presenter and journalist, was a Labour MP from 1974 to June 1986 when he resigned the safe seat of Knowsley North alleging socialist Militant penetration of the local party.
21. Author, journalist and theatre critic (1891–1974).
22. (1911–76); ethnologist, joint founder and chairman of Mass Observation.

**Saturday 27 September**

Lunch with the Senior Steward and other Stewards at the Jockey Club at Ascot.

Lady Trumpington[23] sat next to me. She is a Minister in the DHSS. She told me that she had fixed my pension with a special amendment to some bill allowing for the Chairman of the Gaming Board and of the Levy Board and of the Tote to have a pension. I thanked her.

Of course it wasn't Baroness Trumpington who got the pension; it was eight years' pressure from me on the Home Office.

She is jolly lady and had been a steward at Folkestone.

**Sunday 28 September**

The *Observer* weekend review has its front page and part of the inside devoted to an attack on me by my cousin Honor[24] and also on Moorea. It is full of spite, irrational, contradictory and hardly a fact in it is correct.[25]

Her trouble is that she is getting senile at seventy-six and is obsessed with fury that I proved in the foreword to the Wyatt book[26] that the claim to be descended from Sir Thomas Wyatt the poet is utterly bogus, though she has gone round telling everybody she is all her life. And she is also cross because I wrote in *Confessions of an Optimist* that her mother[27] lived only for pleasure and left my mother to bring up the children although she was much older than my mother when their mother died.

I described an incident when her mother was drunk and her curls, false, fell from her head between us on the sofa when I was a child. I also referred to the fact that her father, [to] whom my father had given his own money to send [him] to Cambridge after their father died at an early age, had taken his money out of the school my father owned at a critical moment and it had to be replaced by Uncle Arthur.

---

23. Baroness Trumpington, Parliamentary Under-Secretary, Department of Health and Social Security, 1985–7, Ministry of Agriculture, Fisheries and Food, 1987–9; Minister of State, MAFF, 1989–92; life peer 1980.
24. Mrs Honor Ellidge.
25. The article told anecdotes about WW's childhood and said that Pericles lived until he was about four years old with Honor's sister-in-law and husband near WW's country house.
26. *The Wyatts: an architectural dynasty* by John Martin Robinson (1980).
27. WW's Aunt Annie (his mother's older sister), Uncle Horace, and Uncle Arthur are described more fully in *Confessions of an Optimist*, pp. 35–6 and 42.

I cannot imagine why the *Observer* thought this drivel was worth publishing but I suppose it is because they dislike me intensely and under Trelford[28] the *Observer* has become a source of malevolent attacks on Mrs Thatcher or anyone who backs her. Also they know I'm close to Rupert.

Robin Day rings from Blackpool where he is dealing with the Labour Party Conference. Wants to know what is the gut question to ask Kinnock about defence and the abandonment of our nuclear deterrent and expelling American nuclear manned weapons.

He suggests Chris Chataway[29] as Chairman of the BBC. Says he was a good Minister, sacking the Chairman of a nationalized industry when he was Postmaster General or the equivalent. He thinks he is far enough away from having been a professional; he's made a lot of money and could do it well.

I pass the suggestion on to Mrs T who is not at all keen, saying that he did nothing about ILEA [the Inner London Education Authority] when he could have done and allowed it to go on, displaying a very wet manner.

She likes very much the idea of my describing the robbing of the rich called by the Labour Party redistribution as *retribution*. That was in the draft suggestions I sent her for her speech.

**Monday 29 September**

Lunch at Vintners Hall for Ian MacGregor and the launch of his book.[30]

Peregrine Worsthorne sitting opposite me at lunch said it was a disgrace that the political establishment were not there. 'It was as great a victory[31] as Wellington after Waterloo, why were they not there?'

I said, 'This is an expedition to sell books as Collins are giving the lunch, not a state luncheon to thank him for what he's done.'

Also opposite was James Hanson. I told him that now he owns Imperial Tobacco he'd better get some proper research done with the

---

28. Donald Trelford, editor, the *Observer*, 1975–93.
29. Former athlete, television journalist and Conservative politician; Parliamentary Under-Secretary, Ministry of Education and Science, 1962–4, Minister of Posts and Telecommunications, 1970–2; he left Parliament in 1974.
30. *The Enemies Within.*
31. The defeat of the miners' strike in 1984–5 when Ian MacGregor was Chairman of the National Coal Board.

backing of Hugh Sinclair, saying that you won't get lung cancer from smoking cigarettes if you eat the right food. He was very interested in it.

Next to him was Charles Wilson and Hanson said he read everything I wrote and liked it very much in the *Times*. I said, 'Say that again to Mr Wilson as he is one of my part-time employers.'

Charles Wilson is coming to the Tote Cesarewitch. He said he's just signed a cheque for some £900 to the Tote. He is one of our best customers. I said, 'For goodness' sake be careful. It's a terrible way to ruin yourself.' He said, 'I get some good returns as well.'

I told him how the bookmakers' shops at the Tote were doing about eleven per cent better than last year which is an indicator that the country must be in a good state as the punters have been losing far more than usual.

We are having a record year with £3,339,000 profits at the end of the first twenty-four weeks. That's after sponsorship of nearly 300k a year and increased payments to help racecourses.

Next to me is this Mr Sherbourne, the Political Private Secretary to Mrs T.[32] He says, 'Of course I know all about you, as we all do at No 10.'

I said, 'I'm a little bit in love with her.' 'I think we all are. She's such an attractive woman. The other day I came back from holiday just as she was arriving from Chequers and she looked really beautiful.'

I told Jeffrey Archer[33] they must do these simple posters with the salient facts.

He asked if I had spoken to Mrs Thatcher about my idea of the posters. I said, 'Yes and she is all for it.' 'Of course you can tell her anything. The rest of us can't.'

---

32. Stephen Sherbourne, Political Secretary to the Prime Minister, 1983–8.
33. Deputy Chairman of the Conservative Party at this time.

**Wednesday 1 October**

During the Tote Board meeting a message to speak to Downing Street urgently. The Prime Minister wanted me to know before the official announcement was made that Duke Hussey[1] was to be the new Chairman of the BBC. I was shattered. I thought it must be Rupert trying to get rid of somebody in his organization of no value to him.

Later Rupert rings in a great state: 'Has she gone mad? What a disastrous appointment. He was quite useless here and the only thing he was fit to do was to run things like the Hampton Court entertainment we had last summer. They will make rings round him. The BBC Mafia must be absolutely delighted.' Rupert only kept Hussey on at the *Times* when he took it over because he is very kind hearted and he had no money, contrary to what is reported in the press. He made him a director to give him something to do but he was useless as a mainstream operator.

He went on to suggest that it was something to do with the Palace, 'An easy way for them to get him a peerage.' His wife is Lady in Waiting to the Queen.

**Saturday 4 October**

Ring Mrs Thatcher. I sense she will be wondering why I have not spoken to her again about her speech for the Tory Party Conference and also about Hussey. We launch into a long conversation about what she is to say. She says, 'What would the media have said if we had started dishing out roses or flowers at our Party Conference?[2] Everyone would have hooted with laughter but the media are so keen on Kinnock

1. Marmaduke Hussey, managing director and chief executive, Times Newspapers, 1971–80, when owned by Lord Thomson; director, Times Newspapers 1982–6; m (1959) Lady Susan, née Waldegrave, Woman of the Bedchamber to HM the Queen from 1960; life peer 1996.
2. Labour had launched the red rose as their new symbol at their conference.

and Labour that they accept it as a sign of Labour unity and fitness to govern.'

When I told her that the Duke Hussey appointment was a bad one, disastrous like the two previous ones, she said, 'I wouldn't have done it if I hadn't had a strong recommendation from Rupert.' I was amazed and said, 'But he rang me up asking me whether you'd gone mad,' and I told her what he'd said.

'Good Lord,' she said. 'Well he told me he was a very strong man, what had happened at the *Times* was not his fault, the Thomson organization had let him down and that he understood communications and would be very good. Otherwise I wouldn't have made the appointment. Tackle Rupert about it. I can't understand what he's doing, why he's suddenly saying this.'

'I have said in the *News of the World* I think it is a bad appointment though I hope I shall find myself proved wrong. I don't think it's a bad thing that I'm seen to disagree with you from time to time.' She said, 'No, excellent.' We returned to discussing her speech.

Mrs Thatcher said more than once what a weak list they had for Chairman of the BBC. The person she has always wanted to be Chairman is me, but if I were I would be unable to write my articles in the *News of the World* and the *Times*. We have both agreed several times that this is more important even than being Chairman of the BBC – to get the propaganda across and to counter the enemy.

**Sunday 5 October**

Charles Price[3] was at Longchamp in the Trusthouse Forte room after the race. Slightly drunk, very pleased when I told him he was the hero of the hour for having put Kinnock straight about the Reagan administration being intensely worried about Labour's abandonment of the nuclear deterrent and of NATO. He kept asking me what horse to back. Could I tell him what favourite would win? I said, 'If I knew that I wouldn't be wasting my time here.'

Lady Trumpington also there at Longchamp. She is puffing away at a cigarette when I introduce her saying, 'This lady is a Minister at the DHSS where they spend a lot of government money telling people not to smoke,' and she laughed and they did too.

---

3. The US Ambassador.

**Monday 6 October**

Still desperately looking for 'Roses, roses all the way' from *The Patriot*[4] and how it goes on. Ring Kingsley Amis who is immediately able to quote me the next line. I say, 'Are there any lines which Mrs Thatcher might be able to use further on?' He says, 'Give me five minutes and ring back.' I do. He has found two or three apposite ones about how he was hanged by his supporters etc.

I give her some more notes about the abolition of the Trade Union Act 1984 which Labour proposes. She says that from the Department of Employment Kenneth Clarke has given her pages and pages of complicated stuff. I say, 'I will simplify it. I'll put it in a form you might be able to use in a speech,' which I did.

Representatives of the Roman Catholic Church, the Council of Churches and Church of England come to the Jockey Club. Not very hopeful about Sunday racing but say that provided we don't ask for the law to be changed their constituents will not kick up a rumpus.

I give them my usual homily on the high moral value of betting and how a punter loses just over twenty per cent a year of his stakes and gets a great deal of entertainment while he does so, and is not beating his wife or getting drunk. I also explained that credit betting is legal on Sundays so preventing ordinary betting shops being open or betting on the course is another piece of anti-working class discrimination because they tend not to have credit facilities – we require bankers' references for them.

**Wednesday 8 October**

At lunch with Petronella I ask her what clothes she is taking to Oxford. 'Not Chanel, I hope.' 'Yes,' she said, 'I'm taking skirts and jumpers like I've got on today.' 'What are you wearing today?' 'Oh, that's from Valentino. Why shouldn't I look smart?' She gets a discount now indefinitely for having worked at Chanel but it hardly brings it down to the level of Marks & Spencer prices. She thinks too much about clothes. That's how Verushka has brought her up. She had a dressing-gown from Dior when she was nine.

---

4. The poem by Robert Browning (1812–89) begins 'It was roses, roses all the way, / With myrtle mixed in my path like mad'; but concludes 'A rope cuts both my wrists behind; / And I think, by the feel, my forehead bleeds / For they fling, whoever has a mind, / Stones at me for my year's misdeeds.'

**Thursday 9 October**

I speak to Rupert who is on his way back to America and California and Australia. After the rejection by the NGA and SOGAT of his final offer he will do no more.

I tackle him about his having recommended Duke Hussey. Strange. He denies it, says he didn't mention his name. He did say someone was wanted who knows about communications. I said, 'Are you sure you didn't say anything about Duke Hussey?' He seemed evasive and giggled a bit. I said, 'Why did she get the strong impression that you did?' He says he doesn't know. I think she is telling the truth and not Rupert. He repeated that the bright intellectuals and the clever people at the BBC will make a fool of Duke Hussey who will be unable to cope with them.

To dinner at George's.[5] A long wait. We got there at 8.15, the dinner didn't start until nearly 9.30. I got fed up with standing and sat down in what used to be his bedroom which is now a kind of ante room. I was quite by myself for a while then Susan Crosland[6] came and joined me and one and two others.

Susan is in a typical female mess about Wapping. She says she's against the printers and how they behave but she has to be loyal to her union, the National Union of Journalists, so she writes for the magazine of the *Sunday Times*, which is not printed at Wapping, but not for the black and white *Sunday Times* which is.

Susan is quite pretty still. She has a sexy mouth. I said, 'Tony would have been horrified by Kinnock's unilateral CND policy,' and she said, 'How do you know? I'm not so sure.'

She is still a devoted supporter of the Labour Party.

I find that Princess Michael has asked for me to sit on her right-hand side at the dinner party of about forty people at three tables.

On her left was David Frost whom I find creepy. On my right was Annabel,[7] one of Jimmy Goldsmith's wives. Poor girl. They've only just had a memorial service for her son who was presumed drowned, he had disappeared for so long. She said she was very close to him, he was like a brother. She had him when she was nineteen. It is the third

---

5. George Weidenfeld's.
6. Journalist, widow of Anthony Crosland, Labour politician.
7. Lady Annabel Goldsmith, née Vane Tempest Stewart, m 2 (1978) Sir James Goldsmith, his third wife.

time only that she's gone out since he disappeared. I held her hand a bit.

She said Jimmy Goldsmith is convinced that Mrs Thatcher will lose the election. I tell her that Jimmy never had any judgement politically, was always writing me daft memoranda saying in ten years or five years, or whatever date he had chosen, the apocalypse would come, chaos and anarchy would reign. He once advised me to get a house with a large walled garden in the country, arm myself with shot guns and grow vegetables enough to keep myself alive while warding off the marauding bands which would be all over the country looking for food.

I remarked, 'I cannot understand that a man so brilliant at making money and a flair for running businesses and putting them together, could be so absurd in other matters.' I reminded her of the dinner party we had been at with Hugh Thomas before he published his magazine *Now!*[8] I had said to him, 'What is it going to be like?' and he produced a copy of the French Paris magazine *L'Express* which he owned and said, 'Like that.' I looked at it and said, 'But this will never do, Jimmy. It's all in French. It won't go down in England.' For some time he didn't understand the joke. What I meant was it was too much of a French style magazine and it would not succeed here, which it did not.

Princess Michael has already begun to find George rather tricky as most people do when he is publishing them. She got a £30,000 advance for her book[9] and has to sell fifty thousand [copies] before she makes any money. Out of the £30,000 he deducted £5,000 to get some kind of historian to check her facts. This man she says was useless and took a passage which she had repeated from somebody else's book and sold her tiny piece of plagiarism of a hundred and six words to *Private Eye*.

The Princess tells me, 'All the men who have loved me have loved me for my brain not my body.' I express surprise and she flings her arm around me.

She looks thinner and slightly less attractive. She says it is because she lost 3 stone in weight over all the rumpus about her father and the allegation that he was a Nazi, to say nothing of the allegations about Mr Hunt.

8. Goldsmith launched *Now!* magazine in 1979; it folded in 1981.
9. *Crowned in a Far Country: Portraits of Eight Royal Brides*.

I ask her why she says that charity openings were boring. She said she didn't. That was taken out of context and put into an article in *Good Housekeeping* and built up to something quite different.

I said, 'I've told you before not to give an interview without insisting on the right to read it before it is published and have anything removed from it which you don't agree with.' I suspect she really said all the things she was quoted as having said and doesn't like the way they look when they come out. She will always get into trouble. She has a nice back and I put my fingers on it. Her skin is pleasant to the touch.

Neil Hamilton, a Tory MP,[10] talks to me about his case against the BBC. They showed a programme in which a number of Tory MPs were labelled as Nazis, or fascists or racist. He was singled out on the most flimsy grounds. He is a decent ordinary kind of man. They said he'd worn Nazi uniform when he was President of the Union at university. But what he had done was to wear some form of Ruritanian costume as a joke. They said he had goose-stepped past the memorial in East Berlin maintained by the Russians. He had not and had witnesses to prove it. Somebody who did actually do that on the same delegation was Jewish and was only doing it as a joke in any case. They said he'd made a lot of foul racist remarks to an Asian lady in a delegation saying immigrants ought to be repatriated and dreadful things should be done to coloured immigrants. The Asian lady said he did nothing of the kind.

'They won't settle out of court because the BBC has all the money in the world from the licence fees.' They are intimidating him by the weight of the rich man against the poor. Already his costs have come to £150,000. If he loses he will be totally ruined, though he's got guarantees for £120,000. Even if he wins in court the costs will be taxed; unless he's awarded about £50,000 damages he still wouldn't cover his expenses. The BBC is behaving like a fascist bully and I promise him that when his case is over, which begins on Monday, we will talk and I will see if I can write an article about it.

I sent an invoice for £2,500 to NERA.[11] I have now rejoined it so the loss from Irwin Stelzer has been made good.

At dinner Princess Michael says how keen Prince Michael is to get involved with the Tote on the ground and to understand racing.

---

10. For Tatton; this case preceded the later allegations of 'sleaze' which were a central issue in the 1997 election when Martin Bell won the seat.
11. See 22 May 1986.

Eventually I find myself trapped into asking them both to Newmarket. I said I hadn't before because it's so far from Gloucestershire. 'But we've got a helicopter.' Oh hell.

**Friday 10 October**

In the evening I rang her at Chequers to tell her she had done well [at the Conservative conference]. 'You looked beautiful, so beautiful that I fell in love with you all over again.' She was delighted. She said that she had been helped in writing the speech but most of all by me. 'You see,' she said, 'I got in it what they were going to do to the trade union law accurately. You put the most into the speech.'

She must have been in some pain. She said that she had now had two doctors to look at her ankle. There is a hair-line crack and they hope it will mend soon. It was from the stumble over a manhole she had on Monday.

She has enormous guts and never complains.

Petronella goes to Oxford with her mother. By the evening she is ringing up to say how awful it is. Verushka says the room is squalid, the mattress of the bed is cut down the middle and torn, she can't work on the desk; it is covered with grease, nobody has cleaned it; it is terrifying and slumlike. Petronella soon ringing up in despair. 'Not at all like *Brideshead Revisited*. Nothing, nothing. Queers and Lesbians. Boys with curly ringlets down to their waists. People wearing boot straps round their wrists.' The food is terrible.

**Saturday 11 October**

I sit in the garden in beautiful sunshine and have my lunch of scrambled eggs there, while intermittently reading *Cat's Cradle* by Maurice Baring.[12] It is almost as well written as 'C' but has his usual pessimistic despairing theme of people caught up by events they cannot control and out of which they can find no happiness.

In the afternoon Petronella comes back from Oxford. She gives me an account of her first night there. Next door through the paper thin walls she heard a boy and a girl making love and grunting all night. The noise of music and rowdy shouting doesn't stop until two in the morning. She has had little sleep. She is a wreck.

Long discussions: shall she stay, give it more of a trial or what? I

---

12. Writer and diplomat (1874–1945); *Cat's Cradle* and 'C' were novels published 1925 and 1924.

say she can leave at once if she likes but she thinks she will give it another few days. Meanwhile there is a possibility of her changing to London University if she can't stand it.

**Sunday 12 October**

Get Noël Annan on the telephone. He was Provost of University College from 1966–78 and Vice Chancellor of the University of London 1978–81. He says at once he will get on to his successor to see what can be done if she really wants to got to London University instead but he says it's all pretty nasty there, with the grubby canteen and fearful food. I say, 'That doesn't matter because she can eat at home and coming home at night would make a lot of difference to her.'

She says nobody at Oxford wants to talk about anything except sex or sport. Noël says, 'Can't she give it a bit of a trial first?' I said, 'Well perhaps for a month.' 'On the other hand,' Noël says, 'the sooner she makes the change it will be easier to get it done if she is really going to.'

**Monday 13 October**

See Professor Thomas at the Royal Free Hospital.

He gives me a long examination – is there any Parkinson's disease in the family? I tell him my brother has had it for years. He says that it is very unusual for two members of the same family to get the same disease. He gives me a series of tests. One is walking across the room putting one foot in front and against the other as I walk. He says I don't do it too badly but I tried hard and I was a tiny bit wobbly. He examined my eyes and large parts of my body. He said, 'Professor Ricci's diagnosis was one I agree with.' I have symptoms of Parkinsonism which is not by any means to say that I have Parkinson's disease or anything like it.

He says my brain is perfectly all right and he reads my articles. My brain should not deteriorate. He then prescribes Sinemet which is exactly what Ricci proposed. I am to see him in six weeks' time. He thinks it may help my walking and arrest any deterioration.

Arnold rings.

I'm sorry for him. He's feeling unloved by the great and in Whitehall. He is being attacked by so many for running a failing business after being praised as the greatest entrepreneur in Britain.

He doesn't understand that doing things like making Jim Prior, an enemy of hers, Chairman of GEC also does not encourage Mrs Thatcher to go on being friendly.

He has enormous intelligence and love of music, usually accurate perception of people but often he is blind. I am very fond of him, he has been a good friend in times of trouble and always will be.

It sounds as though Prince Michael may be difficult with the Tote. Colonel Farmer, his secretary, said to Geoffrey Webster, 'I have to let the Lord Lieutenant know he may wish to meet him when he arrives at the racecourse.'

Queen Elizabeth the Queen Mother is never met by a Lord Lieutenant nor is the Queen, nor Prince Charles nor Princess Anne. They slip in on a low key basis. Oh dear. Maybe I've made a great mistake in putting him on the Tote Board.

Andrew Knight sends round a fifty cigar box of Romeo y Julieta in a bundle. Must have cost over £150.

**Tuesday 14 October**

Dinner with Douglas Hurd and Judy, his wife. She is a largish lady, not unattractive and the sister of the trainer Jeremy Hindley's wife. Much interested in racing.

Douglas Hurd commented on the sudden flood of Asians coming to Heathrow today and yesterday trying to beat the ban on the requirement for them to get visas in their home countries before they will be admitted here. I said, 'That shows very much that they weren't genuine visitors or tourists or just coming to see their relatives and friends.' He said, 'I hope you'll be saying that in the public print.' I said, 'Certainly. I'd already decided to do so.'

Of course Labour wants to remove the visa restrictions and allow as many Asians to come in as like. People from the West Indies too. Perhaps they think it will put up their vote at general elections.

After dinner there was some talk about the next election.

Kenneth Baker says of course the weapon they have against us is the unpopularity of Mrs Thatcher.

I said, 'I think the weapon of the unpopularity of Mrs Thatcher will break in their hands. The nearer it gets to an election the fashion will start to change. People will say she's not so bad after all, she's done very well, she's brave and courageous and knows what she is doing. And then it will be, 'Don't let hold of Nanny's hand for fearing of getting something worse.'

They're both a tiny bit reserved about Mrs Thatcher for their own reasons, being what they call on the wet side of the Tory Party though they are not really wet at all; they are quite sensible and I think both worthwhile though Douglas has not got the calibre to lead the party. Conceivably Kenneth Baker may have. He is clever and adroit and makes a better speech than Douglas Hurd does.

After I had told Douglas that I thought he had made a mistake with Duke Hussey, that he wouldn't be strong enough and he wouldn't be able to control the clever people around him at the BBC, he told me that he thought I was wrong. He had just had a long talk with him with a preliminary report from him and it was quite clear that he understood what was wrong and had got his finger on the correct points and he thought he would do very well.

**Wednesday 15 October**

Asked Sir Ian Trethowan before the [Levy] board meeting what he thought about Duke Hussey's appointment. 'Superb,' he said.

**Thursday 16 October**

I speak to Margaret.

I tell her about Arnold's complaint that the Canadian firm Northern Telephone is being given a contract to fit up Whitehall with internal communications though the official report actually said the GEC tender was a better one. 'Well they wouldn't have done that unless it was a matter of price.' I forbore to say what the hell are you giving jobs to foreign countries for and losing them in Britain by not buying British.

On Reykjavik[13] I said, 'Are we still solidly behind Reagan?' She said, 'Yes. We can't abandon SDI. But I wouldn't mind a fifty per cent reduction of medium range missiles over five years.'

**Friday 19 October**

The attached letter arrives from Margaret.[14]

Robin Day asks me have I heard from The Other Club? I have not.

---

13. Reagan and Gorbachev had met at Reykjavik on 11 and 12 October 1986.
14. 'Thank you for the beautiful lillies [*sic*] and the note that accompanied them. I am so grateful to you. And thank you for all the help you gave me with my speech. Your thoughts were, as usual, invaluable.' The flowers were for her birthday on 13 October.

'Don't say anything,' he said, 'but I think they are going to ask you to join it.' This was a dining club founded by Winston Churchill.[15]

They take themselves very seriously. People like Hartley Shawcross[16] and Jock Colville[17] and Arnold Weinstock, Julian Amery, meet I believe once a month at the Savoy. Membership is by invitation only. I might have found it more amusing if I was younger. Perhaps the invitation won't come anyway.

**Saturday 18 October**

Prince Michael, who rang me yesterday to say he'd got his binoculars ready, sounding like a schoolboy, arrives in his helicopter at Newmarket. He brings two people with him. Can they have lunch, asks the Princess.

One of them is Micky Suffolk.[18] He says we have met before, which is true, once or twice and at Tony Lambton's. I say, 'Oh yes. You always amuse me. You have a name like a public house – Suffolk and Berks.' Princess Michael whispers to me that the *News of the World* say there is 'fire between us. I think he is going to sue them and they may lose a lot of money. There is nothing between us. I don't even find him attractive.'

Micky Suffolk has a fairly pretty wife (his third) but she is not with him.

Isabel says, 'I didn't curtsey to her. I wouldn't curtsey to that cow.' Others, however, do, mostly.

I have to sit next to her because Verushka says so but I didn't want to.

Will I introduce her to Makhtoum? I say, 'There are about six of them and I don't know them.' 'Can't you send one of your minions to fetch him?' I decline.

They come into the paddock with us before the Tote Cesarewitch

---

15. Churchill and F. E. Smith (later Lord Birkenhead) founded The Other Club in 1911 because they were not wanted at a club called 'The Club'.
16. Lord Shawcross, former Labour MP; Attorney General, 1945–51.
17. Sir John Colville (1915–87; knight 1974), Assistant Private Secretary to three prime ministers (Chamberlain, Churchill and Attlee); Private Secretary to Princess Elizabeth before she succeeded to the throne, 1947–9; Joint Principal Private Secretary to Winston Churchill as Prime Minister, 1951–5.
18. 21st Earl of Suffolk and Berkshire; m 3 (1983) Linda Viscountess Bridport, née Paravicini.

as the horses parade round. Prince Khalid Abdullah, my dear sweet little friend who owns Dancing Brave and is a brother-in-law of the King of Saudi Arabia, sees me and comes over to say hello. I introduce him to Princess Michael and Prince Michael and he bolts immediately. I tell her that he has far more money than all the Makhtoums put together but she does not rise.

Bruce Matthews is a guest. He tells the Princess that he is only Managing Director of News International and has nothing whatever to do with what goes into the newspapers. She tells me that after the *News of the World* said she wouldn't be allowed to go to Windsor for Christmas following one of her gaffes (alleged according to her), she bet Rupert Murdoch or the *News of the World* £10,000 that she would be invited because they had roared with laughter at Buckingham Palace at the idea she wouldn't be. The *News of the World* wisely refused to take the bet.

Verushka manages Princess Michael effectively. Though everybody complains about the woman they certainly have much to talk about and I find her a source of jokes which keeps everybody happy.

Off to Hatley Park. Find Jakie in a worse condition then before with Parkinson's disease.

There is a charming and intelligent girl who has a daughter and a child, one of eighteen and one of twelve who are not there, staying with Jakie. V says she knows her way round the kitchen. She is a sculptress of horses and Jakie has a handsome bronze done by her. Her name is Marcia de Savary. She is divorced. Peter de Savary[19] is rich. Jakie says he is quite generous to her. She seems sad. She is a Canadian.

**Sunday 19 October**

We play our annual game of croquet. Jakie gives me five bisques.[20] In a moment of impetuosity I take three at one hoop. He beats me but I nearly catch him up at the end. He still plays well despite his Parkinson's disease.

Jakie loves to call me Lord Toad of Tote Hall. I sign myself Wyatt of Tote Hall in his visitors' book.

Jakie drives us over with our luggage to Victor [Rothschild] in Cambridge. Far from looking ill, he seems much better than for a very

---

19. International entrepreneur in the energy, property, finance, maritime and leisure fields.
20. A bisque in croquet is the right to play an extra turn.

long time. Full of jokes and life. He immediately takes to Petronella and says, 'Come and see me but not with these old people. We'll discuss life and your difficulties at Oxford.' Shades of Harriet Crawley who wrote a novel about her association with Victor and her dismay when he tried to make it non-platonic.[21]

Tess is no longer Labour, not even SDP or Alliance. She says she is going to vote for Rhodes James, the local MP,[22] who is very good locally. 'You mean you are voting for Mrs Thatcher?' and she concedes that she must be doing that.

After Jakie and the de Savary lady have gone Victor immediately wants to know the gossip about them. 'Is he going to marry her?' he asks. I say, 'I asked him that this morning when we were playing croquet and it would be very nice if he did because she obviously has great affection for him, the way she kept popping out and taking photographs of us, knew where his tablets were and fetched them for him, but Jakie told me he hadn't asked her.'[23]

'Are they in love?' asks Victor. 'It depends what you mean by being in love,' I say. 'They are obviously fond of each but I don't suppose they leap into bed and attack each other with sexual frenzy.'

Tell Margaret that Douglas Hurd said he has had a very good report from Duke Hussey which seems to indicate that he knows what to do about the BBC. Ian Trethowan had told me the new appointment was 'superb'.

I say, 'It looks as though once again I've been wrong and you are right.' 'Doesn't often happen,' she says.

Ask her to say a kind word to Neil Hamilton and Howarth.[24] They've been through hell resisting for two and a half years this fearsome libel action brought [about] by the BBC with all the weight of public money trying to intimidate and blackmail.

**Tuesday 21 October**

Dinner at Cavendish Avenue. Leon and Diana Brittan, Irwin and Cita Stelzer, Chips Keswick, Olga Polizzi, Petronella.

---

21. *The God-daughter* (1975); see 4 May 1986.
22. Conservative MP for Cambridge, 1976–92; biographer of Anthony Eden; knight 1991.
23. They married in 1988.
24. Gerald Howarth, Conservative MP for Cannock and Burntwood, 1983–92, for Aldershot since 1997.

Diana Brittan talks about the difficulties of Leon getting back into the Cabinet. Who is to go?

She asked who I thought would be the next Lord Chancellor and I said, 'Michael Havers.' 'Why do you think that?' 'I just do.' She said, 'I think you must know something about it.' 'Oh no, it's just my observation,' but of course I do know something about it.

I said George Younger was expendable, a rather ineffectual Minister of Defence, not a bit bullish or as good at propaganda as Michael Heseltine. Paul Channon is obviously expendable and useless.

Then she said, 'Of course Mrs Thatcher won't be there all that long.' I said, 'Oh? Why not?' She said, 'She'll doubtless win the next election which Labour is making easier but surely eight years is enough for a Prime Minister.' I thought to myself, 'That's the way the wind is blowing, is it!'

Obviously Leon Brittan is aggrieved at his treatment over the Westland affair and I understand that.

Leon is not bad to look at but he's awful on television, unfortunately for him. He has a remarkable brain and I told his wife he is one of the two or three cleverest people in Britain. Fundamentally a decent man.

Earlier in the day Mrs Brigstock had rung up from St Paul's where she is High Mistress in a state of excitement. They had been rung by University College London asking what sort of person Petronella was.

I explained to Mrs Brigstock who said, 'Well it's lucky we gave her a good report. I couldn't understand what was happening.'

Sonia Melchett calls. She says she's had her book[25] accepted by George Weidenfeld, not a difficult feat I should have thought. It is a novel although it's based on her experiences after Julian died. She wanted me to know before an announcement because I helped her with the first book which wasn't bad but superficial, based on telephone conversations between two lovers.

**Wednesday 22 October**

Neil Hamilton rings. I congratulate him on his great triumph[26] and he says the *Sunday Times* have asked him to write an article about it for this Sunday dealing with all the dishonest negotiations and behaviour of the bullying BBC, using their vast resources to intimidate people

25. *Someone is Missing* was published in 1987; *Tell Me, Honestly* in 1964.
26. He won the libel action.

with very little money. The *Sunday Times* only offered him £3,000. I said, 'I think you can get more than that.'

Lunch at the Savoy. David Montgomery tells me that Jeffrey Archer has been observed picking up at least one tart in the street. They[27] have an affidavit from her and are protecting her now and watching her so she does not give the story to anyone else. Jeffrey Archer heard something about this and gave David lunch at Bournemouth and said, 'What are you doing about it? It's all untrue,' and so forth.[28] He keeps ringing him up about it and David Montgomery said, 'I thought the *Mirror* were running it. It's all over Fleet Street anyway.'

Jeffrey said that Maxwell had promised they wouldn't print it and that the *Sunday Mirror* keeps saying the *News of the World* is going to, and he rings up on Saturdays to find out what's happening.

The truth is that the *News of the World* don't feel they've yet got a sufficiently good story. To be seen taking the tart away, having stopped his car to pick her up (they know it was his car from the registration number), may not be sufficient to prevent them being sued for libel. She, however, has told the *News of the World* that she provided Jeffrey with the services he required.

He must be really mad.[29] He is rich. He is by himself in London for the week. His very pretty and charming wife is in Grantchester being a don at two colleges at Cambridge. He could easily get a respectable girl to go to bed with him because many girls would think him attractive because of his power as Vice Chairman of the Tory Party and his riches and his fame, and he is not altogether unattractive.

David asked if I thought the story would do Jeffrey any harm. I said, 'It might do the Tory Party harm which I care about more.' He said, 'I don't think it would do him very much harm because people don't altogether take him seriously.' I said, 'It would probably ruin his political career.'

Perhaps like Tom Driberg,[30] the more dangerous and degrading the

---

27. The *News of the World*.
28. Jeffrey Archer subsequently won his libel case against allegations in the *Star*. In October 1987, he settled out of court with the *News of the World* in an action he brought against the newspaper for inferring that he had slept with the prostitute. He received £50,000 damages and £30,000 costs.
29. If he had he acted in the way alleged.
30. Barred from office as a security risk because of his taste for homosexual 'rough trade', as recounted in his posthumous autobiography *Ruling Passions* (1977).

sex is the more he likes it. I said, 'He might say that he was doing research for his next book, or that he was trying to find out why prostitutes behaved in the way they did. Or that he was like Mr Gladstone wanting to know what made nice girls become prostitutes.'

David said, 'She isn't a nice girl. She's an ordinary hooker who plies a steady trade, hardened.' He says he thinks there will be something about it in *Private Eye* soon, possibly with a story that David Montgomery had been nobbled to hush the story up – which is not true. He just thinks he hasn't got enough to go on. It must be strange to be the editor of the *News of the World*, putting out stuff which could harm the Tory Party which he really supports, and cause a lot of distress, but that's how they sell newspapers.

He said that the Press Council had received another complaint about me but this time it was the headline of the article in which I had replied to the Press Council. 'The headline was not by me,' I said. It was 'A Black and White Case'. If the Press Council is going to pursue things like this they will become even more discredited than they are already. David says nobody takes them seriously in Fleet Street any more and no editor minds being rebuked by them.

The *News of the World* will make £5 million profit this year instead of the £500,000 they managed to make before the Wapping move. The *Sunday Times* is making a bomb, having almost a monopoly of classified advertising, and the *Times* is also making a profit. The *Sun* is running at about £30 million profit. He thinks that the *Daily Telegraph* and *Sunday Telegraph* are not very good newspapers and disagrees with me. He says the *Telegraph* have lost the most to the new paper the *Independent*, followed by the *Times* and the *Guardian*. He thinks the *Independent* is a good newspaper and likes it.

Called on Charles Forte on the way home at 86 Park Lane. Wants me to write an article in the *Times* about the scandal of his not being able to take control of the Savoy Group when he has sixty-nine per cent of the shares. Hugh Wontner controls the 'B' shares which are the voting ones as opposed to Charles' 'A' shares. He has lived for years in a suite of rooms at Claridge's, able to order caviar all day long if he feels like it without paying for anything.

I say I don't know if I'll be able to write the article in the *Times* because they would know that I am a friend of his.

He says if I can't write in the *Times*, could I do some sort of analytical piece like the profound one, as he calls it, that I did in the

*Times* last Saturday on nuclear disarmament and SDI. I take the papers away and say that I'll let him know what I think about it.

**Friday 24 October**

A letter from Michael Hartwell inviting me to join The Other Club. Rang Robin Day who said that he had voted for me. There are fifty members.

It meets ten times a year at the Savoy and dinner only costs £10 a time with champagne and wine.

Amused to find that Callaghan is one of the members who hates me because of my story in *Confessions of an Optimist* about Tom Driberg having grabbed his penis when they were peeing by the side of the road on the way back from a meeting.

Ring to congratulate Kingsley Amis on winning the Booker Prize on Wednesday night.[31] 'Did you get drunk?' 'Yes, and I couldn't find my dinner jacket in the morning.'

**Sunday 26 October**

The news broke in the *News of the World* and was taken up by other papers of Jeffrey Archer's prostitute. The *NoW* played a dirty trick. The editor had told me that the story from the prostitute by itself did not in his view represent a strong enough case to resist a libel action, without corroboration. So they got her to ring Jeffrey Archer and he suggested she should go abroad and he would give her the money. It was a trap. The *NoW* had photographs and the whole details of Archer's emissary handing over the money on a railway platform to the prostitute. They taped the conversations when they went to a bar and the fat was in the fire.[32]

I rang Margaret early and told her that I felt this morning I couldn't write for the *News of the World* any more because it was such a dirty trick. Rupert had not mentioned it to me when he rang on Thursday (but perhaps he didn't know anything about it though Verushka thinks he must have). She said, 'Oh for goodness' sake don't do that. We'll lose our only platform if you don't write for the *News of the World*.'

She thinks it will be a big blow to the Tory Party. 'We can take one or two people running off the normal track but when everybody starts

31. For *The Old Devils*.
32. Archer sued the *Star* for libel about this matter, won the case and was awarded £500,000 damages.

doing it, it's far more difficult to sustain the position. When behaviour like this becomes the norm then the public don't like it.' 'Most of the country is immoral,' I say. 'I don't think they give a damn once they are in the polling booth whatever they may say publicly.'

When Mrs Thatcher came [to dinner in the evening] I told her how Jeffrey Archer tried to silence David Montgomery by emphasizing his influence with her and how 'He could get you to black him or give him an interview according to what he said,' and she remarked, 'Oh lor, how silly of him.'

Robert Kee[33] was deeply impressed by her authority. He got in his plea for the Maguires to have their case re-examined.

As we stand in the hall at the end of the evening as everyone is departing, Arnold offers Margaret documents and papers and says, 'Oh, no, I won't give you this.' She says, 'Well give it me then.' As he fumbles agitatedly, 'I'm so much in awe of you I've even put on the wrong coat for my trousers.' She said, 'I thought it was meant to be some new trendy fashion.' The coat matched a different suit.

The dinner went merrily. At the end at about 11.00 which is later for her than usual because she has work to do, Denis got up and said, 'I want to go home now. My arthritis is giving me trouble.' Meekly she got up. He had difficulty in going down the steps.

**Monday 27 October**

Enchanting Prince Khalid to lunch. The VAT position on his horses is if he keeps one he brought in from abroad for two years here, they make him pay VAT on whatever the price was paid originally for that horse. It doesn't matter if it is a very grand horse like Dancing Brave because the value is so enormous. But with the many horses he has which don't win much it is quite a burden. They don't make him do this in France or in Ireland.

He is more concerned about the vast taxes they try to make him pay on his money here. The Inland Revenue claim that everything he has here is income and should be taxed accordingly even though it may not be true. For example, he may have sold a house or a racehorse and therefore it would be a capital transaction but the Inland Revenue

---

33. Writer and television journalist; he published *Trial and Error* in 1986 about the Maguires (imprisoned in 1976 for handling explosives for IRA bombings and eventually released after a long campaign) and the Guildford Four.

say, 'No, everything you bring in here is your income and you'll pay the full tax on it.'

As it runs into hundreds of millions they must be mad. They don't do this in France where they exempt him entirely from income tax because of all the money he brings in. He says at least he'd like to be able to make some kind of a deal with the Inland Revenue like, 'I'll give you so many millions a year and we'll call it a day.'

I said, 'If you don't succeed with the Inland Revenue (Freshfields are the representatives dealing with a fairly high level man in the Inland Revenue), I'll take it up with Nigel Lawson and the Prime Minister because if you go and others like you go it will be not only a blow to racing in England but to the economy as well.'[34]

**Tuesday 28 October**

Lunch with Cecil Parkinson and Michael Ivens[35] at l'Escargot.

Parkinson tells me that when he was offered a job as Foreign Secretary by Mrs Thatcher after the election he told her that he had to tell her something first. He then blurted out about Sara Keays and the baby and all that. 'Have you been carrying this burden knowing all this during the election campaign?' she asked. When he said he had been, she said, 'Well you can stand pressure very well. That's very remarkable and I admire you for it.' She was not in the least bit censorious. She wanted him to stick it out but it all got too hot.

I asked him whether he would be happy to go back now, after a general election. He said, 'Yes.'

He said that there had always been a majority in the Cabinet since 1979 of people who have been divorced or who have married divorced people. I laughed and said, 'But I think I was the first to point out how strange the morality is which says if you stay with your family and wife that is immoral but if you go off with your mistress that is fine.'

He thought Norman Tebbit[36] was foolish in not devoting all his time to running the Conservative Party machine and getting it straight

---

34. Sheikh Mohammed announced in April 1998 that he was sending 120 of his top horses to be trained in France because of high costs in this country.
35. Director, Aims of Industry, 1971–94; director, Foundation for Business Responsibilities, 1967–92.
36. Chancellor of the Duchy of Lancaster, 1985–7; Conservative Party chairman, 1985–7.

and dealing with propaganda. He keeps wanting to attend Cabinet committee meetings and is hurt if he is left out and insists on his presence being felt at No 10 otherwise he doesn't think he is in the centre of power and [thinks he is] losing out on the leadership race. But if the Tories win, his power will be greatly increased and stand him in better stead in any subsequent leadership contest.

Verushka came back from Oxford with the little possessions Petronella had taken for her room.

In the evening I wept for her lost Oxford and my lost dreams as well as hers. I was so proud of her getting in but she gave up after only a ten days' trial, spending not more than two or three nights in her room there.

**Wednesday 29 October**

A [Levy Board] reception at St James's Palace. Everybody was given rooms to stand in and not to move from, with different coloured invitation tickets. This caused resentment among those penned into one room unable to move or see what [was] going on elsewhere. St James' Palace is pretty and some of the rooms are fine. I wanted the largest room to hold an orchestra and to have the alternative of pink champagne.

Afterwards at dinner with Angela Oswald, the Queen Mother's lady-in-waiting, and Michael Oswald, who breeds for the Queen and is one of her closest friends, I mentioned this and they said, 'How silly. The Queen would have liked the music and why would she have objected to people having pink champagne as an alternative?'

My encounter with the Queen was my normal one. 'Good evening, Ma'am.' A gloomy smile from her and a hand-shake through a white glove. I've never exchanged more than a few words with her and find her impossible to talk to, though Michael Oswald says he chats away with her the whole time on almost every topic. He also said it was impossible that Michael Shea could have known her political views when he authorized the *Sunday Times* to print the notorious article. He has known her for years and closely and she never talks about politics to anyone.

After the Queen and Princess Anne have wandered through the rooms the order was that they came back again to the Council Chamber where members of the Levy Board had to reassemble. We waited for some time with nothing happening then from the opposite direction from which the Queen would arrive, two corgis pranced in. I was hardly able to stop laughing. It was like a *Spitting Image* programme as they wandered around as the advance guard of the Queen.

Princess Michael in her latest television broadcast in America apparently said one of the things she liked doing (she liked cats and didn't like dogs) was kicking corgis. The woman is an uncontrollable ass.

**Tuesday 4 November**

The Wexford Opera Company are brought by Heinz to the South Bank. Tony O'Reilly asks us to go. I don't want to but Verushka thinks it will be full of amusing people, particularly after the opera is over when we have what is called a breakfast at the Savoy.

In the next seats was a cousin of Annie Fleming.

How fast the trees and flowers disappear. Annie, despite her bitchiness, was a dear friend. She and Ian [Fleming] had a son called Caspar and the too familiar tragedy occurred. His uncle,[1] the explorer, kept giving this boy guns, beautiful ones. He had an armoury. He then at Eton got into trouble for seducing one of the maids. Wilder and wilder he became until he committed suicide with one of the guns, his father already being dead.

Is it the parents' fault? Can parents ever do anything about their children who have characters born in them and will behave according to their characters whatever the parents do or say? Advice from parents is not thought much of by children who must learn from their own experiences and, if they have the character, will survive the nasty ones.

**Wednesday 5 November**

Charming man, Mr Alastair Wilson, from BBC Radio 4, who lives in Manchester came to interview me about Stafford Cripps.[2] I liked talking about him and refuting the legend that he was an austere ascetic.

**Thursday 6 November**

To the West Midlands Serious Crime Squad dinner. Three hundred policemen.

I made a few jokes and talked about their problems in dealing with

1. Peter Fleming (1907–71), travel writer.
2. As a young Labour MP, WW was Sir Stafford Cripps' personal assistant on the Cabinet Mission sent to India in 1946 to negotiate Indian independence.

the coloured population, namely the West Indian/Africans. They had first hand experience of them in the Handsworth riots[3] where they rioted, looted and burned when the police went in to catch drug peddlers. I said that many of the West Indians/Africans were lawless, etc. and that I had been censured by the Press Council for saying so.

I noticed two West Indians/Africans among the diners. I said, 'We must try to get more coloured and blacks into the police force because it is the only way to get them assimilated into British society, but I realize their own families and friends revile them when they join if they are black. I salute their courage.'

On the way out I stopped at the table where the two charming black West Indians/Africans were sitting and shook hands with them. They were pleased.

**Sunday 9 November**

Rupert rings on arrival from Australia. We have dinner with him. He says he was worried and concerned about the entrapment nature of the *News of the World* dealings with Jeffrey Archer. 'If, however, I told them not to go ahead with it there would have been a hundred journalists who would have known and who would have reported it to *Private Eye* or elsewhere that I had stopped it in order to help Mrs Thatcher.' His view was that she was well rid of him in any case.

**Monday 10 November**

At GEC Avionics looking at their airborne early warning system which they are desperately trying to sell to the government who are veering towards the American more expensive type which would kill British technology in this area. The Managing Director, a portly man, spends most of the time while talking to me clipping his finger nails. I wonder if he does that with important foreign buyers of British military equipment.

**Wednesday 12 November**

Reception at the American Embassy for what they call the opening of the political season. Archie Hamilton, a junior Minister at the Ministry of Defence to do with procurement, says I'm on dangerous ground writing in the *Times* in favour of the GEC early warning airborne system against the American. He says the GEC version won't pick up

3. In Birmingham.

all the targets like the American AWACS one does. Get in a mild panic and when I get home ring everybody including Arnold to find out what the answer is. Of course what Hamilton says is not true which is typical of the British desire to run themselves down and buy foreign equipment whenever possible even when British is best.

**Thursday 13 November**

Dinner at The Other Club, Savoy. Meet Tony Lambton outside the Savoy who tells me he is coming to dinner at The Other Club after a long absence because he knew I would be there, which I doubt.

Meet the other members present drinking champagne out of magnums before dinner. Lots of little bits to eat well done. Champagne is good. The dinner excellent. I have dressed crab followed by wild duck and a delicious mess of peas. The claret is Beychevelle 1978, good and a splendid year though young. Drink quite a lot of it but avoid the brandy at the end of the meal. Total cost drinks and all now £12.50 which surprised Jo Grimond[4] sitting next to me expecting to pay the long-standing £10.00.

Quintin Hogg[5] is Chairman for the evening and as a new member I sit on one side of him and Jacob Rothschild, another new member, on his left. At seventy-nine his brain is nimble. We have known each other since 1945 when against convention he interrupted my maiden speech with a joke.

Of Mrs Thatcher he says it is quite different having a woman Prime Minister from a man. She is capricious and like he imagines Queen Elizabeth I to have been. You have to handle her not as a man but as a commanding changeable woman and walk delicately. He thinks she has a very good intellect and would have got a First in one of the humanities subjects rather than science. He admires her greatly. The Cabinet atmosphere is not as it is with a male Prime Minister to whom you can say things you can't say to a woman.

Quintin was First Lord of the Admiralty for a few months coinciding with the time of Suez. Mountbatten[6] was discontented about the enterprise and wrote to Quintin with his resignation. Quintin replied he

---

4. (1913–93); former Leader of the Liberal Party; life peer 1983.
5. Lord Hailsham, Conservative politician; Lord Chancellor, 1970–4 and 1979–87; life peer 1970.
6. 1st Earl Mountbatten (1900–79), First Sea Lord, 1955–9; the Suez venture was in 1956.

was ordering him to stay at his post and that it was no time to desert. At this point Tony Lambton sitting opposite said he was writing a book about Mountbatten[7] and that he was a terrible liar.

On my other side Jo picked up the odd comment being made about how intimate I am with Mrs Thatcher and asked me whether I still rang her three times a week. I said, 'I never did but I speak to her quite often.' 'I hope you are making a record of it. It would be very valuable historically,' Jo said. I said no but it is not true as she appears often in this diary.

In the car after dinner, when I gave a lift to Jock Colville, Gordon Richardson (former Governor of the Bank of England) and Arnold Weinstock, some comments were made again about my relations with Mrs Thatcher. Arnold said Woodrow knows everything but he won't tell. 'Quite right,' said Jock.

He then proceeded to relate to me, after the other two had got out, a recent conversation with the Queen. He asked her whether what the *Sunday Times* and Andrew Neil had put in their paper about her attitude to Mrs Thatcher and the government and sanctions was true. 'Not at all, absolutely wrong,' she had replied. He then asked her what she thought of Mrs Thatcher and she said, 'Jock, you do ask the most impertinent questions,' to which he answered, 'Well, Ma'am, I was your private secretary for some years' and she laughed and said, 'I get on with her all right but like all Prime Ministers she won't listen.'

Jacob was saying he was surprised that I was friendly with Tony Lambton. I said, 'Oh, I quite like him.' He said it as we were leaving, and Tony heard Jacob mentioning our quarrel and said, 'Woodrow kept complaining about the swimming pool' and I said, 'It wasn't me; it was you who kept complaining about me. I complained about nothing.' He put his arm around me and said, 'I am very fond of you, Woodrow.' A bit like Judas Iscariot, I felt.

The dinner was jolly. Jeremy Thorpe[8] was there, for the first time in ten years I was told. He was not jolly and looked as though he had AIDS. Emaciated and haggard.

**Friday 14 November**

Tony Morris and Tony Ellis, two of the main energies in the National Working Miners' Committee come to see me. They are the last of the

---

7. *The Mountbattens* published 1989.
8. Leader of the Liberal Party, 1967–76; suffering from Parkinson's disease.

old committee still working for the Coal Board; the others having taken redundancy in disgust at the lousy treatment working miners had from management after the strike was ended.

Tony Morris and Tony Ellis both wanted my help to get them out now from the little management jobs they'd been given with adequate compensation. They were wrecked in their health and lost a lot of money struggling through the strike. They spoke of the most glorious moment they had which was when they came here to meet Mrs Thatcher at a dinner I gave for the working miners and she helped clear away the plates.

**Sunday 16 November**

Ring No 10 and they tell me she is resting and I say, 'Don't bother her. I'll ring her in the morning,' but in an hour she rings back. 'You must be tired.' 'I was a little about 4.00 this afternoon and decided to have a sleep for an hour and now I feel fine. I've got three Boxes to go through.'

She left London at 12.00 noon Friday and got back 7.00 a.m. this morning. She's very pleased that she got what she wanted from Reagan about Trident and the statement on not getting [rid] of all nuclear arms.[9]

I ask her to read my article saying the government must buy Nimrod which was in the *Times* yesterday. I say, 'I'm not asking you to agree with it, just to read it. It makes a few points that haven't been made before.' She said, 'Yes, I will certainly; thank you very much for telling me.'

When I say how good it is about Mark[10] she says, 'Yes, she's a very nice girl. She seems very steady.' She said, 'I thought neither of them were ever going to get married.' I said, 'When is Carol going to?' She said, 'I've no idea. It's something I can't do anything about.' I said, 'No not even the most powerful Prime Minister can impose their will there' and she laughed.

**Wednesday 19 November**

The *Spectator* and the Highland Park Whisky firm gave a luncheon at the Savoy for the *Spectator* Parliamentary Awards of the Year. We were

---

9. See *The Downing Street Years* (p. 473) for Lady Thatcher's account of her meeting with the President at his Camp David retreat.
10. On his engagement to Diane Burgdorf, a Texan heiress.

subjected to a long speech about the awful things the Japanese do with regards to duty on Scotch whisky. Thereafter all went well.

Nigel Dempster, the *Daily Mail* gossip columnist, on my left and Julian Amery on my right. Dempster very ingratiating; that is his policy and approach. Appeared to be keen on racing, having a horse. Invited him to come in after lunch at Newbury on Saturday.

Julian and I lament for a while the death announced in the *Times* this morning of Billy McLean[11] who got septicaemia. Julian has written the obituary of this adventurous man. I first met him in India towards the end of the war. As the European War was ending I met him again in London. He and his wife to be, Däska, who was then married to a Mr Kennedy and was strikingly beautiful, used to meet in a little café, secretly, in Wigmore Street and tell me I mustn't tell anyone about it though I knew nobody to whom I should tell it.

He was attractive and loved all political intrigue but was not much good at politics direct when he was in the House of Commons. His forte was going to places like Albania or the Yemen and trying to whip up support for those fighting the Communists. He was a worthwhile person, slightly younger than myself, and his death made me feel that another of the trees in the forest of my life had been cut down.

Däska is a Yugoslav, of a family which had a few merchant ships outside Yugoslavia when the War began and therefore saved a largish part of their fortune. Her brother put me up for the RAC. He was the only person I knew, apart from Lord Plummer, who belonged to it.

Roy Jenkins was sitting just behind me. He won one of the awards and made the best speech because it was so brief. 'I am grateful, delighted and astonished to receive this award.' It was only a bottle of whisky and some kind of mock medal.

John Smith was a winner of an award. I said to Roy, who was sitting behind me, 'You should have him in your party.[12] He's got a lot of sense and marshals his facts well.' Roy agreed.

John Smith got his award for harrying Mrs Thatcher over Land Rover, Westland, on all of which issues he was actually wrong but he did it well. He is able and intelligent and puts his ideas well.

Nigel Dempster said the horoscopes persistently showed that the

---

11. Lieutenant Colonel Neil Loudon Desmond McLean, Conservative MP for Inverness, 1954–64.
12. The SDP.

Prince of Wales would die before his mother. Would Diana be capable of running the State with her infant son as King William?

**Thursday 20 November**

Social Affairs Unit, Lord North Street, in the evening, run by Digby Anderson – plump and lively with a ruddy face. He is a nutter about food, however, believing that you can eat anything you like plus bags of sugar and salt and it makes no difference. Otherwise sound on almost everything.

Tony Jay was there. He was one of the originators of the *Yes, Minister* programmes.

I asked him whether he thought the BBC realized the nature of the message of his programmes, namely that by attacking bureaucracy and ridiculing Ministers they show that more government is worse and less government is better. He said, 'No they have no idea or they'd probably stop them. They cannot comprehend that *Yes, Minister* and now *Yes, Prime Minister* really extol the free moving spirit and are undermining the concept of socialism and that the state should run everything.'

**Friday 21 November**

Noël Annan comes for a drink. I think Gaby Annan is not too keen on us any more as she seems to have dodged dinner invitations but Noël is as friendly as ever. He is very pleased about getting Petronella into University College, and I was extremely grateful to him.

**Saturday 22 November**

At Newbury I was reluctant to call on Queen Elizabeth because I was mildly irritated that she could come racing on Saturday but not to dinner on the previous Tuesday.[13] Verushka said, 'Oh you must. She will hear you are here and will be hurt if you don't go to see her,' so I did.

She was without quite so much colour in her face as she usually has but lively nevertheless. She said how sorry she was about the dinner; would I ask her for another day; perhaps we could fix one in February? She also said she would like to present the Tote Cheltenham Gold Cup again and she thanked me very much for the book and said how interesting it was. It was *The Follies*, produced by the National

---

13. Her equerry had rung on Friday 14 November to say she could not come to dinner on the 18th because her bad leg had not recovered sufficiently.

Trust. I said, 'Don't forget to look the Wyatts up in the index,' and she said, 'I have.'

Someone commented on my tartan tie and she said it was very nice. I said, 'I wouldn't have worn it if I'd known you were here, Ma'am, because I have not a drop of Scottish blood in me. What kind of a tartan do you think it is? You must be an expert.' She said, 'A McWyatt hunting tartan, of course.'

At the end of the day Brian Cubbon said he'd done quite well with his betting. I said, 'On what principle did you decide your bets?' 'From reading Mandarin in the *Times*. It must be for me, mustn't it?'[14]

Charles Wilson, editor of the *Times*, won on a £5 bet a dual forecast at 134 to 1. He was very pleased. He bets a lot and we extended his credit which may not have been a good thing for him.

Little Flora Fraser[15] was there.

She wrote a book about Lady Hamilton which has sold well. I said, 'Are you a better historian than Antonia?' To which she diplomatically replied, 'I'm not as good as my grandmother, Elizabeth Longford.'

**Sunday 23 November**

Talk to Pericles. The restaurant he is managing, aged twenty-three, in Philadelphia pays him $30,000 a year plus tips at about $5,000 a year. He works from 11.00 in the morning till 12.00 at night. He says it is not like working in a warehouse as he did for GEC's subsidiary in America when he first got there, where one was always watching the clock and wishing the time would pass, because in the restaurant he is so busy organizing the waiters and looking after the customers that he never notices what the time is.

Much happier than he was two years ago. I suspect he will never come back to England which he finds dead and without opportunity for somebody like himself who removed himself from Harrow in the January of the year he was eighteen and, not doing his A levels [which were later that year], has no qualifications.

Edward IV might be amused to know that the boy with the best claim to the throne after his grandfather and mother die – not an Act of Parliament claim but based entirely on his grandfather being the

14. He was Permanent Under-Secretary of State, Home Office, 1979–88.
15. Daughter of Sir Hugh Fraser and Lady Antonia Fraser (Pinter).

senior surviving Plantagenet who, if heredity was the test, would be the King now – has been graduating as a waiter in America.[16]

**Monday 24 November**

Margaret thinks contrary to press comment Robert Armstrong is doing well in Australia and I agree.[17] We both agree that, irrespective of the outcome of the case to try to stop publication of Wright's book on MI5, it is of great importance to have brought the case. We must try to stop the proliferation of secrets from ex Secret Service members who are often pursuing their own quarrels and now appear to be anxious to make money out of them.

She thinks Kinnock doesn't understand the issue at all otherwise he wouldn't be trying to make a party issue out of it.

Last night Michael Tree rang up in a great state. What about this stuff on Victor in the *Observer* saying that he tried to nobble Mr Wright to prevent himself being named as a spy? I say, 'The story has been around for a long time. He was mixed up with the Apostles.'[18] Michael says they're dreadful people, really awful. I say, 'Yes, but I don't think Victor ever did anything treacherous. I'd be very surprised.'

Professor Norman Stone[19] and Mrs Stone, Sonia Melchett and her husband Andrew Sinclair, Harold and Diane Lever, Billy and Maureen Dudley,[20] Andrew Devonshire and Petronella. Dinner.

I have arranged Gazin (one of the first great growths of Pomerol) 1960 for dinner and then wonder whether it is good enough because Verushka says how much Billy likes good wine. I decide to produce a 1925 Château Latour-Carnet, a fourth growth now moved up in the unofficial 1978 classification. But I think I won't open it until about

16. Pericles' grandfather was the 15th Earl of Huntingdon (father of Moorea, WW's 3rd wife); hence Pericles would be the Plantagenet claimant after the deaths of his grandfather and mother.
17. Sir Robert Armstrong, Cabinet Secretary, was sent to Australia to defend in the Supreme Court of New South Wales the British government's attempt to ban the publication of Peter Wright's autobiography *Spycatcher*. Wright, who had gone to live in Australia, had given in the book a detailed account of his experiences working for MI5, naming alleged spies and including allegations of a plot to undermine Harold Wilson as Prime Minister.
18. Dining club in the 1930s at Trinity College, Cambridge, which was a recruiting ground for Soviet spies.
19. Then Professor of Modern History and Fellow of Worcester College, Oxford.
20. The 4th Earl and Countess of Dudley (Maureen Swanson, actress).*

twenty to nine as it will die very quickly and the meat it will be drunk with won't be on the table until about ten past nine.

Billy arrives and says he is not drinking anything, no champagne. He has become a teetotaller. I rush downstairs and remove the 1925 wine from which the capsule had been cut off the top and put it back in the cellar. The Gazin turns out well.

I tried to get Billy to let me have a copy of the famous poem he wrote about Princess Michael and her ghastly behaviour which was leaked by Prince Alexander of Yugoslavia – he sent her a copy he had borrowed from Billy for one night only. She brought legal action and all the rest of it. He said, 'There's only one copy now and that's with my lawyers.' Billy said they'd been offered $100,000 for it by an American magazine. Maureen was a kind of unofficial Lady in Waiting to Princess Michael and they were very great friends until Maureen found she was a serpent.

She said horrible things about her. Maureen Dudley used to be Maureen Swanson the actress and is remarkably pretty still. Billy and I talk a little bit about his one time step-mother Laura who finally fetched up by marrying Bert Marlborough[21] for whom she had been the great love of his life. He said his father had cited four co-respondents when divorcing Laura.

Andrew offers the wet worry that if Labour doesn't win the next election the country may turn to violence and something like civil war. Harold nods sagely and agrees. I say, 'This is total rubbish. Why don't you, Andrew, get the party you now support, the SDP, to assert themselves and replace Labour?' He says, 'They take my money but not my advice.'

After dinner Harold Lever tells Norman Stone how he knew my tutor at Oxford when I was at Worcester – Alan Brown – and that Alan Brown had told him that I must be Prime Minister or there would be something wrong with the country if I were not. Perhaps there is something wrong with the country! I don't think I could ever have become Prime Minister starting with the base of the Labour Party with which I was gradually disenchanted after the 1951 government ended.

Mrs Thatcher said she was sorry she could not speak to me at once

---

21. The 10th Duke of Marlborough (1897–1972) m 2 (1972) Laura Viscountess Long; he was her fourth husband; she had married 1 2nd Viscount Long, 2 3rd Earl of Dudley, 3 Michael Canfield of New York and London.

'but I was having physiotherapy on my finger. It's painful where the wound is and I mustn't let it go stiff.'

**Tuesday 25 November**

A disturbance. Verushka and Petronella were in my library having a drink before dinner. I look up and notice Petronella reading a page of this diary. I am furious and say she must never look at it again and say nothing whatever about it and she is not to know what it is as it is a secret.

Verushka then defends Petronella and starts a great row and says, 'Why do you lock yourself in? Have you got a girlfriend?' I forbore to retort that if I had a girlfriend I would hardly be letting Miss Cook, my secretary, type accounts of her. 'Anyway,' says Verushka, 'I've got a key to your library and I can come in as much as I like. Why do you want to lock me out?' Petronella in floods of tears, Verushka raging away saying I'm not a proper father.

I have dinner by myself; the other two do not come down. I tell Verushka if she doesn't give me her key back I won't go to Italy and she won't be able to take the house she wants. This produces more furious rage plus the proposition that I've promised her lots of money and luxury when we got married and I haven't fulfilled my promise. Also that I am senile and she rang up the doctor who says I must have Parkinson's disease because the pills have made an improvement and I make a fool of myself when I talk to pretty women because they all think I'm an uninteresting old man.

**Wednesday 26 November**

Verushka announces that she hasn't really got a key to my library at all. She just said it to make me angry. I say, 'Well you succeeded in your enterprise.'

There is much more in the newspapers this morning about Victor Rothschild's involvement with the book by Chapman Pincher *Their Trade is Treachery* and his arranging for Wright to be paid a large sum to help Pincher with information. The suggestion floats around that Victor was so involved with Philby, Burgess, Anthony Blunt etc., that he was himself interrogated to establish whether he had been involved in passing on secrets when he was a member of MI5 during the war. It was he who got Anthony Blunt into the Secret Service, who was a great friend of his. I tell Petronella that at lunch time on Sunday with Victor it would be inadvisable to suggest playing a game of I Spy.

Dinner at the Wolfsons. I knew it would be dreary and by God it was.

A side amusement at the Wolfsons is to estimate the value of the pictures in each room. I put it at an average of about £8 million with Impressionist and Post-Impressionist mainly French paintings. I like Leonard but he is a dull conversationalist.

Before dinner I went to see Brian Inglis, former editor of the *Spectator* and a friend of Koestler's[22] for ten years before he died. I am writing the piece about Koestler in the Dictionary of National Biography so wanted to know his views on Koestler's para-psychological activities. Inglis is one of the trustees of the foundation set up in Koestler's name.

**Thursday 27 November**

A pleasant dinner with Edwina d'Erlanger[23] at Claridge's. We pick up Clarissa on the way. I am the only man present. It is a nice old fashioned place and the orchestra with its old world tunes makes me feel nostalgic though I am not clear about what.

I notice Jack Heinz and Drue coming in for some reception the other side. I mention this and Edwina says, 'Jack's been having an affair with a girl called Sylvia. Drue found out about it and immediately headed him away or tried to but she dressed up as a nurse when he was ill and smuggled herself in to look after him or something to that effect.' 'That's very game of him, because he must be about eighty-two.' She said, 'Oh people do carry on at that age.'

He didn't found the Heinz beans empire but he inherited it. He could never have founded it. Nor does he run it: Mr O'Reilly does.

Edwina recalls how she came to dinner at Tower House once when George Brown was Foreign Secretary and sat next to him which she asked if she could do. He talked to her for a bit, was drunk and said, 'I've talked to you, you old hag, long enough; I'm going to the woman the other side who is younger and prettier.'

Not that Edwina wasn't pretty: she was very when young. She

---

22. Arthur Koestler (1905–83), Hungarian-born writer and polymath whose disillusionment with Communism inspired his best work.
23. Widow of Leo d'Erlanger, banker.

nearly married Esmond Rothermere[24] years before Annie Fleming and others did. They remained attracted to each other. I remember going to a house Esmond had in the country with a swimming pool at the bottom, Daylesford (built for Warren Hastings but naturally without the indoor swimming pool). Edwina was there and Esmond was thrilled.

**Friday 28 November**

Slightly startled by a stern formal looking envelope with 'Prime Minister, Urgent, In Confidence' on it. I wondered what I could have done to annoy her. The letter offered me a life peerage and was unexpected as I thought she had given the idea up.

I am delighted because I would like to spend the last few years of my life somewhere round the Palace of Westminster not as a visitor but as of right. I was first there in 1945. I would like to use the Lords and House of Commons Library again and their research facilities, to see old friends and perhaps to take part in a debate or two. I might hear a lot more which could be of value in helping Margaret. I might even be able to help her in the Chamber of the House of Lords but that I don't know.

I compose a letter accepting the offer of the life Barony. Verushka is half pleased saying it won't make any difference to her because she's already Lady Wyatt. I said, 'If I'm allowed to do it you won't be Lady Wyatt any more because I propose to choose the title of Weeford in honour of my family.' They lived there as farmers in their own lands for five or six hundred years and had several houses there. We all came from there, the twenty-eight architects, the sculptors, the painters, the engineers, the inventors, canal builders, the lot. They collected several knighthoods on the way but never a peerage.

I also think how annoyed Honor will be who wrote the vicious article about me in the *Observer* recently; that mildly pleases me.

---

24. 2nd Viscount Rothermere (1898–1978), m 2 (1945–52) Lady Anne O'Neill (1913–81, widow of 3rd Baron O'Neill, née Charteris; she married in 1952 the writer Ian Fleming); m 3 (1966) Mrs Mary Ohstrom, daughter of Kenneth Murchison of Dallas, Texas (Mary Viscountess Rothermere, d 1992).

**Saturday 29 November**

Petronella and I go to stay with the Trevor-Ropers (Lord Dacre and wife) at Peterhouse.[25] The bedrooms are warm when we arrive but the central heating is turned off at night and I got nearly frozen.

Xandra's son Howard-Johnston is staying with his wife Angela Huth[26] and their small daughter, five and a half, called Eugenie. I haven't seen Angela for a year or so when she was at one of the lunches given by the Quintons at Trinity, Oxford. Her first play came off abruptly because Celia Johnson died on the opening night and Sir Ralph Richardson died shortly after. She's now got another one going, put on by a man called Toby Rowlands and I must speak to Laurence Fitch about him for my play.

I mention to her the dinner they gave us when she was married to Quentin Crewe twenty-five years ago. She said, 'Yes it was a christening present from Clement Freud[27] for our son. He said he would provide all the wine and food and cook it all as a present.' I remember that he didn't come upstairs at all, refusing to see the guests. She said, 'Yes but the most extraordinary thing was the next day he came round and gave us a bill for all the wine, the food and his cooking. It would have been cheaper to take everybody at the dinner party to the Mirabelle.' She said she never much cared for him after that.

I think she has been knocked about a bit by life but seems OK now with a dullish husband but quite good looking who is a Byzantine scholar, lecturer and a Fellow of Corpus Christi, Oxford.

We had to wear dinner jackets. The dinner party assembled. Academically there was a fair amount of brain power but a general absence of liveliness.

**Sunday 30 November**

At breakfast we talked about Jesus Christ. Hugh said he thought there was no proof that he existed.

He spoke about how he goes into chapel as Master of Peterhouse. 'I perform my proper duties outwardly and go through the rituals.'

---

25. Lord Dacre was Master of Peterhouse, Cambridge, 1980–7; Lady Alexandra Dacre (d 1997), daughter of Earl Haig, m 1 (1941–54) Rear Admiral Clarence Dinsmore Howard-Johnston.
26. Writer and journalist, m 1 (1961–70) Quentin Crewe, m 2 Dr James Howard-Johnston.
27. Liberal MP (1973–87), journalist and broadcaster, food writer; knight 1987.

'Yes,' I said, 'but where is your heart?' He says he doesn't believe in God, only performs conventionally.

Hugh took us round the college. He's sad to be going. His seven years are up in June. He has quarrelled with the Fellows throughout and made a lot of changes. He took us into the library which he has had entirely reconstructed and got it back from an archaeological society; it is now the largest undergraduate library in Cambridge where before they had only a tiny room. It is very handsome.

Hugh said, 'Did I tell you about the encyclical letter? The leader of the caucus against me wrote to all the Fellows about the choice of my successor, about which I'm supposed to know nothing but I have my spies. He said in his letter, "I was largely instrumental in getting the present Master elected. For this I make no apology. But he has not made us happy. We've had a bumpy ride during the last six years. Now we need somebody who will make us happy."' Hugh says they're a dismal lot and he doesn't think anybody could make them happy.

We were a few minutes late getting to Victor. Marcus Sieff[28] had been staying the night with Lily. He doesn't look very well. He'd brought a copy of his book to be published in January or February. I said, 'Is there lots of sex in it? You've had a lusty love life.' He said, 'No.' 'Then the book won't sell. You're a foolish fellow.' Lily said he'd had a passionate love affair with her before his divorce and just refers to it as a pleasant weekend.

Victor said, 'Please don't start him off on the buy British campaign. He's a frightful bore about it.' Marcus looked mortified. I said, 'Where do your clothes come from?' He said, 'My coat comes from Marks and Spencer's and my trousers and my shoes and my tie.' I said, 'I'm sure your trousers and coat which are both quite smart were specially made for you.' He said, 'Oh no, they're off the peg.' So Victor said, 'Yes. All the M & S suits and coats are made to fit Marcus.'

Victor says he has been badly harassed during the week with twenty reporters squatting outside his house in St James'.

I told him he was quite right to say nothing and should go on saying nothing.

He referred several times to 'that shit Wright' whom obviously he'd been helping with money and he did introduce him to Chapman Pincher. Victor kept saying he was subject to the Official Secrets Act

---

28. Chairman, Marks and Spencer, 1972–84; life peer 1980; the book was his autobiography, *Don't Ask the Price.*

and very conscious of it which I think is true. It is not Victor's fault if Wright gave a lot of secrets to Pincher which he shouldn't have done and that Pincher published them and the government let them pass, although they had a copy of the book two weeks before.

He thought that poor Armstrong had been making a bit of an ass of himself. I said, 'Not at all. You only read the snippets in the newspapers. If you saw the whole thing and were there you wouldn't be influenced by the selected bits in the newspapers trying to send him up and, by inference, Mrs Thatcher.'

Victor said, 'What about his phrase "economical with the truth"?'[29] I said, 'Perfectly sound.' 'You mean he was lying?' 'Not at all,' I said. 'To be economical with the truth means that you don't give any facts which are not necessary.' 'Oh that's very good. I don't know why nobody's thought of that before. Very well put,' said Victor, a high compliment from him.

When I spoke to Margaret in the evening, she had been at Dulwich all day but she said she'd been rung up every half an hour.

I told her that Hugh Trevor-Roper thought she was absolutely right to pursue the [*Spycatcher*] case, win or lose. She said, 'Why doesn't he say so publicly? That would be a great help.' So when I wrote to him the next morning I told him that he ought to say something publicly.

Thanked Margaret verbally for the life peerage. She said, 'I thought it wouldn't do you any harm now,' meaning that earlier when it had once been discussed she was afraid that it might have been not a good idea in relation to my *Sunday Mirror* articles.[30]

I told her that neither Trevor-Roper nor Victor thought that Roger Hollis had been a Russian agent. She said nor did she. She said, 'It's awful for his family, being persecuted after all this time and having his reputation attacked in this cruel way.'

---

29. Sir Robert Armstrong used the phrase when cross-examined in the Australian court.
30. WW moved to Murdoch's newspapers in 1983.

**Monday 1 December**

To Katie [Macmillan] for dinner. Arrived at eight, said she had booked a table at Memories of China for a quarter to nine so we might well have spent half an hour extra doing some work. I had already drunk some champagne thinking I might not get any. We then had a bottle of pink champagne and David her son came in to join us.

Katie is on this new apparatus which automatically discharges your waste matter into a bag. She looked better because she doesn't take any cortisone now. David said his grandfather Harold Macmillan missed her because he liked quarrelling with her.

We then went to Memories of China which is one third owned by her son Adam, the best investment he ever made. Another third was owned by Billy McLean[1] and it seems that Adam may be able to buy that, and the third third is owned by the Chinese who started it up and is the chef.

The food is expensive but very good and I ate too much. I think the bill was about £120. But Katie suddenly felt ill and went and left a cheque for David to fill in but I noticed he paid with his credit card.

Katie is probably going to take the smaller of the two adjacent houses Verushka wants to hire in Italy. Her daughter Rachel, who married a guitar player after living with a hairdresser and who is now divorced, is coming too. It might be quite amusing with various bits of the young Macmillans.

I still feel, 'Oh my God some fifteen to twenty thousand pounds to be spent. What about my little stock of money I'm trying to build up for Verushka to live on when I am dead?'

Poor Katie hardly ate anything before she had to dash off. We went back to her flat briefly and I shouted out to her, 'Katie I love you. I hope you're all right,' but I got no reply and David said he thought she was in the lavatory. Poor soul.

---

1. He had just died; see 19 November 1986.

**Tuesday 2 December**

Go to see Brian Leaver, property agent consultant who is advising Jack Knight on the sale of the Royal Windsor Racecourse. They want £4 million for it though it's only making a total profit of £100,000. They talk about the development potential it might have.

I am keen on it because I want to have a racecourse in which the Tote can whittle down the number of bookmakers; they have an average of fifty-eight a race day at Windsor. If we could do that we could probably multiply the Tote take on course at least five to six times. It might give us a profit of £200,000–£250,000 from the Tote alone. It would be a demonstration to all racecourses [that] if you whittle down the bookmakers you get much more from the Tote as we pay a percentage of the turnover, not the profits, to the racecourses.

**Wednesday 3 December**

The Atlantic Richfield dinner much less boring than in previous years.

The tedious Bob Anderson, now handing over as Chairman of Atlantic Richfield to another tedious-looking man, refrained from making his usual long speech. He said only a few words and then handed over to Henry Kissinger. He was quite good apart from his usual reference to saving the world, a bit like Cicero who could never make a speech without reminding the Senate that he had saved the Roman republic.

Ted Heath made for him a passable speech.

In thanking the organizers and the hosts of the dinner he remarked that 'when the *Observer* dinner began ten years ago it was given at Lincoln's Inn, the Americans believing that the English are committed to high thinking and low living. They discovered their mistake and moved to Claridge's so that the English could indulge what they really like namely high living and low thinking,' adding hastily, 'not that thinking is absent in this assembly.'

Arnold was there. He had an earnest talk with Michael Heseltine who was being equivocal about Nimrod. Afterwards we went into the front part of the hotel and sat down and talked for about half an hour. Arnold was saying how awful the hostility towards him is. Repeating what he had said in the morning about handing over to some whizz kid, he nearly found one tonight, John Harvey-Jones, head of ICI.

I said, 'But he's older than you.' 'Yes, but he might do it better.' I said, 'Do stop talking in such a defeatist way. No one would do it better than you.'

He said, 'All the electronics firms in Japan particularly are doing much worse than we are because there's a downturn internationally in electronics at the moment.' 'Why doesn't your Tim Bell of Saatchi and Saatchi publicize this?' 'He's only just beginning to do this but it takes a lot to turn back all the stuff that has been written against us.' And he complained again that they said he had this huge mountain of cash (£1,600 million) and did nothing with it but whenever he tried to buy something like Plessey he was prevented by the government from doing so.

We then walked to Grosvenor Square and he told me he put in a bid at Sotheby's for some old cigars for me. We stood talking on the steps outside his flat. Suddenly he put his arms round me and said, 'I value your sympathy very much.' I said, 'Arnold I love you and I don't like you to be upset and to retire hurt.'

He said Sara Morrison's dog had died. That was another tragedy.

**Thursday 4 December**

Dinner with Elizabeth Jane Howard.[2]

She is intense and moves with restless nervousness. I tell her she looks more beautiful than ever and she calls it a lovely start to the evening.

Peter Parker[3] and his wife were there. So were Anthony Hobson and his wife whom I have not seen for years. When we were in Wiltshire they were about an hour's drive away and we used to meet often. He was a senior partner in Sotheby's and writes learned books about such subjects as the Renaissance library. He says Hugh Thomas is wrong about the reading room and the new library at the British Museum.[4] The system is so bad you have to wait for days to get a book. People will still be able to use the Round Room.

He recalls that I saved Regent's Park Terraces with John Betjeman. I am delighted that someone should remember what we did. John Summerson[5] was in on it too: I did a television programme on *Panorama* and some other broadcasts.

---

2. Novelist, married to Kingsley Amis, 1965–83.
3. Chairman British Rail Board, 1976–83; m (1951) Gillian, née Rowe-Dutton; knight 1978.
4. Lord Thomas and others were campaigning against the closure of the old reading room.
5. Architectural historian (1904–92).

We talked about what kind of a memorial service we would like. Peter Parker was all for bits of Mozart and a lot of high fangled stuff like that. Anthony Hobson said he wanted among the hymns the one by George Herbert which includes the item about the 'servant with this clause'. To everyone's surprise I knew it better even than Anthony and sang in my unmusical voice the whole of the verse, irritating Verushka: 'A servant with this clause / Makes drudgery divine; / Who sweeps a room as for Thy laws / Makes this and th' action fine'.

I also wanted Macaulay's 'Battle of Naseby' as well with those marvellous lines beginning: 'Oh, wherefore come ye forth in triumph from the north'. And the recessional by Kipling. And if the service hasn't gone on too long already they might finish with 'Land of Hope and Glory', the whole damn lot.

And perhaps somebody could read Marvell's poem, 'This coyness lady were no crime, / Had I but world enough and time.'[6] After all it was written by a clergyman, if anyone were to protest.

**Sunday 7 December**

Asked Victor if he was satisfied with Margaret's statement in the House in which she said there was no evidence against Lord Rothschild and her interview on television yesterday when she said that was clearance that Lord Rothschild never was a Soviet agent. He said, 'Margaret has made me very happy.'

I tackled her about Nimrod: 'I fear there are some prejudiced people in the Defence Ministry afraid to admit their mistakes and that Nimrod was better than Boeing.' She said, 'This is an expert matter and I can only go on advice. I can't make the decision by myself.' I said, 'But I think that the experts themselves are prejudiced and I am told the Boeing wouldn't be ready for three years anyway. Why do we have to make a decision so immediately? It's gone on for years already.'

I told her I had written about it in the *News of the World* and after a bit she said, 'I must drop everything I'm doing now and read the *News of the World*. I will read it carefully. But there have been some critical tests and I'm sure you are not right in thinking that the experts would give me wrong advice out of petty pride.' I pressed on a bit and said that Boeing were only spending all this money and offering all these contracts because they want to drive us out of that type of

6. 'Had we but world enough, and time, / This coyness, Lady, were no crime'– Andrew Marvell 1631–78, 'To His Coy Mistress'.

technology and have the world free to themselves. I think she began to take it a little more seriously after I talked to her but what they will decide I don't know.

In the afternoon Hugh Trevor-Roper rang up. He said he'd taken my suggestion which I'd written to him in my letter of thanks for the weekend that he should declare himself in favour of the principle of trying to stop Secret Service people from writing their memoirs and giving away secrets.

He said, 'I have a difficulty though. Is there a can of worms in the court case in Australia which could affect her?' 'Why should it do that?' I asked. 'Well, there's all this business about a plot in the MI5 to get rid of Wilson. She might have had something to do with it.' I said, 'She wasn't Leader until 1975.' 'What about as a backbencher?' I said, 'No of course not. And the most she ever got to was Minister of Education. She was a serious girl. She wouldn't get in a silly game like that.'

**Tuesday 9 December**

Dinner party at Cavendish Avenue. Michael and Anne Tree, Sir Robert and Lady Armstrong, David and Ninette Montagu, Nigel and Thérèse Lawson, Rupert and Anna Murdoch, Petronella, Chips Keswick.

The dinner was good though the veal was a little fatty, having been bought at Harrods because Verushka couldn't get to Sainsbury's because her car broke down. It was stuffed with apricots and tasted well. The first course was a mousseline of salmon with slices of plaice put in the circles. An excellent watercress sauce. The pudding was difficult to cut because it was circular with apple in fairly large round chunks. It was very good but it nearly went on the floor several times as people struggled to cut it.

A very good Grand Cru Chablis. There was white and pink champagne plus a 1953 Perrier-Jouët before dinner. Two magnums of first class Brane-Cantenac 1964 much admired by those who know anything about wine. Why it was so good is that it has been carefully stored in my cellar and not disturbed for at least four years since it was moved from Conock where it had also been stored for ten in the cellars. A different type of Tokay 1963 of the special grape muscatel. It had a little wig on the top of moss and stuff which collects in the estate cellars in the Tokay region.

Mrs Lawson sat on my right.

She asked who I thought might be leader when Mrs Thatcher goes.

I said, 'But she's not going for ages.' She said, 'Oh she may go sooner than you think, you never know,' indicating perhaps a view in her household that it is time she went. She thought Geoffrey Howe would have the best chance of succeeding. I said, 'If it's soon.' She said, 'Maybe it will be.' She dismissed the chances of Douglas Hurd who was once a rising star but somehow seems to have faded.

She said it was not pleasant being next door to No 10. 'With the connecting door?' I asked. She said, 'Exactly. He can be sent for too easily and she can come through at any time.'

When I said to Nigel after dinner that Roy Jenkins had been a very good Chancellor of the Exchequer and his rule was to go home at 6.00 and tell the others they could do what they liked, therefore having time for the broad decisions and leaving the details to the civil servants, he said, 'He was not a good Chancellor. He was really responsible for the inflation which began in 1970 and continued in the years after and it was his fault.'

After dinner I asked Nigel why he hadn't brought taxes down more below the sixty per cent at the top rate. Surely it is now shown that you have collected more total revenue with lower taxes than with the higher taxes. He said, 'I like that argument but it isn't true. More tax would have come from the top one to five per cent in any case because the salaries of the top earners have been put up so enormously. But still let's go on using the argument.'

Lawson said he thought it didn't matter if there was an increase in inflation now. It would remind everybody before the election how serious inflation is and how awful inflation would be if Labour got back. Rupert and I both said we thought that was a terrible mistake. It would not be helpful to the Tories for inflation to rise again before the election and I said it was also a very narrow view of the future.

I also said 'You're in a dreadful position with wages going up at 8.4 per cent or more and inflation only by 3.5 per cent. We're pricing ourselves out of all the markets.' He said, 'Yes but it's very good electorally,' to which I said, 'Yes but that's not the right view to take in the long run for the country.'

I tackled him about Nimrod and said it was madness to buy the American. He said, 'Are you an expert?' I said, 'As much an expert as any member of the Cabinet is,' which he conceded. He said, 'We'll have to be guided by the experts.'

When I was talking about Nimrod to Nigel, Rupert said, 'He has been using the *News of the World* and the *Times* for propaganda for

Nimrod against the American Boeing.' He sounded irritated. When he left the house he handed us tomorrow's *Times* which had a leading article in which the *Times* has changed its tune and says we should now buy the AWACS system from Boeing. Arnold says it must have been Rupert's doing which it certainly was, as he made them change tack in the few days he has been here. Arnold says Rupert is a director and has a lot of shares in United Technology which makes things for Boeing and AWACS.

Robert looked entirely well after his ordeal in Australia.

He said to Rupert that his sudden buying of newspapers in Australia, including his father's old one, had taken Robert right off the front pages there.

Rupert found Robert much more impressive than Nigel Lawson, which is probably a bad judgement because Nigel Lawson is extremely good.

Nigel thinks the economy is going well and will certainly hold out until after the election, which he regards now as a paramount consideration, and adjustments can be made afterwards. Owing to our curious system of the Prime Minister being able to choose the date of an election, politicians always take a short view. Perhaps they would even if there were fixed terms of four or five years as they approach the end of a term. I said, 'There is no chance whatever of your losing,' and repeated what I had said to John Wakeham about his perhaps being surprised by getting a larger majority than he has got now.

Anna was saying that basically Rupert is very simple and puritanical. I said, 'I know that.' 'He is also very impatient and in some ways cold and remote. That's why I won't show him my books because he would either make some dismissive and cursory comment or not take it in because he doesn't read very much, or with any patience.'

I reminded her how I had asked her sons Jamie and Lachlan what it felt like to be the sons of Rupert when boys at school made comments about his activities not always politely reported in the press. They had explained at considerable length. Rupert was amazed. He had no idea that his sons felt like that and had never had a conversation with them about it.

Anna said she had said to him the other day he must tell the boys about sex. He said, 'Why?' 'Well they've got to know about it. They're in their puberty.' Anna said to him later on that day, 'Did you tell them about sex?' He said, 'Yes. I told them in the lift going down,' so she said he couldn't have told them anything. I said, 'No. I know why.

Because he believes that they know more about it than he does already. He once told me how Jamie had said to Rupert about a girl, "Do you think she'd give you a good blow job?"!'

Robert told me that he like Lawson had to go back and work on boxes late into the night when he left us. I said, 'My goodness. I don't know why you do all that work. I never would.' He said, 'Judging from your book I think you never have.' I thought that was a bit rough. I may give the appearance of being casual and indolent but I think I can truly say I am not entirely.

**Wednesday 10 December**

Billie de la Warr[7] told me that he gets £90 a day when he attends the House of Lords because he has a flat in London. It seems a bit of a racket because he would have one anyway as well as having his farm in Sussex.

**Thursday 11 December**

Rupert rang. Furious at Mrs Thatcher because the IBA had awarded a big satellite contract to Granada and Anglia. He said his wasn't the best entry but he thought it was second best: why does she let her enemies in Granada, with their very left-wing staff as on *World in Action*, get a satellite licence?

I said I didn't know. 'It was done by the IBA.' 'Yes, but why does she let the IBA be run by people like that?' I said, 'I'm not responsible. You're blowing off at me as the nearest thing you can find to Mrs Thatcher.' He laughed. He is a bit like Arnold. They seem to think they can say things to me they can't to her and hope it will dribble back in some diluted form to her.

The Other Club. Sit next to Roy [Jenkins] nearly opposite Bernard Levin, and also on my right is Jeremy Hutchinson[8] who used to be rather left-wing, a barrister. He now belongs to the SDP and is in the Lords. He was once married to Peggy Ashcroft, a connection of Jacob's through his sister, making Jacob his nephew.

Before dinner Peter Walker [Secretary of State for Energy] was very full of himself about the success of the gas share flotation. He attacked MacGregor for nearly surrendering in the coal strike which he said he had been arranging to do secretly with the union leaders and when

7. 10th Earl de la Warr.
8. Life peer 1978.

he, Peter Walker, got to hear of it he managed to stop it, threatening to sack him. This I am not sure about.

During dinner discussion about Proust. Bernard says he's never got past page seventy. His bibliographer will find that all quotations of Proust in Bernard's writings are from the first seventy pages. He asked me had I managed Proust. I said, 'I've several times tried to read a chapter but got no further.'

Jeremy Hutchinson is amazed saying, 'It's absolutely marvellous stuff. How can you say that? And you like Wagner?' and he goes on and on. Roy says, 'I've read Proust three times in English and once in French' which I find very revealing about Roy because Proust was the arch snob and student of social manners. Jeremy says he's only read it twice but both times in English. William Heseltine, the Queen's Secretary, sitting next to Bernard looks bemused by the conversation but laughs a fair amount.

It's a very full house. Willie Whitelaw is there, and the Duke of Buccleuch in his wheelchair; he has to be carried up the steps afterwards on the way out. I hadn't seen him for some time. A pleasant man who ruined his life in a hunting accident. Madness to go hunting and skiing. Whatever is the point of it? It's some kind of a demonstration of virility but too often ends it all together.

Jeremy Hutchinson said that Victor hadn't been to The Other Club for twenty years and when they wanted to make Jacob a member they don't have fathers and sons so they asked him to resign. He was furious and two people had to go and see him, including I think Jock Colville, to persuade him to give it up and not be a dog in the manger but he is so opposed to Jacob, his son, that he didn't want to.

**Sunday 14 December**

Bowden. Arnold depressed. Declares he will leave GEC to someone else to run and live in Switzerland where he is only twenty minutes away from the Milan opera and live on his money. That is if he doesn't get the Nimrod contract. I tell him not to be silly.

Arnold feels he's entitled to see the examination results, as it were, of the tests from the Ministry of Defence experts and scientists. He complains still that they've been rigged against GEC and that they kept altering the specifications because they were determined not to have the GEC product and to say there was something wrong with it. 'If it was so bad ten months ago, why was I urged to put our own money into it to try and bring it to fruition and iron out the faults? What are these faults? George Younger[9] has said that both systems work.'

He says he is seeing Mrs Thatcher on Tuesday. After lunch we run over what he is going to say. He has sheets and sheets of paper. I said, 'How long is the interview?' He says, 'Twenty minutes.' I said, 'Throw all that stuff away. You won't even begin on that in twenty minutes. There is no point in having an argument with her in which she is forced to defend her officials as all governments do. You've got to ask to see the evaluations of the Nimrod and ask to be allowed to comment on them and say whether or not they can be put right within a reasonable time. You need more time don't you?' 'Yes.'

Arnold and I walked around the gardens and the hot houses. In one of them he suddenly said, 'Do you think Verushka would like an azalea?' I said, 'Yes, certainly.' It was an unwonted piece of generosity from Arnold because he likes to sell all his plants and flowers. So I walked around the rest of the garden carrying a pink and white azalea but not a very large one.

I looked again at the lovely old Bath column and the eagle on top which I had given Arnold when I had to leave Conock. He also pointed out again in front of the garage at the side of the house the great stone balls which I had got from the Knightsbridge barracks built by Thomas Henry Wyatt when they demolished it. They had been on one of the entrance gates.

There was a lovely sky. James Wyatt put Bowden in a marvellous position but successors have built up an embankment and put some balustrades in front of the house which prevents the house being seen as it should be from a distance. 'Do you think I should remove that embankment and balustrade?' asked Arnold. 'Yes,' I said.

**Monday 15 December**

Asked her if she'd seen the Trevor-Roper piece in the *Independent* in which he said she was right to go on with the case in Australia. She said, 'Yes, but he spoilt it at the end because like all these academics they think they have to genuflect to the *Guardian* trend of thinking.'

'I had lunch with Arnold yesterday in Wiltshire.' I paused. 'And he was in a great state,' she said. She felt it was not helpful for all this shouting to take place which is going on in the newspapers this morning and yesterday and with Prior on the wireless and I commented that I

9. Secretary of State for Defence, 1986–9.

suppose they think they'd better do the shouting now, before it's too late. I said, 'Arnold feels that he ought to be allowed to see the evaluation made about Nimrod and be able to answer or deal with the points concerned if he can. If he finds that the Boeing thing is really superior he'll say nothing more about it.'

This should put her in a better frame of mind for seeing Arnold on Tuesday.

I told her that Arnold would abandon GEC and go and live in Switzerland if he didn't get Nimrod and get somebody else to manage it. She said, 'That would be a disaster. No one else can run it like Arnold and he would be wrecking GEC by leaving it at this stage. I hope he won't do anything so silly.'

We skated round the question of whether the decision had been made yet but I think it possibly has. She talked rather as though it had been.

When I told Arnold that Rupert had been irritated that I was doing propaganda for GEC and Nimrod he said, 'Don't write any more in favour of it because it's a very important part of your income' (my working for Rupert).

I said, 'I'm not in the least bit concerned about that. I write exactly what I think and have never done anything different. And I shall continue to do so.' Though I might not write much more about this Nimrod business. I've given it a fair bang. And she has put her case very reasonably to me. Probably if I were Prime Minister I would take the same view even though I would prefer to buy British and support British technology.

**Tuesday 16 December**

In the morning, Arnold sounding like a wounded animal, quite bewildered. He says he is going to take out a writ against the *Daily Mail* for the untrue things about GEC mistakes and so forth which have occurred.

I go over with him again the line he should take with Mrs Thatcher when he sees her at a quarter to six this evening. He is taking an expert scientist man from GEC with him. I warn him again not to attack the integrity of the officials: she says they are scientists, not RAF people, who have been doing the evaluation though no doubt helped by the RAF officers.

He's got something going with the French. There's going to be a test which he's had to pay for, £100,000, with the RAF flying the

Nimrod over France on 17th December. He didn't want to pay the money himself to begin with because it's three times the actual cost but he thinks it a good idea. I said, 'If you can get the French to buy it that would be one in the eye for the British government.' He said, 'I also might get the Australians.'

He's hoping for some delay while he gets two so-called independent assessors he's appointed, who are genuine scientists, to look at the whole GEC Nimrod project.

[Later] Glad to hear that Mrs T has been very kind to Arnold though he said she did nothing but listen, likewise George Younger, when he went to see her at a quarter to six and stayed about three-quarters of an hour. Then she had to go and left him with George Younger. Clearly GEC is doomed as far as Nimrod is concerned. She did go out of her way in the House though to say she had every confidence in GEC and about the huge government contracts they had for defence.

Popped into the American Embassy for their Christmas party.

On the way out bumped into Michael Heseltine, more friendly than usual after my attacks on him. He thought the government had probably made the right decision over Nimrod and he had been Minister of Defence when a lot of the work on it was going on.

Back to our dinner.

Mrs Benson[10] is fairly pretty and agreeable. When she came in she was standing with Mrs Metcalfe, also a pretty American. Flavio had put into the ice vase a bottle of pink champagne and taken off the wire, which was foolish of him. Suddenly as they neared the pink champagne which they wanted to drink and I was going to open, the bottle exploded, the cork shot up into the air and the liquid ejaculated. I said, 'On seeing such beauty the bottle could not contain itself and exploded. This sometimes happens in real life.' They thought it very funny.

After the ladies had left Peter Rawlinson talked about the spy trial in Australia. He said that the BBC had asked him to go on their breakfast television and do a piece they have discussing the day's papers which would be full of the spy trial in Australia. He said yes he would come. They then said to him, 'What sort of things will you say?'

He said, 'I'm going to talk about the dishonourable Mr Wright and

10. Wife of Charles Benson, racing journalist.

his disgraceful behaviour and emphasize that the government were absolutely right to bring the case whether they lost it or not.'

At which point the BBC said they didn't think there was any point him coming as they wanted an attack on the government generally. He said, 'I'm coming now because you've asked me.'

When he got there they put him in a corner and took a short two minute interview in which he did express his views but that was all. This is absolutely typical of the bias of the BBC against the government. Duke Hussey has done absolutely nothing so far to improve the situation.

Peter said he gave immunity to Blunt[11] and the Queen knew for four years that this man was a spy. It was essential to keep him in his position at Buckingham Palace looking after the Queen's pictures otherwise Russia would have realized that his cover had been blown. What he told them was immensely valuable.

It was nice of Peter not to want to criticize the Attorney General on TV as he would dearly like to have the job of Lord Chancellor which Michael Havers, an inferior person and very indiscreet, will get because of his loyalty to Mrs T during the Falklands and in general.

Rocco Forte and his wife had arrived to dinner thirty-five minutes late as usual.

**Wednesday 17 December**

To lunch with Mr Saunders the man who runs the Guinness combine. Lunch alone with him. Ronnie Grierson had told him, before the trouble broke about whether shares had been bought irregularly during the bid for Distillers,[12] when he was concerned about the image of Guinness and making of friends for Guinness (apart from their advertisements for their products) and not looking too much like

---

11. The spy Sir Anthony Blunt was Surveyor of the Queen's Pictures.
12. The Distillers' Company turned to Guinness for support when threatened by a takeover bid from the Argyll supermarket group in 1985. WW summarizes subsequent events. Ernest Saunders, Sir Jack Lyons and four others were charged with various offences in 1987 but the first Guinness trial did not open until February 1990. In the end Saunders was found guilty of twelve offences, Lyons of four. In December 1996 the European Court of Human Rights ruled that Saunders' trial had beeen unfair because of the use of evidence given before the inspectors without the right of silence.

technocrats, that he should see me. Now this trouble had blown up Ronnie said it was even more important.

At lunch he told me about the Board of Trade investigation which had been done under the old Companies Act, not under any new legislation, as Michael Howard, the ambitious Minister at the Department of Industry, was pretending. He is deeply worried because Paul Channon is a member of the Guinness family and is the Secretary for Industry and feels that he has to be seen leaning over backwards against Guinness. He said he'd done that already in referring the bid to the Monopolies Commission which was quite unnecessary (that was the bid for Distillers). Now Paul had nothing to do with the investigation but was leaving it to Michael Howard, a Junior Minister.

He said it was stirred up by a Mr Gulliver[13] of Argyll who was bitter at losing the bid battle.

Gulliver had dug around and had been obviously supplying the Board of Trade with information about a concert party in which bids had been engineered in co-operation with other people; and there was the position about a distributor of Guinness products in America who, as I understand it (this was not said to me by Saunders), had been promised that his franchise to distribute would continue if he helped them with the bid; and the distributor had bought just over the five per cent permitted amount of shares without reporting them to the Stock Exchange. Saunders thought it was like Hitler, the power the Board of Trade inspectors have. I said, 'But it's the same for everybody.'

He had written to the Prime Minister saying that he was afraid of the damage being done to Guinness and he didn't think the investigation was being conducted fairly. I said, 'I'm not sure that was wise. What did she reply?' He said, 'She didn't reply.' He just got a brush-off letter from a private secretary. I said, 'That is exactly what I would expect. In a quasi-judicial or judicial matter she will take no part whatever because she herself is a barrister and would never put herself in the position of being seen to influence a procedure being applied under the law.'

He said their results which came out last week were very good. I asked him whether the trouble, which I gather mainly came from this man Boesky who has been giving evidence against everybody in return for not being prosecuted in America, was harming the current business.

13. James Gulliver, chairman, Argyll Group, 1977–88.

He said, 'It's too early to tell but it's probably not doing it any good.' What was my advice?

I thought for a long time. I expect that Ronnie Grierson told him that I knew Margaret though I didn't ask that because I don't want her involved in it.

I said I might consider talking to Robert Armstrong about it on the grounds that I was a bit worried that owing to Paul Channon being the Minister at the head of the Department they might perhaps not be examining the case as fairly and as objectively as they ordinarily would but I would brood upon the matter. He was very grateful.

It was obvious from what he said to me that there had been at least minor irregularities in the way the shares had been bought, building up the position of Guinness to take over.

He said, 'All the City establishment is now terrified.' What they really want in his view is a damning report against Guinness and possibly followed by prosecution against some people in Guinness, leaving all questions of behaviour in the City over the matter untouched.

I told him that my main concern was that justice should be done and that if I felt the situation was veering towards injustice, as apparently it is, I will try to make sure he gets a fair hearing, particularly as to damage a great company like Guinness with their huge exports would be folly if it were done unfairly.

Most of the time at lunch I was trying to decide whether I liked Mr Saunders or not. He is not immediately attractive and I dare say a tough customer. I told him, politicians are naïve about the jungle of commerce and would not believe that people get up to the dirty tricks they do, though if you ask them about how they were diddled out of an office or an election or a post they would be full of the dirty tricks of other politicians.

There was no doubt that Mr Saunders is badly rattled. I felt like any port in a storm. It is a curious situation. The lunch was quite good, dressed brown crab meat and wild duck cooked quite well. I had a glass of white wine and a glass of red, neither anything to write home about but I did get a decent Davidoff cigar.

It was clear from Ernest Saunders that there might have been one or two things that were not quite right in the Guinness bid but I said if it is only trivial things, the authorities wouldn't necessarily have to take any action of a prosecution kind, [they'd] just say it wasn't quite right. But I do not know to what extent he was telling me the truth.

**Thursday 18 December**

Pamela Digby, then Churchill, then Harriman,[14] talked rubbish at Clarissa's lunch. Moving in democratic circles, naturally she has a screwy view of Reagan as stupid and incompetent and now finished. She expects that his illness will mark his retirement to which I replied, 'Why would he go when he's down? He's not the sort of person who'd want to give up when it seems as though he had been forced to do so.'

Arnold Goodman says that Wilson told him four months before he resigned as Prime Minister that he was going to do so because he wanted it made clear to somebody who was credible, [so] that when he did resign (and he gave Arnold the date) nobody would be able to say there was some fearful personal crisis or scandal coming out. Arnold thinks he went because he knew he had an illness coming on. He didn't believe what I thought, namely that he'd been through the dreary round of TUC negotiations again and again and had got fed up with it and he had nothing new to say in politics.

Arnold W rings 11.00 pm. Sounds sad but less depressed than I thought he would be.[15] I tell him opinions are all matters of fashion and I detect there's a move back in his favour but he must pump out the propaganda saying what the achievements of GEC have been. He thanked me for all my support and I said, 'I fear that it was not much good.' to which he answered, 'But at least I know who my friends are and to be supported by them is a big comfort.'

**Sunday 21 December**

At last my Bordeaux piece appears on the front page of the review section in the *Sunday Times*. Truncated but I'm glad to see it.

Margaret ebullient. She is a kind woman. Before I could say anything else she asked me, 'How is Arnold?'

She wondered whether the Gallup poll putting her eight and a half points ahead of Labour which came out on Thursday wasn't a freak. I said, 'It may be slightly freakish but the trend must be right. As I have told you all along, once the British public has got it into their

---

14. She married 1 (1939–46) Randolph Churchill, 2 (1960–71) the American producer Leland Hayward, 3 (1971) the American Democrat statesman Averell Harriman (d 1986); she was US Ambassador to France from 1994 until her death in 1996.
15. It was officially announced that the government was dropping GEC's Nimrod spy plane in favour of the American AWACS system.

heads that Kinnock really does mean to abandon our nuclear defences and get rid of the American nuclear defences they will never wear it.'[16]

She said, 'Its a nice Christmas present, anyway.' I wished her a happy Christmas in case I didn't speak to her again. She said, 'You must wish Arnold a happy Christmas from me and tell him how I feel towards him.'

When I rang Arnold afterwards he was pleased but then started talking about all the people making attacks on him including Peter Levene, the defence procurement man, apparently leaking things to the *Sunday Times*, claiming the Foxhunter [radar] system was no good and all the rest of it.

I said to Arnold, 'Why don't you send her a copy of the letter you had from the Admiral saying how marvellous your new torpedo is and the tremendously high rate of success it has?' He said, 'I can't do that it's marked private and confidential,' so I started laughing. 'Do you really think you can't send something as private and confidential to the Prime Minister? Send her a copy with a letter wishing her a happy Christmas and say she might be interested to see the enclosed from Admiral whatever his name is, which shows that GEC has at least one satisfied customer.' He said he would ask the Admiral's permission.

Great gala at the Coliseum in honour of Lord Goodman. He is retiring as Chairman of the English National Opera though I think he becomes the President.

Apparently John Mortimer had prepared the occasion. He had Leo McKern, who acted Rumpole in the television series, sitting at the side of the stage making ridiculous speeches, 'Ladies and gentlemen of the jury, my client is a Mr X.' This was meant to be funny, referring to Lord Goodman.[17] He then proceeded to try to tell his life, interrupted by various performances on the stage. The words were poor. The music to me was mostly terrible stuff, Verdi and so on, and there was a bit of ballet, I thought badly done, from *Swan Lake*. There was not much amusing in it though at the beginning of the second half they did the barrister piece from *Iolanthe* by Gilbert and Sullivan.

The whole thing finished with a ridiculous pantomime by John Mortimer who is an infantile leftie. The pantomime had such characters

16. Labour had launched its non-nuclear defence policy on 10 December.
17. The reference was to the first time Arnold Goodman came to prominence: as the unnamed negotiator of a strike settlement for the Wilson government he was called 'Mr X' in the press.

as Poseidon Nuclear Weapon and Trident Nuclear Missile represented on the stage. The Arts Council or the English National Opera were seen being denuded of subsidy by the need to keep up these highly expensive nuclear weapons which we were to infer were unnecessary. It all turned out well in the end: Cinderella got her slipper with subsidy on it and so apparently it was OK.

I managed to get to sleep several times but not enough.

**Monday 22 December**

David Somerset enthusiastic about my article on Latour and Bordeaux in the *Sunday Times*. 'One in the eye for Broadbent.[18] Particularly when instead of using those fancy wine words to describe the 1953 Margaux you simply said, "Bloody marvellous".'

**Tuesday 23 December**

Last night a little group of children came singing carols at the door. I went out and among them was a charming looking African origin boy. I asked them whether they were collecting for a charity or for their own Christmas presents. Honestly they answered that it was for their own Christmas presents. 'Good,' I said, 'I would have given you a pound if you had been collecting for one-legged people starving in South America, but for your honesty I will give you two pounds.' I hope they will remember that as an example of honesty being the best policy.

**Wednesday 24 December**

Lunch at the Montagus' new house. It is three rolled into one at the end of a mews. Much money has been spent on it by the previous owners and themselves. The effect was open plan from top to bottom which I found disagreeable. You can be overheard talking at the top of the house by those at the bottom of the house, there was no sense of privacy or intimacy. But for its kind it was well done with some nice pictures and furniture.

John Freeman was there. He is over seventy. He has a child of about sixteen months who presumably will hardly get to know him before he dies. His wife is very plain, Jude. She was Catherine Freeman's social secretary when John was Ambassador in America.

---

18. Michael Broadbent, author of the magisterial *The Great Vintage Wine Book* (1980).

It is his fourth wife. John is now a professor at the University of California in one of the outposts.[19]

John said that when Ninette told him we were coming, did he know us, he said, 'I've known Woodrow for nearly fifty years,' which is true. I said to John, 'I have known all your wives and you have known all of mine.'

We talked a little about Tom Driberg. John thinks from some of the observations he made to John he was definitely a Russian agent and almost certainly was then turned by the British, so must have worked for both sides. He said a significant moment in his life was when he was going bankrupt; he got £50,000 from somewhere which was never explained. I said, 'Do you think Wilson made him a peer to improve his cover story as an agent for the British to lull the suspicions of the Russians?' John laughed, 'There's no knowing why Wilson made the peers he did.'

John has cancer. They will know in a month or so whether he has been cured. He looks gaunt.

Before lunch Christopher Chataway was there for a drink. He had done television with us thirty years or so ago. He then went to be an executive with the Orion Bank where David was Chairman for some time. I have never thought him of much account even though he did run a mile under four minutes when it was unusual so to do.

**Thursday 25 December**

Petronella and I paid our annual visit to the Grosvenor Chapel where John Wilkes is buried. We stayed longer than last year. There was a different clergyman. I put £5 in the collection, surprising myself.

**Friday 26 December**

Kempton Park for the King George VI steeplechase. Sitting next to the Queen Mother watching the racing she says, 'The coming year – will it be all right?' Knowing what she meant, I said, 'Yes. It will be quite all right.'

She was referring to who would win the election, of course. She is much more pro Conservative than the Queen or the Prince of Wales.

---

19. At Davis; Freeman was a Labour MP with WW (1945–50); editor, *New Statesman*, 1961–5; British High Commissioner in India, 1965–8; Ambassador to the US, 1969–71; chairman, London Weekend Television, 1971–84; m 3 (1962–76) Catherine Wheeler, née Dove, m 4 (1976) Judith, née Mitchell.

Queen Elizabeth the Queen Mother asked Verushka how she had met me. She told her, saying she had known me since about 1956 when her husband was still alive though we hadn't seen each other for a few years until after her husband died and Moorea had gone. Then we met again and Verushka said she thought I was very funny. Queen Elizabeth said, 'Yes, isn't he?'

She had been very surprised to see me there on Boxing Day. I told her, apart from the hope of seeing her, I had come because we had put the minimum stake up to £2 in the cheap rings everywhere including Kempton on Boxing Day and thereafter. Complaints and angry shouts from customers had been expected so I had promised to go to Kempton to deal with them. There were no complaints, nobody minded except for one person who said, 'Never mind dear, it's only for Bank Holidays you know,' which it isn't.

I told her I was feeling very ill and couldn't talk sense to her. I had eaten too much last night and drunk too much for two days running and was not functioning properly. 'However,' I said, 'I'm feeling better now under your radiance. You're like a sun lamp.' That pleased her. I promised to let her have *The Piccadilly Murder* and I will also send her *The Poisoned Chocolates Case*.[20]

She likes thrillers of the Agatha Christie kind. I say, 'Anthony Berkeley, author of the one I've just lent to you, also writes very genteel murder stories without people being mutilated and without excessive violence.' 'Genteel. What a good word for it!' she said and laughed.

**Monday 29 December**

She rang back after her hairdresser had finished in the morning.

Asked her about the Green Paper on union reforms. Rapidly ran over the heads on which she must act. She said David Young was away (Secretary for Employment). Would I please send her a note quickly about the points I thought must be covered.

Told her that I had seen Saunders of Guinness and he was concerned they might not get a fair deal because of the British penchant for leaning over backwards to show fairness, Paul Channon being very much involved as a member of the Guinness family. She said, 'I don't think the Board of Trade inspectors are like that.'

20. By Anthony Berkeley, a pseudonym of Anthony Berkeley Cox (1893–1971), also a.k.a. Francis Iles.

I asked her whether I should speak to Michael Howard. She said, 'You can do. He is very good. A very acute Silk.'[21] So I may do that.

I decided to speak to her about Saunders because I don't like to do anything even vaguely behind her back without her knowing in such an important matter.

**Wednesday 31 December**

Day one of being a Lord. Am enjoying it. The *Times* New Year's Honours List has a large headline, 'Life Peerage Goes to Woodrow Wyatt at Head of Varied Field', and I am the first photograph. On the front page they refer to me as the *Times* columnist (there is no mention of *News of the World*).

A telegram from the Duke of Edinburgh: 'Many congratulations on your well deserved honour. Philip.' A letter by hand from Arnold Weinstock, a long one in his own handwriting. Never knew him write such a long one before. Says the main advantage of being a Lord is the free stationery, offset by the disgusting food one is obliged to eat there.

Charming letter by hand from the editor of the *News of the World* saying he is sure it's entirely due to my column, and can they arrange for the logo at the head of my column to carry a picture of me in robes and coronet, photographed by, of course, Lord Lichfield.

The BBC news ring up with what they describe as a very embarrassing call. They have to disinvite me from appearing on the TV *News at One* because they say their space is being cut. It wasn't of course; it is because of the vendetta conducted against me by Alasdair Milne for daring to complain privately and publicly about the lack of impartiality and slipping standards of the BBC.

I point this out in answer to a nice letter I had yesterday from Duke Hussey. I told him I was not asked to any function during the Jubilee celebrations of the BBC though Richard Dimbleby and I were the founder members of *Panorama*; that a few months back I was asked to take part live in celebration shows they put on to talk about being a foreign correspondent for *Panorama* and that ten days or so later I was disinvited as I knew I would be.

I asked Duke Hussey when he has time and inclination to enquire when if ever they are going to take me off the BBC black list. I told him I used to appear quite often on *Any Questions* and after I made

21. Howard was appointed a QC in 1982.

an appearance on *Question Time* Robin Day said it was one of the best ever but I was never asked again. Duke Hussey says he is trying to get across the point about the facts being quite separate from the comment and that BBC correspondents have no right to editorialize, nor do commentators, but it is clearly up-hill work.

Bernard Levin sends a letter round by hand addressed to the Baron Wyatt of Wyatt (in the County of Wyatt). 'Good Lord! You may be a peer of the realm to others but you will always be WW to me. Congratulations. Love, Bernard (Mr).'

James Hanson apparently sitting in Palm Springs has delivered to me by hand a fax copy of a letter to me of congratulations. His envelope and writing paper has his crest and a little coronet on top. Quite elegant. Should I do the same?

Just as we were sitting down to dinner a call from No 10. 'I should have rung you this morning but I was busy with coming up to London because of Macmillan dying.[22] Are you happy? Have lots of people rung you up?' I said, 'Lots,' and told her about Prince Philip sending me a telegram which she thought was lovely. 'Did you hear from Arnold?' 'Yes, he sent a letter round by hand and said the greatest advantage of being in the Lords was the free stationery.' She laughed and said, 'Yes, he would say that. Is he all right? I must see him soon.'

I told her she couldn't have given me a nicer present. 'It's not a present. You have to stir the Lords up and do things.' I felt suitably ticked off. I said, 'By the way, I've sent you the note about what we need to do for further trade union reform.' 'Good,' she said. She also said, 'You'll be sitting on the crossbenches, won't you?' almost as a command. I said 'Yes, I thought it would be better showing some semblance of independence for my articles.' She said, 'Yes, they are very important to us.' I said, 'Of course my vote will always be with you whenever you need it.' 'Yes, I know that.'

So there are my marching orders. We spoke a bit about Macmillan. I said I thought she had been very sweet, almost over-generous. She said, 'No, I don't think it's too generous at a time like this. One can't be anything else.' 'Maurice Macmillan always used to say to me, I hope he dies before they find him out, but you were quite right to speak as you did.' She said she had spoken to Catherine[23] and rung

---

22. The former Prime Minister, Harold Macmillan, had died on 29 December.
23. Macmillan's daughter, married to Julian Amery.

her up. I said, 'That's very sweet of you. Catherine was the one who loved him most and he loved her most.'

I said, 'I'm sure it will be a successful year for you.' She was very chirpy. I knew from the sound of her voice that she'd been having one or two drinks but she never gets drunk. She just gets slightly more lively and trusting. Quite happy and gay. I wish people understood how feminine she is and how kind and feeling, as for instance over Arnold who she knows had this deep blow over Nimrod.

# 1987

**Friday 2 January**

Julian [Amery] called to congratulate me. He asked whether I would like to go to Harold's funeral at Birch Grove [on] Monday. I said I couldn't (I am seeing the Garter King of Arms at 11.00 am that day).

Catherine is very upset. I said Mrs T told me she had rung her and Julian said, 'Yes, I gave her one of her phrases: "one of the great trees of the forest has fallen".' I felt some remorse after speaking to him and started tinkering with my reference to Harold in the coming Sunday's *News of the World* which was not adulatory. It's difficult when you are friends of the family.

When I went to Maurice's funeral, Harold Macmillan said to me, as he sat for once forlorn in a room near the front door, 'Maurice was much cleverer than me' and when I said I couldn't adjudicate on that, he said, 'Well anyway he was much nicer than me. I was always a shit. Maurice wouldn't be one so that's why he didn't get on in politics like me.' I said I wasn't going to adjudicate on that either, though I agreed with him.

**Saturday 3 January**

Another great batch of letters and telegrams. I must sort out some of them and put them into the diary in a heap, the jollier ones.[1]

A lot of discussion about my title. I wanted to call myself Lord Weeford but Verushka complained that would mean changing her name in the shops who wouldn't know her, and changing her name on her share certificates and so forth. Stronger arguments were then produced from various people like Bernard Levin and Arnold Weinstock

---

1. The Queen Mother's, handwritten towards the end of the month from Sandringham, read: 'Dear Sir Woodrow, Many congratulations on becoming a Lord. It is wonderful to think that The Voice of Reason will be heard in the House of Lords (an institution that I venerate) and I am sure that everyone there will look forward to hearing your contributions to the debates.' She goes on to mention two detective books 'for which I send you a thousand thanks'.

that if I change my name people wouldn't know who I was when I was speaking in the Lords.

After a lot of argument I thought the best thing to do was to ask the Garter King at Arms on Monday whether I could call myself and be known as Wyatt of Weeford or Wyatt and Weeford.

Ernest Saunders rings up as a consequence of my leaving a message for him to do so when he got back from Switzerland. I told him that he should get Napley, to whom he changed as solicitor, to insist with the Board of Trade that they investigate all sides of the bid not merely the Guinness side 'as you have told me that Gulliver and Argyll got up to some dirty tricks', to which Saunders agreed.

**Sunday 4 January**

Speak to Margaret.

'I received your paper on the trade unions, excellent,' she said. I said, 'I thought of writing something in the *Times* this week about it.' 'Yes, that would carry great weight.' Once again we are embarking on a little game by which I attack her government to get them to move forward while she approves behind the scenes. I told her that Jim Prior had written to me and in his letter he had said, 'We all knew' (referring to the time when he was Secretary for Employment) 'that you were the source of her information and knowledge on trade union matters but irritatingly she wouldn't admit it.' She laughed.

A call from the self-important Cousin Honor. She wanted me to know that she did congratulate me on getting my peerage. She had been shown a copy of *Sunday Today* where it says that she has not congratulated me. I say, 'You must know how that arises as you have been in newspapers. They asked me whether you had congratulated me and I said "No, there was no reason why you should."'

She then started condescendingly telling me I had a good brain, but ventured into saying that I had been unfair about her parents. At which point I blew up. I said, 'You told a pack of lies in that article in the *Observer*.[2] Pericles was never neglected. He was forty yards from the main house, I saw him every weekend. He soon came up to London and my daughter was also brought up in the same way. It is much healthier to spend your early years in the country basically. Your story was a pack of lies from start to finish.'

Verushka is put out about Jacob's [Rothschild] and Serena's invi-

---

2. See 28 September 1986.

tation to dinner on January 27th, because they have not asked us for five years and are only doing so now because I have just been given a peerage making it look as though I still have some importance in the world.

**Monday 5 January**

A hilarious morning at Garter King of Arms.[3]

I thought our interview would last about twenty minutes at the outside. Not a bit of it. 'I want to be called Lord Wyatt of Weeford,' I said. 'That is not possible,' he replied. 'You would have to be "Lord Wyatt *comma* of Weeford".' I said, 'Why?' and produced *Vacher's*[4] I had gone through on Saturday night marking with an 'x' all those who were called, apparently officially, Something of Somewhere.

He went through them all, or nearly all, saying that some of them were a mistake by *Vacher's* and that's not their real title, there should be a comma [after the name], it shouldn't be printed in *Vacher's* like that at all but with just one name.

He said there was an agreement between the Sovereign and Harold Wilson when he was Prime Minister that the name either had to be completely territorial or just the surname of the person concerned.

I said, 'It was suggested to me by Hartley Shawcross that I should call myself Woodrow-Wyatt.' He said, 'I think that would not please the Sovereign at all because when George Brown became a peer on that basis there was a great deal of argument about it. She said she didn't want to see that precedent repeated.'

He said, 'Have you ever had your name mistaken for another name like, say, White which sounds a bit like it?' I said, 'Oh yes. Tradesmen sometimes do that and call me White. Some people spell it wrong as Whyatt and also people sometimes say when I speak on the telephone think my name's Weir, rather like Viscount Weir.' 'Ah, now we're beginning to get somewhere. There could be confusion.'

He thought about it a very long time and went on discussing the pros and cons and the awful precedent I was creating and the difficulties there might be but finally he went out saying, 'I'm going to go and get a piece of paper and draft something.' I thought he was going to draft an enormous document. He came back with a quarto sheet on which

---

3. Sir Colin Cole had been Garter Principal King of Arms since 1978.
4. *Vacher's Parliamentary Companion*, updated quarterly, lists MPs, peers and senior government and parliamentary officials.

he had written in pencil 'Sir Woodrow Lisle Wyatt, Baron Wyatt of Weeford, of Weeford in the County of Staffordshire'.

He had got Lyle spelt wrongly. 'Oh dear,' he said, 'I've got no slave today, my secretary hasn't come in. I've got to do it all myself.' Well, we agreed that and then he got the name spelt right.

I asked him, 'Am I a Lord now?' He said, 'No, not yet.' 'Prince Philip sent me a telegram addressed to Lord Wyatt.' To which he replied, 'He was usurping the prerogative of the Sovereign. He may be her husband but he has no authority. It is only the Earl Marshal, the Sovereign and myself who can decide anything about these matters.'

We then talked about my coat of arms.

Then he said, 'You can't go yet. Do you want a lunch party? You don't have to have one. But if you do you can have twelve or fourteen if you have it in the dining-room. If you have more than twenty, you have it in the Cholmondley Room. It's convenient to me,' he said, clearly indicating he wanted a free lunch. 'I can wait there with you and we can go out at 1.30 when we have to start rehearsing for the ceremony.' 'Oh yes,' I said, 'That's fine.' So he gets his free lunch.

I asked him if he had got the book by Dr Robinson which I had brought with me, *The Wyatts: An Architectural Dynasty.* He said 'No.' I said, 'Would you like me to give you a copy.' 'Oh very much' so I think I cemented the arrangement. It turned out that John Robinson is some kind of temporary herald or temporary extra part-time herald though I didn't know that John Robinson[5] had got into this queer life as well.

At the end he said, 'When you get your Writ of Summons you must sleep with it under your pillow. You must carry it around changing it from pocket to pocket. On no account must you arrive at the Lords without it because the whole ceremony will be vitiated.'

**Wednesday 7 January**

Loads more letters as on Tuesday and Monday. I despair of ever answering them. Arranging postcards with a picture of Bonython on with stamps to save time on a conveyor belt basis.

Early morning – began to watch England beating Pakistan. At times it looked dicey, in the one day challenge tournament at Perth. Towards the end Petronella reported a call from Duke Hussey, Chairman of the BBC. With one eye on the television and one ear on the commentary

5. Appointed Maltravers Herald of Arms Extraordinary in 1989.

I began by telling him that there was at least one good television programme on BBC, 'I'm watching it now.' He said he was too.

He said he was on his private line. He didn't want to write me because it would soon get around in the BBC. 'I'm horrified by what you told me.'

He is anxious to let me know that he is entirely on my side and is moving as fast and as well as he can though, as I knew, the difficulties are enormous.

**Thursday 8 January**

Ask Eddie Shackleton[6] if he will be one of my sponsors along with Arnold Weinstock on February 4th which is the date that has been fixed for my being introduced into the Lords. He is delighted and didn't think it matters that he is still in the Labour Party (he used to be leader of the House of Lords for Labour governments), and he would look out his Garter chain and badge.

I said, 'Yes, you're very grand and I'll be very honoured.' He said, 'No, it's me to be honoured. We're very old friends and I often tell people how kind you were to me when I was hard up and you used to feed me with breakfast when we were first MPs and what a wonderful friend you've been to me whenever I've been in difficulties.'

He said that when he had become a peer in 1958 Garter King of Arms had tried to sell him a coat of arms. He said, 'But I've got one.' 'Where is it registered?' 'With Ulster.' Garter then tried to make him pay £300 to have the coat of arms proved – though Eddie comes from a Southern Irish family with a coat of arms several hundreds of years old. Eddie said he wouldn't, but he managed to find somebody, the Somerset Herald, to do it for £25 which annoyed Garter considerably.

Harriet, Moorea's half-sister,[7] married Charles, Eddie's son who died very young.

She will not see Eddie any more or any of the rest of the family.

I was fond of Harriet when she was very young and thought her badly used by her mother Margaret, which she was. She was a pretty, clever girl, went to Edinburgh and got a good degree but she was always highly strung and liable to be indignant or difficult.

---

6. (1911–94); life peer 1958.
7. The 15th Earl of Huntingdon (1901–90) m 1 (1925) Cristina, née Casati (Moorea's mother), m 2 (1944) Margaret Lane, the writer (mother of Lady Selina Hastings and Lady Harriet Hastings).

Moorea sent a kindly postcard of congratulations adding, 'The Hon. Pericles will be amused.'

**Friday 9 January**

Having a bath just after 10.00 p.m. when Ernest Saunders rings. Very difficult getting him back again at the Inn on the Park where they profess no knowledge of him but I insist on speaking to the Manager who then gets the unfortunate Ernest Saunders to ring me. Though he is tough and has doubtless been harsh with many, I feel sorry for him.

It had just been announced that he is standing down until the end of the inquiry by the DTI into the Guinness affair. He wanted to tell me immediately and thank me for my advice. He asks me whether he can get in touch with me again to ask for more. I say, 'Delighted.' It seems to me he will not return to be either Chairman or Chief Executive.

**Saturday 10 January**

Driving towards Badminton[8] it gets colder all the while. We pass through patches of snow in the fields. We are in the Chinese set of rooms, very pretty but cold despite the central heating and electric fires. Verushka has a magnificent floating Chinese bed, lacquer Chippendale style. The furniture is likewise. The rooms are very handsome. We are always put in them.

My bedroom has fluted Corinthian columns at the entrance to the alcove where the bed is and a beautiful circular domed ceiling over the bed with octagonals picked out in gold and flowers in the middle with gold centres. There is Chinese wallpaper with peacocks standing in unlikely poses on thin bamboos. The view is splendid.

In the evening Verushka and I decide to light the fires in our rooms but there is not much wood or coal. When David comes to see us off to bed, he vigorously puts coal on Verushka's fire – mine has gone out. The maid who looks after Verushka says in the morning that she has worked at Badminton for thirty years and has never seen these fires lit before. Caroline had the chimneys unblocked.

The bedroom Verushka is in was always used by Queen Elizabeth the Queen Mother when she came for the trials at Badminton. She is so hardy that I suppose she never noticed the cold and certainly would not have had a coal fire when the chimneys were blocked.

8. To stay with the Duke and Duchess of Beaufort.

Archduke Ferdinand (Ferdie) of Austria is here. He is charming, smokes a pipe but has cancer, poor man. If the Pretender, Otto, were on the throne he would be very high in Austria, being Otto's first cousin. He disputes my version of Rudolf's death[9] as supplied via Verushka's great uncle Emile who got it from Rudolf's widow.

He says Rudolf had syphilis, took drugs and was in a dreadful state. He was finished politically and every other way. He had previously asked a tart to commit suicide with him but she had turned down the honour.

According to the Archduke, Rudolf first shot his mistress and stayed alive himself until the early morning when he finally shot himself. He says the rumours and stories about Mayerling are entirely due to the Emperor Franz Josef putting a complete blanket of secrecy over everything. He also blames the old Emperor for the collapse of the monarchy in Austria because he resisted all change and made no attempt to cope with the future. He says Rudolf was intelligent and foresaw the awful things that would happen to Europe if there were a European war.

Ferdinand said that the Kaiser and the Tsar were the only two keen on the war, Russia because of its perpetual territorial ambitions and the Kaiser for the same reason. The Archduke has been allowed to live in Austria for some ten years or so now. Previously the top Hapsburgs were banned entirely.

Saturday night we had dinner in the Grand Dining-room, the first time David and Caroline have used it since they moved to the big house.[10] It is splendid with its large portraits round the walls. Caroline says the carving over the fireplace is Grinling Gibbons. I think that is the carving which John Robinson said to Mary Beaufort was not Gibbons but Edward Wyatt. I must check with him. Caroline says they have some bills saying some carving is by somebody else altogether but they are indebted to John Robinson for identifying the staircase as Jeffrey Wyatt. He rebuilt large chunks of Badminton and made it look as fine as it does now.

---

9. See 18 June 1986.
10. The 10th Duke of Beaufort, David Somerset's kinsman whom he succeeded, died in 1984.

**Saturday 10 January and Sunday 11 January**

We had a tour of the wine cellars after lunch. Very large and long stretching for fifty to a hundred yards around the place. Many cases of excellent wine of recent years: Beychevelle, Cos d'Estournel, Lafite, Latour, Margaux and others. Not much very old as the late Duke was no good on wine, as the man in charge explained. David keeps the wine in boxes correctly so that they can be resold later. He treats much of it as an investment.

David said he would never go to Badminton at all if it weren't for the hunting which is the only thing that saves him from going out of his mind from boredom at weekends. I joined him and the Hunt Secretary in the kitchen for tea on Saturday afternoon while they ate eggs and I ate crumpets with Patum Peperium on them.

Daphne[11] came to lunch Sunday. Sprightly for over eighty. When I compliment her looking well, she points to a newly lost tooth in front. Tells me that Oonagh Oranmore (a Guinness) is now almost destitute from bad investments. She was as lovely as the angel on the Christmas tree when I used to stay with her at Luggala in County Wicklow for Christmas and exceedingly rich.

On return to London I spoke to Margaret. I told her about the Harris poll in the *World This Weekend*. It showed sixty marginal seats which Labour must win to form a government with the Tories well ahead. It also showed that where the Alliance had been in second place at the last election they had no hope of winning any. This is the right kind of poll, not a blanket one but a selected poll in the seats which matter. The results would give Margaret a majority of around a hundred. I think she will improve on that by the time of the election.

We talked about the north/south divide which is unreal. I suggested that there might be some subsidy, however, for those who find work in the south but are a great deal hampered by the difference in house prices even for rent.

She considered it briefly and said that if we did something like that house prices would rise still more in the south.

She was busy working on what she had to say in the House tomorrow about Macmillan. She read out some passage from the last pages of his final volume of memoirs in which he talks about material things not being so important as spiritual ones. We both laughed. I said, 'I should concentrate on the test ban he achieved and starting to

11. The Hon. Daphne Fielding (1904–97), Caroline Beaufort's mother.

get us into Europe which were considerable points in his favour. He also was a patriot.' We talked a little about the enormous effect the First World War had had on him when he lost so many friends in the trenches.

**Tuesday 13 January**

Letters still coming in. Have arranged postcards with stamps to answer most of them in my own writing when the letters are in writing. Dictating letters to those who sent typewritten ones.

It is a mistake for me to drink particularly in the middle of the day. Verushka is right when she says too much claret and port give me lassitude and disinclination for work. If I drink nothing my head is fresher, a sign of old age. I have this battle with my self-indulgence conflicting with my desire to make use of the few remaining years.

**Wednesday 14 January**

Before dinner I went to Carlton House Terrace for a celebration party given by Neil Hamilton and Gerald Howarth to commemorate their successful libel action against the BBC. Mrs Hamilton had a very rough time. She is a little large but blonde, pretty and charming, and agreed fervently when I told her she must be much relieved now.

**Thursday 15 January**

Take my little toe to Mrs Humphreys, the chiropodist, to have the pain ended or lessened. This she does remarking, 'I rarely see better feet than yours. They are a very good shape.' Like Churchill I am proud of my small hands and feet, the only passable features I have. Even wrinkled a trifle, my hands and fingers are almost elegant, as some women say to me to my great pleasure.

Petronella, much happier now she has left Oxford, prances in triumphantly when I get home in the evening. 'I've found a mistake by a historian.' It is a serious historian and she is going to point out his error in her next essay for her new hero Conrad Russell.[12]

---

12. Astor Professor of British History, University College London, 1984–90; Professor of History, King's College, London, since 1990; son of Lord (Bertrand) Russell the philosopher, he succeeded his half-brother as 5th Earl Russell in 1987 and became Liberal Democrat spokesman on social services in the House of Lords.

**Sunday 18 January**

Dinner at Arnold's flat in Grosvenor Square. He has a seventy-two years' lease left. He put it in Netta's name who can throw him out.

The pictures belong to his children's trust.

After dinner we had a long talk about the Jewish religion and Arnold belonging to the hereditary priestly tribe the Levites.

Arnold is not popular with other Jews. He maintains that they [Israelis] have got to have a federal state with the Arabs or let them have a separate state on the West Bank.

Even Isaiah Berlin gets furious with Arnold when he says they've got to reach an accommodation.

In reply to all his critics he's thinking of buying the whole of GEC himself which would cost around £6,000 million. 'Can you raise the money?' I asked him. Yes, he thought he could. He would have to borrow perhaps £4,000 million. I said, 'You'd be in a high risk situation like Rupert.' 'Well that is true but I wouldn't have the bother with shareholders and dividends and having to publish annual statements and reports to be attacked by the press.'

The Prudential Insurance Co have been to see him. They own seven per cent of GEC. They say, 'We know it's very well run. We know that your performance compared with other companies in the same field at home and abroad, even in Japan, is better. But nothing exciting is happening. Why don't you do something exciting?' Arnold said, 'I'm not just going to go in for mergers and all this fashionable stuff which creates no wealth at all. I just have to go on making the place more profitable.'

He told me how he had bid for Telephone Rentals some twenty years ago and he made a final bid saying he would not pay more than 75p and an institution rang him up and said, 'If you'll just pay another 5p we'll accept it and you've got the company.' He said, 'No, I won't. I gave my word that it was my final bid and I'd be cheating those who believed me and sold shares at that price. This is not a code of honour accepted any longer in the City.' Arnold has always refused to behave in the dishonourable way now so prevalent.

Arnold said if he distributed the cash mountain of £1,600 million that GEC has to the shareholders, they'd only get 40p each. So what's the point of it? It earns a lot of interest at the moment.

**Monday 19 January**

Bernard Levin to dinner. Gave him Château Montrose 1967. He once said it was his favourite wine but it probably isn't, any more than primroses were Disraeli's favourite flower which he wrote to Queen Victoria on getting some from her.

Petronella was eventually persuaded to sing when Verushka had gone upstairs about a quarter to eleven. Bernard had never heard her sing before and was impressed by her voice, saying she ought to sing semi-operatic songs, lieder.

Bernard thought Charles James Fox was the greatest politician of the 18th century. I said, 'Ridiculous. He was wrong about everything,' after Bernard had said that he was right about everything. 'Even about not wanting to fight Napoleon?' I asked. Petronella likes Charles James Fox. They both like romantic rollicking characters. Charles James Fox seems a very similar character to Nye Bevan, flashing and spectacular but not enough substance. We all agree however that we would rather have Charles James Fox to dinner with us that night than William Pitt.

**Tuesday 20 January**

Dinner at the Austrian Embassy.

Talked to John Biffen before dinner. He said he only had three hates, believing that one is entitled to a few hates in one's life. His principal hate is Ted Heath. Ted knew that he had voted for Enoch Powell[13] for the leadership and never forgave him. He was much more domineering than Mrs Thatcher ever has been. He would accept no disagreement whereas she not only puts people into her Cabinet who don't think like her but encourages argument because she wants to get the best solution.

It might have been different John thought if Ian Macleod[14] had lived. He was a considerable figure and Ted had to pay attention to him. Also his effect on economic policy would have been much better and they would not have run into the difficulties which occurred under Ted.

---

13. (1912–98); Conservative politician and classical scholar; in 1965 he obtained fifteen votes in the Conservative leadership contest won by Heath after Sir Alec Douglas-Home stood down; he was dismissed from the Shadow Cabinet in 1968 after his speeches on immigration and sat as an Ulster Unionist MP, 1974–87.
14. (1913–70); Conservative minister who died shortly after his appointment by Heath as Chancellor of the Exchequer.

When I said I had known Ted since I was at Oxford and was very fond of him, he could scarcely credit it. I said, 'He's not a bad fellow at heart and is like an animal of the forest, deeply wounded. I know he's too stiff' (to which John agreed), 'but there's something good there.'

Verushka enjoyed the dinner for the Austro-Hungarian Empire atmosphere. There was a large picture of Maria Theresa who was godmother to one of Verushka's direct ancestors and there are still bits and pieces of the beautiful silver presents she gave in this house and some in Hungary. It has been the Austro-Hungarian Embassy at 18 Belgrave Square since 1868.

The Guinness saga splashes on. Heads still roll.

Saunders, as I thought when I first saw him, is likely to go to prison at the end of the day. The government are determined to get some heads to show how anti-corruption in the City they are. So far there's been no electoral backwash but it might turn into it.

**Friday 23 January**

Andrew Stephen who is writing a profile on me for the *Observer* for February 1st on my going into the Lords came to lunch. I gave him some sparkling wine and enjoined him not to write that I was giving him champagne and living in luxury.

He seemed a pleasant young man. He didn't like Andrew Neil (he was on the *Sunday Times*) and he didn't like the way the Wapping move had been conducted, that is why he had left the *Sunday Times* and gone to the *Observer*. He thought Rupert very hard. I explained to him that he was not and he did mind about the people who lost their jobs.

In the morning Verushka went to Stuart Devlin[15] to order and design the trophy for Queen Elizabeth the Queen Mother which we are going to give her after she has presented the Tote Cheltenham Gold Cup on March 19th. She seems to have chosen well. It's going to be an Easter egg about six inches tall. You take off the top and there is a horse, golden, lying in a field of grass and flowers of the Queen Mother's racing colours.

Speak to Bruce Matthews about the meeting I am arranging with drinks for the Big Four representatives to talk to him about the job of

---

15. Goldsmith, silversmith, Royal Designer for Industry.

chairmanship of SIS.[16] He will do it well. I am also grateful to him for getting Rupert to put my salary or whatever it's called up to £50,000 a year.

**Sunday 25 January**

The businessman, Sir Ralph Halpern of Burton's, is plastered over the tabloids and the *Sunday Telegraph* for having a jolly affair with a nineteen-year-old topless model who posed full frontal for *Penthouse*. He appears in distress, apologizing to his wife and eighteen-year-old daughter.

I don't know why Mrs Thatcher gave Halpern a knighthood. She has a weakness for people who make large sums of money quickly and puts it all down to their endeavour and worthwhile enterprise. It is often not. There is a man called Salomon who is a terror whom she likes, Michael Richardson, Sir Jack Lyons. It is dangerous for her.

When I spoke to her today I nearly raised it but decided not to. I will wait until it slips in some other way.

We talk about my article advocating the setting free of Channel 4 which I wrote in the *Times* yesterday. She agrees with it and says we need a new broadcasting policy altogether and she is going to raise this, as well as the Channel 4 item, which she will discuss with Douglas Hurd. So many developments in technology are changing broadcasting rapidly.

She was horrified by the riots at Wapping last night[17] and the intimidation of the police, saying, 'There you can see what Labour would allow again.'

**Tuesday 27 January**

Call on the wily old Isidore Kerman now aged eighty-two. He has new palatial offices in New Cavendish Street. I say, 'You must be a multi-millionaire now.' 'There are a lot of partners here' but he is doing very well out of property, greyhound tracks and all kind of things which have nothing to do with being a solicitor.

He has had his offer for Windsor [racecourse] accepted, though that is not quite the same thing as having the contract signed. Wary to begin with but became brighter when I explained my plan to reduce the number of bookmakers and move the Tote building to the front

---

16. Satellite Information Services.

17. Twelve thousand demonstrated and 162 police officers were injured.

and offered him participation with money from us in his ownership of the horse-race track but perhaps not the greyhound track. He said as soon as he got the whole thing signed he'd be back and we would work out some co-operation.

On to the Clerk of the Parliaments, Sir John Sainty, at the Lords. It was pleasant to be back in the atmosphere. He started showing me round and when we got to the Chamber I said, 'I made my maiden speech here.' He was startled. I said, 'Yes, the House of Commons was bombed out and for the first six years or so of my life as a Member of Parliament we were in the Lords and so I made my maiden speech here in 1945.'

Got myself a photographic pass, something we never used to have for Parliament before.

Able to walk straight through St Stephen's Entrance into the Commons Members' Lobby. Mrs Currie[18] and a Mr Teller, an Assistant Secretary at the Department of Health, waiting for Dr Sinclair and me. 'Would you like tea or a drink?' 'Tea,' I said firmly and we marched off to have some.

She is a sexy, lively lady. Sometimes she put her hand on my arm. Frequently she buttered me up over my articles and how good they were 'and like all good politicians you winnow out the real points,' etc. She is dark with a smooth skin. She seemed to have no hair on her upper lip and I wondered whether she really had a great deal but had it removed by some erasing method.

She was good on her basic facts though misinformed on some aspects of theory and practice. I asked her as we got to the end of the conversation, 'Are you an ally?' She said, 'I'm certainly very interested and I think you can say I'm an ally.' She and the Assistant Secretary (a senior official) suggested a few people Hugh Sinclair might pursue and they would give their blessing. Reasonably hopeful.

She wore a pretty diamond ring with a large diamond and an elegant brooch, gold and bits of diamond. At a table adjoining was the old humbug Fenner Brockway[19] now about ninety-nine. He was smoking a pipe and looked gaga. Not that that would make a great deal of difference to the intelligence of what he says.

Dinner at Jacob Rothschild's, No 30 Warwick Avenue. He used to

---

18. Edwina Currie, Conservative politician, Parliamentary Under-Secretary of State for Health, 1986–8.
19. (1888–1988); Labour politician, journalist and campaigner for peace.

live in No 28 but has joined the two together. It is now a large and luxurious house. He has a Sultan-like bedroom with a switch to raise his television up at the foot of the large double bed. His bathroom has an old fashioned type bath like we used to have in Conock and is splendidly in the centre of the room like ours was.

A lot of marble around. Some sculptures by Richard James Wyatt. Many valuable pictures. The drawing-room is handsome. I noticed the full-length Reynolds lady is still there. It goes from house to house from where they used to live near Pelham Crescent where it was the first picture you saw when the door was opened. As he's got richer it has become one of the last pictures you see.

The hall has various statues and what looks like an ancient Greek battered horse, though one of the chairs, I said to Jacob, must have come from the Clifton Nurseries. 'How did you know that?' I said, 'I've seen the type there before.' (Jacob owns Clifton Nurseries.) The chair was made of marble.

Serena, whom I love, has a separate bedroom and I don't think they have had any sexual relations for a long time. Many find her dour but she's not underneath. She arranges dinner curiously. The first course is a Spanish type pilaff with big prawns, bits of chicken and rice. The second course is cold beef and cold salad. Before dinner there was either the red wine we were going to have with dinner or champagne. The red wine for dinner was in magnums, some kind of offshoot of a Rothschild wine 1982, low average cru bourgeois type and much too young to drink.

There were two tables in the dining-room, one large one and a round one at which I sat next to Serena. Grey Gowrie[20] halfway through dinner came to sit next to Serena. I had asked her whether she thought him attractive and she said, 'No.' He has a pock-marked face but not bad looking. When I asked him why Bron Waugh was so against him he said he thought it was something to do with a girl years ago.

Told me there was an open line telephone on which you could telephone America or anywhere in the Whips' office. 'But I'm not a Tory.' 'No but you'd be quite welcome there I'm sure.' He used to be the Arts Minister which he gave up because he couldn't live on £30,000.

---

20. 2nd Earl of Gowrie, Conservative politician; Minister for the Arts, 1983–5; chairman, Sotheby's International, 1985–6, Sotheby's Europe, 1987–94; chairman, Arts Council of England, 1994–8.

He now works for Sotheby's or Christie's. Jolly and friendly. His wife was not there.

A rough-looking semi-handsome man called Richard Rogers in a pink shirt and sports jacket and no tie. A blonde wife with potentially attractive face but marred by skin blemishes wearing a green shirt. He is a celebrated architect who built the Pompidou Museum with all the pipes on the outside which I regard as a monstrosity but is supposed to be the top in modern architecture. He is doing something at the National Gallery of which Jacob is Chairman.

After dinner Nico Henderson,[21] Jeremy Hutchinson, Rogers and his wife and I stay talking in the dining-room. Jeremy said everybody was finished at sixty-five, that's when old age gripped you, you became idle, you couldn't think properly any more, there should be no judges of that age. He thought Denning[22] was now useless and ought not to be allowed to say anything. He himself said he did little work. One doesn't want to work at that age, he said.

Nico was horrified, saying he felt lots of right ideas came now and he is sixty-six or seven. I said, 'I've never worked so hard before in my life because I feel the years are so few I have to get as much done as I can.'

Rogers also disagreed and said the rule certainly did not apply to artists and Jeremy said, 'It may be they're an exception.' I said, 'Architecture is the greatest art form of all because you have to find the right site, make the house work inside and out and be beautiful inside and out and make it last for centuries.' To my surprise Rogers did not agree, though he accepted that the ancient Athenians took my view. He did not accept my proposition that anyone can paint a picture which is far easier than building a house.

Before dinner Jessica Douglas-Home[23] was standing beside me and joined with me in resisting Jeremy. She's an active girl politically, having taken great interest in the amendments Baroness Cox was promoting to stop political indoctrination in the schools. She said she was going to Czechoslovakia but when she came back she was going to give up politics altogether and just concentrate on her painting. She looked more attractive than when I first knew her. I didn't recognize her, and

---

21. Sir Nicholas Henderson, diplomat.*
22. Lord Denning, Master of the Rolls, 1962–82 (b 1899).
23. Widow of Charles Douglas-Home, editor of the *Times*.

had to be reminded by Serena who she was. Her looks have improved since poor Charlie died – probably getting some sex.

Isaiah Berlin was there and his wife said he is always muddling things up, as he did the letters when he sent mine to Iris Murdoch[24] and Iris Murdoch's to me congratulating us on our recent honours. I like him but Verushka says he is too deaf to be asked to the Queen Mother's dinner. So we are going to try the Austrian Ambassador and his wife who look elegant and he is amusing.

During dinner there was some talk about the Alliance. Jeremy is an SDP member. When the question of the leadership came up and having the two Davids[25] and the difficulty of which was to be the Alliance leader I said, 'Maybe that's not a bad idea. They remind me of the two Ronnies who are more or less indistinguishable when they sign themselves off on the television. They're very popular.'

Verushka said that during dinner Jacob talked about nothing but art and speaks of himself as a great patron of the arts, no doubt from being Chairman of the National Gallery. He appears to pretend that he is nothing to do with making money any more and all that grubby stuff of appearing in the City is no concern of his. I wonder.

**Wednesday 28 January**

The *Sporting Life* announced that Isidore Kerman has not got the Windsor racecourse. Despite lawyers being in touch with each other the board suddenly decided to sell to a mystery buyer. Charles Spencer-Churchill rings to say the group which he is in touch with are going to make a bigger bid than the mystery buyer so all may not yet be lost.

Dinner at Harold Lever's. At the end of dinner the men went into what he calls the library. This consists of a few expensively bound books dotted around elegant shelves with pieces of china in between and in front of them.

Maureen Dudley said she had a twenty-year-old dress on which she simply rejigged to modern fashions. She still looks amazingly pretty and was about to go on a *This is Your Life* programme as a friend of the actor selected, though she wouldn't say who it was.

When I expressed some disbelief in her having an out-of-date

---

24. The novelist; she was awarded the DBE in the same Honours List as WW received his peerage.
25. David Owen (SDP) and David Steel (Liberal) had become joint leaders of the Alliance formed by the Liberal Party and the SDP to fight the 1983 election.

wardrobe, she told me how once for a US trip she borrowed lots of dresses from Princess Ferial, sister of the King of Jordan. She had been the mistress of Niarchos.[26]

She said that the Princess had been poor when she started living with Niarchos but ended up very rich, and that she was extremely pretty.

In Maureen's view Niarchos is everything women like – immense power and all that goes with it. I said, 'He has no power in a political sense or anything which matters.' Maureen said, 'But he can whistle up private aeroplanes and has comfortable houses and dishes out lots of jewellery and the atmosphere is supremely luxurious. He gives the impression of power.'

Harold Lever tried to get me to have a Partagas cigar made by some Cuban expatriates according to the original formula of Partagas. I refused, taking a Monte Christo, saying, 'There is no way in which Havana cigars can be made other than in the soil of Cuba. Everything else tastes like punk, however hard the makers have tried.'

After dinner there was considerable talk about the City shenanigans. Harold pretended he didn't really know what insider dealing was which made me laugh. I dare say he has done a good deal of it in his time though, as he said, it was not a crime until recently.

**Thursday 29 January**

I like The Other Club. The champagne is good. The Château Cantemerle 1978 was excellent. So was the dressed crab and the guinea fowl plus a lentil sauce. This three course meal with first class wine for £12.50 can't be bad.

I sat next to Norman Tebbit and Dick Mabon, a former Labour Minister now in the SDP. Mabon is unreasonably hopeful of winning back the seat he lost by a narrow margin in the last election.[27]

Tebbit was not clear yet when the election ought to be. Neither he nor Mrs Thatcher have made up their minds. I said, 'I'm sure she won't have it until after the four years is up, knowing her views about the public not being asked to vote too soon for parliaments which have a five year span. But whatever you do, don't hold it on Gold Cup Day at Royal Ascot. I only just managed to avert that once before.'

---

26. The Greek shipping tycoon.
27. He failed to do so.

He said his wife[28] was showing slight signs of improved movement but she is never going to recover.

Much of her day is saved from boredom by the long getting dressed and undressed and bodily functions. He felt awful when he lost his temper because he couldn't find his glasses or some trivial matter like that and she overheard him being annoyed and he thinks of the appalling suffering and immobility to which she is reduced.

I told him that the reason Labour hated him so much was that he understood ordinary people and he once led a strike when he was an air pilot. He said, 'Yes. I don't have a public school background. I'm not rich. And no one can associate me with sex scandals either.'

The book goes round to everyone to sign their names. Later the original book was brought in with the founders' signatures heading the first page, F. E. Smith and Winston Churchill. There were some good drawings of members like Arnold Bennett by artists such as Orpen and Munnings. They don't seem to do these drawings any more; perhaps we have no artist.

William Rees-Mogg[29] came to sit by me as the dinner ended. He thought it absolutely right that Alasdair Milne had gone[30] but he couldn't have known of the intention to get rid of him. 'I saw him at a dinner for a departing Northern Ireland BBC governor last night. He was very cheerful and relaxed, obviously not knowing what tomorrow had in store for him.'

**Friday 30 January**

Dinner at the Dudleys. The first time they've had a dinner there for two years. They had the house redecorated, then dry rot appeared and it all had to be done over again.

Barbara Cartland's grandson, eager, fair-haired young Lord

---

28. Seriously injured in the IRA bombing of the Grand Hotel, Brighton, at the 1984 Conservative conference.
29. Editor, the *Times* 1967–81; chairman, Sidgwick & Jackson (publishers), 1985–9; vice-chairman, BBC Board of Governors, 1981–6; chairman, Arts Council of Great Britain, 1982–9, Broadcasting Standards Council, 1988–93; director, GEC, since 1981; chairman, Pickering & Chatto (publishers), since 1981; knight 1981, life peer 1988.
30. His resignation as Director General of the BBC had been announced that day.

Lewisham,[31] greeted me with enthusiasm, telling me he read all my articles in the *News of the World* and agreed with every word.

He then called me Sir. I said, 'You were very flattering up till then. Now will you kindly not call me Sir, it makes me feel so old.' I sent my love to his grandmother who once sent me a book about honey with the inscription: 'Woodrow, this will improve your sex life.'

On my right was Jonathan Aitken's pretty new Yugoslav wife.[32] She has very pretty legs and a round sexy face. I complimented her on her prettiness, her legs and her dress and she said, 'You can't be English.' (She knew who I was, however, having met me before when I'd been to their house.)

She thought passionate sex lasted in marriage more or less for five years. 'How long have you been married?' 'Eight years.' I laughed.

She thought the English extraordinary in their prurient interest in the goings on of Sir Ralph Halpern and others of that kind. In France they take it for granted. Why are the English so amazingly interested? I said, 'Perhaps they are buttoned up and repressed by their wives and of course they are hypocritical. But do not suppose that this is a novelty in English life.' I then told her about the Delicate Investigation into the Princess of Wales (Caroline of Brunswick) and how this was paraded through the newspapers with cartoons, and how all the Prince Regent's affairs were paraded and William IV's. There's nothing new about the English excessive interest in the sexual activities of the rich and famous and well-born.

When Mark Birley shook hands with me before dinner at the Dudleys I felt a little finger in my palm. I said, 'Does that mean you're a Mason?' He said, 'No. I've just got a crippled finger.' I felt ashamed of myself.

**Saturday 31 January**

Eddie Brown [barber] and Mrs Wilson, manicurist, were amused in the morning when I told them a true story about Enoch Powell. There is a very chatty barber in the Commons who never stops telling MPs

---

31. Son of her daughter Raine and the Earl of Dartmouth.
32. Lolicia, née Azucki, m (1979) Jonathan Aitken, Conservative politician, journalist and businessman; MP, 1974–97.

whose hair he cuts about politics and what his views are on the world. Enoch Powell went to have his hair cut by him one day, sat down and the barber said, 'How would you like your hair cut, sir?' 'In silence,' Enoch replied.

**Sunday 1 February**

Put out by a snide profile in the *Observer* evidently written by the young man who came to lunch and who had said in reply to my question, 'Is this another *Observer* cutting up job on me?' that he had no intention of doing so. It is full of the usual journalistic trash about my supposed high living, fine wine and cigars.

There was the repeated ridiculous lie about my father making me eat my food like a dog on the floor, related by my cousin Honor in a previous edition of the *Observer.* I suppose I should have refused to be interviewed unless I saw a copy of the article before it was printed to prevent inaccuracies though not to interfere with any opinion.

The young man had been so charming and I had forgotten that the once reputable *Observer* is now worse than any of the tabloids in smears, untruths and viciousness. The piece was shoddy, shabby and shallow as so much of the *Observer* is now. When I had a kind note from Anthony Howard, deputy editor, about my peerage, I thought the subsequent interview was an olive branch. What a fool I was.

Felt rather low. Didn't ring Mrs Thatcher until twenty to seven when I heard that she had already left Chequers.

Talked to Robin Day about who should be the new Director-General. He says that when Alasdair Milne was under consideration he wrote to the then Chairman, Howard, and said, 'For goodness' [sake] don't. He'll be hopeless.' He thinks Paul Fox aged sixty-one, a highly competent and experienced television man who originally ran *Panorama* and now runs Yorkshire Television would be a good choice. He is against Jeremy Isaacs[1] who he regards as too left-wing, 'a *Guardian* man'. Robin thinks he would put on pornographic films and all kinds of weird leftish stuff and interview terrorists saying, 'Of course we ought to know what terrorists are thinking.'

---

1. Chief executive, Channel 4 Television, 1981–7; general director, Royal Opera House, Covent Garden, 1988–97.

**Monday 2 February**

Speak to Mrs Thatcher just before 8.00 a.m. Tell her that when I rang yesterday she'd already left Chequers but that I hadn't much to say. 'But I always think there's something wrong if you don't ring,' she said.

We talked briefly about the disappearance of Alasdair Milne and I said what a good thing it had been. She primly said, 'Nothing to do with us.'

Speak to Norman Lamont's secretary at the Treasury to try to get figures which I'm not getting from the press office about British overseas assets. Some figures faxed over later in the evening and then Norman Lamont rings saying he shouldn't be speaking to me because the Treasury Ministers are now in their purdah period. I said, 'What do you mean?' He said, 'Because of the Budget.' 'When is the Budget?' It turns out it's not until mid-way through March but he's not allowed to speak to anybody so that if there is any leak he can say he hasn't spoken to any journalists.

Duke Hussey for drinks. He is large but agile despite his gammy leg[2] which he manoeuvres up and down the steps with the aid of a stick.

He had difficulty with Alasdair Milne from the start. When he found out that the programme about Maggie's Militant Tendency, in which two Conservative MPs[3] were libelled and won heavy damages from the BBC in a case which ought never to have been defended, had not been checked by lawyers until the weekend, and then only by BBC lawyers before the Monday programme (*Panorama*), he was horrified. In a newspaper that would have been done immediately, he said to Milne. 'But you don't understand television. The programme had to be advertised in the *Radio Times* and copy for that prepared some weeks before.'

Joel Barnett[4] is working very well with him and he thinks the governors are now not too bad a bunch. They kept absolutely to themselves the arrangements he made with them that Milne was to be asked to sign a resignation letter immediately after the end of the governors' meeting. The Board of Management knew nothing and were stunned. So was Milne. Duke arranged that the post should be open

---

2. He lost a leg in the Second World War.
3. See 9 and 22 October 1986.
4. He had been appointed vice chairman of the BBC Board of Governors in 1986.

to people who apply only until next week so as to stop a revolt occurring. The suddenness with which he acted winded potential strikers and mischief makers and the speed with which the new Director-General was to be appointed made them think more about that. Very clever.

**Wednesday 4 February**

Off to the Lords. A lunch before the introduction ceremony including Roy Jenkins, Robert Kee, Henry Anglesey, Julian and Catherine Amery, Petronella, Verushka, Nicholas and Caroline. Bernard Levin couldn't come because he had 'flu. Arnold and Netta were there, of course, as Arnold was one of my sponsors. The Garter King at Arms sat half resplendent at the table and then began to get agitated as it neared ten to two.

Lots of jolly jokes in the robing room and Eddie looked fine with his Collar of the Knight of the Garter.

Then we went in led by Garter, now in full regalia. We rehearsed twice advancing up towards the Lord Chancellor, stopping to bow at two selected places and holding our hats over our left breasts with me clutching my Writ of Summons. Eventually I got to Quintin[5] and knelt on my left knee and handed him the Summons. I had to about turn and go back to the table where the Crown clerk read the whole of the Patent urging me among other things to be vigilant in my attendance to save the nation in discussing and settling great matters of state. This took a long time. (Roy afterwards said he hadn't realized how vital it was for me to be there to save the state.)

I then had to read out the oath which was short. I nearly forgot to sign the great parchment of the Record of Peers and as it was half rolled up I made a terrible squiggle of my name because I couldn't get my hand over it properly. Then we had to walk back again bowing in appropriate places and go up to a back seat reserved for the junior Baron. There we put our hats on and rose and bowed with a great sweeping of our hats to the Lord Chancellor who acknowledged us by taking off his hat. I nearly put my hat on again at the end and would have done but for a hiss from Eddie, 'Don't put your hat on.' We went past Quintin again, I to shake hands with him, and out to the accompaniment of a loud 'Hear, hear' which Verushka said came

5. Quintin Hogg (Lord Hailsham, Lord Chancellor).

mainly from the Tory benches and hardly from the sparsely attended Labour benches. That was understandable.

I bumped into Harold and Mary Wilson. He glared. She stopped to congratulate me and to say how much she still agreed with my columns, to his evident annoyance. Seeing it she said, 'Perhaps not all.'

I thought that Charles Forte and his wife were coming to dinner on Thursday. When I got in at just gone half past seven, Verushka said, 'What about the wine?'

Eating with them alone was much more fun than when we go to their large dinner parties where you hardly talk to them at all.

He asked me whether I would write leading articles for his newly launched *Time & Tide*.[6] (A letter came the next morning saying I'd be one of a panel of seven writers which means about one and five-sevenths times a year, at £500 a shot for a thousand words.)

Irene knew Malu Casati.[7] She didn't know the history of the family and I explained it all to her in great detail. Irene knew Malu when she was quite young, having known her first a bit in Venice apparently. She used to go to see her in her one large room just off the Brompton Road, and Malu was fond of her.

**Friday 6 February**

Sonia [Sinclair] says that Antonia[8] is now suffering from the treatment she used to give poor Hugh. She made him almost ill with her lovers flaunted under his nose, beginning with David Somerset[9] with whom, instead of having a discreet affair, she blazoned it all over London to Caroline's distress.

When she went off with Harold Pinter she thought it was the great love of her life and all would be romantic for ever. Now Pinter has a succession of girlfriends and Antonia is perpetually consumed with jealousy and anguish. She was never beautiful but attractive as a well scrubbed shining milk maid, plump in the face with a nice complexion. I only kissed her once years ago when we went to Salisbury races where I had a runner.

---

6. Sent to Forte credit card customers, MPs and peers, with a circulation of 150,000.
7. Marchesa Malu Casati, grandmother of WW's former wife Moorea (see *Confessions of an Optimist*, pp. 232 ff.); friend of the Italian poet D'Annunzio; painted by Augustus John; her house in Venice is now the Guggenheim Museum.
8. Lady Antonia Pinter who m 1 Sir Hugh Fraser.
9. Duke of Beaufort.

Jo Janni[10] comes to lunch. Due at 1.15, he arrives at 12.40 and is helped up the steps, still disabled by a stroke of four or five years ago. He wants me to go into some film ventures with him again and get Rupert Murdoch who owns Twentieth Century Fox interested.

A year or so back United Artists invited him to New York and gave him a penthouse and flew him over. He said he had to take a nurse as he couldn't look after himself dressing and undressing, etc. That was agreed. He asked an agency if any nurse would like to go to New York and back. A very pretty girl from Manchester turned up and Stella his wife said, 'Oh she will not be suitable for you,' but Jo hung on and said he thought she would be very suitable. Off they went. The girl was thrilled with New York. She'd never been out of England before and the penthouse and the excitement of the restaurants and the functions filled her with delight.

One evening Jo decided they would not go out to dinner but have dinner in the penthouse at the top of the hotel where they both had respectably separated double bedrooms in the same apartment. After dinner the girl said, 'Would you do me a favour?' Jo said, 'What is it?' and she replied, 'Take me back on Concorde so that I can tell all the nurses that I've been on the Concorde.' Jo promptly said, 'Will you do me a favour?' and she said, 'What?' He said, 'Take off all your clothes and I'll take you back on Concorde.'

At this point in the story he said to me, 'Do you think I was stupid?' I said, 'I don't know till you tell me what happened.' He carried on. 'She went out of the room and came back a few moments later with nothing on but her nurse's cap.' I said, 'What happened then?' and he answered, 'I'm not made of steel. Not bad for somebody nearing seventy don't you think?' I thought, 'Not bad at all, particularly as he's still hopelessly disabled by a stroke and can hardly walk around even with the aid of help and a stick.' He saw her once or twice again in London.

It is sad to see him so disabled. In his vigour he produced many successful films like *Darling*, *Sunday Bloody Sunday*, *Far from the Madding Crowd*, *A Kind of Loving*. In one or two of them I had a share of his share of the profits, I having suggested the film and put up money or merely put up a little money for the option. I lost some money on our last option because he couldn't continue with the film. I'm not sure whether to put any more up. I would prefer it if Twentieth

10. (1916–94); film producer.

Century Fox agreed to do a film and we negotiated something with them direct. He left me a treatment of a Patricia Highsmith book on which he has an option and is sending me a film script of another film which he thinks he can get the option on.

**Saturday 7 February**

David Dimbleby[11] has been suggested as a new Director-General of the BBC. Alastair Burnet at Sandown was the second person to suggest him to me. Could be a good idea though I'm not sure he would be quite on top of the administration.

I was accosted at Sandown by Simon Raven[12] who reminded me how he used to have lunch with me at Tower House years ago. His face was enormously bloated. He looks as though he'll have a heart attack any second. He was one of our guests among the credit customers. He loses a lot of money with us, he tells me, but not as much as he used. He was in debt to the bookmakers so heavily that he had to leave the Army and start writing. I said, 'That's at least one good product from bookmakers because you write very well.' He swayed off heavily laden with drink.

**Sunday 8 February**

I see John Willoughby[13] left over £1 million. Surprising. John Abergavenny[14] told me how poor he was and how wretched it was for him to have to eke out his last months in a tiny room in a cheap nursing home near Notting Hill Gate with poor food. It was he who spurred me on to take him champagne and bottles of wine because I thought he couldn't afford them.

Congratulated Margaret on her rousing speech to the Scarborough Young Conservatives' Conference. Full of good stuff about Labour's defence policy and the need for security on state secrets and so forth.

I told her how I had stopped Dick Crossman when I was Under-Secretary for War going to Germany to interview British Generals and commanding officers.

I knew that Dick was out to find information to rock the government's defence policy. In those days it was not thought an admirable

11. Broadcaster and newspaper owner, son of Richard Dimbleby.
12. Novelist and critic.
13. Lord Willoughby de Broke; see 2 December 1985 and 31 May 1986.
14. 5th Marquess of Abergavenny.

occupation for journalists, however eminent, to try to discover secrets and use them against the nation's security.

**Monday 9 February**

Visit Lords and sit in chamber and vote twice. Astonished to hear precisely the same drivelling arguments that I left behind seventeen years ago.

Bertie Denham[15] says that he will let me know if my help is urgently required to defeat the Opposition in a vote. It would not be proper for him to send me actual copies of the government whips because that would compromise my independence. He takes my telephone number instead which will amount to much the same thing.

**Tuesday 10 February**

Stephen Shelbourne from No 10 rings. 'As usually happens after the week-end, the Prime Minister is much taken with your articles. She asked me to find out from you where Neil Kinnock said what you reported him as saying in the *News of the World* about changing the law to prevent employers succeeding in such situations as Wapping.' I gave him the clue to follow on and he said he thought he would be able to do that.

Verushka says, 'You ought to have been asked to Mark Thatcher's engagement reception. Charles Forte has been. Arnold and Netta have not been and they are very put out.' I said, 'I'm not in the least bit put out. If I had to go to such a tedious reception I would also have to give him a wedding present.'

Lunch.

Professor Russell is slightly reminiscent of his father but a stronger looking face and a sturdier body. He says he got on well with his father as a child but in the interim very badly and well with him again before he died.

The Professor's mother is still alive and with his father dying at ninety-seven he should, as I said to him, top the hundred, however bad the food he ate.

**Wednesday 11 February**

In the Lords sat in my usual place in the front row of the crossbenches. There are only three narrow benches and if there were a big crowd

15. 2nd Baron Denham, Conservative Whip in the House of Lords.

there would have to be an overflow but I don't know to where. About two foot away from me Alec Home was sitting; I noticed that he had on an ancient pair of shoes, crinkled and rubbed. I should think they were forty years old. He is like Lord Emsworth[16] whom visitors to the House mistook for the gardener.

Went to the *Sunday Times* twenty-fifth birthday colour magazine party at the Whitbread Brewery.

Arnold Goodman wants me to write to the *Times* to protest against the BBC doing a programme about John Profumo and Miss Christine Keeler. Ringing the BBC I find that the programme is supposed to be about Christine Keeler but they haven't decided how it's to be done so far. Arnold says it will be a vicious blow against the family of Jack, who now has not only children but grandchildren, and the BBC seems to be out of control. I was mildly amused by this since Arnold usually takes a somewhat over liberal view of the freedom of broadcasting or the press except when it affects one of his clients. He is advising John Profumo.

I duly write the letter but I do not know whether the *Times* will publish it or whether Duke Hussey will take any notice.

A jolly dinner at Robert Kee's in Camberwell. Sit next to forty-three year-old girlfriend, Katy, daughter of Humphrey Trevelyan,[17] whom he intends to marry and she him. She is dark with a semi *belle-laide* face. She has a good figure and nice legs, and a chirpy conversation. Being part of the great historian family Trevelyan, she got a First in History at St Andrews. She is a business manager of the *Burlington Magazine*.

With her father being an Ambassador and a senior diplomat almost as long as she can remember, she is accustomed to having interesting people around and a luxury life in embassies. Like Petronella that put her off discomfort and boring gauche young men without informed conversation. So she never got married though she says that she feels a biological urge to have a child so maybe she will have one with Robert.[18]

---

16. P. G. Wodehouse character.
17. (1905–85); life peer 1968.
18. He married 1 (1948–50) Janetta, née Woolley, 2 (1960–89) Cynthia, née Judah, 3 (1990) Catherine, née Trevelyan, managing director, *Burlington Magazine*.

Robert, previously tied to Cynthia, has told Verushka he no longer was tied to her in any way.

A merry fellow, Frank Johnson,[19] told me he would like to be editor of the *Times*. Nico Henderson asked, 'Why?' and got the answer, 'Because of the power.'

There was a Grand-Puy-Lacoste in magnums 1973. Not bad. It's the same as I bought in a sale recently at Berry Bros.

Next to me on the other side was Miriam Gross[20] who remains married to her husband though they haven't lived together for ages. He is in America, she is in England. They have children. I never recognize her and she always has to remind me that we met at Michael Astor's or some other place. Her looks are faintly reminiscent of Pandora Jones who was once married to Michael [Astor]. Mrs Gross is always less pretty than the last time I saw her which is maybe why I had difficulty in remembering her.

Nico has a very good memory. He recited the headline of the article I wrote in *The Oxford Camera*,[21] 'Oxford Women Are Awful'. 'I remember the name of the lady who replied, "Oh No They're Not," an undergraduate called Douglas-Cameron.'

**Thursday 12 February**

Had a long talk with David Dimbleby advising him on how to deal with his attempt to become Director-General.

He wants to put news at the top and in charge of current affairs because he thinks you can't separate the two. I think he would not be bad as DG. It seems that Paul Fox may be going for it on a time-limited contract. He would have to give up options worth half a million in Yorkshire Television but he might do it in order to show that he was wrongly passed over as Director-General last time. I said to David, 'It seems a very expensive price to pay for pride.'

---

19. Journalist, on the *Times* at this period, later on the *Sunday Telegraph* and editor of the *Spectator* since 1995.

20. Journalist; arts editor, *Daily Telegraph*, 1986–91; literary editor, *Sunday Telegraph*, since 1991; m 1 (1965–88) John Gross, writer and critic, m 2 (1993) Sir Geoffrey Owen, former editor, *Financial Times*.

21. An undergraduate weekly newspaper closed down by the proctors in the spring term 1938; in *Confessions of an Optimist* (p. 73) WW says the article mentioned here was in *The Oxford Camera*'s successor *The Oxford Comment*.

**Saturday 14 February**
Tote Gold Trophy at Newbury. The first running since we took over from Schweppes. Great success.

Prince Michael presented the Gold Trophy which cannot be kept by the winner and Verushka presented the Silver Trophy which can. He was much happier in the absence of Princess Michael who makes him nervous and seem crushed. He said he'd never realized that racing was such fun.

Douglas Hurd was there with his wife. Douglas said why couldn't I get Mrs Thatcher to go racing? Surely she would come if I asked her. Others think it's vitally important to racing she should turn up at the Derby or Royal Ascot. I said I couldn't see any importance in it at all; she's not interested in racing. Douglas said, 'I think she even disapproves of betting.' I said, 'Not too much.' I was thinking she wouldn't have gone on making me Chairman of the Tote if she so thoroughly disapproved of it.

**Sunday 15 February**
She said, 'You have some new peers joining you,' and I said, 'Yes. David Stevens among them,' and told her I didn't like him which mildly annoyed her. 'He's very able,' she said twice in her firm voice. I said, 'Yes he is but I still don't like him very much. I wonder if he's going to speak there?' She said, 'They're supposed to be working peers and they should be voting and supporting the government.' I didn't tell her Arnold said it's not worth having a peerage if people like Stevens get one; but I did tell her I supposed it would keep the *Express* newspapers in line for the election.

'God bless,' she signed off.

Arnold upset. *Sunday Telegraph* has got a story about the Ministry of Defence police investigating alleged overcharging or cheating by GEC in their Southampton operation on defence contracts. Arnold says Levene is his enemy at the MoD and is partly responsible. Apparently the information came from a man who had a nervous breakdown and was getting the sack and Arnold tried to save him when his wife rang up. He then threatened the local executive that if he wasn't given what he wanted he would expose them to the Ministry of Defence, which is blackmail.

He was a very junior person and where there may have been innocent mistakes one way or the other, as there always are in cost plus contracts, there can be no question of cheating by GEC. I know that

Arnold is honest beyond peradventure and would never allow any crookedness of any kind. He is upset because he sees again conspiratorial elements in an attempt to do him down and make GEC's reputation suffer. It's all part of a campaign to get rid of him, he fears.

**Tuesday 17 February**

Dinner with Ronnie Grierson. Somebody asked me what he did and I said, 'He has a farm in Virginia, he is Vice Chairman of GEC, he is Chairman of the South Bank and he has a finger in every pie. But he is also a good man who likes to help where he can out of genuine concern.'

It was about thirty people as they usually have. You had to help yourself, more or less, and there was his own wine from Italy which is not very good, only red, and a filthy vodka and orange drink if you wanted it, which I didn't, to start with. The fish mousse cold to begin with was very good. The curry was about the same as you would get from any Indian restaurant and the pudding was full of cream so I left it.

Ronnie Grierson said he'd been in Boston recently talking to Kenneth Galbraith and he said to Kenneth Galbraith that when he read my book and the bits about India he had not realized before how much influence and input I had had into the Cabinet Mission and Indian independence. 'Did you know that?' Kenneth said, 'Yes, I did know. Woodrow has told me so often.' I thought that quite a funny dig at me but also a question of the pot calling the kettle black from Kenneth who boasts of having done many things, beginning with instituting price control in America in the First World War.

The good-looking John Patten,[22] Minister of Housing, was there. He asked me whether the fish was all right for him to eat. He kept telling everybody that I used to shout at him when he was at the Ministry of Health about eating the wrong food. The lady I sat next to for a time, wife of an official at the Bank of England, said to me when he was out of earshot that he was too good-looking and she didn't like good-looking men. They were altogether too pleased with themselves and he, Patten, looked precisely that. However, he is a competent operator and is bound to end up in the Cabinet.

---

22. Parliamentary Under-Secretary, DHSS, 1983–5; Minister of State for Housing, 1985–7; Minister of State, Home Office, from later in 1987 until 1992 when he entered the Cabinet as Education Secretary.

Duke Hussey said he got my letter about David Dimbleby and he agrees. He said, 'The dirty tricks are colossal and people keep ringing up backing Jeremy Isaacs and sending anonymous letters and saying that David Dimbleby will be no good in administration and the high up people are going around muttering they would resign if he is appointed. Which is exactly what I hope they would do. It would be a marvellous way of getting rid of some of the worst.'

He is in favour of David Dimbleby at the moment. I said, 'Surely you and Joel Barnett can just fix the governors?' He said they would try. I also told him that Edmund Dell[23] had told me that Jeremy Isaacs, who is the Managing Director of Channel 4 where he is Chairman, is no good at administration, so why have him?

Duke Hussey said the Profumo programme was 'way down the line' meaning that it was very far from being produced. He promised me that he was going to stop it. So my letter in the *Times* did some good on Saturday.

Duke Hussey's wife said to me, 'You wrote horrid things about him when he was made Chairman.' I said, 'It's better that I should start that way and come around to saying I was wrong and how well he is doing.' He was slightly embarrassed by her saying this. He is very anxious to demonstrate he really is cleaning the place up. It will be a long job but I think he knows what he is about.

Denis Healey was very friendly to Verushka and in her corner he talked to her throughout the meal. She said he can actually speak some Hungarian. He seems to bear me no ill will for writing such things as that he has lost all sense of honour in supporting Kinnock's CND policy. He just takes it as the small change of politics.

**Sunday 22 February**

To Willie Whitelaw and Cecilia for lunch at Dorneywood. Nearly there saw the Soviet Ambassador's car moving very slowly in front because they were ahead of time as we were. We followed and I wondered whether he thought he was being shadowed by some intelligence unit. He [Mr Leonid Zamyatin] is in his sixties, having begun in the diplomatic service in 1946, greyish haired and with the appearance of being civilized. His wife was a machine-made blonde but pleasant with a round face and had made an attempt to look non-dowdy.

Willie Whitelaw said after they had gone he was a penetrating

---

23. Former Labour minister.

person. I said I hadn't noticed it but Willie said, 'Ah but he was listening very carefully all the time.' I don't think he could have learned much.

At lunch I sat next to Cecilia and Melissa Stevens. Melissa is ridiculous but not unpleasant. Originally she claimed to be Hungarian which she can't maintain in front of Verushka and said rather lamely to her today that when she was very young she went to Yugoslavia where she was educated so she can't speak Hungarian properly.

Melissa told me about her book which is about how women treat their husbands. She had done seven thousand interviews or something of the sort.

I like Cecilia. She is a jolly lady, keen on horse racing which we discussed at some length. Melissa was tying to explain to me that her book was not all about sucking her husband's toes and massaging him from head to foot. I said, 'What a pity. I liked the extract I saw in a newspaper which suggested that it was. I think all wives should treat their husbands like that.'

Other guests were Henry Plumb[24] of the Farmers, just given a peerage, and Patrick Mayhew, Solicitor General, and his wife. Whenever I touched on anything interesting to Patrick Mayhew, such as the raid on the BBC in Glasgow by the police,[25] or the *New Statesman*, or Victor Rothschild, he said, 'That's a very sensitive subject.'

Henry Plumb is just boring.

I promised David Stevens that I would let him have some notes on what I thought of the *Daily Express* after looking at it with that in mind over the next fortnight. I decided I liked him a little better than before. I suppose I have been prejudiced against him because at one time he was offering to help rescue Banbury and then dropped the idea.

At lunch I said to Cecilia that not only will Mrs T win this election but she'll win the one afterwards. 'Good Lord,' said Cecilia. 'Yes, she's only sixty or sixty-one now. She'll only be sixty-five or sixty-six by the time the next election comes.' 'Won't she wear out?' I said, 'Never. It's her hobby. That's where she gets all her energy from. I expect she will

---

24. President of the National Farmers' Union, 1970–9.
25. On 2 February 1987, to remove material allegedly gathered for a banned programme relating to the Zircon spy satellite. The government was also considering action to stop the *New Statesman* publishing extracts from a leaked document on Zircon.

be Prime Minister when I die. The country is not yet ready to do without her. She is an institution in her lifetime like Churchill except it was not much good to him when he was going gaga and she is not. Macmillan was not an institution, nor was Eden, Attlee, Home, Wilson, Callaghan. There is a streak of slight masochism also in the British that they like being bossed around a bit by a nanny while pretending not to but when they need their socks darning, they're back to her pretty quick.'

**Monday 23 February**

Dinner at Margaret Anne du Cane's in her little house in Fulham. Too many people for so small a space.

Some people called Carew Pole from Cornwall were there and I was made to sit next to her so she could talk about Cornwall which was pretty boring. They knew my brother. He stayed with them when he was High Sheriff.

I am always faintly embarrassed about my brother because he is such a fearful name dropper and combines vulgarity with illiteracy, most of which he acquired from his wife who already had false teeth when he met her during the War when she was a chorus girl. Robert, my brother, has taken to ringing up frequently with bits of advice on how to run the nation. Sometimes he puts these on paper and sends them to people like the Prime Minister or the Chancellor of the Exchequer telling them that he is my brother. Though he has a different name from me,[26] he can meet no one without bringing in that I am his brother, somewhat exaggerating my potency.

**Tuesday 24 February**

Long piece on the back of the *New York Herald Tribune* about Arianna Stassinopoulos now aged thirty-six, ecstatic about her social success in America.[27] Bernard Levin was much in love with her at one time and I could never understand why. She is badly built with a face too heavy and a pushy, tiresome nature not backed by real knowledge or brain.

When he came once to dinner when Queen Elizabeth the Queen

---

26. Major Robert Lyle, WW's older brother (d 1989), took the name Lyle as a condition of inheriting in 1949 the family estate belonging to their Cousin Molly.
27. She left London in 1980, and in 1985 married Michael Huffington, Texan millionaire and aspiring senator; they divorced in 1997.

Mother was there Arianna was invited as well. She was so pleased with herself that she arrived thirty seconds before Queen Elizabeth in a taxi, having refused a lift from Bernard. He was furious. So was I – she like the other guests had been asked to be here a quarter of an hour before Queen Elizabeth, which they all did, but she thought herself too grand to bother about it.

**Wednesday 25 February**

At the Tote a call comes through. 'Lord Beaverbrook would like to speak to you'. When I got him I said, 'It's a long time since I heard on the telephone "Lord Beaverbrook wants to speak to you". I loved him dearly.' 'I know you did.' It was Maxwell Beaverbrook, the grandson, now a Whip in the Lords. He is doing it very well and is strikingly handsome. His grandfather would be pleased with the way that he presents the government case in speeches in which he has to cover so many departments.

He rang because I want to make my maiden speech on the Sizewell nuclear power station on Monday. Everyone is nervous that it will be controversial, Bertie Denham, Maxwell Beaverbrook and Alexander Hesketh.[28] I said, 'What would you like me to do? Make a speech about the ordination of women in the Church of England?'

A message from the *Times* that they particularly liked my article this morning and that Mrs John Hislop had rung them up saying that she had done so as well, but was I right about Estonia, Lithuania and Latvia being annexed by the Soviet Union in 1939? She also told them that she disagreed with me often about racing matters.

What an extraordinary woman. She thrusts herself in everywhere. I had to give up going to Sandown at one time and having lunch in the directors' box because I found myself sitting next to her too often.

Her husband is a nice little man, a very brave jockey at one time and a member of the Jockey Club. She never stops talking about the horse they owned once called Brigadier Gerard which they bred themselves and was a great success.

A strange dinner. Arrive at 9 Grosvenor Cottages at nearly ten to eight though we had been asked for seven thirty by Reggie Paget.[29] Greeted by his paramour Marjorie Verulam with whom Reggie Paget

28. 3rd Baron Hesketh, another government Whip in the House of Lords at this time.
29. (1908–90); Labour MP for Northampton, 1945–74; life peer 1974.

cheerfully says he has 'lived in adultery for thirty years'. The little cottage is cold with a tiny fire in the sitting-cum-dining-room. The pictures have partly been painted by Reggie Paget and partly by others. His are bad derivatives of Winston Churchill.

When he was a Labour MP Reggie was Master of the Pytchley and hunted with it two days a week. Then two or three of the other days he hunted with the Quorn and another neighbouring hunt. He would travel up to the House to vote or speak after the hunting was over from Northampton and go back for the next day's hunt.

Enoch Powell was keen about hunting, the joys of which he had heard from a soldier in the Eighth Army when they had to spend a day together and Enoch had said, 'You choose a subject for conversation,' and the man chose hunting. Reggie asked him up to stay with him and hunt with the Pytchley and it was a disaster. That was the longest hunt for years, four and a half hours covering twenty-six miles and Enoch fell off at the first fence. Enthusiastic bystanders put him on his horse again and he fell off another three times before his daughter told him he had to stop and he was taken home within half an hour of the proceedings beginning.

Enoch used to go to hunting on the London underground which had a terminus near a hunt close to London. He would dress in his full hunting outfit to the astonishment of the natives on the train.

Reggie recalled how once in Palace Yard I was so drunk that he refused to let me get in the car to go home but put me in a taxi. Andrew was saying the other night that the stewards at Pratt's are well trained in this way and ask for members' car keys if they seem very drunk and then get a taxi and send them home.

After dinner Reggie took Verushka and me upstairs and we looked at more of his pictures and some of his drawings. He had a very good nude by Augustus John which is exquisite. He had a Picasso lithograph which Tom Driberg left him. Reggie says he couldn't have been a spy because no one would have trusted him with a secret. I agree.

Reggie says he collects £93 or more a day when he is in London from the Lords. He takes £20 for attending and another £20 for secretarial assistance and books, and the balance for having to come to London and be in London because his real home is near Northampton where he has got a shooting box/lodge. He stays in the Lords usually half an hour.

His father was quite rich and to Reggie's surprise left him all his money which after death duties was half a million plus. Reggie being such a decent fellow and not believing in primogeniture shared it with his brother so Reggie got only £211,000 net. It was a lot of money in those days.

I wish my brother had also disapproved of primogeniture and had not taken any notice of my mother's new will, when she was deranged, in which I was cut out instead of getting half her money and half all the furniture and pictures which must have been worth £150,000 or so. And five hundred acres and some houses in Cornwall would have been a nice half share.

Reggie was first cousin to the Mamaine Paget who married Koestler, and her twin sister Celia. We agreed how beautiful they were. When I said Koestler had treated Mamaine badly he said it was what she wanted. She always wanted to serve a genius. I said, 'Well she didn't do it for very long.'[30]

As the evening drew on Reggie's conversation became more perplexing. At seventy-nine this year I think he finds it more difficult to marshal his thoughts, as doubtless I will if I ever reach that age. He had spoken in the Lords that afternoon making the best of a bad job in defending Labour's defence policy, though saying it was absurd to get rid of the nuclear deterrent. He agreed he only stayed in the Labour Party because of old friendships and associations.

It was touching how Reggie kept looking at Marjorie and smiling with love in his eyes. Though eccentric he is a thoroughly good and kind person. He was almost shocked when I said that Harold Lever, ostensibly Labour and taking the Labour whip in the Lords, would be in despair if Mrs Thatcher were defeated. Reggie said he didn't believe it but Harold had to admit it was true under pressure from me.

I told Reggie about my dilemma about the entry in the Dictionary of National Biography about George Wigg. Should I or should I not put in at the end how he had been arrested for accosting women at Marble Arch? Reggie said he thought the most humiliating part of the story was that three of the black prostitutes he had accosted had rejected his approaches. Reggie totally believed the police, as did the Magistrate who only dismissed the case because he thought no crime had been committed. Wigg's defence was entirely based on a proposition that the police had lied, which they clearly had not. In the end I left this bit out of the DNB entry.

Reggie's face is red and his body sturdy. He has enjoyed his life.

30. She was married to Koestler 1950–3, his second wife.

When he announced he had joined the Labour Party after getting tutorials from Keynes and was standing as Labour candidate for Northampton, his father was furious and didn't speak to him for years but nevertheless he did not cut him out of his will. His father had been Tory MP for Market Harborough.

**Thursday 26 February**

The Other Club not so interesting as before. Got there very early, thinking it would be more amusing that way. Profumo very grateful for my letter in the *Times* attacking the BBC for contemplating a programme about Christine Keeler. He was not impressed by the reply of Bill Cotton, Managing Director of BBC Television, that the programme was intended to be about Stephen Ward,[31] as it was impossible to make one about him without dragging him, Jack Profumo, in.

I noticed that Michael Hartwell was pouring the dregs from one of the bottles which had been decanted (they leave them on the table which is a good idea) into his glass of perfectly OK claret. I said, 'What did you do that for?' He said, 'I wanted some more wine.' I said, 'Didn't you see the sediment? Now look at the colour of your wine.' 'Good Lord,' he said, 'That confirms you ought to be on the Wine Committee.'

It turns out the Club does not have large sums of money.

They just have a whip round when they need money for wine.

Bernard very agitated about who [had been appointed] Director-General of the BBC, and popped out to the telephone to try to find out. There was no answer. However, on the way back I heard it was Michael Checkland who had been acting Deputy Director-General since Alasdair Milne went.

The Dictionary of National Biography people are the most niggardly lot in conjunction with the Oxford University Press.

The labour that goes into these Dictionary of National Biography pieces is enormous – each one must take me a full five working days for which there is £100 worth of books at shop price plus £25, which when income tax is taken off comes to something like £10. Yet they still get remarkably good writers to do this slave labour for them.

---

31. The osteopath who introduced Keeler to Profumo as well as to Ivanov, the Soviet Assistant Naval Attaché, precipitating the 1963 scandal.

**Friday 27 February**

Rang Margaret early this morning to tell her that the Greenwich by-election was a problem for Kinnock but not for her.[32] She was inclined to agree.

She was perplexed about the appointment of Checkland as Director-General of the BBC. We both concluded that they simply could not agree on one of the others and took him as what she called 'the neutral alternative'. It could be all right if he works closely with a determined Duke Hussey.

About 11.00 Rupert rings from Sydney to ask what's going on in England.

He said, 'Is she going to have an election now? Isn't it a good time?' I said, 'I don't think she will. She's not dismayed by the Greenwich result. But she doesn't know herself yet when the election is going to be.'

He said he was going for a week to America or somewhere else, then he would be coming to England in March. I said, 'Good. They tell me that when you are away your papers lose a sense of purpose. So you'd better come and tidy them up.'

**Saturday 28 February**

Early today Ian Trethowan tells me that Duke Hussey wanted Dimbleby, that Joel Barnett wanted Jeremy Isaacs. Isaacs had done very well at his first interview, but not at his second. Checkland did very well at his second interview and impressed the governors.

We both agreed it was a crazy way to appoint a Chief Executive – a one day set of interviews. Why didn't Duke Hussey impose his will? The natural thing for the Chairman of a board, as Ian and I both are of boards on which the members are appointed by the government and not by ourselves, is to say that his Chief Executive must be somebody he wants and can work with and to refuse to accept any other.

Arnold rings. A long detail of the speech he was going to make in the Sizewell debate in the Lords on Monday and he wants me to

---

32. On 26 February Rosie Barnes won for the SDP the previously Labour seat of Greenwich in a by-election caused by the death of Guy Barnett; the Tory vote fell from 12,150 to 3,852.

use his points. He had had lunch with Mrs Thatcher who had told him to keep his chin up which he didn't regard as particularly helpful.

**Sunday 1 March**

At the end of our conversation she laughed and said, 'Those are my instructions for the week.'

While I was talking to Margaret, Arnold had been trying to get me. He was in a great state about the *Sunday Times* Business Review publishing an extract from the book of Ivan Fallon (the deputy editor) in which he said that Arnold was responsible for the whole Guinness affair because he had reneged on his undertaking to provide finance for Gulliver to mount his bid for Guinness in August 1986. He wants to bring a libel action. Poor Arnold. An unlucky star is passing over his head.

**Monday 2 March**

My maiden speech quite successful. A nice letter from Noël Annan[1] and another from Maxwell Beaverbrook.[2]

Lord Marshall, Chairman of CEGB,[3] was particularly delighted with my speech and said that I had got all the facts absolutely right. He said to me that if CEGB were allowed to buy its coal at international prices the electricity tariffs would be dramatically cut. But of course they are not allowed to. They have to subsidize the coal industry by government edict and can't import all the cheap coal they'd like.

Someone who seemed displeased was Lady Hylton of Foster. She describes herself as convenor of the crossbenchers. She found me before my speech in the library, fiddling about with it. 'You won't be more than ten minutes, will you?' I said I would try not to be. 'You can't be. It's absolutely forbidden.' Actually I spoke for twelve minutes and took no notice of her.

---

1. 'You broke your duck in an innings in which the elegance of your late cuts was matched by the power of your drives and the severity of your pulling . . .'
2. 'You commanded the attention of the House in a masterful way.'
3. Central Electricity Generating Board – WW's speech was about the nuclear power industry.

Afterwards I saw her sitting at one of the top side benches reserved for crossbenchers fiddling with her pencils as though they were knitting needles and she were waiting for the occupant of the tumbrel to be disgorged on to the platform of the guillotine. An exceptionally bossy woman. She also told me that I mustn't be controversial. However, everyone thought I had been though I had only given what I thought were generally agreed facts.

**Tuesday 3 March**

Lunch at the Centre for Policy Studies presided over by Hugh Thomas. They have a new Director of Studies, a very bright young man, David Willetts,[4] who used to work in the so-called Think Tank of Mrs Thatcher. He was asking what things should the Centre for Policy Studies be concentrating on. I said, 'Let us please have a thorough piece of work on the nature of local government and whether it cannot be reconstructed so that we don't have the situation in which thirty per cent only of the people eligible to vote in council elections are ratepayers or full ratepayers and the rest are voting for their own handouts. One of the troubles is the apathy at local elections. Maybe local elections should always take place on the same day as a general election so that in the same polling booth you vote local and national?'

**Friday 6 March**

Patrick Minford[5] and Chips Keswick come to lunch. Patrick Minford believes that almost the most significant thing that Mrs Thatcher has done is abolish exchange controls. It helped to smarten up British industry, as well as seeing that the North Sea oil money was not wasted but got invested in sensible things overseas.

Chips brings me a box of excellent Ramon Allones which have some agreeable maturity. I chide him for always bringing boxes of cigars and he replies that he smokes three large ones every time he comes to dinner and that should give him an entitlement to eight more dinners. Chips drinks nothing which is his rule at lunch nowadays. He says he has a bonus of £50,000 related to profits, as it were, from

---

4. He became director, Conservative Research Department, 1987–92; MP for Havant in 1992; Conservative Opposition frontbench spokesman on employment in 1997.
5. Edward Gonner Professor of Applied Economics, University of Liverpool, since 1976.

Hambros over the last year. I said, 'Is that all? I thought you were really rich.'

**Sunday 8 March**

Tell Margaret how glad I was she went to Zeebrugge.[6] 'I felt I had to. It was agonizing. There was that child of eight who had lost his parents and grandparents.' I told her that on television she looked very beautiful. 'Oh did I?', sounding pleased, 'How very nice.'

She said she thought industry was doing well in dealing with the unions now and getting better productivity but they still didn't spend enough on research and development.

I told her about my lunch with the Centre for Policy Studies. One of my ideas was that one might have council elections only once for all each time there was a general election. She said, 'But there is a danger that some Labour voters who don't normally vote at general elections would turn out if the local elections coincided because they want to try and make sure of their free hand-outs.'

I asked her why she thought Tiny Rowland disliked her so much. She said, 'I think it's something to do with his not getting Harrods when the government didn't refer the question to the Monopolies Commission and the Arab[7] got it. But that was nothing to do with me. I didn't know anything about it. It was a Trade and Industry decision which I had nothing to do with.'

She added, 'Of course, he's not English.' 'No, not only Tiny Rowland isn't English, nor is Maxwell. They are both as bad as each other. Ted was right when he called Rowland "the unacceptable face of capitalism",' I said and she agreed. She said, 'I've heard that Tiny Rowland is giving money to the SDP. He's enormously rich. Have you heard anything about it?' I said I would try to find out, which I must do.

She's looking for a positive approach in her speech after the Budget. She wants somehow to deal with what she calls the middle class softies who have guilt complexes about earning more than others and crave to be chastised with higher taxes.

---

6. After the cross-channel ferry *Herald of Free Enterprise* capsized there.
7. Mohamed Al Fayed.

Roy[8] rings to say that the Claus Mosers[9] will give us lunch next Saturday when I go to vote for him.

**Monday 9 March**

Young Ned Carson[10] has died, aged sixty-seven. He was the youngest MP in 1945. For a time George Weidenfeld and I and he and his wife shared a house in Chester Square. We were his tenants. She was very pretty and he was tall and darkly handsome. They used to sit in the bath together singing. They were a beautiful couple and he had promise, but there was nothing much there except for his good looks and his charm; said to be similar to those of his father, Lord Carson, but otherwise nothing had been passed on to him. His death woke memories of the hopes of forty years ago and the light-heartedness.

Dinner at the American Embassy. Black tie. Large dinner party with several tables. Sit on the table of Carol Price, the Ambassador's wife. She is quite a pretty, jolly sort of woman in an expensive red dress, her favourite colour, showing more than a hint of plump white bosom.

Verushka brings up a strange woman to me when we are in the drawing-room, pretty and dark. Says, 'This lady is a great admirer of yours.' It turns out she is a columnist at the *Times*, I can't remember her name – Amiel perhaps.[11] She talks to me for ten minutes and I can't get away. She is Canadian and walking out with George Weidenfeld.

Douglas Hurd is there and tells me that the judges have now usurped the role of the executive government: it will be utterly absurd if they are going to decide legally in the courts on each case of an immigrant being denied entry. The courts will be wholly bunged up and the executive won't be able to operate.

**Tuesday 10 March**

The Tote Annual Lunch. Willie Whitelaw sits on my right and Bernard Levin on my left. Willie says he heard I made a very good maiden

---

8. Jenkins, candidate for the Chancellorship of Oxford University, an election in which all MAs of the university can vote if they attend the poll in person.
9. Sir Claus Moser, head of the Government Statistical Service, 1967–78; chairman, Royal Opera House, Covent Garden, 1974–87; Warden, Wadham College, Oxford, 1984–93.
10. The Hon. Edward Carson (1920–87), Conservative MP for Thanet, 1945–53; his father was the celebrated advocate Edward (Lord) Carson (1854–1935).
11. Barbara Amiel, journalist; m (1992) Conrad Black.

speech. Says that the Lords are very good at teasing out the weaknesses in legislation and he usually arranges with the government that two or three amendments they want in any particular Act should be allowed to stand because they are nearly always right.

He thinks she should keep her window open about the election, and relax and not think about it. If she sees a window sufficiently open for a June election, then she should have it.

There is some talk about the Chancellorship election at Oxford. He and Douglas-Home got together and decided to support Ted [Heath] because otherwise he would say there was another Conservative plot inspired by Margaret to do him down.

He is sorry for Lord Blake[12] whom he thinks is excellent, and I say, 'Any one of the three would do it quite well but I hope Roy gets it. I'm supporting him because he's one of my oldest friends.'

**Wednesday 11 March**

Dinner for Queen Elizabeth the Queen Mother.

On her left was A. N. Wilson,[13] opposite me. He turned out amusing, light and intelligent. He recommended some detective stories for Queen Elizabeth by a woman called Caudwell.[14]

I explained to Queen Elizabeth that though his novels are somewhat racy he is a dedicated Anglican to which he assented. She said she was enjoying his *John Milton* which I had sent her.[15]

She was complaining to me about the press and how badly they treated her grandchildren in particular. Rubbish about a split between Princess Diana and the Prince of Wales because they went out separately to dinner one night and things of that kind. She said, 'We are very vulnerable and it is rather fraught having the gossip writers at you the whole time.' She recalled that when she was the Duchess of York nothing of that kind ever appeared in the newspapers.

She was wearing a beautiful necklace which she told me had been given her by Queen Mary. I told her how pretty she was looking which was indeed true. She said, 'I always try to put on something special in

---

12. Robert Blake, historian, Provost of The Queen's College, Oxford, 1968–87; life peer 1971.
13. Novelist, critic and journalist.
14. Sarah Caudwell: *Thus was Adonis murdered* (1981), *The shortest way to Hades* (1984), etc.
15. *The Life of John Milton*, published 1983.

jewellery for you when I come here because I know how much you like it.'

She said, 'Could we have a dinner here with Ted Heath?' She's very fond of him. She said, 'Of course he doesn't like women.' I said, 'Well he likes Verushka because she's continental.' 'Ah yes,' she said, 'I can see that.'

She attacked Roy, saying he was a cheat. I said, 'Why do you say that?' 'He and Owen and his SDP people ought to have stayed in the Labour Party to fight it out. Now they're pretending not to be Socialist but they are. What does it mean? Social Democratic Party means they are Socialists and they're pretending not to be.' I said, 'Well I left the Labour party too you know because it had gone so far left and I thought there was nothing more they could do with it.'

She doesn't like Roy because she thinks he's too mannered. She hates Shirley Williams and mentioned again the awful things she did in destroying the grammar schools. 'But I like the dear old Labour Party,' she said. 'But,' I said, 'it is not the dear old Labour Party . . . it's not like it was when Ernie Bevin was there and Attlee and Co.'

Peregrine Worsthorne also performed well and of course Andrew Devonshire who is always charming and looking all the better for not drinking.

I said to Queen Elizabeth that although the press treated her family very badly these days, 'When Prince Philip's letter, which he had written to the Commandant of the Royal Marines,[16] was leaked to the *Sun*, it really did Prince Philip good. It showed that he was a very understanding and sympathetic father whereas the press had been saying the opposite.' She said, 'Yes, they always try to make him out as a brute. In fact he's extremely kind to his children and always has been.'

Queen Elizabeth said she thought Prince Michael was very agreeable but would I put some push into him, he is too mild. I said, 'I don't dislike his wife. She is quite funny and any man who sits next to her is immediately bowled over.' I told her that Anthony Quinton, who sat next to her at the Tote Annual Lunch at the Hyde Park Hotel, was enchanted by her.

Queen Elizabeth said she was against the ordination of women. She said that the deacons or whatever, and the women who wanted to be priests she met, all seem so aggressive and A. N. Wilson applauded this sentiment.

---

16. Prince Edward had decided to leave the Marines.

She thought Mrs Thatcher was very patriotic. But somehow I think the Queen and the immediate Royal Family prefer Labour governments to Tory governments because they are always so anxious to prove how dedicated they are to the monarchy and push in much larger rises on the Civil List than they would otherwise get.

Queen Elizabeth said that when Stafford Cripps came to a meal during the war he asked for an omelette. There was egg rationing and the Royal Family strictly adhered to all forms of rationing. All the eggs available went in Stafford's omelette and Elizabeth and Margaret watched with horror and fury as Stafford polished off their egg rations for the week, their eyes popping out and making faces when Stafford couldn't see them.

At the end of the evening it was announced that the gas boiler had broken down and the central heating and hot water had ceased. Verushka said this breathlessly in front of Queen Elizabeth who was amused.

I think Queen Elizabeth might not have gone at twenty to twelve if it hadn't been getting cold because of the collapse of the central heating. She was beautifully dressed in one of her chintzy light dresses. She didn't sit anywhere near the gas fire we now have which looks like a coal fire. She prefers to sit on the hard backed settee on the other side of the room.

**Saturday 14 March**

Creepy-crawly letter from Tony Howard.[17] 'Thank you so much for including me in that galaxy of the illustrious at your lunch on Tuesday. I much enjoyed the occasion – and in particular your speech – it took me back to the last time I heard you at I think the annual dinner at Bosworth in 1962. Thus the caravan moves on. PS I'd hoped you would be reviewing RAB (Howard wrote the book) in the *Times* – no complaints against Campbell but I am sure you would have done it more perceptively.'

So having done his unpleasant hatchet job on me in the *Observer* profile he butters me up again but this time I shall not be deceived.

Sunny and not too cold. Oxford was its old romantic self. The midday queue for voting for the Chancellor wound round and round like an uncertain snake, not knowing where its head or tail was. I and

---

17. Anthony Howard, at this time deputy editor of the *Observer*, had written a biography of R. A. Butler.

a very nice American called Price, who had been at Harvard and at Pembroke, and is Managing Director of Chloride where Michael Edwardes is the Chairman, bobbed in and out to make ourselves better positions.

When I actually got into the place to vote I was handed a grubby-looking large piece of green paper. 'What is that?' I asked. The girl who gave it me said, 'It's your voting paper.' One had to fill it in oneself with personal details and having done so take it to the Vice Chancellor who gravely raised his hat and bowed and said, 'Good morning.' He put the open completed voting form into a pile at his right-hand side. No nonsense about secrecy. One's name was on one's vote.

In the queue my instant American friend said that he was going to vote for Roy until he read his election address in a newspaper saying that he didn't think it was his job as Chancellor to raise money for the University. That should be unnecessary, Roy had said; it was for the government to provide the money. My American friend Mr Price said, 'That's exactly what's wrong with this country. They think the government should provide everything. At Harvard where I also was they raised all their money from alumni and others. They would have been ashamed to beg money from the government or depend upon it.'

Roy won not with an enormous majority but enough. Poor Ted was third, about twenty-two votes behind the 2,670 votes of Blake. If only one of those two had stood it was likely that Roy would have been defeated as there would only have been one candidate on the so called right.

Oxford combines ageless continuity with youth and perpetuity. I can never go there without being faintly stirred. I wanted to go to Worcester but didn't. I am still embarrassed by Petronella's short stay there. Silly, but I feel raw and defensive at the thought of seeing Asa Briggs or Harry Pitt.

Outside the Sheldonian were people shoving out an appeal to buy the Opie collection of children's books[18] for the Bodleian. I said to the man in charge at the stall, 'I've written two children's books,'[19] and he

18. Belonging to Peter (d 1982) and Iona Opie, editors of *The Oxford Dictionary of Nursery Rhymes* etc.
19. *The Exploits of Mr Saucy Squirrel* (1976) and *The Further Exploits of Mr Saucy Squirrel* (1977).

said, 'I know. That's why I thought you would be interested in this appeal.'

At the other end after one had voted there was a petition for saving the Playhouse which when I was at Oxford moved from its position near Somerville to a smart new building in Beaumont Street. The girl undergraduate in charge said they had heard they were going to turn it into a leisure centre which sounds terrible. So though I do not believe in subsidizing theatres I signed the petition just the same out of sentiment and memories of some jolly evenings at the Playhouse. Fifty years ago it was the very latest thing in theatres and now to be disused so soon. I gave them a four year covenant for £5 a year.

**Sunday 15 March**

She is looking for the election date gingerly, for some definite indication. She is hesitating about June.

I say, 'You can let it go a bit longer because Labour's going to quarrel more and more now.' 'Do you think so?' she asked. I said, 'Yes, it's getting worse with all these rows about defence and the trouble in the party about the Militants so that will go on helping you. But of course you have to make some strong attacks on the Alliance – who have they got for a government? What are their policies? The whole thing is incoherent. When people get closer to the election they will appreciate it couldn't possibly form a government. As the signs are going now the Alliance will help you by splitting the left-hand vote as they did last time.'

She spoke about the Chancellorship. I told her I had supported Roy, which she knew already, and I had said to him, 'I won't be one of your nominators unless you promise to make sure Mrs T get her Honorary Degree in a decent way.'[20] She said, 'Oh I don't mind about that a bit. It's not at all important.'

**Monday 16 March**

Dinner – Arnold Goodman. Meet David Astor[21] on the doorstep. He is charming and kind but always seems lugubrious and puzzled. It is

20. A proposal before Convocation, the university's governing body, to give Mrs Thatcher an honorary degree had been turned down in January 1985 by Oxford dons, indignant about government policy on higher education.
21. The Hon. David Astor, editor the *Observer*, 1948–75; director, the *Observer*, 1976–81.

as though his high intelligence bothers him for fear of the fearful things it may reveal to him about the world's suffering.

Clarissa also there, as she usually is. She nearly killed herself underwater diving in the West Indies being about a hundred and fifty feet below water when all her bits and pieces enabling her to breathe came off. Being a calm girl she remembered how to fit them on again without panic and saved her life. She was practising underwater diving or swimming when she was staying with us in Italy last summer. I warned her against such foolish practices at her age but she took no notice.

Sir Jack Lyons came into the conversation as a side issue on the Guinness affair. He received some enormous sum of money for 'advice' on the take-over of Distillers – about £3 million. He is under investigation and is obviously crooked. Arnold said he ought to go to jail.[22]

Verushka said, 'We've met them once or twice at Leonard Wolfson's.' Arnold was surprised. 'Leonard is such a punctilious man.'

I said, 'I have not much recollection of her.' Clarissa said, 'She looks like a vulture dressed by Dior.'

**Wednesday 18 March**

Bought myself a racing overcoat. Never had one before. Angela Oswald has always criticized my mackintosh particularly when it is dirty and I go with Queen Elizabeth the Queen Mother when she presents the Tote Gold Cup.

I recorded earlier that Lady Hylton-Foster had looked sour about my maiden speech. A few days later however she came up to me and said that it was very good indeed and it didn't matter about it being controversial.

**Thursday 19 March**

Cheltenham Gold Cup. Sit next to Queen Mother on her right and David Stevens, Chairman of the company that owns the *Express* etc. who has just been made a Conservative peer, sits opposite me, next on her left-hand side.

His company sponsors the Express Triumph Hurdle, that is why he is there. Queen Elizabeth complains of the *Daily Express* this morning

---

22. He was found guilty in 1990 on four charges including false accounting and theft of £3 million from Guinness, fined £2 million but not sent to jail because he was seventy-four and ill with cancer; later his knighthood was taken away from him. See *Requiem for a Family Business* by Jonathan Guinness (1997).

inventing a story that David Somerset is in disfavour with the Queen and she will not go to Badminton any more because she doesn't like him and generally disapproves. As Queen Elizabeth rightly says, and as I know from what David Somerset tells me too, there is no truth in the story. It is sheer invention. I ask him what control he has over his own newspaper and he is mildly embarrassed.

She tells me again the story of the two little Princesses when they were about eight and ten, that sort of age, and Osbert Sitwell thought it would be a good idea for them to know some poetry and poets, and he assembled a few poets, among them T. S. Eliot, and they came and read their poetry. The little girls thought T. S. Eliot was very strange and some of the words peculiar. When he recited *The Wasteland* they giggled behind their hands and Queen Elizabeth was embarrassed.

I told her that I thought of her on Saturday morning when I was voting for Roy Jenkins because I knew she would disapprove. She laughed. She said, 'I always talk too much to you.' I said, 'Oh you mean too volubly?' and she said, 'No. Somehow I seem to tell you everything I think which I shouldn't.'

I told her that Roy was really a very commendable person and how his father was a miner[23] and when Roy went to Oxford he got into a different more civilized world. He was very shy when he went into the House of Commons. The old Labour hands and union members thought that though his father was a miner Roy was looking down on them, but he was really just too awkward. In fact I told her he is a very remarkable man. He knows his defects and he was one of the few people I knew who had improved himself all his life and tried to make himself a better person, and I thought he had distinctly done that.

It had been arranged that when we came back from the paddock a presentation of the egg, which had been designed between Verushka and Stuart Devlin, should take place in the dining-room.

She opened it and was greatly moved. I thought she was going to give me a hug. She had almost tears in her eyes. She said 'Oh it's so beautiful. It's beautiful,' and then she looked at me and said, 'It was your idea.'

She says she has to go to the Royal Film Première very shortly. It's her turn. They take it in turn. They are usually dreadful and the next one is an American one and she's not looking forward to it at all.

There was great applause over my new overcoat.

---

23. Arthur Jenkins became a Labour MP in 1935 and was a Junior Minister.

Angela said, 'Was it expensive?' I said, 'Not very. £195.' 'Oh I call that very expensive.' I said, 'It was made in England.' Angela: 'I'm proud to be seen with you wearing it.'

As we were about to walk out to the paddock for the presentation of the Tote Gold Cup, Queen Elizabeth said to me, 'Last year an Irishman shouted at me, "I hope you live another thirty years."'

We were approaching the podium when an Irishman grabbed her and kissed her, and an Irish voice shouted out, 'I hope you live to be a hundred and thirty,' and I said to her, 'You've been promoted.'

**Saturday 21 March**

Ring Rupert in the afternoon and find he has been here for two days. 'I was just going to call you.' My natural insecurity makes me wonder whether he disapproves of something I may have said to a third party or no longer likes my articles. Sounds cheerful and asks us to supper for Sunday evening.

**Sunday 22 March**

We talked about the coming trip to Russia where she goes next Saturday morning. They are working now at No 10 on what they should say about arms reductions. She feels she can't trust the Russians so long as they repress civil rights and are in places like Afghanistan. I said, 'I go further than that. I won't trust them until they take their troops out of Eastern Europe and the Baltic countries. They have nothing to be afraid of from us.' She said, 'No of course not. The USA are not a first strike country. They would never attack Russia though they seem to be afraid of it.'

I went on to explain that we had never acted as Imperialists in the sense that the Russians do, imposing their ideology. In India we wandered in there by accident and through trade. It was always the unwritten compact that when they were ready to govern themselves and wanted us to go we would. We instituted the Macaulay system of education in universities like Calcutta. We taught them to be free and democratic, educating them on John Stuart Mill.

'Did you know,' I asked her, 'that there were municipal elections in India before there were in Britain?' She was astonished. I said, 'Moreover did you know that a British Indian civil servant started the Congress Party to train them for self-government?' She was unaware of that too. I said, 'It was only Roosevelt who was duped into believing that British Imperialism, which was coming to an end, had to be destroyed and there was nothing wrong with Russian Imperialism, though it would never come to an end voluntarily and has to be brutal and dictatorial as it is based on Communist ideology.'

When I told her I was seeing Rupert tonight she said, 'We depend on him to fight for us. The *Sun* is marvellous. It was the best on the Budget with its headline, "Look What a Lot You Got". We're up against quite a lot now. Tiny Rowland has got the *Observer* and the *Today* and *Sunday Today*.'

She asked me whether I thought the *Independent* would advocate the Alliance. I said, 'It might but if it does, it will only do it in a wishy-washy way. Whittam Smith[24] who runs it ought to be all right.' She said, 'Yes but what about the others, those who are not so keen?' I said, 'Surely he is the head of the thing and he can control it?'

I told her Bernard [Levin] had written to me saying he was doing a programme on Channel 4 on March 30th about the Refuseniks and would it be possible for her to see one or two, highly reputable in origin, in Moscow of those who had not been in trouble with the authorities at all. It would give tremendous encouragement all the way round to the oppressed people in Russia and they would know about it at once.

'We are doing something about this. The Embassy knows all about it. But don't press me about it and push me on it. I don't know what will be possible.' I said, 'I understand. It might be very difficult if you're trying to get somewhere on arms negotiations and then you irritate them. It's OK to talk with Sakharov[25] who is now licensed to criticize but seeing a wider section could be tricky.'

I said to her that sometimes people say to me, 'Why doesn't she go racing?' and I answer, 'I don't think she's particularly interested.' She said she might be interested but not until after the election.

On the election, we talked a bit about the improved results the Tories are now getting in local elections. It is a good augury.

I get the impression she's beginning to harden towards June, dependent on how the local elections go.

A jolly evening. Rupert's butler and wife had given notice because they said there was not enough to do.

---

24. Andreas Whittam Smith, founding editor of the *Independent*; city editor, *Daily Telegraph*, 1977–85.
25. Professor Andrei Sakharov, a leading dissident whom Gorbachev was trying to win over in the two years since he had become Soviet leader.

My touch of insecurity was as usual ridiculous. When I said I want to go to Australia before I die, Rupert said, 'Yes. You must come to the Melbourne Cup. I think it's October or November. Stay with us on the Farm and I will get lots of Australian politicians together to meet you. You'll be able to write articles easily back for the *Times* and the *News of the World* from there. And you would enjoy it.'

When I asked Rupert whether he had ever been to the Melbourne Cup he said, 'Certainly.' When getting divorced from his first wife he went there with forty Australian dollars and started betting. He nearly lost it all, he was down to five dollars. Then his luck changed and by the time he'd finished he'd won £100,000 at that meeting which paid for his wife's divorce settlement. (Rupert didn't have much money in those days.)

As we talked I wondered whether maybe I should write something about Rupert and when I put it to him he said, 'Yes. It could be a good idea.' He talks very freely to me. He says his television stations are mostly beginning to make money in America now but not all of them. He has an extraordinarily lucky touch combined with an instinctive judgement and determination which always bring him out on top.

He mentioned he is seeing David Stevens in the morning. He thought David Stevens wanted to talk to him about printing the *Star* and *Express* at Wapping. I said, 'How can you do that? Haven't you got enough to do with your own papers?' He said, 'No. We could probably fit them in.' I told him I thought David Stevens was an honest man and could be relied upon unlike Maxwell. Rupert said he seems to have broken with Maxwell now and that he had heard Maxwell was running short of money.

I asked Rupert whether he would be willing to get Twentieth Century Fox to look at Jo Janni's outline by Patricia Highsmith for a film. He says yes. But when I ring Jo he is a bit vague. I hope he is all right now and could carry it through if Twentieth Century Fox took it up.

**Monday 23 March**

Norman Lamont to lunch looking pleased and chirpish. His scandal troubles appear to be over. He is doing well at the Treasury and I said I thought he might become perhaps Secretary for Industry as I didn't think Paul Channon would last very long. Norman hopes to be in the Cabinet after the election.

He read what I said about the Budget in the *News of the World*, my criticism that it hadn't gone far enough. He said it was a fair criticism. He had argued with Nigel quite a lot about it. Come the election and the Budget after that, they are proposing tremendous tax cuts particularly for the high earners.

He raised a very interesting subject: the system of paying pensions.

It is absurd that we should pay everybody state pensions even if they don't need them. They should be means tested.

When I asked about the public reaction that they had paid for the pensions, why shouldn't they have them, he answered, 'They have not paid for pensions. What has happened is that those at work now are paying for people's pensions who are not at work. They are not paying for their own pensions because they are not funded.' A future generation will have to pay for the pensions of the people now at work.

With occupational pensions taking over so much and more worthwhile, people should be encouraged to have those and the only state pensions should be for those who are needy and can't get on without them. He says that is only twenty per cent of the pensioners. He is going to let me have some figures on the subject and thinks it would be a good idea if I were to take it up in an article.

Talk to Sir Robert Haslam who succeeded Sir Ian MacGregor as Chairman of the Coal Board.

He is in favour of privatization and would like coal to be privatized as a whole rather than fragmented. He expects to be breaking even before long despite all the difficulties.

Previously he was fifty per cent of his time with Tate & Lyle and fifty per cent of his time with British Steel. He says the difference is enormous. In British Steel or British Coal there was interference from Ministries all day long. Civil servants ask for all kinds of figures and statements and reports which take everybody a vast time to prepare. MPs think they have the right to come and talk to you, which I suppose they do, whenever they want. Even church leaders. 'Even me,' I said, and we both laughed.

He said he was also at Cable and Wireless as a director and once it became privatized the atmosphere changed entirely. When they began to be very successful they got a message from Mrs Thatcher congratulating them for doing so well but they were exactly the same board as before when it was a public board. It was release into liberty which enabled them to get on with the job. Also senior management get higher salaries when it is privatized.

**Tuesday 24 March**

Katie Macmillan and Bruce Matthews and his wife come to dinner. Katie talks volubly, incessantly and irrelevantly and inaccurately on almost every topic. I decide I must learn to say nothing as she prattles on with her rubbish, particularly as she'll be in the other house in August in Italy, not far from us but separate. Though she says she cannot bear her son Alexander and Alexander reciprocates the dislike, Alexander is driving her out to Italy and will be staying with her for the first part of August. They understand each other well and tell their friends what a liar the other one is.

In conversation with Bruce alone it emerges that Rupert is not altogether happy about the *Times* and is pressing hard on Wilson. I'm not surprised. Bruce says the two most dedicated editors are Kelvin MacKenzie of the *Sun* and Montgomery of the *News of the World*.

Bruce is dissatisfied with Schroder in its performance in placing the remaining forty per cent of the SIS[26] shares. There is not even a proper valuation on the worth of the company at the moment. Estimates range from £18 to £26 million. Either way the Tote's five per cent which I secured for them on the ground floor must be worth a lot of money already. Our investment money is converted to loan stock paying twenty per cent interest.

**Wednesday 25 March**

Rupert rings just before going to America early in the morning.

He wants me to send him notes about anything else I feel about the *Times*. He is clearly not quite happy about it.

Waiting outside the Levy Board building after the Board meeting at the bottom of Aldwych looking for Robbie [his chauffeur] I felt some hostility in the atmosphere. I turned round. There was a displeasing blond youth, slovenly dressed, who said to me, 'Are you Woodrow Wyatt?' and I said, 'Yes,' smiling in a friendly way. 'You're a scumbag,' he said and walked off. Perhaps there is something in telepathy à la Koestler. I felt his hate before I saw him and heard his words.

**Thursday 26 March**

Lunch at the *Spectator.*

On my right was Frank Johnson who is enchanting. I told him that

---

26. Satellite Information Services, of which Matthews was now chairman; Schroder was in charge of its flotation on the stock market.

I had told Rupert that he wanted to be editor of the *Times* and Rupert did not think it at all unreasonable but a promising ambition, and that Rupert had said he was writing leading articles now. Frank said that was not quite right. He was going to do it shortly and becoming associate editor to Charles Wilson. I said, 'Hooray.'

We had discussed the Alliance. We somehow have to do this curious job of getting the Alliance into second place without disturbing Mrs Thatcher but being ready to take over from the Labour Party as the acceptable alternative. It had been a remarkable coincidence that a death in Greenwich and a death in Truro[27] had given them a chance for a great boost but I still did not believe there would be tactical voting against Mrs Thatcher. Many may dislike her but they are not in dread of her whereas they really are afraid of Kinnock.

This morning the Vicar of Weeford rang up to say he is arranging about me being able to have a site for my grave and asked if I would come to Weeford on July 4th to open a fête.

The Other Club. At ten to ten Arnold got up and said to me across the table, 'You're going to Pratt's, aren't you?' Knowing what he meant I quickly said, 'Yes.' As he started to go Jock Colville said, 'Oh you must have a girlfriend.' Arnold looked annoyed. After he had gone Jock Colville said, 'Isn't it strange that so big a man as Arnold Weinstock has got no sense of humour and was irritated when I asked if he had a girlfriend? Of course he hasn't.'

Jock Colville said he is writing a book about the Lambtons and would I ring the *News of the World* editor and ask if he could see their archives to go into the famous case when Tony was photographed in bed with two prostitutes, one black and one white? 'Tony is very co-operative and has asked me to stay in Italy.' I said, 'Surely he doesn't want all this raked up?' He said, 'Oh he doesn't mind a bit; he says it's all been published. Why not have it done properly?'

**Friday 27 March**

Arnold in gloomy mood. Shows me papers about the Ministry of Defence police investigation into alleged fraud on contracts from the GEC establishment in Southampton. It seems the Ministry of Defence has gone mad in asking the police to look at contracts simply because

---

27. Matthew Taylor held Truro for the Liberals with a slightly increased percentage of the vote in a by-election on 12 March 1987 caused by the death of David Penhaligon in a car crash.

a profit has been made higher than originally estimated, probably because of increased efficiency or simpler ways of doing the job. Such profits are fully disclosed and [the] MoD gets a share of them. The trouble was started by a disgruntled man made redundant. If GEC had paid him more redundancy money as he suggested they would not now have this difficulty. But Arnold never gives in to blackmail.

Arnold also worried about the alleged deficiencies on the Foxhunter device GEC are preparing for the Tornado aircraft. The front page story in the *Sunday Telegraph* greatly upset him and when I arrive he is on the telephone to Andrew Knight complaining about it. One of his main complaints rests on the fact that it is not stated that GEC is not responsible for the radar on this item of equipment but Ferranti, who are left out of the criticism.

Arnold puts the attacks on him down to anti-Semitism. He says anti-Semitism is rife in the higher reaches of government. 'But Arnold,' I say, 'a number of the Cabinet are Jews.' 'Yes and they're the worst of the lot.' He says the same about Mr Levene in the Ministry of Defence who has been persecuting him, and whom to my surprise last week-end he had down to Bowden. I said, 'Why did you do that?' 'I just thought I'd better get to know him better.' He says his wife was a good Jewish girl who lit the right candles on the right days and they were a very ordinary couple.

We had 1966 La Lagune. An excellent wine properly decanted by the butler. He congratulated me on becoming a peer and apologized for not doing so before. I said, 'Yes, you haven't been here for some time.' He replied that he had been on holiday in Morocco.

Actually he had left some months before to work for the Duke of Westminster where he thought life would be grander and more in the patrician manner which he sought. He returned to Arnold, disappointed by the young Duke's behaviour. The hours were odd, the meals were odd and their friends were distinctly odd. He preferred the more patrician and traditional surroundings offered by Arnold to the unconventional set-up of the Duke of Westminster.

**Monday 30 March**

It is now Monday morning and there is another disturbing report about Foxhunter and GEC on the front page, this time of the *Financial Times*.

Sara Morrison, Jim Prior, Tim Bell and three or four others whose names I can't remember anxiously discussing [at GEC] how to react to the implied allegation coming out of the Ministry of Defence that GEC has let them down over Foxhunter.

I want them to put in any statement they make that Ferranti was making one of the component parts connected with the radar which did not work and it was not GEC's fault at all. David Fletcher, the GEC man in charge of this side of the business, who Arnold says is one of his best people and at the moment is at the Ministry of Defence, is keen to leave Ferranti out. Presumably he has got things going with them which he does not want disturbed.

Eventually David Fletcher rings from the MoD with a draft statement prepared by the MoD and it is put on the loudspeaker telephone so we can all hear. Jim Prior looks at me and says, 'I don't think it's so bad.' I say, 'Quite agree. It's not at all bad.' Arnold says, 'It's terrible.' He then walks up and down saying rather foolish things. Sara says, 'Don't be childish Arnold.'

At the end of the meeting, in which I think I actually did help them formulate their approach, Arnold who had left the room, rushes back, puts a bottle in my hand. It is a 1977 Château Lafite. 'That's your present,' he said. Jim Prior said, 'Good Lord, it must cost about £60 or £70,' and Arnold said, 'I keep some of them here.' Sara said, 'How interesting to see you bribed.' I said, 'If this is a bribe, what is it a bribe to do?'

Tim Bell says he will arrange to meet me as soon as possible. We got on well. He says, 'It will do my image good to be seen with you in a restaurant.'

**Tuesday 31 March**

Gave lunch to David Montgomery at the Lords. I looked up to see Jeffrey Archer leaving with the peer who had been his host. He waved in friendly manner to us both, yet David Montgomery was the man who ruined him with his story about Jeffrey's arranging to pay the prostitute at Victoria Station to leave the country.[28]

---

28. Archer was not in fact 'ruined' by this story; he won substantial libel damages in respect of such allegations.

**Wednesday 1 April**

A party, shepherd's pie and champagne, at Jeffrey Archer's. Mary was not there so don't know who to write and thank.

Agree with John Wakeham, Government Chief Whip, that an immediate election would look too much like cashing in on Mrs Thatcher's Russian triumph.[1] I say we are only talking about the size of the majority. Tories are surprised when I say this.

Tim Bell there so I see him for the second time in a week. The MoD are delaying the GEC Tornado statement and he believes they are going to issue it as an answer to a planted parliamentary question.

Having got some food, I sit next to Ernie Wise[2] and his wife. Both absolutely charming.

He is much taken up with his new project – a musical version of *The Mystery of Edwin Drood*, at the end of which the audience are invited to vote on how the story would have ended if Dickens had finished the book. There are three possible endings they've allowed for and whichever the audience votes for, they get it after the vote. He is the chairman of the proceedings and sings a lot. He was slightly hurt when I said I didn't know he could sing.

I find myself next to a lady with large breasts of which a fair amount can be seen. She is called Pollard[3] and edits *You* magazine, the colour supplement of the *Mail on Sunday*. She is with her husband Nick Lloyd and I wonder whether he has seen the notes I sent to David Stevens on how to improve the *Daily Express* and my criticisms of it. He makes no comment but I notice some of my suggestions are being incorporated.

---

1. The Prime Minister's visit in the USSR was 28 March to 2 April.
2. Comedian, of Morecambe and Wise.
3. Eve Pollard, editor, *You* magazine, 1986–8, *Sunday Mirror*, 1988–91, *Sunday Express*, 1991–4; m 2 (1979) Nicholas Lloyd (editor, *News of the World*, 1984–5, *Daily Express*, 1986–96; knight 1990).

**Thursday 2 April**

Tell her at ten to eight in the morning, 'Bloody marvellous. The most triumphant thing you ever did.' She has been thrilled by the crowds, 'Quite spontaneous,' she said.

Watch Mrs T in the Commons dealing with questions and making her statement after her Russian visit.

Kinnock sounded miserable and carping in response to her Russian trip. The Alliance were much more sensible in crediting her for what she had done, thus keeping in tune with the public mood which Kinnock and Healey had misunderstood.

On the way out saw David Owen again who said, 'She must go on the 7th May. If she doesn't the 7th May council elections will be bad for her. The Alliance will be coming up and she might not look so good.' I said, 'I don't see how she can go on the 7th May because it would look like too obviously cashing in on the Russian trip.' 'I bet you she will go on the 7th May,' he said. 'All right. I'll bet you £5 she won't.' Then he said he didn't bet on such matters.

'How do you think you are going to do?' He said, 'I must remember you're a confidant as well as a journalist. I always believed in a hung parliament.' He said it in such a way that I didn't think he had much faith in the proposition.

When I mentioned this to David Young[4] he said, 'All that David Owen has to do if he wants power is to come over to us and he would have a Cabinet job.'

**Sunday 5 April**

She said that when people are expecting an election decisions are not made as they should be in Whitehall.

I said, 'Surely not so much now because they must be pretty certain you are going to win?' She thought it wasn't so bad as it was in 1983 but it is a factor that government doesn't work as it should do because too many civil servants are feeling that maybe they are doing things for nothing and the new government will come in and change it all.

---

4. Lord Young of Graffham, Secretary of State for Employment, 1985–7, for Trade and Industry, 1987–9; deputy chairman, Conservative Party, 1989–90; life peer 1984.

**Tuesday 7 April**

Arnold pursues me round SIS meetings to ring him. He reads me a short letter he has written to Margaret following a dinner last night with the Pakistan Prime Minister whom he is trying to sell frigates to. She increased the guarantee credit on the order by £100 million.

He wrote a letter of thanks. 'PS,' he had said, 'I'm much happier when we are both on the same side of the argument.' I said, 'Don't say that. You didn't have an argument and it suggests she was wrong in other arguments, and you don't want to strike a nasty note.' Finally I got him to say, 'I am much happier when we can work directly together.'

In the Lords I saw David Stevens. I said to him, 'The *Daily Express* is getting better. Is that due to your intervention?' and he said, 'Yes, I think it is. Nick Lloyd asked me who had I been talking to and I said nobody.'

David Somerset must be very rich. He has a problem with capital transfer tax which in this Budget is to be abolished for money going into or out of trusts. The year before it was abolished for straight gifts. He wants to know whether to proceed with a transfer to his sons from or into a trust on which there would be £2 million capital transfer tax to pay if the new law is not in position.

Norman Lamont tells me it might have reached that part of the committee stage by the election but that if it hasn't they do a deal with the Opposition to pass through the remaining stages on an agreed basis. He and I both thought they would be unlikely to allow this particular concession to the very rich to go without a fight. Prudence, says Norman, would dictate that he wait until it actually becomes the law before taking it any further, which I told David.

**Thursday 9 April**

Decided I must try and earn a bit more money. I'm about £10,000 to £15,000 light of what is really needed, especially with the income tax coming up.

Spoke to Chips about the organization which supplies non-executive directors to companies. He had asked me to sign a reference for him which I did and they thanked me. I asked him the point of his doing this as he has to give the fees to Hambros, whereas I would keep mine. He said he was asked by the Bank of England to do it because they think they should have better non-executive directors on some companies. 'I would like to be one.' 'When I'm signed up and accepted I will recommend you to the same people.' It seems it's quite high powered.

Called in at the Levy Board to look at the Ascot accounts. I was interested to see that in 1985 during the four-day Royal meeting the cost of entertaining royalty was £115,000. On other days when it is not Royal Ascot the costs of Royal entertaining run from about £3,500 to £15,000. I cannot imagine how they manage to get through so much money. When the Tote gives its lunch on Wednesday and Thursday at Royal Ascot in our entertainment room we have about thirty people to lunch and it doesn't cost more than about £1,000 including lobster and champagne and all the rest of it.

They were very fussy at Ascot about letting me look at these accounts, the first time the Levy Board members have been allowed to do it. You have to go to the Levy Board itself to see them. I don't know how they've managed to get away with the secrecy for years – I suppose by pretending the Queen has something to do with it which she does not so far as running the course is concerned.

Pop into the Lords, partly to ensure my £40 expenses is worth £100 as it's tax free, partly to put down an unstarred question to ask the government what they are doing about Sunday racing if anything. In the Lords this leads to a short debate and I can make a speech as long as I like. Others will doubtless join in. It's a good way of testing the feeling.

Däska looking very sad in the evening and aged considerably. Verushka unable to come [to the dinner party] because in seclusion after her latest face lift. Katie (presumably she took her place) who talked very loudly non-stop as usual. Reresby Sitwell was there with his wife. I've met him on and off over the years. He seems to be rather bitter now.

I also made a mistake with Reresby by asking him how the vineyards were which Osbert Sitwell used to have in Italy. He said, 'You're the third person who has asked me that this evening. I sold them in 1973 which is a long time ago.'

He was nowhere near as pleasant and jolly as I remember him being. He seems to have some of the acid of his aunt Edith without any of the lightness and jollity of his father Sacheverell or his uncle Osbert. But I dare say he would do well enough on a railway journey with nobody else in the carriage.

During dinner I asked Paddy[5] what happened to the girl he had the affair with before the War in Transylvania. He said, 'She's eighty-two now. She was ten years older than me and I'm seventy-two. I traced her recently and sent her a copy of the book.[6] Like other Hungarians who lived in Transylvania she was driven out and had to live in Budapest in a house they had there. And they put five other families in and she had a terrible time. She was forced to share a little flat with a ghastly Communistic dictatorial woman who finally she got into such a rage with that she stabbed her to death. But she was acquitted by the Hungarians because all the neighbours said they hadn't been able to understand how she had put up with her for so long.'

**Friday 10 April**

Dinner with Irwin Stelzer at the Connaught.

Irwin tells me that he is getting $100,000 a year for reorganizing the Department of Energy at Harvard University and another $300,000 a year for a consultancy job he has got which is taking him backwards and forwards to Spain at the moment. What with the $18 million he got for his business[7] he must be very rich.

He is now thinking of buying a flat in a converted house in Upper Grosvenor Street for £650,000. He thinks it would be cheaper than staying expensively at the Connaught whenever he comes to England which they propose to do more now.

**Saturday 11 April**

Irwin to dinner at Ken Lo's Memories of China, an expensive Chinese restaurant. I had not wanted to do this but Verushka had said we would give him dinner on Saturday night as he'd be alone in London.

It cost me £95 though I suppose after all his generosity to us I shouldn't grudge it but I get very worried about the money pouring out of my boots on all kinds of ridiculous things.

I was annoyed with Petronella who wanted to have the most expensive menu. I put my menu up in front of my face and say in her ear, 'I've told you before we are going to have one of the set dinners

5. Patrick Leigh Fermor, travel writer.
6. *Between the Woods and the Water*, the second of his autobiographical travel books, published in 1986.
7. National Economic Research Associates.

between the two of us and the others will have their choice. We can all help ourselves to the bits and pieces. Why are you so extravagant?'

She had been very helpful reading my article about Japan.[8] So was Chips Keswick who got a man at Hambros to fill me in with the holdings of Japanese banks in London and the amount of trade they've brought to us from overseas in money transactions.

**Sunday 12 April**

Margaret says how pleasant it is to be away from the House for a week or so.

I say it is a good thing those two Tory MPs have resigned over their dodgy share dealings with BT.[9] She says, 'And one of them – how could he say he was buying shares for his granddaughters? If he was doing that, why didn't he put them in their name, not his own?' 'It was only a minor irritant but it tidies it up a bit for you. Now we've got to get rid of this man Proctor,'[10] and she agreed. 'Yes there are three of them who've been a nuisance.'

She carried on a bit about GATT[11] being so slow: they haven't dealt with the Scotch whisky penal taxation applied by Japan yet. I said, 'Of course other countries must feel badly about us as we've been doing so well out of them,' but she made no comment.

**Tuesday 14 April**

To Scotland, Glasgow. Dash round looking at betting shops. Over lunch discuss with the very bright young Area Manager, Jim Grey, whether an incentive scheme of paying bonuses to those who find us betting shops, or new locations where we can buy or start new ones, would be good. I want to give such people a big bonus, if something eventuates. Brian[12] hesitant as he usually is.

---

8. WW wrote in the *News of the World* on 12 April: 'The Government is an ass over Japan.' He was complaining about the way Michael Howard, Parliamentary Under-Secretary of State at the DTI, had handled Japanese discrimination against Scotch whisky.
9. Keith Best and Eric Cockeram had made more than the one application per person allowed for British Telecom shares when BT was privatized.
10. Harvey Proctor was the subject of newspaper allegations about his private life; he was charged later in April 1987 with gross indecency and resigned four weeks before the general election.
11. General Agreement on Tariffs and Trade.
12. McDonnell, chief executive of the Tote.

Dinner with Alan Hare. We arrive promptly at quarter past eight as instructed. The Weinbergs[13] arrive at 9.00. I ask Anouska, who is pretty and was an actress and now has a large hotel called Blakes employing a hundred and twenty people and a dress business where she employs seventeen, why she is so late. I say, 'I'm very hungry. You've delayed everything.' She said, 'I've been fixing some Japanese. It was very complicated.' The Japanese were rude to the customers when they came for their fittings if their bottoms had got bigger and they would point that out instead of being tactful. However, they were good at sewing and making dresses.

George Thomson,[14] and his wife are there. Over dinner (the table is round) I attack him for his pusillanimity in appointing Richard Attenborough[15] as the new Chairman of Channel 4. I say 'He is a typical old fashioned trendy; left-wing, do-gooding interferer. His film about Gandhi was a disgrace. Why Gandhi was even portrayed as a man with matted hair on his chest, whereas he didn't have a hair to be seen. Not only that but the Viceroy was made to look an idiot, so was Jinnah. The film was absolutely absurd. It doesn't tell you that Gandhi delayed the independence of India by at least ten years and he caused all the deaths. If he had allowed the Government of India Act to work after 1935 everything would have gone smoothly and there would have been no problem at all, not even Pakistan.'

George said he wanted Channel 4 to stay as it was. I said, 'Did you read my article in the *Times* saying it should be privatized? The big ITV companies get a lot of kudos for supplying money which is unnecessary to Channel 4 and then deducting it from the amount of levy they have to pay to the government.' He argued that privatizing Channel 4 would lower its standards as it pursued advertising and higher market ratings. I said, 'Not having advertising has never prevented the BBC from lowering its standards which it has been doing constantly for years.'

Mark Weinberg is deputy to the Chairman of the SIB.[16] He says

13. Sir Mark Weinberg, chairman, Allied Dunbar Assurance, 1984–90, J. Rothschild Assurance, since 1991; knight 1987; and his wife Anouska Hempel, designer and hotelier.
14. Chairman, Independent Broadcasting Authority, 1981–8; Labour politician and former EEC Commissioner; life peer 1977.
15. Actor, producer, director; knight 1976, life peer 1993.
16. Security and Investments Board.

Chips is wrong in believing that the regulations are too detailed and too many and that Chips was never very good at reading. He says insider trading and all kinds of shenanigans have been going on in the City for years and nobody took any notice. Now it's all got to be cleaned up and this is a very good system the government is devising.

We had Forts de Latour 1973 to start with. It wasn't bad but the 1959 real Château Latour was splendid. I drank far too much and felt sickish in the night and woke up with a hangover in the morning. The food was very rich. There was a lot of duck well cooked and crème brûlée and all that kind of thing. I am too greedy and should not have drunk so much. I asked to drink the 1959 Latour of which there were two decanters before the cheese and was allowed to start on it then.

**Wednesday 15 April**

Frank Johnson tells me he is now a kind of deputy editor.[17] He writes leading articles and controls the letters page.

Frank told me that Charles[18] is very timid and will not be tough enough. He watered down his leading article in the *Times* this morning in which he has attacked Baker[19] for being so wet.

To Hambros with Brian McDonnell to talk to Chips and Christopher Sporborg[20] about privatization of the Tote in advance of my interview next week with the Home Secretary, mysteriously described as 'on a one to one' basis. We all feel the position has changed since I wrote to the Home Office with the views of the Board (really mine) earlier this year, saying we somewhat abandoned the idea because of the difficulty of getting enough money out of the operation.

First, we have had profits of around £4 million to the end of the year March 31st 1987 after sponsorship and after writing off some £343,000, which we didn't have to, by way of advancing depreciation further than we need.

Secondly, we have now got a valuable holding in SIS which could come out to be worth £5 million or £6 million in a few years, and is probably worth £2 million now.

Thirdly, the Tote is still going so well on the course that we are

17. In fact associate editor of the *Times*.
18. Wilson, the editor.
19. Kenneth Baker, Secretary of State for Education at this time.
20. Vice chairman, Hambros, 1986–90; deputy chairman since 1990; member, Jockey Club.

getting a take of more then twenty per cent over the previous year at each meeting, sometimes better.

Fourthly, we have new devices on the way for linking our Tote betting shops direct to the pools and with the betting shops containing the changing odds on the Tote Win, Place and Dual Forecasts.[21] They can be instantly compared with the bookmakers' board prices so customers would like to come into our shops, even if they don't have a bet with the Tote, where they can see what choice they really have which they couldn't in any other betting shop. If they don't like the Tote bet they can have an SP[22] bet with us.

Fifthly, it was agreed that the Stock Exchange is now not so difficult about Golden Shares which in the Tote's case would be designed to prevent its ever being taken over by Ladbroke's or another betting shop chain.

Sixthly, it would be acceptable to say in our prospectus that we were always going to maintain at a given level our support to racecourses above the call of duty or commercialism.

**Sunday 19 April**

David Montagu and Ninette come to lunch. I had spoken to David on Thursday when I saw in the newspaper that his son had been sent to jail for being in possession of drugs and for supplying them, but not for profit.

David deeply distressed because he felt the Judge had been extremely unfair in not recognizing that Charles, his son, had been making superhuman efforts to get himself off drugs, which he is at the moment, and had also done an enormous amount of voluntary work with Narcotics Anonymous to help others. He fears that he may have a relapse of some sort in jail because one never fully recovers and the only phrase

---

21. The Tote Win is a Tote pool bet for the winner of a race; the Tote Place is a Tote pool bet for a horse to get a place; the Tote Dual Forecast is a Tote pool bet in which the first and second in a race have to be forecast in either order.

22. It is also possible to bet on the Starting Price of a horse – the odds decided on the racecourse on the day of the race by (at the time of this volume) a representative of the *Sporting Life* newspaper and a representative of the Press Association after consultation with the bookmakers. The SP is given in newspaper results columns and on the media results services. It is the basis for much payment by betting shops and credit bookmakers.

one can use about someone who has been taking cocaine – Charles had been taking a gram a day – is that they are 'in recovery'.

David wanted me to write an article to say how unfair the Judge had been. His defence counsel had said it was absolutely scandalous.

Charles has done no harm to anyone.

Sonny Marlborough's son Jamie[23] had got off with a suspended sentence although he had actually committed a criminal offence in breaking into a chemist's shop to steal drugs. He also pointed out that Boy George[24] had been given a suspended sentence. But Boy George had not been accused of supplying drugs.

Poor David was almost in tears. Ninette on the surface was taking things more calmly. Charles is now in Wormwood Scrubs. They have not been allowed to see him except for once just after he was sentenced when they put him behind a glass screen – 'as though he was going to attack us,' David said bitterly.

Charles is a charming boy about thirty-two years old, good looking. He went on drugs according to his own story when his sister, to whom he was devoted, committed suicide two years ago. They have had terrible bad luck with their children. One fattish girl seems to be the only child of the three who is balanced. She is getting married shortly.

Tried to cheer David up by giving him first a 1964 Dom Pérignon which was excellent, golden but still with its little bit of fizz. Then we had Pontet-Canet 1961. That was superb like rich but dry liquid velvet.

**Monday 20 April**

Bowden.

Susan[25] with her child Clare was there, not yet two. Bright, talks and calls me Mr Bow Tie. Arnold dotes on her as he does on all his grandchildren. He is more cheerful. He is just putting together this great business of Phillips and Picker in America which GEC will own and control and will be the largest medical equipment firm in the world.

We talked about whether people could in fact influence their children, after Arnold had said it must have been bad upbringing by Ninette Montagu and David that caused the suicide of their daughter and their son to be a drug addict. I said, 'I don't agree. Are you saying

23. The Marquess of Blandford.
24. Pop star.
25. The Hon. Mrs Lacroix, the Weinstocks' daughter.

it was my fault that Pericles decided to leave Harrow and go to America?' 'Probably, because you were divorced and that must have unsettled him. He obviously felt he didn't fit in and he didn't like the society of England.' I said, 'However, he is doing very well now. He's getting $35,000 a year and managing a restaurant which is not bad at his age of twenty-three.'

Nevertheless I wonder to what extent it was my fault that Pericles left Harrow and turned against the world and became convinced he didn't have a place in England. I was a bit rough with him before he went back to Harrow in January after that Christmas. He then absconded after a couple of weeks or so. But he had had a very bad report and it was clear he needed to pull himself together. He also resented my ticking him off in front of Arnold Weinstock at Conock over some trivial matter of getting the wrong decanter or pouring the wine wrong or something not important of that kind.

When I rang Downing Street and asked to speak to Mrs Thatcher and the girl said, 'Oh wait a moment, Lord Whitelaw, I'll get her for you,' I kept shouting, 'No, it's not Lord Whitelaw, it's Woodrow Wyatt,' but she didn't hear. When Margaret came on I had to say, 'It's not Willie, it's me' and she laughed.

I told her that I had been talking to Frank Johnson of the *Times* this morning about the Maurice Oldfield affair.[26] It seems he was a homosexual who went in for the rough trade. It also appeared that there had been a report from McNee, who was then Metropolitan Commissioner of Police, which he had given to Willie Whitelaw when he was recalled to do security work in Northern Ireland by Margaret.

I said, 'There's going to be a lot of pursuit of this matter. I think you ought to be ready to know what line to take and if there was such a report, why not say, "Yes there was a report and I was quite satisfied he was not a risk in Northern Ireland from blackmail or any other source"?' and that indeed was true because he wasn't and he did a good job. She was slightly tart and said, 'Do we have to reply to every story that appears in the newspapers?'

---

26. Sir Maurice Oldfield was head of the Secret Intelligence Service (MI6) from 1973 to 1979. According to Hugo Young in *One of Us*, his biography of Margaret Thatcher (p. 459), the Prime Minister formed 'a close and mutually admiring relationship with Sir Maurice Oldfield'.

**Wednesday 22 April**

At 6.00 saw the Home Secretary Douglas Hurd. The government are obviously more interested now in privatizing the Tote and he wanted to know my general feelings about it. We discussed the holding of a Golden Share to prevent anyone taking it over and to enable us to expand and issue new shares without fear of losing control and to develop the business.

**Thursday 23 April**

A shock on the ten o'clock news. Rachel Macmillan[27] dead, last night. She had been mugged earlier on her way home at knife point. £4,000 of jewels had been removed and her credit cards by the three men who posed as mini-cab drivers. She had been able to give a perfectly coherent statement to the police.

Later that night she was found dying by her flatmate who got on to Katie. She had been into drugs and was an alcoholic, poor child. Only thirty-one. Very thin always but pretty. She had a weakness for fairly low level people. I remember a great birthday party – Harold Macmillan's – when her live-in lover hairdresser was there. I made him feel at ease and told Harold that he wasn't too bad. He was enterprising and ambitious and was trying to set up his own business. However, after a while Rachel left him and found somebody else. She had met the hairdresser while she was in Canada. She was married to a man – I think something to do with films – who was no good and they separated.

Only the last time that Katie came to dinner she said she was so glad that Rachel was leaving her flat because she was so untidy and made such a mess everywhere. She had only just gone to this new flat.

Earlier in the day Mrs Thatcher made a very good and full statement about Maurice Oldfield. When I had first spoken to her about the need to do this she had been tetchy. As so often happens she disagrees or reacts unfavourably to begin with, thinks about it, decides you were right and goes and does it.

NERA board meeting at 4.00. Chips is very downbeat. Says it doesn't sound as if we have much of a business. Afterwards Chips said to me that he thought that Dermot Glynn, who is very nice and who is the Chief Executive, had not got enough bite. He doesn't press or fight hard enough for work.

---

27. Daugher of Katie and Maurice (Viscount Macmillan, d 1984).

**Friday 24 April**

Verushka talks at length to poor Katie. She says she has her other children to think of and will still come to Italy and they will stay with her.

In the evening Sabihah Knight came to supper after she, V and P had been to a film. There was talk of Harriet Crawley now aged thirty-eight. She is standing as Conservative candidate at Brent against Ken Livingstone. She announced that she was pregnant by a man she was not going to marry and whose name she would not give. A very pretty girl who I've known the best part of her life. Vivacious, intelligent, flirtatious who laughed at my jokes. Always her standards were too high, perhaps because of the people she met with her father and mother, all intellectual or grand or important or whatever. Maybe that will be Petronella's difficulty.

Some people think it may be helpful to her to be an unmarried parent in Brent where there are two thousand unmarried mothers.

**Sunday 26 April**

Just as I was coming in from a walk I was told Rupert was on the telephone from Paris. Like a jolly schoolboy he told me gleefully that he was celebrating the twentieth anniversary of his marriage with Anna with a weekend in Paris, staying at the Ritz.

Would we have dinner with them when they come to London for two nights, on Tuesday?

We discussed briefly the Oldfield revelations. I told him that I had got on to Mrs T after speaking to Frank Johnson and her statement had been the result. I thought it was excellent and required nothing further to be said. He was laughing and said, 'The *Sun* perhaps was the best with their headline "Tinker, Tailor, Poofter, Spy".'

I told him in confidence that Frank Johnson said that when he wanted to be tougher with leading articles, Charles Wilson was always nervous and wanted to tone them down. I praised Frank to him. He was very grateful for the information. He said he would have Stothard, Wilson and Frank Johnson to lunch or dinner and see what he could do to elucidate and stiffen Charles Wilson up.

She [Margaret] had been deeply shocked by the murder of the judge, Lord Justice Gibson, in Northern Ireland and his wife. 'They are very brave, those Northern Ireland judges. I keep thinking of the pictures of the terrible wreckage of their car.'

On the election I said, 'The pressures are building up for June,' and she agreed. 'But let's wait to see what those local elections are like.'

I told her about my meeting with Douglas Hurd. She was pleased he was thinking along the lines of privatizing the Tote. I said, 'Why not do it? Put it in your manifesto.' (But of course she won't.)

**Tuesday 28 April**

Memorial service for Jack Heinz. Music rather wispy and hymns with no substance. Tiny Hugh Casson[28] gave the address and Alec Home said to me afterwards, 'They ought to have got a box for him to stand on. He's so small you couldn't see him.' Alec asked me when I thought the election would be. I said, 'She won't make up her mind until after the local elections on May 7th but I suppose it will be June 11th.'[29]

Dinner with Rupert and Anna. Also Charles Wilson and his wife Sally who edits *Options*, a women's magazine.

Anna says she wants my advice on her new book, but she's not far enough on yet. She was looking prettier than usual, as she did when they stayed with us at the Strozzato years ago and spent a lot of time in bed.

I asked Rupert what I should tell Mrs Thatcher about his views on the American economy. He said, 'I'm nervous of it. It looks a little bit better from a distance but I certainly wouldn't keep an election waiting for it to get better.'

I told Rupert we must keep in touch and have an input when the election starts, which is most likely to be on June 11th. He said he would come over specially. I said, 'I always talk to her a great deal during the election, commenting on how I think it's going and what I think she needs to do to counter new arguments or situations. We'd value your help.'

**Thursday 30 April**

Tony Morris and his wife, plump and homely, full of their plans for the bar they have bought for £50,000 in Spain near Marbella.

They had brought a parcel in a cellophane bag which they had left outside the Lords dining-room. It was a present for me. I said, 'Shall I fetch it?' which I did. It was beautifully wrapped up with a gold ribbon.

---

28. Sir Hugh Casson, president of the Royal Academy, 1976–84.
29. WW was right.

It was a miner's lamp in brass, pristine and engraved with a message at the bottom: 'To Woodrow. Eternal Thanks. Tony April 1987'. That was not merely because I helped the Working Miners' Committee during the Scargill strike but because I had got Tony far more redundancy (and also the write-off of the mortgage of his Coal Board house) than he ever expected.

I was very touched by the present.

Dinner at Clarissa's. Arnold Goodman there as usual. He talks about Kagan[30] when I say I have not yet discovered which he is in the Lords. 'He came to me about his son who had gone off with his mother to a man she later married.' The son was illegitimate and Michael Astor was the adopting father. Kagan wanted to bring actions against Michael unless he agreed to give him access and also to pay for his upbringing because he didn't want some other man to be paying for his child's education etc. He was full of violence against Michael.

Arnold said, 'You are talking of an old friend of mine, and I cannot help you other than to say to you that if you behave in a quiet and sensible manner I am sure you will he able to see the boy frequently but he has been adopted legally.' Kagan wouldn't listen and fought an unsuccessful action.

All this from Arnold made me wonder if he ever talks about my affairs. I thought solicitors never spoke of what passed between them and clients, even if they are only potential clients. Arnold often talks about Harold Wilson, for example.

Peregrine Worsthorne, a little miffed at my being first a knight and then a peer, said the only thing worth being was Privy Councillor when you are described as the Right Honourable. I said, 'But so am I. Officially the designation is The Right Honourable The Lord Wyatt of Weeford.' He wouldn't believe me. I said, 'Would you like to bet me?' but he withdrew.

---

30. Manufacturer of the Gannex raincoat Prime Minister Harold Wilson always wore; he was made a life peer in Wilson's controversial 1976 resignation honours list, 'the lavender list' typed by Wilson's political secretary Marcia Williams (Lady Falkender) on lavender-coloured paper. Kagan was subsequently imprisoned for evading excise duties.

**Saturday 2 May**

Prince Khalid Abdullah came to lunch [at Newmarket]. He would still like to have a chunk of SIS and I told him to get his man of business talking to the SIS people about it, and Bruce Matthews and even bookmakers as well, if he thought it was a good idea. He likes now to come to the entertainment room at Newmarket for the 2,000 Guineas since he has discovered that he has luck that way.[1]

Afterwards dinner at Stanley House[2] with with Isabel where David and Ninette are staying. Charlie Benson and his wife Caroline come. So do Albert Finney [actor] and his girlfriend Sarah Mason who works for somebody called Robert Fox, brother of Edward Fox, in connection with plays and films. She was not ugly but not especially appealing. I sat next to her and we got along well until the conversation turned to unmarried mothers. I said I thought it appalling for people to bring bastards into the world out of self-indulgence, caring nothing about how the bastard would feel. She called me bigoted and got very angry and more so when I said that the bigots were those who impose their sense of morality on to the unborn who have not been consulted.

I told Sarah Mason about the play I had written and said I would send it round to her and she said she would happily read it. That was before we quarrelled.

Dinner became quite merry. Petronella said something about my singing around the house in a tuneless voice which annoyed [her] mother. Isabel said, 'What is your voice like?' and I said, 'I'll sing you some songs,' which I did, like 'Shuffle off to Buffalo and Craven A / Craven A, Never heard of fornication, / Quite content with masturbation, Craven A, Craven A. / His behaviour at the varsity was most grotesque. He went up and laid his penis on his tutor's desk. / Craven A, Craven A. / Never heard of fornication. Quite content with mastur-

1. See 3 May 1986; his horse, Belotto, did not win this year.
2. The Derbys' house at Newmarket.

bation.' My songs were received with great applause; even Verushka did not seem disapproving.

**Sunday 3 May**

Mrs T bright and sparkling. 'You were very robust again this morning in the *News of the World*.' She said she agreed absolutely with my warning not to be arrogant and approach the election with humility. 'I always do.'

I said, 'Don't forget the fearful lesson of Harold Wilson's conceit in asking people to 10 Downing Street after the election was over in 1970. The voters don't like being taken for granted.'

She was delighted that Rupert had promised to come over especially for the election to keep in touch with me and to have an input of advice and two-way traffic so we can also perhaps tell him what we would like his newspapers to be saying. I said, 'He is one hundred per cent for you.' 'He's marvellous,' she replied.

She said, 'We will talk again this time next week. We'll have to be deciding then. We must have a pow wow about it. We won't be able to leave a decision beyond next weekend.'

**Wednesday 6 May**

Fifteen people to dinner. Never had so many in the house for dinner before.

Flavio and José did the waiting well and efficiently. The Château Brane-Cantenac 1964 in magnums was excellent. People also liked the Spanish Tondonia white wine with the first course. I have never given a Spanish wine at a dinner party before. For a favoured few the Perrier-Jouët 1953 champagne before dinner.

The Mark Weinbergs arrive late as I realized they would. I should have told them to come at a quarter to eight, not eight fifteen.

Anouska sat next to me on my left. She is not so pretty and is older than I had thought at close quarters, with grown up children, one of whom has left university. Her previous husband died, as did Mark's wife. They both had children but the children never got on together in the joint household. She is a clever creature with her dress-making business – she has just been fitting out Princess Margaret with the most fashionable looking outfit she has ever had, a change from her usual dowdy appearance. She has found her much easier to deal with than expected.

They must be immensely rich between the two of them as he owned a large chunk of Hambros Life and sold it for a vast fortune. I find it very odd always at Cavendish Avenue when I have a room full of people immensely rich, yet I have difficulty in scraping by and am almost without capital.

I have always been fond of Sarah [Keswick] though I have not seen her for a year. She is a lost soul, eager but uncertain. She had a terrible car accident once which has left scars on her face but they are not too badly visible now. She has an exquisite little figure with a delicious behind.

After dinner in the drawing-room, Maureen Dudley was talking about Jonathan Aitken and his present wife. He was living with her before they got married and was always playing around. On one occasion he said, 'You're very tired dear, you should go to a health farm for the week-end,' and she thought how kind it was of him. But on the Sunday morning she leaped out of the sauna, saying to herself, 'I wonder what he's up to?'

She belted back up to London. They were living in a house, quite tall, at the time. She went up to the top room and looked into the garden and there were Mr and Mrs Thatcher and Carol, evidently fixing up her engagement to Jonathan. He had his intercom telephone in the garden with him so she picked up the other end in the top room and rang him. She said, 'Look up,' and he looked up to see her. He was startled. She went on, 'Come upstairs at once or I shall come down and make a scene.'

He made some excuses and came up. 'I want to say goodbye. This is the end. I am going,' and he pleaded with her not to, and said it wasn't serious at all. After they had had a good row, he went down and broke the engagement off.

One can never tell what's going on in people's hearts and heads.

Mrs Lamont seemed agreeable and pleasing to look at and had even learned shorthand and typing so that she could deal with her husband's constituency problems.

Earlier in the evening when Amabel came in David said 'How's the millionairess?' She is now very rich, Amabel, Patrick Lindsay having left £4 or £5 million.[3] I don't know if she has a boyfriend, I didn't ask her; she's got quite fat although still pretty in the face. She was angelic to look at twenty or thirty years ago. She never forgot my saying that

3. The Hon. Patrick Lindsay died in January 1986; Lady Amabel Lindsay is the daughter of the 9th Earl of Hardwicke.

she was the stupidest girl I ever met though she seems to have forgiven me.

**Sunday 10 May**

'That makes me very angry, very angry indeed,' she said when I told her that Bernard Donoughue,[4] according to Frank Johnson, has been going round Fleet Street saying the reason she won't have an inquiry into the Wright allegations is because she wants a cover up of Airey Neave[5] who would come out of it very badly.

I told her I was writing every Saturday in the *Times* during the election campaign, so I could keep the muddled egg-heads in order in the *Times* and the masses in the *News of the World*. She said, 'That's marvellous. I'm so glad to hear that.'

Quite a jolly week-end.[6] Johnnie Manners[7] says Dukes have nothing else to think about but sex, they've no work. He says even he, only the younger brother of a Duke, is in very much the same boat. I asked him to tell us about some of his sexual exploits. Mary said, 'Oh goodness, we've heard all about Miss Green before and what you got up to in the motor car.'

This morning I spoke to Monkey Blacker, getting the latest information on Sunday racing about which I am speaking in the Lords tomorrow, my unstarred question.

I said, 'Are you going to be the next Senior Steward? I hope so.' He said, 'I'm afraid the hot money is wrong about that. I'm just going into retirement.' 'What a pity,' I said and indeed it is. It is only because the grandees of the Jockey Club think that Monkey Blacker is not rich enough or socially high enough but he is much more intelligent and competent than nearly all of the rest of them.

After dinner last night we played Slosh, a bastard kind of billiards which I first played with Anne when they lived at Mereworth years ago. Johnnie turned out to be very good. He was drunk but the drunker

---

4. Senior Policy Adviser to Harold Wilson when Prime Minister, 1974–9; former academic, journalist and investment banker; Parliamentary Secretary, Ministry of Agriculture, Fisheries and Food (MAFF), since 1997; life peer 1985.
5. Conservative MP murdered by the IRA in 1979.
6. With the Trees at Donhead St Mary.
7. Lord John Manners, son of the 9th Duke of Rutland (d 1940) and brother of the 10th, m (1957) Mary, née Moore.

he got the more balls he potted. As he was my partner we beat Michael and Esther[8] easily.

Anne tells me Adrian Daintrey[9] is in Charterhouse. We used to stay with Liz von H[10] in Austria and play tennis. He is now eighty plus without money but is happy in a lovely room with view of old courtyard and buildings. Only bachelors allowed and no possessions. He still drinks a quantity and is cuddled by a black nurse. Sadly, he never made the top as an artist.

### Monday 11 May

*Mrs Thatcher announced the general election would be on 11 June.*

Wrote my speech about Sunday racing in the morning. Got to the Lords at a quarter past three believing that business might collapse, as I had been told several times. Instead of which they seemed to add more and more and I wasn't reached until ten past ten, by which time I was restless. There were about seven people in the House only when we came to Sunday racing.

Fairhaven, Senior Steward [of the Jockey Club], sat there but is apparently incapable of speech so he says nothing and never has in the Lords. Rupert Manton, the former Senior Steward, spoke well and supportively. Lord Crawshaw also spoke well from his wheelchair, saying he had been a Church warden and that he didn't think the Church were right about this matter.

Mishcon[11] wound up for Labour with some very flattering remarks to me, so I purred away.

We got a good answer from the government saying they would support a Private Member's Bill from either house.

After it came to an end Bertie Denham, the Chief Whip, asked the nobs of racing who had been present and myself to have a drink with him in his room which he apologized was so untidy. I thought it was

---

8. The Trees' daughter.
9. Artist who painted cityscapes and portraits of his literary friends including John Betjeman, Anthony Powell, Peter Quennell and Paddy Leigh Fermor (in Cretan costume); Sutton's Hospital in Charterhouse is in the City of London.
10. Liz von Hofmannsthal, at Zell-am-See.
11. Lawyer and former member of the London County Council; Opposition spokesman on legal and home affairs in the House of Lords, 1983–90; life peer 1978.

very agreeable. He had an enormous supply of drink and ice and a nice wash basin behind a concealed door. He said he thought it was a good idea for someone to promote a Sunday racing Bill in the Lords and I said I would be willing to do it as Lord Crawshaw had suggested. We will see what happens.

During the conversation he referred to various people who just popped in for a moment or two just to draw their £40 which he thought was not a proper way to behave. He said some Labour people did it, and named one or two, and some Tory ones did it. It seems that the expenses claims are not exactly confidential.

**Tuesday 12 May**

Go to the Churchill Hotel to make a welcoming speech to the Pari-Mutuel Conference – Totes from all over the world.

Quite a jolly dinner party. Jacqueline [Carrus] sat next to me and after a while I ran out of conversation more or less. She is a cousin of Wildenstein, the French art dealer and unpleasant racehorse owner. However, she is charming, as is her husband Pierre who controls the Pari-Mutuel in France. He wants to combine with the Tote in buying betting shops in Holland and Belgium, also putting forward a project to the Germans to run Tote betting shops with SP [starting price] if necessary throughout Germany instead of Ladbroke's who are trying to get the order. There are only fifty-nine bookmakers in Germany but they seem to have leverage on the government.

I gave Sonia[12] my play *A Thoroughgoing Woman* as she is connected with the Royal Court Theatre and says she has some influence.

Andrew Sinclair was there. Gosh that man is dreary, I could hardly exchange a word with him. I noticed he took Petronella on one side towards the end, had her talking to him for about half an hour and Sonia kept looking across to them with a worried look on her face.

Nico Henderson, when the ladies had left the room, was interesting about his feelings on Mrs Thatcher. He had come greatly to admire her. Basically I think he is really an Ian Gilmour[13] wet at heart but he has been so impressed by her that he is now a fan.

He wondered how far she felt the European ideal – not very much he supposed. I said I thought she was better and had been keen on the

---

12. Sonia Sinclair, on the council of the Royal Court Theatre and the Royal National Theatre.

13. Sir Ian Gilmour, Conservative politician and journalist; life peer 1992.

Channel Tunnel. He said he thought she had been dragged into that. I said, 'No, not at all. I used to talk about it to her right from the beginning, saying "I want my tunnel" and when it happened I said, "Ah, now you've got my tunnel" and she said, "What do you mean, your tunnel? It's my tunnel."' I agreed with him that she is not a wholehearted European in the sense that he and I are.

Nico has considerable experience of the world from being Ambassador in Paris and in Washington when he came back and dealt with the Falklands. I think his talents are being wasted now. He gave up being Chairman of the consortium which won the enterprise to build the Channel Tunnel because he said he was no good at financial or industrial matters and somebody else had better take over that. But without him I think it might not have happened at all.

**Thursday 14 May**

Jack Profumo says he liked Wigg, he was a good man. I said, 'Jack, all this do-gooding at Toynbee Hall[14] has gone to your head. You're being a masochistic saint thinking of yourself as Jesus Christ. That malevolent man ruined you for no reason whatever other than his spite and beastliness.' Jack said, 'He felt he had a legitimate grievance because he had been misled by an answer of mine about the Army in Kuwait.'

I replied, 'You merely gave him the answer supplied you by the War Office as he knew perfectly well and had not deliberately misled him at all. It was only an excuse to himself for the way he persecuted you. You must be mad to think that man was good. Here I am still wasting my time stopping the BBC reviving the whole thing in a television series based on some new book about Stephen Ward and defending you all over the place and you say that Wigg was a nice man.'

**Sunday 17 May**

Arnold says, referring to the letter he wrote to Mrs T offering her personal (and he emphasized personal) help with a helicopter or other means of progression or rest for her election tour, he had just got an acknowledgement from her and subsequently got a letter from young

---

14. Profumo was chairman of the charity Toynbee Hall in east London, 1982–5, and then its president. George Wigg led the clamour in 1962 for him to admit the allegations about his relationship with the call-girl Christine Keeler and to resign from the Commons.

McAlpine[15] at the Tory Central Office saying he had seen the letter and would he give a subscription to the Tory Party.

Arnold was ridiculously offended and said she should not have sent him a letter marked personal and he didn't want to give any money to the Tory Party. They let him down and his troubles have been caused by the cancellation of Nimrod and it had been unfair; and why should he support the Tory Party?

I said, 'If you want to have good relations with them and not be thought ill of and mend your fences, you should give £25,000 or £55,000. It's not being paid for by you but by the shareholders.' He said, 'I might do it on my own account for £5,000.' I said, 'That is not enough and it's silly. Your shareholders would have their money well spent for them by keeping on side with the government which is one of their principal customers.' 'It's a matter of principle.' I said, 'I don't know what principle is involved with shareholders and their shares other than hoping that they go up. There is nothing corrupt about giving money to a political party. All the other big firms do it and you will just be thought mean and unpleasant if you don't. Do you want a Labour or an Alliance government?' 'No,' he said. He wants a government led by Mrs Thatcher but he doesn't like the Conservatives. I said, 'Well you will have to lump them along with Mrs Thatcher.'

Then he said Levene, his dreaded enemy at the MoD, had said that as part of the deal in which they go on with Tornado, which apparently they are going to do with GEC, would Arnold make a contribution in view of the fact that GEC had not fulfilled entirely everything they were supposed to under the contract so far. He said he didn't want to do this because that would admit GEC had defects but they had complied with every bit of the contract. I said, 'Well don't do that bit but just give £50,000 to the Tory Party.'

**Monday 18 May**

Dinner with Charles Wintour[16] – seventieth birthday – at Rouxl Britannia in Triton House in Finsbury Square. There was somebody playing a bit of music, about sixty or seventy people there for Charles' umpteenth celebration party of retirement or birthday that he likes

15. Alistair McAlpine (b 1942), Honorary Treasurer, Conservative Party, 1975–90; life peer 1984.

16. Former editor, *Evening Standard*, *Sunday Express Magazine*, *UK Press Gazette*.

giving for himself. They must have run out of speakers to have asked me to make the principal speech, followed by Angus McGill of the *Evening Standard*. I didn't look at my notes so everybody thought I was ad libbing.

Otherwise the evening was fairly boring. I sat next to Audrey Slaughter,[17] Charles' wife, who talked drivel about voting for the Alliance because Mrs Thatcher had done nothing for women. Charles is also voting for the Alliance because he is an ass politically. Robin Day opposite me couldn't believe that they were so silly.

Nor could Mrs Duffield to whom I sat next on the other side. She is a very fat daughter of Charles Clore.

She complained bitterly that when the Queen opened the Clore extension at the Tate Gallery she did not make even a three word reference to the extension having been provided by private patronage. She also remarked that when she put up the last half million for a Constable the other day to save it going out of the country, she got a letter only about three weeks afterwards because Luce, the Minister of Arts, had heard from somebody that she was riled about never getting any credit for private patronage. 'I'd rather give the money to my Jewish old people in the East End. At least they're grateful.'

She wondered why Mrs Thatcher never referred to the enormous amount of private patronage going into the arts. I said, 'That's a very good point. Mrs Thatcher of all people should be welcoming the introduction of private patronage into the arts and a cessation of the total reliance on the government always to provide subsidies.'

Maybe she has a good heart but I don't find her appealing either in what she says or how she looks, Mrs Duffield that is.

**Tuesday 19 May**

Great day at the dentist for about two hours. Poor dear Peter Holford dead from cancer of the lungs at an early age, sixty-fiveish, looked so fit and handsome. New young dentist called Martin who had a practice in Cardiff. Seems well trained and up-to-date.

I asked him the first time I saw him yesterday if he had ever read *You Never Can Tell*[18] which begins in a dentist's surgery in a south coast town and the man only charged half a crown a time. He said yes he had read now, up to halfway through the second act, and it wasn't

17. Writer and journalist, m 2 (1979) Charles Wintour (his second marriage).
18. Early comedy (1896) by George Bernard Shaw.

half a crown, it was five shillings. I said, 'All right multiply for inflation by twenty-two. You should be charging me £5.10 a visit.'

I think he is probably a better dentist than Peter Holford. I think he could have saved the tooth which fell out in the Lords. I felt it wobbling like mad when I put my tongue against it and it suddenly dropped. It had been shaky but I did not expect it to go while listening to a debate. Hastily I hid it in my handkerchief. When I came home I laid it on the table beside Verushka. I said, 'Why did my tooth fall out? Only one of its three prongs was broken. The others looked quite firm.' She was horrified and left the room.

He wanted to do some elaborate work costing £3,000. I said, 'There's no point in that. I shall be dead soon,' so we are compromising on something I hope will not cost more than about £1,000.

**Wednesday 20 May**

When I was talking to Mrs T I passed on Rupert's belief that we should attack Kinnock for being the tri-tax party while the Tories are the cut-your-tax party. 'Appeal to their greed,' said Rupert.

Mrs Thatcher wondered what had become of the *Financial Times* with its hefty praise for the Labour Manifesto. I said, 'It's had a lot of Communists in there for a long while.'

Jacob Rothschild came to see me before The Other Club dinner. We drank some champagne. He wanted my advice on his future life. Should he go on in business or should he seek to branch out into the art world or something similar? He is now Chairman of the National Gallery.

I asked him how much he had been put out by the failure of the merger with Charterhouse and Hambros Life Assurance. He said he had been a bit but had sold off the pieces again which had been good for the shareholders, but it had prevented him having a launching pad for something greater. 'Have you long been losing interest in business?' He said, 'Yes, since that time.'

'What do you want to do?' Clearly he doesn't need the money. I said, 'How much money have you got?' He said, 'Many millions. My children are well provided for.' I said, 'It's not like Rupert who just wants to go on and on buying television stations and newspapers. You don't seem to have that kind of outlook. Do you want to go back to N. M. Rothschild?' He said, 'No, never.'

He thought he would like something different. He said, 'Would Mrs Thatcher give me something?' I said, 'What do you mean, a knighthood or a peerage?' He said he didn't mean that, he meant a job. He was thinking of being chairman of an organization to prepare for the year 2000 which every other country of a major kind is doing. Nobody seems to have thought about it here and he would love to take it over.

I said, 'You mean something like the Great Exhibition of 1851 but a lot more with the arts and so forth?' and he said 'Yes.' I said, 'What an excellent idea. Why don't you write down a plan then I can approach Mrs Thatcher and say let's do it.'

On the way out he asked me what my ambitions were and I said, 'I'm happy writing my articles because I think they do some good in a way I want and have influence. I'm happy having a political input. But of course my career had really come to a stop as far as money making was concerned when Banbury collapsed. As to my political career, there's no future in it except pottering along. I like the Lords but I've been a failure.'

'Do you have any ambition to make money?' I said, 'Well I wouldn't mind making some.' 'Would you like to make a million?' I said, 'Yes.' 'Oh I think we ought to see what we can do about it.' This was very encouraging but nothing will happen because it never does on that kind of a statement.

**Thursday 21 May**

Decided not to go into the Lords today, remembering what Bertie Denham had said.

Dinner at Rupert's. Also present David Young, the blind T. E. Utley who used to work for the *Telegraph* but now for the *Times*, Frank Johnson an associate editor of the *Times*, Kelvin MacKenzie editor of the *Sun*, Bell from the financial pages of the *Times*.

David Young very free in his comments. When I said, 'Why not put Michael Heseltine on to one of the TV broadcasts?' he said it wouldn't do because he was so disloyal and wrecking over Westland. 'He's finished.' I said, 'Well you might at least put him on Robin Day's 9.00 a.m. *Election Call* – he's very attractive to women with his flowing hair and he's playing it straight now, anxious to make his passage back.' Young, who is partner with Tebbit in managing the campaign, agreed this might be a good idea.

David said John Biffen would be out of the Cabinet after the election. (Rupert had previously told me that the Tory Party Central Office were no longer distributing his speeches.) David said that his behaviour when she was in difficulties around the time of the Westland affair was utterly disloyal just when she needed support – Biffen had said they wanted a balanced ticket and that Mrs Thatcher should go after the first two years of a new parliament.

After everybody had gone at about a quarter to twelve and I was trying to get home to bed Rupert said, 'Oh don't go. Come and have another drink and a talk.' He collared Frank Johnson and T. E. Utley who was being taken home by Frank Johnson.

I had told Rupert to talk to Frank Johnson about the *Times*. He then proceeded to do so with me and Utley for an hour or so. He agreed with Frank Johnson that the *Times* was no longer clear and lacked cohesion and its policy was ambivalent and sloppy. The leaders were not definite or well written enough. He also thought that the letters were not sufficient in number. He criticized Charles Wilson for not being strong and getting frightened.

Eventually after planning various new approaches to the *Times* Rupert pointed out to me how he had altered some of the headlines in tomorrow's paper which had already arrived. ('I'm not supposed to interfere of course!')

I took T. E. Utley home who though blind since nine was able to guide us to his complicated address somewhere in Maida Vale.

**Friday 22 May**

Rupert rings at ten past eight. I had only just staggered myself out of bed after getting to sleep around ten past one. I almost fell when I got out eventually and stubbed my toe.

Rupert full of life ringing from the motor car. He said, 'Frank Johnson has a lot of good ideas,' but he didn't think he could ever organize a newspaper and edit it which I was sorry to hear as I hoped he might be in line for it.

**Saturday 23 May**

In the morning I get up early to catch an aeroplane to Manchester. Visit betting shops in Salford and Bootle. Talk to various staff and punters. They say that if people had been able to go straight to the polls after seeing Kinnock's glossy TV ad political broadcast made by the makers of *Chariots of Fire*[19] he would have won easily.

The Alliance seem to be getting more support than is shown in the

---

19. The programme (directed by Hugh Hudson, who had directed *Chariots of Fire*) on 21 May showed Kinnock as a family man and a caring, effective leader.

polls. There is still a good number reluctant to vote Labour because they will leave us without any nuclear weapons, nothing to fall back on in an emergency.

On return from Haydock where I presented the prize for the biggest race in England that day, the Tote Dual Forecast, Rupert rings from the airport. He is just about to catch the Concorde and was in the waiting-room. He says the polls will be all right tomorrow. He giggles away about a story they have about Roy Hattersley[20] in the *News of the World*. He is registered to vote in two places, one at home and one where his girlfriend lives and where he is seen going in and out with his own latch key.

Arnold says to me he has done what I told him to do. He has given £50,000 to the Tory Party from GEC plus £5,000 from himself.

In the *Daily Telegraph* there is a long obituary of Isobel Strachey.[21] They describe her as very beautiful and a good novelist. She was ten years older than me and I had an affair with her during the War after I separated from Susan.[22] She was in some ways vapid and I used her badly, pouring all my distress over Susan into her without much caring about her. I arranged to stay with her on one leave and she had cooked some things which she knew I liked and was waiting for me when I suddenly felt I couldn't go to her place in Oakley Street. Her arms and legs were too long and octopussy. I hurt her badly and unfairly by abandoning her.

Biddy Harrisson (Tom's[23] wife), through whom I had met her, said I had shattered her, and I felt awful, but what could I do? I thought of all these things and her kindness to me which I repaid so meanly when I saw her photograph and obituary; and how instead I had spent some time with Bill Sansom[24] who produced a half Hawaiian girl with whom I went to bed, young with beautiful breasts. Poor Isobel: she was born to be faded, unhappy and ill-used.

---

20. At this time Opposition spokesman on Treasury and economic affairs.
21. Novelist and painter, née Leslie, m (1933–40) John Strachey, painter nephew of Lytton Strachey.
22. WW's first wife.
23. (1911–76); ethnologist, founder of Mass-Observation.
24. William Sansom, writer (1912–76).

**Sunday 24 May**

Bowden. We left early so that I could swim in the heated pool, though it was cold outside.

Tim Bell, formerly of Saatchi and Saatchi and adviser at the moment to Margaret on presentation, was there. I had been pressing Arnold for a long time to take on someone to make his public relations better and improve the feelings about him in the City and in the country. I had said, 'It doesn't matter if you have to pay him £250,000 a year,' and I repeated that in front of Tim Bell who said, 'Please say that again. He's not paying me anything like that.' But he is doing Arnold well and the *Sunday Times* is almost a benefit paper for Arnold today, talking about all the new things he is doing and how GEC is coming alive again.

I said to Arnold, 'I told you that Rupert was not organizing attacks on you in the *Sunday Times*. He has so much to do and so many newspapers he doesn't even know what's going into them. But when I spoke to Rupert he took it on board and now this is the result. So please stop thinking you're friendless.' This was while I was swimming and he was standing by the pool before the others came. He said, 'It's better to feel that you're friendless. Then you can't be disappointed.'

When I got back from Bowden I spoke to her. I said, 'You must appear in at least the last three political broadcasts very prominently. I think there is something a bit disorganized about your campaign. Tebbit is good in some ways but no good at organizing. David Young is much better,' and she agreed.

She said, 'We didn't realize how important these party political broadcasts were.' I said, 'But there are polls which say that enormous numbers of people make up their minds how to vote on the impression they make.'

I said, 'You've got to attack Labour now. I'm worried about the Alliance slipping. They need to come up and bring Labour down otherwise it's going to be too difficult to get a big majority. You've got to show up Labour as being dominated by Communists and extremists, Militants and the like. You've got to attack them on defence and make that issue simple.'

She was pleased when I said that after I finished my book review next day for the *Times* which is on a book by Donoughue about

Callaghan and Wilson,[25] I would spend the rest of the time trying to think things out for her that she might say.

**Monday 25 May**

I wrote the book review with Mrs Wood [secretary]. I then wrote about three thousand words under different headings of things Margaret might say and I attach them here.[26]

There were not any magic phrases because I could not think of any but I will try from now on. She always remembers my phrase 'Pennies do not come from heaven. They have to be earned here on Earth' which she used to great effect.[27]

Tim Bell said to me in the afternoon that she had said she wouldn't have had the election on June 11th if she had realized how disorganized they were and unprepared at Conservative Central Office. She said herself she had made a very bad decision in making Tebbit Chairman twelve months ago and wished she hadn't done it.

Bank holiday. I send the stuff over to No 10 on the fax machine. When all is done I watch Pakistan against England in the third match deciding the Texaco one day series. Before the finish Bruce Matthews arrives to talk about something in connection with SIS. He tells me he had more or less quarrelled with Rupert because Rupert would not allow him to give orders to some inferior Australians who were put there to bring new methods to Wapping.

Bruce says that Frank Johnson is shit when I praise him. I say, 'Why?' He says, 'Because he wrote in the *Spectator* that I ought to have been fired as Managing Director of News International for allowing the *News of the World* to do the story about Jeffrey Archer and the

---

25. *Prime Minister* by Bernard Donoughue.

26. The headings were: Defence ('So long as I am Prime Minister/there is a Conservative Government, the Russians will never tweak the British lion's tail or end a thousand years of British freedom . . . I trust Mr Gorbachev to keep his word. We understand each other . . .'); Taxes ('Higher taxes are an envious punishment for earning more. They diminish the general wealth of the nation. They can never increase it . . .'); Prosperity and International Trade; Trade Union Reform; Immigrants ('Our non-white immigrants are becoming a valuable part of our society . . . But it would be dangerous to them if their numbers were significantly increased . . .'); National Health Service; Education ('Let me make one thing clear about our new plans to improve education. No one will ever be asked to pay a fee for state education . . .').

27. In her 1982 Mansion House speech.

prostitute. How could he say that? It ought to be against all his principles as a journalist to have the management interfering with an editor.'

**Tuesday 26 May**

Morning. Spoke to Mrs T at 7.30 a.m. Before I could get a word out she started to thank me for all the notes and suggestions and phrases and paragraphs I had sent her yesterday afternoon. She was particularly pleased with the bit about trade unions which she said she could not have sorted out for herself in such an authoritative way.

I said that Kinnock had delivered himself into our hands with all that rubbish about fighting in the hills.[28]

David Beaufort rings up in a great alarm. 'I'm sure we're going to lose.' He was reassured when I laughed. I remember his getting panicky like this throughout the last election.

**Wednesday 27 May**

Dinner to celebrate David Stevens' peerage and fifty-first birthday at the Berkeley. One hundred and twenty or so of the dreariest imaginable people assembled.

On my left sits Eve Pollard, editor of the *Sunday Mail* magazine *You*. She is married to Nick Lloyd editor of the *Daily Express*. When I saw him before dinner he said, 'Have you been writing any more letters or giving more advice to David Stevens about the *Express*?' I was a bit abashed. I had only written my notes for David Stevens on the strict understanding that he was not to tell Nick Lloyd where the ideas had come from. But apparently Nick Lloyd had guessed or David Stevens had given me away.

Eve Pollard said it had all been a dreadful mistake, Nick's leaving Rupert. I said, 'Would he like to go back?' She said, 'Yes, I think he would. It was Bruce Matthews' fault.' When Rupert made Nick Lloyd some kind of a General Manager of News International according to her Bruce Matthews wouldn't even let him order pencils and gave him no authority. He was so frustrated he packed it in.

She said, 'We've always been grateful to Rupert for taking us to America and putting Nick into the Harvard Business School.' I said,

28. In a television interview with David Frost on 24 May Kinnock had referred to the efficacy of the Mujaheddin forces in Afghanistan; this had been interpreted as meaning Britain would rely on guerrilla bands or 'Dad's Army' for its defence.

'Would you like me to say something to Rupert about wishing to return?' She said, 'Yes.' I said, 'I will do so if you speak to Nick first and he agrees.' Nick Lloyd says that David Stevens is no good to work for as a newspaper proprietor because he doesn't understand anything about newspapers. He said how marvellous it was working with Rupert who is a born journalist and newspaper man.

My poor brother was there. He still sits on some investment trust which David Stevens runs and in the past gave him an enormous amount of apparently good advice on investment which he never gave to me, Verushka or Nicholas. On the contrary he lost us large sums of money.

My brother was shaking uncontrollably. He obviously has a bad bout of Parkinson's disease now.

David Stevens made a pompous speech though funny on his wife's terrifyingly awful book about how to keep a husband by licking his toes and licking him from head to foot when he arrives home from work, and making a great fuss of him as the hero and head of the house.

I said to Nick, 'I understand from Melissa that the book was put up to auction in Fleet Street and you were the lucky buyer.' Nick and Eve thought that very funny as, of course, he had been obliged to print it which he did, tucking it away as best he could on the back pages.

All around me I see old friends and acquaintances either retiring or dying. Or fading away.

**Thursday 28 May**

Ring Mrs Thatcher at a quarter to eight. Having her hair done and will ring back, which she does in ten minutes. 'I was so glad to have all the material you sent me. When I got back last night at ten o'clock they said to me, "We've written a wonderful speech for you." It was useless. I had to use your material and sit up until three writing another one. I've only had three hours' sleep.' I said, 'My dear darling,' almost choked in sorrow for her. She was also slightly emotional at my obvious distress.

I told her the broadcast political last night was excellent with John Moore[29] putting it over splendidly about all the Hard Left, Militants and Communists in the Labour Party. She said, 'I particularly wanted

---

29. Conservative politician (b 1937), Secretary of State for Transport in the out-going government.

him to do that. He looks so nice and young. I wanted to move that TV one up earlier. I thought it was the time to attack them about that.'

'Reagan was marvellous,' I said.[30] Margaret said 'Yes, and he was so tactful about it.'

I really love that woman. I felt awful about her having such an incompetent staff.

**Friday 29 May**

Rang her at 7.45. 'I thought you looked a little tired last night.' She bristled mildly. 'No, I wasn't, it was the arc lights. Very strong ones at Birmingham.'

I told her that the broadcast last night of Labour on the NHS was fairly effective. I also told her about the nasty sneer that she should have gone on the waiting list for the NHS to get her operation for her hand. I told her that I was going to say in the *News of the World* that Nye Bevan had a private doctor not on the NHS, Dan Davies, and also Barbara Castle had an operation privately when she was a Minister.[31] She said, 'Yes. She explained that she did it because she had to take her despatch boxes into the hospital with her.'

Rupert rings full of beans from New York. Says, 'I think your original prediction she would have much the same majority as before will come true.' He says they will probably have more about Hattersley on Sunday. I say, 'I think it's legitimate because they've started a moral crusade and the family life by presenting Kinnock and his family that way; therefore one is entitled to say are Mr Hattersley's two women compatible with that?'

**Sunday 31 May**

Have a long talk with her in the evening at 7.00. We went through the usual points which need emphasizing like the cheapness of nuclear defence, the Labour Party abolishing the visa system to check immigration and the need for her to go on TV properly. She said the last programme would be more or less entirely her. I said, 'You must be on the one before as well' but I think I'm losing that battle.

I told her we had not done anything like enough about warning the

---

30. President Reagan said on 27 May that if Labour came to power, the US would have to persuade them of 'the grievous error of nuclear disarmament'.

31. In May 1965, when Minister for Overseas Development.

country and the union members who are about to lose all their legal rights. She asked me to send some more material spelling it all out. I said we must have big advertisements in the papers. I had asked Tim Bell to speak about it and he said they've got plenty of money and can afford it, and I was right.

Getting a bit disturbed at the Heath Robinson nature of the Tory campaign.

I still think she will get a majority much the same as she has now but I wish they didn't give me so many heart attacks by their inefficiency and failure to do their homework. The Labour Party have done their homework much better.

**Monday 1 June**

Struggled away to dig out all the facts again from various statements and manifestos of the Labour Party on what they would do to the trade union reform Acts of the Tories. Somehow got it all done in the afternoon and bunged it over to No 10 on the fax machine.[1]

Lunch at the Jockey Club with the Archbishop of Canterbury,[2] the Senior Steward, Sir Ian Trethowan and others. It was to be about Sunday racing. The Archbishop is very slim, slimmer I thought than the last time I met him at dinner with Sir Geoffrey Howe. He looked very neat in a well-cut suit with his purple shirt and a great silver cross hanging from it.

Curious he should be so wet. He won the MC for bravery. But he is pleasant. He reads my articles in the *Times* and even in the *News of the World*. He had read my speech on Sunday racing very carefully from the Lords Hansard.

'My father went blind in the last years of his life. I used to help him put his bets on.' 'Would he have been in favour of Sunday racing?' I asked. The Archbishop answered, 'Certainly.' 'So this is something you could do to honour his memory,' and he laughed.

He said his wife goes racing and he likes racing but he felt that he ought not to go racing now because it would offend so many people. Did I think that was hypocritical? I said, 'No, I don't because you are in a singular position and there is no reason to go racing which is such an unimportant matter to you [but] which might give offence to people who wouldn't understand.'

I then recounted the story of Rosebery being Prime Minister winning the Derby twice during his fourteen months as Premier and how that

1. WW copied his memo to Lord Young, telling him, 'I think we are not making anything like enough play of the fact that the Labour Party intends to abolish all the rights given by Conservative trade union laws. We ought to have great press advertisements and do it on TV speeches.'
2. Robert Runcie, Archbishop of Canterbury, 1980–91.

lost him the Non-Conformist vote in the Liberal Party. So that was why he stopped being Prime Minister.

The Archbishop promised not to make any speeches opposed to Sunday racing. He didn't know how his followers would take it when I introduced my Bill. He did see there was a distinction between that and opening shops. He himself was concerned about Sunday as a special day being further eroded, the English Sunday. I told him I didn't think Sunday racing would erode it but add more leisure activity, particularly as we were going to gear it very much towards the family.

In the morning a lady called Anne Perkins had rung from ITN *Channel 4 News*. They came round to interview me about how I thought the election compared with that in 1959. They had clips of me doing the election Labour Party broadcasts, and Tony Benn, with a particular one of me when I asked my daily question which was a feature of the campaign and we had the Tories rocking. She was charming, tall and attractive. I told her that her hair looked Pre-Raphaelite, which it did and that it suited her.

In the end they only used tiny little bits of me and some of the old clips from the election broadcast of 1959 but it was quite fun.

Before the lunch Monkey Blacker said that Mrs Bridgett Walters was hipped at my presenting the Sunday Racing Bill in the Lords. She said the Jockey Club ought to get all the credit. I said, 'Well actually I began it all before the Jockey Club,' and he agreed and said, 'In any case as somebody said, why bother about who gets the credit as long as it's done?'

She is the public relations or parliamentary consultant (her husband is a Tory MP)[3] the Jockey Club use.

**Wednesday 3 June**

To the Derby by helicopter. Toured the Downs area and Tattenham Corner where we had new betting kiosks in the new structures dotted around fresh areas. I was the only one in this part of Epsom wearing a top hat and morning dress. One girl followed me and asked if she could photograph me. I said, 'Yes, for 50p.' She took the photograph and when I said, 'Where's the 50p?' she didn't give it me and blushed.

Came home to be greeted by a telephone call from Tim Bell saying a Gallup poll showed Tories 40.5 and Labour 36.5. Calamity. The Tories are wringing their hands.

---

3. Sir Dennis Walters.

**Thursday 4 June**

Speak to her early in the morning. 'How are you?' I asked. 'Depressed. Who wouldn't be with that opinion poll in the *Daily Telegraph*?'

I say, 'They are hiding you. They really behave as though you were a liability instead of their greatest asset. You've got to go on the television more. You must go on the one on defence tomorrow night and you must do the whole of the last one. You must appear the whole time on television. It is a waste of your time pottering around supermarkets and schools and standing in empty fields shouting through a megaphone. Labour is running a very slick campaign. They have friends in the media who are helping them. Why haven't you got Gordon Reece?'[4]

She said, 'Well, there's the problem of his being connected with Saunders.' 'That means absolutely nothing. He was only a consultant plying for hire like anybody else. Like a lawyer. You should get him back.'

I told the Tories at Central Office when making one of their TV programmes they have got to put her on among the crowds properly in Russia and addressing either the Russian nation on Soviet TV about nuclear weapons, or standing up in front of Gorbachev saying the same thing at a banquet, or preferably both.

I told Howell James,[5] for him to pass on to David Young and Tim Bell, that David Young must go with Mrs Thatcher to the television studios. Gordon Reece said to me that she needs settling like a horse, highly spirited. She gets nervous if people surround her and crowd her. She must be kept calm. Like Reference Point which won the Derby on Wednesday, she has to be settled and then she gets out in front and she's confident.

During the day Rupert complained that he hadn't been able to get me yesterday. 'You were cavorting with the aristocracy at the Derby.' I said, 'It's the Tote's main day of the year and I have to be there.' He said they are doing two shock issues in the *Sun* about what it would be like under Labour and about Britain being great again and the miners earning £450 a week, and people at Wapping earning £19,000 a year and all the rest of it.

I told Mrs T that. She said, 'Rupert is marvellous.'

---

4. Public relations consultant; see 5 January 1986.
5. Public relations expert at Conservative Central Office for the campaign; later in 1987 he became BBC director of corporate affairs.

I had complained to Rupert earlier that his *Sun* had had no politics on its front page on Monday, Tuesday and Wednesday and on Thursday all it had was a statement by Steve Cauthen[6] that he would leave the country if Labour wins.

I had also told her earlier that it was no good having a Lord (Young) talking about unemployment on the television. He was very nice but no one knows who the hell he is anyway.

They've got themselves very rattled. It is their own fault for not being properly prepared and not realizing that Labour had been preparing itself for this election for eighteen months. They have been behaving as though it was the Labour Party which fixed the date of the election and not the Tories. They have failed to analyse Labour's manifesto which is not so hidden as they pretend. It's all there. You have to refer to the other documents it mentions for the full ghastliness of it. They don't do any homework at all at the Conservative Central Office.

Tebbit is confused and hopeless as an administrator. David Young is too weak and does not understand politics. He's never been in it before. An education in the House of Lords for a year or two acting as Secretary of Employment is not sufficient to understand ordinary people and how their minds work.

**Friday 5 June**

In the evening I watched *News at Ten* and was made furious. They led with a long carefully manicured extract from Kinnock's speech appealing to Alliance voters and wavering Tory voters to vote Labour as the only way of keeping Mrs Thatcher out or getting her out. The ghastly Jon Snow was saying, 'They are very confident. Their private poll is showing them gaining on the Tory Party etc.' We then cut to Ken Dodd [the comedian] jumping about with a feather duster on a Tory platform and then the cameras turned to Mrs Thatcher who was described by the commentator as 'waiting nervously in the wings'. They then only gave a tiny snippet from her speech.

When I complained to Sue Timpson, the producer, she got very cross.

She said, 'Our balance is perfect' and started reading out lengths of times that they gave to Labour and Tories and the Alliance.

---

6. Champion jockey.

I said 'You may have the same length of time covering the parties but Ken Dodd waving a feather duster is not exactly Tory propaganda.'

**Saturday 6 June**

Speak to Ian Trethowan. I tell him I want to speak to Alastair Burnet.[7] He said he should be seeing him at the Oaks[8] this afternoon.

Later on I spoke [again] to Ian Trethowan who said, 'Alastair Burnet knows what you want to speak to him about. He absolutely agrees. He was having a day off and watched the programme himself and he thought it was disgraceful. He was very angry indeed,' so maybe I will not pursue Alastair Burnet any more as I seem to have done the trick.

Nigel Clark was playing tennis with Ian Trethowan. He is a public relations man or something of that kind and has been made a Jockey Club member and owns horses. He has offered a tenth share, one to me and one to Ian, of a horse called Isaac Newton trained by a man called Armitage. It's a jumper. It's been second once or twice but not won lately. We would not have to pay any capital cost, only one-tenth each of the training bills and expenses. I think that's rather a good wheeze. I shall certainly do it if Mrs Thatcher wins the election. Otherwise I may be in Queer Street. For example, they certainly would not renew me at the Tote (Labour hates my guts), and I would lose that important part of my income.

Chips Keswick yesterday gave lunch to Jules Joscow who came here to dinner on Tuesday. He is the head of NERA and deals with it for Marsh & McLennan who own it now in the States. He (Jules) told me that Irwin never had such a large share of it as he pretends to have, and didn't get all the money he pretends he had. Jules thinks having some money has gone right to his head: 'When I first knew Irwin he drank Coca-Cola in restaurants and never ordered wine until I told him how to do it.'

Jules Joscow says he is glad to have me back on the advisory board. Chips said when he gave Jules lunch on Friday at Hambros, he said how marvellous I was and he was going to keep the thing going anyway for five years in London, so Chips said, 'You don't have to worry about your £10,000 a year – he thinks you're wonderful.'

I had been speaking to her every day and did so again in the late afternoon. I told her not to bother any more with these questions

---

7. Associate editor, *News at Ten*.
8. Race at Epsom at the end of Derby week.

about her having private treatment under an insurance scheme. Her trouble is she won't explain that it was because she was so busy as a Prime Minister and won't stop talking about her right to have private medicine like everybody else.

I said, 'Don't bother about that issue any more. We're chasing up what Mrs Castle was up to and also Norman Tebbit told me that Kinnock's mother was given private medical treatment at his expense when she was very ill.'

I once again said, 'You've got to go on the television all the time,' and she detailed all her appointments including David Frost tomorrow. She says, 'Thank you for your wonderful article in the *Times* this morning. It quite cheered me up.'[9]

I said, 'Be yourself. Don't let anybody make you go against your own instincts, not even me.'

I also told her that Heseltine had been very good the previous evening. That was according to Verushka and Petronella though I did not see it myself because I was watching something else. I said to Mrs Thatcher, 'He is no doubt trying to work his passage back but he is doing it very well.'

Half my Saturday was spent ringing editors of the *Mail*, the *Express*, *Sunday Times*, *Sunday Telegraph* to make sure they got it in about Barbara Castle.

We were sitting in the kitchen having our simple supper. I was having warmed up fish pie and a Sainsbury sausage roll which was rather good. Then Henry Anglesey rang in a great state about the election, 'What is going to happen? Will you speak to Shirley[10] and tell her she's got to vote Tory,' which I do.

Then John Sainsbury[11] came on, whose house they were staying in, and asked me about the election and what I thought was likely to happen. I told him much the same majority as before. I said, 'I'm eating your food. It's very good. First class sausage rolls and I had an old fashioned doughnut earlier this afternoon, excellent. You're doing wonders. You're even using unsaturated fats a lot more now.'

---

9. WW had begun, 'Yes, there is a Thatcher factor,' and gone on to compare her with Kinnock: 'In whichever area you look, Mrs Thatcher is strong and Mr Kinnock, who has made his personality the main issue of the election, weak.'
10. His wife, the Marchioness of Anglesey.
11. Chairman, J. Sainsbury plc, 1969–92; life peer 1989.

Everybody's getting very worked up. I never knew an election like it for the terror and panic.

**Sunday 7 June**

She was very good on TV AM with David Frost. Tim Bell told me Frost is a Wilsonian Socialist and is a friend of his (Tim's). He is very rich and feels guilty about it and thinks everybody should vote Labour against Mrs Thatcher so he gave her quite a hard time.

She caught him out by saying, 'Well you have private medical attention for yourself and your family,' and he looked flustered and said, 'Oh, er, yes, but I think people like us ought not to and the National Health Service would be better if we didn't. It's the same as schools.' She then pointed out she went through the state school system herself and it is the Labour Party that has been destroying the grammar schools like the one she went to.

The *Mail on Sunday* and the *Sunday Telegraph* had quite decent bits about the story I gave them about Barbara Castle, and the *Mail* included a statement from me saying that Nye Bevan was never on the NHS himself.

I think the Kinnock gimmick of repeating his glossy spectacular may not have much effect. We have the *Sun*'s shock issues coming Monday and Tuesday which should help. Maybe people will go back to their original intention before the campaign began, as I said to Arnold this morning and as I said on Channel 4 ITN news early last week. If that's the case my prediction that she will get much the same majority will be right.

**Monday 8 June**

Spoke to her at 7.30 a.m. Abscess on the tooth which has been giving her trouble is better now but not entirely.

I said, 'It would be good if you found a spot to say that far from the Tories being divisive, it is Labour which is divisive. Think of the strife there would be on the picket lines while workers and employers were intimidated. Think of the way in which union members would be set against union members because they had been denied secret ballots before strikes. Please don't call it secondary picketing because many people don't know what it means. We have to remember all the time how ignorant millions are. They might think secondary picketing was a new kind of toothpaste or arrangement for cleaning your teeth.'

I continued, 'Please call it picketing by mobs who don't even work at the place they are picketing.' (Later I noticed she got it right on *Panorama*.)

She is also pulling ahead in the best leader poll. Forty per cent think she would make the best Prime Minister and only twenty-seven per cent Kinnock.

**Tuesday 9 June**

The TV AM Harris poll shows Tories down a little bit (42, 35) but I don't think it means much as they take two hundred and fifty out of the sample at the back end and add two hundred and fifty new ones from the day before.

Maybe the stuff about her having private treatment for her hand operation had an effect. It was quite well exploited by Labour. But this morning the *Sun* has huge headlines about Denis Healey's [wife's] private operation. Being interviewed on the early morning television with Michael Heseltine, when a girl asked him about the operation, he said, 'You're trying to throw muck,' and got very, very angry. She said, 'But you started it with the attack on Mrs Thatcher.' He was furious.

Ring Central Office trying to get hold of David Young or Norman Tebbit to point out to them that they are making idiots of themselves over the taxation issue.

The Tories are such fools. They are conducting themselves as though they were having a debate in the House of Commons, slinging complicated figures at each other.

**Wednesday 10 June**

Spoke to her at 7.30 this morning.

I said, 'You did splendidly on your party political broadcast last night. It was excellent.' She said, 'Thank you very much for all your help. I used lots of the stuff you sent round yesterday for me in my speech last night at Harrogate.'

I said, 'Good luck.' and she said, 'God bless you for all your help.'

I still think she could get a majority much the same as she got before. I think there will be a lot of unexpected results. She is still holding above in the main polls and I think any slippage has stopped. The Denis Healey fiasco about Edna going in for private treatment for a hip operation has rebounded on the Labour Party.

A jolly Tote Board meeting. David Montagu remarked that he was surprised that I was so ebullient on the day before the election. Acute nervousness around, yet the MORI poll in the *Times* this morning showed the Tories getting a majority of a hundred. But nobody believes in the polls any more. They have been so confused by marginal polls showing differing results even down to a hung parliament.

**Thursday 11 June** ***Polling day***

Rang Mrs T before breakfast at 7.30 to wish her Good Luck.

I asked her where she would be, what she would do today. She said, 'I'm going to have my hair done and I shall go out to Finchley[12] and then I shall come back and have a bath. Then I shall go to Conservative Central Office.'

I said, 'Don't worry about the drivel and drooling remark you made about people who talk sentimental slop about unemployment.' She said, 'I wish I hadn't said that. It was a slip.' I said, 'Don't worry. Many people think the same and as there are not three million genuine unemployed but about two, they all know the truth of the matter too. It won't have done you any harm at all.' I hope I was right. It was a bit of a bloomer.

She was very tired, as you could see on her face, when she did that interview at lunch time on Wednesday. It was a moment of irritation with all the sentimental claptrap that Labour has been talking. They should not have taken her on a helicopter flight looking at some silly factory and to Southend.

The whole campaign was thoroughly disorganized. The feebleness of the Tory campaign will have cost them at least thirty to fifty seats.

At midday I lost my nerve. I placed a bet for £10 at 6 to 1 with Coral's for a Tory majority of between eighty and ninety-six and £5 for ninety-six to a hundred and six at 10 to 1, believing that they had made such a hash of it they wouldn't get much the same majority as before.

Evening: the great dinner and dance at Cliveden.

In the space before the house a lovely Guards band was playing brassy music as the guests arrived in the rain. I remembered the house quite well from when I used to stay there with Bill Astor.[13] The gardens leading down to the river on the other side were beautifully illuminated and looked like those of a French palace. By the river were the little houses by which I once walked with Bill Astor and he stopped in front

---

12. Her constituency.
13. 3rd Viscount Astor (1907–66).

of one and giggled, saying 'I have a friend called Stephen Ward,[14] an osteopath, whom I let use one of these. He knows a lot of girls.'

There was a very good Lynch-Bages on the tables for dinner as well as an excellent Meursault. The food was delicious. At my table I sat next to Jane Rayne,[15] Annabel's sister, whose birthday Jimmy Goldsmith was ostensibly giving the party in aid of, though he had converted it to an election party with huge screens everywhere.

Then there was David Somerset and on his right Joan Collins and on her right Tony Lambton. I was amazed how much prettier Joan Collins is in real life than in her pictures or on television, and told her so which pleased her considerably. I said to her, 'On your left is the most dangerous man in England and to the right is the second most dangerous man in England. Look out. They would make putty of you.' 'Perhaps I would make putty of them,' she replied with a saucy smile and doubtless meant it.

As the election coverage on television began, I sat very close to a big screen near our table which was at the end of the room and was joined intermittently by various people. Sonny Marlborough sat by my side nearly the whole time. He told me he had bet with Chips Keswick £1,000 that the Tory majority wouldn't be more than fifty and that he didn't mind paying up if he had to. (When I said that to Chips the next morning he said, 'Nonsense. He minds a lot. He's the meanest man in England and I've won £1,000 from him. I shall buy some champagne and send you some bottles.')

Rupert turned up and sat near to us at one stage. When Ken Livingstone appeared on the screen and put down the Labour defeat to the dreadful lies and smears of the media, Rupert cried out, 'That's me!' and was delighted.

I was glad I had extended my bet with Coral's from the eighty seat overall majority range to a hundred and six. At this moment I am not sure whether I have won because she might still just top the hundred and six. I have lost £25 to Andrew Knight when I said that her majority would be within ten of what she has now. I have also lost a few other bets of £5 on the same score but I can't remember with whom they were. I hope that they will remind me or even better forget.

All the time we watched the television various bands and orchestras

---

14. He introduced Profumo to Christine Keeler.
15. Wife of Lord (Max) Rayne, née Vane-Tempest-Stewart, sister of Lady (Annabel) Goldsmith.

Jeffrey and Mary Archer outside the Queen's Theatre in London for the first West End performance of his play *Beyond Reasonable Doubt*, September 1987.

Julian Amery, MP, and his wife Catherine.

Norman Lamont
in 1986.

Douglas Hurd,
Home Secretary,
and his wife Judy.

Nigel and Thérèse Lawson on the steps of 11 Downing Street before the March 1987 budget.

Lord Hesketh (*right*) and Nicholas Soames at a charity tug-of-war outside the Houses of Parliament in July 1988.

WW addresses the Tote Annual Luncheon at the Hyde Park Hotel in March 1988 watched by Douglas Hurd, the Home Secretary, on his right and two former Home Secretaries, Roy Jenkins and Leon Brittan. William Whitelaw, another former Home Secretary, and John Mortimer have their backs to the camera.

*Above right:* Sir Ian Trethowan with the Queen in 1986.

*Right:* WW and Queen Elizabeth the Queen Mother presenting the Gold Cup at Cheltenham in 1985.

Lady Wyatt presents a prize to Lord Porchester as the Queen's trainer at Newbury with WW looking on.

Prince Michael of Kent with WW at Newbury in 1987.

Prince and Princess Michael of Kent at Badminton in 1985.

Lady Wyatt presenting the trophy to Mrs Robert Sangster at the Tote Cesarewitch Handicap at Newmarket in 1988.

Sir Philip and Lady Oppenheimer with the Wyatts at the races.

came weaving in and out, some from the Caribbean in a snake formation beating a bath. There was dancing in a huge marquee and dancing in the hall. At about one o'clock there appeared a buffet laden with hundreds of lobsters and ten tons of cheese, ribs of beef – unbelievable quantities of food, and pink champagne and anything else you wanted to drink. By this time I asked for some Perrier water as that was all I could manage.

I had a long jolly talk with Jane. I told her she is always a part of the furniture of my mind and I remembered how attracted I had been to her thirty years or so ago. She is still extremely pretty and talked of when we went to Battersea and held hands.

David Frost was startled when I saw him at the entrance to Cliveden and told him he had behaved very badly in his interview with Mrs Thatcher on the Sunday.

The surroundings were beautiful and the people I talked to on the whole were amusing but I would have preferred to have been at home watching the election results.

**Friday 12 June**

*Conservative majority of 102 over all other parties (from 144 after the 1983 general election, 137 at dissolution). Mrs Thatcher the only leader this century to win three elections in a row.*

David Tytler[16] rang. Would I please write an article today even if they got it by 6.00? 'The editor said we must have you in tomorrow's paper.' When I protested that it was not the arrangement and I was only going to do the four Saturdays he said, 'Oh please do it.' I said, 'Well I've got to finish my *News of the World* article first,' which I did. I then wrote the *Times* article in about an hour. It was to say that Labour won't win the next election either and my evidence for it. Also that she would still be in charge at the time of the next election.

**Saturday 13 June**

Rang her about half past eight. 'How much sleep did you have?' 'I went to bed at twenty to eleven and got up about seven.' I said, 'Hooray' and she said, 'It's the longest sleep I've had for ages.' She sounded very bright and cheerful which she was bound to do.

She thanked me again for all I had done. I said, 'You would have

---

16. *Times* journalist.

got thirty more seats if the campaign hadn't been badly bungled.' 'As many as thirty you think?' 'Yes, you should have gone on that television much earlier. Thank God I persuaded you to do it just in time and take no notice of all those foolish advisers. Your trouble is not that you don't listen but you listen too much and often to the wrong people.'

Then off to the great wedding of Harry[17] and Tracy Ward. We arrived just as David and Caroline were about to go into the church and there was Daphne [Fielding], the grandmother of the groom.[18] She asked me to help her down the steep slippery slope to the church which I did and we both held on to each other as we wobbled down. I said, 'People will think I'm part of the family party.' As soon as I got to the church door I said, 'You're all right now Daphne,' and let her go.

Chipping Norton has beautiful perpendicular decorated stone columns. I looked with interest at the great swathes of flowers wondering how much they cost. David had complained he had to pay for them because Tracy's father said that was the custom.

Daphne has had a jolly life. When Xan Fielding left her she found a marvellous American lover over the age of eighty but unfortunately he died. Splendid that she at the age of eighty, or seventy-eight I think she was at the time, could still have a sex fling.

In the morning before I left I spoke to Alexander Hesketh.[19] He said some of them are already talking about her not going the whole of her third term. 'It's all these ghastly middle and lower middle class people we have at the top of the party. They can't understand how wonderful she is. There'll be a lot of intrigue against her.'

In the tent I sat for a while next to Jane Rayne. She said, Max had asked her what we had been talking about on the Thursday night when I had sat next to her at Cliveden and she had told him that I had asked her whether she still felt sexy. He had thought this very strange. Once that evening Max had made some remark to Jane, teasing her, and I said 'Be careful you are speaking to the woman I love.' He is very nice but he can never quite make out what I mean when I talk about Jane and how much I loved her years and years ago. Incidentally, she said

17. Marquess of Worcester, son of the Duke and Duchess of Beaufort (David and Caroline).
18. Her first marriage was to the 6th Marquess of Bath; see Biographical Notes under Beaufort.
19. Government Whip in the Lords.

yes, she did still feel sexy and so did Max. I said, 'That's fine.' He is only six months older than me.

Tracy's mother Claire came up to me several times. I said, quite untruthfully, that Tracy looked almost as beautiful as she did, which she swallowed hook, line and sinker, looking very gratified.

Spoke to Jamie,[20] Sonny's son, who had been in the courts and in remand prison over heroin taking. He is now working on the farms. It is curious but I could never tell if anybody took heroin or not.

Christopher Thynne was there, Caroline's brother. He was there with his wife who has got very fat. She used to be a fetching blonde with quite a good figure. They stayed with us once in Italy and they were very jolly. Now the poor boy looks a bit bedraggled and says he is helping his father who greatly wished always that Christopher had been the oldest son and not the appalling Alexander Weymouth[21] who was there in a cowboy outfit. He is quite mad. Alexander locked his father out the very first day after he handed the property over to him to save death duties for Alexander.

Dear Caroline was wearing a greyish dress. She is very fat but quite happy. She keeps reminding me that I haven't sent her some set speeches for her to make at opening fêtes and hospitals and goodness knows what else. I feel guilty about that.

Margaret Anne [Viscountess Stuart] said that Andrew D was in a terrible panic on the day before the election saying, 'What have I done, what have I done? Why ever did I join the SDP? I have to get out of it. Won't it be awful if she loses?'

**Sunday 14 June**

Ring Roy[22] to say how sorry I am that he lost his seat. 'Do you want a peerage?' 'Yes,' was his answer but he wanted to be given it as recognition of his great worth. I said, 'But the normal thing is for it to be recommended by your party. I know she has been difficult at times with the list provided by the Liberals and the SDP particularly but I hope she won't be this time.' He said, 'No, I don't want to be on a list like that.' I said, 'Well, does it matter?'

---

20. Marquess of Blandford.
21. Viscount Weymouth, who succeeded as 7th Marquess of Bath on his father's death in 1992.
22. Jenkins, who did not retain Glasgow Hillhead which he had won for the SDP in a by-election in 1982.

Later I rang her and we had a very jolly conversation. I told her that Roy would like to have a peerage and she said, 'Yes, he's a person of great distinction and has had a marvellous career. Presumably they will strongly recommend it on their list.' Then she added, 'He's very vain you know.' I said, 'Yes, but he is a very old friend of mine. I don't want to hold that against him. I know you have disagreed with him a lot.' She said, 'But that's natural in politics.'

Then she said, 'I thought it was horrifying that they threw him out at Hillhead. A man of such great distinction and stature. It was dreadful,' and added, 'It tells you something about the Scots.' She is very against them for cutting the number of Tory MPs in half at this election. She said, 'If they don't put Roy on their list I certainly will.'

I rang Roy again and told him the gist of the conversation but not about her remark that he was very vain. He was very pleased but he said, 'Of course I don't really want to be on a list.'

I said, 'Why worry about it? If they don't put you on the list she's going to do it anyway. Arthur Bottomley,[23] I had to get her to make him a peer when the Labour Party wouldn't recommend him.'

He quibbled a bit and I said, 'Why are you fussing? It comes to the same thing in the end. You'll get your peerage.' He said, 'Well, I suppose you're right' rather grudgingly, then he thanked me profusely and said, 'You have been very useful to me as you often have been in the past.' I said, 'Well I love you Roy.'

Back to Mrs Thatcher. I said I was sad about Quintin Hogg,[24] particularly as while my age advances I think nobody should ever retire. 'Yes,' she said, 'but I had to make Michael Havers Lord Chancellor. He has been Attorney General for so long and I wouldn't ever let him resign in the middle of a parliament as I didn't want a by-election.'

I told her that it was a brilliant stroke making Peter Walker Secretary for Wales. He'll be so keen to make a name for himself that he'll really do some good. She commented he was now behaving himself reasonably well.

I said, 'You have now got to surround yourself with a Praetorian Guard of people who will always be loyal to you,' and I reminded her of what Gaitskell had said to me: 'Anybody can be loyal to me when I'm right. What I want is people who are loyal to me when I'm wrong.'

---

23. (1907–95); Labour politician; life peer 1984.
24. Lord Hailsham, aged seventy-nine, was not reappointed as Lord Chancellor in the new administration.

I told her there are going to be more Westlands, more disasters and more mutterings in the Tory camp. 'Already I am told that some are saying you shouldn't serve the whole of a third term. We've got to have good stout people in the Cabinet – only those who are going to be steadfast to you. I used to think you could have more diversification but now I don't think so.'

I said, 'I don't blame you for getting rid of John Biffen. He showed he could be very disloyal at a tricky moment.' She said, 'I was hurt by him. When we were in Opposition he twice resigned as Shadow Spokesman because he said he was having a nervous breakdown. Twice I had him back and I put him in the Cabinet and overlooked his curious failure in will power at not sticking to the earlier job.'

On Norman Tebbit she said, 'He'll carry the scar of that Brighton bombing all his life. I didn't want him to go. Whenever he is away from her he can't even attend to business properly. He's always ringing up to find out if the nurses are looking after his wife all right.' She feels very sorry for him but he's still going on being Chairman of the Tory Party for the time being.

I told her that Rupert had said to me on the telephone this morning that he is trying to buy the *Today* newspaper which is losing £400,000 a week. 'It's very secret, not that I think you're indiscreet,' and she laughed and said, 'Oh no, of course I'm not indiscreet.'

I added, 'I don't see why it should have to be referred to the Monopolies Commission because it's losing so much money and a lot of jobs would be lost if Rupert doesn't take it over. He's trying to get it for nothing or at most pay something in seven years if it makes a profit. We look like having another pro Margaret newspaper.' She said, 'Yes, I remember the *Times* didn't get referred to the Monopolies Commission when he bought them both, the *Times* and *Sunday Times*, because they were making a loss.' I said, 'Well the same applies here.'

She said she was having some difficulty in thinking of good younger people to bring on. I told her I was pleased about John Moore who had done very well during the election with his party political about the extremists and looked nice and young and clear. I said, 'I've never met [John] Major who has been promoted to the Cabinet.' She said, 'Oh he's very good. I note that you have never met him and will do something about it.' He's been made Chief Secretary to the Treasury and put in the Cabinet.

I also spoke to her this morning about what to do about Scotland. I said, 'Vaguely I have sometimes thought maybe they should be a separate country, though you would have trouble with the Monarchy.' She said, 'Well you couldn't have different old age pensions both sides of the border. Yesterday when I was watching trooping the colour there were the marvellous Scots Guards and I thought, we can never be separate countries.'

A jolly dinner with Rupert and Lachlan, and the Searbys[25] were there.

He was adamant that he didn't want Nick Lloyd back. He said he and his wife had tried this ploy before. He had taken them to America (I think for two years) and he put Nick through the Harvard Business School and he turned out to be totally disloyal. He only remained as an Assistant Managing Director of News International for about two weeks. It was nothing whatever to do with Bruce Matthews that he gave it up. 'He just was tempted by the idea of having the title of *Daily Express* editor and a lot of extra perks and the money.' He's not a good editor according to Rupert.

I reminded Rupert during the evening how at his request and at my instigation she had stopped the *Times* acquisition being referred to the Monopolies Commission though the *Sunday Times* was not really losing money and the pair together were not.

At dinner somewhere last week Verushka made friends with Charles Sweeny whom I used to know slightly. A great amateur golfer, married to the Duchess of Argyll.[26] His daughter is now the Duchess of Rutland who won't speak to her mother because she is such a tart. He became very interested in Verushka. He rang up on Friday and asked if we would both go to dinner at Aspinall's. I said, 'I couldn't but you go by yourself.' 'Why aren't you jealous?' she asked.

**Monday 15 June**

A lovely surprise. A box of six magnums of Lafite Rothschild 1975 arrived with this letter from David Somerset.[27] The box has never been

25. Richard Searby, chairman, News Corporation Australia, and deputy chairman, Times Newspapers Holdings.

26. Margaret, Duchess of Argyll (1912–93), m 1 (1933–47) Charles Sweeny, m 2 (1951–63) 11th Duke of Argyll.

27. 'As in my opinion you were responsible for winning the general election, you may consider this box of wine scant remuneration compared to what "Saatchi & Saatchi" got for nearly loosing (*sic*) it. However please accept it as a token of my admiration for you as a patriot and counsellor for everything that is best, a man of steel nerves and judgement compared to the gibbering wrecks of myself & Buttercup [Verushka] in anxious moments.'

opened before. I rang Broadbent[28] who says each magnum must be worth £100 and I think that was an underestimate, probably £150, making a total of around £1,000 as a present which was thrilling. He says it has got a lot of tannin in it and it needs to develop more before drinking which means I can't drink it for five years.

Rupert elated by his Milan trip. When I ring him he is talking to some people about *Today.* He rings back. It is now losing nearly £500,000 a week and Rupert is concerned as to how such losses can be dealt with rapidly. This now seems to be the main obstacle to his taking over the paper. Tiny Rowland had no idea what he was doing commercially when he bought *Today.* He got it only as another vengeful weapon to use against Mrs Thatcher whom he hates beyond reason.

Rupert's energy is boundless. This trip he was organizing some links with an Italian who has got hold of a lot of television stations in Italy and is trying to do similar things in France.

I wrote to dear old Quintin.

**Tuesday 16 June**

The routine of Ascot week begins with our having our ritual lunch with Piers Bengough[29] in his entertainment room.

The Tote has a record day. Our cash take is thirty-three per cent up on the year before though it is a dull day with spatters of rain. However, the attendance was up seven and a half per cent.

After the races we go for a drink to Drue Heinz. She is sitting by herself in that great house, Ascot Place. There was a wobbly butler who seems to have Parkinson's, who brought the tea and would have poured it out if he hadn't been stopped. She didn't feel like going to the races. Usually they had a huge house party and later in the summer an enormous party with dancing and so forth as they did last year. However, she was lively.

She told me about her writers' residence at Hawthornden. She set it up. It can take twenty-five writers at a time and they have their own room and lunch is left outside their door; dinner is downstairs and so is breakfast. They are allowed there for three or four weeks at a time if they have to finish a novel or get started on one or need peace and

28. Michael Broadbent, wine expert at Christie's.
29. Colonel Sir Piers Bengough, HM Representative, Ascot, member of the Jockey Club; member of the Horserace Betting Levy Board, 1978–81.

quiet away from their beastly mistress or husband or whatever it may be to get on with the work they want. It sounds imaginative.

Some of these great parties Jack Heinz loved so much were in the garden when the grounds were covered with marquees and swings and roundabouts and all the fun of the fair. They didn't really have a very happy marriage. He with his mistress or more than one, and she with her publishing ventures. I don't know whether she had any flirtations or whatever. Nevertheless, she seems sad and forlorn though she has masses of money. Something has gone from her life.

It is Rupert's last day. He is going to New York tomorrow evening and will not be back until October.

He says *Today* is losing £28 million a year. I said, 'I'm getting nervous about it. How can you possibly recoup that?' The arrangement is that he will pay them back £40–45 million losses they have incurred on it so far. After the end of seven years if he makes a profit with it, a lot of that would be chargeable to tax but it would still leave him having paid something like £25 million for the operation. 'What is your market going to be? Who are you going to get to read it?' He said he had worked it out that so many people buy two newspapers that about ten million people don't buy one at all.

He believes that the *Express* is sinking and cannot now be retrieved and that Nick Lloyd is a bad editor and Stevens knows nothing about newspapers, so he will attack them. He's also going to attack some of the *Telegraph* readers as well as creating what he thinks will be a new readership not in competition with the *Sun*. He wants to make David Montgomery, the editor of the *News of the World*, the editor of it.

He says that a fat Jewish lady (whose name I can't remember)[30] would take over the *News of the World*. She is really tough. I said, 'Is she going to be tough with me?' and he laughed. He said, 'No, you'll like her. You'll think she's marvellous.' I said, 'It won't mean that I've got to go and write my column in *Today*?' 'No, never.'

'Is it going to have any politics?' 'Not overtly but it will say the right things on the right issues' and of course it would come out for her at election time.

I told him I thought it had been a pity they lost Peter Kellner[31] from the *Times* who was now writing very well for the *Independent*.

30. Wendy Henry.
31. Political commentator.

Rupert immediately made a note to remind himself to see if he could get him back again.

**Wednesday 17 June**

Last night I asked Rupert what his relations are with Bruce Matthews and told him I had got him the SIS job. He thought he would do that quite well but he said, 'He is not as strong as you may think. He is unable sometimes to make decisions.'

I asked, 'Have you fallen out with Bruce?' and he said, no, he was still on his main board and he saw him there in New York the other day. I said, 'Well if you had fallen out with him I would have cancelled the invitation for him to spend a few days with us in Italy.' 'Oh no, there's no need to do that.' He's very friendly with him still.

I am enormously fond of Rupert. As I saw him into his car last night I said, 'You have the same effect on me as the injections from goats and sheep, or whatever they were alleged to have, on elderly people like Somerset Maugham[32] when they went to Swiss clinics to make themselves young again. You rejuvenate me every time I see you.'

Rupert feels that Bernard Levin's articles ramble around a bit frequently these days. Conscientiously he tries to read them but frequently doesn't get very far with them. I think Bernard has lost his edge and his enthusiasm for causes and situations. The long sentences used to be wrapped around a lot but now the inside of them begins to contain less.

Rupert also said last night that Maxwell is asking for another £600 million for a rights issue. He thinks that one day Maxwell will go bust in a spectacular manner.

Unexpected and lovely letter from Margaret.[33] She is marvellous.

Young Winston Churchill came in. He put his top hat in the room itself instead of in the cubicle outside. He said, 'It belonged to my grandfather.' I said, 'You could sell it for a lot of money.'[34] He said, 'Yes, that's why I keep it in my sight all the time.' It is black and shiny

---

32. Novelist and playwright (1874–1965); he had ewe-gland injections.
33. 'At the risk of being uncharacteristically formal, I did just want to put on record my immense thanks to you for all your help and wise counsel during these last few weeks. I cannot thank you enough. Yours ever Margaret.'
34. A top hat belonging to Sir Winston Churchill fetched £25,300 at an auction of political memorabilia at Sotheby's on 15 July 1998.

and rather splendid. It must be a hundred years old now but still serviceable.

The Tote have issued marvellous loud gas operated whistles to girls and staff to defend themselves against attackers and I suppose rapists. I let it off in Rosita's[35] ear at lunch. Everyone was startled and Rosita said it had hurt her ear so I offered to kiss it better.

I asked her if she still had no boyfriend. She was slightly evasive this time, making me think she probably has. She made such comments as 'Sonny is always around,' or 'I'm always surrounded by people at Blenheim or elsewhere,' or 'It's so difficult getting up to London.' I said, 'Are you still exorcizing your passions in the hunting field?' She said that was a method she still employed, the hard riding subdued thoughts of sex, and laughed merrily.

**Thursday 18 June**

A charming letter from Quintin.[36] I feel so sad for him.

In our entertainment room today there were the French Ambassador and his wife, and the American Ambassador and his wife.

The French Ambassadress was elegant though not pretty and knew a lot about wine, about literature and art. Also she knew about politics.

We discussed Proust whom she likes and Colette whom I prefer. Instead of saying, 'How can you put them both in the same class?' she agreed that Colette was a genius. Her name is Vicomtesse de Nanteuil. I told her that claret was better than Burgundy because the English had shown the French how to make claret for three hundred years. She did not quite accept this, not even when I said the reason why Burgundy was inferior was because the English had never occupied that region of France.

Once I would have thought it exciting to have tea in the Royal Box. Now I find it something of a boring nuisance. We had to leave our guests and not see those who had been invited in for drinks or tea after lunch. My conversations with the Queen are usually confined to 'Good morning, Ma'am,' or 'Good afternoon, Ma'am,' or 'It's a nice day.'

This time I decided to venture a little more and startle her. Howard de Walden had just won the Gold Cup with Paean, a great victory. I

35. Duchess of Marlborough.

36. Lord Hailsham said, 'I think the crux was Michael's [Havers] pension (especially for his wife). At all events I went quietly.'

pointed at my apricot coloured rose and said to the Queen, 'It only won because I wore this rose (the de Walden colour). I wore it because I'm in love with Lady Howard de Walden.' This is not true though I like her. The Queen almost jumped, but took it quite well and laughed.

Princess Anne had reverted to her usual rude self. When the Howard de Waldens came in after their great Gold Cup victory she turned to some unfortunate courtier, quite high on the staff, and snapped, 'Are they staying to tea?' to which he replied he didn't know. 'Well find out at once. Find out and do your job.'

Verushka saw Princess Diana fooling about in the most childish manner, pulling people's hair and tweaking them. I'm not surprised that Prince Charles is bored with this backward girl who couldn't even pass any O levels. While we were sitting next to Queen Elizabeth the Queen Mother Charles came up and said, 'I'm off.' She said, 'To play polo?' and he said, 'Yes,' to which Queen Elizabeth the Queen Mother replied, 'Good idea.' He looked glad to be getting out of the dreary atmosphere.

Queen Elizabeth spoke mostly to me. I told her about the Archbishop of Canterbury coming to the Jockey Club to talk about Sunday racing. Once again she said she didn't really like the idea and I said, 'That's the only thing you've ever disagreed with me about.' 'The only thing?' she asked. I said, 'Yes.' After a moment she said, 'I think you're right. I have never disagreed with you about anything else.'

They make a great thing of tea in the Royal Box. They have had their lunch before they do the carriage procession which begins just after 2.00. So they must be hungry. There were lashings of strawberries and cream and scones and funny little pastries, and puffed bits of buns with some sort of salad cream in them and all the rest of it. However, tea does not take long as the Queen leaps up to make sure of seeing the next race, horse racing being the only thing she is interested in and knows something about.

When we left the Royal Box at about 5.00 we had to rush back to our entertainment room, say goodbye to everyone, regret not having seen more of them during the afternoon and dash off to the car park. I wanted to get back in time to be able to go down to the Lords to sign on before 7.00.

When I got there I found that the House had adjourned 'at pleasure' at five past six because the supply of peers wanting to sign on had run out. It was to begin again at five to seven. I was just turning to make a telephone call when a great voice bellowed, 'Woodrow' and there was Sonny Marlborough with Sam Vestey. They inveigled me into a shouting conversation. It was like being undergraduates at Oxford. Sam kept shouting out that I couldn't go in first because I was only a life peer and Dukes take precedence. He was even shouting that when we did get on to the crossbenches. I refrained from saying, 'I'm sorry my family didn't make enough money out of corned beef in time for me to have been a hereditary peer,' which is what happened to the Vestey family.

**Friday 19 June**

Rupert rings from New York to say the deal about *Today* is nearly completed. They are writing a letter to the Secretary for Trade saying that it would collapse if he doesn't take it over and jobs would be lost. He will let me know when the letter goes and if any help is needed in making sure the Monopolies Commission is bypassed. I told him that Mrs Thatcher knows about it because I have spoken to her. He says, 'I expect she's spoken to David Young.'

**Saturday 20 June**

Open a betting shop in Chelmsford. Attractive and modern.

On, on, on to Heveningham Hall.[37] Barbed wire in front of the house. Guard dogs. Security man at the gates. You have to let him know you are coming. It turned out Mr Al Ghazzi was quite justified in taking precautions which annoy people in the locality.

I was shown the Orangery door smashed just the other day by vandals who tried to break in. Coadeware designed by James Wyatt had been stolen.

The garden at the back looked a bit of a mess. There were only two gardeners. In front was unkempt just outside the house. But the Park and its prospect are lovely. They've had rotten luck inside the house. When the library was just finished some idiot workman left a blow lamp on or allowed something to catch fire with a blow lamp. They keep having fires in the place. But the rest of the house is being beautifully restored and is now nearly ready. They have still not got the furniture which is being kept at Audley End. Mr Al Ghazzi has spent some £5 million on the house already.

It is magnificent in its proportions and the interiors are splendid.

---

37. Fine example in Suffolk of the earlier classical work of James Wyatt (1746–1813).

The colours are typical James Wyatt. The whole thing done in exquisite taste.

**Monday 22 June**

Dinner at Olga Polizzi's in honour of the birthday of Alistair McAlpine's wife. We are the first to arrive. Before many others come Olga says, 'You are the hero. You saved the election for the Conservatives.' I said, 'What makes you think that?' to which she replied, 'Alastair (he is the Treasurer of the Conservative Party) said you intervened at the right moment.'

When I did talk to McAlpine he said, 'If it hadn't been for you the campaign wouldn't have been changed and put on the road properly. We didn't believe the Gallup poll on that Thursday morning was necessarily a rogue one.' 'I told her she must get the campaign changed at once and herself on television the whole time.' 'That is exactly what she did. She told us it had got to be changed and she was going on the television as you, Woodrow, had said she should. And she insisted on the things being emphasized which you said should be.'

Mrs Neil Balfour, a granddaughter of Bert Marlborough[38] sat next to me. Her mother married an American and I met her once in America. 'Did she ever tell you the story about the foaming toothbrush?' She said, 'Yes, it was a great story in our family.' That was when Bert Marlborough stayed with his daughter in America and came down to breakfast and said, 'There's something wrong with my toothbrush. It didn't foam this morning.' It was then established that the reason was that he was travelling without his valet who always put the toothpaste on the brush for him. It seems that he was unaware that this is what caused the foam in his mouth.

Hartley Shawcross was there. He said Michael Havers was amiable but knew little law. I asked him whether he thought Quintin Hogg was a good Lord Chancellor. He said, 'Not really. He didn't know about the law and was not really up to it.' I had the impression that the only person Hartley thought would have been suitable as Lord Chancellor in this lifetime was himself.

I was talking to the Russell girl who married Neil Balfour[39] and several others joined in about how is David Metcalfe so attractive to

---

38. 10th Duke of Marlborough (1897–1972).
39. MEP, 1979–84; chairman, York Trust Group, 1986–91; m 2 (1978) Serena Mary Churchill, née Russell.

women. He doesn't look prepossessing but his wives have been beautiful including Sally. I said, 'It must be his long nose.' 'What do you mean?' I said, 'Work it out.'

Alistair McAlpine said that Gordon Reece was brought back in the last few days as I had asked Margaret to do. So that worked as well. Thank goodness I intervened when I did and so strongly.

**Tuesday 23 June**

Seem to be about five hundred people at Trinity, Oxford. We all ate in a large tent.

There was no speech though it was the farewell of Tony Quinton, the Master of Trinity.

A number of people were there whom I had not expected to see from the social butterfly life of London, like Sally Metcalfe and Diana Wilton. I asked them what they were doing there as presumably they had not read a book for a long time, to which David Metcalfe retorted, 'I've just read yours, I've bought a copy.' I said, 'Paperback or hardback?' 'Hardback,' he said triumphantly.

Verushka sat next to the Princess of Wales' father.[40] She could hardly understand what he was saying, he was so dumb and incoherent. I remember meeting him before his stroke at a garden party at Buckingham Palace. He was dumb then, too. If the Princess of Wales' children are anything like him it will be good because what we need is stupid people on the throne, not ones who get ideas.

Arranged during the day that the government Whips will have the second reading of my Sunday Sports Bill on Thursday, July 16th. The first reading is next Monday. A lot of work ahead.

The Bill has been expanded to make all sports legal on a Sunday and the betting shops to be open.

The second reading of the Private Members' Bills which start in the Lords are seldom opposed unless they are very contentious. I now have to think of the tactics. I can't exactly slip it in without anybody noticing but it looks as though there is a better chance of it getting through the second reading than I had thought. The fun will start after the Recess in the autumn during the committee stage if we reach it.

---

40. 8th Earl Spencer (1924–92).

**Thursday 25 June**

The state opening of Parliament. We leave very early, much too early, because I am nervous about getting my robes which are reserved for me in the Moses Room.

Rosita looked spectacular with her highly jewelled diamond tiara and her lovely earrings and necklace. We grinned at each other.

Some women were beautifully turned out with their splendid family tiaras. Others had none at all, including Cecilia Whitelaw. Verushka had borrowed a tiara from Sonia [Sinclair], the one which Julian [Melchett] had given her many years ago when they were first married. V had to get it out of Asprey's and pay £100 for the insurance.

I did not mind the waiting. Sitting at that kind of ceremony is the nearest thing I ever get to religion.

**Friday 26 June**

Went to Sonia's at half past six. Shortly after the great Allan Davis[41] arrived.

Allan Davis who was responsible for *No Sex Please, We're British* (has run for seventeen years) is looking for a new play. He said, 'I'm afraid what I'm going to say will probably shock you particularly if you have a dedication to your play.' I said, 'I have no *amour-propre* about it. I am only interested in trying to make a saleable commodity. I will follow your instructions as you are the expert.'

He said, 'Yes, you are a professional.'

He wants the male character completely upgraded. He wants the woman still of course to matter but reduced in scope. He wants it in two acts.

The great asset of my doing a play about politics is that I am so well known. It would be a draw in itself. People would want to go and see what my play was like.

We got on famously. He is a queer but an agreeable one. We will have to have several meetings before I start work.

He said I should take Noël Coward as a model, how he got from one point to another and every five seconds or so, or certainly half a minute or thereabouts, the spotlight came on again and you saw something new and interesting. The dialogue needs shortening in the speeches, considerably.

---

41. B 1913, Sydney, Australia, he began his career as an actor; after war service in Britain he became a director and producer.

I felt he was just the sort of man I could be tutored by. He is charming though quite definite in what he wants which is exactly right.

**Saturday 27 June**

Mr Allan Davis rings up.

I feel quite excited. I had told him the day before that if we really got this play off the ground I would write some more plays. It would be a delightful way to finish my life if I could pull it off.

Allan Davis suggested I look at *Private Lives* as there is a very important scene in the middle, which most people don't notice unless it is produced properly, where they talk seriously about life and love, and see how Noël Coward handles it.

**Sunday 28 June**

Told Margaret that Jacob would like to head up a government sponsored committee for the year 2000. She said she had been thinking of this date and that was why she had appointed Richard Branson to be in charge of the litter clearing and so forth and called it Project 2000 but it had run into the sands.

She said she had thought of Tony Snowdon[42] and I promptly said, 'No good. He may be a good designer but he hasn't got the contacts that Jacob has or the ability to raise money or conceive a great concept like this. It ought to be something like the Great Exhibition of 1851, in one part, with demonstrations of British goods and so forth. That was a great success.' I also had in mind that Sir Matthew Digby Wyatt had been the executant architect and secretary of the Great Exhibition and got a gold medal from Prince Albert.

I agreed with Margaret that we would meet with Jacob after the House had gone into recess and she was less busy, probably mid September. She is now keen on Jacob heading such a committee. I told Jacob to look up how the Great Exhibition was done.

Margaret and I talked about the rates. I said, 'I wish we could start absolutely from scratch as suggested by me in the *News of the World* this morning.'

Local government is not democratic at all. It should all be run by Whitehall with local administrators with a fixed budget from Whitehall administering.

She said, 'But that would be more centralization.' I said, 'No it

42. 1st Earl of Snowdon, former husband of Princess Margaret.

would not, because the central government is elected by a much bigger vote than local government is. We have to destroy the capacity of local councils, particularly left-wing ones, to spend money without any understanding of how to do it or any common sense.'

She thinks it's marvellous about my Sunday Sports Bill which I will be introducing on its first reading tomorrow. She had not heard about it but got very interested. I told her the Home Office had been of enormous help and that it was nothing to do with shop trading but to allow sports to conduct their affairs legally on a Sunday; for example, finals at Wimbledon on a Sunday are quite illegal because they charge for them even though they try to get round it by selling tickets in advance. 'Good Lord, I didn't know that.'

I told her the betting shops would have to be open because you can't have racing without betting and otherwise there would be illegal betting. She was interested and pleased.

**Tuesday 30 June**

Forced to go to dinner to be followed by dance at Nuala Allason's[43] in Cheyne Walk. Wanted to watch Connors[44] and his unpleasant Swedish opponent. Insisted on staying until the last ball had been played and Connors had won.

One of the guests at the dinner was Michael Grylls, a Tory MP. He took me aside at the end of dinner and said did I know what Norman Tebbit was up to? He is entertaining all the new MPs in his room and giving them drinks and buttering them up. 'It doesn't sound as though he had any intention of retiring,' Grylls added. 'He is obviously after her job when he thinks the moment is right.' I remarked, 'Perhaps that was why he was so keen on her not being prominent in the election campaign. He wanted her to have a small majority and then be in jeopardy.'

I see that Allan Davis is about five years older than me, which is encouraging. Geriatrics to the fore.

---

43. Mother of the Conservative MP and writer Rupert Allason.
44. Men's Singles champion at Wimbledon in 1982.

**Wednesday 1 July**

Spoke to Denis Howell[1] who has a lot of sense about the Sunday Sports Bill. He says the blonde bombshell[2] had been ringing him asking whether Mishcon was going to oppose the second reading in the Lords. I said, 'Oh for God's sake, can't she be stopped stirring people up and leave it to us?'

He said he had had a note from Kinnock yesterday asking what was their position (Labour's). Ron Todd had already got on to him from the Transport and General Workers Union complaining about the awful things that might happen to union people if there was Sunday opening of racecourses. He sent a soothing reply to Kinnock saying he would protect the interests of all the workers in the industry.

The Bill is beginning to arouse some interest. The Jockey Club keep on trying to pretend through Bridgett Walters that it is all their idea. It never was. I began the whole project years ago which prompted the Jockey Club to set up a working party in the first place.

The Bill was actually drafted by John Heaton at the Tote, Mr Keith at the Public Bill Office in the Lords, the lawyers at the Home Office and myself.

At lunch time Rupert rings from the hotel in Washington where he was having breakfast in the Jockey Club. He was just off to Australia.

He was agitated about whether David Young will give authority for the buying of *Today* without referring it to the Monopolies Commission. Should he ring him? I say, 'I will ring him and say the speed factor is because Lonrho are not willing to stand the losses more than another day or so and they will close the paper down if they don't get an instant decision.'

When I ring David Young he says, 'If you want to discuss *Today* with me, I'm afraid I can't because I'm in a quasi-judicial position.' I

1. Labour MP; minister with responsibility for sport, 1964–9, former football referee; life peer 1992.
2. Bridgett Walters.

said, 'I just wanted to explain that it is not Rupert insisting on the speed, it is because of Lonrho closing it down.' He replied, 'I would rather not discuss it with you at all, but please give my regards to Rupert.' From his last phrase I deduced that all would be well though he had not said so. I rang Rupert and said so.

Mr Allan Davis comes at 4.00. He brought me a book and a play to read. We sit for over three and a half hours and he makes points about the play, wanting a different beginning and various other alterations. It was enormous fun.

Rupert rings just as the ten o'clock news is starting, saying he has heard that there was a rumpus in the House of Commons when the announcement was made there would be no referral to the Monopolies Commission. All is well though. I asked him anxiously, 'Are you sure you have done the right thing? £38 million is an awful lot to pay for a bust enterprise.'

**Saturday 4 July**

Meeting of the International Nutrition Foundation at Lady Place, Sutton Courtenay.

There is an item on the agenda today which nearly made me weep. We needed £5,000 to start a fund-raising campaign of which there are some hopes in America. Dr Sinclair promptly sold the Fabergé miniature frame given to his parents (his mother was Russian) by a Tsarist Prime Minister. He got £6,500 for it in Switzerland through Sotheby's.

On to Weeford. A garden party at Thickbroom. The house is in some way whitewashed and pebble dashed. It is not like the house in the drawing by Henry Wyatt nor in the water-colour they had there of 1904. John Robinson thinks it must have been a bigger house and a better house originally, as the Wyatts had reserved pews at the front of the church and would not have done so if it had just been a little farmhouse.

We went to the church. Petronella said, 'Why do you want to be buried here? There are only two other Wyatt graves.' I said, 'It's a nice view over the fields.' She said, 'But you won't be able to see it and it's so difficult to get to.'

**Sunday 5 July**

Allan Davis is coming for the last few days in Italy to see how I have performed my holiday task of rewriting large chunks of the play.

**Monday 6 July**

I forgot to speak to Mrs Thatcher until it was too late yesterday. I ring her at twenty to eight and tell her that she is not to worry at all about Biffen's outburst that she was a Stalinist and impossible to talk to and ran the government in the wrong way with the wrong policies.

She said, 'It is very surprising because he didn't want to resign. I had to force him to. He wouldn't go. He wouldn't write his resignation letter because he wanted to stay in the government. Why did he want to do that if he thought it was so awful?'

I asked her whether it would be possible to do something for poor Leon Brittan. She said she would very much like to but he has had his chance. 'He's very loyal but so many people think he comes over extremely badly on television and he is not a good communicator. They find him awful to look at. He's very clever but he is really not an alert politician.'

Dinner party at 19 C. David Somerset, Drue Heinz, Tim Bell and his girlfriend Virginia Hornbrook, Frank Johnson and his girlfriend Miriam Gross, Petronella. Jacob comes in just after ten.

Tim Bell very anxious to establish that he really made all the alterations in the election campaign and was at the centre of everything.

After dinner he was talking away saying, yes, I had rung Mrs Thatcher that morning but she didn't do what I told her to do when she went down to the Conservative Central Office and when he found she hadn't, he had to ring me to get me to ring her again but couldn't get hold of me, so he did it himself. This I simply do not believe. A public relations man anxious to prove how wonderful he is, particularly in front of people like Jacob.

He gets paid a fortune for his services, lucky chap. I do it for love.

Tim Bell's Australian girlfriend has lived with him for twelve years so I said, 'Why don't you get married?' She said, 'We've really never sort of got around to it.' I said, 'You're in a bad position because it may not last and you will have nothing.' She was confident that it would. I said, 'Women have a raw deal in life and you should make sure of your future while you have the chance.'[3] She was quite pretty but not as pretty as I remembered her.

3. They married in 1988.

**Thursday 9 July**

A great dinner party at Max Rayne's house at West Heath Road, Hampstead. Had not been there for six or seven years or more. The house is hideous, having been built by Max, enormously rich, in the sixties style.

Before dinner talk to Richard Luce who is supposed to be in charge of culture as a Minister. I congratulated him on his declaration that the arts must find business and other sponsors and not just rely on the state, though I said I thought it a pity that he did not say that the amount of subsidy would be reduced and culture should make up the balance by sponsors.

I then discovered he was talking to the man who has taken over from Peter Hall at the National Theatre who was looking exceedingly glum.[4]

**Friday 10 July**

See *Serious Money*.[5] Allan Davis has a stake in it but is not the director. It came from the Royal Court Theatre, a trendy, left-wing group of which Sonia is a member of the Council.

It is an attack on the City written by a Communist. It is supposed to be about Yuppies though it is not. It takes its cue from the Guinness scandal and other take-over bids and insider dealings. The result is a travesty of what goes on in the City where 99.9 per cent are honest.

The play was conducted at an enormous pace, people coming on and off in a bewildering manner. There was a large amount in the programme to explain the terms of art which need to be studied pretty carefully by the ordinary members of the audience. Even then I doubt if they would understand it. I couldn't make out what on earth was happening most of the time but one of the females was rather pretty. Each act ends with a filthy song liberally bespattered with 'fuck' and 'bugger' and sexual crudities.

The play was apparently a great success at the Royal Court Theatre where all the comfortably off young people in the area attended and laughed allegedly at themselves.

---

4. Richard Eyre became artistic director, Royal National Theatre, in 1988; knight 1997.
5. By Caryl Churchill.

**Saturday 11 July**

Allan rings to know how I liked the play.

I was slightly nervous that maybe he wants the sort of play I couldn't possibly write. I agreed with him that it shouldn't be like Somerset Maugham or Pinero but it certainly can't be a collection of quick fire unintelligible exchanges, however fast and impressively they are delivered.

Arrive at Badminton for lunch.

I sit next to Anne[6] and Chiquita, first wife of Jakie Astor. Anne is bothered about her book on Elizabeth I. She has written two quite successful books of history. *William IV* was good and *Ladies in Waiting* was not so good. She said she sold about four thousand of *William IV* which I thought was good. She now cannot find anything new to say about Elizabeth I and she has been at it for three years. I suggested there might be some similarities between her and Mrs Thatcher.

Chiquita I have not seen for a long time. I once took her shoe off at a dinner. She used to be very attractive.

We talked about Mrs de Savary of whom Jakie is now very fond. Chiquita says she has money and Jakie should not marry her because his children, including Chiquita's oldest son, would violently protest at more divisions of the family property.

Edward's wife[7] is the daughter of Viscount Davidson, a government Whip in the Lords. She is twenty-nine. She asked how old I was and I said sixty-nine so she grinned and said, 'Soixante-neuf.' I replied, 'But that's not on the menu for you.' She is blonde and lively. I find it mysterious that she married Edward who doesn't do a great deal.

After lunch Tracy[8] sat ostentatiously on Harry's lap in front of the television set. She is pretty but not nice, certainly not as nice as her sister Rachel, the actress.

Caroline, the wife of Edward, asked me where I had met Daphne who is her mother-in-law's mother (Daphne Fielding). I said, 'In the Gargoyle after the War. It was a kind of night club with beautiful mirrors which were supposed to have been made all round the walls from a design of Matisse.' Andrew Devonshire, Freddie Ayer[9] and

---

6. The Beauforts' daughter, Lady Anne Somerset.
7. The Hon. Caroline Davidson, m (1982) Lord Edward Somerset, second son of the Duke and Duchess of Beaufort.
8. Née Ward, who had married the Marquess of Worcester (Harry) on 13 June.
9. Alfred J. Ayer, philosopher (1910–89).

Lucian Freud and such people used to go there and it changed into a place where they have naked girls which was quite agreeable but it started to go downhill.

Poor Daphne has actually been in a loony bin for the last two years. I hadn't realized that. After her birthday party last night she suddenly got up and went, leaving all her presents behind. She thinks she is being poisoned by her maid and also that her maid wants to steal her passport, so she cut it all up into little squares the other day. There is a real streak of dottiness on the Vivian side of Caroline's family.[10]

**Sunday 12 July**

David thinks that Jeffrey Archer must be lying.[11] What a silly country it is, he feels, where you can't just say, 'Yes, I went to bed with a tart.'

I said, 'You mean he should have said that by using a tart he was helping to reduce unemployment and to keep tarts employed?'

I said, 'I only went to bed with a tart once and hadn't even realized she was one. She was a kind of bar girl in Munich when I was eighteen.'

I think if Jeffrey Archer had boldly said, 'Yes, I did go to bed with this tart and why not?' he would have got away with it. He must have been mad to bring the libel action. Even if he wins it, many will think he was lying which, judging from what David Montgomery said to me long before the story broke in the *News of the World*, he must be.[12]

Margaret full of jollity.

She said, 'Don't you think North is marvellous?'[13] I told her that I had been speaking to Pericles in Philadelphia and he said he has taken the country by storm. She said, 'Isn't it wonderful? The people have the right instinct and they are on North's side. They know that Congress has been interfering too much and is wrong.'

'Isn't *Today* different?' she said and I told her what rubbish it had

---

10. Daphne Fielding's father was the 4th Baron Vivian.
11. The jury in the libel case under discussion decided in Archer's favour.
12. Archer won substantial damages for the allegations in the *Star*.
13. Lieutenant Colonel Oliver North, an official in the US National Security Council, with Admiral John Poindexter, National Security Adviser, was responsible for the policy of selling arms to Iran to facilitate the return of American hostages held in the Lebanon. Some of the proceeds of the sale were then channelled to the Contras who were seeking to overthrow the left-wing government in Nicaragua, precipitating the Iran-Contra scandal at the end of the Reagan administration. The revelations led to the resignation of Poindexter and the dismissal of North.

been that the Monopolies Commission not being referred to was a pay-off for Rupert.

She mentioned that we have no paper in Scotland. The Tiny Rowland one is against us and so is the D. C. Thomson paper. Of course in England it's much better, though the electronic media are against us. I said I thought that Duke Hussey is trying to do his best, and she thought yes, he probably was and he might be reasonably effective.

**Wednesday 16 July**

Duke Hussey rang.

He again said that he was looking for something on which to have a row with the government about so that he could make the staff feel he was completely impartial. (I had previously said this to Margaret and she wasn't at all pleased and could not see the reason for it. But I think she understood after a bit of argument.)

The debate in the Lords was generally agreed to be a success. It began about 8.00 and was still going on at 11.00. There was some opposition from the Bishop of Leicester and Brentford, of Keep Sunday Special.

The second reading went through without a division.

**Thursday 17 July**

More progress with the play. Allan Davis is confident that he is going to put it on. He told me that he was angling after the man who does the Prime Minister in *Yes, Prime Minister* and previously *Yes, Minister.*[14]

Went down to the Lords. Many congratulations on the second reading all around which delighted me. Went to the Public Bill Office and thanked Mr Keith for all his help. He went with me to the government Whips' office to Mr Walters who gave us the time for the committee stage of the whole House which is Wednesday October 28th.

Dinner with David and Ninette Montagu.

Conrad Black[15] was there. We had a long talk about Rupert Murdoch whom he kept saying he admired and then said he went down-market with every newspaper he touched and he didn't know

---

14. Paul Eddington (1927–95).
15. Canadian owner of the *Telegraph* newspapers.

anything about running quality newspapers, which is not true. The only quality papers of any merit in Australia belong to Rupert.

He asked why wouldn't I write for the *Telegraph* and for him? I said, 'Because Rupert is an old friend of mine and it would unnecessarily hurt his feelings; because I like writing for the *News of the World* because I'm a preacher.'

**Monday 20 July**

Dinner at the Travellers' Club given by A. N. Wilson and his wife.[16] We had been expecting sherry and a rather don-like atmosphere. Instead there was champagne to begin with, though not very good, and white wine and claret neither of which were very good. Then there was port and brandy.

I sat next to Victoria Glendinning.[17]

Full of life and verve. She has written four biographies about women: Edith Sitwell, Elizabeth Bowen, Vita Sackville-West and Rebecca West. I told her how Rebecca West had warned me at the time I got the Communists out of the ETU that the Communists would never forgive me and would pursue me to try to destroy my political career, which is exactly what they did.

She didn't like Mrs Thatcher and I weighed into her. 'Feminists, and I suppose you're one, should adore Mrs Thatcher. She has shown what a woman can do. She's the most remarkable woman of the century and the outstanding Prime Minister of the century. You should all be very proud. You should be writing about her. Have you not noticed, as an intelligent woman yourself, that you are living at the same time as one of the most extraordinary women in history and yet you run her down?'

To which Victoria feebly replied that she didn't like her politics; she always voted Labour. I said, 'That is ridiculous. Mrs Thatcher is not a Tory. She is a revolutionary. You can't say she's like an ordinary Tory. She is a real radical.'

Petronella said her other neighbour was a very religious man who told her that A. N. Wilson's wife is also very religious. He asked her if she had heard any good sermons lately. Perhaps that's how Andrew and his wife first fell in love as he was very keen on religion.

---

16. Katherine Duncan-Jones, Fellow of Somerville College, Oxford; they divorced in 1989.
17. Author and journalist.

**Tuesday 21 July**

Allan Davis arrives on the dot, if not earlier, at five to ten. Work away at the play.

We waste a time on his telling stories such as Noël Coward after seeing a play by a poet called Maxwell Anderson saying, 'So far as I am concerned Anderson's poetic licence has expired.'

Down to the Lords to give Wendy Henry lunch. She is the new editor of the *News of the World*. She is plump and jolly, thirty-two years old.

She was in a disordered state. 'I had my first call from the boss (meaning Rupert) this morning and he was very, very angry with me.'

'What he was really annoyed about was Princess Diana's drinking habits which we had sent up, saying she drinks an awful lot. He said, "Why can't you leave the poor girl alone? It wasn't very good journalism."' I was surprised because Rupert is usually dead against the monarchy and wants to bash it all the time.

I said, 'How are you getting on with the job?' She said, 'Not at all well. I have no confidence. I don't think I can do it.' I said, 'Don't be silly. You've only just started. Rupert has great confidence in you. I know because he told me so.'

To which Wendy answered, 'Wouldn't it be brave and honest for a woman to say, I was given this job and I know I can't do it.' I said, 'In your case it would be stupid because you can do it.'

We had a jolly chat. I introduced her to Frank Longford[18] before she went and said, 'This is the editor of your favourite newspaper, Frank.'

Frank said, 'My wife used to write a column years ago for the *News of the World*. She used to tell her friends it was really for the *Observer* when she went off to work on it.' Wendy said to me as we went, 'Isn't that typical of that sort of person. Willing to take the money but ashamed to say where it comes from.'

Frank wanted to know who was going to win the Archer case to which of course we did not know the answer. I'd told Wendy that we were going to his party on Sunday and I had to go whether he won or not. She said, 'Oh my goodness, what a marvellous story to be giving a party for his wedding anniversary.' I said, 'You are not to use that. I will not speak to you or talk to you again if you do.'

---

18. 7th Earl of Longford; Labour politician and prison reformer.

**Wednesday 22 July**

Dinner at the French Embassy. I suppose about fifty people. It was in honour of Geoffrey Howe. He was able to meet a number of English people he meets often elsewhere.

I didn't approach him as he was continually surrounded before dinner. However, while I was talking to somebody else he came up obviously wanting a chat.

I said, 'You're a very good Foreign Secretary,' which pleased him a lot. I added, 'But you were also a very good Chancellor of the Exchequer.' He said, 'My greatest achievement was abolishing exchange control which I did in three steps. Margaret was against it, thinking it was too risky and would cause too much difficulty.' I said, 'I didn't know that,' and was extremely interested (because she talks as though it was her idea now).

We've always got on well. He probably knows that I think that if Margaret goes at the right time for him still to be Prime Minister, he would make a good one. He is much tougher than he looks and Denis Healey's jibes about attacking Geoffrey Howe being like savaging a dead sheep indicate either Denis's untruthfulness or inability to recognize the strength this man has.

Geoffrey embraced Verushka warmly when he saw her, giving her smacking great kisses. He is an agreeable man with, I think, an eye for the girls which is not surprising as his wife Elspeth is not precisely erotic.

I then fell into talk with Lord King[19] and Charles Forte. John King was delighted with what I had said in support of his merger with British Caledonian in the *News of the World*. He said that if they refer it to the Monopolies Commission, the deal probably will not go through and British Caledonian will have to sell to the highest bidder and not wait for their company to run down during the inquiry.

Charles Forte kept saying to him, 'If you buy British Caledonian, can I have the hotels?' In the end John King said, 'I do not wish to be a hotelier,' adding hastily, 'Not of course that I think there's anything against hoteliers,' meaning really that he despises that trade. He promised Charles that he would give him first option at the price he wanted them. Charles said, 'Of course it would be a fair price,' and John turned to me and said, 'You hear that, my Lord?'

George Weidenfeld was there. He is now intending to marry Barbara

---

19. Chairman of British Airways since 1981.

Amiel. Verushka warned him against this foolhardy enterprise at his age and previous distinct lack of success at getting married. She is a pretty woman about forty-five, and writes well in the *Times*. She's a Canadian. His publishing I would guess is doing so-so from what he said to me.

Before dinner I saw Jane Rayne with Max. I said, 'I forgot to write a thank you letter,' so I took a little notebook out of my pocket and sat at a table in one of the French Embassy's vast rooms and scribbled out, 'Darling Jane, Thank you very much for the lovely dinner. The garden and the house were beautiful but not as beautiful as you. Love Woodrow,' and gave it her. She was delighted. Max grumbled that I was writing love letters to his wife.

**Thursday 23 July**

Wendy Henry rang. Would it be all right if she followed up the story about Jeffrey Archer having a celebratory lunch or bash at Grantchester on Sunday? I said, 'Oh my God, I knew I should never have mentioned it to you.'

Later she rang that the Judge had just mentioned the twenty-first wedding was last Saturday so she's no longer interested. Hooray.

Dinner at The Other Club.

Hugh Thomas across the table was sitting next to Heseltine, the Queen's Private Secretary. He wanted to know why I wrote for the *News of the World* 'This terrible paper' and lived on immoral earnings. I said, 'I write for the *News of the World* because it has a circulation of five million and probably, on the multiplication system accepted by advertisers, a readership of seventeen and a half million. I preach to them and tell them what I want them to do. I could not get a larger audience. What they publish in the rest of the paper is nothing whatever to do with me. Would you have preferred the *News of the World* not to have carried my articles during the general election but ones by Roy Hattersley? Would you have preferred the *News of the World* to have said that Labour was now the party to support? Who is the hypocrite?' and Tebbit agreed.

On talking about the election I said to Norman, 'I hope I didn't upset you by my interventions. I thought you were getting it wrong at one point.' He said, 'No.' He said it was not his fault she was not put on the television earlier. She had been taking advice from other people and that was what they had told her.

When I was talking with him, I told Tebbit how Margaret had

annoyed me on an *Any Questions* programme when she was a young MP by answering the question 'What did the panel talk about during dinner?' with 'Nobody said anything much, they were all forced to listen to Mr Woodrow Wyatt.' Tebbit said, 'She was right, wasn't she?' and we both laughed.

**Sunday 26 July**

Mrs Thatcher had gone to church, or was just going when I rang at twenty-five past ten this morning. Said I would ring in the evening. We are just off to the Archer luncheon party following his great half million pound victory against the *Star* newspaper.

The Judge's summing up was amazing. He spoke like Dr Arnold of Rugby talking of a prize pupil who had adopted his *mens sana in corpore sano*[20] doctrine to the full. He told the jury that here was this man who had been President of the Oxford University Athletic Association, had run for England, took his son up to London on a Sunday to take part in the Hyde Park marathon, fit, look at him, why would he be in need of rubberized sex? He omitted to refer to the evidence of Adam Raphael, a highly responsible journalist on the *Observer*, who said that Archer had told him that he had met the prostitute. Judge Caulfield's summing up must have been one of the most biased in history. The Judge was an innocent abroad.

Nevertheless, though I think the prostitute was telling more of the truth than Archer,[21] it was probably a good thing that Archer won his case. It may curb newspapers writing about the private lives of politicians and others when there is nothing in them to affect the nation's security or policies.

The Old Vicarage, Grantchester where Rupert Brooke lodged and wrote. Reporters and photographers around the house. They stayed throughout the whole proceedings leaning over the low garden wall.

Mary Archer is on a high, triumph in her eyes as well it might be. I said, 'On no account should you give your half million to charity. Buy a decent car and a yacht or something like that. When the *Sporting Life* had to pay me £10,000 in damages[22] people said "Are you giving it to the Injured Jockeys Fund?" to which my reply was, "No, it's my

---

20. 'A healthy mind in a healthy body'.
21. The jury thought otherwise and decided in favour of Archer, awarding him substantial damages.
22. In 1979.

money and I need it just as much as injured jockeys. It's the only tax free thing you get."'

In the evening David Montgomery rang. He said Rupert had rung and they proposed at the moment to resist Jeffrey Archer's action against the *News of the World*.

My farewell talk with Margaret before going on holiday.

She is in a state of considerable confidence. I told her the propaganda was bad so far about the community charge[23] and that I was going to write an article in the *News of the World* before I went, trying to make it simple, which pleased her.

**Monday 27 July**

David Stevens[24] rang up and spoke to me about whether he should sack the editor of the *Star*. He made such an appalling mess in accusing Archer of going to bed with the tart and printing lurid details, unchecked, supplied by the tart's nephew, which the tart in the witness box said was a lot of rubbish. I said, 'Of course you should sack him but wait until the appeal.'

**Wednesday 29 July**

Start summer holiday as usual by staying with Gingo[25] at Perignano.

Gingo is a great Anglophile. His wife Anna Lu is a Princess Corsini and the family have two palaces within half a mile of each other in Florence and also lots of valuable pictures etc. She is still working in the office in Florence every day, sorting out a division of the estate left by her father who died a few years ago.

---

23. The controversial flat-rate local tax on individuals proposed to replace the rates system.
24. Chairman of United Newspapers which owned the *Star* as well as the *Express* newspapers.
25. Count Sanminiatelli.

**Saturday 1 August**

A long hot drive to Porto Santo Stefano.

The house we are in has about five hectares of gardens with a huge swimming pool at one end, some distance from the house. The bedrooms are tiny. Mine is like a ship's cabin. It has beautiful dark panelled walls but no room to move or to put a table.

I am now sitting in a large upstairs drawing-room, with all the doors shut, where I hope to do enough rewriting of my play to satisfy Allan Davis when he comes.

On Saturday also arrive Alexander Stockton[1] and his mother Katie. They have been sublet the little guest house by Verushka.

On Friday night Gingo showed me a video made by the new lady MP who canvassed often topless here and is a pornographic star. Gingo says there are some twenty videos of this kind circulating in Italy. They cause a great sensation.

She is attractive with nicely shaped breasts and legs. The other parts of her were well displayed and heavily utilized by gentlemen and ladies during the film. Also a snake and its tongue play a significant central part in one episode. She was elected for the Radical Party on proportional representation in Rome. The Radicals are just cocking a snook at everybody and think it very amusing to have pornography represented by this lady called Ilona Staller ('Cicciolina').[2]

As nobody had left food for Katie and her family party, we gave them lunch. Alexander is pleasant, overweight and has already had two strokes or heart attacks though only forty-four. He had to give up drink. He made his maiden speech in the Lords recently. When hearing about the new peerages he was disappointed to learn that Callaghan had not been made an Earl. This used to be the custom with ex Prime

---

1. He succeeded to the title when his grandfather, the former Prime Minister, died, his father Viscount (Maurice) Macmillan having died in 1984.
2. She was elected on the slogan 'Less nuclear energy, more sexual energy'.

Ministers. He was disturbed he would remain the most recent creation of an Earl perhaps for all his life.

**Tuesday 4 August**

Bruce Matthews and his dim wife Sylvia arrive. He is fairly lively and intelligent. He is still on the board of News Corporation which controls Rupert's operations world-wide. He thinks Rupert has made a disastrous mistake in buying *Today*; David Montgomery, the editor, does not know how to make an up-market paper rivalling the *Express* and the *Mail* and in any case there is no niche for one.

He says he thinks Rupert, if he can get it suitably organized, will try to sell it before losing too much more money. The *Times* is still losing money.

Bruce believes Andrew Neil has no judgement and agrees with me it is rubbish to pretend that the freedom of the press is involved when the government try to stop ex Secret Service officers from blabbing about their secrets.

Bruce, who was still in charge at the time at News International, was always against the story the *News of the World* ran about Archer and he didn't know about it until half an hour before the trap was about to be sprung with the tart being paid off at a railway station. However, he did tell them they must not let the tart accept the money, otherwise it would look like blackmail. That was why she returned the £2,000.

Rupert was not at all happy about the Archer story. David Montgomery felt he was compelled to run it because *Private Eye* was going to say that they were not running it in the *News of the World* because of pressure from No 10 Downing Street.

David Stevens is in a great state because he keeps ringing up Downing Street asking to speak to the Prime Minister and she doesn't return his call. I am not surprised. When she made him a life peer I asked her why she had done it as I didn't think much of him and she said, 'He is very able.' I wonder if she thinks that now.

**Wednesday 5 August**

Kind hearted Verushka is having her holiday spoilt by having to look after Katie who has asthma/bronchitis. She has just gone over to their house to give her injections. Last night we had Bitta and Alexander and their two daughters to dinner making nine in all. She feels she must have them into meals because chaos reigns with Katie who cries at Verushka, the whisky bottle in her hand, saying everything in her life goes wrong. Not only did one son commit suicide but then her brother died, Maurice died, her daughter Rachel died of drugs and drink.

She was going to let Jill Hare and Alan sleep in her room and herself move downstairs but she cannot because she is ill. We have to have them in this house which distresses Verushka because there are more people in it than she wants at one time. I hope her great holiday in the year which she looks forward to for twelve months is not going to be ruined.

Started taking today these new white pills produced by Giovanni Ricci.[3] We will discover if my brain improves. It is curious that the human brain has thirty-five times more cells than it needs. You can afford to lose a few million through drink.

**Friday 7 August**

Alexander said to me his grandfather[4] said to him, 'You would do well in politics Alexander. You are a shit like myself. Your father didn't do well because he wasn't a shit.' I said, 'No, your father was a gentleman.'

From time to time Alexander reminds us that his great-grandfather was a Duke[5] by telling some irrelevant story. For example, he said Robert Maxwell rang him up and asked him whether he would like to sell his business[6] now his grandfather was dead. He reported himself as saying to Maxwell, 'My great-grandfather the Duke of Devonshire was rung by a newspaper asking whether it was true that the estate was so short of money it would be handed over to the nation with the house, to which the Duke said, "Rather than have it fall into the hands of the nation I would burn it down myself,"' and that according to Alexander is what he said to Maxwell that he would do with Macmillan rather than sell it to anyone, particularly Maxwell.

Last night at dinner Alan Hare said that he must be my oldest friend still alive. I was certainly his. We thought of the people we used to know before the War and whether we still knew them or whether

---

3. Professor Ricci, neurologist, father of Aliai Forte; see 2 August 1986.
4. Harold Macmillan.
5. His grandmother, Lady Dorothy Macmillan, was daughter of the 9th Duke of Devonshire.
6. Macmillan, the publishers.

they were dead. I met Alan about 1938, maybe 1937. Maurice Macmillan has gone, Hugh Fraser has gone, Tony Crosland has gone; friends I had at school whom I liked were killed in the War or are gone. This morning I thought perhaps Jakie Astor might be slightly earlier and still a friend. Michael Astor was certainly a little earlier but he is dead too. Roy Jenkins I didn't meet until 1944. Julian [Melchett] I think I met before Alan.

Alan is mildly miffed when I tell him that Charles Wintour may be an earlier friend I still see. I met him when he was at Cambridge and I was at Oxford and we were fooling about with *Light and Dark*, an Oxford and Cambridge magazine. I also met Arthur Schlesinger Junior at the same time and still see him. Before he went he told Verushka if I would agree that he was my oldest surviving friend, the next time we came to dinner he would give me one of the very best bottles possible of Château Latour. I think I might stretch a point.

**Thursday 13 August**

The shenanigans at this place have been extraordinary. There was the night when Alexander and Bitta and her children etc. were taking Katie out to dinner when she screamed and yelled at the gate, got out and said she wouldn't go because they refused to let her stay at Birch Grove if she came back to England.

Because Katie said she could not bear the noise David[7] and his friends were making in the small house, Verushka let her come and sleep over here. She then started having meals over here which I find a bore. I cannot say anything to her without her twisting it around and making a silly argument. Her views on politics are inane. They are actuated by a loathing for Mrs Thatcher because Ted Heath, whom she likes and worked for as Vice Chairman of the Tory Party and Chairman of the women's section of it, and Harold Macmillan her father-in-law, were shown to be rotten Tory Prime Ministers compared with Mrs Thatcher.

**Friday 14 August**

This morning, Friday, she comes over and she is talking to Verushka in her bedroom. I came out of the bedroom and called out 'Verushka' and Katie's voice came, 'I'm sorry I shouted at you last night.' I said, 'Never mind,' meaning that I didn't want to see her again. She then

---

7. Her son, the Hon. David Macmillan.

announced she was going back to England on Sunday which we all hope she will.

Verushka again somewhat saint-like took her into Orbetello to book her ticket. Verushka said it was in order to make sure she really did go.

Allan Davis arrived today. I worked like billyo yesterday and this morning to finish the play off before he came.

**Friday 21 August**

John Wilton is nice and more so as you get to see more of him. He is extremely knowledgeable about architecture beginning with the Elizabethan period. Knows all about the Wyatt architects as well. James Wyatt built Heaton Hall for his family in 1772. One of his earliest houses.

Diana I love. But I was surprised to hear her say that she used to gamble heavily until recently. John is very good tempered about paying her gambling debts and having to sell things. She once lost £26,000 in one evening at Annabel's [night club].

**Saturday 22 August**

In the afternoon [of the 18th] Douglas and Judy Hurd arrived.

Talk to him about Sunday racing and explain that the betting shops are not like other retail shops.

He thought she would have to listen to the business managers and he would try to move his colleagues on the subject.

We made progress on privatization [of the Tote] and he said he would talk to Nigel Lawson about it.

Before Douglas Hurd went he asked me again whether he could ring me for advice about his Party Conference speech before he finally decided on it. He fears he is going to be under attack at the Conservative Party Conference in October.

**Friday 28 August**

The play at last is done. It has been given a new beginning, a scene from the second act has been brought up to start the play and then repeated, we hope with effect, in the second act when the audience knows what is all about.

Allan says the first act is very good but the second act is even better which is as it should be, it seems.

**Saturday 29 August**

I hadn't realized that John Wilton would be the Duke of Westminster if young Gerald Grosvenor[8] were to vanish. He has but two daughters[9] and, though a cousin, John would inherit, plus the £500 million or so in the estate. I said, 'We must do something about this.' I thought of an idea for a possible play. A ducal murder in which the young and inane Duke (for whom I have nothing but contempt from what I have heard of him and his feeble worthlessness) is murdered by someone. Naturally it would not be identifiable too closely with the Duke of Westminster.

It seems there was some commotion among the Grosvenors a few years ago which lingers. That was when I wrote a review of a book about Bendor[10] and the *Sunday Times* headed it 'Bendor the Bounder'. Loelia, Duchess of Westminster, one of Bendor's wives, was unhappy and said to John Wilton I must be a Socialist or a Communist. Did he know me? He said, yes, he was a friend of mine and I was nowhere near a Socialist.

He told me he agreed with everything I said particularly about Bendor's fearful treatment of Lord Beauchamp[11] when he got driven out of the country because of his homosexuality. He was married to Bendor's sister who knew nothing whatever about homosexuality; she had a large family with Lord Beauchamp and her life was wrecked. He was ruined by the sheer spite of his brother-in-law because he was a Knight of the Garter and quite a public figure. Bendor was nothing, useless: only fantastically rich.

---

8. 6th Duke of Westminster.
9. A son was born to him in 1991.
10. 2nd Duke of Westminster (1879–1953), m 3 (1930–47) Loelia, daughter of 1st Baron Sysonby; see note, 31 March 1986.
11. 7th Earl Beauchamp (1872–1938); he was an Ecclesiastical Commissioner, Lord Warden of the Cinque Ports (1913–33) and Chancellor of London University (1929–31); the Beauchamps had two sons and four daughters.

**Wednesday 2 September**

Back home again. Spoke to Mrs Thatcher. It was about nine o'clock. She said she was off at half past nine to do her annual Scottish tour including Balmoral.

She wants some thoughts for her Party Conference speech. I said, 'I think you should develop the theme which many of your own Ministers have not yet fully grasped that you have carried through a revolution. Britain will never be the same again. Labour will be either forced to become like the Democratic Party in America or never be in power again. Likewise any other opposition.'

When I asked her about her holiday she said it had been very good. She also said she had been to Edinburgh for the Festival. 'I suddenly realized that no Prime Minister had so far been to the Edinburgh Festival so I decided I would.'

Lunch with Conrad Black in his private dining-room at the top of the *Daily Telegraph* building. On the way up parts of the building seem almost derelict. I suppose they are getting ready for their great move out of Fleet Street.

The room itself where poor Michael Hartwell must have presided over many lunches was not bad. Carved panelling.

He told me of his admiration for Mrs Thatcher, which I knew already. He picked me up on a phrase I used that she should always follow her instincts. He said, 'Yes, that's right. I hadn't thought of that. It's her instincts more than anything else.'

He thinks that Rupert being Rupert is very likely to make a success of *Today.* He thought he had been very harsh with Bruce Matthews, after he had created the great move to Wapping then rejecting him, though no doubt he made some reasonable financial arrangement.

Conrad says he had a lot of option systems in his firm and Andrew Knight was now rich as a result.

**Tuesday 8 September**

David Hart to lunch. Mysterious fellow.

His father was a banker, I believe, running Ansbacher. He got to know Mrs Thatcher and trades on this considerably. According to what he says to me it sounds as though he does have a certain amount of input.

He is a likeable rogue, half Jewish, with some good ideas. He was off to his farm in Suffolk to bring the harvest in after working on his property business during the morning in London.

He writes in the *Times*. Recently he had quite a success when talking about the need for Britain and the West to keep their nuclear deterrents because he prompted some Soviet high military chief to reply in a letter to the *Times*.

**Sunday 13 September**

Sandown conference on Sunday racing. Put the cat among the pigeons by saying that the Jockey Club and racing must see that the stable lads' agreements for minimum pay and consolidated week pay with overtime were met. Also that they must do something about injury funds for stable lads. Otherwise stable lads will go on being opposed to Sunday racing, believing they will get no better treatment as far as promises for extra pay and arrangements for Sunday racing than they have had for weekday racing.

Spoke to Mrs Thatcher who is in fighting form.

I said that I am very worried about the electricity industry and that it must be broken up when it is privatized.

She did not know what to do about implementing the Peacock Committee.[1] I said, 'The proliferation of stations and outlets for television may do much of the work for us. It will be like newspapers. There are so many different outlets we will get a much wider spread of views and types of production.'

I then spoke to Allan Davis. He is very upset. His agent who sits in the passage opposite to Paul Eddington's agent said he didn't like the play. He thought that when the first bit was repeated in the second

1. The Peacock Committee, set up by Leon Brittan as Home Secretary in March 1985, had reported in 1986; in September 1987 Mrs Thatcher held a seminar to discuss the future of broadcasting in the light of technical progress and the need for greater choice and competition.

act that somebody had got the pages typed all wrong, or had misplaced them and repeated them.

**Thursday 17 September**

Dinner at the American Embassy. Food is better than at the French Embassy. The wines are Californian and though drinkable are not of the same level.

I sat at Carol Price's table. She always greets me with great affection and puts her arm round me and squeezes me and asks whether I am behaving myself, by which she means she hopes I am not.

David Owen was there and jolly. He thought that Roy had always wanted to be a Liberal from the start and should have said so and not got a lot of Labour MPs to leave their party thinking they were going to have an alternative form of Labour Party instead of fetching up in the Liberal Party.

Debbie, his wife, I call Miss Ten Per Cent. She corrected me by adding that it was fifteen per cent overseas. I was referring to her being the agent of Jeffrey Archer whose appalling play is drawing big bookings.[2] The Duchess of York this morning is reported as having cried at it which did not make me think it was likely to be good.

Cecil Parkinson sought me out. He said he had been with Mrs Thatcher and Sir Robert Haslam this afternoon (a matter of course which must be kept from the press). She was very worried at the way British Coal was conducting itself apropos Scargill[3] and his overtime ban and the disciplinary code.

Cecil asked me particularly when I next speak to her to say that Haslam is doing a good job which will reinforce his belief and mine that he is strong and not a pushover for Scargill.

Cecil Parkinson also discussed with me electricity privatization and assured me that it would be done in a way I would not disapprove of. I said, 'But I still do not see how you are going to give electricity users a choice between one company and another from which they might get their own electricity. That is the difficulty.'

I had a nice letter from Monkey Blacker, written in his own handwriting as he does not like to use a secretary on sensitive matters in the Jockey Club because they are all against him when he tries to be

2. *Beyond Reasonable Doubt.*
3. NUM leader and member of the TUC General Council; he had led the miners' strike.

liberal and fair on subjects like the stable lads. He tells me that my intervention about the stable lads' bad treatment has properly stirred it up. The next morning at the Jockey Club it was agreed that they must urgently do something to put it all right. I am going to be a trustee of the Stable Lads' Association. Maybe I can help them get a square deal which they are too timid to ask for on their own account.

Duke Hussey not yet acting as strongly as I hoped but at least he keeps in touch, presumably guessing correctly that I pass it on to Mrs T.

**Sunday 20 September**

She is concerned about what she calls the euphoria over nuclear arms reduction.

She bore out my view about the verification, saying that as so many of the weapons the Russians have got are mobile they could hide them anywhere and one would never know where they had gone.

I said, 'Part of the trouble is that Reagan is so anxious to go down in history as a President who achieved something that he is willing to give away positions he should not.' I added, 'Perhaps I had better write an article for the *Times* for Wednesday about this.' (I had been thinking of writing about the NUM and their dispute with British Coal.) She said that would be a very good idea, 'I wish you would.'

We discussed Haslam. I said, 'He is a very good fellow,' with which she agreed. I said, 'I'm glad you think so. The *Times* were very silly in attacking him.' She said it was due to David Hart who sometimes goes too far. He has got very bright ideas but he has to be watched. He is so keen on supporting the Union of Democratic Mineworkers that he does not understand the difficulties British Coal has and being fair and even-handed.

**Tuesday 22 September**

A bad meeting with John Patten[4] at the Home Office. John Patten says, 'Now you've put the idea of privatization into our heads we've got quite interested but we cannot possibly allow in the current mood another state monopoly turning into a private monopoly. We are thinking of breaking it up and putting it out to the highest bidders.'

They cannot see that all betting shops are a monopoly because once they get a licence from the magistrates they are never removed or lose their licence unless they behave badly. They are protected from

4. Minister of State, Home Office, 1987–92.

competition because the magistrates will not allow more than a given number in any area. The Tote, on the other hand, has fantastic competition from the bookmakers and in that sense is not a true monopoly but an alternative form of betting. It would weaken that alternative form of betting to split it up.

**Thursday 24 September**

Lunch with Nick Lloyd at the Savoy where neither of us drank alcohol. He is still hankering after Rupert but I told him quite bluntly what Rupert had said when I told him Nick would like to come back.

Eve Pollard was there having lunch with a thin unattractive spectacled girl, editor of *Cosmopolitan* which specializes in female orgasms. Eve sat down with us for a few minutes before our lunch. She is the editor of the *Mail on Sunday* colour magazine called *You*. She says that the circulation has gone up by a quarter of a million, all due to the new colour magazine, which is possibly true.

We discussed the curious paper the *Star* which has merged partly with *Sunday Sport*. Nick said they think they can get a sale for it by going right down to the bottom but he wasn't sure it would work. You must have more to a paper than just lots of naked women, rather vulgarly posed. It drives off the ordinary women readers on whom a newspaper, however popular, must depend to a large extent.

He went to the first night of the Archer play which has been panned by the critics but apparently adored by the public. He had known Mary Archer since he was at Oxford and 'Jeffrey wasn't'. He finds her a slightly unreal person. Very withdrawn but she is very beautiful. He congratulated her on how pretty she looked at the first night and on her lovely dress. 'Yes,' she said, 'I'm making Jeffrey buy me the right dresses now.'

Had a telemessage from Julian Amery: 'Your article today was the best of many brilliant ones.' He was referring to my *Times* article of yesterday in which I warned against getting rid of our nuclear deterrents or disarming too far. It was the article I told Margaret I would write on Sunday.

**Friday 25 September**

Jill Hare rang enquiring about Rupert's buying of shares in Pearson. I say, 'It's all done in order to remove Alan (Hare) from the Chairmanship of Château Latour and give it to me.' I think she thought I was almost serious but of course that would be ridiculous as I cannot speak French, much as I would like to have the job.

Wendy Henry is a good editor. She rang me Friday evening and asked me to write a different piece, if I would, from the chunk I had about *Spycatcher*. She said, quite rightly, that everybody is bored with it, particularly the *News of the World* readers.

**Saturday 26 September**

The Festival of Racing day at Ascot. Clear, cold and sunny. It was the biggest prize-money day in British racing. The Tote sponsored the richest handicap in Europe.

Prince Michael was without the Princess who feared her nose would be put out of joint because the Princess of Wales was sitting in the Royal Box and was going to present the biggest prize of the day. He asked Verushka why there were so many journalists there; we shouldn't have journalists. She said, 'One of them is the editor of the *Times* and the other is the editor of the *Spectator*.[5] They don't write gossip columns.'

I'm beginning to think he is more of an ass than I thought he was. He told Verushka and Petronella that he wanted to go to Russia because he feels he has a Russian soul. He added that he had grown a beard on purpose to look like the last Tsar, his cousin.

We went to the Royal Box to watch our race which I thought was totally pointless but the sponsors had each been asked to do that and it would really have looked rude if we hadn't done so. I sat next to Princess Diana and Douglas [Hurd] sat on the other side of her.

She was looking pretty, nice hat and coat and skirt. Her legs are not too skinny but very attractive. Her eyes are the bluest I have ever seen. I asked her if she liked the racing which she clearly doesn't and she said, 'Well, it can be interesting.' I said, 'Can you follow it at all? A lot of people pretend to with their binoculars.' She said, 'No, I can't.' The Tote race took place without either she or me looking at it. I didn't even know what had won. When I left and said goodbye to her I complimented her on her dress and hat and her prettiness and said, 'I think you're a glorious girl.' She was delighted.

In the Royal Box was Nicholas Soames. I like him a lot less than I used to. I asked him what he was doing about his Private Member's

5. Charles Wilson (*Times*) and Charles Moore (*Spectator*).

Bill and he confirmed that he had slot number seven.[6] He thought he might get a whole day to talk about it which I doubt.

He said he was getting a lot of help from the Jockey Club. I said, 'That's fine but you've got to realize if you're going to have any success this is not a Bill just about racing. Racing tags along with the other sports. Your Bill must be same as mine but mine has been drafted by the Home Office and this is what the Home Office want and will support.'

He said rather grudgingly he would ring me up nearer the time. I'm not happy about his conducting the affairs of a Private Member's Bill in the Commons. He is loutish and given to apish jokes and I regret having recommended him to Mrs Thatcher for promotion to the Whips' office, advice which she correctly did not take.

He is a close friend of the Prince of Wales which doesn't say too much for the Prince of Wales.

**Sunday 27 September**

Spoke at length to Douglas Hurd about his speech. I had jotted down a number of ideas for him. He said, 'That's a whole speech.'

**Tuesday 29 September**

Margaret has had my notes for a theme for her speech: 'Your usual direct style. A very good angle.'

She wonders how genuine Labour's change of approach is. Some newspapers, she remarks, think it is not very. I said, 'Gould[7] was saying last night on television that ninety-five per cent of their old programme would stand but of course he is manoeuvring around.' She said, 'You mean it's only presentation they're after.'

I am quite relieved that I don't have to do any more speeches for M's Conservative Party Conference. It is a mild strain trying to think up new ways of putting the same thing for her.

I must get myself into a more relaxed frame of mind. I tend to worry that I am not doing something useful and filling the unforgiving minute. It takes the edge off enjoying being alive a little bit.

The *Times* rang up this morning. Said they wanted to use my review of the Wedgwood Benn diaries,[8] published on October 5th, on the

---

6. In the House of Commons ballot for Private Members' Bills.
7. Bryan Gould, then Opposition spokesman on Trade and Industry.
8. *Out of the Wilderness, Diaries 1963–67.*

same day and not wait until the Thursday afterwards, and it might need some rewriting to fit into a feature piece on the page opposite the leaders.

At once this mildly agitated me that I would have to do some more work on it and we were just faxing over the finished piece in any case. These things ought not to fuss me.

However, the *Times* will pay me £500 for it as an extra.

Dinner to play bridge with Sylvia and Bruce Matthews in their duplex in Eaton Place just off Eaton Square.

I thought possibly Bruce was a little drunk. He went on and on about Mrs Thatcher going to the Journalists' Benevolent Fund annual event which she was chairman of this year and which was held at Australia House. How wonderful she'd been answering questions and she said to him, 'Mr Murdoch could have paid for all this fund and the homes it has easily.' He attached some significance to a chance remark which was meant mildly to be humorous I suppose.

How can people be so silly? She makes sarky remarks about Rupert these days which I am not all together surprised at. She particularly complains that Rupert is very stingy with his employees, never giving them share options or decent pay. There is something in that. Rupert is a very tight old-fashioned employer. I asked whether he consulted the board when he made his darts into things like Pearson. Bruce said, no, and if the board asked to be consulted he would say, 'You don't have to be on the board.'

**Wednesday 30 September**

I was so moved by Mrs Tynan's account of the last days of Ken Tynan.[9] I knew him a bit. He was always slightly tortured and an exhibitionist. I was amused by a passage in her book about Alix[10] who when married to me (I was not making love to her) had an affair with Ken Tynan which was the first marital infidelity of his marriage to his wife. [Alix] was horrified when Elaine Dundy rang her up and said, 'You can have him if you want.' He offered to take her away with him assumingly to marry her, which Alix (my wife) was keen on, but nothing happened. He then invited her to lunch and told her the deal

9. (1927–80); drama critic, the *Observer* 1954–63, the *New Yorker*, 1958–60; literary consultant, National Theatre, 1969–73; m 1 (1951–64) Elaine Dundy, novelist, 2 (1967) Kathleen, née Halton, who had recently written *The Life of Kenneth Tynan*.
10. WW's second wife, Nora (Alix) Robbins.

was off and she records to the last Mrs Tynan, who wrote this book, how bitter she was.

Dinner party, Rupert, Anna, Cecil Parkinson and his wife, Chips Keswick, Petronella, Verushka and me.

Mrs Parkinson more pleasing and sophisticated than I'd expected. I thought of her as the builder's daughter, which I think she is, without much social know-how. When I asked her in front of Anna, who was sitting on my left-hand side, whether she had read Anna's novel, she said she thought she had, but it was about two or three years ago when she was going through traumas and what she was reading (about fifteen books a week to keep her mind off it) went through one ear and out of the other. She was referring to the troubles with her husband and Sara Keays.[11]

During dinner we had had some discussion about Fiji.[12]

My feeling was that the Fijians who objected to the Indians taking over their country were quite right. Who wants to find themselves turned into a minority in the country they've lived in for thousands or hundreds of years? Anna said, 'Oh but that's all wrong. It should be democratic. One man one vote.' Rupert shouted from the other end of the table, 'Nonsense.' I said, 'Ho! I don't think the early Australians thought that when they took over from the aborigines.'

Rupert bubbling away about his fourteen or fifteen per cent into the Pearson Group. 'I can't lose. It gives me leverage and I can combine with other groups in it over the take-over bid or anything of that kind. I can only make money out of my shareholding. Meanwhile, I might get some magazine associations.'

I said, 'They won't ever let you own the *Financial Times*.' To which he replied no, he wouldn't be able to own the *Times* and the *Financial Times* under the law because it would be referred to the Monopolies Commission and he would be barred. What he could do, and what he is hoping to do, is to own an American edition of the *Financial Times*.

---

11. Cecil Parkinson's secretary, with whom he had an affair and a child, resulting in his resignation from the government in 1983.
12. In a *Times* article on 21 October 1987 WW explained that the current population of Fiji consisted of 33,000 Fijians (original Melanesians), 348,000 Indians (first brought in by the British to work the plantations) and 37,000 others. Resentment had grown among the original Fijian sector, culminating in a military coup by Colonel Rabuka. On 15 October 1987 the Queen stepped down as Head of State and Fiji ceased to be a member of the Commonwealth.

He says their database is terrific and it's a very good newspaper. He could make money out of it in America that way. Very ingenious.

He's having lunch with Lord Blakenham tomorrow, the unfortunate Chairman. He says he ought to be able to do quite a lot with the *Financial Times* because the family is all divided and a lot of them would like to just get out for the money.

Parkinson was anxious to explain that he was not an idolator of Mrs Thatcher and that he argued with her, stood up to her. He said to me, 'That's often the best way with her. She doesn't really like total sycophants, as you know.'

Rupert says *Today* is picking up circulation well. He thinks Wendy Henry is doing well at the *News of the World* but is rather tasteless. She goes further than he really likes.

Parkinson very much liked the wine. A magnum of Château Ducru-Beaucaillou 1973. It drank very well. Much better than most 1973s. Chips liked it too, as he did the Spanish wine Tondonia which is a remarkable 1975. This is white and one of the best white wines I've ever had. Rupert drank it all the time.

Rupert said how young I looked, much younger than he had seen me for ages. So did Anna. That was fortunate as it no doubt encourages Rupert to have me writing indefinitely.

Parkinson was very funny unintentionally. Petronella told me that after dinner in the drawing-room when she was sitting next to him – that much I saw – he took hold of her hand and hung on to it and said, 'Your nose is so beautiful. I love the way it tips up and you're such a pretty and attractive girl.' Mrs Parkinson couldn't see or didn't see. What a high risk gentleman Mr Parkinson is.

He had been saying earlier at dinner how he liked Jeffrey Archer but his trouble was he was such a gambler. He doesn't seem altogether different from Parkinson although he is a superior person to Jeffrey Archer.

**1 October**

News International has put my pay up by £5,000 a year, or my fees or whatever they are called, to £55,000 which is an improvement though the extra carries heavy tax.

Allan Davis has a party at Cadogan Square. Everyone, almost, is older than me.

Old John Mills[1] was there. He's nearly eighty. I told him he was a great encouragement to me because I am eleven years younger. He asked me what diet I used to keep myself going and fresh in the mind and I told him, but what he really wanted to do was to tell me what his diet was, which is not mixing starch with protein, eating a lot of garlic, vegetables out of the garden and so forth.

**Friday 2 October**

We leave for Paris, the l'Arc de Triomphe and meetings with Pari-Mutuel.

Dinner with Pierre Carrus and Cormier who is taking over from Pierre Carrus. I am sad that he is being pushed out for political reasons. Cormier is a banker and is young and fairly lively. We go to l'Ambroisie[2] in Place des Vosges where Victor Hugo used to live.

I had an excellent pigeon done in some good sauce.

We had Château Lascombes, near the top of the second growth, 1978. Much too young to drink. 'Do the French know anything about wine?' I asked myself for the umpteenth time.

**Saturday 3 October**

A meeting with Pierre Carrus, Cormier and a German.

We are now contemplating a Pari-Mutuel International which would approach the European governments and racing authorities to keep Ladbroke's out and establish ourselves.

---

1. Actor (b 1908); knight 1976.
2. Restaurant given three rosettes, the top rating, in the Michelin guide.

The PMU [Pari-Mutuel Union] is antiquated. They do well only because they have all the outlets in the cafés and seven thousand betting shops as well and bookmakers are not allowed.

In the afternoon we go to Lanvin.[3] A shopping trip. Verushka bought a cape arrangement. My money just seems to flow out and I worry there will be nothing left when I am dead or even perhaps to pay current bills. My heavy tax bill is coming up soon.

**Sunday 4 October**

On the wireless service from England provided in the hotel I heard my defence of the Fijians broadcast in the review of the Sunday papers. A pleasant start to the day.

Lunch was at the Trusthouse Forte pavilion at Longchamp. The lunch itself was extremely good, the best of the three meals I had in Paris.

I had an each way bet (very small) on Tony Bin because I thought the association of Tony Benn, whose diaries I had been reviewing, was too close to be ignored. When I told Arnold my association of ideas he said, 'Well Tony Bin is certainly an outsider like Tony Benn.' But he came in second just the same.

The course looked magnificent. The sun shone, the bands were splendid. The Tote Credit operation was highly successful. Over the two days we took £60,000 but we only get seven and a half per cent back from Pari-Mutuel. However, our expenses are less than half of our return from the Pari-Mutuel so it was a good outing.

When we got to passport control at Heathrow I found Geoffrey Wheatcroft standing looking disconsolate by the passport official. He said, 'I've left my passport behind.' I said to the official, 'It is not a legal requirement.' She said, 'Yes but he has to be identified.' I said, 'I will identify him. His name is Geoffrey Wheatcroft. He writes for the *Telegraph*. Not very well, but don't hold that against him.' He looked somewhat taken aback but could hardly make a fuss as I was helping him enter without a passport.

**Monday 5 October**

Rang 10 Downing Street. Mrs Thatcher was having her hair done. She rang back in about twenty minutes. We had a little chat.

I said, 'I'm worried about the security at Blackpool. I've been

3. Couturier's.

thinking about it for weeks. I'm terrified that there might be some attack on you.' She said she was just thinking about that this morning. She said, 'I am not taking my best bits of jewellery but leaving them behind so there will be something left for the family if there's a terrorist attack.'

More conversations with Charles Forte about getting Pericles a permit so that he can work legally for the Trusthouse Forte Palace Hotel in Philadelphia, running the Café Royal restaurant. Charles says, 'If I had all these international calls about every person I took on . . .' and I finished the sentence, 'You'd be bust and so would Trusthouse Forte.'

I hope we can pull it off for Pericles. He never asks me for help unless in extreme emergency. He is independent and self-reliant, determined to show that he can make it by himself.

**Tuesday 6 October**

Lunch with David Montgomery, editor of *Today*. I urge him to take up really radical causes, pushing Mrs Thatcher with criticism. For example, the whole system of local government ought to be scrapped and started again.

Local government is getting worse and worse as was evident at the Satellite Information Service meeting yesterday. Some local authorities like Camden don't even acknowledge the applications for putting up dishes on the betting shops and it may take a year to get an application accepted which in the end they are not entitled to refuse. The SIS are going to have to put up the dishes without council approval and fight them if they object.

In the restaurant, sitting next to us, was Charlie Wilson editor of the *Times*, and Clement Freud. He wanted to join the Tote Board but I told him there were no vacancies. He got a knighthood. I congratulated him. I can't imagine what they were plotting together, nothing very savoury.

Spoke to Julian Amery. He has been very ill and in an intensive care unit. They stuck horrible things up his behind and he first said, 'Oh I won't mind that because I was at Eton and I know what buggery is.' But he did mind. He was afraid of cancer but he hasn't got it.

Petronella read some bits she started writing for her article which I suggested she could do for the *You* magazine. It is really very good. Funny. She is observant. It is about the ghastliness of young men she meets who take her out. She could be a very good writer but she has to practise and stick at it.

**Wednesday 7 October**

John Robinson and Patric Dickinson to dinner. The latter is Rouge Dragon Pursuivant at the College of Arms. He has a large room there where he sleeps; he has his bed there behind his office desk but he also lives in the country as well with his mother. Naturally knows all about heraldry.

John Robinson is also a Herald Extraordinary which means he doesn't get paid but turns up for grand ceremonial functions which he enjoys.

Patric played the piano. Petronella sang one of her songs to it. He is very sentimental and unmarried. John Robinson is not so sentimental but is also unmarried.

John Robinson gave me some advice about James Wyatt and Salisbury on which I have to speak on Saturday. I also wished to talk to him about Heveningham Hall. He said if I would ask Mr Al Ghazzi next week, when I have lunch with him, whether he would allow him (John) to go up to Heveningham and make a report for me which we might even be able to use with the Ministry as well, he would be very pleased.

It was pleasant to see Patric Dickinson properly again. He was one of Nicholas'[4] friends from Oxford where Patric was President of the Union. He has chosen a curious life in the College of Arms, as he is a very good speaker and could have gone into politics but was not interested.

**Thursday 8 October**

Susan Crosland rang. She had read my review in the *Times* of the Benn diaries and was reminded thereby of the article she wrote in 1965 which so horrified Benn after the interview he gave her that he begged her not to publish it. She wondered whether she could publish it now.

He had called it in the diary the most horrible and bitchiest thing he had ever read. I told Susan she had every right to publish it. It was clear from the diary that he had never made his approval a condition and now he had said such a nasty and untrue thing about her article

4. Nicholas Banszky, Verushka's son.

she owed it to herself to publish it so the world could see how unfair Tony Benn was being.

**Friday 9 October**

Mrs Thatcher's conference speech was workmanlike. It set out in unusual detail various plans for education, Inner Cities and so forth. It became more inspiring towards the end when she spoke about Britain's role in the world and her feelings of responsibility about her third term.

She used several notions and phrases of mine. In particular 'No party dares openly declare it will take away from the people what we have given back to the people.'

I spoke to her when she got back from Blackpool. I could tell from her voice that she had been having a few drinks which she does occasionally after some big event when she has had to screw herself up.

I said, 'You looked marvellous. Your hair was terrific and so was the youthfulness of your face. You get younger all the time. You were at the height of your beauty.' She said, 'Woodrow, were you looking at my face or listening to what I was saying?'

**Saturday 10 October**

Reached Longford Castle[5] at half past four. It is amazingly beautiful being built originally in 1592 and added to and improved by James Wyatt some two hundred years later.

In the hall in which I spoke to a hundred people who had paid £10 a head to hear me, which was embarrassing, there was a model James Wyatt had constructed with all the alterations and building he had planned. This was nowhere near completed. The model cost £32: exactly the same price was the Holbein, which is possibly the most valuable picture in the house.

I made a lot of jolly jokes and defended James Wyatt against the charge of being 'the destroyer', as designated by Pugin.

Among many other things I referred to Charles Wyatt's invention of stucco which is on countless London houses. The Dean, who was clearly very left-wing, but pleasant and intelligent, got his own back on me in his little speech of thanks. 'Stucco,' he said, 'that's really a permanent whitewash.' He was referring to my defence of James. He

5. Seat of the 8th Earl of Radnor, Salisbury, Wiltshire.

also said I made the family interlocking and helping each other sound as though the family were like the Mafia which no doubt they were. In a modest way of course.

I had begun by explaining how I had come to be there through the invitation of Canon Kerruish, my old friend from Oxford, who ought to be a Bishop, looked like a Bishop, beamed like a Bishop, was as clever as a Bishop but unfortunately he was right-wing and had the disadvantage of believing in God.

Isobel, the step-mother and Dowager Countess I suppose,[6] told me how on some historic building committee she got to know Tom Driberg very well and he came to stay with her shortly before he died and before his book was published. He often used to stay with her and she found him very polite, amusing and cultivated.

'If I had known what he was going to reveal in that book (meaning his buggery), I would never have asked him to stay.' She went on, 'My generation never knew anything about that sort of thing. I find it terribly shocking and inconceivable.'

**Tuesday 13 October**

Lunch with Abdul Al Ghazzi. Call on him at his office at 128 Park Lane. He owns the whole building; some is flats and some offices. Decorators and painters everywhere. 'Do I want some coffee?' which is of course the Arab conventional greeting. Impolitely, knowing perfectly well the custom, I said no because we were already late and lunch was at Claridge's.

He was very jolly. Reminded me of Emile Bustani, my old friend who was killed in an aeroplane accident in 1963 and could have been the President of Lebanon. He is immensely rich. He put Roy Thomson, when he, Abdul, was a young man, into oil and that is why the Thomson newspaper empire was able to sustain the *Times* and why it is still a very rich organization. He comes from Iraq and has some family there. He explained about the tribal system and how his tribe are scattered, some in Iraq, some in Kuwait and some elsewhere.

So far he has spent over £5 million on Heveningham Hall. He does not want to put the library back into order again after the fire because he is fearful of the security. The government after five years have still not given him the power to put the footpath on the other side of the

---

6. The 7th Earl of Radnor, m 2 (1943) Isobel, née Oakley (1908–98), widow of R. T. R. Sowerby.

lake. It is just a general right of way and people can wander where they please which they do right up to the house. Because of the right of way he is not allowed to close the gate. That is why the James Wyatt fireplace was stolen the other day from the dining-room.

He thinks it is all organized by one person in particular (whom he wouldn't name) who is anxious to drive him out and then buy the house cheaply himself.

He immediately agreed to John Robinson going up there and making a report to me.

**Thursday 15 October**

Susan Crosland has her article about Benn, which Benn was so cross about, appearing in the *Spectator* this week. She wonders how I can find so much time to read all the newspapers and books that I do. I said, 'I am reading the newspapers by half past seven but I have a lot of time as being old I do not have a love life and that is time-consuming.'

To Wincanton today to open a new Tote betting shop and bar attached to it and a new turnstile, the lot having cost about £100,000 of which the Tote contributed around £50,000, being well in excess of the actual cost of our new betting shop. We do that to help racecourses who co-operate with us.

I have had a lot of letters from *News of the World* readers agreeing with what I said about the Fijians having the right to try and keep Fiji Fijian. Many of them said, 'Look what's happening to us. In many parts of the country the English, the indigenous inhabitants, no longer control their own affairs either in the schools or in the councils.'

**Friday 16 October**

Allan Davis disconsolate. Donald Sinden does not like the play.

He wants me to go and see Jeffrey Archer's play which so far as I can see has no relevance whatever to ours. I shall not go and see Jeffrey Archer's play.

Allan is not willing to do the play as I understand it unless he finds a great star.

Terrible storm overnight.[7] A lovely ash had an enormous branch blown off it into the private road. The brick wall in our garden on to

7. The 'hurricane' which devastated southern England.

the public road has collapsed. I am glad for the moment I am not at Conock. I expect the two hundred-year-old beeches have suffered badly.

**Saturday 17 October**

Tote Cesarewitch day when we give a luncheon. Not as many 'friends' as Isabel describes them on the course. Some have been put off by the weather.

Before dinner, talking to Isabel and John,[8] the subject of guns and violence came up. I said, 'Isabel, you had a terrifying experience.' It was in 1953. She told the story of how she was having dinner alone at Knowsley, John having gone out to some formal dinner. She was eating chicken vol-au-vent and some was in her mouth. Suddenly she heard the door open behind her and a man with a sten-gun came in. All he said was, 'Get up' which she did. He then shot her, the bullet going through the back of her neck and out of the side of her face by her ear. (She showed me the mark.) She had her back to the man at the time because he told her to turn away.

She fell on the floor but was still conscious. She had the presence of mind not to move so he might think she was dead. Her hand was outstretched and she kept on feeling the urge to move her fingers but she didn't. She was also afraid that some of the chicken vol-au-vent still in her mouth might come out. The blood was starting to come at a great rate and she watched it go on to the blue carpet, wondering to herself whether it would reach the next pattern or not.

The butler and footman came in because they probably thought she wanted her next course. The man shot and killed the butler and the footman after telling them to get out which they would not because they saw her on the floor, dying as they thought. He told them, 'I've killed Lady Derby,' and went down and told the cook the same. He shot the cook (male) but did not kill him, and another servant

He then went down to the Lodge to wait for John and he was going to kill him. Fortunately he was caught first. He was in Broadmoor for some time and then he was let out about ten years later. This terrified Isabel. John said to her, 'But he's dead now.' Isabel didn't believe him. Maybe John was saying it to stop her being worried.

He was a man who was employed as an odd-job man. His mother had been in a lunatic asylum so it was hereditary madness.

---

8. The Earl and Countess of Derby owned Stanley House at Newmarket as well as Knowsley in Merseyside.

To this day Isabel cannot be in a room without the door being open. I often wondered why in the drawing-room at Newmarket the door is always left fairly wide open. It is because the door was shut when the madman came in to shoot her and she heard the click of the door opening. She wants to be able to see if anybody is coming to attack her before they get into the room. When she is alone when John is away she locks her bedroom door and she has a little gun which gives her some comfort. She said that for two years she was in a terrible state and John had a very difficult time with her. He is very kind and patient.

There were also unpleasant rumours which went round in London that Isabel was having an affair with butler or footman and had been having one with the odd-job man as well, who got jealous and shot them all. There was obviously not a scintilla of truth in such ridiculous rumours but people were saying it very knowingly.

After dinner John wanted to go on talking when we joined the women in the drawing-room. (There was no port though I asked for it. Very odd.) Isabel wanted to watch Dame Edna Everage and put it on. When a break came for the commercials John turned it off. She said 'Why are you turning it off?' 'Surely you haven't asked people to dinner to watch television?' Then she turned to me and said, 'Do you want to watch it or not?' 'You put me in an embarrassing position,' I said and made no comment. Actually conversation was not all that bright and Dame Edna (whose show I had never seen before) was moderately amusing.

**Sunday 18 October**

Went to an early supper on return from Newmarket to Allan Davis.

Allan Davis was quite amusing about a man he had an on and off affair with for twenty-five years. He said he disagreed with me about the sex wearing out in marriages because he had a lovely time the other day with a man and he actually came and he, Allan, is seventy-five or seventy-four. When I said, 'You haven't been living with him as a married couple would have been living,' he agreed that was the case and there had been several breaks in their relationship.

Allan goes to the Andes at the end of the week. I must try and have my play ready for him by the time he comes back in mid November.

**Tuesday 20 October**

On the wireless this morning it said that the world stock market tumble was continuing.[9]

Verushka in a great state about her shares, which she has mostly in America, because they have gone down at least twenty-five per cent. I tell her not to panic or worry because they will come back again in due course. She doesn't need the money at the moment. Why not hang on?

Generally speaking my little stock of money which was running at about £150,000 has now gone back to less than £100,000, maybe £80,000.

Dinner with David Montagu. Others present were Lord Weir[10] and his Swiss wife. Quite attractive and fair. Two daughters, twenty-five and twenty-three by her previous marriage. Said she didn't think that infidelities in marriage mattered because it was impossible for people to stay at the same rate of loving as when they first got married or to change at the same pace as each other.

He is pretty rich with a big, publicly quoted family publishing business. Deputy Chairman to Jacob [Rothschild] at his St James's Street operation.

Jacob very cross with himself for not foreseeing the crash. Said it upset his sense of professionalism.

Everyone was a tiny bit subdued to begin with. They have all suffered, at least on paper, considerable losses. However, Jacob said he hasn't sold anything or done anything in particular. I asked him what I should tell my readers in the *News of the World* about BP shares. He said, 'Tell them to buy them from the underwriters when they come on sale.'

The dinner was excellent. It was caviar – you could take, as I did, large helpings on blinis with some sour cream sauce which I thought rather spoilt it but David made me take it. There was also smoked salmon to go with it. It was followed by stuffed quails and some sort of ice-cream pudding which I didn't have.

The Krug 1955 before dinner, and we took some in with us, was terrific. The magnums of Lynch-Bages were very good. It was 1959.

---

9. On 'Black Monday' (19 October 1987) there was a sharp fall in the stock market, precipitated by a fall in Wall Street.
10. 3rd Viscount Weir; chairman, The Weir Group; vice-chairman, J. Rothschild Holdings.

But I don't know why David won't decant his bottles before he serves them.

Jacob is getting very worked up about his dinner with Mrs Thatcher. He said, why didn't I ask Tim Bell because he would be very good on the publicity side of year 2000. I said, 'No. I think he is rather boastful and I don't want him running the whole thing from the start.'

He is preparing a memo so he has Griselda Grimond[11] doing research. I said, 'Why don't we get the Prince of Wales to behave much as Prince Albert did for the Great Exhibition?' We both agreed that the Prince of Wales is nowhere near the calibre of Prince Albert who was a very remarkable administrator and what Jacob called 'a serious German'. However, he should perhaps be the patron of the committee and Jacob can be the Chairman.

**Wednesday 21 October**

Spoke to Mrs Thatcher. She got back last night at 10.30 from the Commonwealth Conference and her stay in America, in Dallas with her son. She said he is getting on very well there.

A different note comes into her voice when she speaks about Mark. She obviously dotes on him. I think he is a pretty good wash out. He gives a lot of trouble to his mother. She puts up with it as mothers do with their favourite son or child.

She said she had spoken to a group of forty American bankers who had told her that the real trouble was the big deficit the American government is running. She said, 'People kept urging me to run one here but I wouldn't.'

On the stock market crash she had more or less the conventional view that prices had got exceptionally high and she had been afraid it wouldn't last. The computers are pre-set to sell, as she said, at certain prices, without common sense being involved.

Dinner at the Wolfsons. On the way we were saying that the people are usually very dull and old and it is a dreary occasion. We had been asked in June and reminded several times.

On arrival we found that it was a dinner for the Foreign Secretary [Geoffrey Howe] and his wife Elspeth. Duke Hussey was there and Clarissa Avon and various others – David Stevens and his wife among them. Tony Quinton and his wife Marcelle also there.

---

11. Daughter of the former Liberal leader Lord (Jo) Grimond and Lady (Laura) Grimond.

At dinner sitting one away from me, Leonard Wolfson said he thought the fall in the stock market was very salutary particularly for new investors. I said, 'Really. So you think I should write in my column that the government's campaign to persuade everyone to take part in share buying and become share owners has been much helped by new shareholders losing twenty to thirty per cent of their money, and it is very good for them?'[12] He was rather cross.

Duke Hussey was friendly. He says he likes getting my letters. It keeps the adrenaline flowing. He says *Panorama* is being cleaned up but it takes years to get through the morass of left-wing producers in the BBC. He says they have a campaign against Birt[13] trying to vilify him in every way because he is being tough.

He said that when he first went to the BBC a very attractive lady was put in his way and they hoped he would take an interest and be caught in a trap and found having an affair with her. That would put him in their grip. He was quite serious. I asked him twice, 'Do you really mean that?' and he said, 'Oh, yes. She was definitely trailed in front of me. She was very attractive and "they" wanted to see what the form was. But I resisted the temptation.'

I am quite fond of Elspeth Howe. I congratulated her on her old body the Equal Opportunities Commission at last having done something good by forcing Birmingham to give the same number of places to girls as to boys in their grammar schools and thus forcing other authorities to do the same.

Geoffrey is always very friendly. I think we have a genuine liking for each other but he is not unmindful of the fact that I write a column in the *News of the World*.

David Stevens talked to me long and earnestly about his newspapers. 'What should I do with the *Star*?' he asked. This newspaper has got as low as any newspaper has ever thought of going. Full of breasts and vulgarity and the crudities of sex. I said, 'Is it making any money?' He told me that the circulation is now 1.2 million but he has cut the costs by fifty-five per cent and it is now breaking even and in the coming year will make £1.5 million. 'Is your problem that you wonder whether

12. WW actually wrote comfortingly in the *News of the World* on 25 October, under the headline 'Don't panic!': 'It's not unusual for share prices suddenly to plunge . . . Those who don't sell their shares may have to wait for some time for a recovery. It's bound to come eventually.'
13. John Birt, Deputy Director General, BBC, 1987–92, Director General since 1992.

the social shame of owning such a newspaper is worth the million and a half pounds profit you are making with increased profits to come?' He said, 'Yes.'

'That's a problem you'll have to work out for yourself. If I had something making a million and a half pounds a year I would stick to it.' Of course he is only the Chairman, not the proprietor, but he has a lot of shares in the operation.

David Stevens wants me to arrange [for him] to meet Rupert when he is in England. Rupert, according to him, thinks he is in Maxwell's pocket or is a great friend of his which is quite untrue and he would like to do some business with Rupert. He wants to know whether he, David, might join in the Pearson operation.

**Thursday 22 October**

At The Other Club in the evening Jock Colville told me that he sold outright his diaries when secretary to Sir Winston Churchill in the War years. That was on the advice of Arnold Goodman who said it would reduce his income tax merely to a capital gain. It was not good advice; Arnold Goodman's advice is not always correct. The book sold a hundred thousand copies in England in hardback and all over the world. Poor Jock had sold off all the rights and got no royalties whatever. However, Hodder & Stoughton, whom he described as gentlemen, made him an ex gratia payment, saying that he had been paid far too little, but I don't think it was up to what he should have got if he had had a proper royalty arrangement.

Roy Jenkins said David Owen used to be an acolyte of his and followed everything he thought and did. He said, 'David must either be an acolyte or have acolytes. He can be nothing in between. He cannot deal with equals.'

Roy told me that he now gets £10,000 a time for lectures in various countries but sometimes he does it for about £3–4,000. He reckons to do five or six a year which greatly boosts his income. He says he has a very good agent. He must have.

I hadn't seen Peter Walker since the election. I said to him, 'You have a very good job there as Secretary for Wales. You can do a great deal.' He looked at me mournfully, half smiling and said, 'You know that's not true, Woodrow. There's nothing in the job at all.' He realizes he is finished and lucky to hang on in the Cabinet.

**Friday 23 October**

Lunch at Jacob's office in St James's Place. He has a splendid early 18th century house converted. He has got magnificent paintings. One of Hyde Park 1864 he showed me proudly. Three Rothschilds riding alongside Dukes, the first time this had ever happened to Rothschilds.

His own office is very large. I said, 'What a wonderful place to bring girls.' He said, 'Yes.' 'You can say to them when you've shown them around in the sculpture gallery, "I've shown you what I've got. Now it's your turn to show me what you've got."'

At the lunch Griselda came who is allegedly doing research for the project 2000. She hadn't done any. The paper was Jacob's and was not very good. I made a lot of jokes about it which he took in fairly good part. Then he said, 'Can we be serious?' 'But I am being serious. I can only do it through jokes.'

Jacob has some mad scheme of linking Trafalgar Square, Leicester Square and Westminster Square (meaning outside the front of the Palace) in a great pedestrian complex. He didn't want to have an industrial exhibition as in 1851.

I said, 'Mrs Thatcher will never wear that because she wants to show off what Britain is doing in the modern world commercially. Nor will she be happy about the idea that the government is to provide money. The government provided none for the 1851 Exhibition which was a tremendous success.'

Jacob said, 'I've given you a very good lunch because you said my father's lunch at N. M. Rothschild is so good.' I said, 'Yes, this is excellent.' It began with a grouse soufflé which I'd never had before. I wasn't so impressed with the next course which was goujons of sole fried up a bit with pieces of something or other, but I said it was very nice. The sorbet at the end was rather good, being mango and with slices of mango. We didn't drink much. Just a little white wine.

**Saturday 24 October**

The *World at One* programme, Radio 4, for Sunday rang up. Would I talk about the fall out and the controversies and the implications on racing, jockeys, owners and trainers of the Piggott affair?[14]

I rang Arnold and asked his advice. He said don't do it. 'You would have to attack your friends like John Howard de Walden and others

---

14. On 23 October Lester Piggott, champion jockey, was sentenced to three years' imprisonment for tax fraud.

who have not behaved at all as they should have done, stewards of the Jockey Club, in allowing these extraordinary arrangements of Henry Cecil[15] to be made and other such deals.'

The Henry Cecil letter even asked owners to destroy the letter which he sent them saying there was an extra retainer to be paid to Piggott in cash.

Henry Cecil was fined £2,000 by the Jockey Club.

**Sunday 25 October**

We go to Bowden for lunch.

Arnold in great distress. It is getting bigger and bigger in the newspapers that Marconi is being investigated by Ministry of Defence police looking for evidence of fraud in Ministry of Defence contracts. Also something to do with non-payment of royalties.

I spent the whole day with Arnold while he talked to Arnold Goodman and Michael Lester, his legal director at GEC, and Tim Bell about a statement they were putting out. He also spoke to the people who ran the affair at Portsmouth where this particular Marconi company is situated. It was quite obvious that they know of no fraud at all. There was an argument about royalties but that is a matter of commercial dispute.

The police raid was done with forty vans and forty men, and a crowbar was used to break down a door. All quite unnecessary because Marconi was giving them full co-operation anyway.

We got home very late in Arnold's uncomfortable Rolls-Royce.

The pudding at supper was excellent. A lovely stuffed dish of stuffed prunes. But it is all too rich and I eat too much of it.

**Monday 26 October**

The stock market slide continues today.

In the evening Rupert rings. He puts the trouble down to Reagan's fading away. It began with the Iran Contra hearings in Congress. It was followed by his failure to get Bork[16] made a member of the Supreme Court. Reagan has no effective answer. He is now badly advised by Howard Baker who took the place of sacked Donald Regan.[17] They seem to be entirely adrift. Reagan, Rupert says, has got

15. Trainer.

16. Robert Bork, a conservative judge.

17. As White House Chief of Staff.

to do something to knock the dollar up five or six cents. He ought not to be negotiating with Congress. He should not have any more press conferences as he is very bad at them. A couple of modest decisions were now needed

Rupert also said he would meet David Stevens: 'I can't understand why these people are so frightened of me. Let's have him for coffee one morning at 9.00 when I am over here.'

Tonight we had dinner at Diana Wilton's. Ali Forbes[18] was there shouting a good deal.

When I said to Ali, 'You should write your memoirs,' he said, 'You're always saying that to me and it's ridiculous. You don't earn anything for them, as you know yourself.' This is quite untrue as far as I am concerned because I made some £60,000 out of *Confessions of an Optimist* with the serial rights and everything else.

He was in rather a spiky mood and said I was doddery when I was explaining the Michael Havers situation.

Havers has resigned. He had to be Lord Chancellor for a bit to get the pension for himself and his wife. After years as Attorney General he had not been making any money and had nothing. He has always been loyal to Mrs Thatcher and it was a perfectly reasonable thing for her to make him Lord Chancellor, even though she knew he would not be there very long.

I was saying that he was very loyal and ingenious, good at producing reasons why we were acting within international law 'over Suez', instead of saying 'over Falklands'. He thought that was very funny.

I asked Jane [Churchill] what she would do if she were on a committee to prepare events to mark our entry into the year 2000. Surprisingly she had no ideas at all other than to cover Westminster Bridge with fabric of her making.

Diana said Lord King was chippy. She was referring to his slightly aggressive behaviour in polite society deriving from his humble origins. She said she couldn't understand why this man, who had been so successful at his enterprises, turning British Airways into a company fit for privatization, was like that.

I said, 'Now you surprise me. Of course he is like that. He is in the structure of England with its curious snobbishness and class divisions. He had no formal education other than at state school. He was deeply ambitious. He saw the most respected section of the country appeared

18. Alastair Forbes, journalist.

to be the upper classes and the aristocracy. He resented his not being one of them but determined to become one. He married the daughter of Viscount Galway. That was his second marriage. He advanced in the world. He became a Master of Foxhounds and cultivated royalty and Dukes like David Beaufort. But however much he wants to appear to be secure in his social niche, he never feels subconsciously that he is. Hence his chippiness. The class society of England is extremely interesting. Similar in some ways to the Hindu but more flexible.'

'For example,' I continued, 'when Peter Carrington's[19] ancestor was made a peer, for a long time George III didn't want him to be one because he was a banker from Nottingham called Smith. George III said, "I don't want tradesmen in the House of Lords." Now Peter Carrington, roughly two hundred years later, is regarded as an aristocrat. You can move up and down in English society with ease. You go down if you lose your money. You go up if you make money and cultivate those people who appear to be grand. Why do you think Nigel Dempster and gossip columns of that kind are so avidly followed?'

**Tuesday 27 October**

Lord Mancroft's[20] memorial service in St Margaret's, Westminster.

The address was given by Peter Rawlinson. Sitting far at the back I could hardly hear what he was saying, although he mentioned how witty Stormont was and how much he enjoyed life. He was in fact the worst Chairman of the Tote in its history. I had to rescue it. It was true, as Rawlinson said, he had many talents but he didn't do much with them, other than write quite funny articles for *Punch* and make amusing after dinner speeches. He was lucky to have been a Junior Minister.

**Wednesday 28 October**

A letter from all the grand sports organizations in the *Times* this morning, the lead letter. It urged everyone to support my Bill which has its committee stage on November 5th in the Lords.

Dinner in Room 108, Hyde Park Hotel, given by Johnnie Henderson. It was a conspiracy consisting of Bruce Matthews, Tommy

---

19. 6th Baron Carrington, Conservative politician.
20. 2nd Baron Mancroft, Conservative politician; chairman, Horserace Totalisator Board, 1972–6; chairman, British Greyhound Racing Board, 1977–85.

Wallis, Sir Peter Leng and myself to decide on who to give the forty per cent shares available in SIS.

Johnnie Henderson has got a great thing called Henderson Administration, [worth] about £750 million. He inherited huge sums via his grandfather or great-grandfather, the railway magnate.

He said that he expected that within three or four months half the losses made since the Great Fall would be recovered. It would take a year or so to get back to the old prices.

**Thursday 29 October**

Went to Christopher Soames' memorial service at Westminster Abbey. A remarkable attendance of Prime Ministers and other notables.

We sat in Poets' Corner, a few yards away from the tablet sacred to the memory of James Wyatt with our coat of arms on the top. It made me feel part of the continuing English life.

On my other side sat Lady Gladwyn.[21] She is a descendant of the great Brunel but there is no tablet to him in Westminster Abbey though he was associated with some of the Wyatts in various projects, including the ironwork at Paddington Station.

The service was inappropriate to the nature of Christopher Soames. The hackneyed 1 Corinthians:15 read by Ted Heath about 'Oh death, where is thy sting?'. Nicholas Soames read an appallingly sentimental and tripy passage from *Pilgrim's Progress*. It described the reception Hopeful had on the other bank of the river – in heaven, I presume. I cannot imagine Christopher wanting such a reception, even if he was lucky enough to get one.

I must think about my memorial service.[22] I want the last chapter of Ecclesiastes down to where it says 'Vanity of vanities, saith the Preacher. All is vanity.' And the bit about the lilies of the field. I want someone to sing, if not the entire audience, 'Stand up and fight' from the *Carmen* done by the blacks. I would like Bernard Levin or Roy Jenkins perhaps to do the address. I want music playing as everybody leaves after singing 'Land of Hope and Glory', 'Dear Little Buttercup' from *HMS Pinafore*. If there is to be a second lesson perhaps it should be the parable of the talents. The 'Battle Hymn of the Republic'

---

21. Cynthia, née Noble (d 1990), wife of Lord Gladwyn (1900–96), former ambassador, Deputy Liberal Leader, House of Lords, 1965–88; life peer 1960.
22. See 25 November 1985 and 4 December 1986 for how WW's wishes were carried out at his memorial service on 1 April 1998; Roy Jenkins gave the address.

would be nice. And so would that extraordinary hymn by Herbert which contains the words 'A servant with this clause / Makes drudgery divine; / Who sweeps a room as for Thy laws / Makes this and th' action fine.'

I would not like my memorial service to be as banal and unimaginative as the ones I so frequently attend. Another hymn one could have is 'Did those feet in ancient time' ['Jerusalem'], as it is jolly good.

**Friday 30 October**

Dinner with Rocco Forte. I was asked beforehand, did I mind meeting Sir Jack Lyons and his wife at dinner. That meant that I had to accept otherwise it would have seemed I didn't want to meet him. I didn't want to meet him in point of fact. I find him a dreary uninteresting and rather sub man.

His wife looks like a witch. Naturally she told Verushka that her husband was innocent of the charges against him.[23] It was obvious she would say that but I don't think he is innocent.

---

23. Sir Jack Lyons and Gerald Ronson had been charged on 8 October 1987 in relation to the Guinness case. See note, 17 December 1986.

**Sunday 1 November**

She was in jubilant mood. I told her that I thought ordinary people were not anywhere near as panicky as those at the top in the money scene. They are like the Cabinet in 1940 who wanted to make plans to go to Canada and take the King with them when Hitler was at Calais. I said, 'My soldiers I was commanding in my little platoon at Dover never thought for one moment there was a chance of Hitler beating us.'

I said I hoped she wasn't bothered about the business of David Young and the chairmanship of the Tory Party.[1] Some people are always jealous of the person who has got on rather quickly in the political field, coming to it from outside. She said, 'They should remember how well he did on unemployment and the Manpower Commission and be grateful for it.' I said, 'You've been around enough to know what human nature is like.' She said, 'I don't think that being Chairman of the Party is a full-time job.'

**Monday 2 November**

Peter Brooke was appointed Chairman of the Tory Party. I am told he is quite agreeable and may be a reasonable organizer but no spark. He is a Junior Minister, Paymaster General.

**Tuesday 3 November**

I have always wanted to be in a Dictionary of Quotations. At last I am there. I was sent the *Bloomsbury Dictionary of Quotations*. In it I found 'Pennies do not come from heaven. They have to be earned here on earth.' I wrote that for Mrs Thatcher for a speech at the Mansion House in 1982. She gets the credit but I'm there vicariously.

1. There was opposition to Lord Young, as Secretary of State for Trade and Industry, taking on an extra commitment.

**Wednesday 4 November**

Robert Heber-Percy is dead.[2] He looked like Pan and as he grew older, like an elderly Pan. He was bi-sexual. He never lasted long with a girl and had two marriages of poor success, the second one in particular ending after a few months. He was amusing and jolly. I used to stay with him at Faringdon House before I married Verushka. He usually had some ghastly common semi-permanent boyfriend though sometimes they were reasonably respectable.

He had a housekeeper, greatly devoted to him, whom he used to insult a good deal but she never seemed to mind. John Sutro[3] was a great friend of his and we had lots of laughs and plenty of good drink.

He was very friendly with Lord Berners[4] who owned Faringdon House, pretty and splendid furniture and lots of valuable pictures. I assume they lived together, in a homosexual fashion, though I have no direct evidence. When he died Berners left him everything. He had lent a picture to Tom Driberg. Tom claimed that he had given it to him but it was listed in the inventory and Robert demanded it back which upset Tom.

Robert used to dye his doves multi-colours with a special dye from ICI. They were very pretty as they circled round and landed in front of the house.

Occasionally I went to a small gaming club with him. He once gave me £50 to see what would happen; this was years ago when £50 meant about £300 now. I soon dissipated it.

John Wilton and he had a fantastic row in Majorca when we were all staying with Philip Dunn[5] about thirty years ago. Robert peed all over John and said he was a fool and an idiot and very common. John retaliated by saying that Robert was not a real Percy but only a Heber-Percy and his connection with the Duke of Northumberland was tenuous. It was childish. It was late one night when the weather was hot.

---

2. (1911–87); known as 'The Mad Boy'; m 1 (1942–7) Jennifer Fry, 2 (1985) Lady Dorothy Lygon.
3. (1904–85); film producer; member of an Oxford set which included Harold Acton, Brian Howard and Robert Byron; a gifted talker and mimic.
4. (1883–1950); 14th Baron (Gerald) Berners, musician, painter, writer; see 16 August 1988.
5. Sir Philip Dunn (1905–76), father of Serena (m Jacob Rothschild) and Nell, the playwright.

I don't think Robert ever did anything to contribute to the world other than to give it amusement and live in some style. He once brought a horse into the drawing-room at Faringdon House. It was the house where Malu (Moorea's Italian grandmother) arrived one day to borrow some money or rather be given it by Lord Berners who gave her a regular small allowance, as did many others at the time. She wanted £20 urgently. This was when £20 was worth about £100 today. At the end of the afternoon when they had tea he said, 'Now you need to catch your train back to London otherwise there is no way of getting back,' and she replied, 'Oh, it's all right. I came in a cab from London and he is waiting for me still.'

**Thursday 5 November**

The committee stage of my Sunday Sports Bill. All would have gone well if enough members of the Jockey Club and other peers who support Sunday racing and are connected with racing and racecourses had stayed the course. It was very narrow on the first vote when we had a majority of five. Then our majority disappeared because the Jockey Club type of person decided to go out to dinner because he had expected that the committee stage would start and he was hungry. But the government put in ahead of it a Bill to do with the storm damage in the south of England.

They expect, these peers do, to have everything mapped out for weeks ahead and no change. Their private engagements are too important for them. Even Ailwyn Fairhaven, Senior Steward, idiotically went to a City dinner because his name had been printed on the list of guests, as though that mattered. The vital vote was at 8.45 when we lost the provision to have betting shops open on a Sunday when there is horse racing.

**Friday 6 November**

I went to the Bill Office at the Lords and spoke to Mr Keith. I'm going to put an amendment to the report stage which comes on at 8.00 p.m. on Wednesday, December 9th. We have got to organize a proper whip so we know who is going to be there and who is not.

Last night I was very fed up and couldn't sleep for annoyance and feeling that I had been remiss in not making sure everybody was there, but I had written about a hundred and twenty letters. I didn't realize what frivolous people hereditary peers are.

**Sunday 8 November**

Mrs T to dinner. Jacob there to talk about his ideas for the year 2000. It was a jolly, friendly dinner. She looked very healthy and not tired. She wore an attractive red suit. She had never had pink champagne before and I gave her some which had come from Sainsbury's. She liked it. She also liked the Château Latour 1960 which I said I had produced because Jacob drank too much Lafite Mouton-Rothschild so he should know there were other wines.

She drank neither whisky nor gin nor port at the end of the dinner. She chatted in a relaxed way with no hint of domineering as her enemies are fond of alleging.

On Jacob's plans she remarked that we must concentrate on leaving enduring monuments. With her current interest in city centres she said we should try to encourage the creation of city squares as the old city fathers used to produce – market places like the agora of the Ancient Greeks. Places where people naturally went if they wanted to celebrate something.

To Jacob's idea there should be a repeat of the Robert Peel banquet at the Mansion House for provincial Mayors to come and give their ideas as they did for the 1851 Exhibition, she commented that those were the days of serious substantial city fathers and today the people who run the councils have no ideas worth considering.

She was amazed to learn that the Royal Commission of the 1851 Exhibition still exists, has a large income and over £5 million in capital. It owns all the freeholds of the Albert Hall and the surrounding museums, etc. in South Kensington. It uses its money to promote science, particularly with scholarships which have educated fourteen Nobel prize-winners. I said, 'We must try and do something like that at least.'

Of the new towns, like the Japanese are planning for 2000, she wondered whether Jacob's suggestion would be sufficiently in the centre if it were on land owned by British Gas at Greenwich. She liked the idea that the Great Exhibition had been entirely self-financing, started with a float from the Royal Society of Arts. She was highly interested when I told her that Sir Matthew Digby Wyatt was Secretary of the Committee for the Exhibition at the age of thirty-two and that the Baron Lionel de Rothschild, the first Jewish MP, was one of the treasurers. Jacob said, 'The Wyatts and the Rothschilds were operating again together.' And I thought, 'And in their usual inequality of income and capital.'

The dinner was excellent. She commented on the first course particularly which was an experiment devised by Verushka, haddock and other fish topped by cheese baked in little dishes. She had a second helping of the second and the third course. The second course was veal and wild rice and other nicely coloured and presented vegetables. The third course was an open apple tart plus jam on top which had originally been devised by Verushka and which Teresa [the cook] can be relied upon to do more or less right.

At one stage in the evening she remarked, 'Each family pays £60 a week towards the NHS. If they put that into private health schemes they would get better service and attention. No waiting for hip operations or all the rest of it.'

**Tuesday 10 November**

Cause a mild commotion at the Levy Board by insisting on exposing the details of the bookmakers who pay below the one per cent rate to the Levy Board, thus depriving the Levy Board of hundreds of thousands a year, in fact about a million pounds each year.

Legally it is possible the bookmakers, the big ones, may be able to rearrange their betting shops in such a way that they are in very small groups which don't pay the top rate of levy. But even that is not certain. In any case it is clearly against the spirit of the levy, particularly as they collect one per cent from the punters for it by adding it to their deductions when anybody places a bet and don't pass it on in full to the Levy Board.

**Wednesday 11 November**

Tote Board meeting passes over fairly happily. The Prince [Michael] is there looking smart with a new blue suit. He had a dashing tie. I am wondering whether to recommend his non-renewal. As he was so pleasant this morning I keep changing my mind back and forth. He doesn't come to many Board meetings and doesn't do a great deal.

**Thursday 12 November**

David Hart gives me lunch at Claridge's. I have a poor exchange of cigars with him. I give him one of my pre-Castro large cigars which I got at Christie's the other day for £80 for twenty-five. They were Hoyo de Monterrey. He gives me a new smaller Rafael Gonzalez.

He is a merry fellow but I wouldn't trust him entirely. He was mildly put out that I had not signed a letter supporting the Committee for a Free Britain. I said, 'I don't do that kind of thing because I don't want to have epithets attached to me such as "He must be a fascist" because I joined a thing like that.'

He said, 'Oh it couldn't possibly be fascist, the Committee for a Free Britain, because I'm a Jew.' I said, 'What makes you think that? What about Sherman[6] who tried to invite that amazing man Le Pen[7] to come to address meetings at the Blackpool Conservative Party Conference?'

He says will I try and get a knighthood for Brian Crozier[8] who is nearly seventy and has spent most of his money on *Background Briefing*, an anti-Communist publication detailing little known extremist connections of Labour leaders. He, David, is raising money for that to continue.

'She must fill the Lords with people loyal to her. People say like Paul Johnson,'[9] and he mentioned a few other names. 'And myself,' he said hopefully. I said, 'It would be difficult for her to justify some of those. She could only make me a peer because I had been in the Commons for twenty-one years. She is very conventional.' He said, 'No, it's because you are a friend of hers.'

Dinner with David Stevens and his wife. The food was filthy.

David Stevens is much preoccupied with his relationship with Mrs Thatcher.

'How do I get her to call me David?' he said, 'Shall I say to her "Will you call me David"?' I said, 'I wouldn't if I were you. Just wait until she decides to call you David.'

**Sunday 15 November**

Lunch with Rupert. Less downbeat than when I spoke to him last week. Thinks that Holmes à Court[10] may be in difficulties. His shares have fallen from eleven Australian dollars to $1.90. He doesn't actually go in and run businesses but tends to invest in them and if they don't produce high profits he is in difficulty. But Rupert's scheme is to engender high profits to cover his interest payments. He says that

---

6. Sir Alfred Sherman, journalist, co-founder of the Centre for Policy Studies.
7. French right-wing politician.
8. See 2 June 1986.
9. Writer and journalist (editor, *New Statesman*, 1965–70) who had moved from the left to the right.
10. (1937–90); Robert Holmes à Court, banker in Australia.

business has been better than ever and his shares must go up again because of the growth he has got.

Stevens had said that Rupert wanted to sell the *Times* and would probably sell it to him or Conrad Black. Rupert laughed. He has no intention of selling the *Times* as it is doing quite well.

Stevens had also said at that dinner that David Montagu came and said how much he hated Jacob. He goes into his office at St James' and says, 'You're not earning the money we're paying you. You're not doing anything. There's nothing for you to do,' as though he wanted to get rid of him.[11] And David said to David Stevens, 'Will you give me a job?'

I find this story hard to believe. David M is very proud and would be unlikely to talk to David Stevens like that. Nor do I think that Jacob, though he can be unpleasant, would be quite so tough – though he might be in Rupert's view.

It is true that David Montagu went there to run Charterhouse, the merchant bank Jacob took over, and other enterprises he was hoping to acquire. When Jacob didn't get Hambros Life to put the whole thing together on a better footing, he lost interest and left David out on a limb. David said to me bitterly and with a fierce face, as he was getting into the lift one day at the Tote, that Jacob was a swine and he had let him down and behaved abominably to him. Alas, the world is full of horrid things and people.

Poor Arnold today was upset because the *Sunday Telegraph* had printed a leaked letter that Jim Prior[12] had written to Younger,[13] Minister of Defence. The *Sunday Telegraph* said that the Minister of Defence was furious at getting a letter from an ex-Cabinet Minister former colleague. It was a perfectly reasonable letter in which Jim Prior said would you please make some statement to say that we are still an accredited defence supplier, there is nothing wrong with us at all and the Marconi thing is nothing to do with the main companies.

Arnold said last week the American government suspended a $6 million order until the Ministry of Defence gave them some kind of clearance as a firm they should be dealing with. Arnold says once more he is going to give everything up and leave the business and just devote himself to a foundation promoting music and scholarships in it.

---

11. Montagu was a director of J. Rothschild Holdings, 1983–9.
12. In his capacity as chairman of GEC.
13. George Younger, Conservative politician; Secretary of State for Defence, 1986–9.

**Monday 16 November**

Lunch at the French Embassy for Max Rayne to invest him as an officer of the Legion of Honour.

Max has apparently given a lot of money at the instigation of Jane to the Pasteur Institute in France and done other things of great help to France, on the health side.

As we went in to lunch I said to Jane, 'The long speeches gave me the opportunity to admire your legs again. They're very pretty.'

**Wednesday 18 November**

Dinner Alan Hare Wednesday night. John King present. I like him more every time I see him.

At the end of the evening he said he had been to Oxford that day to talk to the University Conservative Association. He arrived at about 12.15 and they gave him lunch and he gave them a talk. They asked lots of intelligent questions. I said, 'Why ever did you do that? You're far too busy for that kind of activity.' He said, 'I did it because I was afraid of it. To you it would be nothing dealing with undergraduates' sharp questions. But for me it is not a world to which I am accustomed so I must face it because I am afraid of it.' 'Did it go well?' I asked. 'Yes,' he said, 'very well. I think they all enjoyed it. I liked them and I think they liked me.'

He gets up at five in the morning and it was a quarter to twelve before we left.

We began with Forts de Latour 1976. It was good. We then had Château Latour proper, 1964, which was wonderful. That was followed by Château Latour, proper, 1949 which was extremely good but curiously no better to my mind than the '64. However, to drink three different Latour wines of great vintages in one evening is a remarkable experience.

**Thursday 19 November**

The Other Club. Not a large attendance. Bernard Levin was in the chair.

Ian Gilmour on the other side of Nico Henderson, who was next to me, had been saying to Nico's astonishment that Callaghan was a great Prime Minister and we shouldn't run him down. Nico, when Ian had gone, said, 'It's sad how Ian has become bitter and out of touch since he parted from Mrs Thatcher.' There was some question as to why he wanted to stay in Parliament and the answer seemed to be he likes writing about politics and, as perhaps a theorizing surgeon would like to have a base in a hospital, to go and look at it occasionally because he must know that he has no future in politics other than as a fading backbencher.

Nico also said that when he was at Oxford with Ted Heath he was the most amiable and jolly and friendly, joky man. I agreed with him because I remember him exactly the same way. Nico went on to say, 'I have never known anybody change so much in their character. He became what we all know him to be now, when he was Prime Minister. He actually said to me, "I want to be feared." He was far more a dictator than Mrs Thatcher ever dreamed of being.'

Before dinner I had a fairly friendly talk with David Steel[14] about travelling in sleepers on long distances and the Orient Express. He said there was a special steam train which took tourists from America etc. north to Scotland on a several day journey which was very luxurious and very popular. He was thinking what I was thinking as we talked – that he doesn't like me because I'm always so beastly about him in print, knocking his capacity as a leader and minimizing his importance.

Dinner wore on in a jolly atmosphere. Michael Hartwell asked me if I would take the chair at the next meeting which is on December 17th.

Then he suddenly said he had been asked to go out to the telephone.

Jock Colville had died on his way to the Club. That was a blockbuster. We were all stunned. We had been wondering why he wasn't there as he usually is and he has been the person who has kept the Club going and enthused over it and made the arrangements whether for wine or new members or anything else connected with it. He was the last great link with Churchill having been his Private Secretary for several of the War years and afterwards. He was sharp and alert, full of curiosity and kindness.

We discussed how to maintain the Churchill connection. His Private Secretary, Montagu Brown, is in the Club but he was only a Private Secretary when Churchill had retired from being Prime Minister and is a dim miserable fellow, gloomy, with no spark. So he would be no good as Chairman.

I said, 'What about Mary Soames for the Churchill connection? We've never had women.' Somebody said that once it had been sug-

14. Liberal Leader, 1976–88; his constituency was Roxburgh, Selkirk and Peebles in Scotland; knight 1990, life peer 1997.

gested that Mrs Thatcher might have been asked to be a member and Michael Hartwell had vetoed that. It was also said that Pam Berry (Michael's wife)[15] and Mary Soames both wanted to be members and were nearly carried through but Michael again vetoed that. He was always anxious to get away from Pam and couldn't have borne to see her there as well as everywhere else. Pamela of course wanted it because she was a woman of voracious appetite for being at the centre of power and intrigues imagining she had an influence way beyond reality.

A curious evening. I will always remember Jock with great affection. He got a First and was brilliant intellectually. He was also Private Secretary to the Queen for a while as well as Assistant Private Secretary for a period to Neville Chamberlain. As well as to Attlee when he was Prime Minister after the War. He knew everybody and knew everything and wrote very well in his memoirs and in the diary he kept when he was Private Secretary to Churchill during the War. He was born in January 1915 so he was only seventy-two.

**Friday 20 November**

Saw Prince Michael. Highly exercised about what he regards as insulting treatment by the Metropolitan Police who are subordinates of the Home Office and the Foreign Office. They won't give him police protection abroad or on many other occasions.

The official reason is that he is not on the Civil List. This I agree with him is illogical. Princess Alexandra is on the Civil List because she was at one time of an age to do public engagements when there was no other Royal lady of the same age and so she was put on the Civil List. This means that she and her husband Angus Ogilvy get police protection, as indeed does Mark Phillips.

He said, 'But I am a Prince of the blood.' He doesn't get a Civil List because of some rule laid down by his grandfather George V about how far it went down to younger sons of the brothers and sisters of the King etc. He showed me the correspondence with William Heseltine and with Patrick Wright.[16]

In one of the letters Bill Heseltine, the Queen's Private Secretary, says the Queen is very content with the arrangements. I said, 'Do you

---

15. Lady Pamela Berry (d 1982), political hostess, daughter of 1st Lord Birkenhead (F. E. Smith).
16. Sir Patrick Wright, Permanent Under-Secretary of State and Head of the Diplomatic Service, 1986–91.

think that's true?' 'I don't know.' 'Why don't you speak to her?' 'I can't go and talk to her about this problem because between us she is not an easy person to talk to if you bring her a problem. She likes not to be bothered or have any trouble.'

I said, 'Do you think they are trying to get at Princess Michael through you because some of them don't like her?' 'No. It is the same situation as before I married her.'

He said that Douglas Hurd had given him police protection when he went to Geneva for a recent exhibition where he was going in his private capacity and wrote to him afterwards and said he did it on the spur of the moment and now realizes this is a one-off situation. He said Douglas Hurd was coming to see him on Monday. What would I advise and what would I do?

**Sunday 22 November**

Talk to Douglas Hurd. 'It is all about a status symbol,' he said.

I told him I thought it odd that the government doesn't mind him being assassinated abroad but objects to it happening at home. He said that much of it comes down to what the police perceive as a threat. 'I don't think he's in any danger. They like to have whatever other Royals have. The Prince and Princess of Wales, the Queen Mother, the Queen and Prince Philip obviously are at risk. The others are not.' 'Perhaps you can work out some compromise.' He said, 'It all comes from the highest, you know. It's a family matter.'

Arnold Weinstock much more cheerful today. There was a letter from Peter Levene, Ministry of Defence Procurement Officer, in the *Sunday Telegraph* saying the story the previous Sunday was all wrong. However, Arnold pointed out they didn't leave in his letter where he said, 'If you had checked these facts with us you wouldn't have made the mistake you did in your story last week.' I said, 'That was typical of newspapers.'

Arnold asked my advice as to whether he should reopen the merger with Plessey. I said I thought it was a good moment; since the Monopolies Commission turn-down in 1986, a lot had happened. There has been the Wall Street crash and, 'You've just told me that Plessey are doing very badly and can't get by on their own any more. They are losing money. There is the realization from the King merger being allowed with British Caledonian that we have to compete abroad more effectively by bigger units.'

I added, 'Also buying AWACS from America and not Nimrod from you shows that there is plenty of competition in defence supplying for Britain from outside Britain so it would not be creating a monopoly of supply to the Defence Department. With the world perhaps going into a mild recession there will be the need to have a strong joint Plessey/GEC even more.'

Arnold said he thought, too, that Plessey would now like the merger. I said, 'That is another big factor. They were opposed to it before. So I think you should take your own idea very seriously.' He said he would think about it for a couple of months.

Princess Michael rings just before dinner. In a great state. A story in the *News of the World* which I had not seen about some letter going around Whitehall saying the red carpet is not to be laid out for Princess Michael any more at embassies and so forth.

Harold Lever was taken ill Monday last week. He has had to cancel the dinner he was coming to here. It seems serious. I rang Diana to find out how he was and she said, 'He'll speak to you,' which he then proceeded to do for half an hour. He has made a pretty quick recovery though he is not allowed out for another three weeks.

I am very fond of him. However, he threatened that when I have more time he was going to explain to me thoroughly what is wrong with the world's finances. Oh dear.

**Monday 23 November**

Told her that I thought her instinct was dead right in going to Enniskillen for the Remembrance Service yesterday.[17] She said, 'I thought I must show that we were with them.'

She always does the right thing by instinct.

Afterwards she went to Paris to see Chirac the French Prime Minister. 'How did that go?' I asked. 'Quite well. He has his difficulties. But I don't think they really want to do anything about the Common Agricultural Policy.'

She said, 'The trouble is that Germany doesn't want to do anything about it either. I asked Chirac whether he would like the whole issue

---

17. On Sunday 8 November 1987 the IRA had planted a bomb by the war memorial in Enniskillen, Co. Fermanagh, Northern Ireland, killing eleven people and injuring more than sixty assembled for the annual Remembrance Day service.

postponed and not discussed at Copenhagen[18] because he has got an election coming up[19] but he said no.'

She said, 'Chirac will have a very difficult job beating Mitterrand. Mitterrand is a very wily man.'

**Tuesday 24 November**

Every time I go into the Lords I pick up an extra one or two people who promise to support the Sunday Sports Bill amendment about the betting shops being open when there is horse racing on a Sunday.

Now the opponents are saying they are going to raise a point of order about my putting it back in again because it has already been decided by the House. I have had discussions with the Public Bill Office. The opponents are quite wrong 'if you favour the relevant part of the Standing Orders latest edition'.

Went to a large cocktail party with champagne, fortunately, given by David Stevens at No 3 Whitehall Court where they keep a company flat of enormous size. Lots of journalists and low level people there.

I asked Andrew Knight whether he had had a call from Princess Michael on Sunday evening and he said, yes, he did. Sabihah, his wife, was cross with her because she knows her perfectly but when she answered the telephone she didn't say hello to her but immediately said, 'I want to speak to Andrew Knight,' as though she were a servant. However, nothing was published in Monday's *Telegraph*. I don't think they had much of a story.

**Wednesday 25 November**

We have now got sixty-one postcards returned saying that the peers concerned will support the Sunday Sports Bill on December 9th. This should be enough with luck if they all turn up and keep their promise.

The Highland Park Spectator lunch for the Parliamentarian of the Year award. I sat next on my left to Nicholas Soames and on my right to Craig Brown who writes funny things for the *Times* whom I met years ago, as he reminded me, at Sonia Melchett's in Italy. On his right was Diane Abbott, the new black MP. She is a little bit like the Song of Solomon: 'I am black, but comely.' Nicholas Soames was almost drooling about her before she arrived, saying he doesn't know her really but has seen her in the Commons.

18. Next meeting of the European Council, on 4 December 1987.

19. The French presidential election was scheduled for 9 May 1988.

She thinks nothing of Ken Livingstone. Actually admires Mrs Thatcher. I said to her, 'The difference between Mrs Thatcher and Kinnock is this. Napoleon said that genius was an infinite capacity for taking pains and she takes them. Kinnock does not take the same pains and that is why she always beats him at Question Time or in debate. She works hours considering what questions she may be asked at Question Time or any other time and knows all the facts and figures. As well as delivering them forcefully and well.'

Though John Smith isn't in line with her views, she agreed when I said, 'He is your route to power if you are ever going to get it again. He looks good. He's got a kind, honest face. He is highly intelligent and understands what the Labour Party has to do to win the votes.'

At the end of the lunch I was set upon by Mrs Ruddock,[20] the CND lady who used to be Chairman of it. 'Why did you write such a horrid review of Peter Jenkins' book?'[21]

She said, 'I know why you wrote it. It's because he said Rupert Murdoch shouldn't be allowed to buy the *Financial Times*.'

I said to Mrs Ruddock, 'Do you really think that I don't write what I believe?' She said, 'I think you just did it because Rupert Murdoch wanted you to.' 'He had no idea I was reviewing the book. How could he have?'

I suppose it reveals how the minds of that sort of person in the Labour Party work. They think nobody ever does anything other than for some ulterior motive which includes themselves.

I didn't tell her that the book was sent to me at about three days' notice and I began to read it with some hope that it would be good and then saw it was a regurgitation of a lot of old ideas with nothing new whatever and probably plentiful use of notes he had been unable to use in his columns. In fact I have never written anything which I did not believe in any newspaper since I first began to write for them.

You could, I suppose, say that Rupert needs my friendship as much or more than I need his. I was vaguely irritated at this implication of my venal behaviour because I didn't even know what Peter Jenkins' views were on Rupert Murdoch or the *Financial Times* or anything else which might be annoying to Rupert and I wouldn't have cared if I had.

---

20. Joan Ruddock, chairperson, Campaign for Nuclear Disarmament, 1981–5; Labour MP since 1987.

21. *Mrs Thatcher's Revolution: The Ending of the Socialist Era*, 1987.

**Friday 27 November**

Just as I was leaving for the Jockey Club after lunch to talk about the sacking of John Beard, Chief Executive of SIS, I noticed there was something in the letterbox. I pulled it out. It had been delivered by hand and it was a Writ. Ladbroke's were demanding damages for libel. It was because of a letter I wrote to Pierre Carrus on October 13th about their dastardly ways, to help PMU thwart Ladbroke's in Europe with background information. Brian McDonnell rang Pierre Carrus who said somebody must have taken it out of his files. He regarded it as a private letter.

Later it emerged that they were also going to ask for an injunction to make me refrain from repeating the libel.

**Saturday 28 November**

Off to Towcester. It is a crisp sunny morning. We were staying at Pomfret Lodge where Kisty Hesketh[22] lives. That's about a quarter of a mile from the house, Easton Neston, which was built by Hawksmoor in 1702. The family have been there since 1622.

The house is glorious as one would expect from Nicholas Hawksmoor. Alexander said it is the only country house he ever built. The racecourse was built for the Empress of Austria. It is in lovely countryside with a wonderful Decimus Burton style screen and arch in the distance on the top of a hill. That was built about 1820. It was an entrance to the Park at one time.

The Empress of Austria, Elizabeth of Bavaria, was the naughty lady who hunted a great deal in England and was reputed to have had a gentleman friend who hunted with her. Meanwhile Franz Josef had an actress friend he set up in a house in Vienna. The Empress was stabbed in Geneva in 1898 by an anarchist. The two had never been happy together. He died in 1916, having been instrumental in the beginning of World War I which wrecked Europe to this day.

Alexander Hesketh was very generous and agreeable. His wife, Rupert Manton's daughter, is pretty and slim with a figure like a boy, very long legged, with two little daughters. She is fair. Her mother Mimi's face is in hers, and also a touch of Rupert Manton's. Alexander produced the best wine, which he carefully opened and nurtured in the morning, I have ever had on a racecourse. It was Léoville-Barton 1975, one of the very top years. He brought four bottles. I drank so much I

22. Christine, née McEwen, mother of the 3rd Baron (Alexander) Hesketh.

was nearly ill from it, particularly as I had been persuaded to have a whisky mac before lunch by Kisty with whom I had gone on a tour of the racecourse, meeting some sponsors with her.

Charles Wilson and Sally his wife were there. She, with her brothers and sisters, has a farm some twenty miles away. They have fifteen hundred acres or so. They all share it. I told him I thought of writing about the Sunday Sports Bill for my article for the coming Wednesday. He thought that was a very good idea. I have to beat up all these peers and make them understand what the issues are. Some of them may even read the *Times*.

At dinner at Pomfret Lodge, Michael Heseltine and his wife came. When Kisty had asked him he said, 'Do you realize that Woodrow hates me?' and she had said, 'Never mind. Just come all the same.' I sat next to his wife on one side and Kisty on the other. She is not bad, Mrs Heseltine, she turned out to be quite jolly. She said she was not interested in politics and didn't like the constituency which reminded me of Victoria in my play. But she does do all the necessary chores of an MP's wife.

She says she remembers when I was staying in a hotel in or near Coventry and they were staying there, fighting Maurice Edelman[23] years ago in a general election. She liked Maurice Edelman. They knew they couldn't beat him although they were optimistic. Actually Maurice said to me, looking across the restaurant, 'That's Michael Heseltine. He's a pornographer. He publishes magazines with naked girls in them in order to sell them.' I don't think Heseltine would like to be reminded of that now. He's made a great deal of money, extremely enterprising, in publishing.

After the ladies went we had a longish talk about the community charge or Poll Tax.[24] He said it was a disaster. He knew all about it, he claimed, because he had been Secretary for the Environment and he at one time had thought it was a good idea but not now.

He is opposing the community charge because he says it will be desperately unfair to people in the Inner Cities who have hardly got any money at all. It should still be based on something to do with the

---

23. (1911–75); Labour politician and author; this must have been in the 1964 general election for Coventry North constituency.

24. The proposal was to replace the local rates system, paid by householders and based on the value of properties, by a flat-rate local tax on all individuals on the electoral register.

value of the property you live in. The widow who chooses to live by herself in a house paying high rates, that is her affair and it is not unfair that next door there are about ten people in a similar house and they are paying the same rate as she is. He is going to attack it and thinks it is going to be a terrible disaster for the Tory Party because it is going to emphasize the centralization of government which is not a Tory principle. Really the present checks and balances are all right and not all the councils are bad, only some of the lunatic Labour councils.

I said, 'Do you think it's going to lose the Tories the next election?' He said, 'No. You have to have a five per cent swing for that and that hasn't happened since the War. Also the country is prosperous.'

He was emphatic that she was the only person in the Cabinet who wanted it, except perhaps for George Younger.

I said, 'Whose idea was it?' 'Her idea. She got the civil servants to put up a plan or somebody brought her the idea and then they worked on it. And then she railroaded it through the Cabinet. They're all frightened of her and do what she tells them.'

I told him that I had agitated for him to be on television during the general election and he said he knew that he'd been blacked from on high. He was quite surprised that later on in the election he'd been nominated to appear, not in a party political broadcast but in other political programmes by the Conservative Central Office.

**Sunday 29 November**

Spoke to Mrs Thatcher. I told her I had been worried about the report of her fainting at Buckingham Palace earlier in the week. I commented that the usual story was rapidly appearing that she was wearing out and so on, and might not last much longer.

She said, 'I'm perfectly all right.' She didn't actually faint. She had had the Enniskillen thing just before and had been going out in the cold. It was very hot at the diplomatic levee. She says, 'I've got low blood pressure.' 'Well that does make one dizzy sometimes. I have low blood pressure too and low cholesterol. We're both the same type, thank goodness We last longer.'

I told her about Michael Heseltine. She said, 'Poor man. He is all on his own now. It was his own fault.' She didn't really mean poor man. She would never have him back. I said, 'He'll make a lot of trouble. I will have to become an instant expert on the subject and help battle against people who are opposed to the Poll Tax in the

Lords.' She said, 'It's not the Poll Tax.' I said, 'No, but you're lumbered with that name now.'

Of course one good by-product might be that a lot of people won't put their names on the electoral register if it's going to be the method of checking payment of the Poll Tax because they won't want to pay it. As they will be those people most likely to vote Labour, it could be a benefit. I didn't say that to her but I thought it.

When I told her that Michael Heseltine had said that nobody in the Cabinet agreed with the community charge except perhaps George Younger and she was forcing it through against their will, she said, 'How does he know? He hasn't been there.'

**Monday 30 November**

I spoke to Arnold Goodman about the Ladbroke's libel action against me. At first he said, 'Someone been libelling my darling Woodrow? I can't have that.' I said, 'No, it's Ladbroke's who accuse me of libelling them.' He replied, 'That's impossible. Nobody could libel them.'

I gave him a few of the details and he sounded pretty relaxed. He thought it was the sort of thing he would settle with the lawyers concerned whom he knew reasonably well. Ladbroke's would have to be mad to have all this in court, everyone to be reminded [that] they lost their casino licences.[25]

In the afternoon I visited the Tote. I found that foolishly Brian McDonnell, probably egged on by the slightly know-all and immature John Heaton who is Secretary of the Tote – he is pleasant but suffers from the proposition that a little learning is a dangerous thing – had decided they wanted another solicitor whom the Tote Board normally use as well as Arnold Goodman.

I said, 'You're absolutely mad. That would mean two sets of solicitors. Two lots of consultations. Two lots of different opinions. Two counsel. The thing would cost a fortune. Double all the time wasted on it, which is going to be wasted anyway. We stand together. I was acting as an agent of the Tote and you're involved in it because your name was in the letter that I wrote.'

I had previously said to John Heaton, 'The libel action is based on a letter which you passed.' He said, 'I knew you were going to say that.' 'Yes, but it's quite true.' Not that I blamed him for it because

25. In 1979 magistrates did not renew some of Ladbroke's casino licences because of violations of the Gaming Act.

there was nothing really wrong with the letter and all the facts were right.

Pierre Carrus rang me last night to say that it had been sent by one of his staff in confidence to the German racing authorities who must have shown it to Ladbroke's and/or given them a copy of it. As he rightly said, it was a private letter which could not be acted upon in France. And Arnold Goodman said also that it carried qualified privilege unless there was malice. I can't see how they could prove malice. Even if they could, it was justified by accuracy.

Then I went on to the Jockey Club. Ailwyn Fairhaven said he would speak if he had to and started to look sick at the thought of it. The blonde bombshell was there (Bridgett Walters) wearing red stockings, looking very sexy. Mrs Walters is married to an MP, a Tory who was previously married to Duncan Sandys' daughter.

A sad little letter from Prince Michael: 'This is just to say how much I appreciate your coming here the other day. And the trouble you took to put my case to the Home Sec. The resistance is there, all right, but I shall battle onwards! I am grateful. Yours sincerely, Michael.'

**Wednesday 2 December**

A jolly meeting at Arnold Goodman's office. Ladbroke's writ of libel against me. We are going to enter a defence and produce the particulars of the pleading on which we base the assertions in the letter and then see what they do. Arnold says that making an apology which they'd like us to do would make any damages worse rather than better. He can't believe they would ever bring it to court.

We think that not only can we plead qualified privilege of my letter to Pierre Carrus but also justification if the former fails.

Cocktail or champagne party at Sonia Melchett's (Sinclair).

Prince Michael without the Princess. Angus Ogilvy without the Princess [Alexandra]. It was evidently intended to be a grander party socially than the one which Allan Davis told me he went to on Monday.

The French Ambassador said that it was not fair to attack the French for having exchanged an Iranian terrorist to get back some French hostages in Lebanon. He said the truth of the matter was that the prosecuting authorities in France did not think they had a strong enough case to convict the man. That being the case, rather than just let him go without anything in return, they got the French hostages back.

Andrew Sinclair very jolly. Said when he married Sonia a few years ago she had all the money and he was earning little. Now, like Verushka, she has lost about fifty per cent of her money and he is earning very well. This situation seemed to please him as obviously he thought it gave him a stronger end in his relationship. She is somewhat older than he is.

She is very happy with him which is about all that matters. I liked him a bit better last night.

I am not sure how much I like Andrew Neil. I find him an unreal figure with a face of tin which is flexible but doesn't show much feeling. I think he is a man for sensations rather than thought. He is a prey to the fashionable and is not a great editor in the terms of pursuing truth and justice.

**Thursday 3 December**

Dinner party at Cavendish Avenue.

John and Penny Mortimer. Fitzroy MacLean.[1] Noël and Gaby Annan. William and Susan Boyd. Bernard Levin. Susan Crosland. So it was left and right political stance.

I asked William Boyd[2] whether his success and increasing wealth had turned him away a bit from Labour and he said, 'No.' Writers move in a suspended free floating world disconnected with reality. John Mortimer is the same. He says he thought Ken Livingstone ought to be the Leader of the Labour Party.

It never occurs to these people that their continuing prosperity depends on Thatcherism being a success.

Susan [Crosland] remains fairly pretty though the years are telling. She says Andrew Neil had told her he didn't want any more about child abuse in her column this week. Nobody knew what she was talking about because I think hardly anyone reads her column. It's very poor stuff.

She told me that Bernard Levin might not like to see her as she had been cross about something unpleasant he had written about Tony Crosland, politically. On the contrary he was delighted that she was coming and they got on well together. Bernard wore strange red trousers almost like beach ones and a jacket with checks.

I told John Mortimer that I had been writing a play and that Allan Davis had been making me reconstruct and rewrite large parts of it. He said Allan Davis had done very well with his one act plays and made him rewrite but he has not been able to write a play for ten years. He has no further ideas for plays.

Susan Boyd is less pretty than she was when she was at the Oxford University Press; she was the publicist of the Wyatt book they published.[3] She is eager. She told me then she could never contemplate having a love affair, she loved her husband so much. That was ten years ago. I wonder if that remains true? She still has no children and says she doesn't want any. She was very full of the new house they are getting in Fulham.

---

1. Sir Fitzroy MacLean, Conservative MP, 1941–74; commanded British mission to Yugoslav partisans, 1943–5; writer and journalist.
2. Novelist and TV writer; he won the Whitbread Prize 1981, Somerset Maugham Award 1982, John Llewellyn Rhys Prize 1982.
3. *The Wyatts* by John Martin Robinson (1980).

Gaby Annan said she thought of nothing but sex. It was the most important thing in life. I said, 'Do you mean now?' 'Oh yes.' She must be about sixty plus so good luck to her if she is finding people to go to bed with her. She is not unattractive. I was once mildly interested in her but thought she was too Germanic.

After the women had left the dinner table I got Fitzroy to talk about his experiences in Russia. He has just been back there for a couple of months or so making films. He has met Gorbachev three times. Fitzroy speaks perfect Russian. He was first there as a young man in the Diplomatic Corps before the War. He attended Bukharin's trial.[4] Bukharin was a friend of Lenin who was judicially murdered by Stalin.

He says there is definitely a new mood in Russia. He talks to all the people as he goes round. He said, 'When I was first in Russia before the War to be seen talking to a foreigner was to get yourself arrested and shot. Now there's no difficulty whatever.'

He said the Ukrainians still want their independence and they have won a certain amount of autonomy. The Baltic States where he travelled a bit are very bitter. They work a kind of Hungarian system. That's because the Baltic States were only taken over by Stalin in 1939–40. They are like the Finns and the Swedes. They know how to make an economy work.

Fitzroy said of all the friends who had died recently he missed Hugh Fraser the most and I agreed. We both mournfully considered the deaths of our friends and the ones particularly who are dying younger than ourselves. I said, 'I'm trying to make some new friends so that they will outlast me.'

The stock market continues to fall. My brother bought BP partly paid shares at 89p and said they were cheap at the price. He recommended me to buy them which I did at 83p. They are now 70p. There was an article in the *Evening Standard* saying they really are only worth 40p.

I have three thousand of them. What an ass I am. Every time I go into the stock market it is a disaster.

---

4. The last Moscow 'show trial' in 1938; Bukharin was a member of the Politburo, 1919–29; editor, *Izvestia*, 1934–7; at the end of the twenties he helped Osip Mandelstam to get published.

**Sunday 6 December**

Margaret said that it was ridiculous that the heads of government should have been there in Copenhagen discussing set-aside schemes for farmers and such detailed matters as that. I said, 'What are set-aside schemes?' 'Oh that's what they will be paid for not growing anything. They are trying to sneak it in without having agreed the corresponding responsibilities.' She said to them, 'You don't subsidize our inefficiency in industry. Why should you expect us to subsidize your inefficiency in agriculture?'

She is looking forward to her meeting with Gorbachev tomorrow. 'It's quite exciting' and she spoke with that schoolgirl eagerness I love. She said again she had much sympathy with him in his difficulties in getting any reform done but she agreed when I said, 'One has to be careful because if you scratch him right down there is probably still the old Communist Imperialist at heart.'

I told her that I had seen in the papers that she was weakening on the SDI[5] and trying to persuade Reagan to make a compromise. She was indignant. 'Which papers? What nonsense.'

She is seeing Gorbachev at Brize Norton at 11.30 tomorrow. She said, 'The others' (meaning the European leaders) 'are as jealous as hell.'

Shortly after I spoke to her Rupert rang. He wanted to know why she was telling Reagan to compromise on Star Wars.[6] I said, 'She's not. She was horrified when I suggested that to her.'

**Monday 7 December**

John Robinson has been to Heveningham Hall. He says everything has been done according to the instructions of the great experts recommended by the Department of the Environment.

He is sending me a note which I will send on to the Department of the Environment and to Abdul Al Ghazzi.

**Tuesday 8 December**

Party at Rupert's. Politicians and journalists.

Duke Hussey brings Michael Checkland, the new Director General of the BBC, to meet me. He is short. He has an intelligent face. I tell him that I think the BBC is becoming fairer though Brian Redhead

5. Strategic Defence Initiative.
6. The US nickname for the SDI.

still pumps out Socialist propaganda every morning on the *Today* programme.

Hugh Trevor-Roper is there. He says Charlie Wilson is no good as an editor. He left school when he was fifteen and was an office boy. He has no education. 'How can such a person edit the *Times*?'

We repair for dinner to Harry's Bar, that is Rupert and Anna, Irwin Stelzer the host, and Andrew Neil as well as Verushka, Petronella and myself.

Rupert in a larking spirit wants to go gambling. I say, 'You can take Verushka if you like but I'm going home.'

Rupert said that he was at some function the night before when Mrs Thatcher had said to Robert Maxwell,[7] 'Can you tell me what we should do to help Mr Gorbachev?' To which he had replied, 'Why help him at all?'

This morning a silk carpet in a handsome design arrived from Abdul Al Ghazzi as a Christmas present. It looks expensive. We don't know what to do with it. It doesn't look quite right in the hall and it looks wrong in the other rooms.

But it was a noble present.

**Wednesday 9 December**

Before the Tote [Board meeting] David Montagu told me he was leaving Jacob and becoming Executive Chairman of Rothmans. His job at J. R. Rothschild [Holdings] had been a non-job for a long time. So it was probably true what David Stevens said about David Montagu asking him for a job.[8]

A condition of his new job at Rothmans is to give up all other boards. But he got them to make an exception for the Tote Board because he so much enjoys the meetings with myself as Chairman. I am glad he is not going because he is a very loyal friend and valuable at difficult times.

We had the great debate [in the Lords] on my amendment to allow betting shops to be open on Sundays when there is approved horse racing. It was a thoroughly English occasion. To my horror I saw seven

---

7. The former Labour MP, publisher and newspaper proprietor (1923–91) was born in Czechoslovakia; after serving in the British Army during the war, he established a joint company with Ferdinand Springer, Germany's largest scientific publishers, the first of many trade links with the Soviet bloc.
8. See 15 November 1987.

Bishops lined up who had not been there earlier in the day. They had come to vote against it.

The lobbying was extremely effective. We won the vote by seventy-eight to sixty-one.

It was a great moment when I was able to take the numbers to the clerk at the table and find that we had our majority and I could take it to Baroness Cox[9] who was on the Woolsack. She had previously written me a letter saying she couldn't vote for me because of her religious convictions. I thought, 'How strange. Here is what Bernard Shaw would consider to be a new woman, thoroughly libertarian, full of zest for getting rid of censorious and restrictive practices in education and the unions and elsewhere, and yet when it came to the crunch she wanted to leave Sunday as it was because she said she was a Christian.'

George Thomas (Viscount Tonypandy)[10] sat next to me. I said, 'George you're not going to make a speech, are you?' He said, 'Yes.' 'If you do, I shall expose your secret drinking,' and he said, 'Oh I wish I knew something about you, Woodrow.'

Ted Graham (Lord Graham of Edmonton) said it was the only time a three line whip had been issued through the *Times* and started quoting my last Wednesday's article and what I had said about the need to have the betting shops open.

A glorious moment. A little man, mousy, called Earl Attlee, got up. Face slightly reminiscent of his father's. Then much as his father would have done he said, 'I'm not a gambler. I never go racing. I wouldn't go on a Sunday if there was Sunday racing. I wouldn't go to a betting shop if it was open on a Sunday. But if that's what people want to do they must be allowed to do it. It's their choice.' It is extraordinary how like his father that was, though not so clipped and precise and definite.

A very effective little speech was made by Peter Rawlinson who said, 'I've acted for bookmakers. I've acted for murderers. And that doesn't mean I sympathize with either. But I think that there is enormous hypocrisy about Sunday still and we should pass this amendment. I don't like hypocrisy.'

The Jockey Club salvaged its honour. Some nine members who are peers turned up. Not quite the maximum but not too bad. Lord

9. A deputy Speaker, House of Lords, since 1986.

10. (1909–97); Speaker of the House of Commons, 1976–83; he was a prominent Methodist.

Tonypandy said there were more Jockey Club members there than there were Bishops.

In the afternoon at half past four Verushka and Anna Murdoch came to tea. She is very affectionate and rather beautiful although her legs are not her best feature.

Anna told me that she and Rupert went to Aspinall's for twenty minutes after dinner last night. He immediately won £3,000, said that was enough and went home. He is the most amazingly lucky person I have ever known.

**Thursday 10 December**

A fascinating lunch. Eric Hammond,[11] and Phillipa Marks and Dermot Glynn from NERA.

I'm trying to get Eric interested in NERA doing some research work on the lines of propaganding the good things they've been up to. I said that Jimmy Knapp of NUR [National Union of Railwaymen] had already employed NERA to find out what customers want on British Rail. I said, 'If a man like Jimmy Knapp can do that, my darling Electricians' Union can't be far behind.'

He then explained the wonderful things they've been doing in their own private training scheme, using government money which would have gone on the YTS[12] (which provides very few secure jobs for people it trains), to provide really skilled training for their electricians. They've increased the number of skilled electricians enormously by doing this. He said nine hundred electricians are needed for the Channel Tunnel. There aren't any. They couldn't get six hundred electricians to build the nuclear power stations now under planning.

There was a terrible risk of there being no new apprentices. Of course it would have suited the union in some respects, as the demand for electricians would have been so high they could have charged the earth for them and held the employers to ransom. But he felt this wouldn't be good for the future employment of electricians.

He also told me that they are planning a merger with the Engineers Union. It would make them the largest union in the country. Would I say something about it in the *News of the World* this week because on Monday he is on the carpet again over the Wapping dispute. He is being accused by the TUC of breaking an undertaking about recruiting

---

11. General Secretary of the EETPU.
12. Youth Training Scheme, a government initiative.

new members and so forth. If they knew there was a possibility of this giant union being formed and leaving the TUC altogether, they would be very much more circumspect on how they attack the ETU [EETPU] in the General Council.

American Embassy for what they call 'holiday drinks'.

Talked a bit to William Rees-Mogg.[13] Wanted to know what Rupert was up to with regard to the *Financial Times*. Told him, 'Nothing sinister – only the possibility of starting a *Financial Times* in America using the London databases but an entirely American production.'

On to the French Embassy. There was Alan Clark[14] and his wife to whom he has been married for twenty-eight or twenty-nine years. He has a castle near Folkestone and is very rich, being the son of Lord Clark of *Civilisation*. He is the man who gleefully talked about Bongo-Bongo Land in relation to our black brothers.

He asked me whether Mrs Thatcher had a direct input into my articles. I said, 'Why do you ask that?' 'Several times in Cabinet Committee she has said, and has done it for a long time, "Oh, it's a very difficult thing to explain to the public. We must get Woodrow to write something about it."'

I said, 'Not at all. I don't even know Bernard Ingham (the No 10 Press Officer). Sometimes I may mention to her that I'm thinking of writing on a particular topic and she may say, "Oh that's a good idea. I hope you do." Otherwise we never talk about my articles before they're written. Only afterwards.'

No doubt her talking about me in Cabinet committees and in Cabinet is the reason why Ministers are very polite to me – far more than they used to be when I was in the Commons.

He said half her Ministers adore her. The other half are trying to get rid of her.

I sat next to the Ambassadress which I said to her was an honour above my station. On her other side was the Duke of Rutland. On my other side was Mrs Powell, the vivacious Italian wife, dark and attractive, of Charles Powell who is the Prime Minister's Private Secretary from the Foreign Office. Mrs Powell said recently her husband came

---

13. Former editor of the *Times*, at this time chairman of the Arts Council of Great Britain, a director of GEC and proprietor of Pickering & Chatto Ltd, antiquarian booksellers.

14. Minister for Trade, 1986–9; his father, the art historian Kenneth Clark, won acclaim in the 1960s for his television series *Civilisation*.

back home late at night roaring with laughter. He told her that he had been there when I had rung her up after her Mansion House speech.[15] I told her how beautiful she looked.

Mrs Powell said her husband said she obviously adored me talking to her like that.

**Friday 11 December**

A frantic day. I was thrown out in time in trying to rush through the newspapers to find a few items to write about for my *News of the World* column.

Then came news that the Home Office wouldn't back the amendments to the schedule of the Sunday Sports Bill which they had first proposed and I had agreed with the chief opponent, Lord Graham of Edmonton. They said they still didn't work and the Bill therefore wouldn't be complete in the form that the Home Office could back. John Heaton had to go to the Home Office and sort it out.

Later comes an agitated call from Christopher Foster at the Jockey Club. What can be done about next Wednesday night?[16] When is it going to start? Five members of the Jockey Club are having some anniversary dinner with the Queen which she is giving at Claridge's.

I said, 'There's nothing I can do about it. I hope it will only last about half an hour but how can I tell? I can hardly get up and say, "Would everybody kindly finish his business immediately because the Queen is expecting five Jockey Club members for dinner."'

There are endless complications in trying to get a Bill as a Private Member through the Lords. You are not supposed to vote against a third reading by convention but there's nothing to stop people doing it and it has been done in the past.

Milton and Dru Shulman[17] – dinner at their flat in Eaton Square.

Donald Sinden came up to me before dinner. Very friendly. I told him we had altered the play and incorporated most of his suggestions. He said, 'Oh, am I getting a percentage?'

At dinner Sinden was describing the commercials he does using his own voice because it is very distinctive. They kept saying to him, 'Can you do it again?' and he said 'What's the matter?' They said, 'It doesn't

15. On 17 November 1987.
16. The third reading of the Bill.
17. Milton Shulman, journalist; dramatic critic of the *Evening Standard*, 1953–91; m (1956) Drusilla Beyfus, journalist; associate editor, British *Vogue*, 1979–86.

sound like your exaggerated voice on *Spitting Image*.' Of course it didn't because that is not his voice. They just send him up on *Spitting Image* – so he wasn't very keen to send himself up.

Sat next to Dru. I said, 'Did you ever go to bed with Beaverbrook?' She said, 'Well nearly but not quite. When I was going to America he was going to America. I said I would go with him and he booked a great bridal suite or whatever on the *Queen Mary*.' At the last minute she didn't turn up. He never forgave her. She said he was very cruel to the women he had in his life and she did not agree that he was as kind as I thought he was. But nevertheless the women seemed to adore him.

'Do you remember Nurse?' she asked. Nurse was an Irish girl, very pretty, who used to wear white overalls and often came to dinner. He had a French mistress who was devoted to him although he treated her very badly. I said, 'Are you still interested in sex?' and Dru was very surprised. She said, 'Yes, yes. Naturally I am.' She must be pushing sixty now.

Dru is still pretty.

Beaverbrook was over seventy when he wanted Dru to be his mistress. She was twenty-two.

Paul Johnson doesn't really like me. He was sitting one away from me and became rather aggressive about betting. I said, 'You're as silly as a Bishop.' 'Oh all you're doing is trying to take pennies away from the poor working man and make him destitute.' I said, 'That sounds like unregenerate parlour Socialism.'

I think he must earn a lot of money. He never stops writing – well-paid feature articles and his books are successful.

The dinner was merry and we didn't leave until 12.00. The food was good and the beef was nice and underdone. The wine was terrible.

I am very fond of Milton and Dru. They are a part of the furniture of my life. He goes on being lively and she has a job now with the Al Fayed who owns Harrods. She does the house magazine.

The atmosphere is bad there because he sacked the people who know anything about running a store. The old employees can't bear him because they think it's terrible they have got this Egyptian as their employer. He, Al Fayed, adores Harrods because he sees it as entirely England and being part of the monarchy with the Queen and his Royal appointment and all the rest of it.

**Sunday 13 December**

I said, 'I notice that Michael Heseltine is putting himself at the head of the dissidents about the community charge.'

She said of course all those people would have been thoroughly for the community charge if they had still been in the government.

She said there is a great deal of difference between the way hospitals in different regions are run. Some are very good and utilize their resources fully and well and others don't. We've got to get to a state where the hospitals are paid for what they do, that is to say, their resources will be coming from the number of patients and the kind of operations they do. This would introduce some element of incentive to the hospitals.

I said, 'Can't we get an element of tax relief for people who pay for private health care?' She said she might have to do that in the end but she was against adding more to tax relief. 'We have it in mortgages and that is after all one's home.'

One of her most admirable characteristics is her simplicity. She winnows everything down to the salient point. She is thinking hard, harder than anyone in her government, on how to reconcile the needs of patients to the money that can be afforded and give them good treatment.

**Tuesday 15 December**

I had just arrived at Broadway House, Tothill Street, for a meeting with the Stable Lads' Association and the Transport & General Workers representative, before joining in the bearding of the trainers about the miserable poverty wages paid to the stable lads, when an urgent telephone call arrived. It was David Tytler of the *Times*.

As Willie Whitelaw had collapsed with a mini-stroke in a Christmas carol service at St Margaret's Westminster last night, would I kindly write about him and what would happen without him and the importance of the Lords and the legislation coming up and so forth.[18]

---

18. WW followed his brief, analysing Lord Whitelaw's skills and the latter-day role of the Lords in amending legislation: 'He is the best equipped of all Conservative peers to get difficult legislation through the Lords, conceding the odd amendment here and there to achieve the whole . . . The House of Lords is more powerful than for decades because it is wise enough to stop short of serious confrontation while nevertheless making a discernible impact on legislation in a manner often popular . . . This is an area of intricate dancing which is a joy when it goes perfectly and a disaster if there are too many false steps. Lord Whitelaw is a supreme master of the dance . . .'

It made me think of what Shaw said about happiness. If you are busy you do not have time to wonder whether you are unhappy. The antidote to unhappiness is to be full of work.

At No 11 Downing Street [party] Mrs Lawson terribly pleased at my defence of her in the *News of the World* when I said she had only been attacked over her drink offence because she was who she was and ordinarily a Mrs Smith of Hull would have been given a caution and never appeared in court.[19]

On to the Abdul Al Ghazzi party which was full of Arab diplomats.

Abdul was jolly but the party was not exactly sparkling with wit and amusement. Christopher Mayhew[20] was there. He was being unpleasant, telling everybody I knew nothing about politics and I only knew about racing. I know why – because I said in my book that he had been violently anti-Wilson until the moment that Wilson gave him a job in the government, at which point he said Wilson was marvellous and a very decent chap. He's never forgiven me but he can't deny the truth of it. He was always very vain but with not enough talent to back his vanity.

The Jeffrey Archer party was one for mainly journalistic and newspaper people. We should have been going on the Wednesday night. He gives three parties in a row. We went on the Tuesday because of the Sunday Sports Bill being due on Wednesday evening.

Robert Maxwell there. Very friendly on the whole. I asked him why on earth he wanted to own a football club.[21] 'It must be extremely boring mixing with dreary people.' He admitted that he liked wearing his ridiculous baseball hat in photographs and being an actor.

He told me the *Mirror* was doing extremely well. The only paper of its kind going up in circulation. He always says things like that. Maybe it's true for a week or two but I think the *Mirror* is in fact better than it was.

Robert Maxwell is a buccaneer and a crook. His energy splashes bogus charm around. He longs to be popular but, however hard he tries, I think he will never succeed in that.

Mary Archer looking very pretty and now far better dressed in

---

19. She was fined £125 and lost her licence for a year for being two points over the legal alcohol limit when in charge of a vehicle; WW ended his article, 'She wasn't drunk and she wasn't driving.'
20. (1915–97); Labour politician who joined the Liberal Party in 1974; life peer 1981.
21. He owned Oxford United and Derby County.

expensive, fashionable dresses than she's ever been before. She told Nick Lloyd, an old university friend, when she had lunch with him today that she had now got Jeffrey absolutely under control. If he makes any false step she can deal with him. And she passed her hand across her throat. She is the one who triumphed in the libel action.

**Wednesday 16 December**

The third reading of the Sunday Sports Bill. Myself greatly agitated in case the opposition decided to vote against it. I had to keep telling our people like Micky Suffolk and Ailwyn Fairhaven and Rupert Manton and all those who did turn up, which was very valiant of them, that their presence was not wasted even if there was no vote. And indeed afterwards Ted Graham said to me, 'Well, seeing all that phalanx there I realized that there was no possibility of holding the Bill up and so I decided not to make any more speeches.'

So the Bill was automatically put to the vote and passed, the whole proceeding lasting about eight minutes after I had moved some amendments to make the Schedule protecting workers more effective in the terms it was meant to be. So those who were going to the Queen's dance got away quick.

**Thursday 17 December**

I am now trying to see what I can get done in the Commons. Mr MacLean in the government Whips' office said the government has never provided Private Members time since 1979 and was not likely to do so now.

He got me to get Denis Howell to ring him to explain which day would be a good one to sneak in the second reading and perhaps get it on the nod, catch people unawares. We have to use a lot of cunning.

In the chair at The Other Club. Michael Hartwell made a little speech about Jock Colville. He ended by saying that Jock in his diary, which he kept about Churchill during the War years, was not afraid to say that Churchill was a mountebank. I looked at young Winston Churchill's face when he said that and he tried to smile.

Sat next to Quintin.[22] I had to choose my neighbour on the right and he was the one I chose. He said he wouldn't want to live his life again. He had had many sorrows and many disappointments. Many

---

22. Lord Hailsham, former Lord Chancellor m 1 (1944) Mary, née Martin (d 1978), m 2 (1986) Deirdre Shannon.

black moments. He said he had not got over his previous wife's death. And he said he had never got over his half-brother's suicide. That was Edward Marjoribanks[23] who was about thirty-four, a brilliant lawyer. He had written a wonderful life about Marshall-Hall. He said he felt guilty about him and thought about it every day because he loved him.

I said, 'How can you feel guilty about it?' 'Because it was a Sunday in the country and he said to my father, "I'm going back into the house."' He (Quintin) was more interested in himself than in any problem his brother might have. He didn't know he had one so bad. Before Quintin left, which he did earlier than his brother, he didn't lock the gun cupboard. I said, 'Did you normally lock the gun cupboard in that house?' 'No.' 'Then your brother would have thought it an insult if you had.' 'Yes, but if I had locked the gun cupboard, and curiously I thought about it, he would not have committed suicide.'

I said, 'That is foolish. He would have attached a tube to a motor car engine and sat in the car and asphyxiated himself or jumped out of a window or taken some barbiturates or something of that kind.' 'No, I don't know that he would have done. If only I had been with him. I could have stopped him. But I was thinking too much of myself.'

Edward Marjoribanks committed suicide because he had been bitterly disappointed in love. He was also a poet as well as a brilliant lawyer. He was highly sensitive.

I said to Quintin, 'You should write your memoirs.' He said no, he wouldn't do that. There were enough of these, like Harold Macmillan's and Anthony Eden's, boring autobiographies around. I said, 'I didn't mean a book like that. I mean one in which you set out your true feelings and thoughts about your wife and your half-brother and your disappointment at not becoming Prime Minister and your feelings about how life should be lived and how you have lived yours.' We discussed that for a while and he began to think it was a good idea.

I said, 'Can I get Ian Chapman of Collins to talk to you about it? It would make a lot of money which you could leave to whoever you wanted. You would do it extremely well.'

There was a very jolly atmosphere. I felt full of beans. Robin Day

---

23. (1900–32); son of Lord Hailsham's mother by her first marriage; became a Unionist MP in 1929; he published in 1929 his life of Sir Edward Marshall-Hall QC (1858–1927, celebrated advocate and Conservative MP), *Poems* in 1931 and a biography of another famous lawyer, Lord Carson, in 1931.

said I carried the chairmanship off with great aplomb and authority. He seemed to be surprised. I don't know why.

I had to say, among other things, that Michael Hartwell had given sixty magnums of champagne to the Club which was a fantastic gift.

We were talking afterwards about getting some more rancour, as described in the Rules, into the occasions. 'If we get David Steel more often and we had David Owen as a member too, we would have plenty of rancour about,' I said.

I talked to one or two people including William Waldegrave about having Charles Moore and Andrew Wilson as members. Everyone I mentioned it to thoroughly agreed though Jock Colville hadn't when I first raised it.

**Friday 18 December**

Denis Howell told me that Nicholas Soames was going around saying I was a shit. I ought not to have given to him (Denis) the job of picking up the Sunday Sports Bill from the Lords but to himself. I said, 'But he knew all along you were going to pick it up,' and Denis said, 'That's exactly what I told him.' I said, 'In any case Nicholas Soames is such a buffooning elephant he makes a terrible mess of everything. He couldn't begin to handle the matter with delicacy and caution and circumspection as you will if we are going to get it through.'

**Saturday 19 December**

It was a mild day at Ascot.

Just before the fourth race we were told we had to be at the Royal Box.

I talked to Queen Elizabeth the Queen Mother for quite a time and sat beside her. She made a bit of a show from time to time of saying, 'We ought to watch this race you know,' and she pulled out some glasses [binoculars] and said, 'They're not mine. I can't see anything with them.' I said, 'Have you the slightest idea what's going on, Ma'am?' and she said, 'Well not really.' She added it didn't look good if she didn't pretend to be watching. I said, 'I'll try and get you a better pair of glasses. Trust House Forte gave everybody a marvellous pair at the Arc de Triomphe lunch.'

I told her I was reading this book about Oscar Wilde[24] and how badly the country had treated him. She said, 'Yes, it was a fearful

24. Richard Ellmann's biography, just published.

tragedy.' 'When you read this book you see that he was doomed from the start. He was really hoping for some dramatically tragic fate and everything he did led to it. But still the country were vile about him being a homosexual.' 'Yes, they were much too strict about those things then. But now I think they've gone too far the other way.'

I told her about my play and she was fascinated. She said she had met Allan Davis and thinks he is very clever. 'What is it about?' 'It's a little bit about politics,' I said being unwilling to tell her all about it.

She said, 'What a marvellous thing. A new career, to add to all your others, as a playwright.'

After I had been talking to Queen Elizabeth the Queen Mother for a bit, the Queen herself came in. She started talking to me. It is the first time I ever had a real conversation with her. We talked for about ten minutes or so. She wanted to know all about the Sunday Sports Bill. 'Whether the government will give time or not I don't know. I am friendly with Mrs Thatcher and I will try to see what I can do with her.' The Queen said, 'She is not a very sporting lady.' 'No, but she has at last promised me that she will go racing. I've been trying to get her to go for years.' The Queen said, 'Oh that would be a great triumph if you pulled it off.'

We talked about last Wednesday night when she had her dance at Claridge's. She said, 'It began years ago when a number of friends of ours who had all got married in or about the same year decided to celebrate their anniversaries every year at Claridge's.' I gather that somebody else pays for it.

The Queen was in a friendly, gentle mood. I didn't feel the touch of severity I have sometimes felt. It was charming when she said several times to her mother, 'I'm going now, Mummy,' or 'I'm going to do this now, Mummy.'

During the time I was there Michael Oswald[25] came up and took me on one side and said, 'I hope you will agree to this but the new Press Secretary at the Palace, his name is Janvrin,[26] would very much like to have a quiet dinner with you and me because he wants to

25. Manager, The Royal Studs, and husband of Lady Angela Oswald, Woman of the Bedchamber to the Queen Mother.

26. Robin Janvrin, press secretary, 1987–90, assistant private secretary, 1990–5, deputy private secretary, 1996–8; he succeeded Sir Robert Fellowes as private secretary to the Queen in 1998; knight 1998.

minimize the number of mistakes and avoid the jams and difficulties that so often occur in the press.'

I have a feeling it must be prompted by the Queen or Prince Philip and she wanted to have a little talk with me first to make up her mind whether she liked the look of me.

**Sunday 20 December**

Spoke to Margaret. First we talked about Willie. It was uncertain whether he would be well enough to do the job in the Lords the old way. I suggested Humphrey Atkins[27] now Lord Colnbrook. She said she didn't think he had quite the scope or experience.

'The qualities required,' she said, 'are bonhomie and steel.'

'Did you see my Sunday Sports Bill got its third reading?' She said, 'Yes.' (I had already spoken to Douglas Hurd this afternoon and said that I would raise it with Margaret to see if I could persuade her to give some time which he thought unlikely.)

She said, 'You will have to get together a large group and go on pushing and pushing. I don't see any chance of government time this year. We've got masses of legislation coming.'

On the community charge I said, 'We've still got a lot more propaganda to do but I think we're beginning to get it across. This is a matter of paying for services rather than a tax.'

Mrs Thatcher said, 'My father always said that everybody should pay something even if it's only sixpence.'

**Wednesday 23 December**

At the Montagus there was a very good dinner.

Verushka told her part of the famous Chatsworth story. It was the occasion when a party was staying, as we did every year at that time, at Chatsworth as Andrew's guests for the week-end of the St Leger.[28]

Andrew used to love these parties. We would get mildly drunk and play strange games on the billiard table banging balls about with our hands and running round and goodness knows what. There were always vast quantities of marvellous champagne and Château Lafite '61 and the equivalent.

Debo [Duchess of Devonshire] hated these parties partly because

27. Former Chief Whip, Secretary of State for Northern Ireland and Lord Privy Seal.
28. The St Leger is run at Doncaster, south Yorkshire, not far from Chatsworth, the seat of the Duke of Devonshire, in Derbyshire.

Andrew enjoyed them so much and she thought they were distinctly non-intellectual which they were.

On this particular occasion Andrew had been going through one of his bad drinking spells. He had injections or something of that kind to stop him drinking but they hadn't worked long enough and he was in a fairly maudlin state. He was not too good on the Friday night before the St Leger. Debo was getting increasingly cross.

In the morning she summoned all the guests and asked us to leave at once. Her reason was that it would give Andrew a shock and bring him to his senses and cure his drinking. Andrew she always called 'Claude' among her intimates – a strange name and mildly derogatory.

All present, except for Jakie Astor, Verushka and myself, said they would go and quite understood. Jakie said that Andrew was one of his oldest friends and he couldn't do a thing like that. I said, 'I've come up for the St Leger and I'm Chairman of the Tote and that's why I'm here. I'm jolly well going to see it. And what is more I propose to stay as usual until after lunch on Sunday. Andrew is one of my oldest friends.' Verushka of course backed me and Jakie.

Debo was furious.

She drove everyone else off – there must have been about ten of them who sheepishly started to go their ways. Then poor Andrew appeared and began dishing out the badges for the racecourse, and the grouse and the picnic were all being put into the back of the cars. When he offered badges to these friends, they said they couldn't take them, they were not staying.

When I went back to my bedroom Stoker [the Devonshires' son] rang. He said, 'You're one of my father's oldest friends and my mother would particularly value it if you would leave now and give my father the shock he needs.' I said, 'Stoker, I fear I cannot do that. He is an old friend of mine, an older friend of mine than your mother is. I cannot take part in his public humiliation in his own house.'

At dinner that night Andrew was in fairly good condition, just a bit gloomy naturally. Jakie and Verushka and I made jolly jokes and so forth. After we had gone to bed I wondered where Andrew was. I went out to have a look and he was not in his bedroom. I told Verushka I couldn't see him in the drawing-room either. Verushka picked up the story here.

She went into the drawing-room which was in darkness and there was Andrew crying. She sat with him for an hour or so and comforted him and told him it was not so serious as all that and cheered him up and finally he went to bed in a more or less tranquil condition. The next morning he gave her a beautiful silver box and told her that she had saved his life. He had been at that moment totally suicidal.

Jakie wrote later to Debo and got a brush off. I never wrote to Debo. Since that day neither of us, two of Andrew's oldest friends, particularly Jakie, has ever been asked back to Chatsworth. Sometimes I see Debo with Andrew at a distance and then she comes forward and calls me Uncle Woodrow and kisses me with great affection but I can see that she hates me. Andrew is then sheepish.

This conversation all arose from David saying, 'Why did you make Prince Michael a Board member after Andrew had insisted on going?'

I said, 'I wanted somebody who would share in my ceremonial duties. Andrew was very good at it and would go to the Tote Ebor[29] always when I was in Italy and hand over the prize. I hoped Prince Michael would do the same but he hasn't done much.'

I am wondering if I can now get rid of him. David said, 'If you had only asked me before, Sonny Marlborough would have loved to have done the job. He is very keen on horses. He's not a member of the Jockey Club and thinks they are awful.'

**25 December**

I found a Christmas card from the MCC in Australia 1932–33 tour, the great bodyline tour. There they all are in pictures drawn by Arthur Mailey standing on a cut-out of Australia. D. R. Jardine the Captain is holding a lance which carries the words, 'Christmas greetings.' On his right is Bob.[30]

I asked Bob this morning was it worth anything. He said he didn't think it would be worth much. He hadn't signed it. Obviously he must have sent it me at the time. I would have been fourteen.

Nursery tea at Blenheim.[31] All conducted on an old fashioned basis.

Sonny delighted with my joke present of a large china hand which when you put a glass on it moves across the table towards you but when it gets to the edge doesn't fall off.

Part of tea time spent with the organizers, Rosemary Muir (Sonny's sister) and some of her children, trying to fix the treasure hunt for

---

29. The Ebor Handicap, sponsored at this time by the Tote, is an annual race at York.
30. WW's cousin Bob Wyatt, the England cricketer.
31. Seat of the Duke and Duchess of Marlborough.

after dinner. Little rhymes for each clue. Eight clues. There are to be twenty couples, paired together. Forty-three people coming to dinner.

My dressing-room about three times the size of my bedroom in Cavendish Avenue. Verushka's bedroom next door is huge, hung with marvellous tapestries. Our suite is called the Sunderland Rooms. Doors marked in the same passage carry ancient labels. One is called Lady-maid's Cupboard. Another is called Housemaid's Heights. When I looked through the door there were stone steps going ever upwards.

Dinner at a great long table for all but about eight who had to sit at a side round table. It is in the Great Hall with marble floors. A wonderful piece of architecture by Vanbrugh and with the decorations by Laguerre.[32] Thornhill[33] was to have done them but wanted to charge too much. He did some of the other decorations in the house, then they switched to Laguerre who was cheaper. The result is marvellous. The ceiling is concave but doesn't look it.

Masses of lovely flowers. All the grand silver had been brought out. Sonny says he has only got thirty-six silver plates left so there are seven or eight who have to go without them.

On my left sat Rosemary Muir and on my right sat Rosita. On her right sat Charles Price the American Ambassador. Verushka and Carol Price sat on either side of Sonny.

For the second course we had to go up to help ourselves at a semi-buffet where the chefs and other servants were standing behind. When I came back I tried to remove the silver plate as I now had a different plate and didn't want to put it on top of the silver plate, as had been my soup plate. I tried to move it. The butler came and said, 'My Lord, you must put that back. You are supposed to have your next course on the silver plate.'

When Rosemary came back she tried to do the same and was told that she could not. She thought this very funny as she had been born in the house and lived there all her youth and childhood, naturally as a daughter of the Duke. I said, 'I'm so glad you did the same as I did because I thought it was just that I was unaccustomed to eating in marble halls.'

Sonny made a little speech and there was a presentation to a butler

32. French artist (1668–1721) who also decorated Chatsworth, Petworth, Hampton Court Palace.
33. English historical and decorative painter (1675–1734) whose works include the decorations to Wren's hall at Greenwich and the dome of St Paul's Cathedral.

who Rosemary remembered coming when she was seven or eight. He had been there for fifty years. He was a very good looking young man and still was quite good looking. He has never married but he always played the field, I was told. He was given a video.

The butler apologized that he was in his shirt sleeves when we arrived and he went to the car with a maid to fetch our luggage. The house is well equipped with servants, footmen and valets hopping in and out and lady's maids etc. Everything laid out beautifully, unpacked beautifully. The rooms upstairs are warmer than the ones we had when we stayed there five or six years ago for the New Year.

The non-staying guests included Charles Price and his wife and a lot of neighbours.

At the end of the dinner Charles Price insisted on making a speech. He got up and said, 'I would like to say a few words.' Apparently he came last year and did the same. It was excruciatingly embarrassing. It was on the lines of 'Here am I the poor boy from Iowa greatly honoured to be having my Christmas dinner with a Duke and his family and his friends. I never realized what a marvellous time I would have when I came to be Ambassador in Britain and that I would be having a dinner in such a fantastic place. All that is best in England . . .' and so on and so on. The poor man didn't know that he caused his listeners immense trouble in desperately trying to keep a straight face.

It was made worse by Mark Weinberg who was there with a video film camera and when the Ambassador got up to speak he turned the light on it and so the Ambassador became even worse, as though he was addressing some ghastly election meeting in the USA.

I never had a Christmas dinner in more splendid surroundings. I had woodcock. We had had our Christmas dinner the night before with Nicholas and Caroline and their two children.

The treasure hunt was quite amusing. One of Rosemary's sons cheated and stole all the clues at about the number two point so nobody could go on looking for the rest properly.

Sonny had some water bottled with a Blenheim label. He hasn't produced very much and was interested when I told him that in Cornwall we had this vast source of water, millions upon millions of bottles of very good stuff. We were just beginning to sell it. He said, 'It's very costly doing that.' I said, 'I know.' 'What have you started with?' I said, 'It's about £50,000 that my brother has put into it to get it going. We have just started selling.'

Breakfast was a very jolly English country house breakfast. There were fishcakes and I had one. There were mushrooms and bacon and egg and sausages. I had a lot of all of those. Excellent.

Sonny still seems to be pretty rich. He has a very large farm. They live in the big house a few months of the year and they live at Leigh House most of the rest of the year. But the house we stayed in was better and more lavishly run than Chatsworth and certainly than Badminton. It must be the best ducal house going at the moment. The servants, the chef and everything else must cost a fortune.

Mark Weinberg was very full of himself, going to Margaret Thatcher's Boxing Day lunch party. He said of Jacob that, 'You can always tell what your rating in the world is by watching him at a party or reception. He speaks to them all in the order, beginning at the top with the most important person and moving downwards.' He added, 'He has to do that because a banker's job is to have information.' I laughed and said, 'You mean like a superior George Weidenfeld who does the same but more obviously than Jacob.' He agreed.

Before we went Rosita kept trying to stop us going. I talked to her for a bit and she said to me, 'I like that blue tie you've got on this morning.' (It was a blue bow tie with white spots.) 'You wore it at Ascot last summer.' I said, 'Good gracious. How on earth can you remember it?'

She said when Sonny was without a valet, and if they were away without a valet, he gets in a terrible state saying, 'What tie shall I wear? Now help me, you've got to take this seriously.' She says he is very vain about what he wears and particularly about his ties and he spends hours on it.

We had a discussion about liking or disliking people.

Then Mary Rothermere[34] got mentioned. I said that when Verushka and I got married secretly, we went the same night to a ball at Warwick House they were giving and I always had a sentimental affection for Mary.

She said, 'She was horrible. She made poor Esmond give up Daylesford in his old age because it was costing quite a lot of money which she felt was coming out of her inheritance. She was cruel and grasping.' She went on, 'She's also two-faced. I can be very bitchy and catty,' and she held her hands out and shaped them into claws. At that moment her face had a little bit of the look of a lioness which she has got in the way she does her bright coloured hair.

---

34. (d 1992); widow of 2nd Viscount Rothermere.

**Sunday 27 December**

A jolly lunch at Bowden. William Rees-Mogg and Gillian were there. We went for a brief walk before lunch. Arnold showed me some pictures of himself getting the freedom of the City of London and Peter Levene was prominent among the guests. He is something to do with the issuing of these freedoms. His wife was also there. She looked quite pretty.

I said, 'But he is your enemy.' 'No, I don't think he is.' I said, 'You're naïve if you think he isn't.' 'He will certainly drive as hard a bargain as he can with me but I don't think now he is my enemy.'

Arnold said, 'She's a marvellous woman, Margaret.' Just before Gorbachev's arrival for his brief visit he reminded her of something she had taken up with Gorbachev in Moscow. This was that the deal should go ahead by which GEC provided automation for an engineering plant. It had all been agreed before and then nothing had happened and they were about to lose a lot of money. Arnold, never thinking she would have the time at the Brize Norton meeting to mention it, said if she did have the time would she do so? She did and a few days later it came through from Moscow that the deal was now to go ahead and everything was OK.

He said she did the same thing with the Malaysian government when GEC was trying to sell them something big and Malaysia had a policy of not buying British because they were annoyed with Britain about something.

I said, 'In that case I don't know why you query her judgement about the community charge.' Both he and Rees-Mogg were ridiculous about it. Arnold was going to vote against it.

I said to William, 'How would you like it if I came into your antiquarian book shop and you said "This book is £3,000" and I said, "Oh yes, but I'm rather poor. Can I pay you £2,000?" which is what you're asking people to be allowed to do in relation to the services provided by local administration.'

Later I spoke to Mrs T and said that Arnold was thinking of voting against the community charge. She said, 'Good lord, he mustn't do that.' 'No, I'll see to it that he doesn't. He and Rees-Mogg were talking a lot of twaddle about it.'

I talked to her about privatization of the Tote.

She said, 'Now you have three years to do it in and you can discuss it all with Douglas,' and I said, 'Yes.' She said, 'Who owns the Tote?' I said, 'Well nobody does. It's like the TSB (Trustee Savings Bank). The government never put any money into it, it raises its own money. In fact it has been expressly said that the government won't stand behind us if we are in difficulties.'

I said, 'It is not a monopoly and it only has about one per cent of the whole of the gambling on racehorses. It prevents the Big Four bookmakers becoming a total monopoly because they have to watch their step and remain competitive in line with us.' She began to see the point.

**Monday 28 December**

Andrew Sinclair and Sonia plus Allan Davis come for scrambled eggs and smoked salmon, champagne and Tondonia white wine. And some Stilton.

Andrew in a very friendly mood. I'm beginning to like him better. I particularly like him better because he says how good my stories were which I wrote when very young in *English Story* and how fascinating the whole thing is.[35] I said, 'I'll take you upstairs and show you a file on some of these books. But they are all in a great muddle.' We found some letters. One in handwriting from Alun Lewis, quite a long one, some from Osbert Sitwell, Elizabeth Bowen, etc. He thought it all very fascinating. If we could build it up properly he thought he could sell the whole damn thing for £50,000 to some university in Texas which is assembling all this kind of stuff.

In the afternoon I went to Kempton and saw Isaac Newton[36] trailing off at the back. Nicky Henderson, the trainer, thinks he may have got the virus which his stable has had. If he has got the virus then it would be some time before he recovers and can run again. So not too promising.

Sonia said that she was talking to Paul Johnson the other night and she said I was the person with the most influence on Mrs Thatcher. Paul bridled and said, 'Oh, no, not at all. She doesn't take any notice of him at all.' Then he added, 'I see her every week' (which I know not to be true). He was then mildly catty about me.

---

35. WW edited the ten volumes of *English Story* from 1940 to 1950 with contributors including Stephen Spender, Angus Wilson, William Sansom, J. Maclaren-Ross, Alex Comfort and Denton Welch.

36. The horse WW had a share in.

I said, 'Of course it's very funny. It's just like the Court of Queen Elizabeth I. The courtiers, among which I suppose I must include myself slightly, are all madly jealous of each other and run each other down and say they are the only one that counts. And anyone who has access to her tends to blow it up a great deal.' I on the other hand have been trying to minimize it.

**Tuesday 29 December**

The Montagus come for smoked salmon and spinach soup and Sainsbury's champagne and off we go to the theatre to see Jeffrey Archer's play.

I expected to be bored and to hate it. It was a very well told story, raced along pretty fast except for the first act which I found a little bit tedious and nearly went to sleep.

**Wednesday 30 December**

Frank Johnson at the *Times* told me that the three peerages were very dull on the whole and all as expected. Robert Armstrong, retiring from being Secretary to the Cabinet. Lord Donaldson, Master of the Rolls. And the Chief Rabbi. I said, 'Why the Chief Rabbi?' 'Oh he's a very good man at answering all that Church of England stuff about the Inner Cities.'[37]

**Thursday 31 December**

The Honours List. Anthony Powell[38] has got a Companion of Honour. I had recommended a knighthood but I think Companion of Honour is better.

Arnold and Netta to New Year's Eve dinner. Just the five of us at a small table in the dining-room.

He has just made his son Simon a Director of GEC. The poor man hopes he will be his successor when he goes. If he is, I think that would be a disaster for GEC. Simon has not got the ability to communicate with others or to understand them or even sympathize with them that Arnold has. He is somewhat cold. His brain is not good enough. He is no leader. For all his faults, Arnold has a giving-out character which inspires people to like him, though he maintains he is really horrid –

---

37. See 1 December 1985.
38. His novels include the *Music of Time* sequence.

which of course he is not, being a kind-hearted, fair-minded man which I don't think his son is.[39]

At the end of dinner we went up to see my mother-in-law at the top of the house and wish her a happy New Year. She was pleased.

39. The Hon. Simon Weinstock died of cancer in 1996.

# 1988

**Saturday 2 January**

Rang Margaret to wish her a happy tour of Africa as could be possible in such a region.

I congratulated her on beating Asquith's record.[1] 'Not yet,' she said, 'it's tomorrow.'

**Monday 4 January**

Sir Edward Pickering[2] (Pick) and Jonathan Saunders, a legal expert on copyright from Theodore Goddard [solicitors], came to lunch. We discussed at length the Copyright Bill[3] now going through the Lords.

Pick said Fleet Street has only just woken up to the changes it would make, particularly in regard to removing the responsibilities of the editor and giving all kinds of weird rights to journalist staff and otherwise. It is a sort of charter for the National Union of Journalists to stir up trouble by law.

A letter by hand from Douglas Hurd asking me whether I would be willing to serve for another three years as Chairman of the Tote from April 30th 1988. I replied yes.

**Tuesday 5 January**

Tote Board meeting.

Prince Michael sat on my left. He uttered not one word throughout

---

1. For length of time as Prime Minister. She had been Prime Minister since 4 May 1979; Asquith was continuously Prime Minister from 6 April 1908 until 5 December 1916, eight years and nearly eight months. The next record, which Mrs Thatcher did not equal, was Lord Liverpool's, nearly fifteen years from May 1812 until he died on 17 February 1827.
2. Executive vice chairman, Times Newspapers, at this time, and director, William Collins, publishers.
3. *Inter alia* it gave staff journalists as well as freelances the right to assert the 'moral rights' of their work i.e. to be identified whenever their work was published and for their work not be modified unless changes were reasonable.

the whole proceedings, reminding me of what David[4] had said and making me wish that I had never had him there.

**Wednesday 6 January**

Went to a party [given] by Hugh Thomas to celebrate his coming visit to Mexico. Forgot to ask him why he was going to Mexico but there was present the Ambassadress from Venezuela (pretty) and her husband. She was an economist. I had to confess I didn't really know where Venezuela was or much about it.

Talked to Isaiah Berlin. He asked me how long I wanted to live. I said, 'Indefinitely.' He said, 'Would that apply if you had only one eye, one leg, one ear, one arm?' I said, 'Yes, provided my brain was in good condition.' He said that was also his answer but one would never know whether one's brain was in good condition or not and therefore wouldn't be much bothered about it.

**Friday 8 January**

I wish I hadn't been feeling so odd since Christmas. The energy ebbs and flows. It was a tremendous effort doing the article about the new Copyright Bill for the *Times* which they are going to publish on Tuesday[5] as that is the last day of the committee stage in the Lords of the Bill.

**Saturday 9 January**

Went to see *Lettice and Lovage*[6] at the request of Allan Davis. It had three acts. He said my play had to have two acts and we reduced it from three to two. The speeches were immensely long frequently, much longer than anything in my play before I cut the speeches down. However, it was a jolly good play.

Allan Davis tells me that he has some hope of Edward Fox and the play is on its way to him.

Damn, damn, damn. I wish this energy would come back and consistently so. Verushka wants me to see the doctor. Doctors are all

---

4. See 23 December 1987.
5. In the article on 12 January WW opposed the Bill, concluding: 'There is unlikely to be another copyright bill for 30 years or so. To implement this one, ignoring as it does the nature and economics of newspaper and journal production and the changes which advancing computerisation is bringing, would be highly retrograde.'
6. By Peter Shaffer.

quacks. When I wasn't walking properly, Dr Collier sent me to have my brain scanned as though I was a lunatic. It turned out in the end that all that was required was the Sinemet pill recommended by Professor Ricci in Italy and endorsed by Professor Thomas in London.

For some days I have not drunk any wine. That no doubt is contributing to my loss of weight.

I am now down to 12 stone 2 pounds.

**Sunday 10 January**

She asked if I had heard the news about Willie which went out half an hour ago. I had not. She has put Belstead[7] in charge. She said, 'He is very courteous.' 'Yes, he does speak to Their Lordships in a manner which they like but whether he has the skill of Willie is another matter.'

It's very sad about Willie. She said the doctors insisted that he should give it up.

I began to feel slightly younger. Willie Whitelaw is the same age as myself and I don't feel like dropping dead at the moment though I've had a curious lack of appetite since Christmas. Today I was only twelve stone. When I came back from Italy I was just on thirteen stone if not slightly above it. The trouble is it makes me look too thin in the face and more aged than I feel, which is a bit of bad public relations. If I were a woman I would contemplate having a face lift.

I also said to Mrs Thatcher, 'Please read pages eleven and twelve of the *Sunday Telegraph* today. It's about why intellectuals look down on you. All the usual tosh. Peter Hall[8] and people like that.' She said, 'Good gracious. Why is Peter Hall saying things like that? I sat next to him at a dinner not long ago and he thanked me for all I've done for the arts.'

I told her to read the bit that Kingsley Amis had said about her. 'He's a great admirer of yours. A very fine writer. There was a man called Sir J. C. (John) Squire[9] before the War who used to be an old drunk but Tory inclined and he was given a knighthood. Nothing like such a good writer as Kingsley Amis. He really is superb. It wouldn't matter if Kingsley Amis got a bit drunk at the Garrick. Nobody knows about that generally. He is a great supporter of yours and it would

7. Lord Belstead, previously Deputy Leader, House of Lords, was appointed Leader in Whitelaw's place.
8. Sir Peter Hall, theatre, film and opera director; director, National Theatre 1973–88.
9. (1884–1958); literary journalist, essayist, editor and poet; knight 1933.

show that you really do care about the arts, particularly about people who write well.'

She said she would make a careful note about it. I know he'd be thrilled.[10]

I asked her what she thought about the Mellor affair.[11] She said, 'The least said the soonest mended. He's very young.' I said, 'Yes, some of what he said was counterproductive. It is a much more complex situation.' She said, 'Yes, you have to remember the Jews are very talented people.' (She underlined in her words 'very talented'.)

**Monday 11 January**

Lord Ferrers is to be the Deputy Leader of the House. It was a Lord Ferrers who was the last peer to be hanged for killing a servant after a trial by his peers.[12] So in our variegated system one day a murderer, and the next Deputy Leader of the Lords.

How agreeable the Lords is. On leaving the Tote I decided to pop in to the Lords on the way home to see if anything was going on.

Henry Porchester was sitting high at the back among the crossbenchers near Lady Hylton-Foster. When he saw me he came down and said, 'I have my brother-in-law who is the Republican Senator from Wyoming. He has got a very important role in the armaments reductions affair. Will you come and have a drink with him in five or ten minutes?' which I did.

This Senator, Malcolm Wallop, was remarkably intelligent. He says he has an official observer position. He can go to Geneva, Moscow, anywhere he likes and ask questions as to whether the agreement on the reduction of Cruises and similar type weapons has been met or not.

He is terrified that they will try and get the inter-continental ballistic missile treaty signed and ratified before Reagan leaves office.[13] He says the more rush there is, the worse the agreement will be from our point of view.

---

10. He was knighted in 1990.
11. David Mellor (b 1949), Minister of State, Foreign and Commonwealth Office, had been reported as rebuking an Israeli officer about Israeli treatment of prisoners.
12. The 4th Earl (1720–60) pleaded insanity but was condemned and hanged at Tyburn for killing his land steward.
13. The presidential elections (November 1988) were looming.

**Tuesday 12 January**

Andrew Sinclair came to look through the *English Story* files. He thought there was something the University of Texas would be interested in.

He also suggested that I should suggest to Collins to do a volume of the best stories in *English Story* during the forties so I wrote a letter to Ian Chapman. I own the copyrights of all these things.

He also took *Stories of the Forties*, one volume. I had forgotten that I had edited two with Reginald Moore.

I am beginning to like Andrew Sinclair quite a lot. He is warming up and talks about himself and the book he is doing about the forties.[14] He is going to reproduce a number of stories including my story 'Hell's Corner' from *Kingdom Come*.

Dinner with Sir Robert Haslam, Chairman of the Coal Board, and Norman Woodhouse the Public Relations Chief Officer. Just three of us.

We had a long rambling talk. I think Haslam is pretty good as Chairman.

He would not object at all to coal being privatized. But it would really have to be in one unit to make sense. 'Who for example would buy Yorkshire by itself,' he asked, 'with all its problems in its pits?'

He said that one of the difficulties with his operation is that he can't pay board members (executive) more than the Treasury will allow him to. He had a marvellous man in charge of the pension fund but he has gone off to another job where he gets double the money.

His own case is different. He said he wouldn't go for less than what he was getting from Tate & Lyle and his other commercial jobs. Even so he could have asked for more. A man running a business like his should be getting a quarter of a million a year.

He said Mrs Thatcher was very difficult about paying board members more than they get at the moment, probably because the civil servants think nobody should get paid more than they do. And she says Cabinet Ministers get less which contradicts her own market philosophy.

I said, 'How have you been able to improve coal?' and he said it was because basically he has a good management team. He broke up the cosy arrangements his predecessors had with the NUM and let

---

14. *The War Decade: An Anthology of the 1940s* (1989).

them get on with managing for the first time. It's remarkable that they have almost doubled their productivity – though he agreed they wouldn't have been able to do that without the huge amount of money put in by the government for investment in new equipment. It isn't that the miners are working harder but they are actually using the new apparatus they have without so much restriction as in the past.

He thought it was likely that Scargill would win[15] although that was very undesirable. I said, 'From the Conservative point of view it may not be a bad thing if Scargill wins. They'd have their bogey man still. But that might be a short sighted view because my theory is that the more unions get reformed and are representative of their members, the members will tend to vote more for the Tories than they did in the past.'

We mapped out what I might say on Sunday in a last minute attempt to sway miners who read my column.

**Thursday 14 January**

In the afternoon went to the Department of the Environment where I saw Mr Patrick Rock, an official of the Department who is an expert on the community charge. I am trying to find out all about it so that I can write on it in the *Times* and in the *News of the World*. And speak in the Lords on it.

**Friday 15 January**

Beginning to feel better. The *News of the World* article not such a struggle. Finished fairly early which was useful as Abdul Al Ghazzi was coming to lunch.

Just before he arrived Charles Wilson, editor of the *Times*, rang. He thanked me for the copyright article which he thought had been very effective. He then said that he wanted slightly to change the format of his feature page. He wants to have my article and the others writing on that page to be headed Political Commentary so would I kindly attach my articles always to some political hook. I thought that might be difficult with regard to promotions for, say, better investigation into human nutrition. However, I went along with him.

Abdul was in ebullient form as usual. He says his carpet should not have been put on the floor but hung on the wall. But added that would not be possible in this house with all its pictures.

---

15. The election for president of the NUM, to be held on 22 January.

He has done nothing about organizing representation at the Heveningham Hall footpath inquiry on February 9th. In the end I undertook to find counsel to represent him at the inquiry. I spent much of the afternoon getting hold of Maunsell at Goodman Derrick and urging him to look for a counsel which he did very quickly.

I told Abdul, 'You've got to really take this last opportunity and get it done. It's extraordinary that you were not represented at all at the last inquiry.' 'I thought it was a matter for the government.' 'You simply do not understand how democracy works in England. People demand these inquiries. They can give evidence and if the person who wants the footpath altered is not there he simply loses the case.'

When Abdul had gone Miss Cook discovered a bag in the hall. It contained two bottles of 1978 Dom Pérignon champagne and two boxes containing ten huge cigars each of Davidoff Dom Pérignon cigars which are very good.

Later in the afternoon Rupert rings from Aspen where he is lying in bed. He has torn a ligament skiing. Sounded in high spirits. Says he was coming to England shortly.

I told him he caused a stir by buying another large stake in Pearson's and he said, 'Good.' He loves startling people.

He thanked me for my copyright article in the *Times* on Tuesday. He thought it extraordinary that Richard Marsh[16] had done nothing about it.

Bill Adams of the Stable Lads' Association rang.

It was agreed that the lads' pay should go up by ten per cent in the first year beginning now and four per cent in the next year, though it would be higher if inflation went above four per cent.

I think my becoming a Trustee quite shook the Trainers' Federation. Without my having done that I don't believe they would have gone much beyond an inflation rated increase.

**Saturday 16 January**

Dinner at Harold Lever's. The first time he has been up for weeks. He had a stroke – another one. He looked much better than I expected him to be. He was still up and talking when we left at 12.00.

Samuel Brittan, Leon's brother, was there. He is terrified of what

---

16. Labour politician; chairman, Newspaper Publishers' Association, 1976–90; life peer 1981.

Rupert Murdoch may be doing. Sam works on the *Financial Times*.[17] He says they are all in a great tizzy. I said, 'All he wants to do is to get involved with some of your publishing and develop his own thereby. He promised he would never take a majority shareholding in Collins. He could have done easily and legally but he never did. Why should he do any more than he says he is going to do with the *Financial Times* and the Pearson Group?'

He said, 'If you are so confident that Rupert is not going to buy the *Financial Times* would you pay my salary for ten years if he did?' 'First of all, you wouldn't need that because he wouldn't sack you. Second, it's not going to happen anyway so why should I make such a grotesque promise?'

The Prince of Wales and his staff are not very polite. Some weeks ago I sent round to him *The Wyatts: An Architectural Dynasty.* I thought he would be interested in it because of his concern with architecture. This morning I got a letter from an assistant to the Equerry to HRH The Prince of Wales. I was addressed as Sir Woodrow Wyatt. The letter began Dear Sir and was signed Yours faithfully, Flying Officer Susanna Perkins WRAF. That is the last time I shall ever be friendly towards that man. He might try learning some manners from his grandmother.

**Sunday 17 January**

Told Margaret I am worried about the public relations for the NHS.

She is clearly worried about Moore.[18] She says, 'We will have to see what happens on Tuesday when we've got a great debate on the NHS.' I see her difficulty. He has only just been appointed. He was seriously ill with pneumonia. He is not on top of his job. How could she suddenly fling him out?

I told her about Malcolm Wallop the Senator from Wyoming and she was very interested. She said, 'We're watching Gorbachev very closely now. They still keep trying to get something into the treaty which would prevent the Americans doing what they ought to be doing about SDI.'

Spoke to John Walsh, Scargill's opponent for President in the ballot of miners on January 22nd. He thinks he has got a reasonable chance.

---

17. Principal economic commentator, *Financial Times*, since 1966; knight 1993.
18. John Moore, Secretary of State for Social Services, 1987–8; life peer 1992.

He thinks the ballot in most places is more or less secret. I said to him, 'Do they still have the system which they used to have at some pits of asking you to show how you voted before you put the ballot paper in the box?' He said, 'They may do in some places.'

He said that it would all be done by branch officials who are on Scargill's side. Nevertheless there were some people in each branch who would be on his side and would probably check to stop the more outrageous fiddles.

**Monday 18 January**

Dr Collier came. He took some blood from me. I hate that. I can't bear to look at it while it's going on. He tested my urine. That can show quite a lot of things.

I told him that I thought I had some viral infection. I just hoped it wasn't anything more fundamental. I have lost something like 10 pounds since Christmas in weight.

**Tuesday 19 January**

Long meeting at Kempton Park of the Levy Board. We go through the performance of an annual strategy review regarding what is to be done about racing.

Sat next to Ian Trethowan at lunch. He is very friendly. I told him he'd like being in the Lords and he said, yes, he would like that very much. I said, 'You're too young at the moment. Immature. But maybe you will get it later.'

Ian has lots of lovely jobs including being Chairman of Thames Television which must bring him in quite a bit. He is also a Trustee of the British Museum, God knows why, and a Director of the *Times* newspaper. I don't know why Rupert put him there because he can be feeble in a crisis.

Ian said to me that he was glad to hear that I was doing another three years at the Tote. He had been told on the grapevine. I think he keeps in very close touch with Douglas Hurd. I don't fully trust him but he is likeable enough and hasn't done a bad job with the Levy Board.

Spoke to Dr Collier. The tests are very curious about my blood. It seems that the white corpuscles are having a job in keeping up with the red corpuscles. The red corpuscles are dropping into sedimentation. I don't really follow all this but what it means is he thinks I have been fighting a virus, as I thought.

**Wednesday 20 January**

Had a letter from Marcus Binney[19] who is running a thing called *Landscape* in Jersey in which he tells me he is going to write about Heveningham Hall. Wouldn't I take out a subscription to his new magazine? I wrote him a fierce letter telling him he had been purveying a lot of inaccuracies about Heveningham Hall and what Abdul Al Ghazzi was doing there.

**Thursday 21 January**

Maunsell from Goodman Derrick tells me that the case for the footpath at Heveningham Hall is not as clear-cut as I might have thought. He has read the Inspector's report at the last inquiry and he has sent me a copy. He also urges me not to use the figure of £5 million that Abdul Al Ghazzi has spent as the figures he has seen show it is much less than that.

Dinner at The Other Club.

Had a curious argument with Peter Walker about the community charge. He says it will be absolutely useless. The idea of paying out money on social security for the recipient to pass on for their twenty per cent of the community charge won't work. 'What are you going to do when they receive the money on social security and have spent it and won't pay their community charge? Are you going to put them all in prison or send bailiffs to take widows' furniture out?'

But he has always been opposed to all the economic policies of Mrs Thatcher from the start. If he had had his way the Tories would never have won another election after 1979.

I said, 'Do you say all these things in Cabinet?' 'Well, my position is well known.' What he means is he never makes any protest in the Cabinet with Mrs Thatcher but likes to keep on side with his wet friends.

**Friday 22 January**

Still losing weight a bit. However felt very well today.

Dinner party. Irwin Stelzer and Cita Stelzer. The party was really for them. Difficult to find anybody in London on a Friday night but we got Peter and Elaine Rawlinson and Andrew and Sonia Sinclair.

Irwin was very uppish about the attacks on the freedom of the

---

19. Writer on architecture and heritage; president of SAVE Britain's Heritage since 1984.

press, as he saw them, by the government. He picked the wrong person in Peter Rawlinson. Peter said the government has to do everything it can to make civil servants, particularly those in the Secret Services, honour their oaths not to reveal anything they know. That's nothing to do with the freedom of the press.

Elaine asked me, 'What would you do if your father was to come into this room now and you had six hours' conversation with him?' It was a very good question. I often wonder what I would say if I met him again. I don't know what it would be. Would I say to him, 'I'm sorry I didn't get on with you when I was thirteen (that was the year he died) but I didn't realize you weren't as clever as everybody said you were'?[20]

**Sunday 24 January**

Still losing weight. Am down to 11 stone 13 now. I have lost a stone since Christmas. I felt very odd this morning but as the day wore on began to feel better.

Went to the Zoo in the morning with Caroline Banszky and her two little children. Genevra runs about excited. Gave her a helium-filled parrot balloon. There was a charming gorilla mother with a gorilla baby which she was nursing tenderly. The father, a great brute of a fellow, prowled in the background and saw no harm came to his wife and child. A better family than many humans have.

**Tuesday 26 January**

Told Mrs T that her *Panorama* interview with Dimbleby (David) last night was excellent. She gave exactly the right impression that something is being done to improve the Health Service and find out what the hell is wrong with it while not panicking and saying we are going to throw masses of money at it.

She asked if I knew people in the private health service. They want to make sure they get adequate audits of what is done in National Health Service hospitals, whether some examinations are necessary or duplicated, whether the time taken is too long, whether the costs related to it are all awry. They are going to publish, she said, details

---

20. WW's father, Robert Harvey Lyall Wyatt, founded and was Headmaster of Milbourne Lodge private (preparatory) school, Esher, Surrey; see *Confessions of an Optimist*, pp. 26–36.

like league tables with the hospitals in order of the use they make of their money.

I said that I didn't think the nurses were going to win sympathy if they go on strike.[21] She said, 'Isn't it extraordinary that the revolutionaries have now got into NUPE and COHSE?'

I said, 'Did you hear on the wireless this morning that the Royal College of Nursing is going to ballot its members again on whether they should adhere to having no strikes?' She said, 'It's appalling. The whole reason they were given the nurses' Independent Pay Review Board was because they didn't strike.'

Saw Lord Wigoder,[22] Chairman of BUPA, in the Lords. Asked him if he had had any approach from the government for BUPA costs in BUPA hospitals. He said, 'No but we would gladly give them.'

Wigoder told me that at a BUPA hospital in Wales (Cardiff) they had vacancies for heart operations. They got on to the NHS and said, 'Would you like to send some here and we'll only charge you what it costs you to do such a heart operation in an NHS hospital?' In the end the NHS had to decline the offer because they said they had not the slightest idea how much any operation cost them, let alone heart operations.

**Wednesday 27 January**

Rang Margaret.

I told her that I had spoken to Wigoder.

I am feeling much better today. I even drank a little champagne before lunch and some of the Vougeot 1972 burgundy which was excellent.

**Sunday 31 January**

A sunny morning. I rang Mrs Thatcher.

I asked her whether she had done anything about Wigoder and BUPA and she said she had told John Moore. Then she said, 'Remember how during the coal miners' strike we had meetings at your house which helped to get the thing solved and defeated?' I said, 'Yes.' 'Well,

---

21. There had been strikes by nurses belonging to the National Union of Public Employees (NUPE) and the Confederation of Health Service Employees (COHSE) in Manchester and Scotland; the government referred the issues to the nurses' Independent Pay Review Board.
22. Liberal Chief Whip, House of Lords, 1977–84; life peer 1974.

I was just wondering whether we couldn't do something along those lines over the National Health Service. We want to collect some names of private people who could help us who have got ideas and know something about it.' I said, 'Do you want me to arrange something?' 'Not for the moment but I think it would be a good idea a little later on.'

She wanted to know all about the NACODS[23] strike. That's the union of pit deputies.

She wondered whether another union could be formed to do the NACODS job. She didn't realize that they have to give their certificates by law before a pit can be operated.

She was much concerned about the Ford strike. I said, 'Maybe they'll settle it this afternoon.' I told her that I had met a nice black man in the betting shop at Chelmsford who works at Ford. He said that he didn't want to go on strike and the workers would only lose out to their competitors.

Spoke to John Liptrott, General Secretary of the UDM.[24] He said he had recruited three hundred and fifty more members last week because of Scargill's victory. He thought it would be perfectly possible for pit deputies to join the appropriate section of the UDM. He did not fear very much from the action they are proposing to undertake.

On the late news it was announced that the Ford strike was off as I thought it would be.

---

23. National Association of Colliery Overmen, Deputies and Shotfirers.
24. Union of Democratic Mineworkers.

**Monday 1 February**

Dinner with Michael Oswald and Angela Oswald at Boodle's – the ladies' extension.

The Queen's new Press Secretary, who has taken Michael Shea's place, wanted to talk to me and ask my advice.

He is called Robin Janvrin. He has a French wife who is bright and amusing. He is much calmer and less pleased with himself than his predecessor. He thinks all the time of the long-term effect of anything done now on the monarchy.

He thought that there was some intelligent criticism like the one in the *Sunday Times* yesterday when they said that the succession should not go to the oldest son but the oldest child. I said, 'That's a lot of rubbish. Nobody is interested in that.'

He said, 'How can we deal with the Murdoch newspapers?' 'You don't have to worry too much,' I said.

I went on, 'But Rupert is settled against the whole idea of monarchy. He thinks it's out of date and that we should be a republic. However, he concedes that the Queen does a good job and that Queen Elizabeth the Queen Mother is marvellous.'

He said, 'Would there be any point in meeting him?' 'You've got to be very careful. Rupert likes causing a bit of a commotion and we don't want to give him the impression that he is worrying us. However, I will think about perhaps arranging a lunch or a meeting of some sort.'

Michael was very blunt. He said that the *Knock Out* programme was a disaster and should never have been allowed.[1]

Robin was not worried about Prince Edward doing a job in the theatre because he said it did seem like a sensible job and would probably only last about three or four years.

I went on, 'The institution is thoroughly sound. It has been rocked

1. Younger members of the Royal Family had taken part in a special *It's a Knockout* programme on television for charity, joining in tugs-of-war and other frolics.

many times in the past – the Duke of Windsor, the Prince Regent and his ghastly divorce from the Princess of Wales . . . It is part of our history. It's illogical, erratic, but it has its moments of drama and pageantry and makes people feel good. That will not die. Nothing can destroy the institution of monarchy. Not even a divorce between the Prince and Princess of Wales.'

Princess Diana at the moment is turning out to be a great success. We talked about the passage a few months ago when everybody said they were splitting up and couldn't get on together. I said, 'To some extent I thought it was their own fault because they made no effort to be together.' He said, 'I absolutely agree. The Prince of Wales should at least have spent one or two weekends with her during the period he was doing all his reflections apart etc.'

Robin said that Michael Shea denied ever saying what he was reported as having said in the famous *Sunday Times* article when it was put out that the Queen was in strong disagreement with Mrs Thatcher on the Commonwealth and on other matters. I said, 'I don't believe him. Although I think that Andrew Neil tricked Michael Shea, or his staff did, into saying more than he intended or without understanding the effect of what he was saying, nevertheless Andrew Neil assured me that it was all read back and checked with Michael Shea more than once and he passed every word of it; and I don't believe he was lying to me about that.'

I think the Queen is lucky to have got Robin. He is far more thoughtful than Michael Shea and much more conscious of the effects on the Crown that bloomers can make.

**Tuesday 2 February**

Called on John Wakeham, Leader of the House of Commons, at the Lord Privy Seal's office.

We talked about the Sunday Sports Bill. He says there was a dodge which is very secret. Give it another name. Let nobody know what you are up to. He said, 'Michael Cocks[2] knows how to do it. (He is now in the Lords.) I'll speak to him and suggest he speaks to you.'

Norman Lamont[3] rang. 'Have you heard yet from the Home Office on privatization?' I said, 'No.' 'Well you should have done by now. The Chancellor is keen on it. We argued with Douglas Hurd and John

2. Labour politician, Chief Whip, 1976–9.
3. Financial Secretary to the Treasury at this time.

Patten. He said they are not really in favour of Mrs Thatcher's economic policies and wanted not to privatize it. We dealt with the monopoly question which you call a licence, which I agree is so.' He went on, 'I produced the odd figure here and there, particularly you could not be a monopoly because of your tiny share of the market. John Patten said, "You've been got at," but I said, "No, no. I know nothing about it at all other than some facts I have picked up."' My briefing to him was very useful.

Norman also said we have to get a bank to organize it all and to put the question of the bank out for competitive tender. I said, 'But we've got one already. Hambros.' 'Yes, but you have to do this because that is the custom in these cases.'

**Wednesday 3 February**

Petronella had a jolly evening. Douglas Hurd had a smallish reception at Lancaster House for the two hundredth anniversary of Robert Peel's birth. The plaque itself is to be unveiled in Upper Grosvenor Street on Friday. He told everybody that it was Petronella's initiative and she bullied him to get the plaque put up.

**Thursday 4 February**

Dinner with Timothy Rathbone[4] and his wife Sue. Dinner jackets to be worn.

John Wakeham and his wife were there. She was his secretary, or something to that effect, before his wife was killed in the Brighton bombing. She also had worked for Mrs Thatcher. She has just had a baby. There must have been something before because John had not long been widowed when they married.

As Leader of the House he adores all the intrigue and manipulation which has to go on to get business through.

Wakeham says Kenneth Baker[5] understands her very well and gets her to change her mind by making jokes. She quite likes him buttering her up and she says, 'Oh Ken!' and then she lets him change something.

---

4. Conservative politician; MP for Lewes, 1974–97.
5. Secretary of State for Education and Science at this time.

**Saturday 6 February**

Go to Sandown – it is the only course racing out of three today. Queen Elizabeth the Queen Mother comes to see her horse, Sun Rising, in one of the races. It does not run well.

She was thrilled with the binoculars which I had arranged for Charles Forte to send her.[6]

I said, 'He is a very nice, charming man.' 'He wants to get the Savoy.' I said, 'Yes, whose side are you on?' She said, 'I'm afraid I'm on the side of the Savoy.'

That would not please Charles Forte who thinks that Sir Hugh Wontner who controls the Savoy through voting shares, though he cannot command more than about twenty per cent of the non-voting shares, is a villain. His propaganda that Charles Forte will somehow change the character of the Savoy has evidently got across. I didn't argue with her.

I am putting on weight fast. Today I am 12 stone 4¼. Dr Pounder, to whom Professor Thomas sent me, says that the sedimentation rate for my red blood corpuscles has dropped to sixty. It ought to be only half my age, i.e. about thirty-five. Previously it was ninety. He is still not quite happy and wants me to go for another blood test next Thursday. That will be my third in about four weeks.

However, I am feeling extremely well and I cannot believe there is anything seriously wrong.

**Sunday 7 February**

'We read your article in the *News of the World*. Wonderful,' Margaret said. 'Everything is right.'[7] Who are we? She and Denis I suppose.

She mentioned the *Sunday Express* saying the ballot for Scargill had been fiddled, just as I had said. I told her, 'We've got to alter that law to make sure he has to stand again on a proper postal ballot within a year; otherwise he'll be there ten years.'

I said, 'I do hope that you are not going to make the Archbishop of York the Archbishop of Canterbury. Runcie is fairly feeble but Habgood [Archbishop of York] made a terrible speech saying he was against promoting homosexuality in the schools and generally on the

---

6. See 19 December 1987.

7. It was about the nurses' dispute and the NHS.

rates but he did not think Clause 28 was the right way to do it[8] – the classic excuse of someone who doesn't want the law changed.'

She said, 'They only give me two choices and both from the left.' I said, 'I remember saying to you once why did you pick so and so as Bishop and you said, "You should have seen the other one."' She laughed.

She thinks Runcie is not going for some time.[9] I said, 'Don't for goodness' sake promote the Bishop of Oxford[10] as I see was hinted at in the newspapers. He is very good looking, has got a nice wife who is pregnant, but he is very trendy and mixes with all those like Melvyn Bragg and other left-wingers.'

**Monday 8 February**

Saw young Lord Beaverbrook in the Lords. He tells me that we have won on the Copyright Bill. He says the government are putting down amendments to make newspaper employees like any other employees and that moral rights shall not apply to newspapers.

Again I have put on weight. I am now about 12 stone 5. Feel better all the time. Now I am in danger of putting on too much weight.

Dinner given ostensibly by Andrew Knight and his wife at Claridge's. Conrad Black the proprietor of the *Telegraph* newspapers was there. So were Arnold and Netta.

Arnold in a very argumentative and foolish mood.

He talked a lot of rubbish about politics. He said, 'The way they are going to privatize electricity is hopeless.' I said, 'That's because your friend Marshall[11] doesn't like it and doesn't want to lose his power.'

Arnold then started talking about Jim Prior whom he made Chairman of GEC some time ago. He told everybody at the table this was a disaster, that Jim Prior was no good, he was too lazy and he didn't understand the work he had to do, that nobody knew him when

8. Clause 28 of the Local Government Act 1988 outlawed the 'promotion' of homosexuality by local authorities.
9. He retired in 1991 and was succeeded by the Rt Rev. George Carey, Bishop of Bath and Wells.
10. The Rt Rev. Richard Harries.
11. Former Chief Scientist, Department of Energy; chairman, Central Electricity Generating Board; life peer 1985.

he went abroad, it wasn't a bit like Peter Carrington.[12] I said, 'Arnold, you must stop talking like that. You must not do it.' I managed to get him to shut up after a bit. He complained that Peter Carrington had let him down by going off to NATO and now he was going to run Christie's which was a pitiful job for somebody like him. I agreed to the last point.

Conrad Black defended Reagan's record. I agreed with him but Arnold didn't. Conrad said, 'What he did at Grenada when he took the island over from the Communists[13] was correct.' I said, 'Yes, it was one of the few times I had a quarrel with Mrs Thatcher. In the *News of the World* I wrote an article saying that Reagan had been totally right and she wasn't very pleased.'

Arnold also talked nonsense about Mrs Thatcher, saying that she would be thrown out during this parliament by the Tories.[14]

**Tuesday 9 February**

Got up about six o'clock. Arrived at Woodbridge for the start of the footpath inquiry at Heveningham Hall. Air Vice Marshall Howlett was in charge of the inquiry. He is a retired Air Force officer and seems highly intelligent and conducted the affair sensibly.

There were a number of beardies and weirdies all objecting to the footpath being re-routed.

The protesters had got a number of signatures – three hundred and eight – locally. I gave evidence for about fifteen minutes as I described my connections with the house which stemmed from James Wyatt, one of the twenty-eight architects in my family and perhaps being the most distinguished of them all. This was his great interior masterpiece. Probably some of the outside building was done by James as well as all the interiors and the beautiful furniture.

I said that when the Vannecks[15] no longer could afford to stay there, I had correspondence with the family and the proposition was

---

12. Lord Carrington, Conservative Secretary of State for Foreign and Commonwealth Affairs, 1979–82, had been chairman, GEC, 1983–4; he was Secretary General, NATO, 1984–8 and in 1988 appointed chairman, Christie's International.
13. In October 1983.
14. As she was, in November 1990.
15. Vanneck is the family name of the 6th Baron Huntingfield; the 1st Baron was created 1796.

either that the house should be demolished and the furniture sold or the government should buy it.

There was nobody else who wanted to buy it at the time. I got on to the Department of the Environment; Anthony Greenwood was the Secretary of State.[16] I said I took some part in persuading the government to buy it and that I was quite happy everything was all right.

But the government neglected it. The place was full of dry rot. They decided they didn't want to go on with the expense of it as the attendances were not very large and they didn't think it was worthwhile. They sold it to Abdul Al Ghazzi who has splendidly done all the restoration. Unfortunately there was a fire in the east wing and there have been thefts of Coadeware – twenty-four out of thirty-two pieces of exterior decoration in Coadeware were stolen – there was the theft of the James Wyatt fireplace by people coming right up to the window, etc. etc.

I gave it as my view that the house would not be restored again and the works done unless some resolution could be made about the footpath being diverted. There would then be a secure line on which to base a proper security plan by Siemens of Germany.

I had a lovely walk near Snape on the sandy ground much of which was covered in light green turf grown near the sea. And I saw Framlingham Castle with its exterior looking much as it did when it was [built]. It was lovely and I felt happy and free.

**Thursday 11 February**

Dinner at Addison Road with Mark and Anouska Weinberg. A most extraordinary house. Very dark. All floors of dark green marble. Dark green walls, lights very dim. Music playing. Large drawing-room in which we sat for drinks.

The house must have cost a fortune. He is very, very rich having set up Hambros Life and then sold it.

We were talking about *Serious Money* and I was trying to explain the strange play in which there was a lot of singing and obscenity, in which illegal dealings on Wall Street and in the City were attacked and ridiculed. I said, 'There was nothing very funny in it except one joke I remember: "Why is a clitoris like a Filofax? Because every cunt has one."' Anouska pretended to be shocked but wasn't. Everybody

16. 1966–70.

laughed. I then added, 'My problem at the time was I didn't know what a Filofax was.' They laughed again.

**Friday 12 February**

It's extraordinary how one's mind is affected by one's health. When I was in the grip of that bug, I was losing my optimism, my curiosity, my interest, my will to live and fight. Now it's all come back. I think even I might be able to deal with the money difficulties or shortage. Maybe the play will come off. Perhaps I can write another.

I told Dr Pounder when I first saw him at the Royal Free [Hospital], that I knew I could cure myself. He said today, 'Yes, you were right. That's why Mrs Thatcher has long waiting lists because she realizes that most of the patients will be cured by themselves before they get to the hospital.'

**Saturday 13 February**

The Tote Gold Trophy at Newbury. Rain, rain, rain. Racing was abandoned after the fourth race but fortunately the Tote Gold Trophy had been run and was a great success. It is the most valuable handicap hurdle of the year.

William Douglas-Home was there. William said after trying seven years he got *The Secretary Bird* on (very successful) only because it was first acted by the boys at Eton and an agent saw it.

John Howard de Walden was at the lunch. About the most intelligent member of the Jockey Club there has been for a long time and was goodish when he was Senior Steward. He is mentioned favourably in Christopher Hill's book[17] and I must refer to that in my review.

**Sunday 14 February**

Mrs T angry with both the French and the Germans at the European Common Market Summit Conference which ended in the early hours of Saturday morning. She said, 'They have no integrity.' They were plotting behind her back, they were not bringing things forward to her in an honest way.

She was suddenly presented with a proposition which meant she had agreed to a whole series of things which hadn't been written down.

She got a great deal of what she was demanding and to have insisted

---

17. *Powers in Racing*; see 11 December 1985 for WW's meeting with Christopher Hill.

on the whole would have meant that the eleven others would have gone their own way with a separate international agreement, she would not have got the concessions she did.

I said, 'I thought you did very well. You've certainly started the cutting of the subsidies. And you've also got our rebate guaranteed for another five years which was very important.'

I said, 'I'm getting terribly fed up with the Bishops. The Archbishop of York is now attacking the community charge as being unfair. He doesn't know anything about it at all.' She said, 'Oh, the Bishops,' with a long-drawn out sigh. 'I think it would be better if they were disestablished.' I said, 'I agree, and I have said so in the *News of the World* this morning.'

**Monday 15 February**

Entertaining meeting at Lord Goodman's office with counsel Patrick Maloney and Maunsell. John Heaton and Brian McDonnell there about the libel action for damages brought against the Tote and myself.

Arnold is going to see Mr Berwin, solicitor acting for Ladbroke's, and find out what it is they really want. Do they want a long drawn out case which would take years? Or do they want me, as I said, 'to stop rubbishing them'?

John Heaton pointed out that in France they were only asking for one franc damages against Pari-Mutuel but for ten European newspapers to carry advertisements, paid for by Pari-Mutuel, to say that Ladbroke's are really a good and respectable concern.

My weakness is that I have technically broken the law by revealing some of the details of the Levy Board – of the bookmakers', Ladbroke's, Levy payments – though we think it is possible to show that this is really in the public domain from the Ladbroke accounts and their previous misbehaviour. This was publicized in the newspapers when they voluntarily made a very large payment because they had been playing games with ceasing a company before the year end and then saying it didn't have to pay any Levy because it wasn't trading on the operative date when the year ended.

Dinner with Chips Keswick at the Portland Club. This is at the top of the Naval and Military Club in Half Moon Street. To get to it you walk through a room with chintzy sofas and chairs occupied by dowdy respectable males and females probably up from the country, some using the place for a cheap night's stay.

Behind them when you go through the door is a gambling den. The

Portland Club has a hundred members and through the deductions from money gambled, each of them contributes £5,000 a year – or half a million pounds a year for the lot. This is to provide the premises they use and the dinners. Every Monday there is a grand dinner and it was certainly grand last night.

The Château Pavie 1966 (St Emilion) was outstanding. I must have drunk nearly a bottle of it, it was so good. I had no ill effects in the morning. Chips told me that frequently on a Thursday two members club together to give a dinner at a cost of £2,000. I was astonished that there was so much money about.

Chips is Chairman of the Club.

He would very much like a job with the government. He wants to be a Director of the Bank of England. He's quite prepared to give up Hambros. 'I am very rich,' he said. Indeed he is. His money comes from the Jardine Matheson firm as it was originally, of Hong Kong. He is a big holder of their shares. It's usually a member of their family at the head of it in Hong Kong.

**Tuesday 16 February**

Allan Davis has returned from the States.

He enjoyed talking to the blue rinsed ladies in America. He said on return he found Edward Fox is going to do a revival of *The Admirable Crichton* and therefore would not be available for our play. Had I heard of an actor called Leslie Phillips?

Glad to have Allan back. Am very fond of him and of talking about my play. Dreamland with just the hint it might become real.

Nick Lloyd editor of the *Daily Express* and his wife Eve Pollard, now editor of the *Sunday Mirror* after editing the colour magazine of the *Mail on Sunday*, came to dinner.

She is half Hungarian, very lively with an enormous bottom and very thick legs, unshapely. She has a round sexy quite attractive face. Large voluptuous breasts. He is slight and probably disappears when she wraps her arms around him. She is lively and ahead of her husband one would guess in skills. Already she has livened up the *Sunday Mirror*. She says it is not directed against the *News of the World* but against the *Sunday Express* and higher up newspapers in the quality range. She leaves the *People* newspaper to attack the *News of the World*.

We went on until nearly twelve o'clock which was too late for me but what could I do?

**Wednesday 17 February**

John Patten[18] came to the Levy Board lunch. I sat next to him and Ian Trethowan on the other side.

He behaved well. He asked intelligent questions in a precise manner without hectoring. He made it clear to the bookmakers that if they didn't agree to stop playing games with their Levy contributions there could be legislation although that wouldn't be very popular and he advised the Levy Board to keep careful notes and records of everything that went on during the present talks.

He is rather a smoothie. He is ultra ambitious, pleased with his continental good looks but intelligent. Ian asked me what I thought his future was and I said, 'He's bound to get into the Cabinet.' He is of course a closet anti-Thatcherite, as is Douglas Hurd.

**Sunday 21 February**

Margaret delighted with my article in the *News of the World* about waste in the NHS.

I told her that Chips was very keen to do some job to help her in the public way.

She said, 'What sort of thing?' 'Well one thing he would like to do in any case is be a Director of the Bank of England, as his father was.' She didn't know that. She said, 'I'll run off and put it in my notebook. I'll remember that because we must do something about it.'[19]

Lunch at Bowden. Excellent. The Chef from the Gavroche which is rated as the best restaurant in England by the *Michelin Guide* comes every weekend to cook.

Arnold and I went for a walk in the sun. A beautiful day.

He says all the inquiries by the Ministry of Defence police at Marconi Southampton have taken years off his life, he has never been so worried and upset by anything. He said, 'I don't know if somebody down below has done something silly in order to make his profits look better. But I would never do anything fraudulent,' which I know of course is perfectly true.

As we sat in the sun after our walk on the lovely stone seat at the side of the house he said he was worried about money. 'Personally?' I

18. Minister of State, Home Office, at this time; Secretary of State for Education, 1992–4.
19. He was appointed a director of the Bank of England in 1993, when Mrs Thatcher was no longer Prime Minister.

asked. 'Yes,' he said, 'I'm very short of it.' It then transpired that his stud is losing £1.5 million a year and his horses in training are costing £700,000 a year, though his father-in-law pays for half of the horses in training.

I said, 'Why on earth don't you give them up? What is the point of it?' 'I want to win the Arc de Triomphe.' I said, 'You nearly did with Troy.'

I said, 'But why bother now? You've won the Derby. You've won the St Leger. You've won the King George and Queen Elizabeth Stakes twice.'

He said, 'And the Sussex Stakes,' and reeled off a number of other races he had won. 'Well, give it up.' He said, 'No, I like it.'

I thought, 'All matters of money are relative. It is amazing how many people think they are hard up and pressed into desperation from a shortage of money at every level. Myself included.'

Before lunch we discussed the half-million-pounds-plus telephone installation going into our new Tote credit centre at Wigan. Arnold is very anxious to get this for GEC because it would be a feather in their cap.

I explained that he would have to give some guarantees about non-fulfilment as their system was only at work at British airports at the moment and on not such a big scale as Thorn-Ericsson. I told him that the BT consultant had ruled out their own firm but narrowly had given the verdict to Thorn-Ericsson. However, after [he] had been to see GEC operating at British airports he changed his mind.

I said, 'I am in favour of GEC for several reasons. One is that it is British. Two that I am a friend of yours and can jolly well make you send people immediately if anything goes wrong and raise absolute hell. Three that it is cheaper. I hope you are going to agree to a further reduction in price which we must have. Four that it is more flexible – which was agreed to by the British Telecom consultant. Future developments may come along which are of use to us – we should be ready for the future.'

**Monday 22 February**

Putting on weight again now. Have reached 12 stone 9 which is worrying. Trying to take it off again. I am beset by internal explosions. Perhaps I am eating the wrong things. I hope it is not the beginning of another increased sedimentation rate. I don't think so.

I tidied up my speech and rewrote it for the Employment Bill in the Lords.

This Bill deals with further reforms to the trade unions to make double assurance that secret postal ballots are compulsory in electing union executives and that democracy really works. It has some defects, as I said in my speech. I said also that I propose to move some amendments. I pointed out that the January 22nd ballot, in which Scargill was declared the winner in the Presidential contest against Mr Walsh, was gravely flawed and that fraud attended it.

Baroness Turner (works within the ASTMS),[20] was very indignant and said would I repeat these allegations outside.[21] I said, 'I have already stated them in the *News of the World*.'

My speech was a success. It enraged the élite on the Labour benches like Lord Murray,[22] Lord Basnett[23] and the ghastly Professor Peston[24] who thinks he understands everything but understands very little. They sneered when I referred to the *News of the World* but it has more than seventeen and a half million readership – a newspaper read by a great mass of trade unionists who do not read the *Morning Star* or the *Marxist Quarterly* or the *New Statesman*.

Rupert on the telephone from New York. I felt very sorry for him. Owing to the law which prevents people owning a television station and a newspaper at the same time he has had to sell the *New York Post*. It was losing a lot of money and it is good for his business that he has done so but he loved that newspaper. The sale will be completed in a fortnight.

The *New York Post* was always a difficult paper. It has no Sunday edition. It is down-market. It could not get all the advertising it needed. One store owner said to Rupert, 'Your readers are my shoplifters.' But it had the largest circulation in New York.

Newspapers and the noise of them, the drama of them, the

---

20. Assistant General Secretary (1970–87), Association of Scientific, Technical and Managerial Staffs.
21. Outside the House of Lords without parliamentary privilege giving immunity from libel.
22. Len Murray (b 1922), general secretary of the TUC, 1973–84; life peer 1985.
23. David Basnett (1924–89), general secretary, General Municipal Boilermakers and Allied Trade Unions, 1982–6; life peer 1987.
24. Maurice Peston, Professor of Economics, Queen Mary College, University of London, 1965–88; life peer 1987.

immediacy of them, are things which he has to have alive and kicking about him to satisfy his restless, questing nature. I understand it so well. I was heartbroken when I had to give up the *Banbury Guardian*. That was a terrible mistake of mine. I should have sold anything other than that newspaper but I was in a jam. If I had been able to hang on to it and hadn't developed the printing business instead, I would never have lost all my money as well as being able to expand by adding other local newspapers. There is a romance in newspapers.

**Tuesday 23 February**

Allan Davis is trying to get Richard Harris now to take the lead in our play. It's a long shot chance. It would be wonderful if it came off. But I somewhat doubt it.

**Thursday 25 February**

Dinner at The Other Club. Singularly jolly. I took Roy down in the car. The Chairman was William Heseltine for the evening. He is the Queen's Private Secretary. We had a long talk about Robin Janvrin who is his appointee and he hopes will one day succeed him as Private Secretary.[25]

He asked whether I thought that people would be upset if she ceased to be the Queen or head of the various Commonwealth countries. I said, 'It doesn't matter at all. First of all they don't like the black countries. Secondly the white ones will probably hang on much longer than is supposed with the Queen at their head. Look how Bob Hawke was bowled over by the Prince and Princess of Wales on their recent Australian tour.'

It was announced by the Secretary that £2,000 had been collected towards buying more wine for the Club. I gave £50, Roy gave £25. Jacob Rothschild told me he was giving £100 and I said, 'My contribution considering our relative fortunes ought therefore to be 10p.'

Roy told me that Johnny Buccleuch[26] sent only £10 and suggested that we should buy Spanish wine. He is one of the richest men in England, even richer than Andrew Devonshire. Amazing that he could be so stingy.

Roy kept saying how nice it was to have a long talk with me again.

---

25. He succeeded Sir Robert Fellowes in 1998.
26. 9th Duke of Buccleuch.

I am very fond of him. He was very ill a year or so ago. Now his prostate is OK and he can go six hours comfortably without peeing.

Roy likes the look of the House of Lords. He has made his maiden speech and he has got a motion down about there being too much power centralized in the hands of the government. That's for debate next week.

Andrew is decent. Before the end he sat with Jeremy Thorpe, the sad wreck.

**Friday 26 February**

The GEC deal for Wigan is all fixed. £50,000 less, more modern than Thorn-Ericsson. Tried to tell Arnold but he had left for ten days' holiday in Morocco. My trip to Bowden last Sunday was worthwhile.

**Saturday 27 February**

I go alone to Kempton to present the Tote Placepot Hurdle prize of some value.

Have a delicious Cope's fish lunch beginning with a hot lobster soup, followed by a large helping of brown and white crab meat, shrimps, and huge mussels, plus champagne. I had it in the box with Sir Gordon Brunton who is Chairman of the *Racing Post* which also sponsors a race that day. He tells me that the *Racing Post* is losing £3 million a year.

He is glad that we have taken a little advertising with it but we don't buy the *Racing Post* for our betting offices as Ladbroke's does (one thousand six hundred a day). 'Would you give us a discount if we did?' I asked. 'If you don't tell anyone.' It is something I must look into.

Yesterday General Sir Peter Leng, Executive Chairman of the Racecourse Association, was delighted when I told him that our new arrangements for the financial year will give the racecourses just on half our profits in our Tote Cash Division. I asked him whether it would be a good idea to let the Racecourse Association have ten per cent or fifteen per cent of the shares of a privatized Tote for nothing so that they could make sure that they got more money out of the privatized Tote which would become far bigger than today. First he was against a privatized Tote but I explained to him the arguments.

His wife is the daughter of Daphne du Maurier[27] and is writing an

27. Writer (1907–89); m (1932) General Sir Frederick 'Boy' Browning (d 1969).

autobiography. She had an odd childhood. Her rich mother – and her father was rich too – made her dress as a boy and behave as a boy when a child because she had always wanted the son who came later.

Amazing the authoress of many good books, some turned into highly profitable films, should treat her daughter so painfully and shabbily. She is now ga-ga. 'Her motor's gone,' the General said.

**Sunday 28 February**

I gave Mrs T a list of improvements which we must get into the trade union Bill now going before the Lords because they still have not got it right.

1. They need to have the independent scrutineer supervise and send out the votes, otherwise they will be tampered with by the unscrupulous who will print more than are necessary, filling in bogus votes for the candidate they want on the extreme left.
2. They need to make Scargill and such people as the leaders of the Transport & General Workers Union, this weekend declared victors in an extreme left-wing coup in rigged manipulated workplace ballots, stand again within a year or two years of the passing of the Act in a properly supervised postal ballot conducted by the scrutineer.
3. They need to have candidates' manifestos sent out with the postal votes.
4. The need for anonymity for the humble frightened member who has a genuine complaint for the Certification Officer or the new Commissioner to take up: such people are terrified of exposing themselves to victimization from their unions by taking their unions to court or attacking them in public.
5. The need to make sure that the Certification Officer must examine union rules for ballots, including those for elections, and be satisfied that they comply with the law.

She said, 'I've got your instructions,' and laughed. She said they understand and 'they're going to do some of your points at least'.

I asked her whether she could tag the main provisions of the Sunday Sports Bill which would be very popular, on to anything she is doing to improve the Sunday trading laws. 'We don't know what we are going to do yet.' I said, 'No, but when you do get some decisions please try and get my little Bill through, which would be very much liked by the public.'

Mrs Thatcher said, 'My main worry at the moment is the Middle

East and the trouble that may come there.' I said, 'Myself, I never write anything much about the Middle East because all I do is to offend one side or the other without achieving anything.'

**Monday 29 February**

The Banqueting Hall at Whitehall. Inigo Jones plus some additional alterations by James Wyatt. It's very beautiful. The party was for Caroline Moore's eighth birthday. She was born on February 29th. I took her a large package of After Eight mints which she thought was quite funny as did I.

Sonia and Andrew Sinclair were there. Sonia told a story of how George Weidenfeld gave a lunch party recently in New York for Henry Kissinger and John Gross, who used to be the editor of the *Times Literary Supplement* and is now in America, and Barbara Amiel, the beautiful lady, aged about fifty-eight I would suppose, who writes a column in the *Times* and is now doing one of the ghastly diary pieces they have now put on the features page opposite the leaders.

Henry Kissinger spoke very freely and indiscreetly and after he had gone she said to George, who had given the lunch, 'Well that's marvellous stuff for my diary column in the *Times*.' He was very cross. He said, 'You can't possibly put that in your column. It's a private lunch. It's confidential what he said.' George was right. He has been greatly enamoured with this girl and was on the verge at one moment of marrying her.

To dinner at Jacob's – he and Serena alone. There was some wonderful Château Lafite 1966. There was a beautiful Crux Champagne 1964. Then there was a Trotanoy (Pomerol second only to Pétrus) 1964 which was good. I drank rather too much.

Jacob said last time he had lunch with the Princess of Wales was at Cecconi's and at the next table was sitting Rupert Murdoch. (When the Princess lunches in public with any man she always brings a girlfriend with her to show there is no hanky-panky.) After she had gone Jacob spoke to Rupert and said, 'I wish you would be kinder to my guest. Your papers are beastly to her, particularly the *News of the World*, and it's very unfair.' Rupert said, 'Oh, oh who was your guest?' He hadn't even recognized the Princess of Wales.

Rupert muttered something as he always does to the effect that if she behaved herself there wouldn't be any trouble. Rupert is a great prude. He never looks at another woman, possibly because he is so engrossed in his business, and thinks everybody should lead a totally pure life sexually and deserves to be pilloried, if they are at all well-known, in the *News of the World* and the *Sun*, if they don't. That's because they are setting a bad example to the nation.

I am very fond of Serena. I have known her so long now that she is part of the furniture of my life.

She and Jacob were surprised when I said that I first met Victor at Mereworth where Michael and Anne Tree then lived.

Jacob asked whether I thought that Anne Tree and his father had ever had an affair. I said, 'I don't think so. They may have got close to it. Certainly when I used to go there thirty years or so ago to they were very affectionate but I don't imagine that anything carnal occurred. Do you want me to ask her?' Serena said, 'That's the sort of thing only you would dare to do.'

**Tuesday 1 March**

Allan Davis comes to dinner with Petronella and Verushka at the Lords. I took him on a little tour of the Royal Gallery, Prince's Chamber, Queen's Robing Room and so forth. We are looking for a site for the murder if I do this play about a murder in the Lords.

At dinner he produced a present from his American trip. A brown tie for me with the mask of comedy and the mask of tragedy on it which he had got at the Players' Club in New York. He didn't give the ladies anything.

**Thursday 3 March**

Lunch with Chips Keswick at Hambros and with Sporborg. Brian McDonnell also there.

We talked about the privatization of the Tote. Discussed the price we might get. Chips said he was thinking of about £40 million but Sporborg said he thought that was too high, perhaps £25–30 million. We will not be so saleable as some companies because we shall have to have the built-in provision that bookmakers can't get hold of it. Therefore the chances of a take-over are not so great and that is what excites shareholders because they think they are going to double their money quickly.

At 5.45 I went to see Norman Fowler [Secretary of State for Employment] and Lord Trefgarne, who is the Lord dealing with the Employment Bill, and Ritchie, who will also deal with it in the Lords, and the Minister of State, John Cope, and other officials.

Norman Fowler was jet-lagged, having just come back from Los Angeles. But he has accepted at least two of my amendments more or less. He was also almost won over about the need to have an independent scrutineer. It was a very useful meeting. Norman Fowler is lean, quick and chirpy. I like him though many don't. Like most successful politicians he is very ambitious which is as it should be.

**Friday 4 March**

My weight down to 12 stone 8½. That despite my having two enormous helpings of an excellent cod fish pie and a large helping of broccoli done in Gruyère cheese. I cannot account for my weight going up and down.

**Sunday 6 March**

Told Margaret that she was terrific at the NATO summit. It was vital that somebody gave a clear picture of what the policy is and must be. She said, 'Our Generals said that they have got to have some instructions as to how to get on with new weapons and when to do so.' She said, 'The Trident will be in operation – 1993 – but it was started in 1980. You have to plan a long time ahead.'

She was delighted that the *New York Herald Tribune* in its international edition put on the front page that she had taken charge of NATO which she clearly had.

She said, 'At the moment it's all eyes on America and Super Tuesday in the primaries.' I said, 'Yes, it looks as though Bush is winning. I don't know which your favourite candidate is,' and she said immediately, 'Oh, George Bush.' She thinks he is more experienced and steadier and understands how the world works. Clearly she believes that she can get on with him whereas Dole, his chief rival, is a prickly unpredictable character who might behave rashly.[1]

When we had finished talking after twenty-five minutes, she said, 'Thank you,' in a heartfelt manner. I said, 'No, thank you,' because I felt I had got her solidly behind me on the privatization of the Tote and also my trade union reforms.

**Monday 7 March**

Over the weekend Rupert had said he might be able to come to our Tote lunch. Charles Wilson wanted to come but said he had this board meeting of the *Times* newspaper and Rupert might not let him go.

When I spoke to Rupert this morning he said he couldn't come. I said, 'Can Charles Wilson?' He said, 'No, he has to be there at the lunch with the rest of the board. Anyway he takes too much time for his lunch, they all do. It will be a good thing for him to be back at work

---

1. George Bush, Reagan's Vice President since 1981, won the Republican nomination and then the presidency.

earlier than he would be if he came to you.' He was half humorous and half serious.

**Tuesday 8 March**

The annual Tote lunch was a rollicking affair. There were three former Home Secretaries and one actual Home Secretary. About two hundred and fifty people mostly from the racing world.

My speech contained a demand that the government set the Tote free and properly privatize it. Douglas Hurd didn't even blink. When I said our sole right to purvey Tote odds was not a monopoly, I heard him say, 'No, it's a licence.' Evidently he has been successfully brainwashed by the Treasury and Norman Lamont. I hope that we will now start moving towards the privatization.

John Mortimer made a very funny speech.

I then had to go to the Lords to move amendments on the Employment Bill.

We got the one where I demanded that the independent scrutineer should be responsible for printing and sending out the votes to union members for secret postal ballots.

As though I hadn't had enough to do that day, I was rung by the *Times* who want me to write a piece about Maxwell for printing on Saturday.[2] However, they will give me my extra £500 for a piece out of the ordinary way.

The House of Lords is a place I like more and more. Because of its curious nature, without normal rules of procedure and conventions about committees taken off the floor of the House as they are in the Commons mostly, an ordinary member of the Lords can get far more done than a backbencher in the Commons. The Lords' amendments to Bills are taken very seriously and usually survive into the final Bill. The backbencher in the House of Commons is helpless because the party just rolls all over him. But in the Lords you can get people of all parties voting for your amendment.

**Thursday 10 March**

Lunch with the Iraqi Ambassador – Dr Mohamed Sadiq Al-Mashat – at what he calls the best Arab restaurant in London in Hertford Street.

---

2. The peg for WW's article on Saturday 12 March was three books: *Maxwell, the Outsider* by Tom Bower, *Maxwell: A Portrait of Power* by Peter Thompson and Anthony Delano, and *Maxwell* by Joe Haines.

He was very dapper in a beautifully cut suit and blue handkerchief in his top breast pocket. He is highly intense and believes that Britain is helping Iran against her own interests and against those of Iraq. We talked for a long time and I said I would write an article in the *Times*, if I could find a convenient moment, about the Iraq/Iran war and probably say that I want Iraq to win.

We talked about the problem of Israel and the Palestinians. I said, 'The problem is insoluble,' and gave my reasons. Owing to the fact that the Western countries bring their children up on the Old Testament and the New Testament, it seems totally natural for Jews to be in Bethlehem and around Lake Galilee and Jerusalem. It is totally unnatural for Arabs, who had not seen Jews, other than about two hundred weeping at the Wailing Wall, for two thousand years. I understand the feeling of the Arabs who do not know why they are supposed to expiate Hitler's crimes by having their country taken over by Jews.

The Ambassador said several times he would like half an hour with 'Madame'. I said she couldn't do that or two hundred other ambassadors would want the same.

In the Lords this afternoon a very English little debate on an amendment of Jim Callaghan's. To make the copyright of *Peter Pan* extend indefinitely, it having run out at the end of 1987, for the benefit of the Great Ormond Street Children's Hospital who have been receiving the royalties up till now. Callaghan is a nice man at heart and his wife is something to do with the hospital.[3]

Harold Wilson congratulated me on my amendment speeches on the Employment Bill on trade union reform. 'But I didn't agree with all you said.' I said, 'You should have done, you of all people,' but I thanked him just the same.

Two ex Labour Prime Ministers congratulating me on speeches in one week is a record considering neither of them liked me at all when I was in the Commons.

Dinner party at 19 Cavendish Avenue. Chips Keswick, the French Ambassador and his wife, Rupert and Anna Murdoch, the Duke and Duchess of Marlborough (Sonny and Rosita), David Owen and his wife Debbie.

It was a rousing, jolly, talkative dinner.

Chips loves old champagne. We had a Premier Cru Chablis 1983

---

3. J. M. Barrie left the royalties from his play to the hospital when he died in 1937; Lady (Audrey) Callaghan was chairman of the hospital's governors.

to drink at dinner. Then there was 1967 Margaux. That was splendid. The French Ambassador and his wife adored it and kept asking for more. Anna stuck to the Chablis and so did David Owen. He said, 'I don't drink claret any more. We in the SDP don't drink claret. We only drink beer, now that Roy Jenkins is no longer with us. You can print that if you like.' However, he was drinking the Chablis plentifully.

David Owen was in a merry mood, cracking a lot of jokes. I said, 'Your future will be long if you are to get to the top again through the SDP becoming a power. Maybe you should form a coalition at some point with the Tories. Then you might even succeed Mrs Thatcher.' He said, 'That is not impossible.'

Anna was on my left. Talked about her new book which is selling frightfully well in America but not yet published here.[4] She left a copy for us. She is very proud of having a separate activity from Rupert out of which she is making real money. They've already asked to make a mini television series out of her book but she says she has not yet agreed because they haven't proposed enough money. She is pretty tough. She was looking exceptionally pretty last night and young. She must have had a face lift. Verushka said everybody in California has to.

She was full of her new house in California. She wants to know where to buy antique Italian garden furniture made of marble. They're going to Venice in April and she wants to have it shipped out to her.

After the ladies had gone we discussed Mrs Thatcher and Europe. I said, 'She is a genuine European.' The French Ambassador said, 'Yes, she showed it very much at the last summit.' I said, 'I think there is a slight fear that you and Germany are making separate deals particularly about defence.' He said, 'That is not true though it is unthinkable that we would do anything in defence terms which the Germans didn't like,' thus confirming what I had said.

I said, 'It is also a pity that you withdrew from NATO. It makes it more likely for Mrs Thatcher to look towards America.' He agreed about that and said they did feel in the Common Market that she was hedging her bets by relying on America and using her influence with Reagan.

David said, 'It is not generally understood that the French in fact do co-operate in a military sense very much with America.' The

4. *Family Business* was published here in 1988; *In Her Own Image* had been published in the UK in 1985.

Ambassador agreed and said the military connections were extremely close and if there were a war there would be no problems at all. Apart from winning it, I thought.

Rupert told Verushka that it was not true that he didn't recognize the Princess of Wales at Cecconi's Restaurant as Jacob had said. It was that she looked the other way and would not acknowledge him so he wasn't going to bother to get up and greet her.

Chips brought me a box of cigars, Upmann's Connoisseur No 1 bound together by ribbon without labels so that they may mature the better. He is terribly nice.

**Friday 11 March**

A report on the meeting between Arnold Goodman and the head man at Berwin's, solicitors for Ladbroke's. It looks as though they are willing to settle for some kind of a letter from me which need not even be public in which I would say that I don't mean that they are dishonest with the punters and that I won't repeat the bits that they don't like in the letters.

**Saturday 12 March**

Swam at the RAC and had breakfast. They have a good breakfast there and it is only £5.85 including service to which I added 65p, making a total of £6.50.

While I was happily smoking my cigar and reading the papers a call came for me to go to the telephone. Verushka said, 'Rupert has rung twice from Paris. He is very anxious to speak to you about your article in the *Times* this morning about Maxwell.'

I was mildly put out because I had intended to walk up to St James' Square and get some books by Eden Phillpotts[5] out of the London Library. It is impossible to park later. I dashed back home and found that there was no alarm at all. He wanted a chat.

We talked about Maxwell. He thought my piece was 'great fun'.[6] He said, 'Maxwell, though you said you have a liking for him and you made him sound not wholly unattractive, is a "scoundrel on the bottom line",' meaning there is usually something peculiar about his

5. (1862–1960); prolific novelist, poet and playwright.

6. The article was headed 'Maxwell: Tearaway Tycoon – Woodrow Wyatt on the Contradictions of a Supreme Self-Publicist'.

accounting. He agreed with my assessment of his influence on politics which is zero.

Told Anna that her book had kept me awake last night and it was really good stuff. It hadn't really kept me awake. I am not sure how good it is but there is no harm in pleasing people with praise, particularly when the matter is unimportant.

I also told her she was looking very young and pretty on Thursday and full of life. That also pleased her and it was true.

**Sunday 13 March**

I asked her about the stories in the press that she and Lawson had been having an argument about the pound, she wanting to let it rip and he wanting to get it forced down by spending masses of money in the market. I said, 'Are you really having an argument with him about it?' She said, 'Not at all. It simply isn't true.'

**Tuesday 15 March**

Poor Duke Hussey in quite a state. 'I'm embattled.' Almost to a man the BBC resented his recent speech in which he moderately and mildly said that one of the faults with the BBC has been to resent criticism and never to apologize for what it does wrong.

He can't get proper governors because they only get paid £5,000 for sixty days' work a year. He wouldn't mind some centre left ones. I said, 'What about Peter Kellner and John Lloyd?'[7] 'Yes, but they probably wouldn't do it for the money.'

He has high hopes of Paul Fox.[8] He says he has been arranging this move, heralded as a great surprise in the newspapers, for months.

**Wednesday 16 March**

Dinner Allan Davis.

He is a funny fussy man like so many queers. But I like him. Among those present was Derek Granger who was the producer of *Brideshead Revisited*, highly successful, in a television series. He has just done a film of another Evelyn Waugh book *A Handful of Dust*. He said he had no royalty rights in *Brideshead Revisited* which sounded

7. Labour and industrial correspondent, *Financial Times*, 1977–86; editor, *New Statesman*, 1986–7.
8. He had been appointed managing director, BBC Network Television.

unbusinesslike. He had been at Eastbourne,[9] arriving in my last year. He said I was a great figure there which I don't believe. He didn't dislike it as much as I did, saying it had improved a bit after I left.

He is very agreeable and was interested in our play and suggested Anthony Andrews for it which Allan leapt at but I don't know whether he will do [it].

Granger was absurd about Mrs Thatcher, said he couldn't bear her and she was too authoritarian and taking us into a dictatorship.

There was an argument about *Airbase*.[10] Andrew Sinclair kept shouting, 'Was it a good play? That's the only thing that matters. Was it a good play?' I said, 'That is not the only thing that matters. If it is a libellous account of people who are identifiable as a group, it shouldn't have been put out as fact. It should have been done quite differently.' I might have said if somebody portrayed you as a dishonest lecherous swindler, it might be a very good play but it wouldn't necessarily be a desirable thing to do.

**Thursday 17 March**

Gold Cup day at Cheltenham. Stinking cold. My first task is to get to the bottom of what went wrong on Tuesday when the computer blacked out, losing us nearly the whole of one race and the starting of another race. We estimate now that we lost £200,000 by that.

I am seeing ITS [the firm which installed the computer] at the Tote tomorrow, Friday. I shall make a great commotion with them. Fortunately I got hold of them on the Tuesday and made them send the engineers down that night and make sure everything was in order for the next day, Wednesday.

At the end of the day at Cheltenham we had broken several records despite the failure on Tuesday. We got something like £3,200,000 in cash, easily a record.

Poor Forgive and Forget, a previous winner, broke something in his leg and had to be killed. I wondered why that was strictly necessary because he was still standing upright. Couldn't they have taken him away and put him out to grass instead of just shooting him on the scene of one of his earlier triumphs?

---

9. Eastbourne College, WW's public school.
10. Television play about an American airbase in Britain.

After Cheltenham I got dragged out to a supper party at the Garrick. The Quintons giving it.

When I arrived Marcelle asked what would I like to drink. 'What can I have?' 'Anything.' I said, 'I would like champagne.' But there wasn't any. I was most embarrassed. However, she insisted on having some brought which the waiter eventually did. She said, 'I said you could have anything and you asked for champagne. That's your drink and you're going to have it.'

She's a jolly lady, Marcelle Quinton. She wore a very jazzy short dress, gold and black. She said, 'Now nobody can tell what my figure is like because it's hanging so loose.' I grasped her round her waist and said, 'Well, it's a good figure. Nothing wrong with that.' She is fairly skinny.

Arnold was there. Evidently he had not been to the Garrick before and he kept asking where the Zoffanies were; I think somebody showed them to him in the end.

It was a strange gathering. John Julius Norwich[11] whom I find exceedingly dull, heavy. I sat next to his girlfriend who used to be married to Hugo Philipps. Her name is Mollie. She talked a good deal about La Cerbaia which she has taken from Tony [Lambton] for the month of August. I told her it is very small, very simple. The bathrooms are just farmhouse rooms with baths stuck in them. I said that Verushka had furnished and decorated it beautifully and Tony had managed to get the furniture off her at a knock-down price. My books were still there.

'Tony will be very charming to you. He will tell you how beautiful you are and butter you up.' She said, 'I'm too old for that sort of thing.' 'No one is ever too old to be buttered up in that way. On your arrival he will entertain you as the grand seigneur at the big house. He likes new people but then they wear out.'

Nico Henderson sat at a table with a couple of pretty girls which delighted him. His wife was some tables away. I am very fond of Nico. He gets livelier as he grows older. The Berlins were there. Poor Isaiah croaks a lot now because of this cancer or whatever in his throat. But he keeps going well.

---

11. Viscount Norwich, writer and art historian, former diplomat; son of 1st Viscount Norwich (Duff Cooper) and Lady Diana Cooper; m 2 (1989) Mollie Philipps.

**Friday 18 March**

Allan Davis full of Derek Granger's interest in the play. He said it was much better than he expected. 'It is William Douglas-Home with claws on. It's very funny.'

But he is not happy about the end; nor was Richard Harris who wrote a charming letter saying it was not suitable for him but he liked the play very much.

So I have to work on it again. I think I know what the critics mean but I feel a weariness about girding myself all over again to do the rewriting.

In the evening Petronella's History Society dinner at the Russell Hotel. It was a huge ballroom, about eighty people dotted around [at] tables in the far distance from the dance floor where they were going to dance later.

A. N. Wilson very nervous at making a speech in such a huge place with hardly anybody in it. But he did it well, talking about Scott and Tolstoy and others putting history into their fiction. Particularly that is done, he was saying, by people like Tolstoy and Solzhenitsyn when you can't tell the truth about facts in a country like Russia.

Petronella had a row with her mother because she said there was no ticket for her. She felt embarrassed at the idea of having two parents present with students who had no parent there at all.

Talked to Conrad Russell (the Russell Hotel named after his family, of course).

He said he was taking his seat[12] in time to speak against the Education Bill. I said, 'Is that very bad?' He said, 'Very bad.' He is going to take the Liberal whip.

He hates Mrs Thatcher.

He lacks the light touch of his father Bertrand and is much more frightening.

**Sunday 20 March**

I congratulated her on her speech to the Conservative Council which was fairly well reported. She said, 'I used your bit about taxation not being a punishment.' Her speech would have got more coverage if there had not been a horrible murder of two British servicemen in

---

12. In the Lords, as 5th Earl Russell; he succeeded his half-brother in 1987.

civilian clothes who mistakenly got mixed up with an IRA funeral procession.[13] Television pictures of them being torn to pieces.

I said, 'The Budget's fine[14] but I wish they could have arranged that the tax began not at twenty-five per cent but at fifteen per cent in order to make a bigger difference between being unemployed and employed. She said, 'They are now aiming for the twenty per cent standard rate which would make it better.'

I asked her about the row with Lawson again. She said, 'Well there was a difference to some extent and he can't expect to make all the economic policy. He's a part of the government and I'm the First Lord of the Treasury.' There's not any serious difference, it seems, but there was a difference, so I've slightly misinformed my readers in the *News of the World* this morning by saying there wasn't any.

I said, 'He's done brilliantly.' Then she said, 'Yes, but don't let's forget Geoffrey Howe.[15] He started it all off. He cut the top tax from eighty-three per cent to sixty per cent. He put the VAT up to fifteen per cent. All very difficult decisions and unpopular. Nigel has been able to build on that.'

Thus she indicated to me that she is not so pleased with Nigel as she sometimes has been.

On the Ford situation where they withdrew from building a new £40 million plant at Dundee because they could not get single union representation, she said she was certain they won't come back. 'They've blown it, the unions.' I said, 'Yes but it's not the fault of the Engineers who've got proper leaders because for a long time they've had proper secret ballots for elections. It's the T&GW who oppose the single union representation and are still going in for manipulated and rigged workplace ballots. Their leaders are not really representative of their members.'

She said, 'I hope we're getting on all right with your reforms to make it as good as we can' (the Employment Bill). I said, 'I'm still trying.'

I felt a bit tired at the thought.

---

13. This was the funeral of IRA members shot by the SAS in Gibraltar on 6 March 1988.
14. Nigel Lawson's Budget on 15 March had cut 2p off the standard rate of income tax to 25p in the pound and cut the top rate from 60p to 40p.
15. Chancellor of the Exchequer, 1979–83; Foreign Secretary at this time.

She also said that John Major[16] was extremely good as an explainer of the Budget. 'An excellent fellow,' and that both he and Nigel had elaborated it very well on television. But she is still surprised by the reaction of the public against the forty per cent top tax. I said, 'It will disappear when they begin to understand that there is more benefit to the nation than otherwise.' She said, 'There's still a lot of envy.'

**Monday 21 March**

To lunch at 19 Cavendish Avenue, Norman Lamont. He said there really is a rift at the moment between Lawson and Margaret. He resents her interference and saying different things from him about shadowing the Deutschmark with the pound and keeping the pound close to a three mark level.

Norman said, 'Nigel will think very carefully about his future in the summer. He may be tempted to become Chairman of the National Westminster Bank.'

Norman said he hopes Nigel will go on to be Prime Minister after Mrs Thatcher goes but he genuinely doesn't mind if he isn't. He wouldn't mind being Foreign Secretary if there were a vacancy but he doesn't want Geoffrey Howe to feel he is after his job and trying to edge him out because it isn't true. I said, 'What's the point of being Foreign Secretary after you've been Chancellor of the Exchequer?' and Norman replied, 'Because it stands you in well with the backbenchers in the Tory Party who can't understand economics but all fancy themselves as Foreign Secretaries and believe they understand what it is all about.'

Some of the trouble is that Sam Brittan[17] is devoted to his brother Leon, who never got back into the Cabinet after Westland, and is also the closest friend of Nigel Lawson. It looked at one moment as though Nigel Lawson was priming him in the leaking of the quarrel with Mrs Thatcher over what to do about the pound. Norman had to go and see Sam and tell him to pipe down because of course Nigel had not been priming him at all – he is one hundred per cent loyal.

I asked Norman how his love life was. He said, 'Immaculate now. I haven't done anything for a couple of years.' I said, 'I expect you will. You're only forty-six.'

---

16. Chief Secretary to the Treasury at this time.
17. Principal economic commentator on the *Financial Times*.

He too is hoping for some promotion which I dare say he will get at some point.

He said, 'It must have been six weeks since I told you the decision [about the Tote] had been made by Nigel and he had told Douglas Hurd and John Patten.' He went on, 'When you go along there this afternoon all they are going to say to you is that they must appoint a merchant bank and they will have a beauty contest for one; and that the person there will deal with your merchant bank and yourselves and sort out how it is going to be done.'

That in fact is exactly what did happen when I went to see John Patten. They are going to do a serious feasibility study with the intention of taking it out of the government control and power, exactly as Nigel said they were going to. He sounded as though they had been converted, possibly against their will. Anyway it's definite now. Very exciting but it has to be done with some care.

John Patten was much more interested in talking to me after Brian McDonnell had gone about the Criminal Justice Bill and the crime figures which are coming out on Friday. He said would I write something in the *News of the World* about what they are trying to do about crime? I said, 'Yes, delighted. I may even do something later in the *Times*.'

He said, 'I'm a bit like Margaret. She always says, "I read dear Woodrow's column in the *News of the World* and carefully avoid letting my eyes fall on anything else."'

Being very ambitious John Patten clearly thinks it's a good idea to keep on side with me because of my supposed influence with Margaret.

**Tuesday 22 March**

Lord Marshall of the CEGB to dinner. He is tall, large with baldish head, fifty-six years old, with a squeaky voice which is odd coming from so large and powerful a man.

Arnold says he is very tough as well as clever but he had no business experience when he was appointed. After being Chief Scientist at the Department of Energy he went to the United Kingdom Atomic Authority and thereafter became Chairman of the CEGB in 1982.

He is not against privatization of electricity – but against the manner of it. He thinks that the grid system should have been left with the CEGB because the people who generate the electricity ought to have the grid, for they know exactly how much capacity is needed which would maintain the right supplies and therefore do not overbuild new power stations or alternatively have too few. Now he says the statutory requirement to provide electricity will depart from the CEGB and be given to the area boards who supply the homes and factories with electricity.

I said, 'You mean it's like saying that the statutory responsibility for delivering newspapers will be on the newsagents and they would have to deliver them even if the manufacturers don't produce any?' He said the analogy was absolutely right.

I said I might write an article in the *Times* and show it to him first so he could check the facts. He doesn't even want me to tell Mr Baker, whom I'm meeting for lunch next week and who is his Managing Director, that he had dinner with me. I'm meeting Mr Baker because NERA want me to and because we're doing a lot of work for the Central Electricity Generating Board.

**Wednesday 23 March**

Practically every point I wanted in the Employment Bill has now been conceded.

**Thursday 24 March**

The Other Club. Good dinner, duck Bordelaise as a second course. Once again the Château Talbot 1964 which is first class.

Jacob amusing about his connection with Ernest Saunders of Guinness. He quite innocently bought Guinness shares when asked to help the take-over of Distillers but did not ask for or receive any indemnity against loss or any payment for helping them. When the take-over was successful, Ernest Saunders rang him to say how grateful he was, not that Jacob minded because he had made £6 million profit in buying and selling the Guinness shares.

Ernest Saunders said, 'Is there anything I can do for you? You've done me this great favour.' Jacob said, 'Yes. In the board room of Distillers there are two very considerable paintings, one by Raeburn and one by the great Landseer. If you would lend the Raeburn to the National Gallery I would be very pleased because I am the Chairman of the National Gallery.'

When the time came up for the Raeburn to be put in the National Gallery, there was to be a celebratory party Saunders had asked for in return for lending the Raeburn. Jacob had prepared a speech saying how wonderful Ernest Saunders was, what a wonderful businessman and just the kind of person one needs in business. But when he arrived back from America his secretary said, 'Have you seen what's happened?' Jacob said no, and there was the story about the investigation of Guinness by the police. Jacob hurriedly backtracked on his speech and decided against making one but they had to have the party just the same. So he got the party but not the speech.

At the end of the dinner I asked Michael Hartwell to let me have a look at the Munnings drawings in the books kept where the members sign each time they come.

There were several attractive Munnings drawings of horses. Jacob and I looked at them and I said to Jacob, who knows a lot about art, deals in pictures and owned Colnaghi at one time, 'What do you think they're worth?' and we agreed they were certainly worth £2,000 to £3,000 each; the drawings and the book itself, with all the signatures of Winston Churchill and F. E. Smith and David Lloyd George and other famous people, must be worth at least £20,000 we thought. There were William Orpen drawings in it as well.

Before I left I talked to John Smith who was in the chair. I asked him whether Labour would raise the top rate of forty per cent if they ever became the government and he was the Chancellor. He said, 'No, not exactly, but we would have it graded upwards as they do in Germany and other countries. But we would not go back to the old penal rates.'

John Smith is probably the most sensible of those now at the top of the Labour Party. He would be the Chancellor of the Exchequer if they formed a government. Actually they would do much better to have him Leader, as he is essentially a practical man and comes over well with his Scots accent.[18]

The Queen's Private Secretary (Sir William Heseltine) said he didn't like Munnings' pictures of horses. I said to him, 'You, the Queen's Private Secretary, and you don't like Munnings' pictures of horses?' and he said, 'I don't like horses at all. And the Queen accepts the fact that I detest anything to do with horses. When I was Secretary to Menzies (the Prime Minister of Australia) I also had to tell him that I detested anything to do with cricket and Menzies was very keen on cricket.'

---

18. He was elected Leader after the Labour defeat at the 1992 election but died in 1994.

**Saturday 26 March**

To Badminton for the wedding of Anne[19] to Matthew Carr. Cold in the church.

Laura Dudley that was, or a number of other names,[20] Annie Fleming's sister, came and sat in the same pew. She married Bert Marlborough before he died. She smelled of garlic which I didn't like very much and slightly moved away from her but she was very friendly.

Antonia Fraser was there with Harold Pinter. He is balding and her legs are getting fatter.

Once when Antonia flaunted her affair round London not long after David was married and not long after Antonia was married to Hugh Fraser, Caroline was greatly distressed. I did my best to console her. Now she seemed to accept her presence at the wedding with equanimity. But as Diana Wilton says, it destroyed her and ruined her personality, driving her to drink and changing from a slim beautiful girl to a large plain woman.

Antonia was in white. So was Princess Michael. They looked in some ways not dissimilar though Princess Michael is prettier and younger.

John Manners' wife was very amused just after the wedding at the reception when Princess Michael came up to me and gave me several whacking great kisses and said, 'I've got to go and have my photograph taken now with the bride and bridegroom and the bridesmaids but I'm coming to look for you to talk to you.' When she had gone she said to me (John Manners' wife), 'You'd better go hide in the library.' It wasn't any good in any case because she sought me out.

She said didn't I know the Makhtoum brothers, she wanted to meet them. I said, 'I don't know them. I know Prince Khalid Abdullah who is very rich.' 'But can't you find for me some Arabs who would be kind to beautiful ladies?' I said I would think about it.

I said, 'You're keeping out of the newspapers more now. I'm very pleased about that.' She said, 'They're leaving me alone.' I said, 'Yes, but you're not giving them so much opportunity as you used to.' She said to her horror she heard that Micky Suffolk[21] was having at his

---

19. Lady Anne Somerset, daughter of the Duke and Duchess of Beaufort (David and Caroline).
20. Née Charteris, m 1 (1933–43) 2nd Viscount Long, m 2 (1943–54) 3rd Earl Dudley, m 3 Michael Temple Canfield, m 4 (1972) 10th Duke of Marlborough.
21. 21st Earl of Suffolk and Berkshire.

dinner tonight before the dance Taki, a dreadful Greek who went to prison for drug taking and writes a scabrous column in the *Spectator.* I said, 'Tell Micky that Taki is not to repeat anything he hears.' 'I'm afraid to do that because he would make a great joke of it.'

Suddenly I saw Roy Jenkins there. I assume he was a friend of Raymond Carr,[22] the bridegroom's father, who often used to be at Annie Fleming's. I don't think the Somersets know him. I said to Princess Michael, 'Would you like to meet Roy Jenkins?' She said, 'No. I'd much rather talk to you.'

The bridegroom is a painter. He does it for a living so I hope he is good. Though I am sure that David would have given Anne plenty of money because he prefers her to all his other children. Anne looked really lovely. I never saw her so well got up. Usually she looks a bit ungroomed. Her dress was beautiful and her finger nails were clean. I didn't notice if she is still biting them. She is a very clever girl.

I hope she will be happy. She is the most intelligent of the children by far. The boys are all dolts but they are all good-looking.

Henry Bath was in the church sitting between both his wives, Virginia and Caroline's mother Daphne.[23]

**Sunday 27 March**

I asked Margaret if there were still any friction with Lawson over this business about the level of the pound. She said she didn't think so. I said I had heard from somebody who knows them well (I didn't say it was Norman Lamont) that he was last week at least talking of deciding his future in the summer, whether he wanted to go on or not.

She said, 'Of course one of the troubles is he has these two children about nine and he has got to educate them. And he's got no money.'

My object in talking to her like this was to make sure that she makes some conciliatory noises to Nigel and makes him feel loved and not battered about with arguments about the pound.

I said was she disturbed by these forty or so MPs (Conservative) agitating about amendments to the community charge. She said, 'Not really.' 'Of course people like Heseltine who have got nothing to do, now he's cut himself off, are bound to agitate.' She said, 'Well, that's his fault.'

---

22. Historian, Warden of St Antony's College, Oxford, 1968–87; knight 1987.
23. The 6th Marquess of Bath was divorced in 1953 from Daphne (later Fielding) and then married Mrs Virginia Tennant, née Parsons.

She said she doesn't take much notice of what she reads in the papers. And she meant that in relation to Nigel Lawson and what he was supposed to be thinking – 'They are usually wrong' – and I think she takes the same view about Tebbit's supposed ambitions to displace her at some point.

She was bubbling with life.

**Monday 28 March**

Great excitement. We nearly defeated the government on the requirements for a postal ballot whenever there is a national industrial dispute proposed. I had spoken to Gavin Laird[24] in the morning who said his union would agree with it. They have such a rule in their own books. The ETU of course have a postal ballot before every strike.

The margin was only three in government favour. Baroness Blatch is rather sweet but foolishly got herself into the wrong lobby though she was seconder of my amendment. If she hadn't done that the majority of the government would have been cut to one.

I am now trying to think up a way of producing a further amendment on the third reading which cannot be the same principle as was defeated today.

**Tuesday 29 March**

Consulted Mr Keith at the Public Bill Office.

After a long argument we agreed a formula which he was instrumental in producing which made it sound quite different from a national strike and would cover all strikes short of ones proposed by or intended to be organized by the principal executive committee of a union or more than one union.

**Wednesday 30 March**

Lunch with Mr Baker Managing Director of the CEGB. Nice Californian wine but badly overcooked fillet of beef. I went over much the same ground with him as I did with Lord Marshall when he came to dinner.

I said I would probably write an article for the *Times* and let him see it beforehand so as to get the facts right. He said NERA were doing very good work but he wasn't sure that they had the commercial punch which might be required later.

---

24. General Secretary of the Amalgamated Engineering Union.

**Thursday 31 March**

Ian Chapman of Collins rang while I was in the middle of doing my *News of the World* article. He has good news about the idea of doing a volume of *English Story*, the best stories out of the series of ten. They will almost certainly do it.

**Saturday 2 April**

Verushka annoyed that I refused to accept the invitation of AWA, a firm making Totalisator equipment and computers in Australia, to go there. The invitation had arrived by hand on Thursday with an accompanying letter from the Australian High Commissioner. I said I could not accept such an invitation because it meant they wanted me to buy something on behalf of the Tote from them and I don't accept hospitality and travelling from a potential supplier.

Drinks next door with Justus de Goede – Minister at the South African Embassy. Wants me to go with a couple of other peers to South Africa, examine the situation about sports, verify there is no apartheid and then say so in the Lords and in writing, if that is what we found to be true. Again I could not accept such an invitation.

I spent some time pouring over the lists I made with Flavio on Friday of the wine I have. We haven't quite finished doing the original cellar next to the kitchen. There are about a thousand bottles we have checked so far. Some of it is very good. I reckon there must be at least £10,000 worth of wine in that cellar alone. We then have to go over to the mini cellar and see what is there.

**Sunday 3 April**

Isaiah Berlin and his wife were there [at Bowden]. Before lunch I talked to him a bit about history. I said Macaulay was sensational rubbish, always describing people's convulsions and anguish when they were tortured and giving descriptions of their being flogged to Tyburn and the fearful things that happened to them and their groans.

Isaiah said, 'He was accurate. You can't fault him for accuracy.' 'You can fault him for selection,' and he admitted he was biased. I said, 'He wrote the books to make a best seller out of them,' to which Isaiah agreed but he said it was still beautifully done.

Isaiah produced a large match box, an old Swan Vesta I think, and in it he had some biscuits. He takes them everywhere in case there are not biscuits like his when he eats out. In another pocket he had a slab of chocolate made without sugar. Also some boiled sweets. I said, 'What else have you got?' He pulled out pocket books and engagement books and all manner of things.

He is a very jolly man with no malice. He is against what they are doing to the universities in the Education Bill. He said, 'So is Beloff,[1] who is going to attack the government for the first time seriously.' I said was his university[2] – it was started by Beloff without government money – any good? He said, 'No, it was terrible.'

Lady Berlin had a rich husband who died before she married Isaiah.[3] Her family also had a chunk of Perrier. Her family were Russian Jews and lenders of money to the Tsars, very rich. Her husband before Isaiah was a scientist and he was also a lover of wine, as she is.

It seems she has hundreds of bottles of 1945 and 1947 Latour, Lafite, Cheval Blanc, Mouton Rothschild.

After they had gone I walked with Arnold round the garden a bit and then I went and sat with him on a stone seat at the side of the house in the sun. He is very unhappy. He said he did not sleep last night. All the time he is worried about this Marconi Southampton investigation by the Ministry of Defence police alleging fraud.

Later on the telephone I talked to him again. I said, 'Why don't you be a feckless optimist like me. You know I've had lots of troubles and worries and I have always thought, even when I might go bankrupt, that it would turn out all right in the end and it did. That was because I willed it so to do.' He said, 'I can't do that. I'm a pessimist.' 'You really must try.'

**Monday 4 April**

Jolly lunch with the Wiltons. John says he doesn't want to stay with Tony [Lambton] this summer because he doesn't like the atmosphere and it is too hot, and too much inland for August. He is much looking forward to staying with us. I think that is possibly genuine.

Diana disagreed with me that Tony dislikes women, judging from the way he treats them. She says he soon tires of them but he is a

---

1. Lord Beloff (life peer 1981) was Gladstone Professor of Government and Public Administration, University of Oxford, 1957–74.
2. The University College at Buckingham, founded 1974.
3. Aline, née de Gunzbourg, widow of Dr Hans Halban, married Isaiah Berlin in 1956.

success with them because he makes them think they are the only one at the time.

She thinks he will never marry Claire: he dislikes her as much as he dislikes Bindy [his wife] and that he must be hoping that Bindy won't die before Claire because he would then have difficulty in warding Claire off with no excuse left.

Had a slight brush with Margaret. I put to her the case of a woman losing housing benefit abruptly because she has got £9,000 (£3,000 she has saved and £6,000 left by her sister). She said, 'Well, where would you cut the limit off? Our trouble is that we went on too long with these housing benefits. Two out of three households are paying for the third's housing benefits.'

She added, 'Don't become a Socialist.'

I tried to explain that some old people are afraid of having a terminal illness when they live by themselves and they fear that the National Health Service will not look after them properly so they'll need savings. She said, 'They can go into a home. And £6,000 would not buy much in a private nursing home in any case.'

She was prickly and a trifle shirty.

I thought it fairly ironic. She was accusing me of becoming a Socialist while I have been telling her for years that maintaining the top rate of tax at sixty per cent was Socialist and she ought to bring it down to forty per cent.

I think she was irritated with me because I didn't do as I usually do. I hadn't discussed with her how she should deal with the Opposition more effectively on the housing benefit point (and the £6,000 limit), and the arguments for it, instead of plunging in on a seemingly critical basis of what she had done. A failure of tact on my part.

I was slightly perturbed by Margaret's attitude today. It was the first time for a long time I got a hint that she seemed to think nothing she does is wrong or open to doubt. Though maybe I have exaggerated that in my mind.

**Tuesday 5 April**

David Montagu and Peter Winfield[4] [at] the Tote Board meeting said that I was going back on a decision made by the Board to abandon the idea of commercialization or privatization of the Tote.

---

4. Member of the Tote Board since 1981; at this time senior partner, Healey & Baker, chairman, London Auction Mart.

David said he was flabbergasted by my speech at the Tote Annual Lunch. I said, 'If you'd been at the last Board meeting, and you can see the private minute, I said I was going to talk about it, and I did talk about it.'

'But we want to know the terms,' said David. 'That is what is going to be worked out between the government sponsored merchant bank and Hambros our own bankers.'

I had a feeling that David felt it was one thing to be on a grand public board like the Tote, appointed by the Home Secretary, with a special status in racing, and another to be a director of a commercial organization like any other betting organization.

**Wednesday 6 April**

Spoke to Peter Winfield who said he had read the correspondence now but of course it is all right to hold diverse views and he always says when he is of a different opinion. I said, 'Yes, but I am talking about the facts. I have not departed from the policy. And the implication was that I had been.' After a while he said, 'Well, yes, I suppose you're right. I'm sorry you were offended.'

David Montagu always professes great friendship and I think he is genuinely friendly but I always remember that when John Freeman was running London Weekend Television and wanted to amalgamate with Banbury, which would have been marvellous for us and ensure its future for ever, he put his oar in because he was Chairman of the Board, and stopped it. If he hadn't, Banbury would never have collapsed.

Spoke to the Social Security Department. Began to think Margaret had some grounds for being a bit shirty with me. These housing benefits cost £5.1 billion last year. In 1979 one in seven got rates and rents free or with huge rebates on them, and now it is one in three.

**Sunday 10 April**

Margaret started talking about the strange idea that it was reasonable for people to be on the dole or benefits if their income were a little less when they went to work. 'They ought to want to work, and not be a burden on their neighbours and taxpayers even if they get a little less.'

She spoke to me about a man called Ernest Hall[5] who has got something going in what used to be a carpet factory in Dean Clough, Halifax, which went bust. This was a place where all kinds of people could start up enterprises. He, when she went round there recently, told her that they shouldn't expect to be propped up by the government. 'A little adversity is good for us all. That is how I got on.' She was very keen that I should write something about this Halifax enterprise.

When I asked her whether there was any hope still for education vouchers, she said that she thought that what they are doing now, about being able to move your school if you didn't like the one you were in, was a move in that direction because the money moves with the choice. Also that the NHS perhaps could have something of that sort done by selecting the hospital you wanted.

It was she who made the Department of Employment accept my latest amendment about postal ballots before industrial disputes. She said after I had spoken to her last Sunday last week, 'I sent a memo to them saying we've got to have postal ballots for strikes just the same as we have for elections of officials.'

It certainly is much easier to get things done in the Lords, particularly when the Prime Minister is working behind the scenes for you.

**Tuesday 12 April**

In the Lords for about seven divisions in the space of a couple of hours in the late afternoon. Bessborough said he's been in the Lords thirty-two years and they had never voted so often in so short a time before.

It was all to do with immigration. The forces of compassion wanted to make it easier for people to settle here from the new Commonwealth. Those non-compassionate like myself were voting against this notion. I believe that we have quite enough coloured immigrants here already. To allow any more in would be disastrous. They will multiply faster than the indigenous population anyway and we don't want to become like Fiji, with the Indians swamping the country.

To dinner came Harold Lever, his wife, and Diane's sister. Plus Charles and Sally Wilson.

I like Sally very much though she is not particularly attractive, a trifle raw-boned and clumsily built, with a coarse face plus curly blonde (natural?) hair. She edits *Options*, a highly successful monthly

---

5. Pianist, composer and property developer; chairman, Dean Clough Business, Arts and Education Centre; knight 1993.

magazine. She is about to start *Riva* with a £3 million promotion launch. It is to be a weekly covering news with an angle for intelligent women. That is its basis but it will also have other articles of interest to women.

She prefers to work with women in her job. She says women take more trouble.

She interviewed people for a sub-editor's job on *Options* the other day. Two men came and said they had never seen the magazine. Two women came and had studied it properly before they applied for the job.

Harold is more and more garrulous, repeating old stories repeatedly. He lives in the past. On the way out he said to me, 'We have to make a decision, people like you and me with our young wives. Do we hang on to protect our wives or do we die immediately while they still have a chance of getting married again?' Diane was a little shocked.

Sally, despite her being highly independent and with a large income of her own from her editorship, still is bound by the guilt of whether or not she makes breakfast when the children are at school. The nanny doesn't come in until later. You would have thought they could afford resident servants.

**Saturday 16 April**

Julian Amery rang. 'Your article in the *Times* this morning was masterly. It completely demolishes Michael Mates' case.[6] It's better than anything I have seen written or stated by Nicholas Ridley (the Secretary for the Environment in charge of the Community Charge Bill) or the Prime Minister or anyone else.'

I asked him what was the matter with Mates and he said, 'It's rather sad. He has struggled loyally and always supported Margaret Thatcher and never got any reward for it. So he is very bitter.'

---

6. Mates, a Conservative backbench MP, proposed an amendment to the Community Charge Bill at the report stage so that non-taxpayers would pay 50 per cent of the community charge; taxpayers on the basic rate, 100 per cent; and single persons and couples living together, 150 per cent, when their single or combined income reached the 40 per cent income tax band. WW also attacked the idea of introducing local income tax as an alternative to the community charge.

**Sunday 17 April**

Mrs T says the list of those backing the Mates amendment shows all the usual ones with their guilt complexes, their disappointment at not being promoted, those who are disappointed at not being in the government any more.

I said, 'There was a very bad leading article in the *Sunday Times* saying that they hoped the Mates amendment would be carried tomorrow night because that would mean that the government would have to drop the whole bill, go back to the drawing-board and stop this community charge plan altogether.' I went on, 'I never did quite like Andrew Neil.' She said, 'Oh he gets all that from Peter Walker.'

I have had a letter from Humphrey Brooke who was Secretary of the Royal Academy 1952–1968. He knew A. J. Munnings very well and wrote to congratulate me on my review:[7] 'I am confident A. J. consummated neither marriage. I suspect he was of the type, once fairly common according to an experienced GP, who could not perform with a wife until taught by a "tart". A slightly snobbish streak would have inhibited that course.'

**Monday 18 April**

Felicity Lane-Fox has died.

She got polio when she was twelve. She went up and down the corridors of the Lords in her electric chair which I examined with some care one day. She was very friendly and told me with giggles and smiles how much she enjoyed reading my *Confessions of an Optimist*. She had found it all entertaining particularly the accounts of my love life.

What a lively, bright, enthusiastic woman. She overcame or rose above her great disability.

I went into the Commons and heard Michael Mates putting his amendment. He made a good speech for a bad case. He was followed by Nicholas Ridley who made a bad, or at least a below average one, for a good case. He got too involved in details. He needed a broad brush but didn't know how to apply it. I kept wishing, 'Oh God, I'd love to be at that Despatch Box' and could put the whole thing much more clearly and simply, proving that this really is the best answer.

Then went to dinner at the RAC where I acted as the host after we

---

7. Of *What a Go: The Life of Alfred Munnings* by Jean Goodman, in the *Times*, 14 April 1988; WW said according to the book Munnings' first marriage was not consummated and it was not clear whether his second marriage was.

had interviewed a young man for the job of Chief Executive of Satellite Information Services.

After he had gone a set-to occurred. Len Cowburn[8] raised the fact there had been criticism of Bruce Matthews' feebleness in conducting the post of Chairman. Bruce got very indignant and started attacking me. I said, 'Don't attack me. I'm one of your supporters. But I have said to you several times that I thought the board meetings ought to be much more organized than they are.'

His display of petulant bad temper and banging the table saying, 'I'm going to be tough and ruthless then if that's what you want. I'll be an Executive Chairman,' bang, bang, bang, was childish. It made me feel here was a rather weak man, as Rupert had hinted to me, trying to pretend to be strong.

**Tuesday 19 April**

Spoke to Margaret at 8.30 a.m. I said, 'A majority of twenty-five wasn't bad.'[9] She reacted at once. 'No, it was rather good in the circumstances.'

We spoke about the leaks. There was one yesterday, revealed by the Labour Party. Correspondence between the Prime Minister's office and the Secretary for the Environment (Ridley) had been given to the Labour Party.

She said there are a number of dedicated Communists or Socialists in some of these departments. 'It's their creed to leak to the Opposition to damage the government. When a Labour government is in power the Tory minded officials behave properly and serve the government, even if they don't like it, loyally.'

She said, 'There's nothing to be done with the Tories who voted against the government. What is worrying is that they are now a gang. If you look through the list they are all the embittered, the discontented or disappointed people who seem to be getting almost into a group now.'

Allan Davis rang. His latest idea is Vanessa Redgrave and somebody [Michael] Palin she acts with a lot.

---

8. From William Hill, the bookmakers.
9. Against the Mates amendment.

**Thursday 21 April**

A rushed day.

I had to go and talk to Trefgarne.[10]

He said what he wanted to say to me secretly was that the government ministers were divided about what to do about my amendment. We agreed that I would carry on with the amendment, for that is the only way in which the government can have second thoughts in the Commons. When the Lords amendments come back to the Commons, they can alter a Lords amendment but if it hasn't been passed, they can't alter it or do anything fresh about it.

In the evening Saintsbury Club dinner for members only.[11] A dullish crew.

There was champagne, St Marcause 1976 in jeroboams. A champagne I have never heard of and I didn't think much of. Then the Grand Cru Chablis was changed to Clos des Mouches 1979 and it was pretty poor stuff, not half as good as the Chablis we had at dinner last night at home. The Château d'Issan 1964 was excellent. Lovely flavour smell and taste. I liked it better than the Château Lafite 1955 En Imperial. Then there was 1963 port. Then we had ancient rum put in the bottle in 1795. It was truly awful. One of the bottles had got almost black and tasted of metal or something nasty. The other was lighter but both were like firewater. It was obviously horrible rum when it was put in the bottle and it was still horrible rum two hundred years later because nothing happens to a spirit once it is put in the bottle.

A little speech was made by Oscar Wilde's grandson Merlin Holland. A good-looking young man with the fleshy mouth, a little of Oscar Wilde. I knew his father well, Vyvyan Holland, who wrote a book called *Son of Oscar Wilde* explaining the plight they were in when their mother deserted Oscar Wilde and was divorced and the awful difficulties they were in after their father went to jail.

Like his father he is very knowledgeable about wine.

---

10. Minister of State for Defence Procurement, 1986–8.
11. Founded in 1931 by a small group headed by André Simon in honour of George Saintsbury, literary historian and wine connoisseur (1845–1933); its membership consisted of twenty-one 'men of wine' and twenty-five 'men of letters'.

**Saturday 23 April**

I went to see *The Best of Friends*. This is a play about Sir Sydney Cockerell (who created the Fitzwilliam Museum as it is), George Bernard Shaw with whom he corresponded, and a nun, the Abbess of Stanbrook, with whom they both corresponded. It was strange that her two correspondents on whom she was so keen were atheists. The play was based mostly on fact, with very long speeches, which I had been told not to write by Allan Davis who got the last ticket in the theatre for me.

It was the last night and possibly the last time Sir John Gielgud will ever be seen on the stage. He fluffed his lines occasionally but without him the play would have been tedious. There were one or two good speeches for Bernard Shaw talking about plays needing no plots, which was a typical Shavianism considering that his most successful plays were very strong on plot.

The original Sydney Cockerell was by his own admission second rate.

He cultivated friendships assiduously with the famous but didn't think much of his own children. He described his son, later Sir Christopher, as a mechanic, and despised him. He [Christopher] was an FRS and invented the hovercraft among other things.

**Sunday 24 April**

Mrs Thatcher said I must have enjoyed writing my piece in the *News of the World* today. 'You had a great go.' This was about saying the Lords had no business to reverse so important a measure as the community charge, particularly as it was such a major part of the manifesto the Tories won the election on and the Lords are not elected.

'You're too generous in making peers of potential enemies. St John-Stevas is keen to attack the community charge.' She said, 'Yes, most of our strength in the Lords is on the crossbenches.'

I asked her if she had read my *Times* article on Wednesday about the Zola Budd situation and the International Amateur Athletic Federation.[12] She said, 'Yes. It is appalling how this poor girl is persecuted.'

---

12. The 1977 Gleneagles statement on apartheid in sport forbade sportspeople from participating in events in South Africa. Zola Budd had come to Britain as a young athlete, taking British citizenship in 1984. After she had watched an event at Brakpan in South Africa and used the course there for training, she had been debarred in March 1988 from an international cross-country event in New Zealand.

I said, 'We must get rid of the Gleneagles Agreement quite apart from the IAAF stuff. It was designed to make South Africa have their sports multi-racial and now they all are. Even the race Zola Budd was accused of watching was multi-racial. How can we go on with a system which prevents people competing even with blacks in South Africa?' She agreed.

She said about the various bills backbenchers have been rebelling on, she prefers to have the troubles at this stage, early in a parliament, than later on nearer the election. In other words she is following Attlee's maxim – do the unpopular things at the beginning of your term.

**Monday 25 April**

Disaster for me in the Lords. The amendment to get strikes other than national preceded not only by a ballot but by a postal ballot was defeated by about 153 to 17.

Arnold didn't even vote for it though he sat there. He is very weak really. He doesn't want to do anything he thinks may annoy Margaret or against a prevailing mood. Frank Chapple didn't speak for it. Arnold said he couldn't understand it, although he admitted that his personnel man at GEC understood it and thought it was a very good idea.

There was some feeling that I was merely trying to move the amendment that had been defeated on the report stage which is against the standing orders of the House, although there are no real standing orders. But I carefully explained it was quite a different amendment. I told the government that they will be forced to do what I was saying in due course.

**Tuesday 26 April**

In the Lords found Willie Whitelaw worried a little bit. 'Things are looking rather tricky,' he said. 'The way to get the Community Charge Bill through is to make up your mind what you absolutely need to keep in it. In the first round you try and keep everything in (by which he meant the committee stage). Then you have to make up your mind what you might be prepared to sacrifice without damaging the whole Bill.'

I said, 'Are you giving advice to those who have to handle this?' 'We-ell, yes, a little bit. There's some difficulty . . .' He then stopped because he saw Bertie Denham (Government Chief Whip) standing beside us, having approached us very close, to about a foot. He said,

'Excuse me a moment,' as Bertie Denham wanted to speak to him, and I never heard the rest of his difficulties in advising Lord Belstead, the new Leader of the House, and Bertie Denham.

**Wednesday 27 April**

A secret meeting at Cavendish Avenue of the SIS directors to discuss whether Bob Green's[13] nominee, Bill Hogwood, should be made the Chief Executive or whether it should be another candidate, Christopher Stoddart from Newcastle Tyne-Tees Television. I said, 'I vote for Stoddart.' The others all agreed except for Peter George and Bob Green but they were outvoted.

Bob Green has got his knife into Bruce Matthews and thinks he is incompetent and a danger to the company. I wouldn't go so far as that but he has been disappointing in his lack of grip. It would be inadvisable to ask him to go now, first of all because he would cause a commotion and secondly because the placing of the shares has not yet been done and it would presumably put off the investors if we admitted that the original Chief Executive was no good and now that the original Chairman was no good.

Nicholas and Caroline came to dinner. Caroline was rather unpleasant to Verushka. Wouldn't let Genevra wear the pretty dress she gave her. They are frightfully pleased with themselves because they are making so much money. Between them they must have an income of at least £160,000 a year now, but they are cultureless.

**Thursday 28 April**

Went to Groucho Club. Party given by Elizabeth Harrison[14] and her partner who are starting a public relations business. She remains very pretty.

Richard Harris was there, Elizabeth's first husband. He is the one who read my play, said the first act was wonderful. He said he didn't like filming any more and much preferred the stage. I told him we followed his suggestions for improvement and the second act was now different in construction, rather as he was indicating it should be. He asked to be allowed to see it again but I don't think he'll do it.

---

13. Bob Green from Mecca.
14. The Hon. Elizabeth Aitken, née Rees-Williams, daughter of 1st Baron Ogmore (Liberal politician); m 1 (1957–69) Richard Harris, actor; m 2 (1971–5) Rex Harrison, actor; m 3 (1980) Peter Aitken, grandson of 1st Lord Beaverbrook.

He has been very kind to Elizabeth, helping her with her (and his) children.

And helping her with money though under no obligation to do so. He seems a decent man. Tall with hair, light coloured, in a fringe and stooping.

I had never seen the Groucho Club before. It didn't look to me the sort of club I would care to belong to.

I met Sally Ann Howes. She was once the most beautiful girl you could possibly imagine when she was a young actress, daughter of Bobby Howes. I didn't recognize her because she has got so fat. When I went I kissed her goodbye and she said how pleased she was to meet me at last but it was rather too late after all those years to do anything about it.

**Saturday 30 April**

To Newmarket for the 2,000 Guineas and our lunch party. The new room is not as attractive as the old, larger one which was torn down to make way for new stands. But it is pleasant and has been decorated well by Verushka with Jane Churchill's materials for the curtains and wallpaper.

A fairly jolly party. The Oppenheimers were there. Philip I was teasing as being a secret agent going in and out of Russia. He seemed pleased at the idea as I said he looked so respectable and quiet that no one would suppose that he was a James Bond when he travelled round or to Moscow. He does tremendous deals with the Russians over their buying of South African diamonds from de Beers.

He said that the atmosphere in his recent visits to Moscow has changed. For the first time he was invited to people's private flats.

Diana Wilton sat on my left and Isabel Derby on my right. Isabel said, 'I've got a story for you,' and said to Diana, 'I always have to give him a new story.' It was about a man who drove away from a public house very drunk followed by the police and stopped. When he wound down his window to speak to the police, the policeman said, 'We have reason to believe you have been drinking,' and he replied, 'I haven't had a cunt all day, drinkstable.'

Isabel hates the Aga Khan and hoped his horse Doyoun wouldn't win but it did.

Peter Leng, Chairman of the Racecourse Association, was there. I spoke to him about his idea of the Racecourse Association acquiring fifty-one per cent of a privatized Tote. I joined Tommy Wallis in the conversation assuming that, as the RCA's representative on the SIS board with Peter Leng, he would know all about it.

Afterwards Peter Leng complained to me bitterly that I should not have said anything about it in front of Tommy Wallis. He had wanted to go and see Sporborg at Hambros and talk to him without Tommy knowing because he is dead against the idea.

There is much internal politics in the RCA. They are getting rid of Peter Leng a year from June because they think he takes too much on himself without consultation. This may be cited as another example.

Tommy Wallis said he thought it was quite a good idea but he thought Johnnie Henderson would have a better one. I don't think so. Johnnie's idea is for the Tote to borrow the money and link the interest with profits and not get rid of its equity. I am not keen. I want to raise £20 million or so to buy betting shops with to start off with.

After Newmarket we went to Easton Neston.[15] The only private house ever built by Hawksmoor.

The first part had been a wing in Queen Anne red brick, built 1690ish by Wren who was a cousin of the Hesketh family. He was very old at the time and it was finished by Hawksmoor. Then the much grander new house was built alongside the Wren wing and completed in 1702.

Also staying was Geoffrey Ampthill.[16] He is in charge of the Lords dining room. He says it makes a profit. The only subsidy from the government is about £186,000 to cover the cost of the staff when the House is not sitting, particularly in the summer, and their wages still have to be paid. I said I was amazed. I thought perhaps the lobsters were frozen in the £9 dinner or whatever the price is, which we often have on a Tuesday, but added, 'They tasted too fresh.' He said, 'Yes, they come from Canada and I won't have any of them unless they walk live into the kitchen.'

He said, 'One reason why we can make a profit is the elderly peers have got very poor teeth and they don't chew much so they will only have a little part of the set meal, say the plaice or something soft. We make a lot of money on that.'

He said the House of Commons restaurant cost the government £2.3 million last year. It is very badly managed.

Geoffrey Ampthill is the product of a remarkable marriage, his

15. Lord Hesketh's country house near Towcester, Northamptonshire.
16. 4th Baron Ampthill, at this time Deputy Speaker, House of Lords.

succession subject to court actions in which he was said to have been conceived by buggery [not so, see note] and not by normal intercourse.[17] However, he doesn't seem the worse for wear for it. He works with David Stevens and is a director of United Newspapers and Express Newspapers.

Also staying was Michael White, the theatrical impresario and film maker. I last met him with Chips Keswick at lunch at Hambros.[18] I sent him my play and he didn't like it. I didn't mention my play to him again.

---

17. In the Ampthill Peerage Case ([1976] 2 All ER) Geoffrey Ampthill's legitimacy and consequential succession to the barony were upheld. Conception was *ab extra*, not by penetration (but not by buggery as WW seems to have thought). His mother had said, and his father had admitted, 'that he had been in use to lie between her legs with the male organ in more or less proximity to the orifice of the vagina, and to proceed to emission' (*Russell* v. *Russell* [1924] AC 687 at 721).
18. See 27 November 1985.

**Sunday 1 May**

Late for lunch arrived Anne Lambton, Tony's daughter, and a girl called Huston,[1] the daughter of the film director who died last summer, John Huston. I said to her, 'Did you hear your father sing that marvellous song called "September Song"?' She said, 'Oh no, that was my grandfather.' She must have felt I thought her very old. She remembered the words and promised to sing it to me at breakfast.

Anne Lambton is very nervous, smoking cigarette after cigarette. She rolls them herself very thin. She says she does it so she won't have so much to smoke. Her hands are shaking all the time. Quite but not really pretty. Tony's children, even those born of extra-marital beautiful mothers, are on the whole ugly, Rose being the most attractive.

Michael White admitted at dinner that the *White Mischief* film was very inaccurate.[2] I said, 'I don't like this business of mixing fact and fiction.' He said the trouble was he had a young director who was very left-wing and wanted to show how beastly the whites had been before the War to the Africans. I said, 'Why didn't you stop him?' 'I couldn't. I was only the producer.'

The Huston girl was not attractive but pleasant, with long legs and big thighs, hair straight on either side. She told me she was acting in a film by Roald Dahl, *The Witches*.[3] I said, 'What part are you playing?' 'I'm the chief witch.' She struck me as being well cast for appearance though not necessarily by nature.

Claire [Hesketh], Mimi Manton's daughter, is very pretty like her

---

1. Anjelica Huston, actress, daughter of John Huston (1906–87), director of *The Maltese Falcon*, *The African Queen* etc. and granddaughter of Walter Huston (1884–1950), b Toronto, Canada, stage and film actor.
2. Based on the book by James Fox about amorous intrigues leading to murder in the 'Happy Valley' of colonial Kenya during the Second World War; directed by Michael Radford.
3. Directed by Nicolas Roeg, 1989; Anne Lambton, also an actress, was in this film too.

mother and also equally vague. Alexander runs the whole household because she forgets everything.

**Monday 2 May**

I ate another big breakfast. I didn't find any moment by myself to do my diary or think.

Yesterday Alexander took me round a large part of his five thousand acre estate. He is very modern and now employs more people because they mill all their own grain. He has a co-operative with other farmers.

He is also developing houses for what he calls Yuppies at Milton Keynes. He is doing a good job of converting old farm buildings for people like that.

He wants to make an all-weather track. He showed me the hundred acres he would put it on, not on the present racecourse. He thought he might be able to have flat racing, too.

I was very impressed with him. I think he might make a good Minister of Agriculture. I asked him if he would like to be one and he said yes, very much indeed. He is passionately interested in politics and thinks nothing but politics all the time and talks them.

At lunch Mimi Manton came and we chatted away. She told me how in Ireland, where she was born and brought up, she fell in love with a married man when she was eighteen. Her parents got in a terrible state and she then went to England – they got her to go there. Her brother was in the Army more or less with Rupert and she met him, fell in love with him and they have been married for forty years.

She is a delicious creature, wonderfully Irish and like a leprechaun. She thinks we should take all the troops out and let the Irish sort it out themselves. I said, 'But think of all the bloodshed.' 'Yes, there would be bloodshed. But then they would settle on something at the end of it. This way nothing will ever happen.'

There are servants about the house but nobody does one's unpacking.

Alexander worried me because he is getting very fat. Until recently he weighed twenty-two stone. Now he is down to eighteen. I said I would send him a proper diet and he must stop stuffing all that butter and cream, and eating things with saturated fats in or he will have a heart attack. He is only thirty-seven.

At the racecourse was Bertie Denham. I said to him, 'You couldn't pass my amendment about having secret postal ballots before strikes. Now the seamen working for P&O say they are a majority in wanting to accept the terms but the union won't let them have a secret postal ballot.'

Rupert rang from Venice yesterday. He said he thought she oughtn't to attack the IBA in the way she did[4] because it let all the left-wing people say she is too authoritarian, trying to censor everything. I said I didn't think that was quite the point. Geoffrey Howe had wanted a postponement until after the inquest. He said, 'The real answer is to have lots and lots of channels and no authorities overseeing them and let them all get on with it. It would be like newspapers with different voices and should be the same for the news as well.'

**Tuesday 3 May**

Spoke to Margaret and explained I couldn't ring over the weekend as I was staying in somebody's house and it's always difficult. I don't want to be overheard.

I told her that Alexander Hesketh is a first rate farmer and businessman, highly intelligent. Could she make him Minister of Agriculture one day or is it difficult in the Lords? She said, 'No, we can always have one there.' She agreed with me, 'He has a very good way with the young as well as charm.'[5]

I told her that Alexander had said that Prior, Pym and Norman St John-Stevas had written to the Whips' office in the Lords saying they were not rebels. She laughed. She said the first thing Prior did when he went into the Lords was to vote against the government.

She felt that after the murders at the weekend of the servicemen in Holland,[6] the feeling against that programme *Death on the Rock*, in which it was claimed that the assassins ought not to have been shot because they were trying to surrender, had grown stronger.

She was in good spirits.

---

4. Over the showing on 28 April of *Death on the Rock*, about the IRA shootings on Gibraltar.
5. He became Parliamentary Under-Secretary of State, Department of the Environment, 1989–90, when Mrs Thatcher was still Prime Minister, then Minister of State, DTI, 1990–1.
6. Three off-duty servicemen were killed there on 1 May by an IRA hit-squad.

**Thursday 5 May**

Handed Alexander a list of dos and don'ts for eating. Also a box of chocolates for Claire. He looked eagerly at the box of chocolates and said, 'These are my favourites.'

Dinner at No 10 with the Hungarian Prime Minister and his entourage. He is delighted to see Verushka and she talks Hungarian to him. The Hungarians I talked to concede that they cannot equal the wealth of the Western countries if they don't have the same private enterprise system.

They told Verushka that they are no longer Red but Lilac in Hungary.

They said they are terrified of Gorbachev being thrown out for fear of what would happen in Russia and to them.

Mrs Thatcher kept winging Verushka round to speak Hungarian to various people. Just as I was getting going with one Hungarian, the Minister of Industry, she came and dragged us away and we had to talk to the Prime Minister again. He was engaged in an immensely tedious conversation with Dame Judi Dench [actress], one of the most ugly women I have ever seen. She was asking him the cost of the support given to culture in Hungary. The poor man looked baffled and lost for figures. How daft can one be in interrogating foreigners?

**Friday 6 May**

Richard Harris likes my play very much now though still has one or two hesitations about the second act. He says, 'It will be a long runner.' He only wants a play with a short run.

Lee Menzies, who put on the Archer play, likes the play very much and wants to do it. There is now talk of starting it at Bromley. Allan is meeting him on Tuesday. Menzies couldn't before because he had been replacing Andrew Cruikshank (who has dropped dead), the Judge in the Archer play, and going to his funeral.

Allan Davis is excited. He says the climate towards the play has completely changed since the recent alterations. With great reluctance he has now paid the £500 he has owed me since March 21. He tried to wriggle out of it by saying he would have to pay another £500 for a further option six months later and could the dates be changed?

**Saturday 7 May**

David [Duke of Beaufort] rings while I am swimming. Says it is urgent. Will I ring him back. His problem is Eddie [his son] of whom he is very fond. He is in the Priory, a well known place for the rich to dry out from alcohol and drugs.

The *News of the World* have been trying to reach Eddie and they have been trying to talk to David. Evidently they want to write a story. David says it's probably because the Badminton Trials are on at the moment.

I ring Wendy Henry but she's not there or can't speak. I speak to Philip Wrack, the Assistant Editor. I put it to him that he's a very boring young man, Eddie, and that Prue Murdoch[7] is godmother to his daughter and couldn't they leave the story out as he is really of no great interest? He said they have to judge it by what the story is so far as news worth is concerned.

He said, 'How can we have one rule for friends of Woodrow Wyatt and a different one for people who are not his friends?' I said, 'Oh, I thought that was what the enterprise culture was all about,' and he laughed. He said he would see what he could find out, though it's very difficult if they get the impression he is trying to suppress something. It is awkward and it can get handed on to *Private Eye* that they have been suppressing a story because, say, of Prue Murdoch's connection with Eddie Somerset.

**Sunday 8 May**

There was only a small piece on a distant inside page about Eddie. They called him the Duke of Beaufort's heir, a typical journalist hyperbole because his brother, Harry Worcester, is.

Their main story is one they have pinched from the *People* about Major Ferguson, father of the ghastly Duchess [of York]. He has been going to some weird club where they lay on massage by girls who do more than massage. David said, 'I think I was a member of that club a long time ago. Perhaps I could make you a member of it though there's a seven-year waiting list.' I said, 'I expect it's seventy years after the publicity it's got of what you can get with the massage.'

There was a very good interview by Brian Walden with Margaret in the *Sunday Times* this morning. She said she spoke out freely to him and felt she could trust him.

I said, 'I'm glad he emphasizes the fact that you are in no hurry to retire.' She said, 'I've got to wait for a younger generation who are going to do the things that I believe in.'

---

7. Rupert Murdoch's daughter by his first marriage.

I said, 'But you love it anyway, being Prime Minister.' She said, 'Yes, I have a fascinating life. But sometimes I wish I could go out into business and make some money. And have a nice house to retire into.' I said, 'You don't have to bother about that. Remember Collins want to publish your memoirs.[8] You'll get a very large amount of money from them.' She said she wanted a publisher who would publish in America as well. I said, 'That is exactly what Collins would do.'

**Monday 9 May**

Spent much of the Sunday and Monday morning preparing my speech for the Community Charge Bill in the Lords. It wasn't as good as I would have liked but it went down pretty well. Patrick Jenkin[9] made a very good speech. He is the originator of the whole idea. The weight of the argument was certainly in favour of the government. I do not think there is going to be any real trouble in the Lords about this Bill.

**Tuesday 10 May**

Jolly in the Lords for me this afternoon. About five people congratulated me on my speech yesterday. One said it was inspired, another said it was typically robust.

I spoke to Tufton Beamish[10] who is leading the revolt in the Lords against the government's community charge. He tells me his amendment is the first one and it will be on Monday, May 23rd. It is to make the Secretary of State think out a scheme to improve considerably the rebates relating to the ability to pay for those under and above income support level.

Tufton is a fuddy-duddy old soldier, brainless. He thinks he represents old fashioned Tory values of decency but can't analyse them and confuses himself. He's not a rebel and looks like a toy soldier in front of a firing squad, moustache bristling.

Spoke to Allan Davis. He had Lee Menzies in the room with him. He told me he was booking the Bromley Theatre where he said they would give us a good production. They are now just looking for the right actors. The play is being sent to Peter Bowles. They want to see

8. *The Downing Street Years* was published by HarperCollins in 1993.
9. Conservative politician, Secretary of State for the Environment, 1983–5; life peer 1987.
10. 1917–89; Lord Chelwood, Conservative politician; life peer 1974.

if he is willing first. He is quite tall and if he is willing they will try to get Maria Aitken (very tall) to do the female lead.

Mr Menzies said, 'We are now looking for the right people to do *Knowing the Wrong People.*'[11]

**Tuesday 10 May**

Dinner at Cavendish Avenue. Mary Rothermere, Andrew and Sonia Sinclair, Tony and Marcelle Quinton, Robin Day, William and Rachel Douglas-Home and David Beaufort.

On my right Mary Rothermere who is fairly nice though I have mild reservations. Verushka likes her very much because she is an *haute monde* gossip.

On my left Rachel. I urged her to take her seat in the Lords which she said she had done.[12] I said, 'Well you must turn up there. You must come and support the community charge.' She said unfortunately she had taken leave of absence. She had given notice to end the absence but it won't take effect before May 23rd which is the vital date. I said, 'If you came there we could have little teas together.' She thought that funny.

Robin Day, after the ladies had gone, started off on Mrs Thatcher. He ran her down a little bit and said she was too bossy and all the usual cliché stuff. I said, 'She has a high regard for you,' so he began to change a bit.

David is making a tremendous amount of money with the Marlborough Gallery. He is able to run Badminton on a scale far better than the old Duke and keep all these children who earn nothing whatever. He finds that very disappointing.

I am very fond of David. He says that Caroline has stopped drinking whisky. He saw her with a pale drink in her hand and said, 'Is that gin?', fearing the worst. It was a tumbler full. She was very angry. 'No, it's water. And mind your own business about what I drink.' I fear that the poor strain, coming from Caroline's mother and Henry, her father, who is very agreeable but mildly off his rocker, has infected her children except Anne.

David is irritated by Tracy who is married to Harry.

She brings into the house all kinds of Greenpeace people because she has got a notion she believes in that now. He wanted to give them

11. The play's new name.
12. As Baroness Dacre, daughter of 4th Viscount Hampden, she inherited the barony.

the cottage where they used to live (cottage being a euphemism for a largish country house where Arthur Wyatt lived when he was land agent of the Beaufort estate). They won't live there. Tracy prefers everything to be run for her in the big house. She has a crowd of weird friends and David never knows who he is going to find there. He is long suffering.

I think David was the last to go. He always likes coming to dinner at our house perhaps because he meets people with a bit more brains than he has to be surrounded with at Badminton. He and Caroline have really drifted apart now. He can't bear her drunkenness and fatness. Caroline, however, enjoys being a Duchess. David is tolerant.

I talked to Mary Rothermere about Daylesford and why did they leave it. I said, 'Esmond loved that house. There was a swimming pool at the bottom of it which he loved. I used to stay with him there. It was a wonderful place.'

She said, 'We couldn't afford it.' 'You couldn't afford it? You had plenty of money.' 'Yes, but it was very difficult keeping up Warwick House (which is just by St James's Park and Lancaster House) and Daylesford as well.' That made me feel there was some truth in what had been said about her driving him out of the house and getting it sold because she wanted more money for herself when he died which he was about to do within a year or so.[13]

**Wednesday 11 May**

Lunch at Cavendish Avenue. Kingsley Amis, Merlin Holland (Oscar Wilde's grandson), Philip Howard[14] and Petronella. It was really a birthday lunch for Petronella who had not had one.

I gave them only Sainsbury champagne before lunch. Kingsley had his usual half a tumbler full of whisky which he took into lunch with him.

We began with 1961 Bellevue St-Emilion, a great growth but not one of the first great growths. That was of course after the 1984 Chablis which I am using at the moment and which Kingsley liked very much. We moved on to Château Latour 1952 and right at the end we had Château Capbern 1937 St-Estephe which is a cru bourgeois

13. She married 2nd Viscount Rothermere in 1966 as his third wife; he died in 1978, she in 1992.
14. At that time literary editor of the *Times*.

but described in the Alexis Lichine book as worthy of promotion to one of the listed growths under the 1855 classification.

I then gave the Tokay Eszencia 1967. Kingsley liked it but Merlin said it was too sweet and Kingsley entered into a tirade about people who dislike sweet wines and their foolishness. Merlin said, 'I do like very sweet German wines.'

Merlin Holland, when asked why he hadn't changed his name back to Wilde, said, 'It's a declaration against Victorian values which so maltreated my grandfather. Every time people ask me why I didn't change my name back to Wilde I can give this explanation.'

He adored sitting opposite Kingsley Amis and eventually burst out that he had once taken, when in Tehran, all Kingsley's books to read and loved every one of them.

Kingsley was very funny mimicking various people he had met in my house. He gave a somewhat embellished account of a dinner when Ted Heath and Roy Jenkins among other notables were there. He mimicked their voices beautifully. He said, 'They spoke just as though they were on public platforms when I asked them questions about what they thought about current policies and what should be done. Why should they do that? They were among friends. It showed how pompous and shallow they are. They are just as stupid away from the platform as they are on it.'

He mimicked my voice very well. He then mimicked Roy and Lord Wolfson and Ted Heath and the Archbishop of Canterbury, Runcie, whom he knows. He did Runcie, Roy and Frank Pakenham [Lord Longford] fantastically well.

He said once he wrote a review of an Anthony Powell book. When he writes one about a friend's book, he always puts in some little criticism; otherwise everybody would think he was log rolling. He did it on some minor point but Anthony Powell said the next time he met him, 'Thank you for the nice review you gave my book,' and then kept harping back to the very minor query Kingsley had made about one of his characters.

He admires Tony P because of his relaxed and casual manner. He recounted a story of when they were being led by some young producer at the BBC in a discussion. After they began the producer came in and said, 'I don't like it like that at all. I want much more about the meaning of this person's writing and not so much description of the books.' (I think it was [about] Evelyn Waugh.)

Tony simply looked at him and then looked down and said, 'We're not interested in the way you would like it. We're only interested in the way we would like it.'

Kingsley said that was the sign of somebody who was confidently upper class. Somebody like himself, said Kingsley, would have shouted and got angry and said, 'We're fucking well not interested in what you think, you jumped up little pip squeak. We're going to do it the way we want.' That wasn't Anthony's method and his was much more effective.

Somehow we got talking about Elizabeth Jane Howard and I said, 'I can never understand why you married her. She was so intense and severe. I remember when she was staying with us once in Italy and you wouldn't come because you say abroad is bloody like George V, and every day she said "Is there a letter from Kingsley? I must go to the post office and find out if there's a letter from Kingsley." She was absolutely obsessed with your writing to her.' He said, 'Yes, she always was obsessed.'

Then he said, 'Do you know that song "My Old Dutch"?' which he then proceeded to sing. Then he said, 'I've got another version of it.' There were bits in it like, 'My Old Dutch, / We've been apart for seven years, / And it doesn't seem a year too much, / There's no one more I'd like to kick in the crutch.'

He said he didn't like her friends when they lived in that beautiful Georgian house in Barnet. I said, 'There were no pubs there, were there?' 'No, and it was too far for me to get to my club easily.' Now he says that his first ex-wife Hilly[15] just acts as his housekeeper.

When I asked if he'd like to come racing he said, 'Oh yes. But steeple chasing – I don't like the flat. Can I bring her too?' I said, 'Of course.' We decided he would go to Newbury one day when we had a Tote lunch there in our room. Then he said, 'But how would I get there?' I said, 'I suppose we would have to give you a lift.' 'I don't like that word "lift".' I said, 'Well we could lay on transport for you.'

When we were talking about the wine I said they were some odd bottles I found and Kingsley was offended. 'Oh, are we being used as finisher uppers?' 'Oh, no. It's just that there are only one or two of each and not enough for a dinner party.' 'Oh, I see,' rather grumpily.

I thought he looked not quite so bloated as he had done. I was surprised to be reminded he is four years younger than me. We talked

15. She married the 7th Baron Kilmarnock in 1977; Kingsley Amis lived in their house in his latter years.

about Philip Larkin[16] and their days at Oxford. He said Philip was always anxious to show what a hearty fellow he was, playing jazz records and pretending to be a bit of a Philistine but of course he was quite the opposite.

Merlin asked was it surprising that he went to be a librarian at Hull. 'No, absolutely in keeping.' Kingsley thinks his poetry is very good. He thinks Ted Hughes[17] is rubbish. I said, 'Have you got a Ted Hughes poem in one of your anthologies of verse?' Kingsley said he had included one because it was a bit more intelligible than the usual run by Ted Hughes.

During lunch Kingsley Amis agreed with me that Dylan Thomas is no good as a poet. He has not included much of him in his anthologies. A lot of Welsh verbosity.

We had a much longer discussion about the Bible. All took the view that the Authorized version should be taught. Kingsley said, 'It's such a wonderful story. It doesn't matter whether you believe in God or not. To have a concept of Adam and Eve and everything that happened. It is terrific. There's a lot of very fascinating stuff in the Gospels as well. How did they get this idea about Adam and Eve?' I said, 'Well, simultaneously they were getting the same idea in the Mexico area about Adam and Eve. There is that great mural Jack Huntingdon[18] did which is still at the Strozzato.' He too knew about that myth from Mexico. He knows a lot, Kingsley.

We were all pretty well awash (including myself who tried not to drink too much), having consumed three complete bottles of claret, nearly a bottle of Chablis and a large part of a bottle of champagne, some Tokay among the five of us, Petronella drinking very little and Kingsley drinking two large glasses of port. Wondered how I would be able to face the French Embassy later in the evening.

After the Jockey Club I went to the Lords. There has been a salmonella break out and about forty peers and kitchen staff have gone down with tummy aches and vomiting. Fortunately I haven't eaten there lately.

Came back to the house at about a quarter past six to get changed

---

16. Poet (1922–85).
17. Poet Laureate since 1984.
18. 15th Earl of Huntingdon (1901–90), artist, pupil of Diego Rivera; his murals included those at the Casa dello Strozzato in Tuscany.

into a dinner jacket before going to the French Embassy. Decided against having a sleep because I thought I would never wake up.

The dinner was in honour of Cecil Parkinson, why I never discovered.

On my left was the wife of a French banker. She believed in reincarnation and talked at some length about it. On her other side was Peregrine Worsthorne who said he was going to Brunei as a guest of the Sultan of Brunei. I said, 'Whatever for?' He said he had never been there and thought it would be a nice holiday. 'Yes, but you can't accept the hospitality of someone and then write something about it because even if it didn't impair your judgement, people would think it did.'

Peregrine thinks Andrew Neil is a brilliant editor, though not altogether a nice man, and they are struggling at the *Sunday Telegraph*. He thinks that the *Telegraph* on the other hand is doing a lot of damage to the *Times* which must be worrying Rupert. They are going to move the colour supplement from the *Sunday Telegraph* to the Saturday *Daily Telegraph* as part of the drive to destroy the *Times*.

Arnold was there. He told me he must talk to me, he must talk to me. After the dinner was over I talked to him for about ten minutes. The night before he had been at Downing Street. He felt the atmosphere towards him had improved. Would I arrange one of those dinners we had before when he talked away and gave his ideas? I said yes.

I'm mildly doubtful but probably I will do this. He said, 'She is extraordinary. Like Joan of Arc. When she is in her inspired mood, acting as a leader, I feel I could do anything for her.' This is very different from Arnold's frequently expressed annoyance at her disliking him and plotting against him and all the rest of it. He is very up and down.

He says things are going a little better with GEC. 'But of course it's always difficult if people in Whitehall, who are our main customers for many items, believe that we are no longer in favour with her even if it isn't true.'

I had a cigar which was rather damp but I managed to get it alight eventually. I suppose one should be sufficiently grateful that at an embassy you are actually offered a cigar from Havana.

**Thursday 12 May**

To The Other Club. Long talk with Garrett Drogheda.[19] Says Joan is now unable even to play the notes on the piano, can't remember anything, has expensive nurses all the time. He spent more than twice his income last year but he couldn't put her in a home. He went to see one or two and they were horrid. So he has to go on spending his capital looking after his wife. It's very sad for her and for him.

He said being a Director of the *Times* was a position of doing nothing. Rupert takes no notice of them, does exactly as he likes, it's a mere formality. They meet once a quarter and he is finishing at the end of this year.

Tonight we had Château Lafite 1974 which Nico [Henderson], the enterprising new Secretary, had brought from Christie's at £140 a case plus VAT and buyer's commission.

Leon Brittan may take Cockfield's[20] job at the European Commission. I said, 'But you won't make so much money as you're making now.' Roy had been advising him to take the job. Roy said, 'You shouldn't speak so much about money. It is not important. You're a bore about money.'

He had just been telling me about his lecture tours in America, which he doesn't like to call lectures but talks, which his agents said he shouldn't do for less than $15,000 a time. Roy has always been obsessed by money. He used to tell me how much he was getting in tax free salary at the European Commission when he was head of it and how long the pension went on for – a big one tax free after you retired.

**Friday 13 May**

Dinner. Irwin and Cita Stelzer, Harold and Diane Lever, Andrew and Sabihah Knight.

Harold is all for joining the European Monetary System. Irwin said he was not.

I said that this evening I had heard on the wireless Sir Geoffrey Howe had now said at the Conservative Party Conference in Scotland that we should join the EMS, seemingly taking a contrary view to Mrs Thatcher and siding with Lawson in this perpetual argument as to

---

19. See 17 July 1986.

20. Civil servant, industrialist and Conservative politician; a Vice President of the Commission, 1985–8; life peer 1978. Brittan did succeed him.

whether you can or cannot 'buck the market' in holding to exchange rates artificially.

**Sunday 15 May**

Down to Bowden to see Arnold. A beautiful sunny day. We walked among the blazing azaleas, masses of them everywhere and looked at my column with eagles on top.

He is upset that Margaret, in his belief, has been told things which are not true and he is being victimized. He showed me the details of his Spearfish and his Stingray and how the bonuses had been given by the Ministry of Defence for completion of various stages before time. One or two were behind but the net effect was of considerable bonuses. Therefore it was wrong to say they were not doing it at the right speed or efficiently.

When I returned to London I rang her.

She came on the telephone, 'I was just saying to Denis, "Woodrow hasn't rung today. He's usually rung by this time on a Sunday."'

I asked her if there was any serious trouble with Nigel Lawson and Geoffrey Howe. I said Geoffrey Howe had been saying that we must join the EMS at some point. She said, 'No. If we had been in the EMS we wouldn't have had the growth we've been having.'

I told her that Arnold had been very impressed by her at the dinner for industrialists at No 10 earlier in the week. Then he had raised again his worries that people are not telling her the truth about his dealings with the Ministry of Defence. He had asked whether we could have another of our little dinners.

'I did think he was down in the dumps the other night. We can't have him down in the dumps. I'm very fond of Arnold.'

She said, 'Perhaps we could have some others as well. What about Rupert. When is he coming back to England?'

She said she thought the *Sun* had written very good leading articles about Tufton Bufton i.e. Lord Chelwood and his attempts to overthrow the community charge. I said, 'The Lords are getting too big for their boots. I'm surprised at Noël Annan taking part in this move to try and stop ILEA being closed down.'

We chatted away for some time.

'God bless,' she said as we closed down.

She sounded a little bit high. It was about ten past eight. She usually has a few drinks by this time in the evening – not high in the sense of being in any way intoxicated but just a little. Who deserves it more?

**Monday 16 May**

Arnold is immensely difficult. He wants to pick the people who come to dinner so that they all agree with him and he wants to have a clear run to talk for two or three hours about how beastly the Ministry of Defence is to him. Which may or may not be true. Partly true perhaps since Levene became the Chief Procurement Officer and started striking real bargains with defence suppliers. Levene has undoubtedly been saving the government a lot of money.

In the Lords Willie said to me that he was going to weigh in if the Lords passed the amendment about saving ILEA.[21] He was saying that the Lords is going too far in taking action of this kind against a central piece of legislation.

**Tuesday 17 May**

The government got a big majority owing to their successful whipping.

Lady Blackstone[22] was furious with me – I had no business to call the ILEA parents' poll bogus. But I was right. It was based on 72,500 out of 475,000 parents voting and then declared to be all parents, ninety-three per cent in favour of keeping ILEA. What tripe.

Andrew Devonshire's party at Pratt's Club was very dull. One or two people I knew. None of them interesting. I asked him where Selina[23] was and he said she was coming later. That reminded me that when I saw them outside the Savoy last Thursday and had asked Selina whether I should go and see her father she said, 'Oh no, that would make his health worse. It might make my mother cry. You did once before.' I thought not very friendly.

Jack Huntingdon her father is now seriously ill and according to Selina keeps refusing to die. He is one year younger than the century.

**Wednesday 18 May**

She thought Arnold and Rupert would be enough for dinner plus wives. They should come. I said, not meaning he was a wife, 'I haven't

---

21. Originally the Education Bill had provided for the Inner London Education Authority (ILEA) to be phased out gradually but a backbench revolt in the Commons led by Norman Tebbit and Michael Heseltine had made its ending instant.
22. Tessa Blackstone, at this time Master of Birkbeck College; life peer 1987.
23. Lady Selina Hastings, writer.

Roy Jenkins at his investiture as Chancellor of Oxford University in 1987.

Lord Weidenfeld.

Kingsley Amis winning the 1986 Booker Prize.

Lord Forte, his daughter, Olga Polizzi, and his son, Rocco.

Lord (Victor) Rothschild (*top*) and his son, Jacob,
pictured at a reception at the Royal Academy of Arts in 1988.

The Hon. David Montagu and his wife Ninette, in 1988.

The Duke of Beaufort at the races in 1988.

The actress
Maureen Swanson,
married the
Earl of Dudley
(*below*) in 1961.

The Duke of Devonshire inspecting the Worcestershire and Sherwood Foresters Regiment at Warminster in 1985.

The Earl and Countess of Wilton in 1986.

The Duke of Marlborough skiing in Gstaad.

Heveningham Hall in Suffolk.

seen Denis for some time. It would be nice.' She said, 'He would like to come.'

When I told Arnold this he immediately rang back later saying we should have the dinner at Grosvenor Square.[24] I said Why? He said, 'Because you won't have any fresh vegetables. It's a Bank Holiday Monday. We can bring them up.' I said, 'Don't worry. We can do that perfectly well. Anyway it's all arranged now.'

James Hanson told me in the Lords that he had enjoyed my article so much in the *Times* this morning that he had sent it to President Reagan whom he knows.[25]

**Thursday 19 May**

To the Austrian Embassy for dinner.

The Embassy has been the same and furnished the same for over a hundred years – with the same handsome pictures of the Hapsburgs. The food was awful.

A Mr and Mrs Winterton[26] were there. Both Tory MPs. He had been one for seventeen years. He asked me what I did now, 'I assume you're still a press baron.' This was a reference to the *Banbury Guardian* which I have not owned for nearly twenty-five years. He was quite unaware that I wrote once a week in the *News of the World* and fortnightly in the *Times*. What am I doing if a Tory backbencher of seventeen years' standing hasn't a clue as to what it is?

His wife was more clued up.

She spoke of Mrs Thatcher, said she wouldn't listen to anybody and when you go to see her in a little group or separately she just gives you a lecture and you're never allowed to say what you want.

However, Mrs Winterton agreed that there was no possible replacement for her and that she had performed a revolution no one else could have done; and maddening though it was, they have to soldier on with her with the best grace they can muster.

On my left at dinner sat Mrs Radice. She is Polish. Her husband I used to know well in the old Gaitskell days. He is a Labour MP[27] and

---

24. At his London flat there.
25. The article was about Reagan's belief in horoscopes and WW's own horoscope, cast in India in 1945.
26. Nicholas Winterton, Conservative MP for Macclesfield since September 1971, and Ann Winterton, Conservative MP for Congleton since 1983.
27. Giles Radice was Labour spokesman on education, 1983–7.

was Shadow Secretary for Education. He has now been thrown off the Shadow Cabinet with, as she put it, 'further moves to the left'. His future in politics is now zero. He is highly intelligent but not extreme; therefore it is hard for him to make headway.

Mrs Radice says 'Kinnochio', which is what many in the Labour Party call Kinnock, 'can't stay. He is so brainless and footling that they're bound to get rid of him.' 'Who would you like in his place?' I asked. She said, 'John Smith.' I said, 'You're unlikely to get him because he is much too sensible. They should have had Denis Healey years ago and never did. He would have put up a good fight against Mrs Thatcher.'

It was interesting to learn that Kinnock is much more under threat in his own party it would seem than Mrs Thatcher is in hers.

**Friday 20 May**

Rang Margaret early to tell her the article was in the *Times* this morning about the community charge amendment on Monday.[28] I had used her idea that it would be absurd for the Lords to reject the community charge now since they passed exactly the same one for Scotland a year ago. She is very pleased.

She said, 'I've read your speech on ILEA. It was wonderful.' (I had a letter from Kenneth Baker this morning in his own handwriting thanking me for the speech and saying it was a splendid victory.) She said again she couldn't understand Norman St John-Stevas. 'I had no need to put him in the Lords and now he goes and does all this.'

**Saturday 21 May**

Dinner at the Connaught Hotel with Irwin Stelzer, Cecil Parkinson, Mrs Parkinson, Harold Lever and Diane Lever and Verushka.

Cecil Parkinson very lively. We had a spirited argument about his privatization of electricity. I said, 'I still don't see where the competition is coming in because it will make no difference to the consumer, only very indirectly if the generating of electricity becomes a little cheaper.'

---

28. The article was headed 'Hands Off, My Lords – Woodrow Wyatt on Delusions of Power in the Lords'. WW argued: 'It is amazing that Lord Chelwood and his supporters should think that the Lords is now equivalent to the Commons in its rights to block important government legislation and to go further than the Commons by reversing legislation which it has itself already passed.'

Irwin thinks you have to have a very complicated regulatory system to produce the benefits of competition to the consumer.

Cecil Parkinson is quite incorrigible. He kept trying to hold Verushka's hand under the table and she told me that when he went, he gave her a whacking great kiss and said, 'Good night, gorgeous.'

**Sunday 22 May**

It was pleasant going through the Cornish lanes and fields on the way to Bonython. It was in the tin mines around Redruth that the money came originally in 1836 to buy Bonython and the estate my brother now has. The early Lyles were freebooters who wheeled and dealed with the tin mines and made and lost a lot of money. But they kept enough to buy Bonython.

Glad to find my brother much better than usual. They think they have got his medicines right now.

Robert has put Bonython itself and some thirty acres or so around, including the spring and the bottling plant, into a trust with the trust owning fifty-one per cent of the Cornish Spring Water.

Try to get Margaret from Cornwall. She is at a meeting. Left my number. She duly rang back while I was in the bath later washing my hair.

I told her about the bottling plant for Cornish Spring Water. She became interested and said, 'You must let me have some bottles but you must carbonate it.' I said, 'Yes, we're going to do that. It's only a start at the moment.' 'I wish you all great success.'

I told her it was partly being financed out of my brother's sale of his milk quotas which seems a crazy system.

I told her that last night I had had dinner with a few friends and Cecil Parkinson. I didn't tell her that he tried to hold Verushka's hand under the table but I think she might have laughed if I had.

**Monday 23 May**

The aeroplane was late arriving at Heathrow, twenty minutes. Rushed back to Cavendish Avenue, dashed through the speech dictating it rapidly to Mrs Wood, left the house at about twenty past two, went to the Lords for the beginning of the great debate on Lord Chelwood's amendment.

The House was utterly packed. Never seen so many people. When I saw Henry Bath I realized how intense the whipping has been.

Chelwood was hopeless. He mumbled and fumbled.

Willie Whitelaw made a good speech, a bit unctuous, saying how he always made mistakes and all the rest of it but they should not vote such an important government thing down. Quintin Hogg made quite a good lawyer's speech from the constitutional point of view. He would have argued exactly the opposite if it had been an amendment to defeat something important brought forward by a Labour government.

The majority was huge. Something like a hundred and thirty-four.

Tufton Beamish looked bewildered and bemused, poor fellow, bedraggled and unhappy at his resounding defeat.

**Tuesday 24 May**

Spoke to Margaret and said that it wasn't just the weight of the numbers that won the battle, it was the weight of the argument and she would see that only twelve Tory rebels voted for the amendment.

I also pointed out that forty-three crossbenchers voted for us and they are not government supporters or Tory dug-outs.

Saw Margaret in the Commons at Question Time giving my point [that] we won on the argument in the Lords last night. She had looked up the figures for the crossbenchers – forty-three out of seventy-three had voted for the government.

On my way into lunch with Allan Davis and Lee Menzies we met Quintin Hogg coming in the other direction who stopped me and said of my speech yesterday in a loud voice, 'Fine stuff. You never miss.'

Lee Menzies is lively and charming. He said, 'You must have been paying these people to come up on cue to congratulate you.' We drank a bottle and a half of champagne with our lunch to celebrate the start of our partnership. I complained that there was only one thing wrong with the contract – it didn't give me free tickets. Lee explained that it was quite impossible because managements also had to have their cut out of the seat money.

He said that Jeffrey Archer's personal account for tickets was running at £400 a week at one time.

In the evening Irwin Stelzer came to dinner in the Lords with Cita. More champagne drunk.

Irwin said the House of Lords ought to be totally reformed. It ought to be entirely on the basis of merit. That is what a market economy demands. I said, 'Does it really? Do you think people like Lord Weinstock and Lord King would want to be in the House of Lords if there weren't Dukes and Earls and Marquesses around? You'd wreck the market in attracting good people to come into the Lords.'

**Thursday 26 May**
Went to the Lords to make a speech on the second reading of the Bill to privatize steel. I did it out of memory of Desmond Donnelly[29] who had fought with me to stop the nationalization of steel in the 1964–66 Parliament when Labour had only a majority of three.

**Friday 27 May**
Little Angela Oswald's letter in the *Times*. She rightly complained that the *Times* on May 12 had written that Harold Abrahams was the only man to have run round Trinity Quad, Cambridge, during the time the clock struck. It was not him but her father, Lord Burghley. *Chariots of Fire,* which was 'faction', had given the credit to Harold Abrahams. The *Times* had refused to print the letter which she wrote immediately on May 12th until I rang the editor who was very annoyed and looked into the matter and now there is the letter. She will be very pleased. (She was. She sent me a card with teddy bears all over it with the printed message 'For Being Ever So Special'.)

**Saturday 28 May**
To Haydock [racecourse in Lancashire]. The Tote is sponsoring a valuable handicap. Brian [McDonnell] and I fly up from Heathrow. On arrival at the racecourse we meet the Chairman and Tommy Wallis.

We agree roughly what the Tote will contribute towards the great new stands and restaurants they are having in Tattersalls.

For lunch we have credit customers in a restaurant reserved for sponsors. Among the guests who sit at our table are officials from Wigan where the Tote Credit is going to be rebuilt and assembled in a building provided by the council. The Council Leader was there and the councillor in charge of leisure and art. It is a leisure complex building that is being handed over to us, although there are problems about the air-conditioning.

Having buttered them up a good deal, I think we were able to get across that they really had to come forward with a hell of a lot more money to deal with the Wigan air-conditioning plant before we could agree to go to Wigan finally. I explained we were not only going to take bets there on a very up-to-date system of technology through the telephone but also we were going to sell the services to advertisers on TV and elsewhere, and we would have the largest battery of

29. (1920–74); MP and journalist; see 4 July 1988.

telephonists and the quickest operation assembled in one place in the country.

I judged the best turned-out horse with Christopher Poole from the *Evening Standard*. We selected No 1, which won the race, and No 23 we nearly selected was second. It often goes that the best-looking horse and best-turned out one wins. It makes me feel that although I know nothing about horses and don't pretend to, I must have some idea of what a horse should look like. I was quite pleased with myself and only wished that I had a dual forecast on our two selections – or indeed on the winner.

I am very pleased with what they are doing at Haydock and we are willing to pay them over the odds towards the cost of the building: it is going to be very much an arrangement for the future, with a huge screen on which people can watch away meetings and bet on them. It's really going to be an area in which the Tote is paramount with positions everywhere, the best ones, and also on the front, right on to the racetrack – which we haven't always been able to have because of the fact that Tote buildings were mostly put up originally in the late 1920s and 1930s when the bookmakers were allowed always on the rails in front.

**Monday 30 May *Bank Holiday***

Read that Sheridan Dufferin[30] is dead. Only forty-nine. It seems he died of pneumonia which he couldn't resist because he had Aids. He was a sweet, gentle, aesthetic man – a lover of the arts. Good looking with dark curly hair and a sad questing face. He was always charming and friendly and intelligent. I probably met him in about 1960 or 1959. He often used to ask me to stay with him in Northern Ireland. He had an enormous estate there.[31] But somehow I never felt strong enough to make the journey.

He married Lindy[32] a cousin of his. Tall, thin girl with a vivacious face, not exactly pretty but certainly not ugly. It was a tiny bit wrinkled even when she was young. She was angular as well but had enthusiasm, quickness and interest in literature. Also she is a painter.

In early 1963 they were both at a party given by Edna O'Brien [the novelist] when she lived somewhere by the river. It was a drunken long

30. 5th Marquess of Dufferin and Ava.
31. Clandeboye, Co. Down.
32. Née Guinness, in 1964.

party and it was the night I had a fearful motor accident, though I was unharmed, on my way to Conock afterwards. I talked to them both at length. I said, 'Why don't you both get married? You're very well suited to each other.'

Apparently they took this seriously because not long afterwards they did get married. They had been thinking about it for a long while. Unfortunately, he was also interested in sex with males. They had no children. I don't know what happened in that marriage at all really.

Lindy was the girl who said to me at the height of the Profumo crisis – when I had said, 'He shouldn't mind too much about his troubles and his loss of political career. He's pretty well off. He'll be able to live happily.' – 'How much has he got?' 'At least a million pounds.' She said, 'Oh that's nothing at all.' She was speaking as a member of the Guinness family.

Now the title is extinct. He only has an heir to some Irish title, just a cousin aged sixty-four. I don't know what will happen to all the properties. His mother was a Guinness[33] – that's where they got a great injection of money. When she married Judge Maude she insisted on calling herself Marchioness of Dufferin and Ava though she was really Mrs Maude. Sheridan's father was killed in Burma during the War.

Went to Lord's to see if I could watch Middlesex playing Sussex. Met Alan Watkins.[34] He told me he was waking up at 4.00 in the morning and had lost half a stone in weight since the libel action brought against him by Michael Meacher[35] had started. This was running week after week in the courts. I said, 'But I thought the *Observer* was backing you.' 'Oh, yes. But I don't want to make a fool of myself in the witness box. I don't think I did. I think I shall write a book about it.'[36]

He said Meacher hadn't got a chance of winning which I didn't suppose he had. His complaint is that Alan Watkins had written that he had falsely pretended to be of working class origin and that his father was an agricultural labourer when it turned out that he actually

---

33. Maureen (1907–98), one of the 'Golden Guinness Girls', m 2 (1948–54) Major Desmond 'Kelpie' Buchanan, m 3 (in 1955) John Maude QC (1901–86), Conservative politician.
34. Political journalist, at this time on the *Observer.*
35. Labour MP since 1970, at this time Labour spokesman on employment.
36. *A Slight Case of Libel* was published in 1990.

trained as an accountant and went to live on a farm and did very little work ever and was certainly not like an agricultural labourer.

He also accused Meacher of behaving wrongfully in trying to find out from hospital authorities what the politics of the members of the management committees were.

'But how much is this going to cost him?', and he said it couldn't cost him less than £150,000. I asked, 'Has Meacher got that kind of money?' 'No, not a bit.'

I quite like Meacher but he is not a major figure.

Went into the pavilion and waited for the rain to stop without much hope. Spoke to Imran Khan a little. Asked him what he thought about the new election just announced by General Zia.[37] He said he thought it was extremely cunning and clever. He had taken them all by surprise. I asked him whether he would go into politics himself and he said, 'No. It would finish me off. I wouldn't risk it.'

He is a good-looking fellow, quick face, curly hair. Scrub out his colour in your imagination and he would practically be an English matinée idol. That's why girls fall for him.

Went in a Jaguar, with a chauffeur provided by Rupert, to Chequers.

The dinner party, which had originally been intended to be at 19 Cavendish Avenue with Rupert, Netta, Arnold, Verushka, myself and Margaret and Denis, changed a little but not greatly. There was only the addition of the Laings and Carol [Thatcher]. Denis wasn't there. He was off watching some golf tournament.

On the way down we discussed the *Times*. I said I thought there was something wrong with how the letters are run. They are not good enough. Also they don't even publish ones that they should. I explained about when Angela Oswald wrote about her father.

I said the articles on the features page are mostly bad.

Having a gossip column every day by a different person is ridiculous instead of having a proper gossip column of the paper itself.

They are late with their obituaries. This morning they should have had an obituary of Sheridan Dufferin but they had none. Other papers did. But the news coverage is good.

Rupert agreed. He said, 'Why don't you come and edit the *Times*?' I said, 'No, no. I don't want to do that.'

Then he said did I think Nigel Lawson would be a good editor of the *Times*. I hadn't thought of the matter before. My first instinct was

37. President of Pakistan at this time.

to say he wouldn't do it. 'You wouldn't pay him enough. Would you pay him £250,000?' 'No, no. That wouldn't be necessary. I'd give him £125,000 and he would have a pension as well.'

Rupert reasonably said there is no point in his having run the finances of the country and then to be the Chairman of some merchant bank or even a joint stock bank. 'If he changes to being editor of the *Times* he would go on with a great position of power and influence.' It would certainly strengthen the editorial (the leading article) side which is lamentably feeble and wobbly. I began to warm to the idea.

Rupert said, 'Was he good at the *Spectator*?' I think he was as good as an editor but we both agreed he didn't know how to run anything. And he didn't run the *Spectator* managerially well. But he wouldn't have to run the *Times* in a managerial sense, somebody else can do that.

He said, 'This is deadly secret. Please don't give the slightest indication to anybody that I'm thinking of it.' I said, 'No.'

We eventually got into Chequers slightly after half past seven.

I urged Rupert to say to Margaret what he was saying to me in the car about the danger of her seeming too authoritarian in wanting to censor the media, and the appointment of Rees-Mogg[38] to preview TV films for violence and sex and so forth.

It's very interesting that these great men like Arnold blow off to me the whole time about something they disapprove of that she may be doing and expect me to pass it on but they don't have the gumption to say it to her face. Not only on this occasion have I told Margaret what Rupert had been saying and then had to make him say it too.

She immediately gave a lecture about violence and sex on the TV and so on. Not a very helpful wrangle but I think she did get the point that she should take a little care and not seem to want some kind of censorship. Rupert said as she is urging everybody to be individual and be responsible, surely they can be entrusted to see what they like on television.

The biscuit man, Hector Laing,[39] was there. He was against Rowntree being taken over by a Swiss firm. That was because he fears that his United Biscuits could have a similar fate. I said, 'Why did Rowntree

---

38. As chairman, Broadcasting Standards Council.
39. Chairman, United Biscuits 1972–90; director, Bank of England, 1973–91; treasurer, Conservative Party, 1988–93; knight 1978, life peer 1991.

ever sell out?' He said they couldn't help it. It was death duties. This was a point I had not thought of with regard to family ownership.

We also had a discussion about Sunday racing. The *Times* had written a leading article that morning with myself featuring largely in it with my Sunday Sports Bill. I told her she must put it in the new Sunday Trading Bill, if they ever get around to that. She was not altogether enthusiastic at betting shops being open on Sundays but I knew she never was. I think she will be all right if it ever comes to the crunch.

Arnold did get in a lot, he told me, of what he wanted to complain of in his treatment by the Ministry of Defence. He said she didn't know how approving the Service Chiefs had been over his weapons etc. etc. and he is sending her information via Charles Powell. This is a good thing. He didn't seem dissatisfied with the evening; he was put next to her to sit on her other side with Rupert.

At one time we were talking about Reagan.

There was some question of how good a President he has been. She said she thought he had been extremely good and Rupert agreed. He might not have a lot of brain but he has exactly the right instincts. And makes the right broad decisions. He is coming here this week after the Moscow conference is over. Margaret said he didn't want to go again to Brussels (or wherever he went last time) to explain what had happened. He was more at home here. He doesn't really like it with all the Europeans talking foreign languages.

Mrs Thatcher during the argument about whether or not she was being too censorious of the media, particularly the BBC and ITV, spoke of Duke Hussey at the BBC. I said I thought he was making some progress. She said, 'He's making none at all.' She sounded rather cross. 'He's gone native like all the others.'

On the way back to London Rupert said, 'Mrs Thatcher argues exactly like you. She shouts you down and won't let you develop your case.' I said, 'You should stick to it like I do.' It's curious how these great men fold up in front of her instead of maintaining their position and holding on to it.

**Tuesday 31 May**

Celebration – the eighth volume of Martin Gilbert's biography of Churchill published today. It was at Leighton House.[40] A suitable

40. Museum in Kensington, the house of the artist Lord Leighton (1830–96).

setting. I am sure Winston Churchill would have approved of all Leighton's pictures which were pretty good.

At first I could not see anybody I knew. Then I saw Mary Soames (Churchill) who said she liked the biography because it recorded everything Winston did in the period covered by it without comment or analysis but put everything on the record.

Martin Gilbert made a speech which was excellent. It showed how nice and decent he is. He had become devoted to Churchill and also to Randolph who handed the job over to him of completing the biography when he died. He spoke with great modesty and feeling.

Pol Roger had supplied the champagne. It was Winston's favourite champagne. I am afraid I drank some when I shouldn't in the middle of the day. The 1979 Special Vintage Cuvée Sir Winston Churchill was singularly good.

I told John Grigg[41] he ought never to have given up his peerage. It is such an agreeable place, the Lords. And he said, 'I would have liked to be there if I had earned it as you did.' He is an extremely pleasant man who writes not badly but should have not been too proud to make use of the peerage his father got. His father had been Secretary for War during the War.

41. Writer and historian; he renounced the title of Lord Altrincham when he stood for Parliament.

**Wednesday 1 June**

Off to the Derby early.

Did my tour of the Downs and the stands and paddock to see how the Tote people were settling in.

Three lovely balloons or airships hung in the air with the sign 'Tote' and arrows pointing downwards to our Tote position on the Downs. These were much commented on but some thought it read 'Hotel' because of the arrows not being clear enough and some were not quite certain if they were arrows and thought they were exclamation marks.

Willie Whitelaw and John Wakeham turned up. We immediately began a conversation about the Lords. Willie said, 'That was a very good article you wrote in the *Times* this morning. Exactly right.'[1]

Walked for my usual walk with Isabel Derby down to the paddock to look at the horses. She thought that only Red Glow looked a class horse and possibly Doyoun. She hates the Aga Khan who owns it. When the race was eventually won by Kahyasi, the fastest time since Mahmoud won the Derby,[2] owned by the Aga, and his horse Doyoun was third, she was furious. 'The pig,' she said. My bets went for a Burton as usual.

The Tote took a record amount, just over three-quarters of a million. But it is not enough for Derby Day. We ought to be able to take over one million. On the actual Derby itself we were only a fraction up on last year. That was because last year Reference Point was heavily backed and was a clear favourite. But I suppose many of the people who come to the Derby don't really come to bet or know anything about it.

While I was talking to John Wakeham and Willie Whitelaw earlier,

---

1. Under the heading 'Praise the Lords' WW put forward the arguments rehearsed in this journal against an elected second chamber, while suggesting that there was a case for removing the twenty-four bishops of the Church of England: 'Otherwise the Lords should be left, as it is, to jog pleasantly and usefully along.'
2. In 1936, owned by HH Aga Khan III.

Willie said he had told me I could never get Sunday racing with my Sunday Sports Bill with a frontal attack. I said, 'It's a good thing to have had the marker down and have the approval of the government for it,' to which he agreed. He also said that it should be tacked on with some form of Sunday trading and I turned to John and said, 'Will you fix that please?'

Debo Devonshire gave me a false smile and a false kiss and put her arm round me saying, 'Uncle Woodrow' in a loud voice. I felt how much she didn't like me.

Isabel said to me as the Queen's party came into the paddock, 'Look at my husband. Doesn't he look sweet? Dear John.' I said, 'You should be with him. And you would be if you weren't such a Republican.' She hates the Hanoverians.

**Thursday 2 June**

A dinner at the Dudleys with excruciating bores as guests. Maureen Dudley sat on my right. She is the most restless hostess I ever knew. She kept jumping up from the table and telling the hired footman and the wife of the hired chef to bring different vegetables and bring them more quickly and bring the gravy and bring this, that and the other and she repeatedly told them they weren't doing it right.

Even Billy doesn't seem to be as bright as usual. I said, 'Do you do any writing now?' 'Well, my wife makes many demands on me and I find myself doing a lot of chauffeuring and shopping.'

I said, 'You've got a very good brain. Why don't you use it?' and I began to try to inspire him to write some more poetry which he was rather good at.

I have a dreadful feeling that Verushka has invited the Dudleys in some mad moment to stay with us in Italy.

When we left the Dudleys at twenty-five past eleven Maureen Dufferin was sitting down to a game of bridge with some of the men. The poor creature said it would steady her and give her some solace.

Calamity as well as riches is the portion of the Guinness family.

**Friday 3 June**

I attend the unveiling of a plaque to P. G. Wodehouse by Queen Elizabeth the Queen Mother at his house, 17 Dunraven Street, W1. She made a pretty little speech saying exactly the right things. There were some forty people at the lunch afterwards.

There were five two-minute speeches. Nico Henderson made one.

He said he was late because he had been listening to a speech by President Reagan at the Guildhall. He observed that if ever there were a natural member of the Drones Club[3] it was President Reagan. He also said that he found Wodehouse useful to him as a diplomat and Ambassador to the USA. Americans seem to think that Englishmen are a cross between Bertie Wooster and Jeeves. He, Nico, thought he had done the Bertie Wooster part quite well but the present Prime Minister thought that was rather wet and preferred something harder with more brains, like Jeeves.

I tackled him about that after and said, 'Why did you say that? She thought very highly of your performance as Ambassador during the Falklands crisis.' He said, 'Well, she did afterwards but there was a lot of trouble at the time.'

William Douglas-Home who knew Wodehouse said that a typical piece of his writing was: 'She came out on to the verandah and said, "What are you doing, Daddy?" as he sat at his easel. He said, "Painting." There were no secrets between these two.'

The funniest speech was by an American called Heineman who owns the biggest collection of Wodehouse books and memorabilia.[4] As a Sergeant in 1943 in the American Army he was told to go down to Westminster School, which had been turned into some kind of a club, because the Queen was coming to see it. And he, a very short man, stood next to a man called Wing Commander Edwards, immensely tall.

They were all told that when the Queen came in they were to be natural and not be nervous, which was impossible. If she spoke to you, the order was that you must introduce yourself by announcing your name.

'Your Majesty, you came diagonally across the floor and made a bee-line for me. When you got to me for some reason which I have never understood, I introduced myself as "Sergeant Edwards". You then shook hands with the real Wing Commander Edwards who without batting an eyelid introduced himself as Wing Commander

---

3. The club of P. G. Wodehouse's hero, Bertie Wooster; Jeeves was Wooster's matchless valet who solved every problem for his master.
4. James Heineman's collection of 6,300 pieces of P. G. Wodehouse memorabilia was auctioned, following his death, at Sotheby's, New York, on 26 June 1998 for $351,900.

Heineman. Your Majesty, I have been waiting for forty-five years to put the record straight. I am Heineman and he was Edwards.'

It was all very jolly. Lots of drink before and during. In the room before the dining-room, after we had had drinks out in the garden, there were musicians playing old Wodehouse lyrics and songs from his shows. At the end a lady came in and sang Jerome Kern songs with lyrics by Wodehouse.[5] It was all deliciously summery and English and absurd.

On my right sat Tom Sharpe who wrote *Porterhouse Blue* and *Blott on the Landscape*. He says he didn't get much from the television rights of either but he had got quite a lot from people who bought the film rights and then never made films of them. He said he had begun by disliking Mrs Thatcher and now thought she was wonderful.

He said, 'You must keep your menu. It will be very valuable. There are people collecting memorabilia of Wodehouse.' He signed mine and I signed his. I said, 'Your signature will be more valuable on this than mine.' He politely didn't agree.

In Edward Cazalet's[6] two minute speech he spoke of how his mother had been proposed to in the room he was sitting in and Plum[7] lived there. He is the grandson via adoption of Ethel, Wodehouse's wife. Edward Cazalet has collected a lot of Wodehouse money as a result.

Frank Muir[8] wore the most ghastly light coloured suede shoes and a bow tie. He said to Kingsley [Amis] while we were waiting for Queen Elizabeth and I was standing some way away – Kingsley told me – he thought my tie was too loud. What he meant was that it was a nicer tie than his pale pink one, mine being properly red with spots from Turnbull and Asser.[9] However he is a pleasant man who wastes his talent appearing on lots of silly television games.

**Saturday 4 June**

Arnold quite chirpy this morning when I rang him. He says he's got two excellent orders for GEC, one for a power station on the Isle of Wight and the other a great Voice of America project which he won

---

5. Wodehouse/Kern shows included *Have a Heart* (1917), *Oh, Boy!* (1917), *Leave it to Jane* (1917).
6. Edward Cazalet QC; knight 1988.
7. Plum was Wodehouse's nickname, a contraction of his first name, Pelham.
8. (1920–98); writer and broadcaster.
9. Men's outfitters in Jermyn Street, London SW1.

in competition with American firms and firms all over the world. It will give employment for seven years.

He said at Chequers last Monday he found himself confused by Margaret. He said, 'I look on her as a cross between Joan of Arc and a headmistress. When I think she is against me or not approving I feel very down and depressed. When she seems to approve I lie about sopping it up. She's a bit like a Mosaic (meaning Jewish) matriarch.'

How strange that these captains of industry crumple up in front of her. She did say once at Chequers to Arnold, 'Please don't be cynical,' when he made some reply to a point she was making about industry. That's because he gets nervous and says not quite what he means to do.

At Longford Castle.[10] It is magnificent. It is beautiful all the way round and much improved by James Wyatt in the 1790s. Sad that one of his towers got burned internally, though you can hardly notice it from the outside. The great staircase of his was demolished at the same time. But the rest is pretty good.

Jake Radnor[11] loves the house and looks after it with most tremendous care. He is also an excellent guide. Petronella read out a long letter from George Washington to the then Lord Radnor which was full of gratitude for the praise Lord Radnor had showered on him. This is very effective with Americans who get bored by the paintings which must be worth twice as much as the Thyssen paintings. Jake's Holbein of Erasmus is about ten times the size of the one in the Thyssen collection and outstanding, perhaps one of the best surviving Holbeins.

Quite a jolly man, Barney Miller, staying. He plays the guitar and his wife sings to it. Petronella also sang very prettily although Verushka says her voice has now been ruined by smoking cigarettes and she cannot reach any high note now. He runs a cricket team called the Troubadors. He organized cricket in Argentina where they lived for a very long time. He was a Vice President or whatever of Johnson's Wax.

On Saturday afternoon I went to see our betting shop at Salisbury. I also visited the Cathedral.

How they can run a spire appeal without more attention to James Wyatt on the advertising for it inside the Cathedral is unbelievable. There is a huge picture of one of the worst architects in Victorian

10. Salisbury, Wiltshire.
11. 8th Earl of Radnor.

times, Gilbert Scott, who fiddled about a bit with the Cathedral but did absolutely nothing to improve it.

**Tuesday 7 June**

A meeting at the top of the Hilton Hotel in a suite with a view for miles across London. It's owned by Ladbroke's. That is why we are there. Peter George of Ladbroke's, Len Cowburn of William Hill, Mike Snapes of Coral's, and Bob Green of Mecca urgently asked the Racecourse Association representatives, Sir Peter Leng and Tommy Wallis, and also myself, to meet them. They are determined that Bruce Matthews should go from SIS. It is difficult to defend him.

At Monday's Board meeting he was once again feeble and did not appear to have studied the agenda. He did not control the meeting. Tommy, Peter Leng and myself had wanted to postpone a decision about removing him until after the Placing.[12] We thought it would look bad having just got rid of the Chief Executive two months previously. However, we became convinced that there was no hope of the bookmakers, who put up most of the money, ever reconciling themselves to Bruce Matthews.

I was then asked if I would go with Len Cowburn to explain all this to Bruce Matthews about July 7th and get his consent to an amicable parting. This is grim. I dread it: he will be shattered. It was I who originally suggested Bruce Matthews. He has been a sad disappointment having no real guts or drive. I don't know how Rupert put up with him for so long. I remember now how Rupert had been downbeat about him when I spoke to him.

A jolly dinner with Richard Searby (Chairman of Rupert's worldwide outfit) and his wife in their apartment/duplex in Eaton Square which they use on their rare visits to London. She cooked it and I ate too much and drank too much. This often happens to me.

Rupert was there. He arrived early in the morning from America. He is jetting backwards and forwards. He said he was tired. I said, 'You cannot go on like this. You're fifty-seven now and it won't do.' He said, 'That's what Anna says.'

Rupert says that another Cabinet Minister is in dire trouble. The *News of the World* have a story about him going to a hotel which was not quite seedy and not quite respectable opposite New Scotland Yard, taking two tarts to bed with him in the hotel, making such a

12. The flotation of the company.

disturbance that he was asked to leave the hotel and the hotel complained to the police. He then went home and they were ringing him from the *News of the World* at 4.00 in the morning.

According to Rupert he has more or less admitted it to Wendy Henry. On the other hand they may not feel that their story is quite strong enough. He wouldn't say who it was. We spent half an hour trying to guess. I said, 'Do you really have to do this? It upsets her. It makes it more difficult for her.' Rupert said, 'They shouldn't do these things.' 'You're not a Methodist preacher.' Then he said he couldn't interfere with his editors which is partially true. It's impossible to expect editors of *News of the World* to resist a story like this.

The English are extraordinary about sexual peccadilloes with tarts of politicians and prominent people. What on earth does it matter? No love or affection is in the proceedings so it cannot be said that a marriage is being disturbed unless the woman is very silly. It is just a man performing his bodily functions, like going to the loo. He feels more comfortable when he has done it.

After we left at ten thirty-five, Rupert being very tired and wanting to get to bed, we went on to the Jo Grimond golden wedding anniversary. All the usual liberal type people there including Caroline Gilmour who now will barely speak to me. The children gave the party. Laura Grimond said it was remarkable that two cantankerous people had managed to live together for so long. 'Perhaps it's because he is deaf and I won't listen.'

Jo was sweet. There is no harm or malice in him. He has an extremely good brain but made the mistake of being a Liberal. If he had been a Tory or even possibly Socialist he would have been well in the running for Prime Minister and would certainly have held very high office instead of wasting his time as Leader of the Liberal Party.

**Wednesday 8 June**

To lunch at Cavendish Avenue came two people from Collins, a man and a woman in trousers. The woman in trousers (Joanne Robertson) was very bossy but was junior to the man (Simon King). She has made a selection of the stories she wanted from *English Story* in the new volume to be published.

She wanted to make a great show of Stephen Spender's[13] story, very long, 'The Fool and the Princess'. She assumed that I had read every

13. (1909–95); poet and critic; knight 1983.

story in *English Story* over and over again but I couldn't remember any of them, or at least hardly any.

I insisted we had to have one from MacLaren-Ross.[14] I don't know that I am going to battle much about the selection, too boring. She wants Stephen Spender to be asked to write an introduction as well and me to write a preface because she thinks his book *The Temple* is so good and attracting a lot of attention.

I said, 'But he didn't know anything about *English Story.* He was concerned with *Horizon*[15] and he was rather difficult about that story. I can remember now.' Indeed, I found a letter dated 1946 in which I had not in fact been able to make him sell the copyright for any composition as I had all the other authors. I said, 'You'll have to pay him a bit more. But in any case, any people's stories we use, we've got to pay them something. I always did do that if they were reprinted elsewhere.'

The main memory I have of Stephen Spender around that period was that he was much concerned in the board of and editing of a journal called *Encounter.*[16] He pretended not to know where the money came from. It was ostensibly coming via an American, interested in promoting the freedom of the West and destroying the Communists, who had a great flour business. Actually it was coming from the CIA.[17] Stephen always knew that it was not really this man with the flour business who was supplying the money but he pretended otherwise. He was always rather shifty, Stephen Spender. He had a hang-dog way of holding his head.

**Thursday 9 June**

Charles Forte rang. Would I put into punchy language a statement they want to make following upon documents issued by the Savoy Hotel?

He said would it be all right if he gave me £1,000. 'Or do you think you would want more?'

I said, 'It's a question of whether I have time to do it.' So maybe it will be done over the weekend somehow. I will have to fit it in. He

14. James ('Julian') MacLaren-Ross, writer (1912–64).

15. Literary magazine founded by Cyril Connolly and Spender in 1939 and edited by Connolly until 1950; Spender co-edited it 1939–41.

16. Spender was co-editor 1953–67 of the literary/political magazine *Encounter.*

17. Central Intelligence Agency, a department of the US government set up under the 1947 National Security Act to conduct intelligence operations abroad.

said, 'We'll send you the £1,000 but if you think it should be more let me know.' I can't possibly ask him for more. He's an old friend.

He said, 'We must renew our acquaintanceship more. I only ever see you in the House of Lords when you are making one of your marvellous speeches. Why aren't you on our Tory benches?' I said, 'I was instructed to sit on the crossbenches. In any case I'm not a Tory.'

That was a coincidence. Robin Day had just rung up to say that on page 208 of the Churchill book by Martin Gilbert I was described as having joined the Conservative benches. He said I ought to get the publisher to print a correction slip.[18]

**Saturday 11 June**

Arrive at Donhead St Mary late because Robbie took the wrong turnings two to three times.

Michael Tree had gone to Gleneagles to play golf over the weekend. I thought that strange with us having been invited for the weekend. However, there were three people at lunch who looked somewhat elderly. Two of them turned out to be younger than me. One was a doctor who retired when fifty-nine and is now sixty-five. Staying with him was a man who I thought would be boring and seemed rather old but turned out to be Peter Shaffer [the playwright]. He is only sixty-two.

We discussed *Lettice and Lovage*. I told him that I thought everything was brilliant, very accurate to character, wonderful, hilarious but that I did not like the end. He said, 'I absolutely agree. I'm writing another end for it for when it goes to New York and when it is played later but I can't do it while the production is on now.' He says Maggie Smith is going to New York with it.

He has written ten plays since 1958 and only one has not been put on. They've been marvellously successful, *Amadeus* particularly so.

He says that it takes ages for an idea to come to him before a play.

Once he starts a play it takes hold of him. I asked him if he knew what was going to happen throughout a play before he begins. He said 'No. It develops as I write on.' He added that it takes him four months

---

18. WW wrote to Martin Gilbert on 6 September 1993 when the same error appeared in another volume: 'I would not like posterity to believe I ever joined the Tory party which has been anathema to me all my life.' He added, 'Randolph once said to me, when I suggested his father was a Tory, "We've never been Tories. We've only ever made use of the Tory party".'

to get a first draft, writing and rewriting. I said, 'Do you have to do that with the jokes.' 'Yes. Again and again.'

He goes to all the performances for a long time when a play starts on tour. He sits and listens and rewrites and rewrites, adjusting to the reactions of the audience. I thought to myself, 'This is going to be quite an arduous task for me if my play ever gets to Bromley and Bath.'

Noël Coward was very kind to him. He came to see his plays several times and advised him and helped him become a good playwright. I said, 'I met Noël Coward several times. I thought he was a terribly nice man.' He said, 'Yes, he wasn't at all selfish and unpleasant like people thought he was from his plays.' 'Of course not. He was just an observer of life. And he put down what people are like. I thought he was a marvellous playwright.'

We talked about the Cole Porter and Noël Coward songs. He said he liked the latter very much because the words were so good. He said, 'You can't write lyrics like that now. The population isn't literate any more. They don't understand the allusions or what you are talking about.'

**Sunday 12 June**

I was just leaving the dining-room having finished my breakfast when Andrew [Devonshire] said anxiously, 'You're not going, Woodrow? I'm about to light my daily Gauloise.' Last night he had said that he has this one treat every day he looks forward to.

After a few puffs he stopped. I said, 'Is that all you're going to smoke?' He said, 'Yes, that's all I'm supposed to be allowed to smoke in a day.' The poor man cannot drink now and apparently this taking three or [four] puffs of a Gauloise is the only thing he looks forward to. But he is much chirpier than he has been for a very long time because he has stopped drinking.

He asked me whether I went to Pandora's[19] memorial service. I was stunned. I didn't know she was dead. The beautiful Pandora who gave me a Malacca walking stick with a sword inside and had inscribed on the silver band around the top 'The coward does it with a kiss. The brave man with a sword,' from Oscar Wilde. I sat there thinking

19. Daughter of the Hon. Sir Bede Clifford; m 1 (1948–60) Timothy Jones, m 2 (1961–8) the Hon. Michael Astor, son of 2nd Viscount Astor.

of that beautiful ravishing girl. Apparently she had died suddenly of cancer.

She had married in the end a cosmetic surgeon who kept making her look preternaturally young. Poor, dear Pandora. A lovely butterfly who had unhappy marriages but a lot of fun. Golden haired and blue eyed with a perfect figure. One of the girls Tony Lambton showered undying love, gifts and praises on.

She said, 'He couldn't go from breakfast to lunch or lunch to dinner without sex.'

She tried writing a bit herself but not with much success. Her husband, Jones (her first husband), had been a pupil of Tony Crosland at Oxford. He was a son of Enid Bagnold.[20] That didn't last very long. She married Michael Astor. That didn't last many years either. But I think she may have been happy with her cosmetic surgeon. I used to meet them sometimes at occasions like a dance given by Drue Heinz. Michael Astor too, was never happy in his marriages, though I think it went well enough between him and Judy Innes who had been living with the fearful Kagan whose son Michael adopted.[21]

The news about Pandora called back to mind happy days of long ago when there was much laughter. I thought of Bruern[22] where I used to play clock golf with Michael. I thought also of Talitha Pol who was very lovely and married Paul Getty Junior.[23] She was not happy and committed suicide.

Over to Robert Cranborne's house, Cranborne Manor. He is the son of Lord Salisbury. On the way Andrew said, 'I'll tell you a grand telegram that was sent by his grandfather to his son. It read, "Cranborne, Cranborne. Arrive 7.7 p.m. Salisbury, Salisbury."'

We went to see the Empress of Cranborne, a large brown sow. And her daughter, the Duchess, with her nine little piglets. Rather charming as pigs always are if allowed to live under decent conditions, free range in a field. Clean. The sows were friendly.

He is a jolly and intelligent man, very good looking and attrac-

---

20. (1889–1981); novelist and playwright (*National Velvet* and *The Chalk Garden*); m (1920) Sir Roderick Jones (1877–1962); chairman and managing director, Reuters.
21. See 30 April 1987.
22. In Oxfordshire, Michael Astor's house.
23. His second wife (m 1967), daughter of Willem Pol, painter; she died in 1971.

tive. He gave up politics because he was bored in the Commons.[24] He has three and a half thousand acres and there is another three and a half thousand acres at Hatfield which he will inherit.

Andrew says that David Astor whom I regarded as the archetypal wet is now an ardent supporter and has been for some time of Mrs Thatcher whom he regards as perfect. What a revolution she has performed.

In the country I jolly nearly got pneumonia it was so cold.

**Tuesday 14 June**

Ascot first day.

At last the summer. The sun shone warmly yet there was a pleasant wind so that wearing my morning suit which I have had for forty years, of thickish cloth, was not too uncomfortable.

Piers [Bengough] said that we were expected for tea with the Queen after the fourth race. Sometimes we are asked on Thursday when we have a lot of guests and it's inconvenient but one can hardly say one doesn't want to go. Sometimes we are not asked at all. But Tuesday fitted in well as we had no guests, just one or two people hanging around in the Tote entertainment room.

Queen Elizabeth the Queen Mother was full of jollity.

We talked about Castle Coole[25] where she had been in order to open it for the National Trust after its renovation. She thought the colours were probably not quite James Wyatt as they were rather garish and she understood why Lord Belmore[26] was annoyed about it. It's his house, or was until he gave it to the National Trust, being allowed to remain and live there. She said that Belmore and Jennifer Jenkins,[27] who is Chairman of the National Trust, had a brush but then they sat next to each other with her at the same table at lunch and relations began to get better after their public disagreement over the form of the decorations.

---

24. See 26 January and 23 September 1986. He left the Commons over opposition to the Anglo-Irish Agreement. He took his seat in the House of Lords in 1992 and was Parliamentary Under-Secretary of State for Defence, 1992–4, Lord Privy Seal and Leader of the House of Lords, 1994–7; Leader of the Opposition in the House of Lords since 1997.
25. In Co. Fermanagh, Northern Ireland.
26. 8th Earl of Belmore.
27. Dame Jennifer Jenkins, wife of Lord (Roy) Jenkins.

She talked about my article on Reagan and the astrologers.[28] She agreed that there is something in it all though we don't know what. I told her about Brian Inglis' book *The Hidden Power* and about mediums who were so popular in grand Court circles at the beginning of the last century and some way into it. She is not at all sceptical and understands that there can well be paranormal activities about which we know little but which have a potency.

She thought it terrible what the Irish had done about not sending back the terrorist after he was released from prison in Ireland and was due to be extradited to Britain.[29]

We talked about Kinnock's dilemma.

She said, 'I think it was a great pity Roy Jenkins and David Owen and everybody like that all left the Labour Party and let the people who believe in nuclear disarmament and who are much further to the left take over.' I said, 'Well, I was one of those.' 'Oh no, you went by yourself much earlier. I know that. They all went in a group. They should have stayed to fight it out.'

She kept offering me all kinds of cakes and whatnot. She had a chocolate éclair and said, 'It's quite disgusting really.' I did not have one but I did have some raspberries.

On the way to watch the race Princess Michael and Prince Michael came up to me. I was walking towards the viewing space and was just standing at the top of the steps from the room where we had tea when Princess Michael said, 'I have to kiss you while you're on the top of the steps because it makes you a better height for me,' so she insisted on doing that. I nearly fell over and I said, 'I see that you are determined to destroy me in one way or another.' She thought that very funny.

I do rather like her. She has an animal magnetism. She certainly looks a great deal more aristocratic than some of these people in the Royal Family. There is the appalling Duchess of York who looked as though she is walking about in a tent, a yellow one. And from behind her bottom looks three or four feet across. That's not just pregnancy, she is a truly vulgar looking woman, coarse and fat. She was wearing

---

28. In the *Times*, 18 May 1988. It started with Donald Regan's revelation: 'Virtually every major move and decision the Reagans made during my time as White House Chief of Staff was cleared in advance with a woman in San Francisco who drew up horoscopes . . .'
29. A Dublin court had refused to extradite the IRA suspect Patrick McVeigh on the grounds that his identity was not proven.

no stockings and flat sandals. I dare say she is very agreeable but oh my God!

Princess Michael was dressed elegantly and simply. She has style even if she does misbehave. She and Michael were off to Virginia that night. They are going to Hungary and wanted to know a restaurant with gypsy music which is cheap because they have to pay for themselves, though they are staying at the British Embassy and could get their meals there. She is writing a book about Empress Elizabeth of Austria-Hungary. That is why she is going there, to do some research and get some local colour.

On getting back to Cavendish Avenue I find a parcel from Abdul Al Ghazzi. A box of magnificent twenty-five Davidoff cigars and a huge bottle of Remy Martin Xo champagne cognac. I find these presents embarrassing though not unacceptable.

**Thursday 16 June**

Third and last day at Ascot for me.

I had Carol Price on my right and the French Ambassadress Hedwige[30] (that's her Christian name) on my left.

Later at tea time I asked Hedwige, 'Why do you keep pulling your skirt down? You're covering your pretty legs.' She said, 'My skirt is a little too short.' So why did she wear it so short if she had to keep pulling it down? She is a lively girl with a charming manner exuding animal magnetism – not exactly pretty but with a *jolie laide* look.

There was a disgraceful episode during the afternoon. Royal Gait, a French horse which had won the Gold Cup in record time, and easily, was disqualified. Another jockey, Clark, had fallen off El Conquistador. He claimed he had been knocked off and it was the fault of the jockey on Royal Gait which it certainly was not. El Conquistador was collapsing at the time and uncontrollable. I thought it anti-French chauvinism.

It also lost the Tote a lot of money because the delay in announcing the result of the stewards' inquiry meant that many punters were unwilling to bet until they knew whether they had winnings or not, and held up those who wanted to bet as they waited for expected winnings at the windows.

---

30. Mme de La Barre de Nanteuil.

**Friday 17 June**

The cricket lunch. Bob [Wyatt] had never heard of Kingsley Amis though his wife Molly had. Kingsley told him that he was a great fan of his since his boyhood and was very pleased to have met him. Bob was suitably gratified though he had no idea he was talking to one of the great novelists of our time.

Andrew Knight arrived three-quarters of an hour late. He made no apology and said he had arrived earlier than he had to the last cricket lunch he was invited to. I made a mental note never to ask him again to a cricket lunch.

Saw Margaret on the news at the Welsh Conservative Conference. She was absolutely fresh. When she told me this morning she was going to it before she leaves for Canada tomorrow I said, 'Oh, my dear. You'll be awfully tired.' She said no, she wouldn't. And she certainly wasn't. She looked quite beautiful on the screen and answered questions clearly and precisely.

This afternoon Kingsley signed some of my latest first editions. He remarked of *A Case of Samples* [1956] that it is now very rare. He didn't write anything apart from his signature which is a pity because a comment or two makes them more valuable.

He had been put out when I said, 'I have been reading the *Economist* this morning, and Martin's books are more expensive in their first editions than yours.' He said that was because they went into very short runs, unlike his. He doesn't care for his son's writing. He thinks he has got talent but wanders about. I said, 'Yes and he puts in all that conventional sex stuff which is unnecessary for the kind of book he is supposed to be writing.'

**Saturday 18 June**

To Badminton.

Caroline has stopped drinking. She looks much better and more collected. Very much like her old jolly methodical self. I was guilty that I had not written any more speeches for her occasions. She is President or Patron or Chairman of sixty-five organizations in the district.

She showed me the speeches she had written out, beginning with one in 1965. I was very touched by them. I almost had tears in my eyes. She is a sweet girl full of good works and conscientiousness, determined to do her duty as a Duchess and give help, appreciation and gratitude to voluntary and other workers.

She asked for one addition for when she opens hospitals with new equipment. I wrote her one out which went something like this: 'You can have the most modern equipment in the world. But it is the love and care of the staff which makes that equipment doubly useful and gives the patients a feeling that everyone wants them to get well – which in itself is a help to them getting better.'

She liked that very much.

She now has eighty-six scrap books. She started them in 1947.

They are all cut out from magazines and papers about people she knows, or her family. They are probably an important historical record for the future. I'm not altogether happy about being so prominent in them because not everything I have done would I like remembered. She also has a book of people she knows who have committed murders or have been murdered or gone to prison.

We went into Chipping Sodbury together. She said, 'I wanted to show you off where I am President of the local Conservative Association.' 'But I'm not a Conservative.' 'You love Mrs Thatcher.' 'Of course. But that's because she is not a Conservative either. She's nothing like those wets like Ian Gilmour, Jim Prior and Pym. She is a radical making a revolution which horrifies many Conservatives. Though now they see it works.'

We were in a new set of rooms just done up by Caroline. Verushka's bedroom was even more handsome, with glorious white columns, than Caroline's. The bathroom is almost like a yacht with mahogany around the bath and cupboards and on the lavatory seat. I said to David, 'I hardly like to put a tooth glass down by the basin for fear of leaving a ring.' 'Oh, it's just like a ship. It all washes off.' Fortunately David has a lot money which he has made out of his Marlborough Art Gallery and other investments which he has been very shrewd at.

Just before lunch Tom Parr and a German friend whom he lives with arrived. They are well in their middle age, the pair of them. The German has a house near Nice. He was agreeable and jolly.

After tea we looked at Master's[31] grave. The tombstone has been beautifully done. 'Looks very ducal, doesn't it?' Caroline said and pointed to the cushion with his ducal crown on top. One or two other Somersets are buried there. Some of them have been well-known

---

31. (1900–84); 10th Duke of Beaufort; Master of the Horse, Sandhurst, 1936–78; he was succeeded by his cousin the present Duke (David Somerset).

homosexuals and had no progeny. Before the tombstone anti-hunting vandals tried to dig Master up. Kind to animals but not to humans.

I became worried about my agreement with Jacob to take two thousand five hundred of the shares in Colefax & Fowler which is being floated on June 28th. I wondered if I could get out of it. Tom Parr runs Colefax & Fowler. He says they are not shares for a quick return but for keeping.

I rarely have any luck with shares.

**Sunday 19 June**

Before lunch at Badminton we walked to the village which all belongs to David. At the first house on the edge of Badminton Park is a very pretty house with a stone coat of arms (Beaufort) carved in the wall above the front door and the Beaufort portcullis on the gate. It was a charming garden. The sun was very hot and we drank Pimm's made by Mrs Lees-Milne. She and James live there.

David persuaded Master to let them have the cottage or little house when it fell empty. Then Master turned against them, and said, 'He doesn't hunt. He doesn't shoot. They do nothing in the village to show an interest.' It then transpired that what he really didn't like was her whippet which chased his foxhound cubs.

At eighty he writes away still. Excellent books about history and architecture and that kind of thing. He is writing one on the Fifth Duke of Devonshire. He finds it very difficult because he was a bachelor and did nothing disgraceful.

Micky Suffolk's house is Jacobean and handsome.[32] It is being used as a film about war time fliers as a French château because it has his landing strip outside where he landed his aeroplane on Sunday evening while we waited for him.

In the cellar, which is splendid, they have sprayed bogus cobweb on some of the bottles to make ancient local colour for the film. There are masses of bottles of 1982, many of them the best wines, the very best. He showed us Château Grillet and 'Y' which is the dry wine of Château d'Yqem. As I remarked when we drank it at dinner, it had a faint hint of creosote behind it. I found it interesting but would not want to drink much of it. It's wildly expensive.

Micky does not live in the big house but keeps a flat there. When

32. Charlton Park, Malmesbury, Wiltshire.

he was about eight the house was divided up into flats, the big house, and they let them to people from London and local commuters.

**Monday 20 June**

Saw Arnold Goodman in the afternoon. He is very anxious that we should agree to pay Ladbroke's costs on the settlement of the libel action.

His argument is that they could go on dragging it out for years with mounting costs on both sides and then agree to settle it the day before the court case or an hour before it. We wouldn't get our costs which would have come to £200,000–£300,000 by that time.

**Tuesday 21 June**

Abdul Al Ghazzi to lunch. Show him the letter from Nicholas Ridley [Secretary of State for the Environment] saying a decision has not yet been made on the footpath. Then wrote a letter to Nicholas Ridley explaining that the repairs will not be done to the damaged east wing until a footpath is delineated in an area where a security plan can be built linked with it.

Abdul says he would like to meet me at least once a month. He likes the way I make blunt statements. This on the whole is not customary in Arab circles though the Iranians seem to do it a lot but they are not proper Arabs.

He has business interests in Qatar and in Nigeria, both in oil. He has property in a number of countries. He has a training school for tourism and teaching hotel staff in Switzerland which he says is always full and does very well.

**Wednesday 22 June**

At the Levy Board lunch I sat next to Charles Morrison[33] who has just been given a knighthood by Mrs Thatcher. I said, 'Is there any serious revolt against her? Is there any real feeling of unrest?'

'Oh yes. She will have to go by the next election. The country is tired of her. They've had enough of her. They want a new face to carry it all on.' I thought to myself, 'Well there's gratitude for you.' He and wets like Ian Gilmour mutter away about the community charge

---

33. The Hon. Charles Morrison, Conservative MP, 1964–92; m 1 (1954–84) the Hon. Sara, née Long, m 2 (1984) Mrs Rosalind Ward.

and anything else which they like to bat her over the head with but they owe their seats to her.

We had a discussion about national service to deal with football hooliganism. I said I thought the idea of giving everybody a national membership card for a football match was ridiculous. All that it would do would be to drive the hooligans who couldn't get these cards into the racecourses etc. I am actually quite afraid of that.

Charles said, 'But it's your friend's plan.' 'I don't agree with everything she does.' It seemed to surprise him.

I said, 'I ought to have congratulated you before on your knighthood. But it is automatic, isn't it, for a Tory backbenchers who have served a long time?' He said, 'Yes, but normally the period is fourteen years. I've waited twenty-four years.' I said, 'That's for bad behaviour.'

**Thursday 23 June**

T. E. Utley,[34] blind since he was nine, has died. Once I took him home from a party late at night. He guided Robbie as though he was seeing everything. He pointed out the corners to turn on and said, 'Now you turn on the left,' and 'There's a letterbox on the corner here,' and guided us right to his front door. He had a most amazing memory, developed of course by not being able to read. He memorized everything. He had everything read to him and made mental notes and stored them like a computer in his head.

I was not quite comfortable with him. He seemed a little prickly but was doubtless not. It was probably my inability to deal with somebody in a completely normal manner who was so handicapped. He wrote good strong stuff and was an ardent Thatcherite from the start.

It unnerves me to be looked at keenly by a man who can't see you. It also reminds me that if my left eye goes I shall be in the same position as him.

Rupert rang. He is concerned that Lord Young's enthusiasm for the BSB [British Sky Broadcasting], and trying to get the BBC and ITV using their satellites, is going to subsidize his rivals by giving them £30 million a year income, £15 million from Channel 4 and £15 million from the BBC. He is launching this great £199 dish for every home to be able to receive umpteen programmes from Rupert's satellites.

---

34. Assistant editor and leader writer, *Daily Telegraph*, since 1964; previously on the *Times*.

I asked him whether he was worried about the *Daily Mirror* colour. I had spoken to Kelvin MacKenzie, editor of the *Sun*, about it this morning. I told him and Rupert it is much better than the colour put out by *Today*. Rupert said, 'We will have to sweat it out for two years when our colour comes on.' Kelvin MacKenzie seemed pretty confident.

**Monday 27 June**

Didn't get Margaret last night so spoke to her this morning. I said I wanted to tell her how wonderfully well she did at Toronto.[35] I couldn't understand why some newspapers thought nothing had happened. She said, 'Yes. It was one of the best conferences we have ever had. We're all agreed on the type of economic policies we should run.'

Of Kinnock's wild gyrations on defence she said, 'He sounds as though he is getting hysterical.' I said, 'He has no bottom, no depth. There is nothing to be afraid of. People may occasionally say they are going to vote Labour because they are irritated by the community charge or some other change they think is going to hurt them but down below they know that Labour is not fit to govern and cannot be. It would do better if they took somebody like John Smith to lead them but because the Labour Party is what it is they can't.'

Sonia has a party. A variegated crowd. Allan Davis tells me it's the anniversary of the day we met and the place we met a year ago and, 'We're still talking to each other.'

Mary Soames was there. I told her I was answering Edward Pearce [political journalist] in the *Sunday Times* who had said that Winston her father had rotted himself to senile death with drink. She said, 'He painted forty-five pictures after he retired from being Prime Minister in the five years to 1960.'

She said that Montgomery,[36] who never drank, became totally senile for the last ten years of his life though she wouldn't want that printed because it would upset his son. So the idea that drink and senility are connected is not necessarily the case. She said her father certainly faded in the last four or five years of his life. However, he did live to gone ninety which is not too bad.

---

35. The G7 summit, annual meeting of the West's seven leading industrial nations.
36. Viscount Montgomery of Alamein (1887–1976).

We talked a little about the book by Moran,[37] Winston's doctor. He ran Winston down, said he wasn't fit to be Prime Minister in his spell after the War. She said, 'My father hardly ever saw him. He only sent for him when he felt ill.'

**Tuesday 28 June**

A jolly lunch at the *Telegraph*.

A rather handsome building I thought, new, at Wapping. They were objecting to it before lunch because the air-conditioning either makes it very cold or very hot and they can't regulate it. Max Hastings said, 'You can't open the windows.' I said, 'Nobody can jump out then.' 'No, it is a prevention of suicide from the fifth floor.'

There was a good deal of discussion without much point on what would British/American and European/American relations be if Gorbachev delivered a more or less democratic Russia.

When there was a discussion about Russia withdrawing behind her frontiers and troubles in the ethnic minority Russian states, it was said by Max Hastings that he didn't think anybody in Britain or Western Europe would mind a bit if Russia goes on sitting on Eastern European countries. In fact they might be nervous if there was trouble there. I said, 'I'm not sure you are right about that. The British Empire only ruled coloured peoples. The Russian Empire is ruling white people of similar culture to ourselves. They find that offensive even though they might not say so in answer to an opinion poll.'

Tea at the Ritz with Mrs Graham owner of the *Washington Post* and third owner of the *New York Herald Tribune*. We hadn't met for perhaps ten to fifteen years – last at Pamela Hartwell's.

She thinks it is possible that the *Washington Post* may support Bush and even the *New York Times* may do so, though she thought that was less likely.

Before Andrew Knight and Mrs Graham arrived, Nico [Henderson] said I was much missed at The Other Club meeting last Thursday.

'Norman Tebbit was in the chair and there was a great discussion between him basically and Willie Whitelaw as to which was Mrs Thatcher's highest achievement. Tebbit said it was winning the 1979 election. Whitelaw said anybody could have done that.'

I rather wish I had been there to tell them what her finest achieve-

---

37. Lord Moran (1882–1977) wrote *Winston Churchill: The Struggle for Survival* in 1966.

ments were – namely trade union reforms, the revolution of thinking making profit respectable and not a dirty word, rolling back nationalization, making Britain a major country in the world again even if not level with Russia and America, making it impossible for the Labour Party to reverse nationalization, forcing the situation by which the two political parties, if they are to alternate, have to be much more like the Republican Party and the Democrats in America.

**Sunday 3 July**

I told her I thought her Secrets Bill sounded OK.[1] She is pleased at the reception it has got in the press.

I told her I was pleased about her elevation of Parkinson to be Chairman of the committee which decides about public spending in the Cabinet. She was horrified with the *News of the World* leader which made a terrible attack on Parkinson saying he should never have been promoted and should never have been allowed back in public life. 'I wouldn't read the *News of the World* at all if it wasn't for your article.'

I said, 'Rupert is very Puritan and that's why he thinks it is in order to say people in public life ought to behave better and they wouldn't get into trouble.' I also told her that he was married when he took up with Anna who was employed by him as a journalist-secretary so he really hasn't got a very moral platform to stand on. She replied that he sells newspapers on this fearful stuff which is giving a very bad idea to the young that everybody behaves in a scandalous manner.

She mentioned apropos people's private sexual lives that Cecil Parkinson [and] Jeffrey Archer were the most popular speakers in the Conservative Party circuit.

**Monday 4 July**

The Aims of Industry Award. I got the top award which was very flattering. The Chairman made extravagant praises of my activities. Patrick Minford,[2] who got one of the minor awards, referred several times to the evangelical work I did in the *News of the World* coaxing people along and getting them to assert their rights in their unions and elsewhere.

---

1. In the wake of the Ponting and *Spycatcher* cases, the Official Secrets Act 1989 banned any disclosure by present or former members of the intelligence services.
2. Edward Gonner Professor of Applied Economics, University of Liverpool.

There was some talk of Desmond Donnelly[3] who is still remembered as a gallant fellow. What a pity he got into so much trouble over money and women. He committed suicide. But of course it was the Tory Party who wouldn't find him a safe seat. That did for him in the end after he left the Labour Party. I referred to him and our fight to stop the nationalization of steel when Labour only had a majority of three in 1964 and said we delayed it until 1966 when Labour had a great majority. I said we must have saved the taxpayer £300 million by that delay but I never asked for any commission. Quite a good laugh.

Kenneth Baker said he remembered me as a Labour backbencher when he first came to the House. I didn't like being a backbencher. It didn't suit me. And it didn't suit the Labour Party either who were much put out by my activities.

I said to Kenneth Baker afterwards, 'It's very important that you go on caring about what you're doing – the actual job. You are doing it very well.[4] That's the way to become Prime Minister. Not scheme for it and think about how you can get yourself into position for it.'

Kenneth Baker said in his speech (we were in a conference room placarded with notices 'No Smoking'), 'Only Woodrow would come to an award ceremony for the Aims of Industry (which of course is very right wing) wearing a red bow tie and smoking a large cigar.'

So it is my seventieth birthday today. My brother sent me a fax message saying that I was now living on borrowed time and must take life more gently. That doesn't appeal to me at all.

Chips Keswick who couldn't come for the dinner tonight has sent me a case of Krug 1975. Immensely generous of him.

In the evening was my birthday party. Diana and John Wilton, Catherine and Julian Amery, Alan and Jill Hare, David Somerset, Henry and Shirley Anglesey, Michael and Anne Tree. David brought me four bottles of Château Pétrus 1970. They cost the earth, or at any rate some £70 a bottle I would imagine, if not more. Alan Hare brought a bottle of 1949 Château Latour still in its original tissue wrapping.

---

3. Labour MP from 1950 to 1968 when he resigned the Labour whip on British withdrawals from east of Suez; he sat as an independent MP, 1968–70, joining the Conservative Party in 1971.
4. Secretary of State for Education and Science at this time, steering through the Education Reform Act 1988 which would allow the opting out of schools from local-authority control and introduce testing of children at different ages.

Immensely valuable. Julian brought a bottle of Bollinger R D 1976. Diana Wilton brought me a pair of white pants with lipstick kisses all over them and a funny book about hugs, and something else, I can't remember what. Michael said he had a book for me but he had forgotten to bring it. Henry said he was going to send the last volume of his military history book which cost £35, as he pointed out.

Henry was very happy. He thinks it an immensely good idea living at the top of the house at Plâs-Newydd. His son who was once a Trotskyist has now made about £2 million selling a business he built up by the age of thirty-four. He potters along writing, looking after his rhododendrons and azaleas. He doesn't much like coming to London though he comes a bit. He prefers his view across the Menai Straits from his lovely house, largely rebuilt by James Wyatt, though the bottom is occupied by National Trust rooms, open to the public, which he uses when he needs or wants to.

Shirley[5] remains vaguely wet left-wing and as in the past Henry and I assail her for her feeble views. She is a woman who does great work in social help, however. Her brother[6] is Librarian at the House of Lords.

We had the 1975 Krug before dinner, which had been sent to me by Chips Keswick. It was first class. Really very good. We had our usual Chablis at dinner. That was fine. We then had Château Margaux 1967. It was splendid. I opened it at a quarter to seven and it seemed exactly right by the time it was drunk at around twenty past nine.

Abdul Al Ghazzi sent a magnificent clock. A huge carriage clock type. He also sent a very attractive basket of plants which I thought was a strange present for a man on his birthday from another man. I dare say it's an old Arab custom. It's very charming.

Irwin and Cita Stelzer sent four bottles of Mouton Rothschild 1970 which should be pretty good. It must be worth about £70 a bottle.

**Tuesday 5 July**

A foolish columnist called Ross Benson in the *Daily Express*. I sometimes point out to David Stevens[7] his idiot inaccuracies. No doubt he

---

5. Marchioness of Anglesey DBE, at this time chairman, Drama and Dance Advisory Committee, and board member, British Council; chairman, Broadcasting Complaints Commission; trustee, Pilgrim Trust.
6. Roger Morgan.
7. Chairman, Express Newspapers.

hears about this and resents it. This morning in his gossip column in the *Express* he says I sometimes seem confused. He then described my telling the Aims of Industry conference why I came to be called Woodrow.[8] He added I was now a devoted Thatcherite but had been a Labour MP for fifteen years. He couldn't even get that right. It was twenty-one years from 1945 to 1955 and 1959 to 1970.

Went to Allan Davis' drinks party at Cadogan Square.

Allan had asked Diana Rigg and she was there. He dragged me across immediately to talk to her and she was very friendly and I embraced her. When I said, 'The play I wrote for you which you rejected has been largely rewritten. The husband is now much worthier of your being able to turn him upside-down,' she became very interested.

She said she didn't turn the play down. She thought it was very good and very funny but at that time she didn't want to go into a play.

I said, 'You're not giving up acting?' 'Oh, no. I'll go back into it. I like being an independent woman,' meaning that she liked to have her own money. Her husband is pretty rich but she clearly doesn't like to be dependent on that.

She is a striking lady with slight blemishes on her face making her seem more attractive rather than less. The odd little bump, one could hardly call it a pimple. Her legs are splendid and so is her figure. She was wearing a leather suit which by some, I think, is considered to be very sexy though I have never found it so myself.

David Montagu had a dinner party this evening with the guest of honour John Freeman whom I knew first, I think, just after the War. His plain but nice wife, his fourth, asked me what he was like when he was young. I said I must take a long time thinking about that and referred her to the Shakespeare sonnet, 'They that have power to hurt and will do none'.[9] I said he gave me a great feeling of warmth always. She was surprised. She said, 'Everybody always thinks he's so distant.'

'He could have been Prime Minister but he disdained the grubby atmosphere of political life.' She said he has no ambitions. He has been

---

8. He was born on 4 July, American Independence Day, when Woodrow Wilson was President. His mother wrote to the President asking him to be a godfather. 'Surprisingly,' WW writes in *Confessions of an Optimist*, 'this idiotic letter brought a long reply from the President.' He declined, pleading distance and his current responsibilities. ('Such as, no doubt,' WW comments, 'the war against Germany.')
9. Sonnet 94.

Ambassador in America, High Commissioner in India, was a Minister in Attlee's government. He would have held high office if he hadn't resigned with Nye Bevan. He was editor of the *New Statesman*. Then he was Chairman of London Weekend Television. Now he has removed himself from life like an Indian sannyasi. He is teaching in a University in California.[10] He said they live in a little cottage about a mile from the campus. He is very happy though the poor chap has cancer.

I am very fond of him. He is a strange, interesting man with one of the highest talents I have ever known and a disinclination to use them not from laziness but because he is utterly unworldly. He is seventy-four.

He was quite startled when I said of my first wife that he was the first person with whom she had an affair. I said, 'But this is all over fifty years ago.'

**Wednesday 6 July**

A party on the terrace and Cholmondeley Room at the Lords. Alun Chalfont was the peer whose name it was given in though it was for *High Life*. A man called William Davis[11] edits *High Life* for British Airways.

Sara [Morrison] and I sat down at this kind of help yourself buffet lunch. I thought she was looking prettier than she had done for some time. A little less angular.

Fundamentally I think Sara Morrison is a nice woman. She is highly intelligent, genuinely devoted to Arnold. But she is also a genuine enemy of Mrs Thatcher. I suspect that it is a female jealousy that Mrs Thatcher's reached the top of the tree and Sara Morrison, who had political hopes when she was Chairman of the Conservative Women's Association when Heath was in power, now finds every route that way blocked. She and Peter Jay[12] had been agreeing that Mrs Thatcher had to be stopped.

Peter Jay, poor man, is working as a kind of ADC to Robert Maxwell which must be the most humiliating role. He said it did feel

---

10. Visiting Professor of International Relations at Davis, University of California.
11. Author, publisher and broadcaster; later became chairman of the British Tourist Authority.
12. The Hon. Peter Jay, economics writer and broadcaster; Ambassador to US, 1977–9.

as though he had bricks and stones being thrown at him all the time.

John King said that the butlers behind the throne in the Lords told him he couldn't smoke his cigar there. He said, 'Have you spoken to Lord Wyatt and told him he can't smoke cigars in here?' I said, 'That wasn't very nice to sneak on me.' He said, 'They said they had told you.' This was when I had said to him, 'You've now stopped all smoking even of cigars on your aeroplanes. You've given in to the anti-smoking lobby.'

Dinner at Drue Heinz's. Supposed to be in honour of Peter Carrington. Naturally there were about fifty or sixty guests, possibly more. The amount of time you could spend talking to Peter Carrington and Iona, his wife, was a maximum of two minutes. They have just returned from NATO. I told him he had done the job very well. He said he didn't think he had done anything at all and was quite relieved to be out of it. He is now to be Chairman of Christie's. Lord Gowrie is Chairman of the other one, Sotheby's.

Verushka sat next to Lucian Freud who said the thing he liked doing most was having lunch with Michael Tree which he would be quite happy to do every day. He had lunch with him today. He only ate when he felt like it.

Then he said, pointing at Judy Hurd who was sitting opposite at the same table, 'Look at her teeth. She keeps trying to hide them. I think they are false teeth.' He was obsessed by the teeth and referred to them several times. Admittedly they are not very good and are rather like a horse's.

He said he paints any time of day or night, it doesn't matter to him whether the light is good or bad. He does it when he feels like it. He only has four hours' sleep a night.

He began a tirade against the Tote for not taking his bets. He wanted to put £20,000 on a horse before the off and they wouldn't take it. They wouldn't even take £20,000 if the horse was 1 to 4 on. 'Nor will the other bookmakers.' After attacking the Tote for some time he said to Verushka, 'Well I suppose it's not your fault,' which it clearly wasn't.

I would much rather have been sitting with Lucian Freud whom I find interesting. On my right was the boring wife of William Waldegrave who has four children. She has a similar view on food to me, what you should eat and what you should not. She writes cookery books telling people how to do good recipes with food not using saturated fats.[13] Otherwise I found her insipid.

Opposite me sat Caroline Moore. She is a strikingly handsome girl with a very good figure. Her face shines with intelligence, as well it might because she is a don at Peterhouse in English Literature. I asked her whether she was religious and she said yes, very. She went to church always on a Sunday. Very high church, she said. So is Charles Moore. So is A. N. Wilson whom she knows and thinks writes well.

Afterwards I talked for a bit to John Mortimer and his wife Penny who were sitting with Andrew Devonshire. I asked him how his secret society[14] was getting on. This is [the] one that has been paraded in the *Sunday Telegraph*. He said, 'There's really nothing to it at all.' I said, 'I don't think you're going to get very far. You won't dislodge the lady I love very easily.' A group of chumps like Harold Pinter, Antonia Fraser, John Mortimer, and others of that kind are not going to reverse the Thatcher revolution. Though they may have fun imagining they are something like Lenin's Bolsheviks plotting in St Petersburg in 1917.

The French Ambassadress came in after dinner as did a number of other people, Peregrine Worsthorne included. He gets everywhere both before, after and during dinner.

**Thursday 7 July**

Dinner at Cavendish Avenue. Nigel and Mrs Lawson, Arnold and Netta Weinstock, Conrad Black and his wife, Mary Soames, Chips Keswick. Only ten this time because James Hanson got 'flu and could not come.

The Château Lascombes 1959 was first class.

Mary Soames said how much Christopher would have enjoyed it and she nearly cried. And I nearly cried. She is a sweet woman. She has lost the two men in her life who meant everything to her. Her father and her husband. Valiantly she writes on. She says she is leaving her flat in London because it is too large and I think she meant has too many memories. She sat next to Conrad Black and as she was leaving I asked her what she thought of him. 'The biggest bore unhung,' she replied.

---

13. Caroline Waldegrave had founded, with Prue Leith in 1975, Leith's School of Food and Wine.
14. A group of writers who met for political discussion at the Pinters' house

Conrad Black asked endless questions of Nigel who was in an exceptionally amiable mood. Conrad lapped up all the answers like a schoolboy.

Nigel has an interesting head. It is an 18th century kind of head, full of intelligence, quizzical, and determined. He promised to make the Home Office get a move on about privatization of the Tote.

Arnold naturally went on at him after dinner after the ladies had left about all his defence contract problems. Nigel looked at him coolly and said, 'The truth of it is that for too long the defence contracts have been given out carelessly. They are more expensive than they need be. You are now naturally suffering from competition and less wastefulness.' Arnold did not look pleased but it is true. He has been able to get away as have other British defence contractors with a great deal.

We ranged over a wide area. Nigel said there is nothing to fear from the Commission imposing taxes on us that we don't want. They have to be unanimous. The VAT provisions only follow when there has been a directive agreed on. He is not fussed about the deficit. He thinks, as I do, that it will be likely to take care of itself. He pointed out that a very large part of it is due to our import of capital goods needed to improve our industry and not just consumer goods at all.

He does, however, believe we will be able to keep our currency more stable if in the EMS. We would not have to have exchange controls. He thinks it would prevent our pound bobbing up and down in a damaging manner.

He talks very fluently and with authority. It is agreeable to hear a man with such command of his subject and able to simplify it.

Mrs Black[15] is pretty. She has a twelve-year-old son. They have been married for ten years. She wants to send him to a school in England because they are going to live in Highgate. Chips suggested Eton. I said, 'That's hopeless. Why not send him to Westminster? Or Highgate?' She thought it would be difficult to get him in. I said, 'I've no doubt something could be done about it if you let us know.'

We discussed relations between No 10 and No 11. Mrs Lawson said, 'They are like an old married couple. They are devoted to each other but they have their squabbles.' Nigel says he doesn't want to be Prime Minister. She wants him to earn some money. She thinks

15. Conrad Black's first wife (1978–91), Shirley Gail Hishon; they had two sons and a daughter.

something of the idea that he might be editor of the *Times* which is highly secret and which we didn't refer to by name. She obviously thought it was a promising idea, as it should be if it has a large enough salary and a decent pension.

They are going to have a holiday at Blaby in their little house with a small garden. I said, 'What will you do?' She said she would do the garden, cook and make love.

Mary Soames smoked a cigar. Arnold smoked one too. I haven't seen him smoke one for years. He had been put off by his doctors.

I think Conrad Black had no idea that Mary Soames was Churchill's daughter. Otherwise he would have been more polite to her.

When I first knew Nigel Lawson about thirty years ago he was quite handsome. He is now better looking again. He works eighteen hours a day. He is basically a good man. He cares about the country. He has done little to make himself well off.

**Saturday 9 July**

At Lingfield John Howard de Walden came in after the race in which his horse Arden had run extremely badly. I had previously said to Gillie Howard who came a bit before him, when she complained their horses were doing badly, that I had noticed he was not so high up in the winners' league this year. John said he was so fed up with his horses he wanted to shoot the lot. Thus is racing. The triumphs of the Derby two years ago which he won[16] is overcast by the failures of the present.

**Sunday 10 July**

Had wondered whether to ring Margaret. I had little to say. I wanted to ask her about the seven SAS men in Gibraltar and mention the oil rig disaster.[17] I thought it was not enough to trouble her with. However, when I did ring her we talked away for twenty minutes.

We talked about the need for instant decisions as in the American ship which shot down the Iranian Airbus. And in dealing with IRA terrorists.

A little later Arnold rang from his car. He felt that Conrad Black was pretty good, having an encyclopaedic memory for history. He wants him to go on a board of a company in Canada of which GEC

---

16. He won the Derby with Slip Anchor in 1985.
17. The Piper Alpha North Sea drilling rig had exploded on 6 July with the loss of 167 lives.

owns just over half. He has agreed in principle. He also wants Nigel Lawson to take Jim Prior's place as Chairman of GEC if he leaves the government. I said, 'Would you give him a decent pension and salary?' 'Oh, yes. I would have to give him the rate for the job that he would get in the City.'

I didn't tell him that the *Times* editorship was in view if Nigel was interested. I think he would prefer it to being Chairman of GEC, though I did say to Arnold at least the vibes would be right if Lawson was Chairman of GEC and not Prior.

**Tuesday 12 July**

A large dinner party with David Metcalfe. Sally his wife looked very pretty. She is brown with a lot of freckles.

Conrad Black and his wife were there. I like Conrad but I am not convinced that he has much of an intellect. He obviously has a very good business brain or at least one must assume so: he has acquired the *Telegraph* newspapers so young.

Eventually, after the ladies had gone I found myself sitting next to Lord Antrim[18] who immediately said, 'Are there any signs of Mrs Thatcher's megalomania abating?' I felt irritated and hammered away at him. He uses the same hairdresser, Mr Brown, at the Waldorf Hotel, as I do. I thought the efficiency of Mr Brown was about the only thing we would agree on.

**Thursday 14 July**

The Other Club – Pichon-Lalande 1970 excellent.

Sat next to Peter Shore.[19] He is a nice man. He says it's the first time in twenty-five years that he has been out of touch with the top leaders of the Labour Party.

He said he had a lot of Bengalis in his constituency. Hugh Gaitskell had been blind to the perils of unlimited immigration.

I teased Paul Channon, Minister of Transport, and told him of Auberon Waugh's aim to get all the political columnists to write a combined attack on Peter Bottomley, the Minister in his Department, who is obsessive about drinking and the connection with road

---

18. 14th Earl of Antrim.
19. Labour politician; Secretary of State for Economic Affairs, 1967–9; for Trade, 1974–6, for the Environment, 1976–9; shadow Leader of the House of Commons, 1984–7.

accidents. Paul said, 'Unfortunately there are some statistics coming out tomorrow about the increase in road deaths which are not very helpful. But then of course Peter Bottomley goes miles over the top. He ought to be found some safe and quiet job in another Ministry.'

Suddenly there was the most tremendous crash. Quintin by shifting about in his chair (he is not light these days) had broken off one of the legs. A new chair was brought. Robin Day was in the Chair and instead of using the gavel he began to use the broken leg. He said, 'This now has become a treasured relic of the Club.'

**Saturday 16 July**

AGM of International Nutrition Foundation at Sutton Courtenay.

The place looks dreadfully unkempt.

Hugh Sinclair is desperate to try to get some permanency into the Foundation so that it will carry on after he is dead.

He brought a long letter that he drafted in the night in which he offered to give Jimmy Goldsmith lunch with various professors and Fellows at Magdalen.

I said the best thing is for Hugh, myself and the Chairman to have a separate lunch or whatever with Jimmy first to seek to persuade him.

Somehow I have to prevent Jimmy Goldsmith from actually seeing the place.

I am nervous, too, of the distinguished Chairman, Sir Brian Windeyer,[20] coming. He is eighty and doddery.

Other members of the Council arc amazingly important. Sir Richard Doll[21] who used to run the BMA. He is now running cancer research and is retired. Sir Francis Avery Jones.[22] Sir Edward Pochin.[23] I sit there with about ten professors and high level medicos with strings of degrees and am the only person who doesn't understand immediately all the medical and scientific references.

---

20. (1904–94); Professor of Radiology (Therapeutic), Middlesex Hospital Medical School, University of London, 1942–69; Vice-Chancellor, University of London, 1969–72.
21. Honorary Consultant, Imperial Cancer Research Fund Cancer Studies Unit, since 1983; first Warden, Green College, Oxford, 1979–83.
22. (1910–98); Consulting Physician, Gastroenterological Department, Central Middlesex Hospital, 1940–74.
23. (1909–90); director, Department of Clinical Research, University College Hospital Medical School, 1946–74.

Richard Doll is very sceptical of Hugh's theory that a proper diet would mean you were much less liable to lung cancer and other forms of cancer. He didn't object to us investigating it and trying to get people like Rothmans and Gallaher to finance schemes to go further into it, though he thought it was unlikely that Hugh's hypothesis would be proved. I think he may be wrong here. Hugh sticks stubbornly to the proposition that the Japanese, who are heavy smokers, didn't get lung cancer until they started eating the same sort of foods as we in the West eat.

Hugh is much interested at the moment in the beneficial effects of fish oil on diseases like multiple sclerosis, rheumatoid arthritis and the skin disease psoriasis. There is a tablet called Mexapa which he believes has very good effects on preventing coronaries and all these diseases I have just written about. He thinks it has a very good effect on the brain too.

You can get them in health stores. Mexapa belongs to Imperial Foods and Hugh thinks that James Hanson has not the slightest idea of the potential value of this product and how much money can be made out of it. He would like the Nutrition Foundation to be employed to do research on the subject. I will speak to James Hanson.

We went to *Boris Godunov* on Saturday evening and sat in the Royal Box. We had to wear dinner jackets. The host was Sir Alex Alexander who is part Hungarian, part Czech, of Jewish origin. He came to England with nothing and has made a fortune. Good luck to him. He is Chairman of Lyons. A nice man but not highly intellectual or amusing. He is Chairman of the Covent Garden [Royal] Opera [House] Trust which is why he had the use of the Royal Box.

It was all good, thump, thump, loud music. It is one of the few operas I really quite enjoy. The putting of the words against the singers above the curtain is a great new idea. I don't know why it wasn't done long ago. One could really follow the drama, such as it is, as it unfolded.

George Weidenfeld was there with his girlfriend, Barbara Amiel. She looks pretty with a full white bosom.

George once nearly married her but has now gone off that notion.

**Sunday 17 July**

Mrs Thatcher thought that the Cleveland Report[24] by Justice Butler-Sloss,[25] who is a lady, was not all that good.

I said, 'Child abuse is a real problem.' She said yes, but she is not convinced it is as big as people are making out.

I commented on the *News of the World* doing sleazy stuff about Justice Butler-Sloss's husband having tarts in Kenya where he is a High Court judge. I said I thought it was totally unnecessary and I don't know why Rupert allows this sort of thing. She said, 'But unfortunately that is their style.' Then she said, 'The *Sun* is the paper that is very good to us, wonderful.'

She had a stinking cold still. I asked her if she was taking ascorbic acid. She said yes, she had been taking ten grams every morning. I said, 'Well when you've got this heavy cold you should take a couple of grams every few hours. It will help to kill it off. That's what I always do.'

When I said that David Young had handled the actual business of the Rover affair well in the Lords, she said Kenneth Clarke had done his part extremely well in the Commons, handled it splendidly.[26] From which I surmise that he is now due for some promotion: into the Cabinet perhaps.

**Monday 18 July**

Ayr – presenting the Tote Spring Handicap prize.

Jimmy Reid was there. He said it was eighteen years ago that I interviewed him on *Panorama* standing on the dock side at Clydebank, when he was a Communist shop steward and leader of the most difficult section of the trade union, preventing progress and promoting strikes in the shipbuilding industry. Now he is quite different. Writes for the *Sun* in Scotland, makes television programmes about Russia for

---

24. The *Report of the Inquiry into Child Abuse in Cleveland in 1987* was about 121 children diagnosed between January and June 1987 as having been sexually abused and taken into public care.
25. Dame Elizabeth Butler-Sloss, a judge of the High Court Family Division, sister of Lord Havers (Lord Chancellor, 1987).
26. British Aerospace was bidding for the Rover Group which it bought in August 1988; Lord Young was Secretary of State for Trade and Industry at this time; Kenneth Clarke was Minister for Trade and Industry, as well as being Chancellor of the Duchy of Lancaster – he was already in the Cabinet (see 26 July 1988).

Channel 4, highly critical of what they are doing even now under Gorbachev. He has gone right round the clock and is now pro Mrs Thatcher.

**Wednesday 20 July**

At Levy Board lunch sat next to Clive Whitmore, now Permanent Secretary for the Home Office. Had a good opportunity to propagand him about the need to privatize the Tote.

In the afternoon the great play reading. Mr Salmon from Bromley, who manages that theatre, Lee Menzies, the thirty-five year-old up and coming manager who is going to be the producer, Allan Davis the director, Laurence Fitch my agent. The eight actors were professionals; only two of them, however, were really reasonably top actors. One was Simon Williams who played a prominent part in *Upstairs, Downstairs* and the other was a lady who is in the *Mousetrap* still.

The reading went extremely well. I thought to myself, 'This is a better play than I thought it was.'

The man from Bromley, Lee Menzies and Allan Davis were delighted. Diana Rigg has now got the play and Allan Davis is writing to her to urge her on.

When it was all over I gave them champagne out of silver mugs which they all enjoyed. The man from *Upstairs, Downstairs*, Simon Williams, said he would like to be able to say he had been in at the start of this play and hoped he might be associated with it some more.

**Thursday 21 July**

Coffee with Solly Zuckerman[27] and brandy at the Bishops' Bar. He talks at length about the collapse of the Zoo finances and how foolish they have now been to take £10 million as one last payment and then to be on their own.

He recalls the days when he used to raise money for the Zoo and I was on the Council. He said he raised the equivalent of about £40 million for charity: it was a marvellous asset. There is no way by which the Zoo can pay by having a menagerie viewed by the public. The days when people flocked to the Zoo are gone with so many alternative entertainments, safari and wild parks and all the rest of it.

The vital thing is to keep the research going. He thinks the Zoo

---

27. Lord Zuckerman OM (1904–96); Chief Scientific Adviser to HM Government, 1964–71; president, Zoological Society of London, 1977–84; life peer 1971.

should say to the government that it will close the menagerie down unless the government takes over the running of it.

He says he has been writing his memoirs and I appear in them as having refused to stay in his very comfortable house in Birmingham in Edgbaston when I used to visit my constituency, preferring to stay in the heart of my constituency in a back-to-back house with an outdoor lavatory and no bathroom and where you shave in the kitchen sink.[28]

**Friday 22 July**

The wedding of the Hare boy and Lizzie Amery.[29] A lot of old friends I suppose at the wedding but they didn't look particularly interesting, most of them.

Robert Cranborne was there. I always find him jolly. He kept coming over to talk to us and escaping people like Katie Macmillan.

She asked Verushka whether I would ever forgive her. On hearing this I said, 'Never' but I gave her a perfunctory kiss.

Her son Alexander was there, sheepishly by himself. He only stayed briefly. His mother said, 'You must come.' He is in the newspapers as separated from his wife,[30] having had a long-term lover, Miranda, the daughter of Lady Mancroft by her previous marriage. She has been married to several people including Peter Sellers.[31] He is such a pompous idiot; he made a long statement to the Nigel Dempster column about it, saying he hoped Bitte, his wife, who is an angelic woman, would find somebody nicer than he was, etc. etc.

I never liked that fellow anyway. He is always telling the newspapers

---

28. WW's first constituency was Aston in Birmingham (1945–55). Roy Jenkins was the other contestant for the Labour nomination. At WW's memorial service Lord Jenkins said that WW used to say that he, Woodrow, won the nomination because the night before the vote WW stayed with the secretary of the party in a back-to-back house, whereas Jenkins stayed at the old railway Queen's Hotel, famous for the gleam of its chandeliers: 'If he was right, it was a considerable feat to lose to Woodrow on the grounds of being too sybaritic.'
29. Alan Hare, son of the Hon. Alan Hare and Jill Hare, m Elizabeth Amery, daughter of Julian Amery and Lady Catherine Amery (née Macmillan).
30. Lord Stockton and his wife divorced in 1991.
31. Miranda Quarry, m Peter Sellers, the actor (1925–80) as his third wife (1970–4).

that Mrs Thatcher wants him in her government. I should be surprised if she did.

**Sunday 24 July**

To the Hurds for lunch not far from Burford. A pleasant house with a front door and porch not in the centre. Three levels of window on one side and two on the other. It is basically an old farmhouse over four hundred years old. The lack of symmetry makes it attractive.

Andrew Osmond and his wife were there. Douglas and Andrew had been in the Foreign Office service together in Rome years ago. They began to write books together which were moderately successful.[32]

After lunch we walked to the big house of the village where the gardens were open. Interlocking gardens with beautiful yew hedges and topiary. Attractive. We sat in one of the sections and Douglas then proceeded to talk about the three board members I wanted him to renew the appointments of. He queried Frank Chapple – he's rather old and been there a long time. I said he was extremely active and was of great value to us.

He agreed to let the three stay on and didn't press for Kitson.[33]

Spoke to Margaret. Told her we had been to lunch to the Hurds and that was why I hadn't rung her earlier. I said, 'I always have some reservation and doubt about him.' She said, 'I don't think he goes very deep in thought. And he doesn't make the strong decisions.' I said, 'Yes, but I have other doubts. I'm not sure how far he supports us.' She said, 'He is not a believer.' That is the first time I have heard her use that phrase. It used to be he is 'not one of us' which is a very good description of Douglas' attitude. She said he goes along with what happens but he distances himself.

I asked her about the current commotion caused by Alan Walters,[34] who was her economic adviser and may be coming back again, making criticisms of Nigel's handling of the interest rates and the pound. She said, 'Alan Walters is a very sweet man but very naïve politically. If a

32. Thrillers: *Send Him Victorious* (1968); *The Smile on the Face of the Tiger* (1969); *Scotch on the Rocks* (1971); *War Without Frontiers* (1982).
33. Sir Timothy Kitson, Conservative MP, 1959–83.
34. It had been announced on 17 July that Alan Walters, Professor of Applied Economics at Johns Hopkins University, Maryland, US, had returned as economic adviser to the Prime Minister, a position he had held 1981–4.

journalist rings him up and asks him a question he innocently answers it saying what he thinks.'

She said she didn't think that Nigel was all that put out about Alan Walters' remarks. But she said, 'It really isn't any good trying to intervene to prevent the pound going up and down.' She went on, 'Three times the amount of our reserves cross the London currency exchanges every day. How can we possibly do anything solid by throwing our reserves into a battle to keep the pound at one level or another? The reserves wouldn't last.'

She said Alan Walters had been very upset when Sam Brittan had attacked her taking Lawson's side very much in public, and then attacked him.

I commented on Ted Heath's ridiculous attack on her appointing Leon Brittan in place of Lord Cockfield. I said, 'He only does himself enormous harm and looks sly petty and deranged. It does you no harm.'

I referred to the ridiculous front page in the *News of the World* in which Fiona Wright, the girl who had the public affair with Ralph Halpern, claimed that he had told her that he had 'goosed' Mrs Thatcher at No 10. According to her, he said he had pinched her bottom and put his hand on it and she didn't mind a bit. 'I don't know why Rupert lets the papers print these silly things.' She said, 'Yes, he is such a Puritan.' She got that description from me. I was amused to have it coming back again.

While I was speaking to Douglas I said that Piggott should have been fined and not imprisoned. Douglas had been concerned about taking away his OBE and obviously had been compelled to do it.[35] I said, 'He got the OBE for his services to and in racing. The fact that he committed fraud on the Inland Revenue has no connection with whether he was a good jockey or not. Can't you let him out now?'

Douglas Hurd said, 'It's very difficult. He is there as an example to others who commit these VAT and other frauds on the Inland Revenue. It certainly seems to have frightened a lot of trainers and owners and other jockeys into behaving properly,' and he disagreed with me that a larger fine would have been sufficient. It was imprisonment which had frightened everybody in racing off malefaction.

---

35. The announcement was made on 6 June 1988; Lester Piggott had been sentenced to three years' imprisonment on 23 October 1987.

**Tuesday 26 July**

Spoke to Margaret. Said I thought her Cabinet changes and ministerial changes first class.[36]

She said she wanted to get them out of the way now instead of having all this speculation in the summer which made people anxious and was very hurtful for them. I said, 'I know how you agonize when you have to say to somebody, "You must go".' She said, 'Yes. It is awful because they come in and they don't know whether they are going to be promoted or whether they are going to be sacked.'

Kenneth Clarke, as I thought when I spoke to her a while ago,[37] and she praised him, got what was in effect a promotion. He was already in the Cabinet. He now gets the much more important job of Minister of Health. And still in the Cabinet of course. She obviously thinks very highly of him now.

Then she suddenly said, 'Going back to that matter you started talking to me about on Sunday night . . . I haven't really read it properly but it is absolutely terrible. I have had an abject letter from Ralph Halpern saying there is not a scintilla of truth in what was reported as to what he is supposed to have said to Fiona Wright about pinching me.'

She went on to say, 'I don't know how Rupert can do this. He says he supports us but he doesn't. This is a most hurtful and wounding thing to go into his newspapers. It means I can't see either of those editors again,' obviously referring to *News of the World* and the *Sun*. The *Sun* is also playing it very big as they did yesterday and they have done it again today.

I said, 'But he does really support you. He thinks you're marvellous.' Doubtless she will calm down but she is pretty irate at the moment. I am puzzled as to what I should say to Rupert, if anything. It really makes no difference to Rupert. He simply repeats that the public like these sort of stories and he has to publish them. In any case I know he dislikes Halpern a lot and thinks he is a wrong kind of person, and she shouldn't have such people to 10 Downing Street and give them knighthoods.

---

36. The DHSS was split between Kenneth Clarke (Health) and John Moore (Social Security); Anthony Newton became Chancellor of the Duchy of Lancaster.
37. See 17 July 1988.

She said, 'Why does he have such a dreadful woman as the editor of the *News of the World*? Women can be very bitter and nasty about other women and that is what she is being about me. She must be a very unpleasant person.'

Poor soul. It really is very aggravating to be talked about in a Rupert newspaper in the way they have been doing.

**Tuesday 26 July**

Rupert rang about half past six. I told him that Margaret was not at all pleased with what they had been saying re Halpern and herself in the *News of the World* and the *Sun*. He said, 'It was tasteless I agree, but she shouldn't consort with such people.'

**Wednesday 27 July**

To Italy. Exhausted after fitting in my *News of the World* article for Sunday and my *Times* article to be published today.

Got to Gingo's.[38]

**Saturday 30 July**

Anna Lu is still sorting out her chunk of the estate left by Prince Corsini – they have two palazzos in Florence. Poor girl, to have no descendants to follow on when she and her husband are dead.

It's like Camillo Casati, also a Marchese. He was Moorea's half-uncle by the second marriage of her grandfather after he had divorced the famous Malu Casati.[39] He had one daughter by a previous wife who was a night club dancer; then Camillo divorced her on the grounds he never intended to marry her. When I said, 'What does that make the daughter?' it was not a popular question.

His second marriage produced no children. Camillo was a voyeur and his wife, very beautiful, had to pick up good looking boys on the beach in Ostia and bring them back to their grand apartment in Rome. Then Camillo would film and photograph them in various poses. She warned him that one day she might fall in love with one of them, and she did. He asked the young man to come again, he was a student. Then while they were cavorting around he shot

---

38. Count Sanminiatelli's, on their way to the villa they had rented for August.
39. See note to 4 February 1987.

the student, shot his wife and shot himself. That was the last Marchese Casati.

I looked up the Casatis in an old Almanac de Gotha.[40] The family had been very ancient and prominent in Milan and Rome. What a waste.

40. A Who's Who of international royal families, first published in 1763; after a fifty-four year gap it was again published in 1998, for the first time in English.

**Monday 1 August**
We arrived at Mrs Reinhardt's villa overlooking Porto Ercole, high in the hills but you can see the sea and one of the great Spanish forts very well. A beautiful swimming pool with wonderful views also.

It is a well arranged house. I am sitting in the library. It belonged to her husband. He was Ambassador in Rome but died young. They built the house themselves and arranged it splendidly with jolly good American plumbing.

**Tuesday 2 August**
Mary Rothermere and Soup Campbell arrive.[1]

**Friday 12 August**
Came back from swimming to find the Hares and the Wiltons in our bedroom standing around Verushka who was lying on the floor. She had fainted. She had fallen down from the top of a flight of brick stairs, highly polished, while reaching up to look and see what the weather was like because we were going on a boat trip that morning. She had broken her wrist. They had carried her to the bedroom but could not get her to the bed because she was in such agony.

An ambulance came. We went to the Orbetello emergency ward. Waited for a long time. The hospital looks extremely scruffy and dirty. Notices up saying 'No Smoking' but all the doctors and the staff wander around with cigarettes in their mouths and ash dropping on the floor.

She was X-rayed and the wrist was smashed in two places. She bravely refused to go into hospital and have a general anaesthetic before the traction began to pull it straight first. As we waited outside the room where this grisly operation was performed, a man was screaming as though he was being tortured by the Gestapo. I went in with her. They wouldn't let me stay when they began. I heard her

1. See note on 20 May 1986 for 'Soup' Campbell James.

scream once or twice but she preferred that to staying in the hospital which she hates. We didn't like the look of the hospital anyway. Her arm was then put in a huge and heavy plaster. Still in great pain. Her holiday is ruined. Gone in a flash.

**Saturday 13 August**

The swelling in her fingers was terrible and the pain was very great.

Diana drove us to Grosseto Hospital which was a much more modern hospital. They cut open the cast a bit to relieve the pain of the swollen fingers. She is not sleeping and has to have the huge heavy weight up like a policeman stopping traffic all night. The doctor at Grosseto said that was not necessary during the night, it was more important for her to have sleep.

**Sunday 14 August**

Alan Hare and Jill took our hired car to Spoleto to see his great-niece. She is the great-granddaughter of Lord Iveagh. Her mother, Henrietta Guinness, committed suicide from post-natal depression and perhaps because she was aware she had made a fool of herself by marrying an Italian lorry driver.

The father is very protective and insistent on keeping his daughter. He has the legal custody. The father, the peasant, has refused to take any money from the great Guinness family. The child will be a multi-millionairess. She knows nothing of England. She speaks only an occasional word in English. She is now ten. She has been brought up in the local village school in Italy. She will come into her fortune not much aware of the world in which people have such vast sums.

Alan says she seems to be happy but as time goes on she will doubtless be thinking of a wider world and trouble will ensue.

When Soup Campbell and Mary left on the 9th it was amazing to see how frightened he was of her.

She is getting fat and looking more like a beetle every day. She pays all the huge bills of their travel. He has a little money. He has a house with a Chinese cook in Washington but I think he also suffered badly in the October crash.

He was man of minor distinction in the CIA, basically operating overseas, being attached to various embassies. He has read a lot. He is a bore unfortunately and talks a great deal about his life. All the time he was getting hold of John Wilton while we were playing bridge, telling him the story of his life and family. He has a cousin called Edward James who lived in Sussex, an eccentric American.[2]

Mary is not a very nice woman. She is very friendly and gushing but not much sincerity about it. She thinks of nothing but parties.

**Monday 15 August**

The Wiltons, sadly, depart. Last year they left a day late to Tony's [Lambton] and he talked about it bitterly for days.

I am always surprised that Diana persists in saying he is very fond of me. I told her that I can never forgive him for the way he treated Verushka three years ago. She had the contract which he had asked her to extend for another four years or five. He then got us out of the house by being extremely disagreeable during that August.

So many of her little possessions are left there and mine. There is still what is now a valuable picture of an artichoke by Rory McEwen.[3] He painted beautiful vegetables and plants. He had signed this one to me – 'To Woodrow from Rory McEwen'. They are now selling for £2,000–3,000, I gather, if not more.

We discussed Tony's success with women. She said they liked him because he gave them unremitting attention and flattered them. He has a feminine streak. He makes them believe they are the only person he has ever loved. I said, 'Yes, there was that Talitha Pol[4] who was very pretty and had a little starlet job in Yugoslavia; and he went and stayed at the hotel and sent her huge bunches of flowers about every two hours and showered her with presents.'

Diana said that is exactly what he used to do and most women would succumb. I said Pandora had told me that she thought he was stunning-looking in his shooting clothes and carrying his gun and he gave the same treatment to her.

Diana said she didn't believe he had ever really loved anyone. He might have loved Debo (the Duchess of Devonshire) a bit. Debo still adores him and he was the love of her life.

---

2. (1907–84); a patron of the surrealists and modern ballet, his house was Monkton at West Dean near Chichester; he was born in Scotland though of American descent and educated at Eton and Christ Church, Oxford, where he co-edited *Cherwell* with John Betjeman; he was married briefly to the dancer Tilly Losch.
3. His daughter Christabel married Lambton's son Edward in 1983.
4. She married John Paul Getty Jr in 1967; see 12 June 1988.

I said I thought he was capable of considerable kindness mixed up in his cruel streak.

He likes to have rows with people – it amuses and interests him. She said she was dreading going there because now he does nothing but complain about all his children, one after the other, and their husbands.

With Claire [Ward], his long-standing mistress, he has row after row and tells her how fat and awful she is in front of everybody. But his lingering decency won't let him expel her from the place. He would never marry her, not even if his wife dies. He would then find some other reason for not marrying her.

**Tuesday 16 August**

Jill Hare at breakfast told me about Robert Heber-Percy's[5] last years. I was unable to see him much after I was married to Verushka twenty-two years ago.

He was a strange man. He had a long-standing boyfriend called Hugh Carruthers for thirty years. Then Hugh had a row with the cook (German) called Rosa whom I remembered well as amusingly subordinate and a very good cook. When Hugh had a flaming row with her Robert decided he preferred his good cook to his long-standing homosexual partner and Hugh was thrown out to live in penury in a tiny cottage somewhere, where he died of cancer soon after.

Robert had married 'Coote' Lygon[6] when she was seventy and he was over seventy. He then made her cook for him when Rosa left. (Rosa could not bear the new wife. When they came back from honeymoon she had not even made the bed or tidied her room.) So the new bride, aged, was put to being a cook which she did not much care for. After a while they separated and Rosa came back.

However, Coote Lygon had tried to stop him gambling. He had to sell two Corots for £300,000 to pay his gambling debts at Ascot. He was a mad gambler.

He left his house [inherited from Lord Berners] to a granddaughter whom he suddenly got to like. She was a granddaughter by his first wife Jennifer Fry.[7] He did have a nephew, Alan Heber-Percy, to whom

5. See 4 November 1987.
6. Lady Dorothy Lygon, b 1912, youngest daughter of the 7th Earl Beauchamp.
7. Jennifer Fry subsequently (1949–85) married Alan Ross, poet, and editor, the *London Magazine*.

he thought of leaving the house but he didn't think he cared for it enough. Alan was the man who ran off with Susan Blandford when she was married to Sonny.[8]

When he died and they came back from the funeral – Jill went to it – the heiress had had the doves all painted purple and black and let them loose in the garden after the funeral was over. So she seems to have deserved the house.

Robert had a friend in the village, a carpenter with whom he went into business as an undertaker. Faringdon perhaps is more a town than a village. His partner was away on holiday and Robert had to arrange a funeral at short notice. The body was to be cremated at the Oxford crematorium. When the service began the clergyman came to Robert and said, 'I'm afraid, Mr Heber-Percy, you've filled in the forms all wrong. The corpse in the coffin is designated as you, not the person who has died.' A terrible confusion. He had to rush back with Hugh Carruthers who drove very fast, and get some more forms and fill them in correctly. When they got back fifty minutes later the congregation, bemused, were still singing hymns.

I told them how Tony had complained at Alec Douglas-Home, who was then Foreign Secretary, not tipping him off that he was being followed by the Secret Service as he drove in his ministerial car up and down with Norma Levy, the procuress, and about what was going on.[9] Tony was very bitter that he did not warn him. I said it was difficult for Alec because he was Foreign Secretary and if he had warned Tony, they would have realized that somebody had tipped him off and there would have been a lot of investigation, and he would have been in a very embarrassing position. Tony's complaint was that Alec was his cousin[10] and he should have been prepared to break the rules. I think Alec is too honourable for that. Anyway he must have thought what an idiot Tony had been.

Pericles with his Nicaraguan friend Maria arrive.

She is forty-five. She is a grandmother. Her first marriage ended after two years when her husband was killed in a car crash. Her second

---

8. Now 11th Duke of Marlborough (m 1 (1951–60) Susan, née Hornby).
9. Lambton resigned from office as Parliamentary Under-Secretary for Defence (RAF) and from Parliament in 1973 after photographs of him with Norma Levy were offered to the press.
10. Lord Home's mother and Viscount Lambton's father being sister and brother, children of the 4th Earl of Durham.

lasted for ten years when the husband left her for a younger woman. She has now been shacked up with Pericles for about a year and a quarter. Pericles is besotted by her. He tells me that she is the most beautiful girl he has ever seen. So love really is blind.

They have discussed marriage. My final words to Pericles on the subject were, 'Why marry? You can see the age difference. It's bound to end in disaster. You will feel trapped at some point.'

He brought me some American and Dominican cigars. It was very kind of him. I have been trying to smoke some but they are awful.

**Thursday 18 August**

Allan Davis arrives. He has a list of criticisms – new ones. There is work to be done.

**Monday 22 August**

Marchese Corsini's house for a party. He has fabulous botanical gardens built by an ancestor in the 1860s. He is descended in one part of his family from Baron Racasoli who was a famous Foreign Secretary and a helper to King Vittorio Emmanuel in the Risorgimento.

France and England agreed to help the King unite Italy if he would send a contingent to the Crimea. This he did and the Marchese's ancestor lost a leg there but took thirty-seven prisoners. He was allowed to bring these Russians back to Porto Ercole where they built these fabulous botanical gardens climbing up the hill behind the villa.

They have some trees which are alone in Europe. The Germans during the War removed many of the labels. He would like Kew Gardens to relabel them. David Mellor, the new Minister of Health, was there a few days ago and said that he would ask Kew Gardens. I said I would nudge David Mellor to send somebody out.

Racasoli was the Foreign Minister who began the production of Chianti Classico in its modern form when he found his wife dancing too long with a subaltern at a state ball in Rome. He said to her, 'We are now going home.' He drove her to Brolio in his carriage and kept her there for the rest of her life. He then too spent a great deal of time there developing the wine into the present Chianti Classico and keeping an eye on his wife at the same time. She paid a big price for a few dances with a subaltern.

All our activities are greatly curtailed because of Verushka's wrist smashed in two places, and also her thumb broken.

We have been to the hospital twice with the usual wait for several hours.

**Friday 2 September**

Arnold had a rotten holiday. He got a detached retina while at Deauville. Flew back and forth to the hospital; they did something to him which affected his blood pressure. When he got back to Deauville somebody trod on his toe and broke it. He sounded distinctly uncheerful.

**Sunday 4 September**

Asked Margaret how much holiday she had had. 'Seven days.' I said, 'You're incurable.' We both laughed.

She said she had had to come back early because of the shooting of the soldiers by the IRA in Northern Ireland.[1]

She asked me whether I thought the TUC would expel the Electricians tomorrow [at the TUC conference]. I replied it was virtually certain. Eric Hammond had written an article in the *Mail on Sunday* saying that was what was going to happen and they were not going to climb down and they could not now. Bill Jordan of the Engineers is making remarks about trying to persuade Eric to stay but I don't think that will have much effect. It's just that Jordan wants to look as though he is trying to do something about it. But I said that the Engineers will probably follow not long after.

She said she didn't read the *News of the World* any more and therefore had not read my article today. She has it cut out, as well as my article in the *Times*, and given to her immediately. 'But I can't read the *News of the World* any more. It's such a filthy paper.'

She agreed that I must go on writing for the *News of the World*, however ghastly the rest of the paper has become.

I told her that I had written in the *News of the World* about the hypocrisy of India over Graham Gooch being unacceptable to captain the English cricket team because he has played in South Africa. I said,

---

1. An IRA ambush bomb on 20 August at Ballygawley in Co. Tyrone had blown up a bus carrying British soldiers, killing seven and injuring twenty-eight.

'They've got a hundred million Untouchables yet they have the cheek to talk about other people's racial behaviour.' I went on, 'I'm writing a similar article again in the *Times* for Wednesday.' She said, 'Good,' and was pleased.

**Tuesday 6 September**

At dinner we went to Cecconi's with Nick Lloyd and his wife Eve Pollard. They were in a jolly mood, so was I. Poor Verushka was rapidly tired and with a strained face from the pain in her arm from carrying it about.

Eve Pollard and Wendy Henry, the editor of the *News of the World*, frequently talk to each other on a Saturday night. They discuss what's in the other one's paper, each having received a copy at about 7.00 or 8.00 in the evening and having time to adjust their own later editions according to what they want to pinch from each other. Wendy will say, 'Do you mind if I lift such and such a story from the *Sunday Mirror*?' If Eve is very keen that she should not, she will say, 'Well, it's a rather dodgy one. I don't think I would risk it if I were you. We're not quite sure of the facts.'

These two are great rivals and not dissimilar in amply bosomy size. They are very matey, tough madams of Fleet Street.

Eve stalls when she gets a leading article Maxwell wants to publish and leaves it until it is too late for it to go into the press if it is particularly silly. She gets on with him well at the moment because her circulation is going up, having gone up two hundred thousand. She enormously admires Wendy Henry who has now got the *News of the World* circulation up to five and a half million and is uncatchable by the *Sunday Mirror.*

**Friday 9 September**

A call from Buckingham Palace. The Press Secretary Robin Janvrin wants advice and reassurance that he has done the right thing. He had told William Heseltine, the Queen's Private Secretary, he would ring to ask me.

Last week the *News of the World* ran on its front page and on to an inner page a preposterous story saying that the Queen had agreed not to have some IRA terrorists proceeded against when she was in Holland for fear that this would expose the Dutch royal family to reprisals.

He said, 'Do you think we should make a denial?' 'Let me think for a moment.' After thinking I said, 'No, if you make a denial they will try and justify it by first of all printing the denial and then saying something like, "We had the story from two people in Holland and somebody else in Germany and they are all very reliable people. But we can't give our sources." In other words much more will be made of the story than would otherwise have been.'

**Sunday 11 September**

Bowden Park. Find Arnold down in the dumps. He is feeling and looking below par. The eye is not right yet after the detached retina. The drugs they gave him in dealing with it reduced his blood pressure so low his heart began to suffer. He is tired of being attacked for GEC not doing the right thing.

Nothing seems to please the institutions and the analysts. GEC shares yield over five per cent now which is high for his kind of industry.

At lunch I sat next to his three-year-old granddaughter Celia. A pretty child and chatty. I asked Arnold whether it was worth talking to a child of three because it would never remember what you said. He replied that he thought three-year-old children did remember somewhere in their minds what had been said to them. It was part of their process of education. He could definitely remember things that had happened to him when he was three.

Lunch as usual was good and not so rich as it sometimes is. There was an excellent Château Giscours 1966.

I asked Arnold why the horses ran in Michael Sobell's[2] name and not his. He said, 'Originally he had a half share in them all. He likes to see his name as the owner although he doesn't go anywhere near the horses and hasn't seen any of them for twenty years.'

Arnold says that he made £1.5 million net profit, his father-in-law, in his dealings with horses which had all been arranged by Arnold and Simon. I asked Netta what he does now at the age of ninety-six. 'He just sits in what he calls his four walls (at Sunningdale) and thinks about the world.'

Arnold quickly added, 'He also devises schemes for upsetting as many people as he can.' Netta said that he was very pleased when Clare, that's the granddaughter by Susan, said 'shalom' to him. Clare is being brought up as a Jew. That pleased him a lot.

---

2. Sir Michael Sobell (1892–1993), Lady Weinstock's father.

Arnold said, 'I can't think why. He's always been an atheist.' Netta said, 'But he's not feeling like that now. And he wants to go to Israel.' I said, 'Yes, when you get older you go back to your roots.' He is now quite alone, his wife having died. Netta says he has never been kind to anybody. I said, 'But he was kind to your mother.' 'Yes, in a sort of way. But only as an appendage.'

Arnold thinks that Michael Sobell's main intent since he married Netta has been to find ways of annoying Arnold. He said, 'He doesn't like Simon at all.' I said, 'But he ought to be proud of him.' Netta said, 'He's not. He resents him having had the education that he never had.'

For the umpteenth time I thought happiness is a matter of temperament and not of vast riches. A good digestion, good health and an optimistic outlook are a much more reliable passport to happiness. Arnold is hardly ever happy nowadays, much less than when I first knew him, and Netta is unhappy too.

'What did you think of her new face lift?' Verushka asked. 'I never noticed it' I answered. So what was the use of that expense except to make her feel better about herself?

**Monday 12 September**

The fearful news of Andrew and Randall Crawley both killed in their own aeroplane. They were clever, athletic and immensely good and close to their parents. Virginia, their mother, was killed in a car crash in 1983, with Aidan driving who was also severely injured. Now poor Aidan has lost two sons as well, aged thirty-nine and forty-one.

Strange that they are dead and I am alive. They are dead in their full vigour and beauty.

Wrote to Prince Michael and Princess Michael of Kent. When I got back from holiday I found a handsome crocodile cigar case from Asprey's with my monogram, which Jack Huntingdon did for me years ago, in gold on the front. My birthday is on the same day as his. Next year I had better remember to give him a birthday present.

Lunch at the Garrick with Frank Johnson who is principal associate editor of the *Sunday Telegraph* and embarrassed by the title because people laugh at it. He is third in command, not second.

The food at the Garrick is rather good. The consommé was OK. I had a beautifully cooked grouse, my first of the season.

We had a château bottled Grand-Puy-Ducasse 1979 which was cheap and excellent.

As we ordered expensive items I got nervous and said, 'Is this all right?' He said, 'Yes, Conrad Black is paying for it.' Then he said, 'Peregrine Worsthorne once gave dinner to Evelyn Waugh at the Garrick. Evelyn Waugh kept saying, "Do you think Michael Berry will be willing for us to have such and such an item?" or "Do you think Michael Berry will run to another brandy?", assuming that Michael Berry who was the proprietor of the *Telegraph* for which Peregrine was working was paying the bill. At length Peregrine got frightfully cross. "Look here. I'm paying for this dinner. It's my invitation and nothing to do with Michael Berry." "Oh goodness," said Evelyn, "why didn't you tell me? I must help you financially with it," and started showering pound notes on to the table and falling all over the floor with Peregrine desperately trying to pick them up.'

Frank adores Peregrine and is ambitious. He also declares his love for Rupert. He might make a good editor but I doubt it – he's much better as a writer.

To the Home Office to see John Patten and his officials. A great palaver over nothing. It was merely to tell us that they had appointed the bank, Lloyds Merchant Bank, to represent the government to carry out the feasibility study into ways in which the Tote could be privatized.

**Tuesday 13 September**

The SIS board meeting. Just before it Sir Peter Leng, Chairman of the Racecourse Association, asked if we were serious about privatizing the Tote. I told him in confidence about the announcement to be made on Thursday.

He said he would like to raise money from the Racecourse Association to buy the lot. I said, 'We wouldn't allow that.' 'Why not?' 'We don't want to be controlled by the Racecourse Association. But we would be interested in a large shareholding.'

Likewise Johnnie Henderson and Tommy Wallis very keen to get in on the act. Johnnie Henderson has got some crazy scheme by which we wouldn't be properly privatized at all but raise the money on loan geared to profit. I don't like this.

In the evening Chips Keswick came to dinner. He said we want to look out for a lot of sycophants and flatterers. Why the Racecourse Association and Johnnie Henderson and people are interested in having a very large stake is that they see the Tote as a cash cow – which it is; it is a very good business generating a lot of cash. 'They would want to distribute it immediately into racing whereas you would want to keep it to a great extent developing the business into the future,' he said. 'You don't want any one big shareholder to dominate you.'

We sorted out our objectives. One – to maintain our connection with helping racing. Two – to develop the Tote. Three – to develop our business into something really big so that racing will in fact benefit more, even though all our profits were not going into racing by any means.

A message from Allan Davis that Alec McCowen, the actor, is willing to reread the play again with its alterations.

**Friday 16 September**

The Home Office statement about the feasibility study to privatize the Tote. We even had to have a long meeting at the Home Office about our own tiny statement. They didn't want us to mention Hambros as our advisers at this stage.

The young man, Stephen Barrett, Head of Corporate Finance of Lloyds Merchant Bank, appointed by the Home Office to do the study, seems reasonable but he was nervous at making it look as though there is a protagonist and an antagonist if Hambros is mentioned at this stage. Reluctantly I agreed but I made up my mind on Wednesday, when he comes to the Tote, to give him and the Home Office man in charge a lecture about the government not owning the Tote and our not having a monopoly but an exclusive licence and so forth.

**Saturday 17 September**

On the whole the announcement was well received. The *Sporting Life* was a bit dodgy. They got hold of Jeremy Hindley, brother-in-law to the Home Secretary, who said he didn't want the Tote privatized. He dislikes me because he runs the Trainers' Federation. By becoming a trustee of the Stable Lads' Association I forced them to pay more to the downtrodden stable lads. I think he also echoes the Home Secretary's residual dislike for me.

**Sunday 18 September**

Mrs Thatcher says, 'I see you backed Prince Charles over violence on TV[3] as I do.' This was his speech condemning the gratuitous showing of violence in videos, films and particularly television which he said must have some effect on standards of behaviour.

3. In the *News of the World*.

We spoke a little about the economy, saying it is one of the difficulties that when we are going ahead faster than our competitors in growth we become very vulnerable to imports. We're a lovely market for them. She said, 'Yes, but in Japan and France they have a national ethic feeling, they won't buy foreign goods if they can avoid it.'

She also complained about the low ratio of saving we have in this country.

'Although our productivity is going up it is still not going up as fast as other countries,' she said.

Oh dear. I don't think we're going to slide back again but it is a tricky situation for a month or two.

**Monday 19 September**

Arrived Aberdeen about twenty past ten wearing my summer South African suit. It was hot. We saw our new betting office at Stonehaven. Very elegant in the square.

Then on to Musselburgh racecourse in Edinburgh. There it was a Tote day with every race sponsored by the Tote. I presented the trophy and the prize to the winning owner of the main Tote race.

On the way Mr Siers, our Scottish and Northern Development Manager, talked to me about wine. To my amazement I discovered he knew a great deal about claret. He has a bottle of Château Lafite 1961. He paid £50 for it. I said, 'It must be worth £200–£300 now.'

He gets £14,000 a year and is able to lay in stocks of very good vintages of wines. I am delighted to find an employee with fellow feeling about claret.

**Wednesday 21 September**

Levy Board meeting. Stoker Hartington[4] there for the first time. He surprised me by being much more intelligent than I thought and also quite authoritative when he dealt with the National Stud, asking a number of intelligent questions and putting forward a number of sound ideas.

My article setting out the basic conditions for privatizing the Tote so far as the board is concerned in the *Times* today.

In the afternoon Mr Barrett from Lloyds Merchant Bank came to the Tote. I'm beginning to think he is a snake.

---

4. The Marquess of Hartington, son of the Duke and Duchess of Devonshire; Jockey Club member.

**Thursday 22 September**

We went to a charity preview of *Dry Rot*. The Tote had taken an advertisement in the programme of this play about bookmakers: 'Bet with the Tote. It never welshes.'

It is put on by Lee Menzies, Allan Davis' partner in my play. I thought it extremely unfunny, quite out of date, but I raised a laugh here and there. Brian Rix is fairly sprightly despite his age and acted extraordinarily well. I have £500 in it. I think my money is distinctly shaky at the moment. But maybe I am wrong.

**Friday 23 September**

John Heaton tells me that the little squirt Stephen Barrett asked questions such as, 'Do the staff hold the Tote Board in contempt?' He told a group of quite senior staff, about eight of them, that the Tote does not own the Tote but the government does. 'You can take it from me,' he said. This is in flat contradiction to what the Prime Minister and Chancellor of the Exchequer believe, as I told him on the telephone later.

He also asked to see all the Board minutes which I am not going to let him do. It is nothing whatever to do with Lloyds Merchant Bank and it wouldn't be if they were trying to buy a business, and in a sense if the Tote is privatized that is what the public will be doing.

I rang Richard Fries at the Home Office, the civil servant in charge, and complained mightily. I said I wanted written terms of reference of what he is supposed to be doing for his report.

After he had reflected on the questions that Barrett had been asking, Fries said, 'I think that's strong support for the idea there should be written terms of reference.'

My feeling is that this little pip squeak is trying to lay the Tote out like a fish on a slab and dissect it. He thinks he is the only person who is entitled to express views, though he had never heard of the Tote until a few days ago.

I said, 'I must see the report before he sends it in to the Home Office. I have to see whether it is feasible or not. It's no good him sending in a report which we are going to totally disagree with and there is going to be an explosion about.' The government actually is wasting an enormous amount of money for no reason at all.

Later Stephen Barrett rang me. Very apologetic. Said he had been misunderstood though I don't think he could have been but he maintained he was. Could he meet me for coffee or lunch? I said, 'You can come here for lunch on Monday,' which he is going to do.

**Saturday 24 September**

The Tote Festival Handicap race at Ascot in the Festival of British Racing which is now held annually.

David Montagu and Ninette came to the lunch. So did the man from Lloyds Bank and Richard Fries and another Home Office official. The Home Secretary came in after lunch. He referred to my article in the *Times*. He said it was 'very firmly expressed views about the Tote but elegantly written as one would expect'.

Douglas was very friendly as was Judy his wife. They came into the paddock with us and she helped judge the best turned out horse before our race.

David absolutely backs the position of the Tote as set out in my article. I think the tour of the various visitors from the merchant bank and the Civil Service, which I laid on with Mr Sexton in charge of Ascot that afternoon, probably opened their eyes quite a bit as to the absurdity of trying to break the Tote up.

We watched the race in the Royal Box. I sat next to Princess Margaret and David on the other side. The usual utterly meaningless crazy and circular conversation when you can't think of anything to say.

I have just been rereading a review by Francis Wheen in the *New Statesman* of *Confessions of an Optimist* [published 1985]. He was contemptuous and sneering and unpleasant, as I suppose an unreconstructed Socialist should be.

He has just written to me asking for help with the biography he is writing of Tom Driberg and saying also that Jim Callaghan denies the story which he told me of Tom holding his penis and peeing at the side of the road when returning from a Labour meeting one night. Tom grabbed it and said, 'You've got a pretty one there,' according to Callaghan.

He now pretends the incident never happened. But he described it to me with great amusement at the time so I think he must be wrong about that. Our memories are selective. We push aside anything we don't want to remember if we find that convenient.

I was going to write to Francis Wheen in a fairly helpful manner but now I look at his review again I shall write and tell him that I feel sorry for Tom that he should have got so unpleasant a biographer and

I shall do nothing to aid him in destroying Tom's character which he doubtless intends to do.

Drue Heinz came to the lunch. She was delighted to find A. N. Wilson, Charles Moore, Nicholas Shakespeare,[5] Merlin Holland, all connected with the literary world there. I told her it would not be just the ordinary racing crowd. She is into racing, having just sold Chillibang which she bred herself to the National Stud.

I like Drue Heinz very much.

She really cares about writing and has got her Ecco Press and magazine and her house where writers can stay free and just sit and write away without anybody interrupting them. I wondered how she managed to get Jack Heinz to marry her who always had an eye for the girls and was doing so right up until the end. I was looking at her legs on Saturday and they really are like piano legs or what used to be thought of as piano legs. She has not got an elegant figure and never has had.

Bruce Matthews says that he is very worried about Rupert. He fears he has overstretched himself with Sky which is losing a vast amount of money. It doesn't get enough advertising and is not seen by enough people. However, he says if anybody can get it right Rupert can.

**Sunday 25 September**

Harold Lever said he thought that Mrs Thatcher's European speeches last week were wonderful.[6] It was totally wrong that people said she was attacking the European ideal.

I said, 'Why don't you write to the *Times* and say that? I can tell her that. I shall be speaking to her later.' He got very nervous and said, 'I don't want to commit myself to that at the moment. I might think of it.' He is afraid of annoying his Labour friends because he is still a member of the Labour Party in the Lords and takes their whip.

Spoke to Mrs Thatcher.

We discussed the appalling situation about Thames Television putting out the programme[7] with bogus evidence making trial by tele-

---

5. Novelist and journalist; at this time literary editor, *Daily Telegraph*.
6. Her Bruges speech, defining Britain's attitude to the EC ('We have not successfully rolled back the frontiers of the state in Britain only to see them reimposed at a European level, with a European super-state exercising a new dominance from Brussels'), was on 20 September.
7. *Death on the Rock* on 28 April.

vision over Gibraltar. It had been revealed last week that the witness who said he saw the SAS man murdering an IRA terrorist on the ground was lying and he retracted his evidence. He said he was pestered to give false evidence by Thames Television and a solicitor who drew up a statement which he never signed and never saw before it was broadcast.

I said, 'Typical of Ian Trethowan, Chairman of Thames Television, trying to defend the action of the programme team which only went out there to find things to discredit the SAS and the government.' I went on, 'And as for the IBA, they are a disgrace in allowing that programme to go ahead when you and Geoffrey Howe were asking them to postpone it until after the inquest.'

She said, 'We have to think of who is going to take over from George Thomson[8] at the IBA.'

First I suggested Rees-Mogg but she said he was feeble as the Deputy Chairman of the BBC. Then I suddenly said, 'Why not Alun Chalfont? He's very tough. He knows about politics. He knows about broadcasting.' She said, 'What a good idea. What a good idea. I will ask Douglas Hurd what he thinks about it and see whether we couldn't do that.'

She wants me to help with some ideas for her speech at the Party Conference. They are getting down to doing something about it next weekend. She said, 'We've got to deal with this materialistic attack. Bryan Gould[9] was going on about that. And the Church of course keep saying we must relieve poverty and when we do they say we're making everybody materialistic.'

**Monday 26 September**

Stephen Barrett came to lunch with a young man called Manners who is going to work on the privatization project with him. Brian McDonnell and I put him in his place. Told him he couldn't see the Board meeting minutes. And we required a written terms of reference before he could proceed any further asking all kinds of questions. And I wanted to know the questions he was going to ask outside finance, legal and technical matters.

I said I would raise with the Board whether they wanted to be

---

8. Lord Thomson of Monifieth, life peer 1977; chairman, IBA, 1981–8; life peer 1977.
9. Labour spokesman on trade and industry at this time.

spoken to separately on their views on privatization but the Board's policy is as set out in the *Times* article and he knows it very well. There seemed to be a suggestion he wanted to divide the Board. He was somewhat apologetic.

Afterwards Brian and I spoke to Richard Fries at the Home Office. He agreed there would be written terms of reference and they would do them by the end of this week. He also said we could have the terms of reference altered if we did not agree with them and they agreed to our points.

He also agreed that we should see the draft report that was to go in to Ministers at the Home Office so that there wouldn't be a collision. In one way and another it seemed a satisfactory lunch. However, I don't trust Mr Barrett.

Went to the Hambros flat in Wilton Crescent for a dinner with Johnnie Henderson and Tommy Wallis. Christopher Sporborg and Christopher Balfour with Chips on the Hambros side. It was quite a merry dinner. I got a bit drunk.

It was agreed that Hambros should draft their own instructions and send to us for agreement. We have to get in first and set up our notion of a structure for the privatized Tote. They are going to value the business themselves. We should take no notice of what Lloyds Merchant Bank say in their report in this respect.

The gist of the talk was that maybe it would be best if racing did have a large interest because that would make it easier to get the exclusive licence continued. It would be more for the benefit of racing if racing was drawing dividends from the operation.

On the prospect of success for our notions, Christopher Sporborg said, 'She (meaning Mrs T) owes you one.' I said, 'What for?' 'For all the stuff you write in support of her in the *News of the World* and elsewhere.' 'She owes me nothing. I'm in love with her.'

**Tuesday 27 September**

In the morning wrote a possible extract for a speech for Margaret. It was about a so-called materialist society being really a generous society.[10]

---

10. Under the heading 'The Generous Society' WW began: 'I am proud that people are better off than they've ever been before. Our opponents including some in the churches – and we have many blinkered opponents there – think it is a cause for shame.

**Friday 30 September**

Arrive in Paris on the 4.30 aeroplane from London. Long delays. We left the house at half past two and did not reach the hotel until nearly eight. How I long for the Channel Tunnel which maybe I shall not live to see.[11]

---

'We are accused of creating a materialistic society. One of greed in which everyone thinks only of himself and not of his neighbour.

'But greater prosperity is the passport to freedom of the individual and liberation of spirit . . .

'The British people now give over £9,000 million a year to charities, Oxfam, Save the Children Fund, Band Aid Trust, Cancer Research and the rest.

'They haven't become greedy and "materialistic". As they become better off they help others still more. As the general wealth goes up the nation's deep-rooted generosity prompts more giving. If that is the result of a greedy materialistic society let's have more of it . . .'

11. He did; it opened in May 1994.

**Saturday 1 October**

Long talks at the Pari-Mutuel. Brian McDonnell and I got a lot of useful information. We had to tell them that we had settled the Ladbroke libel action and they said they hadn't settled theirs and they were prepared to fight it if Ladbroke's would not withdraw the case.

We told them that Ladbroke's so terrifies the other big three bookmakers that William Hill and Mecca had come to us proposing a consortium if we would back them to oppose Ladbroke's in Europe, which we hoped Pari-Mutuel would join.

They said they would certainly like to discuss it so we got something done.

We also established exactly what happens to the money made out of Pari-Mutuel betting insofar as racing is concerned. French racing gets about £180 million a year out of it. The government also does pretty well.

Lunch at the Plaza Athénée.

There were three old men sitting with three young girls. The girls were there for the money and it was not difficult to guess what the men were there for.

Verushka did her usual tour of dress shops. I said I couldn't afford to spend more than £200 or £250. Eventually she bought a curious but very pretty lace bow with a camellia to put on her hair, at Chanel.

Her arm is very painful and naturally got worse during the journey.

**Sunday 2 October**

I don't think I shall go to Paris again for the Arc de Triomphe. It is so much walking about and although Paris streets are splendid I find them tiring. I'm not very keen on traipsing around dress shops either. I think I've seen all the museums I want to in Paris. The Bois de Boulogne, however, looked very pretty.

Go to see Arnold in his box. His first conversation was to tell me [about] British Aerospace. Though he arranged the introduction for them to see the Malaysian government, they then said to the Prime

Minister of Malaysia, 'You realize Arnold Weinstock is a Jew, don't you?' and so on.

He told me Aerospace have done the same thing in Saudi Arabia to try to reduce GEC's orders but it didn't do any real harm there.

The Aga Khan came up. He was hoping that Kahyasi, his horse, would win. It had two pacemakers. Well it didn't.

It's strange that this descendant of Mahomet who is regarded as divine by his followers should be an owner of hotels and a great tourist attraction centre in Sardinia.

Tony Bin won. I backed it last year, as Arnold's brother-in-law reminded me. Foolishly I didn't back it this year. I backed it last year because I had just been reviewing Tony Benn's idiotic diaries.

**Monday 3 October**

Mrs Thatcher delighted with the suggestions for the speech I sent her titled 'The Generous Society'. She wanted to know where I got the figure of £9,000 million contributed to charities every year. I said it was some time in the summer and I had read it. She thought the Treasury might be able to help her with the figure but I think I had better have a look too.

I congratulated her on her speech about the environment.[1]

She said, 'We have a very good record on the environment. After all it was the Tories who brought in the Clean Air Act.' It was indeed. It was old Gerald Nabarro[2] but the government supported him.

I said I was so angry with the BBC Radio 4 Brian Redhead man who sneered away and said she was only doing it to catch votes and she didn't really believe in it at all. I don't know why these people are allowed to editorialize on the BBC.

**Tuesday 4 October**

Board meeting, Tote. The first since the Home Office announcement about privatization.

I wrote a stern letter to the Home Office afterwards setting out the Board's position and unanimous agreement that while we are very much in favour of privatization it must be with the caveats in my *Times* article. I also explained their views about the questions Barrett

---

1. To the Royal Society.
2. (1913–73); Conservative MP, instigator of clean air legislation 1955–6 and the Thermal Insulation (Industrial Buildings) Act 1957, etc.

had been asking and saying that no employee of the Tote would be seen by anybody from Lloyds Merchant Bank without a senior executive being present.

Also at the Board meeting we agreed that the minimum stake would now be £2.00 whatever the bet – in other words the £1.00 each way option has gone.

There will be resistance by the public to begin with, as there was when we raised the minimum stake in September 1985. However, I don't think the resistance will last long. The number of each way ticket sales will drop but the value of them in cash will rise even at the beginning.

There shouldn't be much resistance at the racecourses this time for they know a higher turnover means they get more from the Tote because they are being paid on a percentage basis of the turnover.

**Friday 7 October**

Rupert rang. When I asked him whether he thought that Bush would win he said, 'It's not certain.' He's sure it is nothing to do with Quayle's allegedly poor performance against Bentsen in the Vice Presidential[3] public television debate. He thought it was that Bush lacks the cutting edge and that Dukakis is very mean and will stop at nothing to get the Presidency. I said, 'I still think Bush will win.'

I told him, 'This is very embarrassing. I wanted to talk to you about what News International pays me. I have spoken to Mr Stehrenberger about it. Perhaps you would like to talk to him about it.' He said he'd see him today. I don't know what he will say about my thinking I should be paid £75,000 a year.

I think I'm worth it. I write once a week in the *News of the World*. Once a fortnight in the *Times*. I do a lot of book reviews in the *Times*. I help sometimes with the government when there's something connected with the papers or somebody wants to get something through to Mrs Thatcher, etc. and I really do think if Jean Rook gets £64,000 a year plus a Jaguar for one rotten article in the *Daily Express* every week, it's time I got paid more.

My pay has been bedevilled by me being a friend of Rupert and

3. By this time the vice-presidential candidates were Senator Dan Quayle (Republican) and Senator Lloyd Bentsen (Democrat); the presidential candidates George Bush Republican), then Vice President to Reagan, and Michael Dukakis (Democrat), Governor of Massachusetts.

him arranging the original change-over from the *Sunday Mirror* to the *News of the World*.[4]

**Saturday 8 October**

Went to Ascot. Horrid rainy day. A lunch at Nicky Beaumont's, the Clerk to the Course. The lunch was good, cold: potted shrimps and huge prawns and smoked salmon and lots of rather nice pies and turkey and pork and beef and so forth followed by raspberries. The white wine was fairly nice.

I sat next to a Mrs J. J. Warr who referred to her husband as JJ[5] all the time and spoke of him as though he was a God, the wisest man in the country. He had a message when he was playing golf to say the Indian government must have an urgent answer immediately about something to do with the English cricket team (which they did not like the look of because some of them have been to South Africa). He said, 'Tell them I have to finish my game of golf first before I ring them back. I'm not going to hurry.' She thought this was marvellous, as though he were Francis Drake reinvented.

She went on, on, on, on, on.

Piers Bengough says he wants to see me to talk about a generous contribution towards some rebuilding Ascot are doing. 'If you give us another kiosk in the mezzanine area and let me have a permanent kiosk in the Erridge Bar, instead of the makeshift one we have had to close because of the roughhouse that occurs there and frightens the girls, then I'll be more favourable.' He said, 'We don't bargain like that.' I said, 'Well I do. Why don't you?' 'We're above that sort of thing.' 'I'm not.' Ascot is amazingly pleased with itself.

**Sunday 9 October**

*In Cornwall visiting his brother*

The sky clears a bit as the day wears on. There are gusts of wind, very strong. The house faces south-west, unusual for Cornwall. Usually the houses face north-east because the south-west wind is the prevailing one, but Bonython is different.

Went to tea with Bob [Wyatt] and Molly. Poor Bob fell over a cliff

4. In 1983.

5. Deputy chairman, Clive Discount, 1973–87; president of the MCC, 1987–8; chairman, Racecourse Association, 1989–93; member, Jockey Club, since 1977.

edge the other day. He insisted on climbing over a parapet which was put up to stop people slipping down that part of the cliff.

Their house at Helford is attractive in a rambling way. They have little money. His pension was never index-linked. They subsist on that and on old age pension and little bits of money he has collected here and there. She is seventy-three, he is eighty-seven.

He doesn't drive as well as he used to either. He clipped Robert's car trying to get into too narrow a space where it was stationary when he took me down to Helford. The trim came off the Rover – which is now eleven years old.

I was sad in his house. There was the great England cricketer, cheered once by thousands, now just painfully going through a day with his bad back and his bad hip. Pictures of him in his triumphs are around the walls but they are not much good to him now except to remind him of things past. He is now the oldest surviving English Captain and test cricketer. He said his 39,000 runs in first class cricket were made at an average rated 29.3 an hour – must be faster then they bat today.

**Monday 10 October**

David Stevens said he would like to talk to me. He said Robbie, my nephew, had tried to get him interested in a consortium in China to operate out of Hong Kong, trading companies. He said he investigated the company around which it is to be built and found that they don't have any profits of their own, only the profits put in by the parent company which is diminishing year by year and it looks like the company is thoroughly in decline.

Robbie had told him that Mrs Thatcher was a great personal friend of his and gave her as a reference. When David rang Downing Street she was, as he said, 'a bit narked' about it. She couldn't remember him. Said she didn't know him at all. The fact of the matter was that in order to help Robbie in 1984 I got her to see a delegation from the Chinese Trade Section of the Chinese government and Robbie took them in to see her. That was all.

Robbie gave Henry Kissinger as another reference. David rang his office and got a very downbeat message saying they didn't have anything to do with Robbie now.

On hearing all this from David Stevens I told Robert [WW's brother] that Robbie must be stopped going to Hong Kong and playing the fool. He will obviously sign some agreement, one of those joint and several guarantees, and be made liable for the lot by a lot of con men. And the rest of the Bonython land will be sold.

I have little tugs at the heart when I see so many scenes from my childhood. Nevertheless, I do not think I want to be buried in Cury Church. The family association with it is doomed. At least the church that James Wyatt built at Weeford should be looked after for a century or two.[6]

**Tuesday 11 October**

I have spoken to David Stevens. I have spoken to Robbie. He has promised to withdraw from this crazy consortium and disentangle himself completely.

He then thanked me for my intervention. I said, 'I thought you would be annoyed.' 'No, you've saved me from doing something very foolish.' What a strange boy.

When I rang Stehrenberger at News International he said the compromise was £65,000 a year, not the £75,000 I asked for. At least it is an improvement of £10,000 on last year and it begins with effect from the 1st October. Rupert had said to me, 'Are you in financial difficulties? If you're ever in financial difficulties let me know.' I said, 'No, I'm not in financial difficulties but dresses cost a lot.'

To which he had replied, 'Well my wife's are costing a lot now too. She was very polite and nice to me at 6.00 in the morning the other day. She was wearing a very expensive new fur coat. However, she made $200,000 out of her new book. It's not great writing but at least it shows she can earn money.'

Len Cowburn and Bob Green of Mecca came to lunch. We discussed at length a joint approach to the Pari-Mutuel with a view to forming some kind of group to oppose Ladbroke's in setting up betting shops in France and in Germany and elsewhere in Europe.

In the morning I wrote a new bit of possible speech for Margaret. It was called 'Socialism is not Dead'.[7]

Dinner at Chips Keswick's. His brother Henry[8] was there. He talked

---

6. WW was buried there on 13 December 1997.
7. It began: 'Our union reforms have increased democracy in unions a hundredfold,' and reviewed the recent Conservative employment legislation.
8. Chairman, Matheson & Co. since 1975; m (1985) Tessa, Lady Reay, daughter of the 17th Baron Lovat; she became a political adviser to Kenneth Clarke MP 1989–95 and in 1995 executive director of the Centre for Policy Studies.

very intelligently about the need for everybody to support Mrs Thatcher.

Henry's wife Tessa is a budding parliamentary candidate. She was in the last election without success. She has been a councillor in Kensington. I think she is whole-heartedly for Mrs Thatcher.

We had some very good burgundy white and red, partridge and wild duck each. It was really an excellent dinner. I'm not quite so keen on burgundy as I am on claret, therefore I did not note properly the names and the years, though I think they were both 1982. I drank too much of it, naturally.

Henry ought really to be given something useful to do. He is able. He has spent his period in Hong Kong as taipan at Jardine Matheson in which the family own a tremendous amount. He thinks that the future of Hong Kong will be good but that we ought to allow Hong Kong immigrants into this country if they've got a couple of hundred thousand pounds.

We're not doing it because we don't like to discriminate in favour of the Hong Kong Chinese for fear of upsetting blacks and Asians from India and Pakistan. We are quite mad because these people would give a tremendous fillip with their enormous hard work and ingenuity to the British economy.

He says the Chinese might make a mess of Hong Kong through not understanding capitalism while thinking they do. He said but it must be in their interests to keep it going. All the indications are that they will. And that the government did get the best deal it could.

Showed Chips the terms of reference the Home Office have given to Lloyds Bank and told him he has got to keep it very much to himself which he will do. The Home Office for some extraordinary reason didn't want us to show them to our merchant bank which is ridiculous – how can they help us if they don't know what the terms of reference are?

Chips is dead against all these new regulations in the City which are supposed to be guarding integrity. He thinks you can't guard integrity by law. The scoundrels always find their way round it. In the meanwhile honest people are prevented from doing their jobs properly.

**Wednesday 12 October**

Three from Banbury where they now run the Cherwell Valley press in the old WW Webb Offset printing works. They bought the old Goss machine from the receivers which is now twenty-four years old and is running splendidly. I gave them tea in the Lords.

It was wonderful to hear how well they are doing. All the restrictive practices have gone which ruined us, forcing us to go into liquidation. They said that all the workers then wanted to agree to the flexi-working which they now have at Banbury in the new outfit.

I am going to try to help them – I already get a commission on *Coal News* and *GEC Topics*[9] – to find more work. They are writing to me with details of house magazines and so forth they would like to get.

Dinner at the American Embassy. Due to arrive at 8.00 which we did on the dot but we were among the first four to be there. Naturally we didn't get dinner until a quarter to nine. I always say to Verushka we never will get dinner to time there so why go so early? We had to stand about in this tiresome way drinking champagne and eating little bits and pieces.

Lady Richardson, wife of the ex Governor of the Bank of England,[10] talked to me about Charles Price the present Ambassador. She said, 'He's not much good, is he? They never are, these Ambassadors. He's going soon. I suppose there will be a new appointment when the new President takes over.' I said he wasn't as bad as some of them. He did get the message across that America was friendly and helpful. The real work is done by the Minister, as it used to be done by Ed Streator.

I found myself sitting next to the Duchess of Wellington[11] on my right. She is extremely plain, rather fat. She talked at some length about her love of gardening which she does vigorously, and the weeding she enjoys greatly.

She said, 'I go to Spain three or four times a year.' I said, 'Oh, you're a Duke there too, aren't you.' She said, 'Yes.' Once the Republican government had tried to end the arrangements made with the First Duke of Wellington saying that it was a gift from the King and they had now ended the monarchy. They proved through their lawyers that it was a gift from the government.

I told her about the Duke of Wellington on his horse by Matthew Cotes Wyatt which the Queen had removed as soon as he died because

---

9. House magazines.
10. Gordon Richardson; life peer 1983.
11. Wife of the 8th Duke; his Spanish title is Duke of Ciudad Rodrigo and Grandee of Spain 1st class; WW was on the Council of the Zoological Society with him.

she didn't like it stuck on Constitution Arch, although he loved it dearly. She asked me what had happened to it and I said that it was bought by subscription of all ranks of the Army and is now at Aldershot.

The dinner was in honour of Peter Carrington who has just retired from being in charge as Secretary General of NATO. Presumably he selected the guests. I felt quite flattered that we were included among them but a lot of them were a little bit rum who were there.

I've always liked him. He has a great deal of charm and quickness though not a deep brain, as is evidenced by his book.[12]

After dinner I had quite a long talk with the French Ambassadress.

I complimented her on her animal sexuality. She said, 'But I'm forty-three.' 'You're just beginning.' She was pleased.

**Thursday 13 October**

To the National Theatre, the Lyttleton Theatre, with Allan Davis.

The play was interesting. David Hare in his *The Secret Rapture* depicts the women well. The play goes off the rails at the end and is too full of tired old out-of-date political cliché attacks on Mrs Thatcher which detract from its merits.

In the interval we go to this private room run by the Manager and I have a Campari. John Mortimer tells me a nice story which he says will amuse me.

At the Blackpool conference he went to speak to the Fabian Society. In the taxi on the way there he is accompanied by the earnest Chairman (whom he calls Chairperson – oh heavens, oh heavens). He mentioned to her 'the Society of June 20th' and she said, 'What is that?' Actually it was what they now call the gathering which met at Antonia Fraser's house on the 20th June last to try to build up the intellectual base to attack and destroy Mrs Thatcher.

Anyway, in the taxi this woman asked him why the Society of June 20th was named as it is. So he said, 'Oh, don't you know? It was named after a group formed in 1865 in Luxembourg by some revolutionaries who were making a coup to overthrow the government. They were all caught. They were idealistic intellectual revolutionaries. Their punishment was to be exiled to Paris where they live out their days drinking champagne in La Coupole.'[13]

---

12. *Reflect on Things Past*, which WW was reviewing for the *Times*.
13. Paris restaurant.

He thought he had been quite amusing. When the meeting began, the Chairperson got up and said he was a leading member of the Society of June 20th which was named in honour of the June 20th coup in Luxembourg and repeated all he had said to her as a joke in the taxi but in utter seriousness.

**Friday 14 October**

We arrive at Isabel's, Newmarket.[14] Ask for a cup of tea which she thinks odd. It was twenty past six, why didn't I have a drink? I said, 'I prefer tea.' 'But tea was at half past four.' I said, 'How plebeian.' I got my cup of tea.

We then went to the Tattersalls sales where John was selling a filly he bred. The sale ring building is very pretty with its domed ceiling. It was darkish by the time we got there and the lights in the yard made everything look romantic as the horses walked round waiting their turn to come into the sale ring. I felt sorry for the little yearlings.

After dinner we were talking about Lester Piggott. I said I thought it was very odd that the Jockey Club had been so quick to say that he could have his licence back when he comes out on parole a few days from now. How could they say that a convicted criminal, who had cheated so badly the Inland Revenue and is obviously nothing more than a crook, was a fit person to have a training licence? Why not just leave it with Mrs Piggott?

John said, 'They haven't quite said he can have his licence back yet. But they have got near to it. It's because others in the Jockey Club connived at and condoned his behaviour with the Inland Revenue by making him extra cash payments.'

Before I went up to change for dinner I rang Margaret but she wasn't there. She rang back just before dinner. I told her that her speech was the most effective Conference one she had made. 'You gave the speech in a very relaxed way but it was full of meat; the content was excellent, and the delivery was excellent too. You looked marvellous.'

She said, 'I found some red roses here for me.'[15] (She was in Downing Street.) 'It was very kind of you.' I said, 'Not at all. I'm

14. The Derbys owned Stanley House at Newmarket as well as Knowsley.

15. It had been her birthday on 13 October; she wrote on 18 October: 'Thank you for the lovely flowers which you sent me for my birthday and for your very kind note. I was most touched that you should have remembered. And thank you, too, for your help in sending me pieces for my speech. Yours ever Margaret'.

in love with you.' She giggled. She thanked me for the pieces I sent her. 'You see I used the "generous society".'

I also said, 'I loved it when they all started chanting, "Ten more years." You looked very moved.'

She takes enormous trouble with her clothes now. It was rather touching how she had written to some American journal which had voted her into the top internationally best dressed women. She sent them photographs with notations on the back of when she had worn different clothes. She has certainly not lost her femininity and has mastered the art of wearing the right clothes. Today she wore a blue suit with a beautiful diamond brooch.

She looked superb when she made her speech. She cleared her throat, however, numerous times. This came across on the microphone with a bit of a tiny thump. Before next year I must remember to tell her not to do that, but I didn't like to say anything about it last night.

Charles Benson[16] was bursting with a story about Porchester (Carnarvon)[17] and Dick Hern.[18] Dick Hern has been very ill. On the weekend after the Arc de Triomphe he returned home (where his young manager/assistant does a lot of the work – however, Charles Benson said he still does all the work sheets, makes the entries and gives all the instructions necessary to train the horses). They had a lease to the end of next year but Porchester asked him to leave the Ilsley stables immediately. He offered them to William Hastings Bass. When he heard that it was only because Dick Hern was being turned out, he said he wouldn't go into them.

Porchester is still trying to get rid of Dick Hern because he thinks he is finished, although he desperately wants to go on training and his mind is working perfectly and his energy is good despite his accident.

Isabel said, 'He's a dirty little Jew.' I said, 'Why do you call him that?'

'There is Jewish blood in the family.' 'But you say that about all Jews.' She said, 'Pretty well.' 'Would you say it to David Montagu's face?' 'Oh yes,' she said, 'he wouldn't mind a bit.' I said, 'You're

16. Racing journalist.
17. 7th Earl of Carnarvon, Honorary Racing Manager to the Queen; son of the 6th Earl who discovered Tutankhamen's tomb with Howard Carter in 1922.
18. Principal Private Trainer to the Queen and trainer for other owners including the Makhtoum brothers; his winners include Brigadier Gerard, Troy and Ela-Mana-Mou; he was seriously injured in 1984 when fox-hunting.

outrageous.' She laughed. I said, 'You're the only person I know who makes such appalling racist remarks.'

However, it appears that Porchester is behaving very badly.

I should like to hear Porchester's side of the events. I find it hard to believe the cruel unwarrentedness of trying to throw Dick Hern out with nowhere to train.

**Saturday 15 October**

The Tote Cesarewitch was run today. Charlie Benson had told us all to back Nomadic Way and it duly won. I hadn't believed Charlie Benson because he gets so much wrong and I didn't back it.

Robert Sangster, when we gave him the prize, said he had had £2,000 on it at 20 to 1. I said, 'That's almost as much as the first prize.' He then said would I receive the people from Vernons Pools, which of course he has now sold. 'They would like to take over the Tote.' I said, 'I'll certainly see them but I don't give much hope of such an arrangement.'

Mr and Mrs John Patten were there at lunch. She is rather pretty and attractive. When I told her that she was very pretty, she said, 'Well, you're very attractive.' I said, 'That's ridiculous for somebody of seventy.' 'Not at all. You are a very attractive man.' So that was a nice bit of flattery. She really is a very pretty girl, with rather a nice hat.

Adrian Daintrey[19] died at eighty-seven. I never went to see him at Charterhouse. It was something I was meaning to do every week but somehow never got around to. Now it's too late and I feel ashamed. He was a dear, sweet man. He had a mild success as a painter but was never outstanding. I have one or two little drawings he did of me.

Saturday night we were talking about another painter, Lucian Freud. John Bowes Lyon[20] said that when he painted the small picture of Michael Tree he charged only £125,000 instead of his normal £150,000. I said, 'But that's extraordinary. He shouldn't have charged him so much or even charged him at all. He told Verushka the thing he most liked doing in his whole life was having lunch with Michael Tree which he did frequently.'[21]

He said the picture he did of Debo Devonshire years ago only cost

19. See 10 May 1987.
20. A director of Sotheby's, 1970–80.
21. See 6 July 1988.

about £5,000. Now it must be worth £180,000 or £200,000. There is one of Bindy Lambton with her arms outstretched which is in her house in the King's Road. Tony Lambton is now claiming that it belongs to him as he has been paying the insurance. That sounds typical Tony.

I think Robert Sangster is somewhat changed. You can see defeat behind his eyes. He has lost countless millions trying to keep on top of racing. He has to have a couple of classic successes every year, major ones, in order to keep up and he has not been having them.[22] He sold himself out of Vernons Pools which was started by his family but even that has not covered his racing expenses.

**Sunday 16 October**

Radio 4 quoted from my remarks about Margaret in the *News of the World* this morning, about her speaking with the authority of a superb world leader and with no complacency. I had also said she was the best Prime Minister we have had in this century or the last.

It is pleasant to stay with Isabel. The house is comfortable, not too large a size. The bedrooms are nice and big. Verushka had a bathroom attached to hers and so did I have one attached to mine. The butler unpacks one's clothes and repacks them and lays out what one is going to wear in the evening. There are maids, a kind of lady's maid on our floor. She does the same for the ladies. They bring breakfast. She helped Verushka dress with her bad arm. It is a very civilized life.

When we were talking about John Wilton, John Derby said, 'He is the most useless person who ever lived.' I said, 'He is full of charm and knowledge.' 'Yes, but he's never done anything.'

He then went on to say how he had built up his own safari park at Knowsley and they take about £1.7 million a year if not £2 million a year from visitors. I thought that was very good. He's worked hard to make that go. They have a restaurant and so forth there as well. So he hasn't just frittered away his fortune by any means. He has preserved something. It's sad that they don't have a son but only a nephew to pass it all on to.

Edward Hulton has died. Poor man. He was successful in a way

---

22. He was leading winning racehorse owner in 1977, 1978, 1982, 1983 and 1984, with winners of the Derby, the Irish Derby, the French Derby, the Arc de Triomphe, the Ascot Gold Cup, the 1,000 Guineas, the Goodwood Cup etc.

because he started *Picture Post*[23] which was excellent. But he was of limited capacity and brain. He had a fearsome Russian ex-Princess wife[24] at one time who was very good-looking, wild and extravagant. Eventually they got divorced because she was going through so much of his money.

The thing which hurt him most was when he was at Oxford and his father, who was a Baronet, died. Immediately his name in the doorway to his rooms was changed to Sir Edward Hulton. He then had to delete it on discovering that he, Edward, was illegitimate. It was a great blow to his pride. But he did do well to get a knighthood on his own account.[25]

John Bowes Lyon says that Prince Charles is currently at Balmoral with his girlfriend. He may be presumed to know. Charles Benson says that Princess Diana had an affair with the King of Spain.

There was some talk on Friday night at dinner of the future of the Royal Family. I said it would last intact but it couldn't take too much of vulgar people like Miss Ferguson and her sleazy father. I suppose that poor Diana faces a life of boredom with her husband now that the sex has worn out and she will look for consolation elsewhere. Maybe that won't matter. It seems she is already doing it.

**Monday 17 October**

Saw Willie Whitelaw in the House who says he is writing his autobiography or memoirs.[26] He has just got to the Falklands. He has spent a lot of time on what I thought he said was his failure at the Palace. I said, 'I didn't know you failed there.' 'No, I mean Fagin. He is the man who got into the Queen's bedroom.'

Supper party at Drue Heinz's. The smallest number of people I have ever seen at her house. About twenty. She said, 'It's very kind of you to come. It's a literary party.' Stephen Spender was there and his wife whom I haven't seen for years so we all embraced affectionately.

We talked a little bit about old times after the War when Natasha claims that Stephen was wholly innocent of knowing that CIA money

---

23. Photo-news magazine, 1938–57.
24. Hulton m 2 (1941–66) Princess Nika Yourievitch, daughter of Prince Serge Yourievitch, Russian sculptor.
25. In 1957.
26. *The Whitelaw Memoirs*, published in 1989.

was behind *Encounter* when we used to write for it or work for it, or do something for it.

Not that it matters a damn. I can't see why the American government shouldn't help finance magazines to preserve the democratic way in Europe. It looked a bit dicy at the time.

I thought Stephen looked rather young but he is seventy-nine.

Margouch was there. She was once married to the painter Gorky.[27] She has lived substantially as his widow on selling his paintings but she says there are now only two major ones left. She shares them with the children.

She and Xan Fielding[28] (once married to Daphne Bath) live in Spain. He is writing a book about Billy Maclean there. I said I thought he might find it a bit heavy going. He believes that the part in the book about the Yemen will be the most interesting and genuinely thinks that Billy Maclean saved North Yemen from falling into the hands of the Communists.

Xan still looks sprightly. I reminded Margouch how she came years ago to the House of Commons with me, wearing nothing on her feet. She said she remembered it. I had been having supper or dinner at her flat with a party. 'I think Michael Astor was there, you were probably keen on him at the time,' I said. She said she had had some association with him.

'Oh dear. Should I apologize now for not having shoes on?' I said no, I didn't mind. 'I just warned you your feet would get cold.'

Geoffrey Wheatcroft was there. I don't know how Drue can think of him as literary. I think he is just a lout. He talked at some length to Verushka who said how nice he was afterwards. I reminded her he was the man who arrived three-quarters of an hour late – or was it an hour – when invited to a set lunch at Newmarket.[29]

The food was absolutely revolting. Some kind of mousse not done well. It was followed by a nasty steak and kidney pie. Then came a summer pudding which had very little variety of fruit in it. I cannot understand how she can serve such food. I suppose she thought as it was a literary party, literary people wouldn't notice what they ate.

---

27. Arshile Gorky (1904–48), American abstract expressionist painter, born in Turkish Armenia; his daughter married Matthew Spender, the Spenders' artist son.
28. (Major) Alexander Fielding (d 1991), travel writer.
29. See 19 October 1985.

**Tuesday 18 October**

Lunch with Abdul Al Ghazzi at the Connaught. Still feeling rough from a stinking cold. I've been dosing myself to get rid of it with ascorbic acid and some lozenges as I also have a sore throat.

He says he is going to start restoring once again the Library at Heveningham.

We discussed the situation in Jordan and Israel. He thinks that if Labour wins in Israel they may decide to make the Palestinian area autonomous and it can join up with the bit in Jordan which the King has already said is autonomous as far as he is concerned.

As we were finishing lunch, in came Irwin [Stelzer] looking, I thought, rather menacing. Obviously he had been told I was with an Arab which he thinks is terrible. I introduced them to each other and made Irwin sit down and talk rationally as best he could about Israel and the Arabs and they got on tolerably well.

Then Abdul said, 'Of course with our money in oil and your brains we could make a wonderful thing of the Middle East. We need each other.' Irwin softened a little bit.

**Wednesday 19 October**

A nice letter from Margaret[30] thanking me for my help with her speech for the party conference which she made last Friday.

**Thursday 20 October**

Norman Lamont to lunch. 'Why does the Tory Party always have to be radical?' he asks, 'Surely it should consolidate? Surely the Conservative Party is not in favour of change, change, change?' I said, 'It has to keep its momentum. Any government has to. Once it looks as though it's run out of ideas a government starts to falter.'

I asked him whether there was any trouble now in the Tory Party about wanting Mrs Thatcher to leave. He said, 'Oh, no. They now think she's solid. Geoffrey Howe realizes he is much the same age as her and he can't possibly succeed her unless she is eliminated.' I said, 'Well, she could always be murdered. It was a damn near-run thing at that Brighton conference four years ago.' He thinks if that were to happen Geoffrey would still have a chance of becoming leader.

---

30. '. . . As ever, your ideas and suggestions were immensely pertinent and you will have seen that we took up many of these in the speech. With warmest good wishes. Yours ever Margaret.'

In the evening I took Philip Siers,[31] the Scottish Development Manager for the Tote, to the Saintsbury Club because of his interest and fascination with good wine and claret. He loved it all.

We sat opposite Alexis Lichine, one of the world's great authorities on wine.

He said Mouton Rothschild had got into the top five by virtue of the prices they commanded. 'That is not the right way to judge a wine. When Château Pétrus is announced everybody faints and murmurs and says "Oh how wonderful" simply because it is so expensive. But it isn't all that wonderful.'

The wines were Corton-Grancey 1966 and Hospices de Beaune 1959. The white wine was much too sweet, the Ayler Kupp Spätlese, though I suppose it would have to be.

There was some 1863 Old Malmsey, Solera. It wasn't bad. The brandy, 1962 but bottled in 1981, was pretty good.

I do hope he enjoyed his evening. I think he will remember it possibly all his life.

**Friday 21 October**

Arrive in Venice.

Hotel Cipriani is on the Giudecca. It is a large hotel, with swimming pool. The rooms, however, are very small; at least the first one we had was.

We went to Harry's Bar which I had not been to for ten years or so – since we were last in Venice. A lady introduced herself, not all that old, as Harry's daughter, meaning the daughter of Harry who started it, Harry Cipriani, and gave rise to their imitations or multiplication all round the world.

**Saturday 22 October**

To St Mark's Square – the same as ever but it was sunny and warm and the music played. We ate sandwiches.

I think the decoration, Byzantine, in and outside St Mark's is ghastly. There are all those mosaic pictures with their dreadful gold. They were vulgar when they were put up or made and are still vulgar now. They are reminiscent of municipal town halls in the north of England in the 19th century. The mosaic on the floor at St Mark's is another matter.

---

31. See 19 September 1988.

So are the arches and the exterior elevations, and the horses from Constantinople.

The Stelzers arrive in the afternoon.

Cita and Irwin wanted us to go to Torcello on Sunday but I didn't want to go. It's an hour's journey and there is only one church[32] to see there and another restaurant, a Cipriani one, to get stuffed in.

**Monday 24 October**

A great party for Cita's birthday. This took place in the Hotel Cipriani.

There was an interesting student of art and architecture who has written books about Venice and other Italian architecture. He is married to a cousin of Jane Stewart [Lady Rayne]. He was hired by Cita for a fortnight to take her round privately conducted tours of Venice. She certainly works hard at her culture.

I gave her two old books now out of print about Venice. He had told her that one of them in particular was a very fine book and I will now get the companion to it for her.

On Monday before the party we went to the Lido on a water-bus. It was very crowded on the way out. We went and had a look at the Excelsior Hotel and at the beaches which I remember well in the days of Arthur Jeffries[33] in 1959.

He used to go out there in his private gondola which was shortly followed by another gondola carrying all the food for lunch in his splendid tent.

The beach was deserted today. It was too cold to swim and all the huts are closed down. The Excelsior Hotel had some ghastly kind of business conference on. Seaside places in the winter look dismal.

It seems every year the Wolfsons stay at the Gritti Palace where they have an apartment with kitchenette. This is in August. Every day they go out to the Lido where they have lunch at the Excelsior Hotel and sit on the beach. I think that is triumphantly dreary. Only the rich could waste their money so boringly.

---

32. Cattedrale di Santa Maria Assunta with its wondrous twelfth-to-thirteenth century mosaics.

33. 'A picture dealer of American origin and rich', *Confessions of an Optimist*, p. 266.

**Wednesday 26 October**

Went to a sad little party given [for] Monty Levy, for a long time a sub-editor at the *News of the World* – twenty-six years. He has been in Fleet Street all his life in that kind of a job. He lamented the days when the *News of the World* had hard news and did exposés of crooks instead of just going in entirely, as he thinks, for show business and royalty. He is taking early retirement, aged I think sixty-one, or he may have been asked to go, it wasn't quite clear.

I thanked him for all his kindness and patience to me when I ring him on Saturday mornings or Friday evenings and want to alter a word here or a line there. And also for his patience while I make the necessary word cuts that frequently arise. I feel quite sad that this Saturday will be the last Saturday I shall be dealing with him.

Long tiresome conversation with Allan Davis. The man is stingy and miser-like. Because he has not yet succeeded in finding the right people as he regards them for the play, he wanted to wriggle out of his contract with me to take another option from the 24th September for a year for the price of £1,000. When asked by the agent, did he not want to renew the option, he said, oh yes he did want to, but he didn't want to pay for it.

Finally he grudgingly agreed that he would pay £500 for six months and then afterwards with Laurence Fitch, my agent, that he would agree to pay the £500 now and then in six months' time pay the next £500.

I fear now the play will never be put on. He has lost his enthusiasm for it.

He is now becoming slightly shrewish as queers often do. He said, 'I didn't want to tell you but the last actor who saw it and read the play and rejected it said he always knew straight away in the first ten pages if a play wouldn't be any good, and he knew after the first ten pages of yours it would be no good.' I forbore from saying to him that the first ten pages were entirely his idea, beginning the play with a scene which is repeated later in the play.

I fear I have wasted my time now on that play. And a good deal of money on entertaining Allan Davis in Italy two years running.

After the Monty Levy party I went to a Claridge's party given by Sears. I told Verushka this would be full of bookmakers.

Sears owns William Hill. Actually, since Norman Tebbit became a Director of Sears, it has become full of politicians and so forth.

Tebbit suggested I should get on to Margaret and ask for a deputation of Norris McWhirter,[34] himself and me to go and see her about this bias in broadcasting left over from the present Broadcasting Act which enables bias to be included in programmes and to be balanced over a series. This is apropos of my article in the *Times* recently on the subject.[35]

Afterwards we had dinner with the Wolfsons at Claridge's instead of going home. I sat next to Lady Young, David Young's wife. She is a fairly basic person who actually believes that Harold Wilson was busy selling the country out to Russia when he was Prime Minister.

I told Ruth I had been to see her haunt at the Lido. She said they didn't have lunch every day at the Excelsior, only one day in three.

I feel everything is running against me now. The play is gone, nothing matures, I have been getting a bit depressed about the privatization coming out the wrong way, which would mean the end of my hopes. It doesn't seem worth going on with the new play I started.

**Thursday 27 October**

The Other Club for dinner. Before we began Michael Hartwell said that Callaghan had resigned in protest against rude remarks I had made about him in a review of his memoirs. I said, 'On the whole I was quite nice about it. I only said that he and Harold Wilson were the two worst Prime Ministers of the century, or words to that effect. I don't know why he should object to that very much in view of the Club's rule that nothing is to interfere with asperity of party politics etc.' He said Callaghan had said he could not remain a member of a club with me.

Then Robert [Cranborne] told me a story about James Callaghan when he was Foreign Secretary and he went to Oman and went round with the ruler and was shown his farm, his cattle and so on. He said, 'Why don't you have any pigs?' so the Sultan said, 'Well, there are technical difficulties.' Callaghan said, 'I'm sure our Minister of Agriculture could help you with any technical difficulties.' The ass didn't realize that Muslims don't eat pig. Then later when Jim was Prime Minister the Sultan came to 10 Downing Street and the first course

---

34. Co-founder and editor of *The Guinness Book of Records*; chairman, Freedom Association; twin brother of Ross McWhirter, murdered by the IRA in 1975.
35. On 4 October under the heading 'Beating Broadcast Bias' WW had called for impartiality within a single programme rather than across a series, to be applied to the BBC as well as the IBA.

was melon with Parma ham which one of the Sultan's aides ate thinking it was raw beef. Julian said Callaghan should have vetted the menu but as he didn't know Muslims don't eat pig it would have made no difference.

Then David Steel[36] said, 'If I resigned every time Woodrow had written something rude about me, I would have been resigning all the time. Perhaps now I'm no longer Leader he won't write anything rude about me any more.' There was a good deal of laughter about all this. He is deeply glad to have given up the thankless job.

Then Willie Whitelaw fell to talking about how Margaret became Leader of the party. He was Chairman of the party and couldn't possibly have done anything other than support Ted Heath who had made him Chairman. He had been away in Northern Ireland as Northern Ireland Secretary and he hadn't realized how things had drifted against Ted Heath, and nobody realized how far until a few days before, with Du Cann (Chairman of the 1922 Committee) playing a double game. Then Willie went on about Ted's crazy behaviour in never accepting anything from Margaret or accepting her hand of friendship. She even went to call on him at his house in Wilton Terrace. I said, 'That was a total disaster,' and he said, 'Yes.'

We discussed whether the new system they had of getting the MPs to vote on the Leadership instead of allowing a Tory Leader to emerge as in the past was a good one. Willie agreed she would never have 'emerged' as Tory Leader.

He said also what had gone against Ted was the way in which he got rid of Alec Douglas-Home after the 1964 election. He should have waited a bit. And Ted should also, after the defeat in 1974, have said, 'Let's have an election again in about three years' time. I'll stand in it.' He might have won.

Willie said that Ted was a very good person to serve, he was a good Prime Minister. He then said that if Margaret lost an election she probably would be out. I said, 'I think if she lost an election she wouldn't want to go on being Leader of the party anyway.'

At our end of the table we had been talking about Marcia Williams[37] briefly. Robert Cranborne asked if I thought she was sexy. I said, 'Oh yes. She definitely had a lot of animal sexuality about her.' He was

---

36. Leader of the Liberal Party, 1976–88.

37. Harold Wilson's political secretary.

surprised. He asked if I liked her. I said, 'I've always liked her. She is very amusing. And full of jolly gossip.'

We were trying to think of some younger, left-wingish members.

There is a man called Tony Blair[38] who is bright on the Labour side. And also another called Gordon Brown. But others were not quite sure if these people were clubbable or not.

Later Harold Wilson left the dining-room with me. He was quite lost. He didn't know where he was going. His eyes looked very puffy, poor fellow. He kept mumbling to me, 'Very good to keep The Other Club going, we have to keep it going. It's very good.'

When we got him to the front entrance on the Strand side he wandered about looking for his car. We got out and tried to help him back into the hotel. A nasty, rough-looking fellow turned up, who I suppose is the driver given him by the government for his detective. Harold didn't know what he was doing when he was not around. Poor old chap. I began to feel very sorry for him. He's not all that much older than me, being born in March 1916.[39]

Netta Weinstock, Verushka and Diane Lever had all had dinner together in what they idiotically call The Other Other Club.

**Sunday 30 October**

To Arnold's at Bowden.

Before we left I talked to Arnold at some length about the Jockey Club hopes and intentions as far as the Tote is concerned. They want to set up a racing trust, give me a five or seven year contract, whichever I might prefer, pay me a commercial salary, not interfere with the staff, in fact not interfere with anything. Johnnie Henderson had previously said I could be a member of the trust.

Arnold thinks it is terribly important that racing should own the Tote and that racing might be on its way at last to getting some kind of a Tote monopoly. I said, 'We'd certainly get more co-operation from the racecourses and perhaps they'd begin to starve the bookmakers a bit.'

I said, 'Where is the money to come from for us to buy the betting shops I want as well as advancing technologically?' He said, 'The Jockey Club has got tens of millions of pounds and masses of acres of

38. First mention of Blair, the future Labour Prime Minister, and Brown, the future Labour Chancellor.

39. Harold Wilson died in 1995 after a long illness.

land around Newmarket.' He thought their racecourses were run very well by Racecourse Holdings Trust.

I said, 'Of course if it was the Jockey Club which gathered all racing interests together, it would make it much simpler to give the exclusive licence we want in perpetuity.' It was his opinion that we would never raise all that much in a public flotation because of all our intentions to make so many presents, as it were, to racing. I said we could sell the betting shops for £80 million to Ladbroke's tomorrow, if we wanted to, but I haven't the slightest intention of so doing. The Tote must hang together, the Credit, the betting shops and Tote Cash on course.

I asked Arnold about Dick Hern.

Arnold said, 'Oh well, Dick Hern wrote first of all and said he didn't want to go on training, that he wasn't capable of doing it any more. Then he changed his mind. But of course he is not capable of it. He can't feel the horses' forelegs so he can't train.' I said, 'But there's a perfectly good assistant there who can feel the horses' legs for him.' 'Oh, that's not the same thing at all.'

I said, 'But he's got a lease until the end of next year.' 'Yes, that's the problem. We can't get rid of him until then.' He said, 'Of course the Queen is involved in it.'

Verushka knew nothing about this story and when she heard Arnold talking like that about Dick Hern she was very surprised. She remembered how there had been a great dinner with Willie Carson and Dick Hern after Troy had won the Derby[40] and Arnold had said Dick Hern was the greatest trainer alive, undying friendship and all the rest of it. I said, 'That's how life is. When people are down a bit they are deserted.'

Of course Dick Hern did train Troy, trained Ela-Mana-Mou and a horse Arnold had which won the Oaks and the St Leger.[41] So having said to Isabel I would like to hear Porchester's side of the story when we were at Newmarket staying with her, I think I've now heard it and I don't think it's very satisfactory.

Petronella spent the day reading the newspapers. She is trying to think of subjects for a column she is doing for the *Sunday Telegraph* next week while Auberon Waugh is away in Spain. She says she has

---

40. In 1979, owned by Sir Michael Sobell, Netta Weinstock's father, trained by Dick Hern, ridden by Willie Carson.
41. Sun Princess, in 1983, owned, trained and ridden as above.

read twelve of Auberon Waugh's columns. She found them much duller than she had realized.

She agreed with a number of his things like about smoking but she did not want to cover the same ground as him. I said, 'That is right unless you can make some new point about it, and say "as the usual occupant of this column might have said", or words to that effect.'

She is understandably very thrilled at being asked to stand in for him while he is away. It's quite an achievement.

Spoke to Margaret. She was pleased with what I had written about child benefit in the *News of the World* today, saying that it was absurd to give it to people who don't need it. I said, 'You must change that.' 'I cannot do it until after the next election. But the pledge did not mean that we were going to maintain it at the same level and up it all the time to cover inflation.'

I talked to her about my conversation with Norman Tebbit on the bias in broadcasting – the argument they can balance one biased programme with another, even if it is not the same subject.

She said, 'There's no point in you and Norman and Norris McWhirter coming to see me about it. I know your views already. I'll have to get on to Douglas Hurd and find out what's going on.'

**Monday 31 October**

Alexander Hesketh says his long hoped-for son, now his heir, was born on Margaret Thatcher's birthday. Did I think it would be a good idea to ask her to be a godmother? I said, 'I think it would be excellent. Even if she doesn't come, she would be very touched and it doesn't have an element of sucking up and so forth because of the coincidence of the birthday being the same. I think she would be pleased at being asked.'

**Tuesday 1 November**

Saw Douglas Hurd alone with John Patten and a little secretary taking a few notes. They wanted to talk to me about my letter of October 4th, written on the instructions of the board, making the various complaints about the behaviour of Lloyds Merchant Bank and laying down various rules that the Tote wanted to be observed.

He said, 'I just wanted to talk to you about your thunderbolt,' waving my letter. I said, 'Thunderbolt? I thought it was very mild. It was only written on the instructions of the Board.' He laughed. He doesn't believe that the Board give instructions to me. When I mentioned this to Brian afterwards he said 'That was true for once. The Board did ask you to write the letter and say what you did say.'

Anyway, after a longish conversation I agreed to ask the Board if they would be willing to see the bank people individually which they previously rejected on the ground they didn't want to be divided and ruled.

He said, 'All the options are open. There may be a management buy-out. There may be other things suggested.' I told him what the Jockey Club and racing interests have in mind but said they would have to pay for it because I want to get some equity into the show so that we can buy betting shops more easily without having to borrow. He said he understood all that.

He found it quite interesting that racing interests may have, say, a majority shareholding. I said, 'It would then be easier to justify the exclusive licence.'

It all went off very amicably. I really thought the whole meeting was rather pointless because he could have rung me up and cleared the point in about two minutes flat two weeks ago.

I said, 'I am amazed to hear that they consider they have been blocked or can't get on with it.' John Patten said, 'Yes, it's costing us a lot of money. We are paying them on a meter basis.'

Then Douglas got worried about Hambros. I said, 'Well Hambros have got to advise us and if there is any flotation I want them to conduct it.' He said he understood that but he didn't want them to come in too early and start a conflict with Lloyds Merchant Bank. I don't know why the merchant bank are so ruddy touchy. I didn't tell him I had already shown Hambros the terms of reference which the Tote Board had accepted.

Later in the Lords I bumped into Willie Whitelaw. He said, 'Your friends the bookmakers are being very difficult, making the Levy Board go to the Home Secretary for arbitration on the new rate of Levy.'

I said, 'It's Plummer's[1] fault. He used to appease the Big Four by taking them a shopping list and saying would they be agreeable to the Levy going up a bit so racing can pay for the things it needs. The right way to do it is a percentage, a fixed one, on the turnover and then the Levy Board can decide how to spend it.'

I also had exactly the same conversation with Douglas Hurd as we went along to the lift, for he is the Home Secretary and has to arbitrate. I told him what I thought and I think we will get something rather like what Ian [Trethowan] and the Levy Board want.

I also said to Willie, 'I don't think Margaret realizes there is such a thing as a Levy. She would have a fit if she knew.' He said, 'No, she doesn't know anything about it. I never mentioned it to her all the time I was Home Secretary or in the government with her. I kept it away from her.'

I said, 'That's the way it's got to be because if she ever found out that this special tax is being collected by one industry alone and an industry which is bursting with millionaires and horses worth £20 million when they go past the winning post at the Derby, I think she would be horror struck and take the thing away immediately.'

Today I feel much stronger, more optimistic that we will be able to get the Tote done much the way I want to. It's all to do with having sleep and not feeling tired and not drinking too much. When I drink a bit too much now it has a very bad effect on my brain and my whole attitude. It lowers my confidence.

**Thursday 3 November**

A motley collection to dinner. Ali Forbes, Johnnie Henderson and his wife, Geoffrey Ampthill, and the Wiltons.

---

1. Desmond Plummer, Conservative Leader, Greater London Council, 1967–73; chairman, Horserace Betting Levy Board, 1974–82; chairman, National Stud, 1975–82; chairman, Portman Building Society, 1983–90; life peer 1981.

Ali Forbes, presumably getting a little bored at one stage, began to dominate the conversation from the other end of the table. I didn't mind a bit because he is amusing. He told a new Churchill story.

It was that when Tom Driberg the famous homosexual got married, Winston Churchill said, 'Poor woman. She won't know which way to turn.'

Ali also maintains that Harry Cust is Mrs Thatcher's grandfather. He was related to the Brownlows who live at Belton near Grantham and was connected with or saw a lot of the Rutland family at Belvoir.

Lady Diana Cooper always agreed, as Ali said, that Harry Cust was her father, he having had an affair with her mother the Duchess of Rutland. Cust was a lively fellow, once an MP, who died at the age of fifty-six in 1917. For four years he edited, brilliantly, the *Pall Mall Gazette.*[2] He was a great conversationalist and dazzled the society of the time and its ladies. No pretty women were free from his attentions.

According to Ali, Thatcher's grandmother worked at Belton and was seduced by Harry Cust. Her daughter married Alderman Roberts, Mrs T's father. Ali used to say to Diana Cooper, 'Can't you see it in her face? Look at that wonderful complexion. It's like yours. Both of you have that Cust skin.' He says that Diana was inclined to agree with him.

When I come to think of it is extraordinary how her complexion and face has a great similarity, with its wonderful skin, to Diana Cooper's, whom I knew well.

Catherine Henderson was at school with Thatcher at Grantham High School between the years of nine and eleven – exactly the same age as Margaret. I said, 'Were there such rumours when you were there?' She said not at the time. She used to go to tea with Alderman Roberts and the family and Margaret used to go back and have tea with her.

Her father had a big engineering concern in the neighbourhood called Barford's – her maiden name was Barford. She said Thatcher never forgot her and when talking about her to somebody she knew the other day said, 'Oh yes, her husband died and she got married again.'[3] Whenever she sees Thatcher she is greeted by her with pleasure and memories of old times. She said Margaret worked very hard, much

---

2. From 1902 to 1906; he appointed H. G. Wells drama critic.
3. She was the widow of Lieutenant Colonel John Monsell Christian when she married Johnnie Henderson in 1976.

harder than the others but was also very good at games like hockey and so was by no means unpopular.

She said that later in the district the stories arose that she was really the granddaughter of Harry Cust though of course that would not make her illegitimate as her mother was properly married to Alderman Roberts.

Ali said, 'Look how she has got all that Cust silver now at No 10 Downing Street. She persuaded them to lend or give for the use of the Prime Minister.' I said, 'It's Brownlow silver.' He said, 'No, not all of it.' Harry Cust was quite rich. He actually became the heir to the Brownlow Barony[4] but died before he could succeed to it.

Ali said he liked that kind of gossip.

I said, 'I think a lot of impetus behind the story that Thatcher is the granddaughter of Harry Cust comes from people who can't believe that a woman born in such circumstances could have such style, brains and elegance without her being descended closely from somebody who is upper class.'

However, it may be true. Margaret undoubtedly got her resolution and her work ethic and her convictions from her father but where did she get her instinctive understanding of politics and her flair for presentation of her case? It must have come from somewhere. Maybe it did come from Harry Cust.

**Saturday 5 November**

Margaret. Told her she looked beautiful during her Polish tour and they gave her a very good show, even on the BBC as well as on ITN.

I said, 'You managed it as a really top statesman. You knew that Solidarity[5] wanted you to say the shipyards shouldn't be closed and you dealt with it very delicately, not to seem to be interfering with the government.' She said, 'Yes. I've learned how to walk on a tightrope.'

She talked about the narrow vote by which the government won on teeth and spectacles on Tuesday evening.[6] She said, 'I was in despair.

---

4. Created in 1776.
5. The trade union moment which, under Lech Walesa's leadership, after the Gdansk shipyard strike in 1979, challenged the Communist government; in 1989 it became part of Poland's first non-Communist government for forty years.
6. The government majority was cut to eight on the plan to introduce charges for eye tests.

I've never felt so low. Do you know that some of those Tories actually wanted us to lose?'

**Sunday 6 November**

A book fair in aid of the Macmillan Trust for nurses. They have homes where they look after cancer cases etc. for free. Clearly a worthy cause.

Pretty, blonde Rachel Dacre[7] with her powerful personality and determination organizes events to raise money for them. They have to be found £400,000 a year. She has an annual book fair at the Spread Eagle Hotel in Midhurst.

The authors sit there signing their books and are asked to forgo their royalties. I never wanted to go because I knew nobody would want to buy my books.

We arrived just over an hour late. Rachel said, 'Oh the great crush and rush has gone,' but it wasn't quite true. My table was next to Robert Morley's.[8] He was selling his paperback of his latest book like hot cakes. A few bought mine. More than I expected actually. But I felt very embarrassed.

He, Robert Morley, was a terrific salesman. He kept hiding his books under the table and putting out two or three and saying, 'Hurry up, hurry up. Only a few copies left,' and all that kind of sales talk.

He is very jolly with a pleasant wife. He says he had been told for his Tote credit account he is now no longer to ring Reading but to ring Wigan. Why have we moved it to Wigan? I said, 'To make it more efficient. You'll find when you dial the number you are answered quicker than your Reading one would.'

At the end Rachel said that four hundred people had been to the book fair. This was nearly a hundred more than last year. Well for sure I won't be going next year. I find it hideously embarrassing.

One lady asked me whether it was more difficult to write for the *Mirror* and the *News of the World* or the *Times* or the other way round. She supposed it must be more difficult to write for the *Times* and the *New Statesman*. I said, 'On the contrary, that's much easier. You have to be more disciplined, more careful in your thoughts and express yourself better when you write for a popular paper if you want to get anywhere.'

This immediately reminded me of my fury with the *News of the*

---

7. Baroness Dacre, wife of William Douglas-Home.
8. (1908–92); actor; he published *The Pleasures of Age* in 1988.

*World* this morning. Monty Levy has gone and the new dispensation of sub-editors hacked my column to pieces without consulting me and made a damn nonsense of my principal item.

I was utterly livid and brooded on that most of the day. Particularly as I had told Margaret yesterday what was going to be in it. She must have thought I was off my rocker it was done so badly, the way they cut my piece about charges on teeth and spectacles. I kept revolving in my mind some massive missive to Philip Wrack who is deputy editor and in charge.

While at the book fair Robert Morley said he had given up acting. He said that acting was quite different now from what it was thirty years ago. Then the actors tried to sense the reactions of the audience and respond to them and jolly them along. Now they just give what they regard as the definitive interpretation of the play and their part, and to hell with the audience and whether they are responding or not.

**Tuesday 8 November**

The debate on teeth and spectacles in the Lords. The government won with modest comfort. Worked on my speech in the morning. I had to fight to get it made, so many people were jumping up and down. However being on the crossbenches helps.

I had a lot of congratulations on it, one or two people saying it was a great help in swaying some of the doubters. The government had put on a three line whip. When these not usual attenders come from among the peers they can't always be relied upon to vote for the government when they have heard the arguments.

Alec Douglas-Home said to me in the lobby, 'You have an inconveniently long memory for the Labour benches.'

I had referred to Nye Bevan being the first person to want to put on charges in the National Health Service in 1949 and quoted him as saying to the Parliamentary Labour Party, 'Something has to be done about cascades of medicine pouring down British throats. And they're not even bringing the bottles back!'

The Lords is a much more agreeable place to speak in than the Commons. There is no nonsense about Privy Councillors taking precedence or grand ex-Ministers, Chancellors of the Exchequer and Foreign Secretaries and ex-Prime Ministers. Everyone is dead equal. When there is a conflict among people who want to be heard, as there is no Speaker, shouts go up for whom those present want. I was rather pleased to hear shouts not only from the crossbenches and the government side but even from the Labour benches for me to be allowed to speak.

In the division lobby Alec D-H said to me, 'The whole thing was really about the constitution. It wasn't at all anything to do with the actual merits or demerits of the charges themselves. It was a constitutional issue how far the Lords can go in chucking out Commons amendments to their amendments which the Commons had rejected twice.'

I pretended to agree with him but this was highly hypocritical because I had just been talking to a Tory peer who said, 'Of course I don't agree with this business of relying on the constitutional issue. I think the matter ought to be on its merits.' I had said, 'I agree with you. It's much better to win the arguments than to give in and rely on blackmail threats of what ghastly things might happen to the Lords if they don't do what the Commons want.'

So within the space of two minutes I gave a completely different answer to the same proposition. I couldn't be bothered to disagree with Alec, particularly as he had been so polite about my speech.

**Saturday 12 November**

It was lovely autumn sunshine as we drove to stay with the Trees near Shaftesbury.

Jakie's[9] daughter and her daughter from the local girls' boarding school were there. The thirteen-year-old girl had a weekend off. She said that Jakie was much worse with his Parkinson's disease now. However, in the Dower House, where he has moved, there is a covered swimming pool which he uses a lot. She says the new wife, Marcia, spends a lot of the time at night up and looking after Jakie who is in pain, poor fellow. He sounds as though he is getting as bad as my brother now.

We went after lunch to look at Michael Tree's new venture. It is a little factory on a disused RAF airbase. It makes Tôle goods. They are made out of tin. They are beautifully designed and he has put a lot of his skill, learned at Colefax & Fowler, into them. He showed us a rather curious lamp with a tulip on top which Mallett's are now selling in Bond Street at £1,500. Many of the items are much cheaper. He will make what anybody wants, as well as producing what he thinks will sell. Very enterprising. He is not at all a fool.

9. Astor.

I was disappointed when the subject of Dick Hern came up to find that Michael is inclined to agree with Arnold Weinstock and the others who want him to stop training.

He does not like Porchester who controls the West Ilsley Stables.

Michael said that Carnarvon,[10] wrote to Porchester in the War and said, 'Now don't ever volunteer for anything. That's how you get killed.' He wrote that Oliver Lyttleton,[11] whom he had met recently, had his son killed because he was always going forward and being brave.

**Sunday 13 November**

At breakfast Anne told me a story which Sophie, Andrew's daughter and her niece, had told Anne. She had before her recent marriage a boyfriend called Hugo. He knew Fergie, now Duchess of York, very well. He said to her, 'What shall I call you now?' 'In public you must call me Ma'am. In private you can call me Red Bush.'

That girl, the Duchess of York, is incredibly vulgar.

Anne said that the reason why Fergie stayed in Australia with Andrew was because she is terrified of losing him. She thinks he will find other girls immediately when she is not there.

Before lunch we went over to a house near Blandford.

Staying [there] were Edward Cazalet and his wife, Camilla Gage as was. He has just been made a judge. I like him very much. We talked about the P. G. Wodehouse lunch when Queen Elizabeth the Queen Mother came.[12]

On the way back Michael said that it was her father in the House of Lords, Gage,[13] who when asked why there was such a good attendance when the Lords debated homosexuality but nobody was there when they debated the fate of badgers replied, 'There are no badgers in the House of Lords.'

When I got back to London I rang Margaret. Told her I had been reading over the weekend a long document called Project 88 which was produced under the auspices of two American Senators and a large number of experts. It had been given me by Irwin Stelzer. It's all about

10. The 6th Earl Carnarvon, who died in 1987.
11. 1st Viscount Chandos, Conservative politician.
12. See 3 June 1988.
13. 6th Viscount Gage (1895–1982).

the trouble ahead, the dangers to the world of global warming up and breaches in the ozone layer and toxic wastes and all the rest of it.

I said, 'I was wondering whether to send it to you. But it's very long.' 'Oh, please send it to me tomorrow morning. I'll read it on the way over to America.' (She is going to see the new President [George Bush] and say goodbye at a banquet to Reagan on Wednesday.)

I said, 'You have so much to do. I wonder if you have forgotten about the question of TV bias and the theory that it is possible to balance one programme in a series with another?' She said, 'No, I did not forget about it. I spoke to Tim Renton.'[14]

She said, 'He was hopeless. He said at the Home Office they were going to stick to the position as outlined to Norris McWhirter and Julian Lewis. I said to him, "These people are our friends. They know what they're talking about."' 'Why won't he budge?' 'Well, you know what people are like. Once they've taken up a position they don't like to admit they are wrong, particularly if they are a civil servant.'

I said, 'It sounds then we have to mount another of these operations in the Lords to make sure that the Lords change it when the Bill comes up. As we did on trade union reform and other matters.' She said, 'Yes, you will have to do that.'

It's funny that she remains the only real opposition to her own government. She sometimes looks upon them as though they were an entirely different group.

**Monday 14 November**

Dinner party at Cavendish Avenue. Lord and Lady Stevens (Chairman of Express Newspapers) Jeffrey and Mary Archer, Alexander and Claire Hesketh, Nicholas Shakespeare, Robin Day, Clarissa Avon.

The Stevenses arrived before the Archers. When the Archers came in there was a terrible tension in the atmosphere. Mary Archer took Verushka on one side and said if she was asked to sit next to David Stevens (which she was originally arranged to do), she would leave the house. Jeffrey Archer said he nearly left the house on seeing David Stevens.

This was because of the story the *Star* carried, which they got from the nephew of the tart, in which it was alleged that Archer had been to bed with the girl. But Jeffrey got £500,000 damages. During the

14. Minister of State, Home Office, 1987–9.

whole evening Mary was very cold when she looked at or spoke to Lady Stevens (Melissa). Jeffrey Archer said very little even at dinner after the men had left, though he talked quite animatedly to his neighbours, Claire Hesketh on one side and Petronella on the other side. Obviously there will be a lot of talk around that we made a terrible gaffe asking them both together though I don't see why.

On the way out I said to Jeffrey Archer, 'But David Stevens didn't know what had been written in his newspaper. Proprietors never do. They just have to pick up the debris afterwards. Anyway you got £500,000 damages.' He said, 'Yes. But we didn't take your advice. We gave it all to charity.'

David Stevens and his wife were still there after the Archers had gone. They both remarked on Mary Archer being quite the tougher one of the two. When she saw the Stevenses, her face was like marble.

Nicholas Shakespeare was among the last to leave. He is a strange young man. He arrived late from Wapping saying there was a bomb scare, which is true, an unexploded bomb from the Second World War. He arrived in brown shoes looking very sloppy and an untidy sports jacket and blue-ish trousers. I don't know why he can't put on a proper suit when he goes out to dinner. He can't be all that poor. However, he is amiable and amusing and knows a lot about literature.

During the day two pheasants arrived from Abdul Al Ghazzi which he had shot at the weekend at Heveningham. Also a bottle of champagne from him, a Moët & Chandon première cuvée. Amazingly generous.

**Wednesday 16 November**

Dirty work at the cross-roads department. Levy Board meeting. Decision to be made as to which courses are to get all-weather tracks out of the three which applied. One is supposed to be in the south and one in the north.

Muddle, who used to own Lingfield and sold it for £8 million, makes his presentation. It is dependent on his being allowed to take over the lease of Nottingham Racecourse Holdings Trust which belongs to the Jockey Club. They have forty-one years left to run. They have no money to put in an all-weather track.

Ron Muddle says he will put £6 million at least into it out of what he made out of Lingfield. He is not even certain he needs the £1 million from the Levy which is available interest free. He will only make about

£300,000 a year out of the project but nevertheless he wants to do it. He is mad keen on racing and has made a lot of money.

The Jockey Club are bitterly against Muddle because he is common, a self-made man and does not in any way defer to the grandees of the Jockey Club. Nor is he a converted or honorary gent such as Arnold Weinstock. They can't abide him. They have been putting every obstacle in his way, saying they would not allow the lease to be transferred to him, or Nottingham Council say they can't assign the lease – they own the racecourse freehold.

He can't be relied upon, they say, not to sell the whole thing as a building site if he got an offer of £25 million.

I say, 'We could stop him. The lawyers could work out covenants by which he wouldn't be allowed to do that.'

I say, 'This is an extraordinary position. Here is a man offering to put £6 or £7 million into racing and you're refusing it because you don't like him.'

The Jockey Club members, Stoker [Hartington] and Michael Wates, blenched as did Andrew Parker-Bowles who is the Steward of the Jockey Club in charge of the all-weather track. They retired from the room for about twenty minutes to reflect and get in touch with the headquarters of the Jockey Club.

When they came back Michael Wates was quite white in the face. He said, 'I think it would be helpful if the Chairman of the Levy Board wrote to the stewards of the Jockey Club to say that if we don't have Muddle it looks as though we might not have an all-weather track at all. And to say the Levy Board ask the Jockey Club to reconsider the whole situation.'

Lunch at the Gay Hussar with Charles Moore.[15] Eat a Hungarian sausage (hot) first. I then had goose and Hungarian potatoes and red cabbage. Mad. Hopeless at overeating. But I only had sparkling water.

Charles Moore wants me to write a memorial about Queen Elizabeth the Queen Mother for when she dies.

But I'm not sure that I will. I am wondering whether I should write it for the *Sunday Times*. I am not sure that I really want to capitalize on Queen Elizabeth. Maybe it should wait until this manuscript is published, if it ever is.

He says Conrad Black of the *Telegraph*, who now owns the *Spectator*, is very good at not interfering in the slightest way. It is quite

15. Editor of the *Spectator* at this time.

independent of the *Telegraph* operations. He is a good editor and I complimented him on the liveliness of the *Spectator*.

Today it was announced that Arnold is bidding together with Siemens of Germany for Plessey. Last time GEC bid for Plessey it was rejected by the Monopolies Commission.

**Thursday 17 November**

Arnold on about his bid for Plessey. Convinced there is a conspiracy against him as usual. The *Times* has come out against it and he thinks that's because Gordon Reece, who was Public Relations Adviser to Margaret for a long time, is acting for Plessey and they will spend any amount of money they can to block the bid by Siemens and GEC.

**Sunday 20 November**

Wedding. Elizabeth Wolfson, Leonard and Ruth's daughter. Married to a young property man they said. He was not handsome; she looked lovely, very pretty.

Ballroom at Claridge's.

Leonard disagreed with my saying that the GEC and Siemens bid should be allowed to go through.

I said, 'I think it's because you feel as I do about the Germans still. You can't forgive them.' I went on: 'I was eighteen when I went to Germany in 1936 and I knew what was going on. A young Jewish boy tried to get me to help him leave the country. He knew what was going to happen. It is ridiculous to pretend that the intelligent or reasonably informed German didn't know exactly what was going on.'

Mrs Thatcher rang back about 9.00 when I was eating what I had cooked for myself in the kitchen, sitting there with Aileen who is a kind of part time au pair girl from Peru who helps out Flavio and Teresa and looks after my mother-in-law when they are away at the week-end.

Margaret was very chirpy. She was so touched by Reagan giving her the banquet.

I asked her if she had done anything about Alun Chalfont being Chairman of the new IBA type commission. She said she tried to get him but they wouldn't have him because he was seventy.

She does not succeed always in getting her way. It's difficult to override Ministers again and again and again. Actually he is only sixty-nine. He's pretty sprightly.

We talked a bit about Estonia, Lithuania and Latvia. I said, 'This is a real test for Gorbachev's determination to move the thing towards democracy.' She said, 'I don't think he will let them go free but he may well give them much more freedom within the system.'

**Tuesday 22 November**

To the Forte Gala Dinner. This is Charles Forte's eightieth birthday. The Grosvenor House had about a thousand guests or more. They said the dinner raised £100,000 and it was £100 a ticket – that would make at least a thousand people.

Charles Forte had got no end of people to give wine, cigars, little china boxes with the menu printed on the top. Big suppliers had donated all these products. The Nestlé Company had produced Ashbourne Mineral Water because Charles knows that Mrs Thatcher likes to drink English mineral water and not foreign ones.

The chef from the Ritz Hotel, Madrid, supervised and prepared the first course which wasn't bad. A mosaic of foie gras and artichokes and truffles but it wasn't all that marvellous. The next course was the work of the chef at the George V in Paris. A fillet of turbot with chicory which was OK but not remarkable. The next was some stuffed *pintadeau* [guinea fowl] done by the chef of the Grosvenor House itself. The last course was some kind of autumn fruits mess-up, with chocolate all over it (pieces of chocolate), prepared by the chef of the Hôtel des Bergues from Geneva.

Before the dinner began about a hundred and fifty people were selected to be upstairs in the special reception suite for Princess Anne and Mrs Thatcher. I talked to Willie Whitelaw who was talking to Peter Jenkins[16] when I came up to him. I put my hand on Peter Jenkins' shoulder and said, 'Have you forgiven me yet?' and he said, 'No, I shall never forgive you.' I said, 'You can't go on not forgiving people.' Then I turned to Willie, 'If he wasn't talking to you now he'd walk away, turning his back on me.' Willie looked very startled but Peter agreed that was exactly what he would have done.

Mrs Thatcher came in and I spoke to her quite a bit. She said, 'I hate these big parties, don't you?'

I said, 'Are you going to make a speech?' She said, 'Yes, the usual thing. First of all they persuaded me to come. Then after I had agreed to that they said, "Will you make a speech?" So I was trapped and had to say yes. But that is the last thing on earth I want to do tonight.

16. (1934–92); political columnist; see 25 November 1987.

I've been making speeches all week in Washington and the House of Commons just now, I don't want to make another one.'

Eventually, when she did make it, it was extremely funny.

She referred to Charles Forte taking her on a dry ski slope in some Forte enterprise. 'That was the last time either of us went steeply downhill.'

While we were talking Charles Price came up. She said, 'Do you know Woodrow?' 'Oh yes, I know him very well. He's my favourite horse tipster.' Thatcher replied firmly, 'Well he's my favourite politician.' I thought that was rather nice of her.

I said I was very sorry that Charles Price was going and she said the same. She said that Reagan seemed to be quite pleased at going underneath, and so did Nancy. She was surprised they were very relaxed about it and obviously thought they had had enough and it was time for him to have a rest.

Then Robert Maxwell came up. He is a terrible lout. He wanted to tell her, oiling away to her, that when he bought Macmillan's in America the Americans said to him, 'This is terrible. We're losing one of our great publishing houses to Britain,' and he said, 'No. Do you remember Harold Macmillan talking about selling off the family silver? Well, I've bought his silver back again, I've brought it back to Britain.' So we politely laughed and said that was clever of him. Maxwell hates me because I don't pull my punches when I write about him.

When we went to go down to dinner Verushka said that a man had come up to her from the hotel and said that we were no longer on table C which was a nice table in the middle, just near table A where Princess Anne and Margaret were sitting and had jolly people like the Keswicks and the Whitelaws, David Young and so forth on it.

The hotel man said to Verushka, 'You've been moved to a very nice table. It's a House of Lords table,' as though, for God's sake, we wanted to sit with people from the House of Lords whom I can see every day.

I was furious. I took it as one of the most insulting things that had ever happened to me: to have a printed seating and table plan in which one's name is on the table concerned where one is to sit altered at the last minute by the hotel servants. I don't know who was responsible for that. Probably Rocco who is frightfully pleased with himself and thought perhaps there were some grander people who came at the last minute who should be sitting at his table. Anyway it made me feel that

I really am on my way out now because he is such a snob and would only have demoted me if I was of no account any more.

When the dinner was over and the speeches were over Olga came up to me and embraced me warmly. 'Talk to William,'[17] that's her new boyfriend, 'about Rupert Murdoch. He is writing a book about him.' I was dragged over to William Shawcross. I said, 'I don't know anything about Rupert Murdoch though I'm a friend of his.' I don't particularly want to feed information to that young man who may do a hatchet job. He wrote a horrible book about Kissinger and he is obviously trying to write a horrible book about Rupert Murdoch.[18]

Charles Forte made a speech, far too long. He kept on saying how much he loved his wife and how marvellous she was.

Then came the cutting of the cake ceremony which was preceded by a fanfare of Household Cavalry trumpeters, or Life Guard trumpeters, with their great banners and so on, all looking very royal and regal. I thought that was somewhat overdoing it for vulgarity.

Then we had Vera Lynn who sang the most appalling song, 'from all the women especially, and Irene Forte, to Charles Forte'.

One of the lines was, 'I tremble when you speak.' On the way out I pinched Rosita Marlborough's arm and said, 'I tremble when you speak,' so she laughed.

Actually Vera Lynn does sing fabulously well for a woman of seventy-one.

So ended an evening which began with some amusement and ended with my being absolutely livid with rage.

I was so angry that I couldn't sleep and kept waking up in the night. By the morning I was deciding I wanted to change the venue of the annual Tote Lunch in March to the Savoy Hotel from the Hyde Park Hotel which is a Trusthouse Forte hotel.

Perhaps Robert Maxwell had something to do with it – he may for all I know even have bribed the hotel staff because we would have been sitting at the same table as him and he hates me. Maybe he asked that we should be removed.

It is odd that the Fortes suck up to Maxwell and have, ever since the Norman Lamont affair when there was a fight outside Olga's house between Norman Lamont and her boyfriend and it all got into Nigel

17. The Hon. William Shawcross, writer; they married in 1993.

18. *Kissinger, Nixon and the Destruction of Cambodia* was published in 1979; *Murdoch: Ringmaster of the Information Circus* in 1992.

Dempster's column[19] and it made it look as though she was having an affair with him.

She rang from her father's office to get me to tell her father that she wasn't having an affair with Norman Lamont. He got Maxwell to write a story to say that the suggestions there was anything improper going on and there was anything in the suggestion that Olga was having an affair with Norman Lamont were all lies.

**Wednesday 23 November**

Rupert rang. We talked for half an hour.

He asked me whether I thought that Arnold would get his way about the Plessey bid. I said, 'The signs are more favourable. He asked my advice on whether he should go and see or tell Mrs T about it before it happened and I said "Yes, though she will say its quasi judicial, it won't do any harm"; and he had an interview with her at Downing Street at quite short notice and explained it all.'

I said, 'He was a bit peeved at the *Times* attacking the proposed merger between Siemens, Plessey and GEC. But it makes sense. We can't go on with tiny little groups like that trying to beat the Americans and the Japanese firms.' Rupert said he absolutely agreed, and hadn't I noticed the *Sunday Times* came out in favour?

(When I spoke last night to Charles Wilson on this point he said he hadn't been there at the time, he was away, and he would not have written such a leader himself in the *Times*. I must remember to tell Arnold that.)

He said, 'Gorbachev is arriving on the 13th. Maybe there will be a great party. Will you be going?' I said, 'I don't know. Possibly not.' He said he would like to go and I said I would ask her. He said, 'Can't you ask somebody else at No 10?' 'No, if you want anything done you have to ask Margaret.'

I told him that William Shawcross wanted to interview me about a book he is writing about him. He said he had heard it was only about global communications etc. 'I was told it was a book about Rupert Murdoch by his girlfriend Olga Polizzi (Charles Forte's daughter) last night.' I went on, 'Do you think I should talk to him or not?'

After a bit of discussion we decided that I would see him and we could find out the line he is taking. I said, 'I told him that I know no secrets.' He said, 'There aren't any.' 'Exactly.'

---

19. In the *Daily Mail*; see 26 November 1985.

I asked him how his new Sky channel was going. He said, 'Very well.' He is quite confident about it. He is going to have about four stations, I gather. One is going to have international news all the time, a proper news service. I said, 'It will be an antidote then to the BBC and to a lesser extent to ITN. You will probably be impartial.' 'Oh yes.' 'And if there is a Falklands War again you might even be on our side.' He laughed and said, 'Yes, absolutely.'

He sounded very perky. He said they do the Thanksgiving Day properly like Americans. Anna is very keen, saying the children are Americans now and must be brought up in the American customs. I said, 'That's absolutely right. You have to conform. Do you feel American?' He laughed. I don't think he does a bit really. I think he just feels himself as a free floating international body.

A jolly lunch with Wendy Henry and Philip Wrack. The Savoy Grill.

I mentioned that I had bumped into Cecil Parkinson on the way in.

Wendy said, 'I think he's barmy.' I said, 'Why?' 'Considering the position he's in, he says such extraordinary things. I met him at a party somewhere and he turned to a person who approached us and said pointing at me, "Let me introduce you to the best bosom in Fleet Street."' She does have an ample bosom but thought it strange that he should talk like that.

She said he is obsessed with Sara Keays and if you are alone with him he talks on and on and on about it. Not about being in love with her but he is afraid she will haunt him all his life and there will be explosions like mines on the road. He also talks about how badly she has behaved. Wendy says she thought he had behaved just as badly, if not worse.

I got the impression that people who work for Rupert respect him. But I wasn't sure how much they loved him. He is fairly tough. I sang his praises and said what a decent fellow he is, open and honest, not like Maxwell who is very evil. Wendy said, 'Yes, you do hear things suggesting that Rupert is not always honest but I have never found it so or believed them.'

**Thursday 24 November**

The Other Club at the Savoy for dinner. Talked to Quintin on my right and Bernard [Levin] opposite me.

Everyone around had been engaged in some sort of libel action. Bernard had been on the receiving end of one. Quintin had acted in them. David Stevens had just settled with the *News of the World* for suggesting he was having an affair with some old friend of the family during the last election. Norman Tebbit sitting on the other side of Quintin was at the receiving end of a libel action from Sara Keays. I myself had won a libel action against the *Sporting Life* and the *Star* [1979] and have just settled one with Cyril Stein of Ladbrokes who brought one against me. We agreed it was almost impossible for a tabloid successfully to defend a libel action.

Norman Tebbit said Sara Keays is refusing to settle the libel action she is bringing against him because he said in his book that she had broken an agreement not to say anything because of the settlement made by Cecil Parkinson. Her ground is that settlement had not yet been finally completed before she did go public in the *Times*.

**Sunday 27 November**

When I was put through to Margaret she immediately began by saying, 'I see you've had a very good go at bad behaviour in the Commons today. Jolly good.'

I mentioned Irwin's point, which I put into the *News of the World*, about it being unreasonable for consumers of water to have to pay extra to enable the water suppliers to make sure that it is pure. I said, 'It's not the drinkers of water who make it impure, it's the people who put fertilizers and effluent into it.'

She said, 'That is true but it's also manure and sewage. It's going to be a great thing, this water privatization.' She waxed lyrical for a while. 'It's going to do a great deal of good for the environment, improving the quality of it. And we've got to get all the surroundings for the water improved and the water itself and so on.' I love her almost girlish enthusiasm.

I asked about whether there is going to be a reception for Gorbachev. I said that Rupert had asked if there was one, he would like to be asked and I thought it would be a good idea.

She said there is going to be a luncheon in the City, she thinks. And there may be a dinner at 10 Downing Street. I said, 'Well, perhaps you wouldn't want to ask him to a dinner?' 'Oh yes, why not? We've got to have somebody from the press there. I'll write it down at once. I'll look into it.'

I said, 'Perhaps you might like to come to dinner with him on the 15th though maybe you don't go out to dinner very much?' She said, 'Well, actually I was going to go out to dinner tonight with Arnold but I have had to cancel it because he has put in a bid. Not that we would have talked about the bid at all.' I said, 'Yes, you're quite right. If it got into the press people would think, "Ah, some favouritism going on."'

As she was signing off I said, 'I think on the whole things are going fine.' She said, 'Yes, apart from the trade figures.'

As she was saying goodbye I was suddenly amused by the thought of a huge article in the *Observer* magazine this morning called 'Margaret's Kitchen Cabinet'. There was a photograph of me among a number of people and it says about me that I am one of the people who claim access to her. But I don't claim access to her at all. I keep it very quiet. She is always giving it away. It went on to say it is said that I can ring the Prime Minister at any time and have her on the end of the telephone, but whether she takes any notice of what I have said when we ring off is another matter. I thought, 'Usually she does sixty-five per cent of the talking. It's a question of whether I take any notice, not whether she does.'

Dinner at Arnold Weinstock's flat in Grosvenor Square. Netta is very proud of the redecoration by Colefax & Fowler with pleated silk on the walls matching the lampshades and the beautiful Aubusson carpets. It certainly is a considerable improvement on how it looked before.

Henry and Jeannie Porchester were there. He said Dick Hern will go on training until the lease runs out at the end of the next year. Then he supposes the decision will have to be made as to whether he can go on training because of his physical disability. The stables belong to the Queen and she has all her horses in training there. She doesn't want to move them to Newmarket or elsewhere because members of her family live along the route to West Ilsley or nearby and she likes to pop in there when she is on the way to see them.

**Monday 28 November**

Went to the gargantuan party which Edwin McAlpine gives annually for men only at the Inter-Continental Hotel. Must have been six hundred people or so. Vast quantities of food, oysters, crab claws, huge prawns, hot things, cold things. Champagne flowing. People sitting at tables guzzling away, though it was only a quarter to six when I arrived.

Spoke to Ian Chapman who is fussed about his defence of the take-over bid from Rupert.[20] I said, 'Don't get too bitter or cross because it may come off. Rupert is very fond of you and thinks very highly of you.' He said he thought very highly of Rupert but it wasn't right that he should (a) make such a low offer and (b) want to take it all over. He doesn't want to be run from New York, etc. etc.

I'm not clear why Rupert wants to take control of Collins. He says he likes to be in control of anything he has a large chunk of; and the other factor, which is mooted abroad, is that he needs the cash flow of the profits to support his other enterprises which are taking a lot of interest payments to pay off the borrowings.

**Tuesday 29 November**

Rang Isabel Derby to see if she and John would come to dinner with Rupert on the 15th. She said, 'Oh is that my favourite platonic lover?' when she picked up the telephone. I said, 'I hope so.' She is coming but he is off shooting somewhere in distant parts.

A postcard from Allan Davis in America saying that Lee Menzies is out there putting on the Archer play and that he is still OK with us for our play. I got a memorandum sent round by him to unlucky backers of the appalling *Dry Rot.* He said in it that he had another thing coming on in the spring he hoped, and he hoped that that would be well compensating for any losses on *Dry Rot.* I hope he means my play.

Dinner party at Cavendish Avenue. Andrew Devonshire, John Bowes Lyon, the French Ambassador, Elizabeth Harris, the Stelzers, the Worsthornes, the Rees-Moggs.

After the ladies had gone into the drawing-room, seven of us remained. William was delighted that I had remembered his book about the gold standard[21] in which he had said that inflation had remained steady from the 1660s to about 1946. He said actually it went down nine points during the period if you took one hundred as the benchmark.

William was asked what he thought about the new broadcasting possibilities of many more stations for television. He wasn't all that keen and started talking about the standards being lowered. Andrew Devonshire said, 'Yes, but they always say that, as Bernard Levin

20. Murdoch was bidding for William Collins, the publishers, of which Ian Chapman (Senior) was chairman and group chief executive.
21. *The Reigning Error: The Crisis of World Inflation* (1974).

pointed out the other day in the *Times*. When ITV first came in everybody said it would lower standards. Now ITV are complaining that if we increase the number of television stations it will lower the standards.'

At this point William said Reith had done wonders for the British. The BBC had maintained and introduced high standards. People spoke better, they were far more disciplined, there was less hooliganism because the standards of the BBC were all-pervading. I said, 'It's incredible that you could believe such a thing.' The BBC didn't begin until about 1928. People didn't have television until after the War, not until 1955 in any serious manner, or the sixties. Radio sets were not prevalent for a long time after the BBC began. The idea that the BBC is a kind of nanny to the nation, ordering it to have higher standards than it wants, seems extraordinary.

The party got broken up because the Worsthornes decided to go at what seemed to be early to the others. The French Ambassador said, 'Why is everybody going?' That was at twenty to twelve. I wasn't sorry to see Mrs Worsthorne go. She is short and ugly and boring and I think French or Belgian.[22] Never says anything of interest.

Andrew continues to look well because he is still not drinking. Before dinner when I was offering people old champagne, new champagne or pink champagne he said, 'Woodrow your hospitality is so lavish that it might almost be thought vulgar.' I said, 'At Chatsworth you put bottles of Château Lafite 1961 around on the table, letting everybody help themselves and ordering new ones before the last is finished.' 'Oh yes, you helped drink the last 1961.'

**Wednesday 30 November**

At the Quintons found myself sitting next to Mrs Worsthorne again. I had asked where I was sitting and Marcelle told me, and my face fell. I said, 'I like Vanessa Thomas on my other side but I'm not very keen on that one.' 'Oh, well, there you are. You're stuck with it.' I thought, 'To hell with it. Why did I come to this bloody dinner?' It was in the Garrick Club.

Vanessa talked about her father (Gladwyn Jebb)[23] and how she had found him very forbidding and sarcastic as a child. She was glad he

---

22. Claudie Worsthorne, Peregrine Worsthorne's first wife, was Belgian; she died in 1990.
23. See 29 October 1987 for Lord Gladwyn.

had lived longer so she got to know him later on in life and found him delightful and was a person she was very pleased to have as a father. I said, 'I wonder what I would say if my father came in now? He would be a hundred and twenty-one.' I like Vanessa. She is a lively girl.

Peregrine Worsthorne called out from the other side, 'Have you had your invitation from Downing Street for dinner with Mr Gorbachev?' I said, 'No. I don't imagine I shall be getting one.' 'Oh, I'm sure you will,' he said looking very triumphant that he has got one as editor of the *Sunday Telegraph*.

But of course I won't get one. When she asks the press she means editors and so forth. I suppose that means, too, that she will be asking (or Downing Street will be) Rupert as requested.

**Thursday 1 December**

Caught the train to Leeds at King's Cross at 7.50 a.m. Never feel the same getting up at that time. Too early to shake down my brain these days and want to go to the loo but can't on the train which I don't like. Tried at the betting shop in Leeds which has a smart new face lift with exceptionally clean lavatories for the staff and nicely tiled. Still it didn't work.

We went on to York. We've just bought four new betting shops there. One was in what used to be a working men's club, enormous.

One of the shops in the mining area had an amazingly pretty girl as Manageress. She said she'd been there eleven years. There were two women in that shop. The Manageress says she has no trouble with the customers, mostly miners. I'm not surprised she does exceptionally well because she is so agreeable. Tall, fair haired, nice legs, trim figure. I didn't notice any wedding or engagement ring on her fingers.

**Sunday 4 December**

Margaret less inclined to blame Haughey, the Prime Minister of the Irish Republic, than I thought she would be for the failure to extradite Father Ryan to Britain.[1]

I said, 'We're not doing our propaganda correctly about Northern Ireland. Many people abroad think it's the same sort of situation as Estonia, a nation struggling to be free. We're not getting the point across that here the great majority in Northern Ireland, two-thirds, consistently vote for staying where they are and not to join the Irish Republic.'

I asked her about the National Dock Labour Scheme. I told her I

---

1. See Margaret Thatcher's *The Downing Street Years* (p. 413) for her explanation that the Belgian Cabinet were afraid of reprisals in Belgium if they extradited Patrick Ryan, a non-practising Catholic priest, to Britain.

was writing a long article in the *Times* about it.[2] I said, 'This is a disgrace. It's the last bastion of unbridled union power. They've lost at least half a million jobs. If the scheme by which the dockers must be employed on the register in the scheme ports was abandoned, at least fifty thousand more jobs would be created, etc.'

I went on, 'I'm thinking of bringing in a Bill in the Lords to end the National Dock Labour Scheme.' She seemed a bit alarmed.

She said, 'It's all right for you to write articles about it. But we can't do it in this session with electricity and water.'

I was mildly amused. She is running away from the Dock Labour Scheme.

I then said to her, 'Rupert never got his invitation to the Gorbachev dinner on the 13th.' 'Oh, well Charlie Wilson had been asked and I did say to them that the owner will be here, he should be asked. But I must go and do it again.'

Then I said, 'Do you think you could get me in as well?' 'Oh, no, Woodrow. There are only sixty-six people altogether and there are sixteen reserved for the press side.' By this I presume she meant editors. I thought to myself, 'Humph, humph. Mine is the most widely read political column in the country with five and a quarter million people buying the *News of the World* every week.'

However, I didn't press the point. I think perhaps I have gone a little too far proposing that I should be invited as well. Usually she understands that the mass readers are more important than the small readership of papers like the *Sunday Telegraph* where the editor has been invited.

**Tuesday 6 December**

Dinner at Cavendish Avenue. Micky Suffolk and his wife Linda were among the guests. As he has given me magnificent wines in his house in the summer,[3] I thought I should return the compliment. We had the usual Geoffroy Chablis 1984 which is good. Before dinner I gave an

2. This was published on 14 December 1988 headed 'Unload These Passengers' with a cartoon by Richard Wilson of dockers idling. Perhaps reflecting this conversation, WW wrote: 'Uncharacteristically, the Thatcher administration accepts all this crippling restrictive legislation passed by its predecessors. Those who attempt to persuade the Government to repeal the Dock Labour Schemes are repelled like the Argentines invading the Falkland Islands.'
3. See 19 June 1988.

oldish champagne for those who appreciated it, the Heidsieck Special Diamant 1964. It was not really the best but Micky Suffolk liked it. The claret was Calon-Ségur 1961. There were three bottles. Each tasted slightly different. They had been unmoved in the cellar since we came to this house in 1970. I now have five bottles left. It was terrific.

We also had the Heine 1963 brandy. Micky Suffolk had some of the Muscatel Tokay and also I gave him some 1967 Tokay Eszencia. So he had a spiffing time.

Tony Quinton talked about the British Library.[4]

I didn't know until this evening that Lenin had worked in the British Library Round Reading Room just as Marx had but under an assumed name – Dr Richter I think it was. They have his card still.

Jane Churchill sat on my left.

She is doing very well with her shops. She tells me she now has six. I said, 'You only had four the last time we talked about it.' She thinks there is going to be a slight slowing down in her sales as Lawson's measures to stop people spending take effect.

She likes Michael Tree and thinks he is a marvellous salesman, tramping up and down the streets of New York trying to sell his Tôleware. He sticks at it. I said, 'Yes. Don't forget that his money all comes from Marshall Fields, the greatest store in Chicago. It was started by his family. They are not afraid of getting stuck into the retail trade.'

Fourteen is too many. We have to add a piece to the table and put a ruddy great white tablecloth over it. Also I am always in danger of running to four bottles of very good claret. Fortunately I got away with three this time.

Earlier today I rang Rupert's secretary at the *Times* to ask whether he had had an invitation for the Gorbachev dinner on the 13th December.

She replied, 'Oh yes, we've been rung up about it but we have not had a formal invitation. It is at 8.15.' I said, 'But that is the invitation.' She said, 'But Mrs Murdoch has not been asked.' I said, 'No of course she hasn't. There are no women going to be there. There are only sixty-six people in the entire fifty-five million people in Great Britain going to be there.'

4. He was chairman of the board, British Library, 1985–90.

**Sunday 11 December**

Congratulated Margaret on ringing the *Today* programme at 6.00 a.m. last week when she heard the news that Gorbachev was returning to Russia and not coming to Britain because of the Armenian earthquake. She was very chirpy about it.

She went on to say, 'It was so appalling. The Russians didn't seem to be organized properly. Nobody seems to know what to do. They are all waiting to be told.'

I said, 'I'm very worried about Gorbachev. Like you I want him to do well and to succeed but I think he's got fearful problems on his hands in trying to get anything moving. It's going to be ages.' She said, 'The arms reductions he's announced[5] are really nothing at all hardly.'

We have agreed all along about Gorbachev. Since the first time she met him she thought he was somebody she could do business with, as she has said publicly. I have been giving her the same view since before that first meeting.

I said, 'When I saw Duke Hussey the other day he seemed quite relieved about the [broadcasting] White Paper. It's given him a certainty of a few more years at least.' She said, 'Their licence goes on until 1996. But of course they ought to be on a subscription basis.'

**Monday 12 December**

Went to the Jeffrey Archer party in their flat at the top of a high building on the river opposite the Tate Gallery with Parliament and Big Ben in view. We could read the clock clearly.

He was wearing the most peculiar blazer and a pair of grey trousers. I said, 'Are you going rowing on the river?' He said, 'No,' and pointed to the blazer. 'This is Somerset County Cricket Club, and the tie is the same.' I think he is partly mad.

Not so many people as usual but it is one of three gigantic parties, Monday, Tuesday and Wednesday, for Christmas. Shepherd's pie and Krug champagne. I also had a mince pie.

Mrs John Patten was there. She is very pretty. I had forgotten who she was. She came up to me looking different, I suppose because she wasn't wearing a hat. Very chatty and very friendly. We talked about her job where she is a kind of management consultant. She says she has to go out to work to afford a nanny and to supply some of the income of the household. She is clever as well as bright and attractive.

---

5. At the United Nations on 7 December 1988.

She said she was not a feminist and was delighted at Petronella and what she writes which shows an anti-feminist turn.

John Patten was there. I asked him whether he had studied the letter I had sent in. He said it was the same sort of thing that Johnnie Henderson was talking to them about at Newmarket. They found it very interesting. I said 'I think those are the lines we ought to proceed on.' He was very non-committal.

Before he went he came and found me and said he had got some crime figures coming out on Thursday, could he send them round to me in advance? I might use them in the *News of the World*. I said, 'Do they show a rapid increase in improvement in productivity in crime?' jocularly. Deadly serious he said, 'Oh, no, it shows a reduction in crime.' He hadn't realized I was making a joke. I think he is fairly humourless.

I talked at length to Bitte Stockton. She said she had had a rotten year and a half since they came to stay at the house we had in Italy in 1987. She said she had suspected but did not know until they got home that Alexander had a girlfriend. I said, 'But he's got rid of her now, hasn't he?' 'Well, I don't know. He may have done. I'm not quite sure.' She had contemplated divorce[6] but she didn't like to break up the family for the children's sake. She has two little daughters aged six and eight.

She said, 'They remember you and they often talk about you and the game you played, "Knock at the Knocker. Please take a seat, Mr Jones," etc.' She asked if I would go and have lunch with her and see her little daughters again who often spoke about me. Well at least I made some impression on two members of the female sex.

Bitte is very pleasant. Still not at all bad-looking.

They are selling Birch Grove if they can. So far they cannot get any reasonable offers.

I said I thought it was very sad. But actually the house is the ugliest one I can imagine. Built in 1920 or so by Lady Dorothy who should have had good taste, knowing Chatsworth and all that,[7] but it was built in a deplorable mock kind of Queen Anne.

Alexander was particularly pleasant. He has always been an oily fellow.

Lee Menzies was there. He is still hoping to get our play on the

6. The Stocktons divorced in 1991.
7. Lady Dorothy Macmillan was the daughter of the 9th Duke of Devonshire.

road. He said, 'At the moment the play is with George Cole.' He is something to do with *Minder* on television.

I talked to Malcolm Rifkind who is the Secretary for Scotland.

Now he says Labour councils in Scotland are desperately trying to economize and tell everybody that, for example, in Glasgow where it was going to be £500 a head the community charge is coming down to about £300, nearer the national average. I said, 'So it is having the effect we wanted. Making councils spend less and be more careful. And more efficient.' He said, 'Yes, it is.' 'We're getting the message across then at long last. It is not the government that sets the community charge but it's the local council.'

I said, 'At last then there is going to be a tiny little bit of real democracy in local elections. But I personally would get rid of all local government.' He said, 'That's the next stage.' 'Well, I can say that but you can't.'

**Tuesday 13 December**

Rupert rang. I began immediately by saying to him, 'Are you ringing up to say you have to cancel your party tomorrow night because you've lost £1 million through the libel damages you had to pay to Elton John for the *Sun*?' 'Oh, no,' he said, 'No, no. There's no need to do that.' I thought to myself, 'Has nobody got a sense of humour in this bloody country now?'

He said Kelvin MacKenzie went too far, he should have been more careful. He is the editor of the *Sun*. He then said, 'I think it's a good thing that people have got to take more care now. The tabloids including my own have been going too far and not taking enough trouble to check the facts. It's right that they should be reined in and not be so reckless in attacking people.'

I said, 'How are you getting on with the Ian Chapman thing?'[8] I mentioned he had been deluging me with stuff, one in my capacity as an author and the other in my capacity as, I suppose, someone who writes in the newspapers. I said, 'I throw it all in the wastepaper basket.'

I told him how I had met Ian two or three weeks ago at a party and had said to him, 'Be careful. Don't get too bitter in this conflict because when it all comes to an end Rupert may well get hold of Collins and if you're too much estranged he may want you out where

8. See 28 November 1988.

otherwise he would want to keep you.' I said to Rupert, 'That from my distant scene is how I view human nature.'

He laughed. He said, 'You're a wise old bird. You're quite right, of course. The thing has got so embittered now that where I would have kept him before, and put in a better Managing Director to aid his weaknesses, which are that he is very bad at management, I won't feel the same.' I said, 'That is what I was warning him about.'

Drinks at the American Embassy. Almost the first person I saw was the Archbishop of Canterbury who was very friendly, asked how Sunday racing was getting on and said, 'I never interfered. I said nothing, as I said I would.' I said, 'Yes, you were very good about it.'

Later Petronella came up to me and said, 'Will you introduce me to the Archbishop, I want to ask him a question. Does he believe in predestination?' So I introduced her and she asked her question. He said no, he didn't really. I said, 'The Arminians didn't believe in predestination.' 'Oh no, they don't,' he said, 'They're lovely people. I went there you know. The Armenians are having a terrible time, being attacked by the Turks and so on and so on. Now they've got this fearful earthquake.'

Petronella and I didn't know how to keep a straight face. He had confused Arminians who were the people whose doctrine about non-predestination was followed by Archbishop Laud.[9]

Petronella then asked him about Archbishop Laud. 'Are you a theology student?' 'No, but it comes in my period, the Civil War, in my history course at University College.' He got very interested. Petronella said to me afterwards, 'He kept looking at my bosom.'

Princess Michael was there. I hardly recognized her because she had done something to her hair and it looked almost like an 18th century wig, greyish. I was summoned over to speak to her which I naturally did. I said, 'How are you getting on with your book?' She said, 'Oh, quite well.' It wasn't quite ready yet. It was supposed to have been but it is not. I said, 'What is it about?' 'Oh, it's about royal mistresses.' 'Have you included yourself?' I asked. She laughed and said no. 'It's only about mistresses of Kings. I haven't had one yet.'

9. Arminius (1560–1609) was a Dutch theologian; the Arminians believed that 'by God's eternal decree all who believe in Christ shall be saved and, therefore, predestination is conditional'.

**Wednesday 14 December**

Meeting with Chips, Christopher Sporborg, Johnnie Henderson and Christopher Spence, and Isidore Kerman and Peter Leng, the last four representing the racing interests. David Montagu, Brian McDonnell and myself represented the Tote.[10]

I think we were working out some quite successful schemes for trustees to be set up and for money to be made available to the Tote at low interest of five per cent over fifteen years, with a profit element attached which could take it up to seven per cent or even twenty per cent if things went well. That's all right because that would be a dividend to racing instead of to private shareholders.

David said we didn't want the Jockey Club to be trying to tell us what to do because they were not always very bright with their own affairs after all.

David is always sour that he was not made a member of the Jockey Club.

Then I went to lunch with Nicholas Soames. I felt sorry for him. Because he is now separated from his wife he has lost a lot of income.

This meant that he has got to earn some money and last September when Mrs Thatcher said would he like to be a Whip, which is what I had told her a year or so before he would like to be, he had to reply that he couldn't afford it. He said she was very understanding.

He is devoted to her.

We talked a bit about Randolph whom I liked very much. We discussed his method of upbringing. He was spoilt because he was accustomed to seeing all these great people being with his father and being ribbed by him, and tried to do the same himself; and he got used to that kind of level of conversation. I said, 'To some extent that has happened to Petronella.'

'Yes. She is accustomed to people speaking with great wit and knowledge and distinguished people at your house and so she doesn't think much of the conversation of people her own age.'

On Randolph he said, 'Once his father couldn't go to see the Pope for some audience that had been arranged and he said "Will you see my son instead?" The Pope said, yes he would. Randolph for once in his life was tongue-tied and couldn't think of what to say. He was overawed by the Pope and the ceremonial and how you had to

10. Keswick and Sporborg were from Hambros; Henderson and Spence from the Jockey Club; Leng from the Racecourse Association with Kerman as solicitor.

approach him and all the rest of it. Finally the conversation languished and he said to the Pope, "Do you know Evelyn Waugh?" and the Pope, who only spoke Italian, basically toyed with the name and so on and said in his accented English, "No, I do not know him." "Pity," said Randolph. "He's a Catholic too."'

He said Randolph was always very keen on girls and had great success with them because of his tremendous charm. I said, 'Randolph was always an extremely exciting person to be with. A great friend. A very good heart. Prone to great rudeness particularly when drunk. He would ring one up, too, in the middle of the night and say, "It's Randolph here." I would say, "Do you know what time it is?" and he would say, "Oh never mind the time. This is serious."'

Nicholas said during the succession battle to Harold Macmillan he decided to ring up Alec Douglas-Home in Scotland about 11.30 at night. Elizabeth, his wife, answered the telephone and went away to fetch him. In those Scottish baronial castles they only have one or two old servants crawling among the vast number of rooms. They don't have live-in pre-War style and at that time of night the butler wouldn't answer.

As he waited for Alec to come to the telephone Randolph remarked to Alan Watkins [journalist] who was there with him at the time, 'These people live like coolies.'

He said that his father had left five hundred long Lonsdale cigars to his brother Jeremy and himself each. I said, 'What happened to Winston's cigars?' 'They were all left to my father. There are still a lot of them about in boxes and cupboards.' I said, 'They are very valuable now. They are all pre-Castro.'

I don't like the idea of divorce or breaking up family, particularly when they are young. Pericles was only about one when I was divorced and putting a child between two parents who are separated, they tend to play one off against the other and have an unsettled life.

In the Lords I bumped into St John Fawsley as he calls himself now [Norman St John-Stevas]. 'That was a very nice party with your friends last night,' he said meaning the American Embassy. Why he should call it a party of my friends I don't know. When I saw him there he addressed me as 'my child'. I asked him whether that was because he thought I was so young or if he was speaking in his capacity as a would-be Roman Catholic priest.

Failed to get to Leon Brittan's farewell party before he goes as a

Commissioner to Europe. Felt very ashamed. Actually forgot about it. It did clash, though, with Rupert Murdoch's party but I did not want Leon to feel that I didn't pay so much attention to him now he is no longer in the Cabinet and on his way to Europe.

Rupert Murdoch has a huge party. Anna very warm in her greeting. She doesn't use the English style of kissing one on the cheek but full on the mouth.

Saw Douglas Hurd at Rupert's party. I asked him if he had read the letter I had sent to him giving the Board's views that the best solution to the privatization would be for racing interests to take over the Home Secretary's role and raise the money we needed to expand themselves. He said, 'I just pass these things on.' 'What without reading them?' 'No, I did read it actually,' but he was not saying anything. I suppose he feels in a quasi-judicial position.

Carol Price and Charlie Price came in. It wasn't long before I was told that they had asked Anna to go to their dance on Thursday evening which is the night of our dinner party. Hurried conference – Verushka and Anna – and Charlie Price said, 'Oh, I thought you'd been asked.' She said, 'No, we didn't have an invitation.' 'Oh, that was a mistake. You were on the list. We'll send round invitations to all your guests for tomorrow's dinner and they can all come to the dance.'

I thought this was a bloody outrage, wrecking my dinner party where I had carefully got Kenneth Baker and Robin Day to talk to Rupert. Rupert looked dejected about the proposition but he said, 'Anna wants to do it and I suppose I have to please her.' 'But I'm an old man. I don't want to go gallivanting to dances at the American Embassy at past midnight. I've got to write my article the next day.' 'Oh, you'll manage that all right.' He seems to think I've got unlimited energy.

Anyway it was eventually agreed the whole dinner party would be told to wear dinner jackets except for Robin Day who will be coming from his BBC *Question Time* programme and those who wanted to would go on to the Embassy.

Then on to Arnold Weinstock's for dinner. David Beaufort was there, very friendly. He always calls Verushka 'Buttercup'.[11] The French Ambassadress was also there, also very friendly. The French Ambassador ditto.

---

11. From the song 'Dear Little Buttercup' in Gilbert and Sullivan's *HMS Pinafore*.

After the ladies had gone Arnold was talking absolute bilge, saying human beings never made any difference to the course of events. I said, 'Do you think Mrs Thatcher made no difference?'

The food was very good but too elaborate.

Also present was Pamela Harlech.[12]

She was particularly agreeable this evening. She is quite a good looking woman still. She disliked the Kennedys and thought they were a frightful wash out but David got very cross with her when she started saying that one day so she never said it again. When David died – he was killed in a car crash when he was drunk driving back from London – she was lucky not to be in the car with him.

Teddy Kennedy[13] rang then and insisted on coming to the funeral. She said, 'It's only a tiny little church and you'll have security people and all the rest of it. I don't want you to come.' But he insisted and she could not resist any more.

Of course the Kennedys were very keen on David Harlech.

When he got there he was frightfully rude at dinner the night before the funeral, got very drunk and said, 'Why can't we have a dance?' She said, 'Teddy, tomorrow is a funeral. This is not an occasion for a dance tonight.' 'Oh, it's all so very dull.'

She said her brother was at university with him and was there when he was expelled for cheating in his examination. She said, 'The ridiculous thing about it was Teddy was so lacking in intelligence that the person he hired to do his papers for him was very dim and didn't do them very well anyway.' She thinks the Kennedys, all of them, were deeply flawed. And it was lucky for Jack Kennedy's reputation that he never served his full time as President because he was actually doing nothing at all except for talk and womanizing.

**Thursday 15 December**

A jolly dinner at Cavendish Avenue.

The conversation was somewhat noisy, particularly after dinner. You had to shout quite hard to talk over Robin, as Rupert had remarked. Rupert is confident that his four new television stations on

---

12. Née Colin, American-born journalist, widow by his second marriage (1969) of 5th Baron Harlech (1918–85), Conservative politician, Ambassador to the US, 1961–5.
13. Senator Edward Kennedy, younger brother of President John Kennedy (1917–63) and Robert Kennedy (1925–68), US Attorney General.

the recently launched satellite will pay off though Kenneth Baker and Robin were sceptical, thinking there are too many channels already. I am a little sceptical but I dare say Rupert will be proved correct again.

He has already added two hundred thousand to the circulation of *Today.* He says it will start making money when it reaches seven hundred and fifty thousand. He thinks there is no reason why it shouldn't, it is a steadily improving newspaper.

During dinner Anna said she thought the *News of the World* was 'sleazy'. She is not very proud of it or of being associated with it. I said, 'I've no objection to being associated with it. I find all the stories jolly and earthy and in any case the larger the congregation the better. I feel like Salvation Army boss, General Booth, who when attacked for getting his money from crooked capitalists said, "I don't care where the money comes from, I'll make it holy."'

Robin said at one point the only reason Kenneth Baker was there for dinner (in front of Kenneth) was that I thought he might be Prime Minister. We both laughed. Actually it was because it was difficult to get anybody else from the Cabinet as most of them seem to be going to the dance at the American Embassy.

Some of us went on to the American Embassy. We went in Rupert's car. There was only room for three in the back so Anna had to sit on his lap, which I said was very romantic. They seemed pleased at the situation – Anna particularly so.

It was a gargantuan party, all kinds of low level people there, insignificant and tatty, as well as some more substantial figures.

George Weidenfeld was there with his pretty and well-dressed dark Jewish Barbara Amiel. I couldn't help wondering how they get on in bed considering his enormous size – he must weigh twenty stone at least and cannot move about very much.

Cecil Parkinson was quite reckless and started making up to Petronella again saying, 'If you want to know anything about energy please come and see me,' then suddenly noticed his wife listening and added hastily, 'in my office, of course.'

It seems unlikely that Petronella would be interested in the technical details of the Electricity Bill and energy generally. His excuse was that she had talked about the dangers of windmills providing electrical power when she did a substitute column for Auberon Waugh in the *Sunday Telegraph*.

Charlie Price was the person I asked to look after Petronella when we left. He said, 'Yes, she's my age group.' He kept coming up to her it seems, holding her hand and saying, 'Are you all right?' but at least he did take some trouble about her.

**Sunday 18 December**

During the night I had the most scaring indigestion, pains across my chest. I kept eating Boots' double indigestion tablets.

I overslept and it was half past eight before I got out of bed and then I decided to go and swim and try and wake myself up. I felt ghastly.

When I came back I still felt ghastly. I read the newspapers as usual, making little notes in my head and on paper. But I began to deteriorate. I had no breakfast, just tea. I had no lunch. I went to bed about ten past one and did not get up again until half past five or later. I got my room into a fug and tried to sweat it out. I still felt groggy. My disordered body made my soul shrink to nothing and my spirits disappear and my energy and enthusiasm vanish.

By the time the evening came I was just faintly beginning to recover. I managed to read through a lot of this manuscript and put some odd literals right. But I was still feeling low.

I then had two scrambled eggs on a piece of toast and a little consommé and began to feel stronger. In the morning just before lunch time I had a temperature of 101. By supper time it was only just over normal. By the time I went to bed it was a tiny bit below normal. Thus my powers of recuperation still remain.

It was all I could do to ring Margaret. I was hoping she was not there when I rang about 6.00 as I did not know how to gear myself up and talk sense. She was not there and I left a message that I had rung.

At 10.00 in the evening she did ring and I was in some state of good order to talk to her.

We talked a lot about Edwina Currie.[14] I said I was very sorry for her having to go. Margaret said, 'She's right really you know.' 'I know but she overegged it.'

I said, 'She wouldn't have had the effect she did if the public had not been uneasy about eggs. There's been a lot of talk about salmonella for some time.'

---

14. Parliamentary Under-Secretary of State, Department of Health; she resigned on 16 December 1988 over her outspoken remarks about the risk of salmonella poisoning from British eggs.

'We had to do something for those egg producers' – she was referring to the millions they are now going to give to help in compensation for their lost business as a result of Mrs Currie – 'because these poor people were just coming up to Christmas and looking forward to having a good Christmas – and their families and staff – and suddenly they found themselves ruined.'

She really does have a compassionate nature.

She said, 'The Epping by-election was extraordinary.[15] Labour got nowhere and the other people, Paddy Ashdown and the David Owen lot, clearly had nothing to offer. Paddy Ashdown doesn't know anything about politics and makes all kinds of observations which are wide of the mark.'

Then I said to her, 'If David Owen[16] came to you and said he would like to join up with you, would you give him a job in the government?' She said, 'Well, not straight away. I don't think I would do it straight away.' That was interesting. She clearly wouldn't mind him joining up with her and would do something about him. 'He was very good on the Northern Ireland terrorist business,' she said. I said, 'He's wasting his life now. It's so tragic. He's got real ability and it ought to be used.'

**Monday 19 December**

Lunch at Trusthouse Forte. This was in the Candide Suite at 90 Park Lane. It was Charles Forte's annual Christmas lunch for a number of friends, basically business. I think I had been asked because he must have heard that I had been offended by being removed from the table at his great eightieth birthday affair at which I had been printed in the programme to sit.

On Charles Forte's left was Norman Tebbit. I sat on Norman Tebbit's left. Norman said it wasn't often that he was to the right of me these days.

He said he wouldn't want to come back into politics again unless

---

15. On 15 December 1988, following the death of Sir John Biggs-Davison; the Conservatives held the seat with their share of the vote reduced by 21 per cent; Labour came third with the same percentage as in the general election; the situation was complicated by there being separate Liberal Democrat and SDP candidates (winning 26 and 12 per cent of the vote respectively but together nearly the same as the Conservatives); Ashdown had been elected leader of the merged Social and Liberal Democrats in July 1988.
16. At this time leader of the separate SDP.

Margaret was run over by the proverbial bus and he didn't like the look of the person he thought might get the job and destroy the work they've done.

There is a growing feeling that Mrs Currie was badly treated and was got out by the farmers' lobby who still are far too powerful, as Norman Tebbit said to me.

Peter Thorneycroft said she had split the party down the middle. He was very much in her favour. He loved the things she said and her courage and her colour. 'Who else would have said, giving advice to businessmen going abroad, that they could resist the temptation of extramarital sex by taking either their wife with them or a good book?'

**Tuesday 20 December**

Went briefly to the features page (OpEd) party at the *Times*.

Norman St John-Stevas (St John Fawsley) was there, as he is everywhere. We talked briefly about the lunch at Charles Forte's the day before and I said Norman Tebbit had told me he would write a column in the *Evening Standard* in the new year. This was mildly malicious of me because Norman writes one himself at the moment and I could see he was alarmed he might be losing his place.

At dinner were William Shawcross and Olga Polizzi. They came because William is her boyfriend and he wanted to talk to me about Rupert Murdoch.

He brought me a book he had written about the Shah which is not yet published in this country.[17] He also brought me friendly greetings from his father Hartley Shawcross, of whom I am very fond. I told William he could have been Prime Minister if he had been prepared to go through the drudgery of the Commons in opposition and if he had not begun, as I did at about the same time, to feel that the Labour Party was on the wrong track – though I think he thought so before I did.

At about half past nine Flavio came in and said, 'Mr Rupert Murdoch wants to speak to you.'

I asked him what had happened about Wendy Henry, editor of the *News of the World*. He said, 'It was amazing. It was after the party, on the Thursday, the next day. There was a meeting and I said to her I thought she was very good but she went overboard too often and put in all the sexy sensational bits merely for their own sake, forgetting

17. *The Shah's Last Ride*, published here in 1989.

that the *News of the World* should be a morality play and that was its strength. It is only supposed to expose bad behaviour in order to discourage it. Not to reveal it in a way which might make people think it was OK.'

She got in a terrible state and said, 'You've got the wrong editor,' to the amazement of the others present. She has now gone to be deputy editor of the *Sun* where he thinks Kelvin MacKenzie can keep her under some form of control. He said the new lady[18] is very good.

He told me he was ringing me from his flat in the midst of a long three-cornered discussion between Harper & Row and Ian Chapman of Collins and himself about his take-over bid. He said, 'There is a half-an-hour break now while everybody is considering their position.'

I told him that William Shawcross was here having dinner. He said, 'When I was at Oxford on Sunday having dinner with Harry Pitt[19] there was a man called John Roberts there. He is a don or a Fellow or an academic of high repute.[20] He said he knew William Shawcross very well and that he was fundamentally a good person. That makes me think I might reconsider my refusal to see him. You can tell him if he rings in the morning I will see whether I have now changed my mind.'

I tried to explain to William Shawcross that it wouldn't be a very exciting book in my view because he is not a person like Beaverbrook or Northcliffe who showers anecdotes and many jokes and behaves in an eccentric manner so there is a lot of colour to write about. In fact Rupert is very modest and doesn't say a great deal except to people he is very friendly with. It is moonshine that he is horrible to his employees. He merely removes those who are absolutely incompetent who should have gone long ago. He often keeps on ones he thinks have given good service in order to give them an income when he thinks they wouldn't find anything else at their level to do.

He said, 'Of course he's much better than Robert Maxwell.' I said, 'There is no comparison. Maxwell is a crook and Rupert is not. I have never heard of any dishonest thing he's ever done. It is also ridiculous to say that he is some hick from the hinterland of Australia. His father was a distinguished newspaper correspondent and newspaper owner and his mother is a very civilized lady.'

By the end of the evening he was saying he thought he had better

18. Patricia Chapman.
19. Fellow of Worcester College.
20. Warden, Merton College, 1984–94; governor, BBC, 1988–93.

expand the book into the whole question of people having these vast communication empires and what it meant to the world. I said. 'I think that is a more sensible approach. Rupert is an illustration of that.'

I explained that the reason why he did it is the same as a tennis player who likes to go on playing tennis better and better. I said, 'He sometimes alarms me with the things he takes on. When I ask him if it will be all right, he says he has worked it out on the back of an envelope and I have hardly ever known him wrong. He is an exciting person in what he does. He has terrific energy and curiosity and his extraordinary ability to have in his head so many business details and so many different businesses whether newspaper, television or airlines or satellites or whatever, all round the world.'

I went on, 'He doesn't in fact interfere much with his editors because first of all he doesn't have time. He can't possibly read all they've put in their papers. Or know in advance. But he does have a feeling for newspapers which other proprietors today do not. And so he is a good person and a real newspaper man to work with.' I said, 'If he found an editor who was continually no good and losing money when he ought to be able to bring a paper round, he would no doubt put pressure on him until he went. But that would only be the sensible course of action to take.'

He asked about Harry Evans.[21] I said, 'That was very sad. And I blame myself. I had recommended him to Rupert as the editor of the *Times* but I think he was going to do it anyway. I thought he would be able to manage it. He had a genius for doing the *Sunday Times* which was more like a magazine. He was highly extravagant and overpaid and over-hired people. When he got to the *Times* he didn't have the kind of gravity or depth which was needed to bring the *Times* up to the level of credibility that it should have. He improved the typeface and the layout and then he again hired lots of people without telling Rupert and wasting lots of money. But it was nonsense to say that Rupert gave him instructions. He was always asking Rupert what to write about, say, the Budget and Rupert would say, "You're the editor. Don't ask me. Do what you think is right."'

I said, 'Rupert undertakes more and more enterprises in the same way as your father, Olga, buys more and more hotels and restaurants. They can't stop because it is their compulsive activity.'

---

21. Editor, *Sunday Times*, 1967–81, of the *Times* 1981–2.

**Wednesday 21 December**

Wrote a letter to the Archbishop of Canterbury in reply to the note he sent me accompanying a speech he made about tourism.[22]

He is a cheery old card. And I like him more progressively.

I go down to the Lords and Lord Blake begins to make his speech about the Mappa Mundi[23] and all kinds of other things. Then he launches an attack on Abdul Al Ghazzi, saying, 'What's happening to Heveningham Hall?' Roy Jenkins did the same.

I was so cross that I added my name to the speakers for the debate. I rounded on Abdul's critics and said we ought to be grateful to him instead of vilifying the poor man.

Pat Gibson[24] who was sitting next to me said, 'You practically had me in tears about the poor Abdul and all his vicissitudes.' He had originally been going to make a similar attack about Heveningham Hall and I told him not to but to wait until he heard what I had to say.

The government seem to accept what I said so I think the trouble is over. But it was a tiring afternoon.

**Sunday 25 December**

At 11.30 last night Petronella and I arrived at the Grosvenor Chapel at South Audley Street where Wilkes is buried. There was a Schubert Mass in G. There was a choir with nice voices. There were carols. It was like a Roman Catholic Mass with practically no difference that I could observe.

In the evening we went to a dinner given by the Metcalfes at 15 Wilton Street. It was very gay on the whole. Very kind of them. There were lots of family there and lots of nice presents, old champagne as well as turkey etc. of course. And curious kind of hot stuffing more like gruel. We were given presents. I got a torch and a pen.

At the buffet dinner where we all sat round if you could find a

---

22. WW queried a passage in the Archbishop's speech which said that it may be 'demeaning for young people to be trained only for jobs that are low paid, insecure and which carry inevitable overtones of servility', citing his son Pericles' experiences and success in the restaurant business.
23. There was a public campaign to raise the money for Hereford Cathedral to keep it.
24. Chairman, National Trust, 1977–86; former chairman, *Financial Times*, Pearson Longman etc.; life peer 1975.

chair, in the dining-room away from the table, Barbara Amiel came and sat next to me. I have never spoken to her properly before.

It turns out that her mother got divorced and took her from England to Canada and was married to another man. One day she came back from school aged fourteen to find all her belongings packed up with a note telling her she was now on her own. The man her mother had married had decided to vamoose. She was put in some place with a cheap room and had to start work as a waitress in a bar to see herself through school. She got herself to university and did well. She was editor of a magazine there in Canada and wrote lots of articles, etc. She has been married, I think twice. Then she came to England.

I asked her how she was getting on with George.

I said, 'I thought you were going to get married to him at one time.' 'That's a very personal question.' 'I've told you about my divorces and so forth. It's not all that personal.' But she became very nervous and started writing rapidly in mirror handwriting which she did very well on bits of paper that were around. I could see she was very neurotic.

She asked me, should she go out with a man who is two months younger than herself. She is forty-eight which surprised me. She looks much younger. I dare say she has had a face lift or two. She is very elegant and beautiful as well as writing a good deal of common sense in the *Times*.

She said she didn't like the idea of getting involved with a younger man.

After reflection I said, 'You should give it a whirl. I can't see that any harm can come of it.'

I suspect she gets very involved and complicated with any man who falls for her.

**Saturday 31 December**

In the evening went to 15 Well Road, the new house that Andrew and Sabihah Knight have built for themselves. She has designed it herself on the style of Punjabi Muslim architecture with windows and arches appropriate.

It is very agreeable. And very comfortable.

The two girls, Amaryllis and Asfahaneh, were in great giggles of delight at the joky presents brought, an expanding snake and something which turned into water and other jokes and fireworks.

All very larky. Unfortunately I spilt my coffee over the brand new carpet in the drawing-room. Soda water was procured. I was dismally distressed. However, they took it all very well.

The last few days I have been so busy rewriting and rewriting again chunks of my play. Allan Davis has been to dinner twice and is apparently happy. He is now aiming to get it put on at a repertory company somewhere and send selected critics to watch it and hope they will say it is a great hit and then it can be brought into London with more famous actors in the leading parts.

It has been a busy Christmas period.

# *Chronology*

**1985**

| | |
|---|---|
| *14 October* | NUT rejects latest local authority pay offer |
| *19 October* | Nottinghamshire and South Derbyshire miners vote to set up Union of Democratic Mineworkers |
| *15 November* | Anglo-Irish Agreement signed; Ian Gow resigns from his Treasury post in protest |
| *21 November* | Reagan and Gorbachev discuss cuts to nuclear arsenals and medium-range missiles |
| *1 December* | Church of England report 'Faith in the City' on inner-city deprivation |
| *13 December* | Westland helicopter company announces rescue deal by US/Italian consortium; Michael Heseltine, Defence Secretary, encourages European alternative bid |

**1986**

| | |
|---|---|
| *9 January* | Westland affair – Michael Heseltine resigns |
| *13 January* | Leon Brittan, Trade and Industry Secretary, admits letter received from British Aerospace |
| *24 January* | Westland affair – Leon Brittan resigns; start of printworkers' strike at Wapping |
| *28 January* | Publication of community charge Green Paper |
| *3 February* | Government discloses negotiations to sell Austin Rover to Ford |
| *10 February* | European bid for Westland fails |
| *12 February* | Police clash with pickets at Wapping |
| *25 February* | President Marcos of the Philippines overthrown |

| | |
|---|---|
| *4 March* | Launch of *Today* newspaper |
| *19 March* | Duke of York and Sarah Ferguson engaged |
| *4 April* | Murdoch offers print unions Gray's Inn Road printing plant and a compensation package |
| *11 April* | Labour wins Fulham by-election |
| *14 April* | Sunday Trading Bill defeated on second reading |
| *15 April* | US raid on Libya using British bases |
| *24 April* | Duchess of Windsor dies in Paris |
| *28 April* | Chernobyl nuclear disaster |
| *3 May* | 175 police and 150 demonstrators injured in clashes at Wapping |
| *8 May* | Liberals win Ryedale by-election |
| *21 May* | Government reshuffle. Kenneth Baker replaces Sir Keith Joseph as Education Secretary |
| *3 July* | Peacock Report published on future of broadcasting |
| *10 July* | Sir Geoffrey Howe's visit to South Africa to press for reform ends |
| *23 July* | Wedding of Duke of York and Sarah Ferguson |
| *3 August* | Special Commonwealth summit on South Africa in London |
| *29 August* | Death of Stuart Young, chairman BBC Board of Governors |
| *21 September* | Liberal Party Assembly votes against its leadership for a non-nuclear defence policy |
| *1 October* | Labour Conference votes for a non-nuclear defence policy; 'Duke' Hussey appointed chairman, BBC governors |
| *7 October* | Conservative Conference on 'The Next Move Forward' |
| *26 October* | Jeffrey Archer resigns as Conservative Party Deputy |

| | |
|---|---|
| | Chairman after newspaper allegations that he paid a prostitute to leave the country |
| *27 October* | 'Big Bang' computerization of the City; launch of the *Independent* newspaper |
| *13-16 November* | Reykjavik summit on nuclear weapons; Mrs Thatcher visits Reagan at Camp David |
| *17 November* | *Spycatcher* court case begins in Australia |
| *25 November* | Lt-Col. Oliver North sacked in US over Irangate |
| *1 December* | DTI announces investigation into possible misconduct over Guinness takeover of Distillers |
| *19 December* | Government decides to buy US AWACS spy planes rather than GEC Nimrods |
| *29 December* | Death of Harold Macmillan (Earl of Stockton), former Prime Minister |

**1987**

| | |
|---|---|
| *9 January* | Ernest Saunders, Guinness chief executive, resigns |
| *29 January* | Alasdair Milne, BBC Director General, resigns |
| *2 February* | Police raid BBC offices, Glasgow, for material on Zircon spy satellite |
| *5 February* | End of Wapping printworkers' dispute |
| *26 February* | SDP/Liberal Alliance wins Greenwich by-election from Labour; Michael Checkland appointed BBC Director General |
| *6 March* | *Herald of Free Enterprise* capsizes at Zeebrugge |
| *13 March* | Liberals retain Truro in by-election |
| *28 March* | Mrs Thatcher in Moscow |
| *16 April* | Harvey Proctor, Conservative MP, charged with gross indecency |
| *7 May* | First charges against Ernest Saunders in the Guinness case |

| | |
|---|---|
| *11 May* | Mrs Thatcher announces date of general election |
| *11 June* | General election: Mrs Thatcher wins third term with majority of 102 |
| *13 June* | Government reshuffle: Michael Havers succeeds Lord Hailsham as Lord Chancellor, John Moore moves to Social Services |
| *24 July* | Jeffrey Archer wins £500,000 damages in libel suit against the *Star* |
| *30 August* | David Owen forms separate SDP after SDP vote to merge with Liberals |
| *11 September* | Government announces plans to abolish Inner London Education Authority |
| *23 September* | Government loses Australian court case to stop publication of *Spycatcher* in Australia |
| *30 September* | Keith Best, former Conservative MP, sentenced for multiple applications for Telecom shares |
| *8–12 October* | Sir Jack Lyons, Gerald Ronson, Ernest Saunders and others charged in Guinness case |
| *11 October* | Reykjavik summit between Reagan and Gorbachev about nuclear arms reduction |
| *16 October* | The great 'hurricane' storm |
| *19 October* | 'Black Monday' on the Stock Exchange |
| *23 October* | Lester Piggott, champion jockey, jailed for tax evasion |
| *26 October* | Lord Mackay becomes Lord Chancellor |
| *8 November* | IRA bomb at Enniskillen |
| *17 November* | Community charge ('Poll Tax') plans announced |
| *24 November* | US and USSR agree on intermediate range nuclear missiles |
| *7 December* | Mrs Thatcher meets Gorbachev at Brize Norton |

| | |
|---|---|
| *8 December* | American–Soviet agreement to abolish medium- and short-range nuclear weapons |
| *17 December* | Second reading of Community Charge Bill |

**1988**

| | |
|---|---|
| *4–8 January* | Mrs Thatcher tours Africa |
| *10 January* | Lord Whitelaw resigns because of ill-health |
| *24 February* | Cecil Parkinson announces plans to privatize CEGB |
| *3 March* | One-day strike by nurses and health workers |
| *6 March* | Three IRA members shot dead by SAS in Gibraltar |
| *15 March* | Nigel Lawson's Budget cuts standard rate of income tax to 25 per cent, top rate to 40 per cent |
| *17 March* | Ford pull out of plans for Dundee plant because unions refuse a single union deal |
| *19 March* | Mob murders two soldiers at Belfast funeral of IRA members shot in Gibraltar |
| *18 April* | Defeat by twenty-five votes of Michael Mates' report-stage amendment on the Community Charge Bill |
| *21 April* | Government announces pay changes for nurses |
| *28 April* | Geoffrey Howe, Foreign Secretary, fails to stop Thames Television's *Death on the Rock* programme |
| *9 May* | François Mitterrand re-elected French President |
| *2 June* | Australian court finally rules against government appeal in *Spycatcher* case |
| *10 June* | Michael Meacher, Labour MP, loses libel action against the *Observer* |
| *13 June* | Extradition of Patrick McVeigh, IRA suspect, refused by a Dublin court |
| *29 June* | Government publishes proposals for amending the Official Secrets Act |

| | |
|---|---|
| *6 July* | Piper Alpha oil rig explodes – 167 dead |
| *14 July* | Conservatives hold Kensington in by-election but with majority of only 815 |
| *17 July* | Alan Walters returns as economic adviser to Mrs Thatcher |
| *19 July* | House of Lords throws out government proposals to abolish free eye tests |
| *22 July* | Leon Brittan appointed UK EC Commissioner |
| *25 July* | Government reshuffle: DHSS split between Kenneth Clarke and John Moore |
| *29 July* | Paddy Ashdown becomes Leader of SLD |
| *30 July* | Mrs Thatcher begins tour of the Far East and Australia |
| *20 August* | IRA bomb at Ballygawley kills eight soldiers |
| *5 September* | TUC expels the EETPU (electricians) |
| *20 September* | Mrs Thatcher's Bruges speech on Europe |
| *26 September* | SLD change title to Liberal Democrats |
| *6 October* | Lord Young, Trade and Industry Secretary, announces government plans for privatization of British Steel |
| *11 October* | Cecil Parkinson announces Conservative plans to privatize coal |
| *13 October* | Law Lords allow publication of extracts from *Spycatcher* in British press |
| *1 November* | Government majority cut to eight over charges for eye tests |
| *7 November* | White Paper on Broadcasting |
| *8 November* | George Bush elected US President |
| *17 November* | Mrs Thatcher visits US |

| | |
|---|---|
| *25 November* | Belgium refuses request to extradite to UK Patrick Ryan, IRA suspect |
| *16 December* | Edwina Currie resigns over British eggs and salmonella |

# *Biographical Notes*

*Names in italics are of people WW mentions in this volume.*

**Amery, Julian** (life peer 1992) b 1919, Conservative politician, son of Leo Amery (Conservative politician and writer), m (1950) *Lady Catherine Macmillan* (d 1991), daughter of *Harold Macmillan*, 1st Earl of Stockton, Prime Minister 1957–63. One son, three daughters (*Elizabeth*, b 1956, m (1988) Alan, son of *Alan Hare*). Secretary of State for Air, 1960–2, Minister of Aviation 1962–4, Minister for Housing and Construction, DoE, 1970–2, Minister of State, FCO, 1972–4.

**Amis, Kingsley** (1922–95, knight 1990) novelist, poet, critic and *bon viveur*, m 1 (1948–65) *Hilary* (*Hilly*) née Bardwell (two sons, one being *Martin*, also a novelist, one daughter). She married 2 the 7th Baron Kilmarnock; Amis lodged in their house for his latter years, lunching regularly at the Garrick Club. He was married 2 (1965–83) to the novelist *Elizabeth Jane Howard*. During the period of this volume he published *The Old Devils*, winning the 1986 Booker Prize, *The Crime of the Century* (1987) and *Difficulties with Girls* (1988).

**Archer, Jeffrey** (life peer 1992), b 1940, Conservative politician and best-selling author, m (1966) *Mary*, née Weeden, scientist, at the time of this volume Fellow of Newnham College, Cambridge, and 1976–86 Lector in Chemistry, Trinity College, Cambridge; she was also a director, Anglia Television, 1987–95. Jeffrey Archer was MP for Louth, 1969–74, and Deputy Chairman of the Conservative Party, 1985–6. He published *A Matter of Honour* in 1986 and *A Twist in the Tale* (short stories) in 1988. His play *Beyond Reasonable Doubt* was at the Queen's Theatre in 1987 and his 1984 novel *First Among Equals* was televised in 1986.

**Astor, Major Hon. Sir John Jacob** (*Jakie*), b 1918, Conservative politician, MP 1951–9, 4th son of 2nd Viscount Astor, m 1 (1944–72) Ana Inez (*Chiquita*), née Carcano (d 1992), 2 (1976–85) *Susan*, née Eveleigh, 3 (1988) *Marcia de Savary* (m 1 Peter de Savary). His brother the *Hon. Michael Astor* (1916–80) m 2 (1961–68) as her second husband *Pandora* née Clifford (she married 1 Timothy Jones, son of Sir Roderick Jones of Reuters and the writer Enid Bagnold) and m 3 (1970) *Judy*, née *Innes*. His brother the *Hon. David Astor*, b 1912, was editor of the *Observer*, 1948–75. 'Jakie' Astor was a member of the Tote Board 1962–8, of the Horserace Betting Levy Board, 1976–80, and Steward of the Jockey Club, 1968–71 and 1983–5.

**Avon, Clarissa** (*Countess of Avon*), b 1920, widow of the 1st Earl of Avon (Sir Anthony Eden (1897–1977), Prime Minister 1951–5, his second marriage; they married 1952), and niece of Sir Winston Churchill.

**Beaufort, 11th Duke** (*David Somerset*), b 1928, chairman, Marlborough Fine Art Ltd, since 1977. He succeeded his cousin the 10th Duke ('Master') in 1984. Married (1950) Lady Caroline Jane Thynne (*Caroline*), daughter of the *6th Marquess of Bath* and the *Hon. Daphne Fielding* (1904–97), writer. (Daphne Fielding, daughter of 4th Baron Vivian, m 2 Xan Fielding, travel writer; she was famous for her beauty, affairs and courage in breaking convention; her books include biographies of Rosa Lewis, Emerald and Nancy Cunard, Iris Tree and Gladys Deacon, 9th Duchess of Marlborough.) Caroline, who died in 1995, was Petronella's godmother. Badminton is the Beaufort seat. The Beauforts' heir is the *Marquess of Worcester* (Harry), b 1952, m (1987) *Tracy Ward*, b 1958 (daughter of the Hon. Peter Ward, son of the 3rd Earl of Dudley, and *Claire Ward*, née Baring, Tony Lambton's companion); their other children include *Lord Edward Somerset*, m (1982) the Hon. *Caroline* Davidson, daughter of Viscount Davidson; and *Lady Anne Somerset*, writer, m (1988) *Matthew Carr*, younger son of *Raymond Carr* (historian, Warden, St Antony's College, Oxford, 1968–87, knight 1987).

**Black, Lady Moorea**, See Note on Woodrow Wyatt, p. xv.

**Brittan, Leon QC** (knight 1989), b 1939, Conservative politician; Chief Secretary to the Treasury 1981–3, Home Secretary, 1983–5, Secretary of State for Trade and Industry, 1985–6, when he resigned over the Westland affair; appointed UK member of the European Commission 1989 and since then a vice president; m (1980) *Diana*, (m 1 Dr Richard Peterson), member of Equal Opportunities Commission since 1989, deputy chairman since 1994; younger brother of *Sir Samuel Brittan* (knight 1993), principal economic commentator, *Financial Times*.

**Cranborne, Viscount Robert**, b 1946, heir to the 6th Marquess of Salisbury, m (1970) *Hannah*, née Stirling. Conservative politician, MP,

1979–87 when he left the Commons over opposition to the Anglo-Irish agreement. Entered the House of Lords 1992, Parliamentary Under-Secretary for Defence, 1992–4, Lord Privy Seal and Leader of the House of Lords, 1994–7, Conservative Shadow Leader House of Lords since 1997.

**Crawley, Aidan** (1908–93), politician and journalist; Labour MP, 1945–51, Parliamentary Under-Secretary for Air 1950–1, resigned from Labour 1957 and became Conservative MP, 1962–7; editor-in-chief, Independent Television News, 1955–6; president, MCC, 1973. M (1945) *Virginia Cowles* (d 1983), writer; their two sons *Andrew* and *Randall* were killed in an air crash in 1988; one surviving daughter, *Harriet*, writer and politician.

**Derby, Isabel, Countess of,** JP (d 1990), née Milles-Lade, m (1948) 18th Earl of Derby (*John*) (1918–1994). No children. Their houses were Knowsley in Merseyside and Stanley House at Newmarket, Suffolk. Lord Derby was a member of the Jockey Club.

**Devonshire, 11th Duke** (*Andrew*), b 1929; he succeeded his father in 1950, his older brother having been killed in the war; m (1941) Deborah (*Debo*) née Freeman-Mitford, daughter of 2nd Baron Redesdale, writer; their eldest son and heir is the *Marquess of Hartington* (*Stoker*) b 1942; daughters, both writers, *Lady Emma Tennant* and *Lady Sophia Morrison* (m 1 (1979–87) Anthony Murphy, m 2 (1988) Alastair Morrison); his sister *Lady Anne Cavendish* m (1949) *Michael Tree*. Conservative Parliamentary Under-Secretary for Commonwealth Relations, 1960–2, and Minister of State, CRO, 1962–4; he joined the SDP at the period of this volume. He was a member of the Tote Board 1977–86 and chairman, Thoroughbred Breeders' Association, 1978–81. Chatsworth is the Devonshire seat.

**Dudley, 4th Earl, William** (*Billy*), b 1920, son of 3rd Earl and his first wife. (The 3rd Earl married 2 (1943–54) *Laura*, née Charteris (d 1990), her second marriage; she m 1 (1933–43) 2nd Viscount Long, their daughter being the Hon. *Sara Morrison*, m 3 Michael Canfield of New York and London, m 4 (1972) 10th Duke of Marlborough (d 1972). Laura's sister *Anne* (*Annie* 1913–81) m (1952) *Ian Fleming*, the writer, having married 1 3rd Baron O'Neill and 2 (1945–52) 2nd *Viscount Rothermere* (*Esmond*, d 1978). Rothermere m 3 (1966) *Mary* Ohrstrom née Murchison of Dallas, Texas. Mary Rothermere died in 1992.) 'Billy' Dudley m 2 (1961) *Maureen Swanson*, the actress.

**Fielding, Daphne,** see under Beaufort

**Forte, Charles** (life peer 1982), b 1908, was Chief Executive, Chairman and President of Trusthouse Forte and Forte (which he began as a milk bar in Regent St in 1935), retired 1996; m (1943) *Irene*; the Fortes had five daughters and one son. *Rocco Forte* (knight 1995), b 1945, m (1986) *Aliai*, daughter of *Professor Giovanni Ricci* of Rome, one son, two daughters; chairman and chief executive, RF Hotels, since 1996, Forte, 1983–96. The Fortes' daughter *Olga*, hotelier, formerly director of Forte and managing director of design, m 1 Alessandro Polizzi (d 1980), m 2 (1993) the Hon. *William Shawcross* b 1946, writer, son of *Lord* (*Hartley*) Shawcross (Labour Attorney General, 1945–51).

**Goodman, Arnold** (1913–95, life peer 1965), solicitor; founder, Goodman Derrick and Co.; Master of University College, Oxford, 1976–86; director, Royal Opera House, 1972–83, chairman, English National Opera, 1977–86, president, National Book League, 1972–85, chairman, *Observer* editorial trust, 1967–76, director, *Observer*, 1976–81, etc.

**Hare, the Hon. Alan** (1919–95), son of 4th Earl of Listowel, m (1945) *Jill*, née North; their son Alan m (1988) *Elizabeth Amery*. Oxford friend of WW; chairman, *Financial Times*, 1978–84, chief executive, 1975–83; director, Pearson Longman, 1975–83, *Economist* 1975–89, English National Opera, 1982–8; president, Société Civile du Vignoble de Château Latour (owned by Pearson), 1983–90.

**Henderson, John** (*Johnnie*), b 1920, chairman, Henderson Administration, 1983–90; Lord Lieutenant of Berkshire, 1989–95; member of the Jockey Club.

**Henderson, Nicholas** (*Nico*) (knight 1972), b 1919, diplomat, Ambassador to Poland, 1969–72, Federal Republic of Germany 1972–5, France, 1975–9, Washington 1979–82; chairman, Channel Tunnel Group, 1985–6; director, Hambros, 1983–9, Eurotunnel, 1986–8.

**Hesketh, Alexander, 3rd Baron,** b 1950, m (1977) the Hon. *Claire*, daughter of 3rd Baron *Manton*. Conservative politician, a government Whip in the House of Lords, 1986–9, Parliamentary Under-Secretary DoE 1989–90, Minister of State, DTI, 1990–1, Government Chief Whip, House of Lords, 1991–3.

**Howard de Walden, John, 9th Baron** (*Johnnie*), b 1912, m 2 (1978) Gillian (*Gillie*) Viscountess Mountgarret. Member of the Jockey Club

(Senior Steward 1957, 1964, 1976), racehorse owner (including Slip Anchor 1985 Derby winner).

**Howe, Geoffrey** QC (knight 1970, life peer 1992), b 1926, m (1953) *Elspeth*, née Shand JP (deputy chairman, Equal Opportunities Commission 1975–9, subsequently chairman, Opportunity 2000, Broadcasting Standards Council, BOC Foundation, and president, UNICEF UK). Conservative politician, MP, 1964–6, and 1970–92. Reached the second ballot in the 1975 Conservative leadership contest and was made Shadow Chancellor of the Exchequer by Mrs Thatcher after she won. He was Chancellor, 1979–83, Secretary of State for Foreign and Commonwealth Affairs, 1983–9, Lord President of the Council, Leader of the House of Commons and Deputy Prime Minister, 1989 until his resignation in 1990, precipitating Mrs Thatcher's fall.

**Hurd, Douglas** (life peer 1997), b 1930, Conservative politician, eldest son of Lord Hurd (life peer 1964, d 1966, farmer, Conservative MP 1945–64, and agricultural correspondent of the *Times*), m 1 (1960–82) Tatiana, née Benedict Eyre, m 2 (1982) *Judy*, née Smart (sister-in-law of racehorse trainer *Jeremy Hindley*). After leaving the diplomatic service in 1966 he joined the Conservative Research Department and in 1968 became Private Secretary to *Edward Heath* when Leader of the Opposition, continuing when Heath became Prime Minister. He entered Parliament in 1974 and although closely associated with Heath became Minister of State at the FCO, 1979–83, in the first Thatcher government. At the time of this volume he was Home Secretary (1985–9) and thus responsible for legislation about betting and opening hours, and for the Tote. Subsequently he was Secretary of State for Foreign and Commonwealth Affairs from 1989 until 1995 when he retired from Parliament. He also writes thrillers, some with *Andrew Osmond*.

**Jenkins, Roy** (life peer 1987), b 1920, politician. His father, Arthur Jenkins, was a south Wales miner who became a Labour MP and junior minister. Roy Jenkins entered Parliament as a Labour MP in 1948, having lost the selection for Aston in 1945 to WW. He was a reforming Home Secretary, 1965–7 and 1974–6; Chancellor of the Exchequer, 1967–70; Deputy Leader of the Labour Party, 1970–2. After failing in the Labour leadership contest on Harold Wilson's resignation, he became the first British President of the European Commission, 1977–81, presiding over the creation of the EMS. He left the Labour Party with *David Owen*, Shirley Williams and Bill Rodgers, the 'Gang of Four', in 1981 to form the SDP, becoming its first sole leader, 1982–3. He won Glasgow Hillhead for the SDP in a by-election in 1982, remaining its MP until his defeat in the 1987 general election. Elected Chancellor of the University of Oxford in 1987, he became Leader of the Social and Liberal Democrat peers in 1988. He married (1945) *Dame Jennifer*, née Morris, (chairman, National Trust, 1986–91) and has written biographies of Balfour, Dilke, Asquith, Baldwin, Truman and Gladstone.

**Lambton, Viscount Antony** (*Tony*), b 1922, disclaimed his peerages 1970; m (1942) Belinda (*Bindy*), née Blew-Jones; one son, Edward (m (1983) Christabel, daughter of *Rory McEwen*, painter), five daughters including *Anne*, actress. Conservative MP, 1951–73, Parliamentary Under-Secretary, MoD, from 1970 until 1973 when he resigned after photographs of him with a prostitute were offered to the press. Owner of Villa Cetinale near Siena, Italy, and La Cerbaia which the Wyatts used to rent.

**Lamont, Norman** (life peer 1998), b 1942, m (1971) *Rosemary* née White. Conservative politician. Merchant banker at N. M. Rothschild & Sons, 1968–79, non-executive director there 1993–5, director, Jupiter Asset Management. MP from 1972 until 1997 when defeated in the general election. Minister of State, DTI, 1981–5, Minister of State for Defence Procurement 1985–6, Financial Secretary to Treasury 1986–9, Chief Secretary to Treasury 1989–90, Chancellor of the Exchequer 1990–3.

**Lawson, Nigel** (life peer 1992), b 1932, m 1 (1955–80) Vanessa, née Salmon (who m 2 Sir Freddie Ayer, philosopher, and d 1985), 2 (1980) *Thérèse*, née Maclear. Conservative politician and journalist (*Financial Times*, *Sunday Telegraph* and editor, *Spectator*, 1966–70). MP, 1974–92, Chancellor of the Exchequer, 1983 until he resigned in October 1989 over differences with Mrs Thatcher about Europe and the EMS. Director, Barclays Bank, since 1990.

**Lever, Harold** (1914–1995, life peer 1979), m 3 (1962) *Diane* née Bashi. Labour politician. MP, 1945–79, Financial Secretary to the Treasury 1967–9, Paymaster General, 1969–70, Chancellor of the Duchy of Lancaster, 1974–9; chairman, SDS Bank, 1984–90.

**Macmillan, Katherine Viscountess DBE** (*Katie*), née Ormsby-Gore, widow of Viscount Maurice Macmillan (1921–84, Conservative politician, Oxford friend of WW and son of Harold Macmillan, 1st Earl of Stockton, Prime Minister 1957–63). Mother of 2nd Earl of Stockton (*Alexander*) b 1943, m (1970–91) Birgitte (*Bitte*), née Hamilton, succeeded his grandfather in 1986; *Adam* Macmillan, b 1948; *David* Macmillan, b 1957; also Joshua, d 1965, and *Rachel*, d 1987. The family estate was Birch Grove in East Sussex.

**Marlborough, 11th Duke** (*Sonny*), b 1926, son of 10th Duke (Bert) by his first wife (*Laura* Duchess of Marlborough, d 1990, was his stepmother, see under *Dudley*), m 4 (1972) *Rosita*, née Douglas. His heir is the *Marquess of Blandford* (*Jamie*). The Marlborough seat is Blenheim Palace, Woodstock, Oxfordshire.

**Montagu, the Hon. David** (1928–1998) (succeeded father as 4th Baron Swaythling 1990), m (1951) *Ninette*, née Dreyfus; son *Charles*, b 1954, daughter, b 1956 and daughter, b 1952, d 1982. Merchant banker: chairman, Samuel Montagu, 1970–3; chairman and chief executive, Orion Bank, 1974–9; chairman, Ailsa Investment Trust, 1981–8; director (latterly deputy chairman), J. Rothschild Holdings, 1983–9; chairman, Rothmans International 1988–98. Member of Tote Board for twelve years. Also director, *Daily Telegraph*, 1985–96, British Horseracing Board, from 1993.

**Murdoch, Rupert**, b 1931, newspaper and media proprietor, son of Sir Keith Murdoch, Australian newspaper owner, and Dame Elisabeth Murdoch; educated Geelong GS and Worcester College, Oxford; first marriage dissolved 1956, one daughter Prudence (*Prue*) m Crispin Odey at the time of this volume; m 2 (1967) *Anna*, née Torv, novelist, separated 1998, two sons, Lachlan and James, one daughter, Elisabeth. Chairman since 1991 and group chief executive since 1989, The News Corporation, Australia; director, News International, UK, since 1969 (chairman, 1969–87 and 1994–5); chairman and president News America Publishing; director, Times Newspapers Holdings, since 1981 (chairman 1982–90 and since 1994); director, HarperCollins Publishers, since 1989, British Sky Broadcasting, since 1990; chairman and chief executive officer, 1992–6, then director, Twentieth Century Fox. His UK newspapers include the *Times* and *Sunday Times* (acquired 1981), *News of the World* (1968) and *Sun* (1969). His newspapers supported Harold Wilson (Labour) in the 1970 general election but in 1973 switched to the Conservatives and back again to Labour in 1997. He is a US citizen.

**Oswald, Lady Angela**, b 1938, née Cecil, daughter of 6th Marquess of Exeter; Woman of the Bedchamber to Queen Elizabeth the Queen Mother 1983–97; m (1958) *Michael Oswald*, b 1934, manager, The Royal Studs,

Sandringham, Norfolk, 1970–97, director since 1997; president, Thoroughbred Breeders' Association, since 1997.

**Parkinson, Cecil** (life peer 1992), b 1931, m (1957) *Ann*, née Jarvis; Conservative politician, Paymaster General 1981–3; Chancellor of the Duchy of Lancaster, 1982–3; Secretary of State for Trade and Industry from June to October 1983 when he resigned on the revelation that his secretary Sara Keays was pregnant with his child. He returned as Secretary of State for Energy, 1987–9, for Transport, 1989–90. He was Chairman of the Conservative Party, 1981–3.

**Polizzi, Olga**, see under *Forte*

**Quinton, Anthony** (*Tony*) (life peer 1982), b 1925, m (1952) *Marcelle*, née Wegier of New York, sculptor. Philosopher and broadcaster (*Round Britain Quiz*). Fellow, All Souls College, Oxford, 1949–55, New College, Oxford, 1955–78; President, Trinity College, Oxford, 1978–87; member, Arts Council, 1979–81; chairman of the board, British Library, 1985–90.

**Rothermere, Mary, Viscountess**, see under *Dudley*

**Rothschild, Victor, 3rd Baron** (1910–90), succeeded uncle in 1937, m 1 (1933–45) Barbara, née Hutchinson, 2 (1946) Teresa (*Tess*), née Mayor. Scientist and banker. Prize-Fellow, Trinity College, Cambridge, 1935–9; in military intelligence during the War; chairman, Agricultural Research, Council 1948–58; Assistant Director of Research, Dept of Zoology, Cambridge, 1950–70; chairman, Shell Research, 1963–70; Director General and first Permanent Under-Secretary, Central Policy Review Staff, Cabinet Office, 1971–4; director, Rothschilds Continuation (chairman, 1976–88), N. M. Rothschild & Sons (chairman, 1975–6); chairman, Royal Commission on Gambling, 1976–8.

Succeeded in 1990 by his eldest son by his first marriage, *Jacob Rothschild* b 1936, m (1961) *Serena* (elder daughter of Sir *Philip Dunn* (d 1976) and sister of *Nell Dunn*, writer), one son, three daughters including *Hannah*, b 1962, and *Emily*, b 1967. Banker; chairman, St James's Place Capital (formerly J. Rothschild Holdings), 1971–97; chairman, Trustees National Gallery 1985–91, National Heritage Memorial Fund, since 1992, National Heritage Lottery Fund, since 1994.

*Evelyn de Rothschild* (knight 1989), second cousin of Victor – their grandfathers were brothers – succeeded Victor as chairman of N. M. Rothschild & Sons. Chairman, Economist Newspaper, 1972–89; a director, *Daily Telegraph*, 1990–6 and since 1997; chairman, United Racecourses Ltd, 1977–94; member of the Jockey Club.

**Sinclair, Sonia,** b 1928, née Graham, m 1 (1947) the Hon. *Julian Mond*, later 3rd Baron *Melchett* (grandson of the founder of ICI, chairman British Steel Corporation from 1967, d 1973), m 2 (1984) *Dr Andrew Sinclair*, b 1935, writer and former academic, his second marriage. Her books: *Tell Me, Honestly* (1964), *Someone is Missing* (1987), *Passionate Quests* (1991). She has been a board member, Royal Court Theatre, since 1974, Royal National Theatre, 1984–94. Andrew Sinclair's books include *The Breaking of Bumbo* (1958), *The Red and the Blue* (1986), *Spiegel* (1987), *War Like a Wasp* (1989); he edited *The War Decade, An Anthology of the 1940s* (1989) and has been managing director, Timon Films, since 1967.

**Soames, Hon. Nicholas,** b 1948, son of *Christopher Soames* (1920–87, life peer 1978, Conservative politician, Ambassador to France, 1968–72, Governor, Southern Rhodesia, 1979–80; chairman, ICL, from 1984) and *Mary Soames DBE* (daughter of Sir Winston Churchill; writer, chairman, Royal National Theatre, 1989–95). M 1 (1981–90) Catherine, née Weatherall, m 2 (1993) Serena, née Smith. Conservative politician; MP since 1983, PPS to Minister of State for Employment, 1984–5, to Secretary of State, DoE, 1987–9; Parliamentary Secretary, MAFF, 1992–4, Minister of State for the Armed Forces, 1994–7.

**Somerset, David,** see under *Beaufort*

**Stelzer, Irwin,** b 1932, m (1981) Marian Faris Stuntz (*Cita*); American economist and journalist living partly in London. President, NERA (National Economic Research Associates), 1961–85; director of regulatory studies at the American Enterprise Institute for Public Policy Research, Washington; columnist, *New York Post* and *Sunday Times* (since 1986).

**Stockton,** see under *Macmillan*

**Swaythling,** see under *Montagu*

**Tree, Michael** son by his first marriage of Ronald Tree (d 1976, Conservative politician who m 2 *Marietta* (1917–91), actress and US representative to the UN Human Rights Commission), brother of *Jeremy*, racehorse trainer; m (1949) Lady *Anne*, née Cavendish, daughter of the 10th Duke of Devonshire, sister of the 11th Duke (*Andrew*).

**Trethowan, Sir Ian** (1922–90, knight 1980), joined BBC, 1963, from newspaper journalism (political commentator) and Independent Television News (1958–63); managing director, radio, BBC, 1969–75; managing director, television, BBC, 1976–7; Director General BBC 1977–82; director, Barclays Bank 1982–7; chairman, Thames Television, from 1987; director, Times Newspapers, from 1982; chairman, Horserace Betting Levy Board, 1982–90.

**Trevor-Roper, Hugh** (life peer 1979, Lord Dacre), b 1914, m (1954) Lady Alexandra (*Xandra*) Howard-Johnston, (d 1997, daughter of Field-Marshal Earl Haig). Regius Professor of Modern History, Oxford University, 1957–80; Master of Peterhouse, Cambridge, 1980–7; director, Times Newspapers, 1974–88.

**Ward, Claire,** see under *Beaufort*

**Weidenfeld, George** (life peer 1976), b 1919, m 1 (1952) Jane, née Sieff, m 2 (1956–61) Barbara, née *Skelton* former wife of *Cyril Connolly,* m 3 (1966–76) Sandra Payson Meyer, m 4 (1992) Annabelle, née Whitestone. Publisher; founded Weidenfeld & Nicolson, 1948, chairman since then of it and associated companies. Member, South Bank board, since 1986, ENO board since 1988, trustee National Portrait Gallery, 1988–95.

**Weinstock, Arnold** (knight 1970, life peer 1980), b 1924, m (1949) *Netta,* daughter of *Sir Michael Sobell* (chairman of Radio and Allied Industries, television set manufacturers, and racehorse owner, d 1993); son *Simon* (1952–96), daughter *Susan,* b 1955. The electrical group GEC bought RAI and its management team, making the Sobell and Weinstock families GEC's largest shareholders. Weinstock become a director of GEC in 1960 and then managing director from 1963 to 1996, building GEC into one of Europe's major electronics companies and a principal defence supplier to the government. Sits as an independent in the House of Lords; Honorary Master of the Bench, Gray's Inn, since 1982; trustee, British Museum, since 1985. Racehorse owner and breeder, member of the Jockey Club; owns Bowden Park, Wiltshire, a James Wyatt house.

**Wolfson, Leonard** (knight 1977, life peer 1985), b 1927, son of Sir Isaac Wolfson (founder Great Universal Stores, d 1991), m 1 (1949–91) *Ruth,* née Sterling, m 2 (1991) Estelle, née Feldman, widow of Michael Jackson. Chairman, Great Universal Stores, 1981–96. Founder trustee and chairman, Wolfson Foundation.

# *Appendix on Racing*

**Horserace Totalisator Board (the Tote)**

The Tote was set up by Act of Parliament in 1928 to provide an alternative means of betting other than with bookmakers and to give financial support to racing.

The term 'totalizator' originates from the machines used for the aggregation of bets under a 'pool' system of betting, whereby an organization acts as stakeholder to enable people to bet between themselves. The Tote's original name under the 1928 Act was the Racecourse Betting Control Board, changed to its present name by the Betting Levy Act 1961. The Tote was allowed high-street betting offices with betting at starting prices in 1972, eleven years after high-street betting offices were made legal for ordinary bookmakers.

Today the Tote offers a full betting service to all fifty-nine racecourses in the UK. Its 1997 annual report, the last with WW as its chairman, states that on average two-thirds of the Tote's profits go back into British racing, £7.9m in that year. By 1997 it had 209 high-street betting shops and was Britain's fifth biggest bookmaker, running the world's largest credit betting operation.

The chairman of the Tote Board is appointed by the Home Secretary and he approves the appointment of Board members. WW joined the Board in 1975 and in May 1976 was appointed chairman by the then Home Secretary Roy Jenkins. He was reappointed by all subsequent Home Secretaries until his retirement at the end of July 1997 at the age of seventy-nine.

WW succeeded Lord Mancroft as chairman and was succeeded by Peter Jones, a director of the British Horseracing Board and a council member of the Racehorse Owners' Association. Members of the Tote Board in 1997 included Christopher Sporborg, deputy chairman of Hambros and finance steward of the Jockey Club.

Members at the time of this volume included Prince Michael of Kent, the Duke of Devonshire, Frank (Lord) Chapple, Mrs Patricia Hastings, the Hon. David Montagu (later Lord Swaythling), John Sanderson and Peter Winfield. On the staff were Brian McDonnell (chief executive since 1981),

John Heaton (secretary from 1983 – he succeeded McDonnell as chief executive in November 1996) and Geoffrey Webster (public relations director since 1976).

During this period WW was concerned to improve the efficiency of the Tote's operations with the introduction of computerized betting systems on the racecourse; the completion of Tote Credit's new high-technology headquarters at Wigan; and the modernization of its high-street betting shops. He was active in persuading Parliament to allow betting on Sunday racing and attempts to achieve the privatization of the Tote in a way which would best benefit racing and preserve the Tote's exclusive licence for pool betting.

WW was also an *ex officio* member of the Horserace Betting Levy Board, a director of Satellite Information Services (Holdings) and a trustee of the Stable Lads' Welfare Trust.

**Horserace Betting Levy Board**

Established in 1961 by the Betting Levy Act to levy money for the benefit of racing. It works by taking a percentage of turnover from all bookmakers (including the Tote) who in turn pass this charge to the punters along with betting tax.

Sir Ian Trethowan (former Director General of the BBC) was chairman of the Levy Board 1982–90. The chief executive at this time was Tristram Ricketts (subsequently chief executive of British Horseracing Board). Other executives included Rodney Brack (finance director, now chief executive in succession to Ricketts). Former chairmen included Lord (George) Wigg, Labour politician, and Lord (Desmond) Plummer, Conservative Leader of the Greater London Council.

The money raised by the levies goes towards prize money, improving racecourses, technical services at racecourses, training of stable staff, veterinary research, improvements to breeding, security, and grants for point-to-point races.

United Racecourses (Epsom, Kempton Park and Sandown Park) was at this time a subsidiary of the Levy Board. Its chairman 1977–94 was Sir Evelyn de Rothschild.

The Hon. Sir Edward Cazalet (Mr Justice Cazalet) was chairman 1977–88 of the Horserace Betting Levy Appeal Tribunal.

**The Big Four bookmakers**

At the time of this volume the 'Big Four' were Coral (represented by Mike Snapes), Ladbroke's (Peter George), Mecca (Bob Green), and William Hill (Len Cowburn).

**The Jockey Club**

The oldest regulatory body of racing in the world, the Jockey Club 'sets and maintains standards for racing'. Its rules and the supervision by its stewards govern the state of the course, starting procedures, discipline on course, the determination of winners and enquiries.

Jockey Club members are elected for life. Those mentioned in this volume include the Hon. Sir John 'Jakie' Astor, Colonel Sir Piers Bengough, General Sir Cecil Blacker, Nigel Clark, the Duke of Devonshire, Lord Fairhaven, Louis Freedman, the Marquess of Hartington, Mrs Priscilla Hastings, John Henderson, Lord Howard de Walden, Sir Freddie Laker, Sir Evelyn de Rothschild, Sir Michael Sobell, Christopher Spence, Christopher Sporborg, Michael Wates, Lord Weinstock and HH Prince Khalid bin Abdullah (an honorary member).

Christopher Foster was secretary of the Jockey Club, 1983–90, and has been executive director since 1993.

The Racecourse Holdings Trust, the Jockey Club's subsidiary established in 1964, owns and operates twelve racecourses including Aintree, Cheltenham, Newmarket (and since the time of this volume Epsom, Kempton Park and Sandown Park). Tommy Wallis (d 1992) was its managing director, 1975–89.

**Pari-Mutuel**

The first system of betting by means of a totalizator was introduced in France in 1872 and became known as the pari-mutuel. Hence the name of the French equivalent of the Tote. Its chairman at the time of this volume was Pierre Carrus, succeeded by André Cormier.

**Racecourse Association Ltd**

All fifty-nine UK racecourses belong. Its chairman at the time of this volume was General Sir Peter Leng, and John Sanderson was a board member.

**Satellite Information Services**

Bruce Matthews (executive of News International, d 1996) was its first chairman at the time of this volume; John Beard its first chief executive, succeeded by Christopher Stoddart. Board members included representatives of racing organizations – Bob Green, Len Cowburn, General Sir Peter Leng and Tommy Wallis are mentioned.

# *List of Abbreviations*

| | |
|---|---|
| ACAS | Advisory, Conciliation and Arbitration Service |
| ANC | African National Congress |
| AWACS | Air Warning and Control System |
| BSB | British Sky Broadcasting |
| BUPA | British United Provident Association |
| CEGB | Central Electricity Generating Board |
| CND | Campaign for Nuclear Disarmament |
| COHSE | Confederation of Health Service Employees |
| DHSS | Department of Health and Social Security |
| DoE | Department of the Environment |
| DTI | Department of Trade and Industry |
| EC | European Community |
| EETPU | Electrical, Electronic, Telecommunication and Plumbing Union |
| EMS | European Monetary System |
| ERM | Exchange Rate Mechanism (of the EMS) |
| ETU | Electrical Trades Union |
| FCO | Foreign and Commonwealth Office |
| GATT | General Agreement on Tariffs and Trade |
| GLC | Greater London Council |
| IAAF | International Amateur Athletics Federation |
| IBA | Independent Broadcasting Authority |
| ILEA | Inner London Education Authority |
| IMF | International Monetary Fund |
| INF | Intermediate-range Nuclear Forces |
| MAFF | Ministry of Agriculture, Fisheries and Food |
| MCC | Marylebone Cricket Club |
| MoD | Ministry of Defence |
| NACODS | National Association of Colliery Overmen, Deputies and Shotfirers |
| NERA | National Economic Research Associates |
| NGA | National Graphical Association |
| NUM | National Union of Mineworkers |

| | |
|---|---|
| NUPE | National Union of Public Employees |
| NUT | National Union of Teachers |
| PPS | Parliamentary Private Secretary |
| RAC | Royal Automobile Club |
| SAS | Special Air Service |
| SDI | Strategic Defence Initiative |
| SDP | Social Democratic Party |
| SIB | Security and Investments Board |
| SIS | Satellite Information Services |
| SOGAT | Society of Graphical and Allied Trades |
| SP | Starting Price |
| TGW | Transport and General Workers' Union |
| Tote | Horserace Totalisator Board |
| TUC | Trades Union Congress |
| UDM | Union of Democratic Mineworkers |

# *Index*